Employee Development

SECOND EDITION

Rosemary Harrison is chief examiner: employee development, the Chartered Institute of Personnel and Development (CIPD), a Fellow of the CIPD, and a leading academic and writer in the field. After graduating from King's College London with an honours history degree, and after some years as a training officer in the National Health Service, she lectured in personnel management and organisational behaviour at the (then) Newcastle Polytechnic, where she was for many years course leader of the Institute of Personnel Management's professional qualification programme. She was subsequently director of the Human Resource Development Research Centre at Durham University Business School. She is currently carrying out research at the University on 'Knowledge development and the strategic direction of the organisation'. She is an experienced consultant and a regular speaker at conferences and universities in the UK and abroad. Her books have an international readership.

The Chartered Institute of Personnel and Development is the leading publisher of books and reports for personnel and training professionals, students, and all those concerned with the effective management and development of people at work. For details of all our titles, please contact the Publishing Department:

tel 020 8263 3387
fax 020 8263 3850
e-mail publish@cipd.co.uk

The catalogue of all CIPD titles can be viewed on the CIPD website:

www.cipd.co.uk/publications

PEOPLE AND ORGANISATIONS

Employee Development

SECOND EDITION

ROSEMARY HARRISON

Chartered Institute of Personnel and Development

This book is for my father
John Park
Born 30 December 1907
Died 11 April 1995

© Rosemary Harrison 1997, 2000

First edition published 1997
Reprinted 1998, 1999
Second edition published 2000
Reprinted 2000

Design by Curve

Typeset by Fakenham Photosetting Ltd, Fakenham, Norfolk

Printed in Great Britain by
The Cromwell Press, Wiltshire

British Library Cataloguing in Publication Data
A catalogue record of this book is available from the British Library

ISBN 0-85292-877-7

The views expressed in this book are the author's own and may not necessarily reflect those of the CIPD.

Chartered Institute of Personnel and Development, CIPD House, Camp Road, London SW19 4UX
Tel: 020 8971 9000 Fax: 020 8263 3333
E-mail: cipd@cipd.co.uk
Website: www.cipd.co.uk
Incorporated by Royal Charter. Registered Charity No. 1079797

Contents

LIST OF FIGURES   vii

LIST OF TABLES   viii

EDITORS' FOREWORD   ix

PREFACE TO THE SECOND EDITION   xii

ACKNOWLEDGEMENTS   xvi

PART 1   SETTING THE SCENE: HRD IN CONTEXT   1

1 Developing people: meanings, origins and reality   1

2 The national training framework   23

3 The national educational framework   39

4 International comparisons   60

PART 2   MOVING INTO THE ORGANISATION: THE BUSINESS PARTNERSHIP   79

5 The strategic framework   79

6 'Adding value'   96

7 Setting and achieving outcomes   117

8 Handling the politics   132

9 Establishing roles and standards   148

10 Organising the function   167

11 Managing finance, marketing and records   187

12 Harnessing new technology   203

13 Training and development in the smaller organisation   219

PART 3   DEVELOPING PERFORMANCE IN THE WORKPLACE   237

14 Developing individuals' performance   237

15 Learning design and delivery: Stage 1   261

16 Learning design and delivery: Stages 2 to 4   278

17 Learning design and delivery: Stages 5 to 8   296

18 Specialised training and development   317

PART 4 BUILDING FOR THE FUTURE 333
19 Developing careers 333
20 Developing managers 359

PART 5 ENHANCING STRATEGIC PROGRESS 379
21 Building strategic capability 379
22 Managing the knowledge-productive
organisation 397

REFERENCES 419

APPENDICES 444
Appendix 1 The CIPD's Professional Standards for Employee Development 444
Appendix 2 National Vocational Qualifications (NVQs) 448
Appendix 3 Comparison between 1995 national education and training targets
for 2000, and 1998 national learning targets for 2002 450
Appendix 4 The comprehensive and the problem-centred approaches to
identifying and analysing organisational HRD needs 451
Appendix 5 TDLB Standards: 'Standards and Qualifications for
Training and Development' and 'Functional Map' 457
Appendix 6 A seven-step appraisal process 459
Appendix 7 What role does the management development process play
in your organisation? 462

INDEX 465

List of figures

Figure 1 Route maps for readers xiii

Figure 2 HRM and the business 87

Figure 3 The wheel of HRM and the business 88

Figure 4 Linking HRD to a Trust's strategic and
business planning cycle 93

Figure 5 A model of training and development's impact
on workplace performance. Source: Harrison,
R. (1999), *The Training and Development Audit*,
p9. Cambridge, Cambridge Strategy
Publications. (Reproduced with kind permission
of the publisher.) 102

Figure 6 The organisation as a system 160

Figure 7 The experiential cycle of learning (based on
Kolb, Rubin and McIntyre, 1974) 239

Figure 8 The Clinical Directors' Programme – first
cohort 299

Figure 9 The key capabilities of the organisation and
its strategic progress 384

Figure 10 Continuous improvement process at Hydro
Polymers, 1997 (with acknowledgements to
Steve Cleary, Total Quality Co-Ordinator) 411

List of tables

Table 1   The seven aims of national training policy listed in
the White Paper *Education and Training for the
21st Century* (1991)   25

Table 2   Five steps to ensure that HRD operates within
the strategic framework of the business   85

Table 3   Matrix to identify training and development
role and contribution to the business.
Source: Harrison, R. (1999) *The Training
and Development Audit,* p8. Cambridge,
Cambridge Strategy Publications. (Reproduced
with kind permission of the publisher.)   101

Table 4   Five steps in producing HRD plans at unit level   108

Table 5   HRD as a partnership process   115

Table 6   Rationale for involvement in the audit process.
Source: Harrison, R. (1999) *The Training and
Development Audit,* p16. Cambridge,
Cambridge Strategy Publications. (Reproduced
with kind permission of the publisher.)   127

Table 7   A typology of HRD roles   150

Table 8   Basic annual running costs of a training
department   191

Table 9   Cost of a trainer day   192

Table 10   The performance management process and a
corporate learning programme   248

Table 11   Eight stages in the inception, design and
delivery of planned learning events   262

Table 12   Some media and methods of learning   303

Table 13   Integrating organisational and career
development   345

Table 14   Building HRD into the business   414

Editors' foreword

People hold the key to more productive and efficient organisations. The way in which people are managed and developed at work has major effects upon quality, customer service, organisational flexibility and costs. Personnel and development practitioners can play a major role in creating the framework for this to happen, but ultimately they are dependent upon line managers and other employees for its delivery. It is important that personnel and development specialists gain the commitment of others and pursue professional and ethical practices that will bring about competitive success. There is also a need to evaluate the contribution that personnel and development approaches and processes make for organisational success, and to consider ways of making these more effective. Such an approach is relevant for all types of practitioner – personnel and development generalists and specialists, line managers, consultants and academics.

This is one of a series of books under the title People and Organisations. The series provides essential guidance and points of reference for all those involved with people in organisations. It aims to provide the main body of knowledge and pointers to the required level of skills for personnel and development practitioners operating at a professional level in all types and sizes of organisation.

The series has been specially written to satisfy the professional standards defined by the Chartered Institute of Personnel and Development (CIPD) in the UK and the Republic of Ireland. It includes a volume designed for those seeking the Certificate in Personnel Practice (CPP), which often provides an access route into the professional scheme. The series also responds to a special need in the UK for texts structured to cover the knowledge aspects of new and revised National and Scottish Vocational Qualifications (N/SVQs) in personnel and training development.

Three 'fields' of standards have to be satisfied in order to gain graduate membership of the CIPD: (i) core management (ii) core personnel and development and (iii) any four from a range of more than 20 generalist and specialist electives. The three fields can be tackled in any order or, indeed, all at the same time. A range of learning routes is available: full- or part-time educational courses, flexible learning methods or direct experience. The standards may be assessed by educational and competence-based methods. The books in the series are suitable for supporting all methods of learning.

The series starts by addressing core personnel and development and four generalist electives: employee reward, employee resourcing, employee relations and employee development. Together, these cover the personnel and development knowledge requirements for graduateship of the CIPD. These also cover the knowledge aspects of training and development and personnel N/SVQs at Level 4.

Core Personnel and Development, by chief examiner Professor Mick Marchington and his colleague Adrian Wilkinson, addresses the essential knowledge and understanding required of all personnel and development professionals, whether generalists or specialists. Practitioners need to be aware of the wide range of circumstances in which personnel and development processes take place and consequently the degree to which particular approaches and practices may be appropriate in specific circumstances. In addressing these matters the book covers the core personnel and development standards of the CIPD, as well as providing an essential grounding for human resource management options within business and management studies degrees. The authors are both extremely well-known researchers in the field, working at one of the UK's leading management schools.

Employee Reward, by chief examiner Michael Armstrong, has been written specially to provide extensive subject coverage for practitioners required both by the CIPD's new generalist standards for employee reward and by the personnel N/SVQ Level 4 unit covering employee reward. It is the first book on employee reward to be produced specifically for the purposes of aiding practitioners to gain accredited UK qualifications.

Employee Relations, by chief examiner Professor John Gennard and associate examiner Graham Judge, explores the link between the corporate environment and the interests of buyers and sellers of labour. It also demonstrates how employers (whether or not they recognise unions) can handle the core issues of bargaining, group problem-solving, redundancy, participation, discipline and grievances, and examines how to evaluate the latest management trends.

Employee Development, by chief examiner Rosemary Harrison, is a major new text which extends the scope of her immensely popular earlier book of the same name to establish the role of human resource development (HRD) and its direction into the next century. After reviewing the historical roots of HRD, she considers its links with business imperatives, its national and international context, the management of the HRD function, and ways of aligning HRD with the organisation's performance management system. Finally, she provides a framework that sets HRD in the context of organisational learning, the key capabilities of an enterprise and the generation of the new knowledge it needs.

Employee Resourcing, by Stephen Taylor, has also been designed specifically to address the CIPD and N/SVQ standards in the area. The author draws upon his wide academic and personnel background to produce a book that examines practical issues but takes into account material from an extensive literature review. He presents readers with a series of options, encouraging them to consider those that are most appropriate in the specific circumstances of their own workplace. This results in a book that is both very readable and extremely comprehensive in its coverage.

Although each of these books is carefully tailored to the CIPD and N/SVQ standards, Malcolm Martin and Tricia Jackson's *Personnel Practice*, now in its second edition, is focused on the needs of those studying for the Certificate in Personnel Practice. This also gives a thorough grounding in the basics of personnel activities. The authors are experienced practitioners and lead tutors for one of the UK's main providers of CIPD flexible learning programmes.

In drawing upon a team of distinguished and experienced writers and practitioners, the People and Organisations series aims to provide a range of up-to-date, practical texts indispensable to those pursuing CIPD and N/SVQ qualifications in personnel and development. The books will also prove valuable to those who are taking other human resource management and employment relations courses, or who are simply seeking greater understanding in their work.

Mick Marchington

Mike Oram

Preface to the Second Edition

The first edition of this book reached a strong market of experienced practitioners. It is also a core text for students on CIPD and many other academic programmes with an emphasis on human resource development (HRD). Figure 1 suggests routes through the book for these different sets of readers.

The first reference point for CIPD students should be, of course, the Institute's Professional Standards in Employee Development. These are reproduced in Appendix 1. All the CIPD's Professional Standards are currently (mid-2000) under review and many themes in this book reflect issues being raised during that consultative process.

CHANGES IN CONTENT

Those who are coming new to responsibilities for developing people as part, or all, of their role need a broad-based understanding of the contribution that they will be expected to make to the organisation. They also need mastery of a sufficient body of operational expertise to enable them to practise competently in a variety of organisational settings.

This second edition has been expanded to incorporate more material to help such readers. More self-checks are included throughout, and all chapters (except those in Part 5) conclude with a review of the chapter's learning objectives through a set of short questions. Most are taken from past professional qualifying examination papers set by the CIPD. Guidelines related to these questions can be found in the Chief Examiner's Report on the examinations in question, published by the CIPD. The questions should be useful for all readers, not just for CIPD students, because they represent the type of on-the-spot queries about developmental issues that human resource professionals constantly have to face.

Those who are established in their HRD roles need to keep up to date on emerging trends and issues, and to be knowledgeable about good practice and about ways of ensuring 'added value' in their operations. This second edition contains a complete updating of the chapters on HRD's wider context and on current practice in the field, as well as those on national vocational education and training policy and systems. There is a special focus on HRD as a value-adding process (Chapter 6), and a new model of HRD in the business has been produced to aid the

Figure 1 Route maps for readers

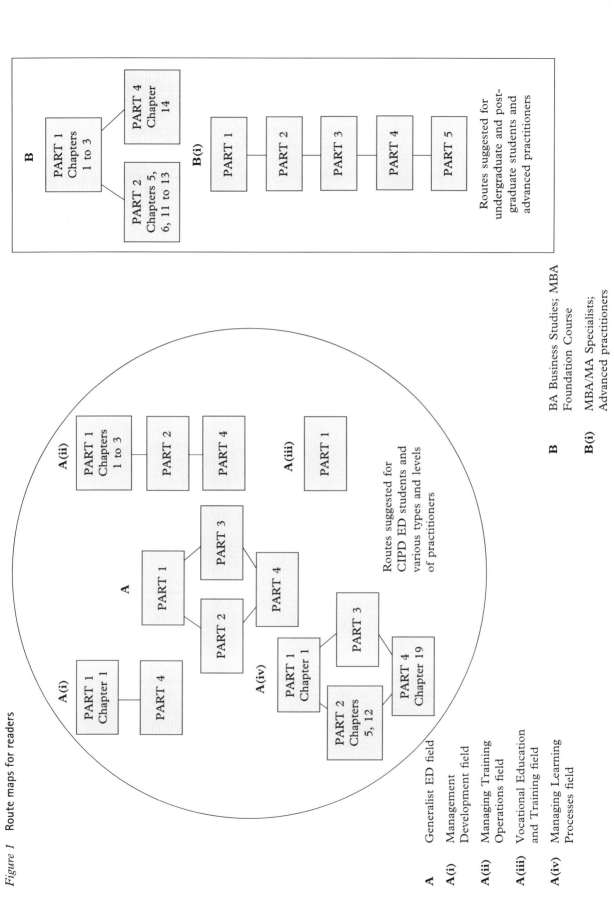

A	Generalist ED field
A(i)	Management Development field
A(ii)	Managing Training Operations field
A(iii)	Vocational Education and Training field
A(iv)	Managing Learning Processes field

| B | BA Business Studies; MBA Foundation Course |
| B(i) | MBA/MA Specialists; Advanced practitioners |

setting, achieving and auditing of HRD that will help to drive the organisation forward (Chapters 6, 7 and 14). A new chapter (12) looks at some of the major developments in electronically based learning, because this will be a primary learning mode for the foreseeable future. Part 5 – intended for senior practitioners and those studying for master's-level qualifications – is now more clearly distinguished from the rest of the book and its two chapters, one of them new, give themes of knowledge development and strategic progress a fully integrated treatment.

CORE HRD TASKS

Although the core tasks of those in full- or part-time HRD roles may not change greatly over time, their prioritisation, focus and complexity does. This second edition places emphasis on the need for those who hold HRD responsibilities to:

- act as business partners in the organisation, and also as citizens of a wider professional community. This need to give due weight to both business and professional roles, to be able to identify any resultant tensions, and to know how to act when such tensions arise reflects many concerns in the field. It is recognised in the conceptual framework now being proposed for all the CIPD's Professional Standards.

- produce outcomes that 'add value' for the organisation as well as for individuals. That term may grate for some, but it is inarguably the case that simply achieving effective and efficient operations is no longer enough. Developmental processes and initiatives must be perceived by organisational stakeholders to produce significant returns on investment by making a real difference where it matters most for the business.

- know how and when to harness new technology to learning, and be able to take a lead here. As is explained in Chapter 12, this is a field from which training practitioners continue to be accused of 'running away'. In an increasingly knowledge-based economy, with a government committed to using new technology to drive access to lifelong learning for all, those entrusted with learning and developmental responsibilities must grasp the challenges that new technology presents. And if they do not, their own future is bleak.

- both through the use of new technology and in other ways, contribute to the development and management of knowledge – another field in which, as yet, few personnel practitioners appear to be playing a significant role. Knowledge development has many implications for the HRD process and forms a central theme in Part 5 of the book.

KEEPING UP TO DATE

With a changing field like HRD, whose parameters are wide in scope, it is essential to keep up to date. At the end of each chapter, useful reading and other information sources are noted but readers should regard these as a starting- rather than a finishing-point. Academic human resource development and human resource management and strategy journals provide an essential reference point for intellectual debate, current research and the development of new theories and practice. Professional journals should always be used to check on emerging knowledge, events, surveys, reports and accounts of good practice. They are particularly accessible for students and for busy practitioners, and for that reason the CIPD's journal, *People Management*, is drawn on regularly throughout the book.

Rosemary Harrison

CIPD chief examiner: employee development

April 2000

Acknowledgements

All real-life material reported in the book relates only to situations current at the time. Unless otherwise indicated, comments on such information are my own, and do not represent any official views in or by the organisations concerned. I acknowledge with thanks the organisations that have allowed me to publish accounts of their business and human resource policies and practice – in particular, Cummins Engine Co. Ltd, Darlington, and Hydro Polymers, Newton Aycliffe.

I am grateful to Cambridge Strategy Publications for permission to reproduce in Chapters 6 and 14 material from *The Training and Development Audit*, R. Harrison, 1999. I am also grateful to Dr Alan Rutter, University of Northumbria, who gave me the financial insights that have continued to prove invaluable in Chapter 11; to the HRD consultant Nicki Fonda who first suggested to me the idea of linking HRD with the strategic capability of the firm; and to my colleague Professor Joseph Kessels, University of Twente, Utrecht, who inspired much of my research into organisational learning and strategic capability. I thank the Foundation for Corporate Education in the Netherlands and the University of Durham's HRD Research Centre for funding that enabled me to undertake research into HRD and strategic capability that underpins this book. My appreciation goes also to Anne Cordwent and Chris Jackson at CIPD Publications for their support of my work on this second edition.

Above all, I am indebted to my husband for his patient and good-humoured encouragement.

Part 1

SETTING THE SCENE: HRD IN CONTEXT

1 Developing people: meanings, origins and reality

LEARNING OBJECTIVES

After reading this chapter you will:

- understand what 'employee development' means
- be aware of how, historically, the development of people has become a key organisational process
- be aware of the main present-day trends, issues and tensions in human resource development (HRD)
- be aware of pitfalls involved in researching its practice.

DEVELOPING PEOPLE: WHAT DOES IT MEAN?

What is 'employee development'?

What is 'employee development'? In its organisational context, it is a process to help people acquire and maintain the competence and commitment that will:

- improve performance, quality, customer service and long-term organisational progress
- aid recruitment and retention, and stimulate and support continuous individual development
- help to enhance the skill and knowledge base of the organisation and of individuals.

Developing people is therefore a critical process whose most powerful contributions to the business are to do with productivity, performance, knowledge development and organisational progress. Its greatest benefits for individuals are to do with personal competence, growth, adaptability and continuous employability.

What are some key terms?

There are many terms that recur in the field of development of people. The following are chosen at this point simply because they tend to give particular problems to entrants to the field, whether students or practitioners:

Business	This is a term used loosely to describe any organisation, private or public sector, for-profit or not for-profit, voluntary or employing, that needs to make efficient and effective use of its resources in order to ensure adequate return on its assets, survive as an organisation, and make continuous progress towards achieving its long-term purpose. The term 'business goals' can refer to corporate or unit goals.
Development	This term is used to denote learning experiences of any kind, whereby individuals and groups acquire enhanced knowledge, skills, values or behaviour. Its outcomes unfold through time, rather than immediately, and they tend to be long-lasting.
Education	Education's primary purpose is to develop in an integrated way an individual's intellectual capability, conceptual and social understanding and work performance. It therefore means more than simply developing their technical expertise or task competence. Used in a narrower sense, 'education' can also mean a course, programme or learning event that (usually) involves a period of study organised by an educational institution.
Human Resource Development	Although this book is entitled 'Employee Development' in order to conform with CIPD Professional Standards terminology, I prefer through most of the text to use the term 'human resource development'. This is because I believe that it is a term that better suggests a process whose scope takes in everyone who works for an organisation, not just those who are its employees. More is said about this at the start of Chapter 5.
Learning	This term indicates any experience or event whose outcome (whether or not intended) develops or changes people's knowledge, skills, values or behaviour.
Training	This indicates planned instructional activities. Sometimes (the text will make clear when) it is used to indicate other developmental activities and processes also.

What is the ED context?

At national level, the changing economic backcloth and the increasing globalisation of businesses mean that by the year 2001 most of the national training policies, initiatives and institutions established in the late 1980s will have been scrapped. At government level there is now a strong emphasis on the need for everyone to achieve basic learning targets, and for all individuals to have equal access throughout life to opportunities for learning that will benefit themselves and the economy. There is greater integration of vocational education and training (VET) provision and of national employment policy, and the Government is constantly trying to find ways of ensuring that employers do more to close skills gaps that are holding back the economy. There is an increasing recognition of the fundamental role that planned learning at individual, organisational and national levels must play, if sustained economic growth and societal well-being are to be achieved.

In its efforts to stimulate that growth and well-being, national education and training policy is trying to come to grips with the human implications of the developing knowledge economy. By 2010, it is likely that around 30 per cent of job growth will be in knowledge-based jobs. However, many companies in Britain are still producing low-specification products that need only low-level skills. In such companies, training in those skills is often the only investment made to develop people. It is not enough. If Britain is to compete successfully in the kind of global-based knowledge economy typified by mergers early in 2000 between Time Warner and America OnLine, and between Vodafone and Mannesman, then there must be a more effective drive for the long-term education and training that will develop knowledge workers and the support staff who can provide the infrastructure that those workers need.

What is the practice?
There are many sources of information about the current state of practice, although all are based on different samples and different approaches to research. A useful starting point is the report commissioned by the IPD from Roehampton Institute, examining how trainers both within and working outside organisations saw their work (Darling, Darling and Elliott, 1999). The CIPD's annual training survey, carried out in conjunction with the Centre for Labour Market Studies at the University of Leicester and started in 1999, is another valuable data source, which is building up through time. The main trends tending to emerge from other surveys as well as these include what has become a 'commonplace' drive to link training to strategic business objectives, and 'a reduction in direct training, greater emphasis on facilitation and consultancy work, a shift towards a more strategic approach to training, and a growth in coaching and mentoring' (Cannell et al, 1999: 48). As will be seen in Chapter 12, one of the most rapidly developing trends is the harnessing of new technology to training and learning.

Looking at the developmental process within organisations, in some there is a clear trend to produce 'bundles' of well-integrated developmental and other human resource practices in order to drive the business forward. There is much discussion about this important issue, which will be explored further at a later point in this chapter.

Whatever the growth areas in HRD, disturbing failures in developmental provision across public and private sectors are regularly highlighted, with human resource practitioners frequently attracting blame for these. In 1999/2000 alone there were damaging reports on training in the prison service, the Metropolitan Police, the care sector, and in hotel, catering, rail and agriculture workforces. To take one example: the Health and Safety Commission's report on the 1997 Southall train crash in which seven died was highly critical of training procedures in rail companies across the country. The criticism related to failure to focus on key areas of skill and knowledge needed by drivers, to lack of consistency of practice between drivers, to absence of any centralised core training programme, and to lack of a unified training record system (Cooper, 2000). These are faults that typify criticisms more widely. They damage the profession and they damage the HRD process, reducing its credibility and its potential to achieve value for the organisation. As we shall see subsequently in this chapter, sometimes the criticisms are valid, but sometimes they mask a more complex reality.

Why is there concern for 'integration'?
The development of people should always be understood, and be treated in practice, as part of a wider human resource (HR) process in the organisation. It must be well integrated with that process in order to be effective – yet often it is not.

Also, if the wider HR process is not itself well integrated with business goals and policy, then developmental strategies and operations will continually be impeded. For many commentators, this is where the real problem lies. They see an ongoing failure of the HR function overall to 'prove its importance to the bottom line, and to gain recognition from chief executives' – a failure for which, again, practitioners are frequently blamed (Walsh, 1999). In part, the blame actually lies elsewhere, in excessively high expectations of HR at board level. In part, though, the failure is due to the perception that 'the HR function lacks enough business sense or experience' (Walsh, 1999, drawing on a series of reports published in 1999 by different bodies). Despite the fact that the great majority of organisations now have HR representation at board level – 72 per cent according to the Institute of Directors report in 1999 (*ibid*) – in too many of them HR policy is not linked to corporate goals. In areas critical to the business, such as staff turnover, succession planning, and preparation for roles of company directors, HR strategies are too often absent (*ibid*). The HR profession aspires to be at the leading edge of change, yet, for example, in the vital field of knowledge development and the management of knowledge workers, it does not appear to be taking a lead. Indeed, many practitioners demonstrate little interest or expertise (Scarbrough, Swan and Preston, 1999).

Why is 'business partnership' important?
This is a term used widely now in HR literature and practice. It has become a major theme in the Chartered Institute of Personnel and Development's current national consultative process to produce updated Professional Standards. Applied to those with responsibilities for the development of people, it is a way of emphasising that they

cannot achieve their tasks on their own. They must build and sustain partnerships with HR colleagues, with management, with unions, and with other stakeholders in development across the organisation, in order to achieve a shared perception of what HRD must achieve, and a willingness to work together to achieve it. Unions have an increasingly important role as partners in the HRD process, as the UK moves into an era of statutory union recognition. For example, the issue of employers being legally obliged to provide staff training (see Chapter 2) is one that can be expected to move rapidly up the union agenda.

How can development 'add value'?
One of the accusations most frequently levelled against HRD is that its operations are no more than sporadic reactions to crises, making no essential difference to the organisation, its products or services, or its people. In other words, that the development of people does not 'add value'.

To add immediate value – that is to say, to create by its initiatives and the outcomes it achieves more that is of value for the business than was there before, in ways that produce high returns for the cost of those initiatives and outcomes – the development of people must be business-led. To add value over the longer term, it must be strategic. Neither is easy, but both can be done, and we will look at ways of achieving a strategic and a business-led approach to HRD in Chapters 5 and 6. 'Fit' is critical here. If developmental initiatives are to bring real benefits for the organisation, they must convince as being relevant to business goals. It is not enough to espouse the importance of that link – as training practitioners now overwhelmingly do (Darling, Darling and Elliott, 1999; Stevens and Ashton, 1999). Practice must demonstrate that it exists – and on that there is less evidence, as will shortly be seen.

What does the role involve?
Whether the HRD practitioner is working wholly or only partly in that field, and whether they are a specialist or a line manager, internally or externally based, there is no single role that they are likely to take on, but a variety that vary widely according to context. For example, in a small or medium-sized organisation, even a newly qualified personnel professional may have to plan and organise the developmental process right across the business. They may have no specialist HR support to help or manage them in their work.

In larger organisations, such new professionals will usually (although not always) be less isolated, perhaps working alongside unit managers but being functionally accountable to a senior HR professional or manager. Like line managers with developmental responsibilities, they may have to plan and organise the provision of HRD in the workplace, and drive the HRD process there. Those more experienced and expert in the field will have to be equipped to advise on, organise and evaluate unit-wide or corporate HRD strategies and plans, to employ and oversee training providers, and generally to run – or help to run – an efficient, effective, 'value-adding' HRD function.

All those who hold HRD responsibilities – whether those practitioners are newly qualified HR professionals, or training and development specialists with many years of experience to their credit, or line managers for whom this is only one aspect of their role – by virtue of their responsibilities, are accountable to the organisations for which they work, to the people whose development they seek, and to the wider professional community to which they belong.

Generalised developmental responsibilities are identified in the CIPD's Professional ED Standards (Appendix 1). They involve tasks that must be pursued in an integrative manner, not as if they were discrete operations. They must also be pursued with a clear understanding of what is most appropriate and feasible, given the organisational context in which each professional has to operate.

What qualities are needed?
All who hold developmental responsibilities must:

- secure recognition and support for the development of people as a critical organisational process whose outcomes can increase the value of people as organisational assets

- aid the building of effective and enduring partnerships with stakeholders in the developmental process

- win credibility and support by bringing to the performance of their tasks at all times an expert and ethical approach – in other words, by being a professional

- raise awareness of any ethical issues and dilemmas arising from the facilitation of learning and development, and identify how these can be tackled

- constantly develop their own expertise and knowledge.

Developing people as a business process

Go back over the questions that have just been raised in this section. Identify any issues that you find difficult to understand, and use these as the basis for discussion with others (in your organisation and, if you are a student, with tutors and fellow students) in order to get a stronger initial grasp of what human resource development means and involves at the practical level.

Next, an exploration of development of people in a wider context. How did it start, as an organisational process? And what is its current state of play? First, some history.

HRD: A HISTORY OF NEBULOUS HARMONIES

It has to be admitted that, in no matter what capacity the professional works, the study and practice of HRD will never be easy or straightforward. Its history, meaning and organisational role are complex. Its organisational boundaries are unclear. The needs it serves are often contradictory. The demands made on the function by 'the business' can be unrealistic, and they are never amenable to black and white solutions. For many reasons, as this book will demonstrate, practitioners find sustained success hard to achieve. Yet for all that – and perhaps in part because of that – it is surely one of the most exciting of HR processes. I hope that some of that excitement comes through in this book, whether readers are new to the field or experienced travellers in HRD's bewildering but fascinating territory.

A sense of history is vital in seeking to understand the human condition. The same is true for the history of HRD's present role in organisations, and is also an aid to our reflection on the kind of future role it might fulfil. A historical perspective is a path to wisdom, enabling us to develop an informed view and to argue persuasively about the kind of contribution the development of people should make to the good of society, of the organisation and of the individual.

To start with a quotation, written at the end of World War I:

> The controlling purposes of education have not been sufficiently particularized. We have aimed at a vague culture, an ill-defined discipline, a nebulous harmonious development of the individual, an indefinite moral character-building, an unparticularized social efficiency, or, often enough, nothing more than escape from a life of work.
>
> (Bobbitt, 1918: 14)

The quotation was pointed out to me by Professor Joseph Kessels, a leading academic and consultant in the field of corporate education in the Netherlands. For him, it conjured up thoughts of the failure of organisations to take full advantage of the opportunities learning can offer. For me, it was the phrases 'nebulous harmonious development' and 'escape from a life of work' that caught the eye. The seventeenth-century alchemist Thomas Vaughan spoke of how 'the liberated soul ascends, looking at the sunset towards the west wind, and hearing secret harmonies'. But Bobbitt referred to 'nebulous' harmonies, and certainly the two concepts do seem far apart: the organisation tying human effort to the bottom line, current or envisaged; the individual seeking transformation through the realisation of human potential.

'Harmony' is the crucial word here. Since harmony is the product of the resolution of tensions, it should not surprise us that the history of HRD is one of a continuing search for a satisfactory balance between responding to the needs of the business and those of the individual. In the 1990s there were claims that the tensions were being resolved, but, as will be seen in this chapter, that is now in doubt.

Meanings

> Strategic human resource development is the identification of needed skills and active management of learning for the long-range future in relation to explicit corporate and business strategies.
>
> (Hall, 1984: 159)

Hall, a respected American writer, saw HRD as integral to an organisation's strategic progress, and this strategic element is core to HRD's meaning. In the USA, the term 'HRD' first came into common use in the 1970s, but its focus then was somewhat generalised. It was defined as

A series of organised activities conducted within a specified time and designed to produce behavioural change'.

(Nadler, 1970: 3)

By the early 1990s, a more strategic orientation was evident, with claims that 'HRD people have been charged to blueprint and lead the way to organisation and individual renewal' (Burack, 1991: 88). By this time, the HRD field had developed in the USA into a recognisable profession.

In the UK, HRD's organisational status and meaning have always been less clear. In a survey commissioned in 1998 by the Institute of Personnel and Development, training and development practitioners were reported as being:

affected by the confusion of meanings and boundaries between such terms as human resource management, human resource development, training, learning and development.

(Darling, Darling and Elliott, 1999: xii)

To some extent, the choice of any descriptive term is arbitrary, given the variety of meanings attached to the developmental process. In a paper introducing 18 definitions and theories of HRD from the USA alone, an American researcher commented, perhaps wearily, that 'HRD is a vast area of practice and knowledge' (Weinberger, 1998: 75). One of the leading HRD scholars in the USA pronounced in 1992 that 'there is still no universally accepted definition' (Nadler, 1992: 104). Many attribute this to HRD's interdisciplinary nature, but the causes go deeper, and it is at this point that a brief review of the history of organisational HRD is relevant.

Early origins and foundation years
For those who see the HRD process as being synonymous with 'training', HRD's historical starting point is clear. During World War II, training as a field developed a business profile in both the USA and the UK, and in the UK training officers came into being as a distinct category of staff (Niven, 1967: 95). G.R. Moxon (1943) extended parameters by linking education with training to form one of the 'six categories' of personnel management work in the UK. By 1996 the professional field had officially broadened to incorporate HRD at levels 4 and 5 of the newly produced national occupational standards in training and development.

However, the development of people who work in and for an organisation encompasses far more than merely 'training', and others view the period of the 1950s and 1960s as the true historical starting point of HRD (Stead and Lee, 1996: 48–9). Throughout that time in the USA the developmental process was being popularised by the work of such organisational psychologists as Argyris (1957), McGregor (1960), Likert (1961) and Hertzberg (1966). In the UK, meanwhile, research of a different kind was being undertaken at the Tavistock Institute of Human Relations. The focus was on organisations as socio-technical systems, the interaction of whose human and technical elements determined the overall behaviour and effectiveness of the organisation (see, for example, Trist and

Bamforth, 1951). This view of organisations as open systems added another dimension to the development of HRD practice, because it drew attention to the centrality of learning as a process to ensure an organisation's survival in its environment. Subsequent work on 'learning organisations' was influenced as much by this groundbreaking research (Reid and Barrington, 1997: 408, 409) as by the work of American psychologists in the same period.

The work of those psychologists did, nonetheless, have a powerful impact on subsequent transformational theories of many HRD apostles of the 'learning organisation' (Senge, 1990; Pedler, Burgoyne and Boydell, 1991; Nonaka, 1991, 1994). Yet influential although it undoubtedly became in that way, the research carried out in the USA in the middle years of the twentieth century was itself essentially a continuation of much earlier work that had been done by social scientists and managers like Mayo (1933) and Taylor (1947). That work was imbued with the imperative of managerial efficiency (Butler, 1986: 119), being posited on rational, systematic forms of management and organisation that would lead to mutuality of interest between management and worker. It is in this early work that the true origins of organisational HRD are to be found, and in locating them here, we can glimpse already those inherent tensions in purpose and values that became more apparent subsequently.

The business imperative
As the HRD field developed, the underlying managerial imperative became steadily stronger. This can be seen in the ways in which HRD research and theory in the middle decades of the twentieth century came to underpin the contingency-based models of strategy that emerged in the 1970s and 1980s. Those models sought to couple human resource strategy with business strategy in order to achieve competitive advantage.

Tight-coupled 'hard' HR models came predominantly from the Michigan School. They were heavily influenced by the work of strategic management writers such as Galbraith and Nathanson (1978) and of HR specialists such as Fombrun, Tichy and Devanna (1984). The models relied on a close interconnection between business strategies, organisational structure and HR processes of selection, appraisal, rewards and development. The approach was rational and deterministic, with an emphasis on social engineering. Its roots lay in social systems theory. It has been dismissed by Mabey and Salaman (1995: 46) as 'a fantastically idealized picture: in reality achieving it is extremely rare'. The difficulty lies in the dependency on clear and detailed business strategy which, in real life, is often lacking; or that may be different in its reality from what is espoused; or that may be of poor quality; or that, if inappropriate, may by its very existence be counter-productive for the organisation.

A 'soft' HR approach was typified by the Harvard School's 'mutuality' model. That model preserved a close relationship between business strategy and HR strategy, but the aim was to install certain fixed HR elements, and to achieve certain universal goals, regardless of the particular organisational context. The desired outcome of this 'high-commitment' developmental approach was to produce resourceful humans rather than having to adopt an overtly controlling approach to the management of human resources. However, the model's elements involved did not in practice sit comfortably with one another, and the unitary frame of reference was riddled with internal contradictions (Guest, 1990; Harrison, 1993: 58–63). The model was rooted in the work of the earlier American organisational psychologists, and was flawed by the same uneasy mix of scientific management and a genuine idealism about the 'perfectability-of-man' in the workplace (Butler, 1986: 119).

By the 1970s in the USA the business imperative had become the strongest force behind HRD theorising. By then, human capital theory (Schultz, 1961) was widely known, largely due to the writings of the economist, Becker (1975). For Becker, people were organisational assets whose economic value derived from their skills, competence, knowledge and experience. Investment in training and education led to increased productivity, and thence to increased wages and business earnings. HRD was, therefore, a value-adding process. Becker stressed the beneficial outcomes for individuals, and the value of education in helping to create a more numerate, literate and informed society. For him, education and training offered performance improvement and social transformation at one and the same time. The possibility of tensions arising from such a duality of purpose appeared to escape notice.

The emphasis on performance improvement has continued to dominate HRD practice in the USA. Business management there has been fundamentally influenced by the business education process and (as has just been noted) two of the most distinctive themes in American business schools – systems thinking and the 'science' of business strategy – emphasise the role of human resource management (HRM) and its functional areas as supporting business strategy and performance targets. An emphasis on performance is also understandable in an economy where the cult of short-termism in business strategy has led to a pervasive philosophy emphasising bottom-line pay-off. Nor does such an emphasis invariably override individual interest: the acquisition of skill can be a strong personal motivator in a thriving domestic economy with a deregulated labour market, a highly mobile labour force and a high rate of job creation, where unemployment is lower than in most competitor countries.

None the less, to those anxious to preserve the individual orientation in HRD activity, the need for a carefully balanced approach here was obvious. The Academy of Human Resource Development was established in the early 1990s by a group of HRD academics who were concerned at what they perceived to be the narrowness of focus, commercial thrust and restricted research base of the influential American Society of Training and Development – itself a distinct body from the Association of Human Resource Managers in the US. Since then, the Academy's membership has grown apace, and it has strong partnership ties with the more recently established University Forum for HRD in the UK, whose network of over 25 member institutions conducts research and provides postgraduate master's-level HRD programmes.

In the UK, HRD's historical development has been more *ad hoc* and fragmented than in the USA, but here too a more performance-driven approach for HRD had begun to gain ground during the 1980s, notably in larger organisations. A sustained period of recession had been accompanied by a collapse in manufacturing. That collapse hit older industries particularly hard and led to large-scale unemployment for almost five years. There was a slow rate of industrial modernisation, and the abolition of most of the Industrial Training Boards in the early 1980s was followed by a rapid decline in the country's skill base as apprenticeship numbers were slashed. The interrelated outcomes of these crises, especially in multidivisional organisations with their emphasis on rationalisation and focus, all highlighted the need for performance improvement and skills development. At the same time, much publicity was being given to training strategies being practised in competitor countries to increase the asset value of the human resource (for example, Institute of Manpower Studies, 1984; Coopers and Lybrand Associates, 1985; the 'Handy' Report, 1987). In most other European countries, HRD was taken far more for granted than in the UK as an important business process, due in large part to national vocational education and training policies that, in turn, emerged from very different economic, educational and societal infrastructures.

Finding a strategic role
By the late 1980s, the interest among many business strategy academics was turning to the unique capabilities of an organisation as sources of its competitive advantage, critical in explaining variations in its performance in its environment. This managerial view of the firm was part of a growing preoccupation with the strategic management process (Teece, Pisano and Shuen, 1994). It led to a particular concern throughout the 1990s to clarify the role of HRM in the development of human capability and to thereby improve the contribution to be made by HR processes – including HRD – to the business.

In 1991 the American writers Noel, James and Dennehy saw HRD positioned to become 'a significant player in the strategic change process'. How?

> HRD professionals must work with top management, focusing on the organization's strategic initiatives and seeking ways to leverage the development of employees to achieve these objectives, in creative and impactful approaches.
>
> (Noel, James and Dennehy, 1991: 19)

The professional must identify the key strategic initiatives to which the organisation is committed and build developmental programmes around these. De-layering and downsizing, for example, may achieve a leaner organisation, but it will not be a more productive one unless managers have been trained and developed to understand the new organisational structure in which they will have to work, unless they can become effective managers of teams rather than of individuals, and unless they can 'delegate, eliminate unnecessary work and procedures, and create an environment of risk taking' (*ibid*: 17).

In the USA and the UK in the last two decades of the twentieth century, despite constant exhortations by consultants and academics that HRD should be more closely aligned with business strategy, such an alignment proved hard to discern on any significant scale (Keep, 1989: 117–19; Storey, 1992: 16; Rainbird, 1994: 87; Keep and Mayhew, 1994; Skinner and Mabey, 1995). At national policy level, though, some progress was being made as government attempted to break the old pattern of a 'stop-go' approach to VET. Strategic VET objectives were established, reforms in the vocational qualifications system were set in train, and an implementation framework was produced at national, sectoral and local levels (as will be detailed in Chapters 2 and 3). The business-focused Investors in People (1990) Standard was established and became one of the few national training initiatives to gain and sustain any notable support in the field. By the closing years of the century, research was beginning to yield indicators that human resource and training issues were moving centre stage in the constant search for competitive edge (Darling, Darling and Elliott, 1999: 5).

The value of a historical perspective

In what ways can understanding of HRD's history aid understanding of its present organisational situation? In an organisation with which you are familiar, how has HRD developed over the years, and what light does this development throw on its present status and focus?

HRD: PRESENT CONTEXT AND TRENDS

The national and global context: trends, policies and practice

Mirroring the USA situation, the UK's low-wage economy, consistently low inflation rate, deregulated labour force and relatively low level of unemployment are now widely praised. In countries hitherto noted for their long-term investment in development of people – notably Germany and Japan – short-termism is creeping in as economic structures crack in the face of global pressures, and as high-cost labour hits inward investment and company profits and forces fundamental reappraisal of organisations' employment policies. The large-scale adoption in the UK of the multidivisional pattern of organisation structure, and the tendency of corporate head offices to emphasise control rather than development, often further inhibit developmentally focused HR strategies (Sisson, 1994: 21). At the same time, management's power over employees has been boosted by a relaxation of employment legislation and – at least in multidivisional organisations – by a marked increase in organisational restructuring and harmonisation of terms, conditions and pay grades.

Such trends can encourage a controlling approach to HRM that reduces HRD to its most operational and short-term component – training to boost current performance and remedy immediate skill deficits. Indeed the true state of HRD remains somewhat unclear. In 1998 the National Skills Task Force in its first report highlighted, as had so many such reports before it, a 'major skills deficiency' (Whitehead, 1999). The UK continues to perform weakly in international comparisons in both training and educational attainment (Darling, Darling and Elliott, 1999: 7). Ministers continue to voice concerns. The old problems do not, after all, appear to have been resolved, but they are at least being confronted. At the time of writing (early in 2000), the Government's review of the UK's national training policies, initiatives and institutions has led to their overhaul and to a new implementation framework to achieve goals of 'lifelong learning' for all (see Chapter 3).

The organisational context: fit, focus and integration
At organisational level, concerns are more with the here and now of HRD activity in the workplace. Disturbingly at that level there continue to be regular criticisms of training provision. These relate particularly to weaknesses in training planning and design, in national vocational qualification (NVQ) workplace assessment, in the use of new technology, and in the business relevance and strategic impact of HRD initiatives. Contextual factors can be significant here. Making initiatives more business-focused is difficult in those organisations where business strategy itself is unclear or absent. Adding value is likewise problematic where HRD policy is not supported by relevant HR practice in the workplace, or when HRD is a stand-alone function. Trends to decentralise, de-layer and downsize sit uneasily with commitments to 'invest in our people' and 'empower the workforce'. The downside of the 'flexible firm' – cheap, vulnerable and easily manipulated workers – puts a question mark against the kind of role that HRD is really playing in organisations. Yet when all such barriers to the credibility and effectiveness of HRD have been acknowledged, it is still too often the case that HRD practice is singled out for criticism. After all, the task of HRD practitioners is not only to execute HRD operations in the workplace. It is also to identify and advise on barriers to the promotion of relevant HRD strategies, and to help determine how best to tackle them. In this, they must have an awareness of the need for focus, integration and consistency in what they do and in what they recommend should be done. It is in these more holistic aspects of the HRD role that practitioners are often found wanting.

Focus and fit are critical if HRD is to help organisations to successfully compete on quality as well as on costs, respond convincingly to ever more knowledgeable and demanding clients – especially in the expanding service sector – and retain the people that constitute its future human capability. HRD strategies, like those for other HR processes, must also be sensitive to the increasingly wide range of employment contracts in organisations. They must cater for diversity in all its forms, so that HRD policy and practice is fair, accessible and relevant to all individuals as well as meeting the needs of the business.

There are now a number of indications that organisations are more aware of the importance to the business of good HR practices, and of the need to find those that fit well with organisational context and are well integrated to make a powerful impact on employee behaviour and performance. This push for focus, fit and integration emerges as critical to business performance in a number of recent research studies carried out in the UK and USA:

- Open University report into management training and development, 1997

- IPD's Performance Management Survey, 1998

- Workplace Employee Relations Survey, 1998

- Reports on 'bundling' of HR practices.

Open University report into management training and development, 1997

Management development (MD) has the potential to improve the performance of an organisation and its strategic progress. Until recently in the UK there was little to suggest that this potential was being widely realised (Sisson and Storey, 1988). However, in 1997 the Open University published its third report since 1987 into development and training of managers in the UK (Storey, Edwards and Sisson, 1997). It provided 'the largest and most representative picture of management development in the 1990s, covering management education, structured training and also more informal processes such as mentoring and self-development' (Storey, Mabey and Thomson, 1997: 28). The researchers found that management training and development had increased substantially, not only in formal but also in informal modes. Alongside this, there was a clear move away from rigid, proceduralised MD systems to more flexible, tailored approaches that fitted the needs of the business at the time. The strongest triggers for training and development were found to be internal, not external, factors, particularly corporate strategy and support from the board. Without such a favourable context in these respects, developmental initiatives faced often insurmountable barriers.

IPD's Performance Management Survey, 1998

Other indications of the success of focused and integrative approaches, this time to performance management and development, emerged from an IPD survey, reported by Armstrong and Baron (1998). The database was admitted to have limitations, but that is common in such studies. The real significance lay, as it did in the OU survey, in comparisons with past, similarly based surveys. The reported emphasis had switched markedly from rigid, formal systems and procedures to more processual approaches, to a concern to find what was fit for purpose, and to a more developmental focus for performance management.

Workplace Employee Relations Survey, 1998

Information indicating a more business-focused and integrative developmental approach in relation to employees generally was found in the fourth Workplace Employee Relations Survey (WERS), the biggest of its kind in the world and the fourth in a series that began in 1980. Mark Cully, principal research officer at the Department of Trade and Industry, pointed out that many of the 16 practices identified in the survey went back to the 1930s, and that data on them were difficult to interpret because of wide variations across organisations (Cully, 1998). Others have many reservations to make about the WERS research approach, particularly because the surveys cover very diverse workplaces where employee relations issues differ radically (Schonfield, 1999). However, what is of real value is the comparisons that can be made with the similarly based 1990 and 1998 surveys.

In that respect, commenting on the attention devoted over the past decade to 'high-performance, high-commitment or high-involvement work practices', what the researchers found to be new was the operation of these practices in conjunction with strategies for employee involvement, and the regularity and consistency with which over half the workplaces surveyed were operating a significant number of the practices. In those 'definite groups of practices', HRD approaches figured prominently. Training, team-working, supervisors trained in employee relations matters and problem-solving groups were together associated in what the researchers perceived to be 'a model of direct employee participation in decision-making' (Cully, 1998).

Others have disputed the strength of the practices across organisations. However, there are parallels between the WERS report and IPD research findings discussed in the next section. Comparisons can also be usefully made with practice elsewhere. For example, in Japan, one of the features found in the 1980s to explain the relative effectiveness of business strategies within organisations was the degree of integration and coherence between training and development, manpower planning and deployment systems (Storey, 1991). In the UK, a study by the Universities of Lancaster and of Wales (Fox, Tanton and McLeay, 1992) showed the value to be gained from an HRD infrastructure in the business that interacts positively with other HRM policies and processes as well as with overall business strategy; it was this interaction that, in the study, enabled HRD to make its fullest contribution to the long-term financial performance of the business.

Reports on 'bundling' of HR practices

There is a considerable body of research now to show the importance of integrating HRD with HR practice more widely in order to provide 'bundles' of practice that aid organisational performance.

A 10-year longitudinal study of over 100 UK manufacturing companies, carried out by researchers at the London School of Economics and the University of Sheffield, aimed to find factors that principally influence company effectiveness as expressed in financial performance. In a 1997 report on the research (Patterson et al, 1997), clusters of HRM practices were seen to account for 18 per cent of variations between companies in productivity and 19 per cent of variations in profitability. The researchers found this to be 'the most convincing demonstration ... in the research literature of the link between the management of people and the performance of companies'. Compared with the other four domains significant in productivity variation (R&D, technology, quality and strategy), the clusters of HR practices were the most powerful in predicting changes.

Relevant to discussion here, the most important point to emerge from this research was the need for relevance and integration – the choice and interrelationship of HRM practices – in order to ensure impact. The most significant groups of practice were developmental and included:

- acquisition and development of skills (where the integration of selection, induction, training and appraisal practices made the impact)

- job design (where practices to do with skill flexibility, job responsibility, job variety and use of formal teams made the impact) (Patterson et al, 1997: 15).

In the USA, Mark Huselid's substantial longitudinal research (Huselid, 1995; Guest, 1998) and research carried out by MacDuffie (1995) point in the same direction. Huselid claimed that it is the choice from a range, albeit limited, of possible 'bundles' of HR practices that can boost business performance (expressed primarily as company market value) and so give competitive advantage. He stressed the need to be 'idiosyncratic' when making that choice. In each situation choice should be determined by the bundle of practices that is the most feasible for the business and the hardest for competitors to copy. Patience is needed to find practices that fit well together, each reinforcing the other and often having to be introduced pragmatically through time until, through trial and error, the 'bundle' that best suits the purpose and circumstances emerges.

As Guest observed (1998), questions remain about what to include in the different types of 'bundle', how long any choice will remain valid for purposes of competitive advantage, and how and why the bundles have their impact. Nonetheless, this 'bundling' approach seems to approximate to a considerable area of HR, and HRD, practice now being reported in the UK. In the initial results of Guest's research programme in this area (MacLachlan, 1999), using a database that included 1,278 organisations drawn from the WER Survey, he claimed to have found a clear association between a bundle of 17 HR practices and financial success, with financial performance increasing most when 12 or more of these practices were used.

Evidence gathered during the IPD's 1999 training and development survey reinforced such findings, both in positive and negative ways. On the positive side, it showed a move towards informal and continuous learning among UK companies, and away from more-formalised developmental approaches often seen to be less fit for purpose, and it indicated the spreading use of a bundling approach, with four high-performance skills bundles predominating. On the negative side, the most frequently used bundles were those to do with working more intensely at the individual level – 'working harder but not smarter' (Stevens and Ashton, 1999: 31). Only 1 per cent of organisations in the survey practised all four skill bundles, while only 28 per cent used two or more sets of skills (*ibid*). Where the approach was to do mainly with improving individual skills rather than 'group-based, quality-based or broader types of skills', the organisations 'were less likely to link the reasons for this development to business objectives and finance' (*ibid*).

In all of these research findings, what is important is the actual – rather than the claimed – focus, fit and integration of practices in developing and reinforcing unique and productive patterns of work behaviour. Performance will be enhanced 'by systems of practices that support each other and that have a mutually reinforcing effect on employee contributions to company performance' (Patterson *et al*, 1997: 15). The causal routes from HR practices to performance appear to be:

- increases to employee skills and abilities

- promotion of positive attitudes and increases in motivation

- expansion of employees' responsibilities so that they can fully utilise their skills and abilities (*ibid*: 13).

The conclusion suggested by all of these findings is that if HRD is to yield value for the business, then it must support, and be supported by, other HR policies and practices that in their turn are well aligned with the organisation's strategic goals rather than just with individual or team performance targets. It must aim for integration of learning and working in ways that produce more flexible organisations, rather than just more hard-working individuals and teams.

Researching HR practice in organisations

Find out more about the studies reported in this section by getting information about their authors' account of their research samples and methodology. How do the studies compare in these respects, and, reflecting on your conclusions, on which reports would you now place most reliance?

Strategic tasks

Three strategic tasks have been proposed for the training function:

- to identify and implement training programmes that explicitly support strategic plans, thereby establishing a competitive advantage rooted in employee competence

- to provide training that equips important managers to plan strategically, to think strategically and to understand key strategic issues

- to become involved in the formulation of strategic plans, either directly through personal participation or indirectly through senior management (Catalanello and Redding, 1989: 51).

Applying this reasoning to HRD more widely, there should be HRD strategies and initiatives that not only support current business policy but also inform and support longer-term strategic goals. There is a linkage to be made here between HRD and what can be described as 'strategic capability'. This will be discussed in detail in the final part of this book but can be described in outline as follows:

> Strategic capability provides the vision, the rich and sustained learning and knowledge development, the integrity of purpose and the continuous direction and scope to the activities of the organisation that are needed to secure long-term survival. It is based on a profound understanding of the competitive environment, of the resource base, capacity and potential of the organisation, of the strategy process, and of the values that engender commitment from stakeholders to corporate goals.

The importance of learning is clear in this definition. In the USA, Nadler (1980) interpreted HRD as the entire range of educational, training and development facilities available in an organisation that enhance the learning processes essential to an organisation's capacity to change. The idea of regarding HRD as a set of processes that can stimulate the acquisition of new organisational knowledge is of particular value when related to the concept of the 'learning organisation' promoted by writers in many different countries over more than 20 years (for example, Argyris and Schon in the USA (1978; 1996), Swieringa and Wierdsma in the Netherlands (1992), Senge in the USA (1990), Nonaka in Japan (1991) and Pedler, Burgoyne and Boydell in the UK (1991)). Although, as will be seen in the final chapter, the 'learning organisation' never seems to have materialised on any wide scale in practice, the concept has never the less been an important stimulus to planned learning and development initiatives in many organisations. There is a strategic role for the HRD function here, in finding practical ways of implementing the ideal into durable workplace reality. The aim should be to promote learning strategies that generate organisationally valuable knowledge and capabilities, together with valued benefits for individuals. Operating on the basis of mutuality of interest, learning and developmental opportunities should be provided at work that aid the business and can enable individuals to explore their attitudes towards career and personal life and to acquire a portfolio of experiences that will promote their personal goals. It is in this sense that Hall (1986: 252) saw development as helping the individual to become 'truly one's own person – self-directed, self-aware'.

Developing for employability
One of the most important outcomes of HRD for the individual can be employability security. The business case for this can be summarised as follows:

- Employers increasingly need a workforce that can deliver 'higher productivity, work more efficiently, give reliable and customer-oriented service, be innovative and accept the need for continuous personal development and improvement' (Taylor, 1994, reporting points made by Robbie Gilbert, the CBI's employee affairs director, to a conference at Warwick University School of Industrial and Business Studies).

- Obtaining long-term commitment of employees in the current climate of employment insecurity is bound to be difficult.

- Trust must be developed, so companies will have to be more candid about explaining to employees the demands facing them in their joint need to secure business growth.

- 'In future a measure of the good employer is not necessarily one who pays the highest rate but who keeps workers' skills, and hence their employability, up to date' (*ibid*).

Through a greater focus on employability security, it may be possible to resolve HRD's historical tensions. It has already been noted that there is no inevitable conflict between the achievement of business goals and meeting social ends, although the tensions inherent in such an attempt need to be openly acknowledged. For example, a number of organisations work with employees and their representatives to develop positive policies around disengagement. Such policies can cover mentoring, coaching, personal development and career planning, achievement of national occupational qualifications, pre-redundancy and pre-retirement planning, strategic partnerships with outplacement consultants, and redeployment and retraining initiatives. Such activities can be integrated to produce a strategy for building up and retaining valuable skills and experience for the organisation, while also giving support to individuals at critical transition points in their working lives.

Practices to improve employability

In your own organisation, how far – if at all – is 'employability security' offered through HRD initiatives? What kind of practices are proving most valuable here?

At the heart of such policies there lies a drive for skills flexibility. This drive is crucial to the success of employment policy in a competitive global market, on both economic and social grounds. In a 1996 report, the Paris-based Organisation for Economic Co-operation and Development (OECD) praised Britain for being one of the few countries that, through its labour market flexibility, had successfully tackled the problem of high unemployment (Segall, 1996). The report noted that unemployment in Europe averaged 11.5 per cent, compared with less than 8 per cent in Britain, and the widening of earnings differentials characteristic of Britain was in this context seen as a positive factor, enticing workers into jobs and encouraging them to upgrade skills. On the other hand, Europeans had little incentive, once unemployed, to seek new work because of the high level of job protection legislation and benefits provided by the state, and the 'excessive' minimum wages and administrative extension of wage agreements.

In the USA, despite its much more dynamic rate of job creation than other Group of Seven leading industrial nations, income disparities between the better-trained and educated and the less well-trained had widened dramatically by the mid-1990s (Graham, 1994). It was the skilled who got the good jobs, the unskilled who remained the economy's underclass. For all governments, working to increase the employability security of those in and out of work continues to be of critical importance, because of the need to directly influence a situation where 'whole segments of the population have been virtually shut out of the job market' (*ibid*: 4).

RESEARCHING HRD

Finding the evidence

What, then, of those nebulous harmonies with which this chapter began? A glance at history has shown us that, through time, some have become less nebulous. We can see signs of a greater awareness of the kind of relationship between the learning of individuals on the one hand, and the performance of the economy and of the particular organisation on the other. This can prove fruitful for all the parties. The crucial question at this point, however, is this: have the main tensions inherent in HRD as an organisational process been resolved? Has real progress been made?

Sceptics remain. Bratton and Gold (1994) believed that the machine model of organisation still dominates western industrial society, leaving little place for the consideration of attitudes, feelings and personal development. They claimed that, in many organisations, learning and training are subservient to accounting procedures that call for tangible outcomes for investment – usually short term. Similar conclusions were arrived at by Ewart Keep (1999: 35), deputy director of the Research Centre on Skills, Knowledge and Organisational Performance, established by the Economic and Social Research Council in 1998 at the University of Oxford. Commenting on the Department of Trade and Industry's white paper on competitiveness, Keep observed a need for less emphasis to be placed on strategies to increase skill supply, and for more concern for forms of 'job design and work organisation that maximise the contribution people can make to business performance'. He cited research that had just been published by the London School of Economics' Centre for Economic Performance, indicating that for many people jobs were 'impoverished, monotonous and deskilling'. Other research, including that done by the Institute for Employment Studies, has led to similar conclusions, showing how often, especially in relation to those employees in managerial and less-skilled jobs, 'companies do not make the best use of the skills that their employees already have. Supplying more skills may not change this' (*ibid*).

So, the tensions may remain. There is little point in merely boosting skills if the forms of work organisation in which many have to work do not allow them to use those skills to the full. Also, and more often than is immediately apparent, learning can be pursued by powerful parties as a means of social and work control. It is easy to mask such an aim by cloaking it in socially attractive and inclusive learning approaches – open learning, personal learning plans, teamwork, continuous development, empowerment and growth for all.

If such concerns and suspicions are justified – and we shall return to this issue in our final chapter – then we can expect to find that even where there is a formal commitment at the highest levels to becoming a 'learning organisation', as well as the structures and production systems to support that intention, the old tensions are still there under the surface. In that event, HRD may only by accident offer the individual any real escape from – or more accurately through – the life of work into some enriched personal existence.

There is something else to consider here:

> The appearance of what we do is different from the intention with which we do it, and the circumstances at the time may not be clear.
>
> (St Augustine's *Confessions*, Book 3:9)

In the HRM literature there is often little hard information about actual practices in real contexts. Too many case-studies 'tend to exaggerate the degree of change. They bestow upon it a coherence and neatness that distorts reality. Moreover, they rarely give details of the real difficulties encountered' (Storey, 1992: 17). Storey told of visits to companies heralded in the literature as having made radical innovations, 'only to discover that the "breakthrough" was viewed as a peripheral trial, was hardly recognizable to the participants on the ground, or had been abandoned altogether'. So the mundane appearance was very different from the exciting intent. He also found that the real circumstances at the time were not clear. In trying to establish the 'reality' of HRD in organisations, there are big issues of methodology to be resolved: what information sources to approach, and how to collect, analyse and interpret data so as to capture the intention, the appearance and the reality, accurately illuminating the circumstances prevailing at the time.

Escaping from or to the life of work?

I end this chapter with a quotation that takes us back to its start. Gilley and Eggland (1989: 354) concluded their book by observing that in HRD the trend is to move away from 'nice to know' subjects towards supporting business goals. Then they wrote: 'However, in response to changing values in the work force, these will be re-examined ... There is a need for HRD programs relating to employees' lives outside the work environment.' There is an increasingly diverse range of issues at the individual level with which HRD practice should be prepared to deal. Many of these issues are not strictly to do with the employer – yet they cannot be disregarded if the employer wishes to retain and develop the core workforce, since they affect people's drive and capacity to work. Gilley and Eggland cited the case of employees who want to know how to deal with complex situations involving high levels of personal stress and responsibility, and of possible HRD responses to meet those social needs. They observed that as demographic trends result in steadily ageing workforces, HRD initiatives may have to help valued employees to acquire coping skills to adjust to constantly changing home environments.

There are other social needs that are already coming within the scope of HRD in some organisations. In the last decade in the USA, there was only a small population available for entry-level jobs. In consequence a number of companies developed training programmes for the hardcore unemployed to remedy that recruitment deficiency (Goldstein and Goldstein, 1990). Low educational standards among young entrants to employment can require organisations to add basic skill and literacy training to their traditional range of job-related programmes. In a similar way, the development of analytical, problem-solving and team skills are frequently part of induction and basic skills programmes for new graduates whose university education, in the view of their employers, has not adequately equipped them with these basic work-related competences.

Such social issues, that have so direct an impact on people's life and performance at work, are becoming more, not less, pressing as HRD moves into the new millennium. They take us back full circle to where we started. It is growing ever more difficult to draw a clear line between life at work and life outside it – and that casts yet another perspective on Bobbitt's quotation, presenting a fresh challenge to those with a controlling influence over the learning and development of people in organisations.

CONCLUSION

Having read this chapter, you should now:

- understand what 'employee development' means

- be aware of how, historically, the development of people has become a key organisational process

- be aware of the main present-day trends, issues and tensions in human resource development

- be aware of pitfalls involved in researching its practice.

To test yourself against these objectives, what five-minute answers would you give to the following questions?

- What are the most powerful contributions that employee development can make to the business and to individuals?

- What 'bundles of HR practices' exist in your own organisation, or what kind of bundles would you recommend should be introduced?

- Explain two or three problems that, as a researcher, you would expect to face when seeking to establish the reality of HRD in an organisation.

USEFUL READING

PUGH D. S. (ed.) (1971) *Organization Theory: Selected readings*. Harmondsworth, Penguin.

VROOM V. H. *and* DECI E. L. (eds) (1970) *Management and Motivation: Selected readings*. Harmondsworth, Penguin.

WALTON J. (1999) *Strategic Human Resource Development*. Harlow, Financial Times and Prentice Hall.

2 The national training framework

LEARNING OBJECTIVES

After reading this chapter you will:

- understand the main trends in, and pressures upon, national training policy and strategy between 1989 and 1999 (see endnote relating to Scotland and Wales)

- be able to evaluate the effectiveness of implementation of policy during that period, and issues for the future that it raised

- be able to explain the value of vocational qualifications at national, organisational and individual levels.

THE VISION OF NATIONAL VOCATIONAL EDUCATION AND TRAINING

A vision of national vocational education and training (NVET) embedded in lifelong learning was set by the Conservative Government in 1991. The vision was – and remains – that:

> everyone has the opportunity and incentive to continue learning throughout life, and that the economy has the skills it needs to meet and beat the best in the world.
>
> (Employment Department Group, 1991: 28)

The Labour Government that came into power in 1997 shared that vision, defining lifelong learning in its 1998 Green Paper *The Learning Age* as the continuous development of the skills, knowledge and understanding that are essential for employability and fulfilment.

> Investment in human capital will be the foundation of success in the knowledge-based global economy of the 21st century. That is why the government has put learning at the heart of its ambition.
>
> (DfEE, 1998: 1)

If this quotation strikes a chord, it is the chord of human capital theory, popularised in the 1970s by Becker, and the inspiration of so much organisationally based human resource development theory and practice in the USA (see page 10). The parallels are clear in the 1998 Green Paper *Lifelong Learning* (DfEE, 1998a). It claimed that nothing could be more important than such learning for the future of the economy, for social cohesion and the development of individuals' potential. That paper stated Labour's determination to create a learning society, with participation in learning throughout life as the norm.

Because this vision of learning, whose purpose is both economic and social, is rooted in human capital theory, it is not surprising that it raises the same questions that were discussed in Chapter 1: can such duality of purpose be achieved? If so, how, and at what cost? These are questions that have dogged NVET policy and practice throughout the latter part of the twentieth century. They continue to do so. It is yet to be seen whether one government can succeed where others have failed, ending the confusion and the stop-go pattern of reactions that have characterised NVET activity for so long.

Between 1964 and 1981 there had been no evidence of any meaningful vision guiding national training policy (Harrison, 1992: 45–54). Movements into and away from a regulatory framework all coincided with fluctuations in wider economic and social problems and with changing governmental approaches to dealing with them. From 1981 onwards there was a clear attempt by government to provide a meaningful 'cradle to grave' vision for NVET together with a consistent long-term policy in relation to training for employment. To date (early 2000), the delivery of that policy has relied on the decentralised, voluntary and market-led system introduced in 1989. As the new Labour Government began a review of that system in 1997, many believed that it must be replaced. The belief appeared justified when, in 1998, a radically new system was announced (see p52).

To understand the reasons for that change and its implications for the future direction and delivery of NVET policy, it is necessary to look at two areas, which will be integrated at the end of Chapter 3. The first, covered in this chapter, is concerned with goals, policy and strategy for post-16 national training provision, including national vocational qualifications (NVQs), up to 1999. The second, covered in Chapter 3, is to do with national educational policy and practice, with developments in NVET strategy between 1997 and 1999, and with the new integrative framework for NVET proposed for implementation in 2001.

NATIONAL TRAINING POLICY: 1991 TO 1999

Aims
In 1991, as Table 1 (opposite) shows, seven aims were established for national vocational training policy. Let us look at some of the big issues that they raise.

What are the incentives for individuals?
There is far less to encourage individuals to invest in training than there is in many competitor countries, notably Germany, where increases in wages and career prospects are linked to training and qualifications and where young people are not distracted by high-pay temptations. However, since the early 1990s some important progress has been made by government to encourage both unemployed and employed individuals to participate in work-related learning.

Table 1 The seven aims of national training policy listed in the White Paper 'Education and Training for the 21st Century' (1991)

1 To ensure that high-quality further education or training becomes the norm for all 16- and 17-year-olds who can benefit from it.

2 To increase the all-round levels of attainment by young people.

3 To increase the proportion of young people acquiring higher levels of skill.

4 To ensure that people are more committed to develop their own skills throughout working life, and more willing to invest their own time, money and effort in doing so.

5 To help the long-term unemployed and those at other kinds of disadvantage to make their full contribution to the economy.

6 To ensure that trainers and teachers remain responsive to the needs of individuals and business, working closely with business and widening individual choice.

7 To encourage and increase employer commitment to training by having effective enterprise plans that complement work.

In 1992 tax concessions were introduced for those pursuing vocational training courses. By 1997 training credits were available for every 16- and 17-year-old leaving full-time education, enabling them to 'spend' up to £1,000 purchasing further vocational training or education of their choice. The pace accelerated under the Labour Government. The first one million individual learning accounts (ILAs) were available in 1999, and ILAs are now open to all. They offer holders 20 per cent discounts on certain courses and on spending of up to £5,600 a year. There are discounts of up to 80 per cent off the cost of key courses such as computer literacy, and firms can claim tax relief on their contributions to employees' ILAs. To concentrate money on those needing it most, the 1992 vocational training relief was to be abolished, with the higher rate of relief coming to an end in April 2000 (*People Management*, 1999).

A major step in establishing a legal framework of individual rights related to work-related education and training was taken quietly with the passing of the Teaching and Higher Education Act 1998. It established the right of working teenagers between the ages of 16 and 17 who have not attained a certain standard of education and training to paid time off in order to study for specified qualifications. In 1999, the right was incorporated into the Employment Rights Act 1996. In 2000, a substantial financial grant was established for students from the poorest homes, claimable on a weekly basis over two years. The range of allowable courses under the legislation is wide, and includes vocational as well as educational qualifications. The only criterion to satisfy is that they must enhance applicants' employment prospects (Aikin, 1999).

The practical effects of this law are uncertain. It may deter some employers from employing young people. Employers may also refuse to contribute to the cost of courses (since the law does not deal with costs), thereby making such provision meaningless for many. However, it marked a significant step in a new direction, attempting to tackle a problem stubbornly resistant to solution (Marchington and Wilkinson, 1996: 52–7).

In 1998 a much more well-publicised initiative, the 'welfare-to-work' programme 'New Deal' – administered through the DfEE's Employment Service – was introduced by the Labour Government. Its practical details, incorporating subsequent amendments, are easily summarised:

> Any unemployed person between 18 and 24 who has claimed jobseekers' allowance for six months, and anyone aged between 25 and 50 who has been unemployed for a year, automatically moves into the New Deal programme. For some disadvantaged groups such as disabled people, lone parents and ex-offenders, entry may come sooner. There is also a special financial incentive for the unemployed over 50 to join the scheme. Entry involves an initial assessment interview, followed by a short gateway period during which participants are helped to improve their employability. Those not employed by the end of that period then have options, each with its timescale of between six months to a year, and including subsidised work-based training, voluntary work and self-employment (also with training support). Further aid is given if participants remain unemployed at the end of their option, and there is financial aid to ease the transition when moving off benefits into work. Employers have an incentive (currently £75 per week) to take on New Dealers. The Employment Service provides personal advisers to help all those on the New Deal programme.

New Deal is claimed to be the first employment scheme to have actively promoted equality of opportunity and outcome for people of all ethnic and racial groups (Smith, 1999). That has been disputed, given the continuing inability of minority groups to achieve equality of treatment and opportunity in the employment market (Johnson, 1999: 56). On a wider front, there were early signs of employer disillusionment at low-quality New Deal recruits, lack of support from the Employment Service and too much red tape (Rana, 1999). More will be said about the programme below.

Despite such attempts by government to provide more incentives for individuals to invest in training, and support for them when doing so, problems remain. The older unemployed and ethnic minorities, whatever their qualifications, have particular difficulties in finding work. That is not likely to change quickly. Youth unemployment is highly sensitive to fluctuations in the national economy: regardless of young people's qualification levels, the trend rises sharply whenever overall unemployment rises. The wider question therefore remains: how far do any incentives for individuals make a significant difference to their motivation to acquire skills and qualifications when the latter are still not tied to a universal reward system?

What are the incentives for employers?
What indeed? Short-termism still dominates the financial base of most organisations and the structure of industry generally in the UK. This is understandable in relation to organisations employing less than around 250 people, for reasons outlined in Chapter 13. But what of the larger organisations, of which only 3,000 between them have been estimated to account for 37 per cent of jobs and 43 per cent of total turnover (Becket, 1996)? For them, the forces at play are more complex. Large-scale domination of businesses by the financial sector and accountancy profession continues to inhibit investment in

training. There is also increasingly aggressive intervention by shareholders in the boardroom (Waples, 1999) and this can have the same adverse effect.

There is a persistent overreliance by employers on market forces to provide their skill supply. In 1999 a report by the London Skills Forecasting Unit (set up by the London Training and Enterprise Councils) highlighted skills shortages in key areas of the city's economy. In the sectors where low-paid workers formed substantial elements of the workforce, training was inadequate despite skills shortages. This was particularly true in the manufacturing and the hotels and catering sectors, both vital to the national economy. In areas of acute skills shortages, employers persisted in the view that investment in training was not worthwhile for them: the market would supply the skills they needed (Whitehead, 1999a). Severe skills gaps, in consequence, remained.

What about skills supply?
Throughout the periods of the 1964–1981 levy grant system (Harrison, 1992: 45–54) and of the Training and Enterprise Councils (1989–1999), national skills supply remained inadequate to meet needs. Late in 1998 the Labour Government revised some national training targets downwards, possibly because of insufficient progress in skills acquisition (see Appendix 3). Concerns increased with the 1999 publication of the competitiveness White Paper and of a report for the government by McKinsey & Co. consultants (Whitehead, 1999b). By the mid-1990s there were still acute skills shortages, particularly in information technology, engineering and certain sectors of finance. The 1996 skills audit by the DfEE showed only 30 per cent of the country's workforce to be skilled at level 3, compared to 75 per cent in Germany – and 'trends show that by 2010 70% of all jobs will require level-3 skills or above' (Chris Humphreys, head of the National Skills Task Force, quoted in Gracie, 1999). To refer to just one more in the steady stream of such reports, one published by the Trade Union Congress in 1999 revealed that the UK had more poorly qualified employees and fewer young people in training than most of its European competitors (TUC, 1999).

The New Deal programme was fundamental to the Blair administration's policy of targeting training provision on those who need it most and aligning NVET closely with skill supply needs. It is too early to be certain what kind of impact the programme will have on skill supply, and in tackling deep-rooted unemployment, but three years on from its inception, reports are not promising.

In 1999 one major report highlighted a clear gap between the standard of training provision for New Dealers and the superior provision for other employees, and this was seen to echo problems that dogged the Youth Training Scheme in the late twentieth century. The loss by such employers of their weekly subsidy for failure to meet their training obligations of one day per week for New Deal recruits had not proved a sufficient deterrent, and it was feared that this kind of neglect could lead to the emergence of a 'training underclass' (Rana, 1999b). The main offenders were small employers 'engaged in low-skill, low-productivity work, where there was no existing training culture' (*ibid*). New Deal, in such cases, was simply being used as a way of recruiting cheap temporary labour. Since around one-third of all jobs in this country are in firms with fewer than 20 employees, half of all jobs are in firms with fewer than 100 employees, and small companies account for 23 per cent of gross domestic product (Becket, 1996), this represents a serious problem. Of course, many small enterprises do provide good informal training that is not officially recorded. Never the less, there are grave skills deficits in the economy overall, and small businesses suffer from them disproportionately (Gracie, 1999), so they need to be encouraged to do more to improve them.

The 1999 New Deal report urged a significant increase in the training of New Deal personal advisers, and a reduction of their workloads. This seemed unlikely to be enough to change deeply embedded anti-training attitudes, and in 2000 a report by the National Institute of Economic and Social Research, commissioned by the DfEE, showed that only 10 per cent of successful New Deal job placements were due to the programme itself (Smith, 2000). In conditions of falling unemployment, the rest would have occurred naturally in any case. More damning, of the 191,000 people 'placed' in jobs since New Deal began, more than 50,000 were back on benefits within three months (*ibid*). Furthermore, training in New Deal continues to be criticised widely. Smith quoted figures showing that only just over 10 per cent of the first batch of New Deal entrants completed their training courses.

How can progress be achieved?
Given all the evidence of failure to make progress in tackling the country's worrying skills gaps, the 1999 Trades Union Congress report recommended a legal framework of obligations and of financial incentives for employers to provide training and lifelong learning (Rana, 1999a). It concluded that without that, reliance on market forces, employers' goodwill and the motivation of employees to train would not bridge the formidable skills gap.

At the launch of the third report from the National Skills Task Force early in 2000, the Secretary of State for Education and Employment indicated that as long as the Blair administration remained in power there would be no return to a levy-grant system (Rana, 2000). He confirmed that a partnership between individuals, employers, trade unions and government was the aim. Certainly that is in line with the administration's philosophy of stakeholder partnerships to achieve a learning society. Acting on one of the recommendations of the influential Moser Report (DfEE, 1999), the NSTF report called instead for a statement of workplace development, setting out the roles and responsibilities of employers and individuals. Signed by the Confederation of British Industry, the British Chambers of Commerce and the TUC, it would say who would pay for training and when (Rana, 2000).

The NSTF report appeared to be a compromise between those urging for legal obligations to be put on employers to train, and those preferring voluntarism. The TUC believes that voluntarism will not be enough, although its general secretary welcomed the 'recognition of the value of partnership in the workplace' (*ibid*).

The Basic Skills Agency (BSA), introduced by the Labour Government, does plan two innovations that are significant: one to design quality standards for training organisations that provide basic skills in the workplace, the other to use business-experienced 'brokers' who will offer companies practical advice. To help ensure that the plans work, the University for Industry (explained in Chapter 3) is to aid implementation, and the National Training Organisations (see later in this chapter) will help the BSA to run pilots in six sectors (Mackinnon, 1999). It will be important to track the progress of these initiatives, since they have the potential to make a real difference to skills shortages at the workplace level.

Incentives to invest in training in your organisation

What, if any, incentives and policies are there in your organisation (or one with which you are familiar) for individuals to invest in training? What steps could be taken, and by whom, to encourage a higher level of participation?

NATIONAL TRAINING STRATEGY: LATE 1980s TO 1999

Strategy

From the late 1980s to 1999, national training strategy was one of reliance on a voluntary partnership at local, sectoral and national levels between government, business, training and education organisations, individuals and the broader community. Strategy also identified the national vocational qualifications (NVQ) system, introduced in 1986, as the route whereby Britain should at last begin to successfully tackle its continuing problems of low vocational standards and critical skills deficits.

Its implementation framework
At national level

Since 1986 there has been a real effort by government to achieve a workable national framework for NVET. In that year the Manpower Services Commission (MSC) assumed a central role, aiming for 'an integrated, national strategy for managing change in education and training across the entire age range – from school to the mature, even advanced, ages of adult working life' (Keep, 1986, quoting Bryan Nicholson, then MSC chairman). However, its monolithic structure proved unequal to the task, and in 1990 the Employment Department assumed responsibility to the Secretary of State for training, enterprise and education functions at national level, whilst the Training, Enterprise and Education Division (TEED) handled the performance contracts of the Training and Enterprise Councils (TECs).

This did not resolve the issue. The Department of Education and

Science remained responsible for policy and planning in the educational sector, and in 1990 Jack Straw, then Shadow Education Secretary, referred with relevance to 'the black hole in government policy caused by almost total lack of coherence and co-ordination between the Department of Education and Science and the Department of Employment' (*Personnel Management Plus*, 1990). In 1994 the two departments were merged to create the Department for Education and Employment (DfEE), which was to hold responsibility to the Secretary of State for education, training and enterprise planning – a welcome step forward in simplifying and integrating the whole structure. A business-led National Advisory Council on Education and Training Targets (NACETT), established in 1993, assisted the Secretary of State in setting national training and learning targets, and in co-ordinating the TEC network. Not all confusion was eliminated. Enterprise planning is also a responsibility of the Department of Trade and Industry (DTI), and although responsibility for statistics relating to employment and unemployment rest with the Office of National Statistics, training statistics remain with the DfEE.

Another national body, the business-led and government-supported Investors in People (IIP) UK, was established in 1991 to promote the IIP standard nationally. The standard was introduced in 1990 by the Department of Employment to improve the links between training and business goals. IIP was to be administered through TECs (see below) and it was, from the first, vital to their task of improving business effectiveness (see Marchington and Wilkinson, 1996: 173–8). It will be discussed in more detail later in the chapter. Another major task at national level since the mid-1980s has been the oversight of national occupational standards and vocational standards linked to them. This aspect too will be reviewed at a later point in the chapter.

At sectoral level
Until 1998 industrial training organisations (ITOs), independent and led by local employers, identified and monitored key skills needs and training requirements in their sectors and encouraged investment in training and in NVQs. They were not conspicuously effective in their role, and in 1998 they were merged with occupational standards councils to form state-owned but employer-driven national training organisations (NTOs) under an NTO National Council. This ensured more integrated control over vocational educational and training (VET) initiatives at sectoral level. The NTOs, financed by the DfEE, became key players in the Labour Government's reforms of post-16 education and training. In the 1999 White Paper, *Learning to Succeed* (to be described in detail in Chapter 3), it was announced that they would act as funding sources for the new local learning and skills councils, operating alongside the regional development agencies (RDAs) set up by the Labour Government in 1998.

At local level
The cornerstone for delivery since 1989 has been the TEC system. *Learning to Succeed* announced that the TECs would be abolished in

2001(see Chapter 3), but it is important to understand their aims and operation, since much value did emerge from the 10-year system.

The Training and Enterprise Council (TEC) system
In 1989, 82 TECs were introduced to form the cornerstone of the NVET framework at local level in England and Wales. Their equivalent in Scotland and Northern Ireland are Local Education Councils (LECs). Hereafter we shall refer to 'TECs' as a shorthand for both, since although there are differences in the legal and administrative constitution of TECs and LECs, their public roles are essentially the same (see endnote to this chapter). They were legally autonomous bodies that controlled the public funds allocated to them, could raise private funds, and were employer-driven in the sense of being dominated in their membership by senior executives from local private-sector organisations. Their purpose was to interact with local organisations to regenerate the community and stimulate business growth, particularly through reskilling programmes.

TECs operated under a national TEC Council. They were responsible to government for national training programmes, and local partnership initiatives focused on four key areas: opportunities for young people, opportunities for the unemployed, promoting training for the employed, and stimulating business growth. Business organisations like Chambers of Commerce and the Confederation of British Industry (CBI) often formed the nucleus of a TEC, which was thereby able to build on existing local communications and training networks.

The TEC system constituted a radical innovation to ensure that training became a vehicle for reskilling individuals, regenerating local economies, and improving national skills shortages. Through them, the aim was to make national training policy sensitive to local needs, informed by an active partnership of local interests, and able to make a real impact on business growth across the country. However, throughout their existence, TECs struggled to fulfil their strategic role as they confronted three major problems:

- *The role itself had in-built tensions.* TECs were accountable not to the local community but to central government for their major funding. This complicated their task of ensuring greater local involvement and of fostering local regeneration. From the start, too, they had a massive workload related to developing NVQs and to taking over and running national training programmes through years of constrained public spending and high unemployment.

- *The TECs' local structure was confusing.* Large employers had to deal with as many TECs as those employers had sites in different regions (and with as many non-statutory training organisations as there were different sectoral groups). Allied to this, many TECs corresponded with local authority rather than local economic boundaries, especially within large conurbations. This reduced TECs' ability to improve supply to meet local needs in their areas and to meet the training needs of local companies in areas where labour was very mobile. On the other hand, if they became too preoccupied with meeting local needs, then they could risk overlooking needs of national importance.

• *The IIP standard did not make its intended impact on business leaders.* In 1999 a report by the Centre for Research in Employment and Technology in Europe found the standard to be bridging the skills gap between the UK and its competitors, with nearly three-quarters of IIP companies having experienced improvement in productivity as a result of gaining accreditation. Yet for many employers, doubts remained. They mainly concerned the need to focus more on the quality of training, on customer satisfaction measures, on results rather than merely on targets and processes, and on reduction in IIP bureaucracy (Rana, 1999c). In April 2000 a revamped standard was introduced by IIP UK, focused on results rather than processes. The main changes, summarised by Rana (2000a), are as follows:

• more straightforward language

• a focus on results, not processes, by assessors

• 12 instead of 23 performance indicators

• an explicit commitment to equal opportunities

• more flexibility in the way companies and assessors can provide and assess evidence

• more feedback by assessors

• IIP-accredited organisations to have a choice of a yearly audit or reassessment every three years

• a reduction in paperwork for employers.

It is likely that IIP from 2001 onwards will be delivered through Business Link and the new learning and skills councils, but that kind of operational detail is as yet unclear. IIP's future seems assured, but uncertainty surrounding its impact throughout the TEC years raised further doubts about the TECs' own effectiveness.

Making IIP more relevant to the business

What are the main changes introduced in the new IIP standard, and why have they been made? In your view, are they sufficient to make the standard fully relevant for all types and sizes of organisations, or would you propose any others?

By the mid-1990s, the TEC system at national and at local levels had become tangled and poorly co-ordinated. After the Labour Government came into power in 1997, confusion about the future of the TECs increased. In 1999 the Government created eight regional development agencies (RDAs) described by Hetherington (2000) as 'business-led quangos charged with improving the economic performance of regions'. It was unclear how TECs would fit into the new employment and regional economic structure that was now being created, and how they would adapt to the national shift in focus from getting the jobless into work to improving workforce skills levels (Gribben, 1997).

In 1999 a damning report on the TECs' training provision by the Training Standards Council 'confirmed earlier findings that about half of the public and commercial organisations providing government-backed training have at least one area of their provision in need of immediate improvement' (Whitehead, 1999c). In that year, the Government announced in its White Paper *Learning to Succeed* its plans for the future delivery of NVET policy (see page 54). As we have already seen, they included the abolition of the TEC system. Yet many of the proposals built on the TECs' achievements, which have not been negligible. To summarise some of these:

- TECs made a vital contribution to regional regeneration, particularly through aid to small firms, attraction of private sector inward investment, and stimulation of business competitiveness.

- Through their links with local business communities, they were able to make IIP and NVQs, two initiatives crucial to achieving a flexible and skilled economy, known to a wide and powerful audience that could not have been reached as effectively by other routes.

- Because they were not government, many took risks that government itself could not take and were entrepreneurial in ways that often brought real economic benefits to their local communities (Latchford, 1999).

However, their funding and audit arrangements, their duality of purpose (caught always between the pull of local needs and the tug of national training priorities) and their tangled structural arrangements hampered them in their tasks and made them increasingly prone to criticism. By 1999 their time had run out.

Evaluating the 10-year TEC system

Do some research into the ways in which your local TEC system operated between 1989 and 1999, the aims it served, and the outcomes it achieved. On the evidence you find, and the wider reading that you have done, should the TECs have been abolished?

The NVQ system in England and Wales (for Scotland, see page 38)

The establishment and development of the system
Vocational qualifications are those that relate directly to a person's competence in employment. By 1986 less than one-third of the UK labour force held vocational qualifications, compared to two-thirds in Germany and significantly less than in other competitor countries. There was a fundamental need for reform.

The National Council for Vocational Qualifications (NCVQ) was set up in 1986 by the Government as an independent body, sponsored jointly by the Secretaries of State for Employment, and for Education and Science, for Northern Ireland and for Wales. Its main role was to produce a national framework incorporating vocational qualifications that met national standards of occupational competence within a simple structure of five levels. Links were established with all the awarding bodies in the UK (at that time, around 250 examining bodies and 150 industrial training bodies) and with the European Commission. The longer-term aim was, and remains, to have a harmonised European system of vocational qualifications, with consistency of standards across Europe in all occupations and professions.

The introduction of the NVQ system in 1986 offered Britain for the first time in its history a structure of occupational qualifications comprising agreed national standards of competence across every recognised occupational area (a more detailed explanation of NVQs is given in Appendix 2). NVQs are intended to be the 'currency of the labour market', and the NCVQ will only accredit qualifications which, by conforming to national employer-led Lead Body Standards, meet employment needs (Department of Employment, 1988). Since performance in the workplace, or activities that realistically simulate it, is integral to the NCVQ assessment system, that system relies on a close partnership between colleges, training organisations and/or employers. For organisations, the introduction of NVQs has clear implications for their appraisal schemes and also for the identification of training needs and the design of training courses in order to ensure that they meet job-related needs and can achieve NVQ accreditation.

NACETT (see page 30) was established in 1993 by the Government in order to speed up the introduction of NVQs and give them a stronger profile with employers. Its role related to NVQs was to monitor progress towards targets, publish an annual report and advise the Government.

Causes for concern
In 1996 one of the key reports on NVQs appeared – the Beaumont Report. It surveyed the first 100 NVQs/SVQs and found widespread employer support for the NVQ/SVQ concept and a general acceptance that the benefits of the system outweighed its costs. None the less, the report produced a formidable series of recommendations to tackle deficiencies to do particularly with a costly and imperfect delivery system, excessive bureaucracy and jargon, inconsistency in funding arrangements, and differences in the interpretation of standards by key parties across the system (Beaumont, 1996: 7).

A major blow to NVQs' credibility came in October 1996 when a study by the Centre for Economic Performance (a government-backed watchdog body) condemned the whole system, set up at a cost of more than £100 million, as having achieved almost nothing (Clare, 1996). The study concluded that although the Government's intention had been to rationalise the structure of vocational qualifications, it had simply added to its complexity, displacing some traditional qualifications, particularly in such areas as clerical and secretarial work, and hairdressing. There was also heavy criticism of the GNVQ system (see Chapter 3).

Reductions announced in 1998 to some national educational and training targets (see Appendix 3) and the extension in their timescale raised further doubts about the progress being made by the NVQ system. Such doubts may be unfair. NVQs are popular in certain industries that previously had few recognised qualifications, for example, the retail industry, where their take-up has been extremely high. But there is undeniably a fear that, through time, the NVQ system will deteriorate into a mass of standards set at very low levels that have no equivalent across the rest of Europe.

Despite the employer-driven nature of the NVQ system, many employers see NVQs as irrelevant to their in-house needs. Take-up has been faster in educational institutions, but many still run traditional and NVQ routes in parallel, and there are problems to do with delivery. The system was meant to ensure progression from education into work and qualifications for those in work. In practice, the settings offered by educational providers are seen by many employers to lack credibility, and the cost of providing an NVQ route in a college is so high – in terms of staff training, time and materials – that, as resource constraints and work overload bite harder into the educational system, the feasibility of offering that route comes into question for many centres.

There is also conflict between employers and educationalists concerning the whole concept of competence gained in one setting being transferable to another, and of ability to do a series of discrete tasks being a valid indicator of ability to do a whole job. With the advent of the Qualifications and Curriculum Authority in 1997, responsible for overseeing the whole national qualifications system, employers feared that the design of NVQs would be modelled on the educational needs of 16- to 19-year-olds rather than on the skills needs of adult workers in employment. The latter was the originally intended focus of the NVQ system, and it remains crucial to the competitive capability of UK businesses that it should be retained.

Areas of progress

Despite such ongoing criticisms, by 1997 over 85 per cent of all occupations offered NVQs within a national framework showing interrelationships between qualifications. Standards can thus be compared between different jobs on the same level, so that the individual can see how he or she could use his or her skills in different areas of work. Many corporate, medium-sized and smaller organisations in the UK are making acquisition of NVQs part of the strategic development of their workforces.

NVQs in a pub chain

You, the training director of a national pub chain want to make NVQs available to all of its 25,000 full- and part-time staff in order to attract and keep high-calibre people. You are proposing that five different NVQs should be offered at Level 1. This would enable staff to train in a variety of skills. Employees should need only two or three months to complete the first NVQ, leaving the rest for completion within seven or eight more months. Staff who gain NVQs would receive pay increases, on the basis that improved competency merits a financial reward.

The company could go on to expand its range of NVQs into Levels 2 and 3 and could develop its own training materials accredited by City and Guilds.

You are convinced of the value of NVQs as a way of accrediting the competence of employees, and of motivating them to acquire qualifications. Also, you are leading a project to gain IIP accreditation, and your local TEC, when advising on the IIP standard, has placed a major emphasis on the value for your chain in training to NVQ standards.

You expect to be opposed in the above proposals by a number of pub managers and their staff. What arguments will you use to support your proposals?

Feedback notes

On present evidence you should collect specific examples, especially those most relevant to this kind of organisation, from the local TEC and from DfEE and National Training Awards publications). You can say that in many organisations, no matter how big or small or in what sector of employment, NVQs have:

- improved profitability and economic performance by raising performance standards and giving employees a better understanding of, and ability to do, tasks central to their work in the organisation

- developed a more adaptable workforce, enabling and encouraging updating and modification of skills through the credit accumulation and transfer system

- led to increased individual motivation, understanding of competency standards and commitment to the organisation

- helped to improve recruitment of competent staff by using the universal standards embedded in NVQs as guidelines for selection

- led to clear and consistent goals being set across an organisation or units of it for continued learning and development; these goals, when used as part of employee development strategy in an organisation, can make a powerful contribution to improving business performance

- by building NVQs into its HRD and career planning systems, helped the organisations to retain valued employees.

CONCLUSION

Having read this chapter and completed its reviews and self-checks, you should now:

- understand the main trends in, and pressures upon, national training policy and strategy between 1989 and 1999 (see endnote relating to Scotland and Wales)

- be able to evaluate the effectiveness of implementation of policy during that period, and issues for the future that it raised

- be able to explain the value of vocational qualifications at national, organisational and individual levels.

To test yourself against these objectives, what five-minute answers would you give to the following questions (dates in brackets refer to the IPD qualifying examination paper in which a question appeared)?

- What are the main aspects of the revamped Investors in People standard that support the claim that it is a 'business efficiency tool'?

- Briefly outline the TEC or LEC system by early 2000, and give **four** reasons why you think that system should **either** have been retained **or** have been abolished (May 1998, adapted to update).

- List some of the benefits that N/SVQs can bring to an organisation using them as part of its employee development strategy (May 1997).

USEFUL READING

The following contain detail that it has not been relevant to include in this chapter. They should be referred to by those needing a deeper knowledge and understanding of the NVET system:

HAMLIN B. (1999) 'The national context' in J. Stewart, *Employee Development Practice*. London, Financial Times and Pitman Publishing, pp22–61.

HEVEY D. (1997) 'The UK national (and Scottish) vocational qualification system: state of the art or in a state?' *International Journal of Training and Development*, Vol. 1, 4. pp242–58.

REID M. A. *and* BARRINGTON H. (1999) 'An institutional perspective', in M. A. Reid and H. Barrington, *Training Interventions: Promoting learning opportunities* (6th edn). London, Institute of Personnel and Development, pp33–57.

NVET information should be regularly updated by referring to sources such as:

- the CIPD's publication, *People Management*; this contains reliable, accessible and up-to-date information, as does the www.people management.co.uk website

- the quality press – and especially the Sunday 'heavies' and *The Financial Times* – for their regular articles and editorials on matters relating to the field of secondary and tertiary education, and national training; *The Times Educational Supplement* and *The Times Higher Educational Supplement* should also be regularly consulted

- local libraries, chambers of commerce, TECs/LECS (after April 2001, Learning Skills Councils), all of which have valuable up-to-date information and examples of good practice in the field.

There are many websites that offer helpful information on national training policy and initiatives, including the following:

- until 2001, Training and Enterprise Councils or their equivalent bodies in Scotland and Northern Ireland (www.tec.co.uk)

- learndirect's website at www.ufiltd.co.uk

- the Department for Education and Employment website at www.dfee.gov.uk; it is a source of comprehensive information about NVET policy and progress.

ENDNOTE: NVET IN SCOTLAND, WALES AND NORTHERN IRELAND

There has not been the scope in this chapter to describe or evaluate NVET policy and systems in Scotland, Northern Ireland or Wales, but CIPD students in those countries are expected to be familiar with them so that, when responding to examination questions on national training policy, they can relate their answers to their own country's system. The following note gives some generalised information only.

Scotland
Scottish LECS have differed from the TECs in England and Wales in their operations and in the scope of their responsibilities, mainly because of differences in educational and funding systems in Scotland. In regard to NVQs, the Scottish system has proceeded more smoothly than that in England and Wales for a variety of historical, educational and geographical reasons, but particularly because 95 per cent of NVQs are awarded by one body, the Scottish Vocational Education Council (SCOTVEC), which also has the accrediting role held by the NCVQ in England and Wales. All standards and the Scottish highers (the equivalent of A levels) are also awarded by a single body, the Scottish Examinations Board. Since 1985, SCOTVEC awards have been delivered and assessed in modules that can be taken by anyone, at any time, in school, in further and higher education, and in or out of work. Employers accept a series of modules rather than whole certificates as entry to certain jobs. Finally, the Scottish NVET system under devolution is likely to be significantly different from that in England and Wales, since the Scottish parliament has complete responsibility for devising and implementing education and employment strategies, and for the delivery system (Johnson, 1999a).

Wales
Responsibility for training in Wales was transferred from the Secretary of State for Employment to the Secretary of State for Wales in 1992. In July 1999 the Welsh Education Minister announced radical plans to reform post-16 training and education in Wales by integrating the Welsh further education funding council and TECs within more broadly based bodies, and establishing a national council for education and training in Wales, underpinned by 'community consortia' for education and training (Whitehead, 1999d).

Northern Ireland
The equivalent body to the TECs is the Training and Employment Agency, with the Economic Development Network providing special services for smaller enterprises (website at www.ednet-ni.com).

3 The national educational framework

LEARNING OBJECTIVES

After reading this chapter you will:

- understand the main thrust of vision and policy for the education system in England and Wales since the mid-1980s

- understand major problems involved in achieving an integrated system of post-16 national vocational education and training (NVET)

- be able to explain and evaluate the Labour Government's main aims and direction for national vocational education and training policy and strategy since 1997.

INTRODUCTION

The vision guiding current national vocational education policy is one of lifelong learning through a variety of routes that will increase individuals' employability and self-fulfilment, and contribute to national economic growth.

In May 1995, revised national education and training targets for 2000 were published in the Conservative Government's second competitiveness White Paper. These stressed the need, in order to improve national competitive capability, for more individuals to reach existing targets, for core skills to have a special focus, and for new targets for the achievement of high-level qualifications (Appendix 3).

In 1998 the Labour Government reduced some of those targets (now called 'learning' not 'training' targets, to distinguish lifelong learning from sporadic training) and extended the period for their achievement to 2002 (Appendix 3). Targets relating to core skills for those aged 19 and over were dropped. It is unclear whether this was because such skills were taken to be incorporated in the learning targets for 11- and 16-year-olds or because the targets had been judged unrealistic. However, reductions in targets and the extended timescale raised doubts about how far progress was really being made in improving national educational standards. To understand the issues here, it is necessary to outline how the educational system has operated since the first radical reforms of the late 1980s.

EDUCATIONAL POLICY FOR SCHOOLS: 1985–2000

Conservative Government policy: 1985–1997

Since 1985, national education policy under both Conservative and Labour Governments has been dedicated to improving standards, coherence and quality of educational provision, and to developing integrated and universal technical, vocational and academic pathways in a system hitherto dominated by the latter.

Up until 1997 the Conservative Government's educational strategy focused on:

• progressively introducing a national educational curriculum and ultimately linking it to the national vocational qualification system

• improving vocational education in order to clarify and expand choice, to raise standards of attainment, and to promote parity of esteem between academic and vocational qualifications

• creating a new post-16 vocational education and training sector.

This strategy was dominated by attempts to break local education authorities' and educationalists' grip of the education system, which was decentralised to ensure a greater responsiveness to market forces.

Introduction of GCSE: 1985

In 1985, in a radical introductory step, the General Certificate of Education (GCE) and the Certificate of Secondary Education (CSE) were replaced by a single General Certificate of Secondary Education (GCSE). Its aim was to offer the majority of 16-year-olds the chance to acquire an accreditation of their five years of secondary education. This was followed by various interventions to help children acquire vocational skills, knowledge and experience in their formative years. With the exception of the establishment of City Technology Colleges, such interventions were costly and largely unsuccessful. Much more was needed in order to overcome the fundamental ills of the educational system.

Educational reforms: 1988–1997

The most fundamental overhaul of the state educational system since the Butler Education Act 1944 began with the Education Reform Act 1988. Then and thereafter, government sought to systematically transform educational standards and delivery in the primary and secondary educational systems, and to overhaul the governance, funding and management of schools, particularly through a dramatic reduction in the powers of local education authorities. By 1997, when the Conservative Government fell from power:

• All children in state schools had to meet standard assessment targets of a national curriculum at the ages of 5, 7, 11, 14 and 16, covering both core and foundation subjects, in a move intended to encourage competence and establish firm links with the National Vocational Qualifications (NVQ) system.

• All schools, state and independent, were to be judged by measurable and publicised outcomes related to these nationally set targets. They had to publish examination results, national curriculum test scores, truancy rates and leavers' destinations in a standard form, the details being summarised annually in local and national league tables.

• Schools could opt out of local authority control and obtain their funding direct from the Government. These grant-maintained schools had significant freedom to select their pupils as they saw fit. Important control was retained at centre, particularly through a national agency for schools that gradually took over from LEAs wherever schools opted out. However, school governors and heads now had major managerial responsibilities.

• The Secretary of State could submit plans to close down surplus schools and refer them to a public enquiry, as well as close failing schools or hand them over to private sector bodies to improve their results.

• Every state school in England and Wales (27,000 in 1988) was monitored once every four years by teams of independent inspectors whose reports were published; school governing bodies had to tell parents how they propose to act on the inspectors' findings.

• All 16-year-olds had to stay in school until the end of the summer term instead of leaving at Easter without taking their final exams, and all parents had to receive an annual written report on their children's progress.

Policy development under the Labour Government: 1997–2000
Structure and control
With the advent to power of the Labour Government, the pace of change increased, but one central strand of Conservative strategy was undone. The School Standards and Framework Act 1998 brought back grant-maintained schools under the local education authority umbrella. Grammar-school status could also be abolished wherever a public ballot supported this. The impact of this legislation is now in doubt, following the use of the ballot for the first time early in 2000. It led to a decisive majority vote in favour of retaining selection at Ripon Grammar School, North Yorkshire. Subsequent government pronouncements on the fate of grammar schools have so far (by April 2000) been muted, with the Secretary of State for Education and Employment, David Blunkett, professing no intention to oversee their destruction.

At national level, structure and control processes relating to schools remain in a state of some confusion. On the one hand, the changes introduced from 1988 on have improved the chances of all children to participate successfully in further or higher education – a development that, if sustained, offers the hope of producing real long-term improvement in national skills supply. On the other hand, under both Conservative and Labour Governments there has been more centralisation, mainly by nationalising the curriculum, but also – under the Labour Government – by returning significant power to local education authorities (LEAs). The national curriculum and the regular assessment of children across all age ranges dominates teaching time, producing heavily increased teaching and administrative workloads. It, and the power of LEAs, have raised concerns that the system does not permit sufficient educational diversity, choice or quality. In an attempt to achieve more efficiency, in 1997 the School Curriculum and Assessment Authority that had been set up only four years earlier, in 1993, was replaced by an overarching Qualifications and Curriculum Authority that incorporated coverage of the whole NVQ system. However, the bureaucratic complexity of the attainment and assessment system remains.

Standards

Meanwhile, the drive went on to improve standards. The Labour Government continued the Conservatives' attack on the child-centred 'discovery' approach to primary school learning that had been prevalent from the late 1960s. It introduced national literacy and numeracy standards, and these and other initiatives have led to a rise in standards in all subjects and across most schools – admittedly from a base that, before 1998, was very low. However, the gap between the best and worst is widening, according to the Chief Inspector of Schools in his annual report published in 2000 (Clare, 2000). One 16-year-old in seven leaves school every year without a basic grasp of English and maths. Sir Claus Moser's independent National Commission on Education (NCE) has through the years revealed the same disturbing trends, and also the extent of the difference that still exists between educational attainments of children in Britain compared with their European counterparts.

Staff resourcing policies

Heads and their staff working at the coalface have to cope with many pressures. They must increasingly manage and work in teams, battle with constrained resources, meet rigorous and constantly changing educational targets, keep up to date with teaching methods, and struggle for a favourable place in the league tables in order to attract and retain sufficient student numbers. Few welcome being brought steadily within a performance management process, and the Government's attempts to introduce performance-related pay across the teaching profession are being strongly resisted. More welcome are the substantial increases to salaries introduced in the early years of the 1997 Labour Government in order to attract and retain high-quality teachers, and to encourage more of them to work in inner-city schools. Staff development is also a high priority, and heads and aspiring heads must now undergo nationally organised training to reach common standards of capability. In March 2000 the first director of the new national College for School Leadership was announced.

Educational policy, and its outcomes at local level

Summarise and compare the main changes described thus far in education policy, that have been made by Conservative and Labour Governments since 1985. What impact do these changes appear to have made in schools in your locality?

The plight of failing schools

Across the whole of the primary and secondary educational system, one problem remains intractable: that of failing schools. There is a significant educational underclass in the UK, just as there is an underclass in its labour market system (see page 27). Any increase in the former leads inexorably to an increase in the latter also. The NCE's annual reports have catalogued the widening educational gaps between richer and poorer, and between north and south, as well as deep-rooted gender and ethnic disparities related to educational attainment. Educational league tables have focused further attention on such gaps, through their exposure of about 400 schools that persistently fail to rise from their position at the bottom of the pile.

Most of these schools are located in inner cities where some of the worst socio-economic conditions in the UK place formidable barriers in the way of any attempts by schools to reduce high truancy rates and improve academic outcomes. Well-publicised cases of closure of failing schools, or of their handing over to private consortia to run, have demonstrated that the problems remain grave. The best-known attempt by the Labour Government's Standards and Effectiveness Unit to tackle the problems – the establishment of 25 Educational Action Zones, launched by the Labour Government in 1998 with heavy funding and private backing – has had little success so far. Nor has the government's 'Fresh Start' programme, under which failing schools can be closed and then re-opened under 'inspirational' heads – three out of 10 of whom resigned in March 2000 without having achieved any turnaround in their schools.

In March 2000 the Secretary of State for Education and Employment, David Blunkett, announced a radical break from government policy on three fronts (Blunkett, 2000):

• Government would encourage the establishment of new foundation or voluntary-aided schools in areas where there was local demand.

• It would also allow more existing independent schools to become part of the publicly funded education system.

• Most radical of all, it would allow the replacement of failing schools with City Academies: the 'City Academies' initiative.

Under the third front, hundreds of failing schools would be offered in their entirety to businesses, churches, voluntary bodies and philanthropists, who would be able to take over control from local education authorities, employ and determine the pay of teachers, and depart from the national curriculum (Clare, 2000a). Modelled on the Conservative Government's highly successful 15 City Technology Colleges (CTCs) set up in the 1980s, which rapidly achieved substantial support from business sponsors, these academies must, however, admit pupils across the whole ability range and achieve performance targets set by the Government. As with the CTCs, the 'sponsors' must also make significant capital investment in the schools, to match or exceed government funding. The first were to open in 2001.

The City Academies initiative came from 10 Downing Street rather than from the Department for Education and Employment, and – given its return to policies and principles of the previous Conservative Government – it was appropriately announced first by Blunkett in the conservative press: the *Daily Telegraph* (Clare, 2000a). In 1999, the Labour Government had ensured that grant-maintained schools 'lost their status, autonomy and a sustained proportion of their funding' (Johnson, 2000). Now, the same government was to give City Academies elite status, a high level of autonomy from both LEA and government control (although the academies would remain in the state system), and major injections of government as well as private sector funding. The initiative was initially dismissed by teaching unions as a panic reaction to the perceived failure of the Fresh Start initiative, and viewed by many business leaders as welcome but too small to make any real difference (Judd, 2000).

However, Blunkett made no apology. He presented this U-turn as a 'new approach to diversity', and 'a way of helping to raise standards in inner-city areas' (Blunkett, 2000). He pointed out that already secondary schools in six major cities were by then part of the Government's 'Excellence in Cities' initiative – a £350 million programme to provide improved education in such areas – and that by 2003, one in four secondary schools would have specialist status.

City Academies will take some years to prove themselves. After all, CTCs took over 10 years to become firmly established. The academies represent a brave attempt to tackle inner-city problems. However, their scope at present is narrow. Many perceive that it is local education authorities that are the real barrier to progress in the 'vast majority' of schools (*Daily Telegraph*, 2000: 29), many retaining a large proportion of funding that should be going to schools and disbursing it for other purposes. Will they keep their present power? In the light of the City Academies initiative, perhaps not. Such is the determination of this government to ensure an educational infrastructure that can at last lead to a reduction in the persistent deficiencies and disparities in the economy's skills base, a 'frontal assault' on local authority power over the system cannot be discounted (*ibid*). In much of the overall vision and thrust of educational policy, the two governments since the late 1980s have thought and acted alike. It will be interesting to see how far, in the area where they so strongly differ – LEAs' power and control – Labour's policy will be sustained or will change through time.

Achieving national standards in failing schools

Find out how failing schools are being treated in your local area, or one with which you are familiar. Are real improvements in educational standards being achieved? If they are not, what seem to be the barriers here?

REFORMS IN POST-16 EDUCATIONAL PROVISION

Conservative policy: late 1980s to 1997

The Conservative Government's intention in the late 1980s and the 1990s was to create a unified framework for the provision of education and training for post-16-year-olds, applying to it the same principles of local autonomy and competition in an open market that underpinned parallel reforms taking place in the national training system and in the primary and secondary education sector. Throughout this period the providers of post-16 provision – bewildering in their number and complexity – were subjected to rapidly escalating changes resulting from expansion in student numbers, government legislation and by official enquiries.

Legislative reform

Under the sweeping changes produced by the Education Reform Act 1989 and the Further and Higher Education Act 1992:

- all universities, polytechnics and major colleges of higher education came together within a single structure for higher education, with power to award their own degrees, thus ending the binary line that had divided universities from other major higher education bodies for 25 years

- new quality assurance measures were introduced, including external scrutiny by a quality audit unit developed in essence by the educational institutions

- remaining further education and sixth form colleges were given independent corporate status, and funded by the Government through two Further and Higher Education Funding Councils; funding was disbursed on the basis of numbers of students enrolled and completing courses.

The General National Vocational Qualification: 1993

In 1993, the introduction of the GNVQ system on a pilot basis across Britain represented a major step in the Government's efforts to ensure parity of esteem between the academic and vocational pathways. A basic pass in a GNVQ equated roughly with two grade-D A levels. The hope was that GNVQs would be chosen by students who were enrolling for A levels because there was nothing more suitable, or were dropping out of school or college at 16, or who were pursuing other, less valuable, vocational courses. If successful, the GNVQ route would help to end the multiplicity of qualifications and establish the GNVQ itself as the market leader in the public mind. It would also offer a more consistent standard of assessment than most of its precursors.

Early GNVQ results were inconclusive, but there were ongoing concerns about what many perceived to be a decline in the quality of the A-level standard. The difficulties involved in trying to ensure consistency in assessment across the number of examination boards operating in England and Wales, and to ensure comparability of standards across the very wide ranges of A level or 'equivalent' courses that different examination boards offer, cast doubt on the meaningfulness of official A-level statistics. Results can improve, yet real standards decline, in a situation where examination boards are many, assessment frameworks differ, choices in examinable topics examined vary, and coursework can account for up to 20 per cent of marks awarded, or none (Burghes, 1997). In 1996 the Government announced that A-level standards were to be overhauled in order to achieve a return to more rigorous standards set in the past.

The Dearing Report on post-16 vocational qualifications: 1996

In March 1996 the Dearing Report revealed that despite earlier reforms to the vocational qualification system, the traditional academic/vocational divide was still in place and was 'damaging to the national interest and to the optimal development of the wide range of talents among young people' (Clare, 1996a). The review set out a new national framework of qualifications to take the place of the existing 'jungle' of academic, applied and vocational examinations.

The need for urgent action was reinforced by the publication in 1997 of a London University Institute of Education report into the GNVQ system. The report was based on a four-year study of that system, and was backed by the Further Education Development Agency. It was bound to powerfully influence government thinking.

The report covered intermediate and advanced awards. It found that although the GNVQ had become an accepted route into higher education as well as preparing teenagers for employment in a limited number of fields, the courses did not represent a broad preparation for employment or satisfy the requirement for parity with academic qualifications (O'Leary, 1997). The conclusion of this highly critical report was that 'GNVQ's problems stem not from its vocational nature, but from a failed attempt to straddle the divide between academic and job-related education' (*ibid*).

Further reforms: 1997

In 1997 a range of initiatives was introduced to achieve syllabus change, improve teaching quality, set new performance targets, reduce the number of examination boards and ensure a wider diversity of qualifications. The sweeping changes included:

- an AS level to credit one year of A-level study, allowing greater breadth of study (treated subsequently by universities as equivalent to half an A level)

- key skills added to the curriculum and incorporated in national learning targets

- the relaunch of Youth Training as National Traineeships (a particularly welcome proposal, and one that promised to offer a clearer route into GNVQs and modern apprenticeships)

- revision and relaunch of the National Record of Achievement to promote lifelong learning (a step heralded by Rover Group's education and careers manager, John Berkely, as capable of making 'perhaps the single greatest difference to promoting and sustaining the idea of lifelong learning')

- merger of the Schools Curriculum and Assessment Authority (responsible for GCSEs and A levels) and the NCVQ into a Qualifications and Curriculum Authority, to achieve an administratively more integrated national education and vocational training system.

The Dearing Report on Higher Education: 1997

Long before the Conservative Government lost power in 1997, there were many statistics to indicate that the higher education system was flourishing. To take just a few illustrative statistics:

- By 1992 the number of full-time students in higher education had reached a record level of 436,000 and the proportion of school-leavers going to university was 31 per cent.

- In the same year, one in three young people had embarked upon a degree or diploma, compared to only one in eight in 1979.

- Forty-one former polytechnics and colleges already had university status by 1992, and in the decade up to 1992 full-time students at the new universities and colleges had doubled, while older universities had experienced a notably less marked rise of 40 per cent (Authers, 1994).

- In 1993 the Government capped growth in numbers until 1998, but by mid-1994 university provision covered almost as many 18-year-olds as in Germany and the USA. The university market was being 'flooded' with new courses to 'woo students who had never thought about higher education' (Scott-Clark and Rayment, 1995).

Yet there were some worrying signs. Pressures on resources were severe. For the universities, pressures of a different kind came from the Higher Education Funding Council, which operated different assessment processes relating to the quality of research and of teaching. To achieve excellence in both seemed increasingly impossible as resource constraints and the burden of additional numbers entering the system brought into conflict longer-term ends to do with research, and teaching coherence, and short-term ends to do with funding and status. Here, as across the whole post-16 educational provider sector, the same drift of standards being experienced in the primary and secondary sectors was feared to be developing.

In 1997, the last year of the Conservative Government's life, the Dearing Report, *Higher Education in the Learning Society*, identified the key role of higher education in enhancing UK competitiveness and 'nails its colours to the mast with its sure commitment to lifelong learning and widening participation' (Gareth Roberts, chairman of the Committee of Vice Chancellor and Principals, quoted in *The Times Higher Education Supplement*, 25 July 1997: 8). It was to shape future national educational strategy in fundamental ways:

- It identified the stakeholders – individuals, the state, employers and providers of education and training – and called for a new contract between them so that historic boundaries between vocational and academic education would disappear, and increasingly active partnerships, involving sets of mutual obligations, would be forged between higher education institutions and the worlds of industry, commerce and public service.

- It proposed a framework for qualifications and the role of the

Quality Assurance Agency in guaranteeing benchmarks and regulating minimum standards.

- It recommended an Institute for Learning and Teaching to promote quality standards and accreditation of teachers, to review staff development policies with a view to performance-based teaching, and to train panels of trained external examiners to ensure nationwide comparability in degrees.

- It also proposed a clear distinction between higher education and further education missions, and tightened restrictions on, and controls over, franchised courses in further education.

Labour Government policy: 1997–2000
The immediate impact of the report on the new Labour Government's educational policy was to convince that more money was needed to maintain high-quality higher education, that rationing of places should cease, and that extra money would have to come from students and their families if the necessary improvements were to be made possible. However, the Government ignored pay structures, and this meant that critical issues related to staff training, reward and motivation were unresolved, and continue to place barriers in the way of change.

The likely impact on further education was unclear. The Dearing target of an overall 45 per cent growth in participation in higher and further education offered the prospect of real expansion for the further education sector, and this was welcome news. However, the new Labour Government did not accept Dearing's socially controversial recommendation of a common £1,000 fee for all students, whether paid up front or borrowed. Instead, it decided to waive tuition fees for poorer students while axing maintenance grants in favour of a loan maintenance package. There were fears that the proposals would not meet the funding gap acknowledged by the Government, and that any extra money raised by the student loan scheme would not go into higher education but would be funnelled off elsewhere.

The Quality Assurance Agency (QAA), set up in line with Dearing's proposals, was welcomed, although it had only three years in which to sort out and oversee a national framework for qualifications and threshold standards for degrees, with the prospect of funding linked to those standards. Within the national framework, NVQs at Levels 4 and 5 were seen to have the potential to integrate with provision in higher education, and colleges and universities would have an enlarged role in delivering and assessing NVQs. The QAA would also have a key role in allocating degree-awarding powers – and their removal – working in partnership with HEFCE. However, failure to achieve these tasks would almost certainly mean direct government intervention.

Feedback notes
- There are many stakeholders in lifelong learning, each with their own set of interests. At international institutional level, UNESCO adopted lifelong learning as its mission in the 1970s, and the European Community espoused it in the early 1990s. Global initiatives followed, including the World Initiative on Lifelong

> **Lifelong learning: the stakeholder challenge** (*with acknowledgements to Gill Homan and Sue Shaw, Department of Management, Manchester Metropolitan University, whose 2000 paper suggested this self-check exercise*)
>
> Identify the main interested parties, or stakeholders, in lifelong learning as a positive way forward for individuals and for the economy. Then take the higher education sector as one sector of provision of lifelong learning opportunities: who are the stakeholders within that sector, and what are their different agendas?

Learning and the European Lifelong Learning Initiative (Homan and Shaw, 2000: 1). In the UK, government, organisations, individuals and the education sector, together with awarding bodies, training consultancies, and others are all interested parties (*ibid*), and within each are further stakeholders, each with ends to serve and a contribution to make. 'The list of professed interested parties is almost endless' (*ibid*: 6).

• Higher education as a sector consists of at least four distinct stakeholders: the long-established universities; universities created in the 1960s from old technical colleges or built on greenfield sites; the new universities created from the former polytechnics in the 1990s; and higher education institutions without university status but operating within the field of professional education. Each has its own view of what it has to offer to lifelong learning, and what it may – or may not – gain from responding to its challenges. Each has its unique characteristics, culture and history.

> Whilst government and policymakers in higher education may promote the rhetoric of lifelong learning, the reality at operational level is very different. It is there that the management of resource issues and the tensions between delivery and quality have to be reconciled...further complicated by the challenge that lifelong learning presents...across all aspects of programme content, delivery and assessment.
>
> (Homan and Shaw, 2000: 20)

Further and higher education: some current issues
The vocational pathways
In 1998 the Universities and Colleges Admissions Service reported an extraordinary increase in the number applying to university or college with GNVQ as their main qualification from 9,380 in 1995 to 29,757 in 1997 (UCAS, 1998). This accompanied decline in demand for traditional degrees as distinct from vocational courses. At the same time, the number of courses offered by the new universities created since 1992 – which tend to produce more vocationally oriented courses than the old – were predicted to exceed those by older universities for the first time in 1998 (Graves, 1998).

However, although post-16 participation rates have increased, likely impact on national skill supply is unclear. It is particularly worrying that applications to universities and colleges for the physical, material and environmental sciences – fields vital to the economy – have continued to decline, dropping by 26 per cent between 1995 and 1997. Meanwhile, freedom of student choice means that many who graduate fail to find jobs commensurate with the class of their degrees, skills shortages in crucial areas continue, and many employers complain that the educational system is not adequately equipping young people with the skills that they need for the world of work.

The social pattern of university provision

Over the past few decades the social mix of university entrants has remained almost unchanged, despite state funding. Given that the 1997 Dearing Report estimated that graduates earn on average 17 per cent per year more, throughout their working life, than non-graduates, the wider implications of this failure to achieve a more balanced pattern of university provision are profoundly disturbing.

In 1993 Peter Drucker, the American management guru, was highlighting the twin challenges facing education: the economic and the social. He emphasised the primacy of knowledge as the basic economic resource of a country and the new currency of the workplace. He identified the key role of the 'knowledge worker' in society and observed the need to ensure the dignity of the less intellectually gifted service workers who would also be essential in post-capitalist society (Drucker, 1993). Yet in this country, the social discrepancies that the 1993 Moser Report (NCE, 1993) identified in educational attainment remain. The question he asked then still requires an answer: in the knowledge society, how can those who are educationally disadvantaged join in fully, not only at work but also as a citizen?

There are options about how to improve the social balance, for instance, by extending the Individual Learning Accounts system to give people the power to spend as they wish instead of continuing the system that funds educational institutions from the centre, on the basis of student numbers. Businesses could also increase their spending on higher education, 'fostering excellence and improving the life chances of poorer people' (Jay, 2000). Yet so far, the ILA system has not been changed in that way, nor have employers' attitudes altered. They have never gone down the educational spending road in any significant numbers – for, as we saw at the start of Chapter 2, what incentives are there for them to do so?

Perhaps more to the point, until more socially disadvantaged individuals have the ability to gain the necessary entry qualifications, the social profile of university applicants is unlikely to change. That in turn means that primary and secondary education must do more to enable the educational underclass (page 43) to gain and sustain real equality of access to good quality educational provision. And so we return to the start of this chapter: the link between the quality of the primary and secondary education system and national skills supply.

Adult learning

The current education system still lacks the flexibility needed to give adults adequate access to learning throughout their lives rather than just for three years after leaving school. For such access to become a reality, there must be easy transfer between universities, regular availability of career breaks, and continuous opportunity to follow courses while working. By 1994, about 85 per cent of UK universities had some system of credit accumulation, or plans to introduce it, but there is still much ground to cover before the vision becomes a reality.

There is a basic barrier to access by all adults to learning opportunities on equal terms: those who can study full-time receive direct financial support from the public purse, but those who study part-time have to pay their own tuition fees and study costs. Employers do little to help, since they continue to give minimal support for part-time undergraduate study, and variable support for professional and postgraduate study (John Daniel, vice chancellor, Open University, quoted in *The Times Higher Education Supplement*, 25 July 1997: 8). This threatens to perpetuate the thrust of UK educational policy that prevailed throughout the twentieth century, when it was directed most powerfully at children and young adults prior to entering work. Yet the need for adult participation in education is now acute. In the rapidly developing global knowledge economy, people will have to be helped to change skills, jobs, even careers, many times in the course of their normal working life. Lifelong learning, provided in new, less costly and more accessible ways, and covering social and intellectual as well as practical skills, is no longer an optional aspiration. It is a national necessity. Yet early in 2000 during the Lords debate on the Learning and Skills Bill, Baroness Blackstone said that the primary thrust of the new Learning and Skills Councils (LSCs) would be aimed at 16–19-year-olds. Her comments were made in response to urgings – supported by the Institute of Personnel and Development – for statutorily based Workforce Development Committees in the LSCs. It seems that, despite its importance to the national economy, adult learning will be left mainly as a matter for local discretion. (I am indebted to Roy Harrison, the CIPD's training and development adviser, for drawing my attention to Baroness Blackstone's remarks.)

Leadership and management issues
The long-term success of educational providers at every level is heavily dependent on leadership and managerial skills. Those who direct educational institutions must perform a demanding dual role of providing quality services and acting as major employers. Local providers and local employers must collaborate closely in activities to do with profiling and assessment of pupils and students, careers guidance, and the design and operation of sandwich courses and work experience. All providers must also ensure open access and non-discrimination. In response to these pressures, industrial, business and professional interests have become increasingly dominant on governing bodies, but this does not invariably lead to an increase in boards' effectiveness.

Educationalists at the workface experience pressures similar to those facing their colleagues in the schools system. They must increasingly manage and work in teams, carry budget responsibilities, generate revenue for their organisations and fight for position in the market place. They must acquire or improve those skills against a backdrop of expanding workloads, a constant squeeze on funding, a fight for

> **The local educational institution**
>
> Take an educational institution with which you are familiar, in the
> further or higher education system. What seem to be the main pressures
> on that institution, and what efforts are being made in it to widen access
> to lifelong learning opportunities?

educational standards, and salary scales that are a cause of bitter
complaint.

THE NEW STRATEGY FOR POST-16 EDUCATION AND TRAINING

1998 – Announcing radical change

In 1998, two Green Papers heralded a radical change in
government strategy across the whole NVET territory. One was
The Learning Age (DfEE, 1998), the other, *Lifelong Learning*
(DfEE, 1998a). The first announced the need for new patterns of
delivering and achieving learning targets, and for a national
culture that would stimulate and support lifelong learning and
individual initiative in relation to that learning. The second put
some flesh to those bones. The main changes that they proposed
were these:

* clear national skills and qualifications targets and the building of a
  clear qualifications system that would give equal value to academic
  and vocational learning

* doubling of basic adult literacy and numeracy provision by 2002

* raising of the standards of post-16 teaching and learning, and the
  involvement of further, higher and adult education in provision of
  lifelong learning opportunities

* expansion of further and higher education by an extra 500,000
  students by 2002 (90 per cent, or 450,000, likely to be in further
  education, 10 per cent, or 50,000 in higher education)

* a new University for Industry (UfI), to be launched in late 1999, in
  order to link businesses and individuals to information technology-
  based education and training; the UfI would be underpinned with
  a national learning grid to carry high-quality networked learning
  and information services to schools, libraries and museums at low
  cost

* new forms of delivering learning and better advice and information
  about learning opportunities, especially through a *'learndirect'* free
  telephone helpline to provide a national information service about
  learning

* support for learners, including personal learning accounts, the first
  1 million of which would be opened in 1999 (but no information
  has been forthcoming subsequently as to quite how government
  will 'strongly encourage' employers to put money into employees'

ILAs, other than subsequently granting tax relief on their contributions

- involvement of business, employees and trade unions in developing workplace skills, and supporting education through unions with a £2 million employee education development fund (Court, 1998: 6)

- promotion of Investors in People, particularly in small firms, so that it becomes a general industry standard (around 29,000 UK companies, covering almost one-third of working people, were by then involved in IIP)

- promotion of continuous professional development across all the professions.

Strategic intent was clear. It was crucial practicalities that remained uncertain.

The University for Industry (learndirect)

From your own research, what *is* the UfI? And what are some of the main resource implications that it raises?

Feedback notes

- The UfI (now branded 'learndirect') is not a university in the conventional sense. It will not offer its own qualifications, and it is not exclusively for industry, but 'the heart of its mission is to tackle the chronic lack of basic skills, which … handicaps national economic competitiveness' (Kingston, 1999: 1f). Through a network of 1,000 'learning centres' run by a consortia of bodies – employers, unions, voluntary groups and so on – in accessible (rather than traditional educational) locations, its aim is to cover learning at every level from elementary to postgraduate. The Internet and the Web are to become key learning tools, enabling learners to interact and learning packages best suited to each individual to be easily accessed. In late 1999, on target, the UfI opened 70 development centres nationwide as a pilot for its official launch in September 2000. There is more about the UfI in Chapter 12.

- UfI plans beg large resource questions. Development centres will only be able to realise their potential when fully operational IT and support systems are established. The UfI has no funding of its own to disburse. It can act only as a broker, attracting people to learning and pointing them to the most relevant provider. Although it has secured funding from the Further Education Funding Council until 2001, the future thereafter is uncertain (*ibid*) because the FEFC's role is to be taken over in that year by the new national learning and skills council. As yet there is no information about the resources that higher education will be given to do UFI work (Court, 1998: 7).

- Learndirect helpline will operate to help people to make the right learning choices, with advice about qualifications to be given in easily understandable form. Again, this raises practical questions. Will it tend simply to redistribute students, steering many to UfI centres rather than to traditional further education institutions (Kingston, 1999: 4f)? Will it confuse, rather than clarify, the territory of post-16 education and training?

How will 'The Learning Age' and 'Lifelong Learning' be implemented?
Learning to Succeed White Paper and legislation: 1999

In July 1999, after an unexpectedly protracted two-year consultation period, the DfEE produced its *Learning to Succeed* White Paper to explain how the changes heralded in the two 1998 Green Papers would be implemented (DfEE, 1999a). The White Paper announced that a new implementation framework to integrate all post-16 educational and training provision would be put into place after April 2001. The main proposals were:

- The (by now) 72 TECs across England would be scrapped in favour of a single, central government body, the national learning and skills council (NLSC) working through 47 local learning skills councils (LSCs). There would be a new council for education and training in Wales.

- The NLSC would be responsible for planning and delivery of all post-16 education and training up to but not including higher education. It would take over the role of the Further Education Funding Council (to be abolished), and so be responsible for funding the further education sector. A training budget five times as big as the one previously allocated to TECs would be operated by the LSCs, and the NLSC's combined budget for both systems (education and training) would rise to around £6 billion.

- The NLSC would provide demand-focused, integrated information, advice and guidance services in post-16 training and development to achieve lifelong learning, and would advise the Government on the national learning targets. The intention was to reduce red tape and incoherence in post-16 provision of education and training – a big problem that the TEC system had confronted.

- It would fund Modern Apprenticeships, National Traineeships and other TEC training programmes. There would be a new youth programme called Connexions, with dedicated personal advisers for young people to ensure motivation and relevant support.

- The LSCs would take on responsibility for training and also for further (but not higher) education. They would be the NLSCs' operating arms, working to its national learning targets but with the flexibility and freedom to link planning and provision to local needs. It has subsequently been announced by the Education and Employment Minister that a typical LSC will have a budget in excess of £100 million to fund over 100,000 learners.

- In order to ensure local relevance, employers would have the single biggest representation on LSC boards at both national and local level, 'joined by trade unions, government and other voluntary groups' (Rana, 1999d: 33). Together, this group would make up the

40 per cent proportion of representation from 'employment'. Thus, although employers themselves would not be in a majority on LSC boards, it was intended that their presence, and the locally based operation of LSCs, would give flexibility to respond to the needs of the local labour market.

- Responsibility for work-based learning for unemployed adults would be transferred to the Employment Service, to 'integrate these programmes with the New Deal and offer a one-stop shop to claimants' (Roy Harrison, 1999: 70). The NLSC in partnership with local education authorities would develop arrangements for adult and community learning.

- A new independent inspectorate would cover all work-related learning and training for those over 19, to ensure coherent provision with high standards. A separate inspectorate, the existing Ofsted, would cover 16 to 19 provision in addition to its schools' inspection responsibilities.

- There would be an 'entitlement to learning' code for further education students, and those completing their course of study would receive a single end-of-study qualification.

- There would be much-needed cuts in bureaucracy and delivery costs. These should achieve greater efficiency and save at least £50 million.

In November 1999, the Learning and Skills Bill to implement the White Paper was announced in the Queen's Speech. It set out the statutory structures underpinning the English and Welsh Learning and Skills Councils. The main thrust of the *Learning to Succeed* proposals now seems certain to be enacted, with the new NLSC likely to be in place by April 2001.

Moving on

Summarise the main proposals in the 1999 White Paper *Learning to Succeed*. How far do they appear to offer a realistic way forward in the implementation of NVET strategy and the avoidance of the TEC system's shortcomings?

Feedback notes
- Roy Harrison, CIPD adviser on training and development, welcomed the White Paper proposals as offering a 'coherent and balanced system of funding academic, vocational and work-focused learning, together with recognition of unit-level attainment' (Roy Harrison, 1999: 69). He believed the proposals could lead to parity of esteem and treatment for the different routes to lifelong learning.

- Employers were uncertain. Many feared that the new structure will prove too centralised and rigid (Rana, 1999e). They also feared that they would no longer have a real role to play, and that their hard work and leadership throughout the TEC decade would be thrown away. Few may wish to serve on local boards 'if they see them as mere talking shops controlled by the national council' (Rana, 1999d: 33). Latchford (1999) commented that the NLSC, like the new small business service, is a government agency. It therefore differs significantly from TECs in its constitution and in the way it can operate. It has a duty of local consultation, but 'local flexibility is likely to be suppressed by the detail of implementation' (*ibid*). Such agencies can become 'safe, inflexible rule-followers' (*ibid*). The Confederation of British Industry has advocated a devolved, employer-driven system with access to local spending power.

• Unions had by now become closely involved with work-based training, through initiatives such as the government-backed Union Learning Fund. They welcomed the 1999 White Paper proposal because it included them on the boards of national and local LSCs, whereas they had been excluded from TECs. However, its policy officer, Bert Clough, felt that employer domination of the new system could lead to a short-term and narrowly focused view of skills needs that might ignore national priorities (Rana, 1999e).

• There are further concerns. The transference of training for unemployed to the Employment Service may divide training provision between that for the employed and that for the unemployed. This would be counterproductive at a time when many are moving repeatedly between spells in and out of work as the employment market experiences rapid and continuous change (Roy Harrison, 1999: 70). Government has also failed, as it failed with the TEC system, to recognise the importance of securing the expertise of human resource professionals at the strategic level within this new organisation (*ibid*).

For educationalists, there were particular worries:

• The NLSC was to establish a clear regulatory framework for post-16 provision. This made colleges wonder what impact this would have on the autonomy that, in 1992, was passed down to them. At this point (early 2000), important detail of the roles and powers of LSCs as they relate to colleges has yet to emerge. Information about the fate of sixth form colleges, and whether there will at last be a common funding structure across all 16 to 19 provision, is also unavailable until April 2001 (Tester, 1999: 3F). And will the power of intervention of the NLSC be greater than that of the Further Education Funding Council (*ibid*)?

• The omission of higher education from the proposals is puzzling, and the intention to have two separate inspectorates to oversee quality of provision seems likely to confuse unless they each 'abide by the same rules to avoid a repeat of the present system of duplication and wasteful bureaucracy' (Tester, 1999: 3F).

• Above all, how are all these proposals to be paid for? In 1998 an extra £165 million was provided by the DfEE, but that was to come largely out of anticipated income from student fee contributions introduced in that year. For higher education in particular, there was frustration at the absence of a 'realistic analysis' (Court, 1998) of how to afford the involvement in workplace learning urged on the higher education system by the Green Paper, *The Learning Age.* There was uncertainty about how to cope with the additional numbers of students due to enter the system by 2002, and about how to improve the links between higher and further education on the one hand and employers and individuals on the other.

- The Green Paper required existing education and training institutions (to) 'transform themselves'. By 1999, the vice-president of the Committee of Vice-Chancellors and Principals of UK universities was able to report that 'only half our applicants come direct from school or college. The other half are mature and with a great variety of qualifications and life experience' (Floud, 1999). This was surely a sign of progress towards the national vision of lifelong learning. But how real a sign? As the Association of University Teachers pointed out (Court, 1998), 'such a transformation needs adequate human and physical resources and the co-operation of those the government is asking to deliver lifelong learning'. So far (early in 2000) crucial information is lacking.

NVET – CHALLENGES AHEAD

In the UK, the NVET system has always been flawed by its exposure to political short-termism and expediency. Educational provision is still beset by complex problems of disparities between academic and vocational pathways, poor standards, multiplicity of providers, resource constraints, tensions between forces of centralisation and decentralisation, and intractable 'underclass' problems. The achievement of work-related skills and the intellectual development needed to underpin them, the advancement of learning to sustain the cultural life of society and its innovative capability, and the role of education in ensuring societal well-being – such needs do not sit comfortably together. The strains grow as the needs intensify.

Tackling these issues means that the Government must ensure:

- a powerful integrating vision driving NVET policy overall, which can be realised, resourced and sustained at the practical level

- coherency, collaboration and integration between educational providers who between them offer a wide variety of routes to lifelong learning

- improved standards of educational attainment across the whole educational system, and the significant reduction of the 'underclass' problem, in schools, in further and higher education, and in the employment market

- a better balance between the tackling and achievement of immediate and longer-term aims, to ensure that NVET adequately serves social as well as economic ends.

It is these concerns that explain the many reforms in the NVET system since the late 1980s. At this point, early in 2000, it is the practicalities related to the most recent announcements that pose the unanswered questions. Crucial details on learning skills councils' allocations, funding and other related issues are the subject of two consultation documents, one in January 2000, the other in May 2000. Until their outcomes are known, it is impossible to assess how far the changes are likely to be successful, and to what extent government commitment to lifelong learning convinces as reality rather than rhetoric.

CONCLUSION

Having read this chapter and completed its reviews and self-checks, you should now:

- understand the main thrust of vision and policy for the education system in England and Wales since the mid-1980s

- understand major problems involved in achieving an integrated system of post-16 national vocational education and training (NVET)

- be able to explain and evaluate the Labour Government's main aims and direction for national vocational education and training policy and strategy since 1997.

To test yourself against these objectives, what five-minute answers would you give to the following questions? (Dates in brackets refer to the IPD qualifying examination paper in which a question appeared.)

- Outline some major pressures that have been experienced by the tertiary (higher and further) education system in Britain in recent years, and briefly assess their likely consequences (May 1999).

- Outline **three** initiatives produced by government since the late 1980s to improve the plight of failing schools.

- Briefly explain the Labour Government's proposals in 2000 to launch 'City Academies', outlining their rationale.

USEFUL READING

HEVEY D. (1997) 'The UK national (and Scottish) vocational qualification system: state of the art or in a state?' *International Journal of Training and Development*. Vol. 1, 4. pp242–58.

REID M. A. *and* BARRINGTON H. (1999) *Training Interventions: Promoting learning opportunities*. 6th edn. London, Institute of Personnel and Development. pp33–57. (Provides information up to April 1999 only, and therefore does not cover *Learning to Succeed* and subsequent developments.)

The information in Chapter 3 will need to be regularly updated. The following are recommended as particularly helpful reading:

- the quality press – and especially the Sunday 'heavies' and *The Financial Times* – for their regular articles and editorials on matters relating to the field of secondary and tertiary education, and national training

- *The Times Educational Supplement* and *The Times Higher Educational Supplement* and similar regular reviews

- local libraries, chambers of commerce, TECs/LECS (after April 2001, Learning Skills Councils) all of which have valuable, up-to-date information and examples of good practice in the field

- the Department for Education and Employment website at www.dfee.gov.uk; it is a source of comprehensive information about NVET policy and progress

- information about the University for Industry (now branded learndirect) can be found through learndirect's drop-in centres, through www.ufiltd.co.uk, and through the free helpline 0800 100 900.

4 International comparisons

LEARNING OBJECTIVES

After reading this chapter you will:

- have a context for understanding the international – and especially the European – scenario relating to vocational education and training (VET)

- understand the key differences between national vocational education and training (NVET) systems in major competitor countries and the UK

- be able to assess what lessons such comparisons offer both for UK Government policy on VET and for human resource development (HRD) policy in individual organisations.

NVET: A FRAMEWORK FOR UNDERSTANDING

We have seen in previous chapters that the development of people operates within a context of vision and strategies of the organisation and, ultimately, of the nation. The same is true when we seek to understand HRD on the international stage: the basic context is still one of vision, policies and strategies. In this chapter a straightforward conceptual framework is presented. It involves three interacting parameters: the socio-economic, the labour market and the educational.

The first part of the chapter deals with the European framework for NVET. Next come some cross-country comparisons. Finally, lessons are drawn for the UK and for individual organisations.

VET POLICY IN EUROPE

The socio-economic parameter

The Single European Market (SEM) has two aims (Hendry, 1994: 93):

- the removal of all artificial barriers to the stimulation of trade within the European Community (EC)

- the improvement, by means of their restructuring and inter-nationalisation resulting from that stimulation, of European firms' competitive capability in the global market.

These two aims involve tensions between economic and social interests. The European Commission's vision of VET is one of many powerful contributors to the development of the EC, meeting a range of social and economic public policy objectives (Commission of the EC, 1989: 3). This vision may seem essentially the same as the vision for VET policy in the UK, but the way in which policy is formulated and implemented across most of the EU is very different from the UK's non-regulatory approach.

At Community level, the Directorate General for employment, industrial relations and social affairs holds responsibility within the Commission for training. Policy is executed by a Task Force on Human Resources, Education, Training and Youth. An advisory committee for vocational training and an education committee meet regularly with union and employer bodies to discuss training as part of the 'social dialogue'. 'Social dialogue' is an important term. It refers to a process involving the social partners in training policy in order to encourage employers to contribute to long-term profitability and economic performance rather than training only for immediate needs. This dialogue enables stakeholder interests, in the shape of organisations representing employers and unions, to agree on policy that is informed by practical knowledge and expertise, and increases the likelihood of successful implementation. Together, the Community's social partners have produced a series of joint Opinions endorsing the importance of education and training within the SEM (Rainbird, 1993: 185). Most member states (apart from the UK) mirror this Community-level approach by having some form of regulation of the VET system, and by incorporating employer and trade union interests into the policy-making process.

The labour market parameter
A four-fold labour market matrix
A country's labour market, like an organisation's, can be divided broadly into two segments (van der Klink and Mulder, 1995):

- *primary*. Entry to this segment requires professional qualifications and sometimes specific vocational training. People in the primary segment of the labour market (or organisation) usually enjoy favourable terms of employment and working conditions, relatively high job security and good promotion prospects.

- *secondary*. In this segment most jobs involve routine manual work, and what training there is tends to be focused on improving productivity on the job, not on opening up career paths for individuals. There are few, if any, of the advantages enjoyed in the primary segment, since there are minimum training requirements, poor terms of employment and little job security.

The labour market itself has two sectors:

- *external* – people waiting for employment, including relatively large numbers of school-leavers, the unemployed and women returners

- *internal* – comprising the human resource base of the organisation, where employee resourcing policy can produce an integrated flow of people into, through and out of the organisation, with a particular focus on performance management, personnel development, career paths and an interlinking HRD policy.

Use of this four-fold matrix can show the extent to which a country's labour market links its educational system to its business needs. The matrix can be applied to an organisation's internal labour market and educational system in the same way.

The links between employee resourcing and development policy in your own organisation

Use the four-fold matrix described above to examine your own organisation and to identify employee resourcing and development policies and issues.

Record on your matrix approximately what proportion of your organisation's employees is in the primary sector (highly qualified/professional/highly trained and skilled employees) and what proportion is in the secondary sector (semi-skilled and unskilled). Then, looking at these two sectors, record the kind and proportion of employees in each to be customarily recruited from the external labour market, and to be customarily recruited from internal sources.

What does your completed matrix suggest to you about your organisation's recruitment, development and retention policies? Does it indicate any need for change?

Europe's routes to competitive advantage

Although competing on efficiency and low costs are two possible routes to competitive advantage, their benefits can cancel each other out in net terms. It is the quality route, focusing on high added value, which promises to minimise the immediate costs of the SEM and to maximise its longer-term benefits. That route involves 'capital investment in new production techniques and products, an expanding knowledge base, and a more highly skilled workforce' (Hendry, 1994: 98). A high-skill strategy requires a strong and successful VET drive. Without this, a large proportion of the labour force will remain trapped in the secondary segment of the labour market and it will not be possible to sustain a drive for quality and innovation.

The UK, like Spain and Greece, is disadvantaged in a drive for long-term quality, being competitively strong only in some (perhaps one-third) of its industrial sectors. Germany, on the other hand, possesses competitive strength in most of its sectors, with 73 per cent of its employment in the primary segment of the labour market. Another source of disadvantage for the UK is that its large firms distribute significantly more of their profits to investors and significantly less to employees than do such firms elsewhere in Europe. This means that employees have less sense of ownership, and also that there is a lower level of investment in those areas that fuel innovation and growth – research and development and HRD – than is the case generally across the rest of Europe. Typical consequences of this culture of short-termism and of shareholder domination in the UK include a low level of average wage and of productivity, reflecting and reinforcing lack of adequate investment in education and training for skills and in employee rewards.

Hendry (1994) pointed out that in the UK's low-wage economy, which is also more internationalised than any other economy in the EC, workers are particularly vulnerable. Internationalised companies require strong social controls in order to avoid exploiting low-wage economies, but the UK has consistently resisted the Social Chapter's attempts to provide such controls.

It would be easy to conclude from the above comments that in a European Community where the quality route is the one being chosen by the majority of countries, the few that, like the UK, are low-wage economies with relatively unregulated labour markets are likely to lose. However, there is another viewpoint that puts the UK's labour and VET policies in a rather different perspective.

Achieving a flexible labour market

It was always predicted that there would be job losses on a major scale in the first few years of the SEM's existence as administrative barriers came down, but the position was expected to correct itself after about six years. In reality, unemployment rates across most of the European Union (EU) are still high, averaging over 8 per cent in early 1997, and job creation has been low. However, economies like the USA and the UK which have deregulated labour markets and more labour flexibility have generated more service-sector jobs than Continental Europe has. Many of these jobs have been part-time, and many taken by women (Wolf, 1994). These countries have also achieved lower youth and female unemployment rates. The USA has the additional advantages of a thriving domestic economy and a mobile population, and so does not have the persistent divide between high and low unemployment regions characteristic of Europe and of the UK.

The EU also suffers from poor export performance and slow growth of output. An important factor here is its heavy labour costs, to which three major contributors are protective labour legislation, relatively high taxation, and a flabby and highly bureaucratised public sector. The steady appreciation of European currencies against the US dollar has added to the EU's competitive disadvantage.

These failures to achieve the expected benefits of the SEM are putting increasing pressure on a hitherto highly differentiated labour market across Europe. Signs of convergence are becoming evident. Country differences rarely explain comparative competitive advantage, since weaknesses in one area of practice tend to cancel out gains in another, leaving the total package of labour costs, flexibility and skill levels similar across Europe (Goodhart, 1994). Now, as Balls and Goodhart have identified (1994), wage restraint is becoming a trend across Europe. There have been few signs of significant social dumping – a process that involves such measures as lowering wage costs, cutting social benefits, increasing hours of work and reducing restraints on employers. Reductions in direct wages and job cuts have occurred but by 1997 were proving to be the consequence less of a deliberate dumping policy or of the feared cheap labour/low-cost competition from Far East countries, but more a consequence of technical and organisational change.

Flexibility is the real issue here. Rising real wages and failures in training and education systems are leaving European countries ill equipped to compete with the USA and Japan in future high-tech products, in the same way as cheap imports from low-wage developing countries are undercutting the expensive products of European manufacturers of medium- and low-tech goods (Balls and Goodhart, 1994). As the shift towards more sophisticated technology grows in advanced economies and as fewer, better-educated workers are employed in manufacturing, wage and labour flexibility become vital for Europe. Failure to adjust is in time bound to lead to high and persistent unemployment.

This suggests a need for more labour market deregulation in the EU. It needs to be sufficient to give the necessary wage and labour flexibility but not enough to threaten the level of job security needed to maintain workers' commitment. Many commentators feel that the labour market models of the UK and the USA are proving more relevant for the future than the tightly regulated Germanic model spreading across the Netherlands, Belgium and France. In the decade up to 1997, the UK achieved faster growth in productivity than its European partners, and in the USA's highly deregulated labour market job creation has remained strong. In both countries the wages of the skilled have steadily climbed, and in the UK average earnings rose more steeply in the year from January 1999 to 2000 than in any other period in the previous seven years (Thornton, 2000).

However, there is a downside here. In an article summarising research undertaken by academics at Sheffield Hallam University, funded by the Economic and Social Research Council, Paterson (2000) noted that although official UK figures now showed record numbers of people in work, joblessness at a 20-year low, and an expansion in vacancies, the number of economically inactive men (those neither in work nor registered as unemployed) now appeared to exceed by two to one the number registered as unemployed. (Female participation in employment, on the other hand, was rising steadily.) Whatever the reasons for this kind of situation, the implications are worrying, especially because a substantial proportion of the long-term male sick are highly skilled manual workers. It must also be remembered that, because of its poor training record, the UK lacks the large pool of skilled workers essential to competitiveness and has much more ground to make up in that direction than most of its competitors.

The plight of the unskilled underclass
In Chapter 3, we saw the plight of the educational underclass, and noted its potential implications for the economy. For those emerging from that underclass into semi-skilled or manual jobs at best, unemployment at worst, the future is bleak. To be unskilled in today's global market place is to belong to the most vulnerable of groups in the labour market. Employment creation inevitably favours the more highly skilled workers, and in 20 countries across Europe there is strong evidence to indicate that the labour market has an overall bias

against less skilled or lower-paid workers (Wood, 1994). The underclass consistently forms between 10 per cent and 20 per cent of all earners, and its plight is growing, particularly with the influx of the cheap unskilled labour that gives Third World countries their competitive edge. In any country, the size of the underclass will not decrease unless basic educational standards improve – the cause of the concern of educationalists and government in the UK. Meanwhile, those left within it are falling ever further behind (Marris, 1995).

In the UK and the USA the effects have been worse in this respect than elsewhere, even though in terms of per capita earnings unskilled workers have done better over the past decade than in mainland Europe (Marris, 1995). Whether, as in the UK, the unskilled tend to form the bulk of the unemployed or whether, as in the USA, they tend to form the bulk of the very poorly paid, they consistently fare worst in the competition for jobs and wages. Their lack of a good basic education compounds their vulnerable position.

There needs to be an investment in training that will give core workers sound basic education and the opportunity to invest and reinvest in workplace skills. Although in terms of good basic education Europe overall compares favourably with the USA, it compares unfavourably with Pacific Rim countries; and at higher educational level it also compares unfavourably with the USA, only 30 per cent of young Europeans moving into tertiary education, as opposed to nearly 70 per cent of young Americans.

In the UK, Conservative and Labour governments have been attempting to overcome these problems since the late 1980s, and there are signs of slow improvement. NVET policy aims to improve both the basic education system and vocational training while also trying to ensure, through a national system of vocational qualifications and closer partnership with unions and employers, the removal of occupational barriers in a hitherto rigidly divided labour market.

'Training as social engineering won't work'

Consider the following arguments that underpin the belief that 'training as social engineering won't work', and then provide an opposite viewpoint.

'Profit comes first, then training', said a *Daily Telegraph* editorial in 1996, continuing with the argument that in a period of steady growth and low inflation, such as was then being enjoyed, the provision of training by employers rises naturally without the need for government intervention, because successful companies spend money on training when they can afford it. Naturally they are wise to reduce investment in hard times, because training adds to costs, and in hard times rising costs are not affordable, leading usually to higher unemployment. Therefore the Government should focus its investment not on improving national vocational training schemes – which in any case have high drop-out rates and are ill equipped to meet the real needs of industry – but on improving the basic educational system (as in Japan and the USA) so that young people have the necessary standards of literacy and numeracy for skills development in-company when they enter the labour market.

Smith (1996) believed that training as social engineering will not work: the role of training is to improve the labour market position of those who receive it, not to change the unemployment figures. He observed that Sweden spends four times as much on training as a share of national income than Britain, but it has a higher unemployment rate, which extensive national training programmes, especially for young people, have not dented. On the other hand Britain has grown faster than Europe in recent years despite a poor VET record. He concluded that investment in training can make a real difference to emerging economies, lifting them to a position where they can compete internationally, but that thereafter it has little impact on competitive capability.

(*Sources*: D. Smith, 1996: 8; the *Daily Telegraph*, 1996: 19)

Feedback notes

- The claim that 'Training as social engineering won't work' is too simplistic. The strongest argument for a higher level of investment in VET in the UK lies not in a claim that it will reduce current unemployment or lead directly to job creation, but that it is essential to the economy's long-term and sustained growth, and to reduce the disparities between skilled and unskilled in competition for well-paid jobs.

- Without a larger pool of high-skilled, well-educated workers, an inability to raise the UK's general level of competitiveness will hold back its chances of strong and sustained economic growth.

- Without a strong and flexible primary labour market segment and adequate investment in research and development, the economy cannot generate the innovation that will provide the means for future growth.

- Without better basic education and adequate vocational training, those who are unskilled will continue to form the bulk of the unemployed and underpaid in UK society. They will also constitute a major barrier to the more flexible labour market essential to competitive advantage. National investment must therefore focus equally on educational reform and on providing a strong national vocational training and qualification system, with free access for those in the secondary as well as primary segments of the labour market.

The internal labour market

Good human resource development policies in organisations can do much to improve the pool of skilled labour locally and nationally. However, if – as is so often the case – there is a rigid division of labour within an organisation, it then becomes very difficult for manual workers to acquire the professional competencies that could gain them entrance to the primary sector of the labour market (van der Klink and Mulder, 1995). New technologies, and especially the Internet, are increasingly providing the impetus to integrate hitherto rigidly separated categories of work, but for that to happen, employees must be able to acquire the necessary competencies. If their educational background is weak and their grasp of practical skills poor, then retraining may be impossible. When that happens a company will be forced to maintain its division of labour, buying in the requisite skills but not resolving the fundamental weakness of a workforce that cannot respond rapidly and creatively to market changes because it is so segmented and inflexible.

Inescapably, therefore, the lack of an adequate VET system will lead to a labour market geared mainly to the manufacture of comparatively cheap mass products, because that is what it has the competencies to produce. In such an economy there will be a declining demand for skilled employees. This, in turn, reinforces lack of investment within organisations in the vocational education and training that could produce more people capable of entering the primary rather than the secondary labour market segment. Caught in such a vicious cycle it is not surprising that British companies have not been keen to invest in HRD, and that the internal labour market is not generating sufficient skills needed by the economy.

The following case-study is based on a real-life company. Answering the question will help you to review the material covered so far in this chapter.

Case-study: Sentex Engineering Company Ltd

What are the basic issues underlying training and development at Sentex?

Context

Sentex Engineering Company Ltd, formed in 1950, manufactures small, high-quality electronic machines for use in a specialised field. Six years ago the business was operating in a narrow and declining market in which its product was a high-quality mechanical specialist machine. However, after a management buy-out and the development and piloting of a prototype electronic machine, a more multifaceted machine was produced. This rapidly captured the British market and moved successfully into the wider European market. Now, the firm has captured about 40 per cent of the world market within its specialised sector but faces increasing competition as it seeks to expand its European market base. With the world population for the specialist product rising, the aim for Sentex is growth by acquisition and diversification.

Corporate strategy

The firm has a strong vision of trail-blazing, excellence and world-class products. The MD's style is open and discussion-based, but he believes that participation in strategy is best restricted to those at the top unless there is genuine difficulty or failure to agree. He has set one long-term corporate goal, which relates to the need for continuing growth. Within that goal the directors annually draw up shorter-term objectives for their own functional areas and agree with their staff on how these can be achieved. Particular issues such as product reliability, quality and standards are targeted over an agreed timescale.

Strategic strengths and weaknesses

The major strengths of the firm are its 300 employees, especially the management team and certain key individuals; excellent basic products; good tools and machines; strong capability in research and development (R&D) and engineering; a first-class network of licensees; and a secure financial base.

Main weaknesses arise from the fact that the firm has been very slow to make the transition from mechanical to sophisticated electronic manufacturing and is still trying to master the complexities of operating in an international market.

Human resource management issues

The MD has not until now felt the need for an explicit HR strategy. Now, however, human resources are becoming a priority issue because the firm must have more flexibility of skills. Currently, the main skills shortages are in R&D, where there is also very high turnover. There are also regular shortages in production and services. In the component assembly area such problems are tackled by buying in. The assembly operation is amateurish, and there is no mechanism for ideas for improvements coming from the shop floor. The new manager there takes the view that anyone who performs inadequately after basic training must leave, and that any but job-related training is an unaffordable cost to the business. Service staff are particularly difficult to obtain. They also take years to train in the variety of skills they need and have to be away from home for up to nine months of the year, making training difficult. Training has been limited to only a few of this staff's skill areas; for the rest, they have to pick things up as they go along.

The MD sees a bigger and more strategic investment in training as an urgent priority. However, with the company developing so fast, it is difficult to foresee exactly what training will be needed. Staff are continually firefighting, and usually they are so busy that time off for training cannot be found.

Feedback notes

Significant issues relating to the development of Sentex's workforce include the following:

- Sentex has chosen a high-quality route to competitive advantage and is operating in an increasingly competitive international market. It therefore needs to build a workforce that is flexible, without any rigid division of labour, and with well-educated employees who either already possess or who have the potential to acquire the competencies needed in a rapidly changing situation. This has obvious implications for recruitment, selection, pay, training and continuous and career development systems.

- Some of the trends noted under the heading 'Human resource management issues' are worrying in this respect. It is clear that there are tensions between the need for cost efficiency and high immediate productivity, and the need to develop skills and competencies for the future. Since that future is unpredictable, investing in an integrated, well-educated workforce will be essential, with strategic thinking and creative behaviour encouraged in every worker.

• On the other hand, there are favourable signs: an MD who is committed to a more strategic investment in training and development, a vision focusing on world-class excellence and long-term growth, and high-calibre employees. In such a situation an expert HR manager can make a strong case for a better balance of the short and the longer term in HRD strategy, and especially for interventions to improve the vocational attainments and competencies of the workforce. There must also be a drive for management development to ensure managerial style and skills better suited to achieving the high-quality, world-class goals essential to the success of the business over time.

The educational parameter

A country's educational system determines its levels of basic education and also the acquisition and potential to acquire work-based competencies. That system can be either full-time or dual (van der Klink and Mulder, 1995: 159).

• In the *full-time system* students do most of their training at a state (or independent) institution of study – a school, college or university – and least in-company. In such a system the main emphasis will be on obtaining theoretical qualifications. Funding is likely to be split, the state helping to resource external provision and the employer carrying the main responsibility for funding training in employment. The UK system is of this kind.

• The *dual system* is a partnership in which vocational training is largely provided on the job with less, but complementary, provision in institutions of study away from the company. In such a system there is bound to be a dominating emphasis on students' obtaining the practical competencies they need to practise their profession. Theoretical qualifications will be focused on acquiring knowledge that will underpin such competencies. Funding is likely to be shared between state and employers. The German system is of this kind.

The socio-economic and labour market contexts described earlier in the chapter explain why the European Commission in its educational policy must do two crucial things:

• improve the level of basic education in certain states

• spread scarce skills more efficiently across the Community and increase the stock of those skills. Greater mobility will make the labour market more efficient, and so the Commission is working for common vocational standards, transferability of qualification and student exchanges.

Feedback notes

Some of the main weaknesses are:

• separation of VET roles in the UK system between the state, employers and educational establishments

---

Skills deficiencies in the UK: some causes

On the basis of your reading so far in this chapter and in Chapters 2 and 3, outline some of the weaknesses that differentiate the UK's VET system from those of the EU and other competitor countries and help to explain its persistent skills shortages.

- lack of incentives in the UK for individuals or organisations to invest in VET
- far fewer numbers and proportions achieving craft-level qualifications and technical qualifications in the UK than in most competitor countries
- a labour market in the UK in which a high proportion of the workforce tends to be trapped by rigid division of labour and high demand for a low level of skills
- a narrow base of skills and knowledge in the UK, limiting employee flexibility.

INTERNATIONAL COMPARISONS IN VET

Within as well as across countries, NVET systems are influenced not only by socio-economic, labour-market and educational differences but also by differences to do with legal systems, history and tradition, and work-related values and other cultural dimensions. Meaningful comparative data are difficult to obtain. That said, there are still insights to be achieved by some generalised comparisons. These will need to be regularly updated, using the kind of information sources noted at the end of the chapter.

Vocational qualification rates
In Germany, 75 per cent of the population is skilled to craft level, whereas in Britain the comparable figure is only 30 per cent. In Britain too, 20 per cent of adults are 'without qualification, literacy or numeracy' (Gracie, 1999, in conversation with the head of the National Skills Taskforce). Reports from the independent National Institute for Economic and Social Research continue to show that the UK still lags significantly behind many competitor countries in terms of its basic education and training. This means that once young people enter the labour market, they are likely to have access only to the secondary segment and to remain trapped there. The need for dramatic improvement is the greater because of changes in jobs that will take place over the next 20 years. Higher-level professional, scientific, technical, managerial and administration jobs will continue to grow fast, and the proportion of knowledge workers continue to increase, against a backdrop of an ageing workforce where there will not be large inflows of new young workers because of a demographic downturn likely to continue for at least two more decades.

At this point, comparison with the situation of France in the 1960s is instructive. At that time France had more acute problems of skills shortages and educational levels than the UK faced at the end of the 1980s. There was also, as in the UK, a widespread reluctance of employers to take a lead in the vocational training of young people. In the 1970s and 1980s the pace of technological and skills change in the French economy was great, yet France managed to equip her workforce to cope effectively with all the demands that faced it. The key to success was the use of government-set targets of vocational attainment using full-time education to provide courses leading to the combined craft and general education CAP certificates. 'A coherent range of qualifications means that practically the whole ability range can gain nationally recognized qualifications which are frequently rewarded by higher pay' (Steedman, 1990). A set of vocational A levels was added in the late 1980s, based on the craft-level CAP (equivalent to City and Guilds craft certificate and several GCSE passes) but still able to lead to higher education. Subsequently there were concerns about CAP, and new legislation in the early 1990s aimed to improve the quality and flexibility of apprenticeship in France. The similarities with curriculum and other VET reforms in the 1990s in the UK are obvious.

Vocational education and training
Although the school-leaving age across Europe varies from 14 to 16, there is already a major emphasis on extending full-time education and training to the age of 18 in Sweden, Belgium, Luxembourg, Greece and Ireland. There is a similar emphasis in France, but there both full-time vocational and apprenticeship training are important for the age group. In Germany and the Netherlands, part-time attendance at a school or college is compulsory up to age 18. In Denmark the emphasis is on young school-leavers moving into the apprenticeship system, as it is in Germany where, however, the term covers most jobs that 16-year-olds can be employed to do. In the UK in 1990 only 53 per cent of children were staying on in school or college, but by 1994 the figure had reached nearly 73 per cent and it has continued to rise subsequently. However, in 1995 it was estimated that only 50 per cent of such UK students could be considered to be in vocational training, compared with 80 per cent in Germany (Smith, 1995). As has been seen in Chapters 2 and 3, the present Government is trying to boost this percentage significantly with its new NVET policy, but it will be some time yet before the practical effects begin to make themselves felt across the economy.

In Greece, vocational education can start at 15. In France, technical subjects can start at 13 or 14, as they can in Belgium, Luxembourg, Ireland and the Netherlands. By 1986 only 15 per cent of young French people left full-time education without completing a vocational course, and more than 70 per cent of 16- to 18-year-olds were staying on in full-time education, compared with just over 30 per cent in Britain (Steedman, 1990).

In the UK, vocational education starting at 14 is still struggling for effective integration with mainstream academic pathways (see Chapter 3) but attempts to develop a unified sector of VET for the 16- to 18-year-old age group are beginning to bear fruit. This has been aided since the early 1990s by tying national funding for youth training heavily to attainment of National Vocational Qualifications (NVQs) and to success in job search.

Occupational standards

In most EU countries (except the UK) youth wages are low until a significant level of vocational qualification has been achieved. In most competitor countries, too, occupational training is tied to the attainment of national standards, and it is widely assumed that young people without a degree will be vocationally qualified. In Germany the aim (achieved in 1984 by over 90 per cent of its young people) is that none without a satisfactorily completed apprenticeship should enter the labour market. It is also illegal in Germany, as it is not in the UK, to stop youth training before it has gone full term, or to stop the off-the-job element during the training period.

There has been growing concern since the late 1980s in a number of European countries (for example, Greece, France, the Irish Republic and Portugal) to improve the legal framework governing apprenticeship. Some have introduced more flexibility at local level to vary course length and content to suit local needs (for example, the Netherlands and France). Even in Germany, the dual system that remains a model for the rest of Europe has attracted criticism relating to inflexibility, length, its overtheoretical nature and the lack of co-ordination between examining bodies, leading to inconsistent standards (Incomes Data Services, 1993: 64). The UK, then, is not alone in its struggle to improve occupational standards.

Continuous learning and development

In our major competitor countries there is a wide acceptance of the need for continuing education and training in order to ensure advancement and adaptation. In Germany and France, local chambers of commerce make available training for employed workers, and in most countries there are now arrangements to train the unemployed – often, too, to help those likely to become unemployed. In the UK under the Labour Government, a series of radical measures are being announced in order to implement national policy on lifelong learning (see Chapters 2 and 3). However, it remains the case that the distinction between education and training, like the distinction between vocational and non-vocational education and training, is more marked here than in most of our competitor countries.

Coverage of industrial training

Per head of the workforce Germany was by the mid-1980s training each year twice as many mechanics, electricians and construction workers, and even more office and distributive trade workers, as the UK (Prais and Wagner, 1981; Prais, 1985). In the UK, managerial and supervisory training tends to receive the highest level of investment, followed by technical and professional training, and then by blue-collar worker training. Our clerical training has traditionally been poor in both quantity and quality compared with France and Germany (Steedman, 1987). This uneven coverage of the training investment in the UK raises the likelihood of a serious shortage of skills in the middle and lower ranks of workforces, which in turn can impede the implementation of technological change and more flexible work patterns.

Training for manual workers in the UK has been almost entirely in the form of apprenticeships, with the cost carried by employers. Since the 1990s, both Conservative and Labour governments have made significant attempts to reverse the disastrous decline that occurred in manufacturing (as in other) apprenticeships between 1964 and 1986, starting with the introduction of the Modern Apprenticeship scheme in 1993. As we saw in Chapter 2 (page 27), there is still much ground to be made up before national skills shortages in key areas of the economy significantly diminish.

Investment in VET
Inter-country comparisons of levels of investment in VET are particularly fallible because of the differences in the way data are collected and analysed, and because relatively little is known about in-company investment and its outcomes. Evaluation of the effectiveness of training, for example, is weak in most European countries (although, interestingly, stronger in the UK). It is therefore impossible to know much about the true value added by investment in training in those countries. In this section, only the most obvious differences between key countries are outlined.

Most of our competitor countries invest substantially in education and training, sharing the cost between the main stakeholders. German employers voluntarily bear the burden of most of the cost and effort involved, working closely with unions and the authorities to provide a high-quality and rigorously administered and controlled NVET system. In Japan the costs are shared by the education system and the employer, with only limited state-sponsored public-sector provision. In France collective agreements usually link pay to vocational and technical qualifications, and small means-tested allowances are available to pupils in secondary and tertiary education.

In the UK the cost of industrial training is carried mainly by employers, but there is a state-funded primary and secondary education system. The government now exercises significant control over the funding of schools as it attempts to develop an education system offering more integrated and comprehensive academic and vocational pathways and more sensitivity to market needs. Recent funding changes in the further and higher education sectors mean that students are having to bear an increasing share of the costs both of fees and of maintenance.

In Sweden the state pays for the integrated upper secondary school; in Italy, France, Belgium, Luxembourg and the Netherlands the state pays for full-time training. In both France and Germany apprentices receive only a modest income, whereas in the UK starting wages at 16 years old can be high, and until recently (with the Modern Apprenticeship scheme) they have not been tied to vocational qualifications.

The French have a training tax, set at a minimum level of expenditure (1.1 per cent of total payroll) to be invested in training by qualified trainers. As was the case with the now defunct British levy-grant system, it has been widely felt to lead to irrelevant training. It has not played any central part in the successful building up of a skilled, highly qualified workforce.

In the USA the ethos of individual initiative and of the innate value of education and training means that individuals invest highly in them, and companies give support where needed. They try to fit training around production in order to minimise lost output costs. The system is less formalised than in Germany, the pressure on employers to provide training coming more from individuals. In 1983 a framework of locally based Private Industry Councils (PICs) was set up, responsible for local implementation of the Job Training Partnership Act, which involves distributing funds for training redundant and disadvantaged unemployed workers. PICs, like the British Training and Enterprise Councils that were modelled significantly on them, have met with mixed success.

After World War II Japan, Germany and the Netherlands rebuilt their education systems, and students today in their schools lead the world in advanced maths, science and other technical subjects. In Japan and Germany teaching is a highly paid and prestigious profession. In Germany teacher training is rigorous and operates at a high academic standard, every type of school requiring its own kind of training course. In the UK, by contrast, teaching has until recently been a relatively poorly paid and low-status profession, with questionable standards of teacher training. Our secondary education system has not focused adequately on science and technology pathways, and this has led to a critical undersupply of teachers in those subject areas and to poor teaching standards. Under the Labour Government especially, a series of steps have recently been taken in the UK to remedy these problems. These steps, still ongoing, include reforms to teacher training, higher salaries especially for younger, well-qualified entrants and those working in inner-city areas where socio-economic problems create special difficulties for the educational system, and moves towards a performance-related pay system (a controversial measure that is proving hard to drive forward).

The USA tends to invest more money on buildings and administration, relatively less going on teacher salaries. There has been much concern at poor standards of teaching and attainment, especially in relation to maths and science instruction, but participation of young people in the American university system is very much higher (at around 70 per cent) than in European countries overall.

Feedback notes

At national level the main needs are for:

- *improved basic educational standards.* OECD statistics in 2000 showed that the proportion of those aged 16 to 19 who were not attending school and were not employed was 19.4 per cent in the UK. That was higher than in 13 other member countries, over three times the rate in France and four times the rate in Germany (Clare, 2000b).

- *an effective, competence-based qualification system.* The Government has sought to establish three routes into the world of work: a work-based route through NVQs, the General National Vocational Qualification (GNVQ) A-level route, and the 'academic' A-level route. Success is proving difficult, and there is a need to learn from practice across most other European countries. Both a

---

Lessons to be learnt from international comparisons

Looking at key differences between NVET in the UK and in leading competitor countries, what are the main needs that emerge for the UK at national level?

---

practical and a theoretical grasp of tasks must be developed and tested – preferably by external examiners in order to ensure uniformity and consistency of skill standards – before a qualification is awarded.

- *adequate investment across different sectors of training.* A formula has still to be found to ensure such adequacy, particularly in the field of craft and technician training.

- *testing to be more rigorously linked to the needs and characteristics of the workplace.* This should be not only in terms of standards reached but also in terms of reliability, punctuality and quality.

- *education and training for flexibility.* When future patterns of demand for skills are so unpredictable, flexibility of skills at an early age is vital. This can be achieved only by a good basic education, together with well-integrated academic and vocational pathways. This also gives young people a wider career choice. Modern apprenticeships and current developments in the NVQ field may right the balance in the UK in due course, but as yet there is much progress to make.

- *continuous development of the workforce.* On the Continent, adult education and training are taken seriously by individuals, employers, trade unions and governments alike. In the UK, it remains to be seen whether the present Government's undoubted commitment to lifelong learning and continuous development both in and out of work (as articulated in the 1999 White Paper *Learning to Succeed*; see Chapter 3) can win the support needed by top employers in order to bring about real change in the workplace.

- *stronger stakeholder involvement in VET policy and its implementation.* As was shown in Chapter 3, a new framework will be in place by 2001. Details of its resourcing are currently unclear. Unless resourcing is adequate, it is unlikely that the new framework will be any more effective than the old was in linking strongly together the main stakeholders – individuals as well as employers and Government – in the formulation and implementation of national labour and training policy.

- *due focus on the long-term.* In the UK employers are expected to carry a heavy burden of responsibility for training. In the recent past this has been typified by government's assumption that they would take charge of delivering Government training for the unemployed through TECs/LECs, and of training for the employed by signing up to the IIP standard. As was seen in Chapter 2, progress in both those areas has been less than was hoped. It seems clear that, if these responsibilities are left mainly to employers to carry out, then short-termism will increasingly dominate. If that happens, then the country's available workforce will not be adequately prepared for the future, and the current geographical and socio-economic disparities in the availability of, and access to, training will continue.

At organisational level it is essential to reduce rigid divisions in the internal labour market and enhance basic education and occupational standards in order to achieve higher quality, flexibility and added value. There is also a need for improved management styles and competencies, especially in those operating at international level (Whitfield, 1995). Meeting such needs will achieve social as well as economic ends. It will give an improved capacity to secure competitive advantage and the innovation essential to growth. Finally, it will help those in lower-level jobs to improve their skills and so to be able to compete on more equal terms for entry to the primary segment of the internal as well as external labour market.

CONCLUSION

Having read this chapter and completed its reviews and self-checks, you should now:

• have a context for understanding the international – and especially the European – scenario relating to vocational education and training (VET)

• understand the key differences between national vocational education and training (NVET) systems in major competitor countries and the UK

• be able to assess what lessons such comparisons offer both for UK Government policy on VET and for human resource development (HRD) policy in individual organisations.

To set yourself a final test, what five-minute answers would you give to the following questions? (Dates in brackets refer to the IPD qualifying examination paper in which a question appeared.)

USEFUL READING

HAMLIN B. (1999) 'The national context', in J. Stewart, *Employee Development Practice*. London, Financial Times and Pitman Publishing, pp22–36 (for information on NVET in competitor countries up to 1999).

The information in Chapter 4 will need to be regularly updated, especially by reference to:

- the *International Journal of Training and Development*, Oxford, Blackwell

---

- Identify and briefly analyse **three** of the main differences between the UK's national vocational education and training system and those of competitor countries. (November 1997)

- Briefly explain **three** ways in which the 'unskilled underclass' are vulnerable in the UK.

- Why are European countries generally failing to achieve sufficient skills flexibility to compete in the world markets?

- the quality press – and especially the Sunday 'heavies' and *The Financial Times* – for their regular articles and editorials on matters relating to VET in Britain and competitor countries, and to patterns of employment and movements in the economies of those countries

- (for students) your university or college library, whose staff will advise you on relevant publications and websites

- the business section of your local public library, whose information officer will be able to direct you to up-to-date sources of information (especially on the Internet) on HRD in competitor countries.

Part 2

MOVING INTO THE ORGANISATION: THE BUSINESS PARTNERSHIP

5 The strategic framework

LEARNING OBJECTIVES

After reading this chapter you will:

- understand the meaning of 'strategic, business-led' HRD

- be able to identify the presence or absence of a strategic framework for HRD in an organisation

- understand the factors inhibiting or enhancing the ability of HRD to make a strategic impact on the business

- understand the concepts of working as a 'business partner'.

STRATEGY TERMINOLOGY

In this chapter I want to look at the strategic context needed if the HRD process is to serve longer-term corporate goals as well as help to achieve immediate business targets. First, a guide to some basic terminology used in this and the following chapter.

Business-led HRD is development aimed at the achievement of current business goals. Business-led HRD can also make possible a widening choice of business strategies as people at various levels of the organisation begin to realise their full potential. Business-led HRD must be a dynamic process, continuously interacting with the cycle of business change. For a real-life case-study illustrating all these points, read the story of Hydro Polymers in the final chapter of this book.

Strategic HRD is development that arises from a clear vision about people's abilities and potential and operates within the overall strategic framework of the business. It was explained in Chapter 1 that throughout this book the tendency will be to use the phrase 'human resource development' (HRD) rather than 'employee development'. This is for three principal reasons:

- 'HRD' better conveys a scope of developmental policy that can extend beyond those who work in the organisation to those who, although not legally its 'employees', none the less make an essential contribution to its success – for example, voluntary and contracted-out workers and suppliers. Responding to the learning needs of these stakeholders is an important way of acknowledging mutuality of endeavour and of interest. Such learning networks also help to stimulate new ways of thinking that can be essential to an organisation's future progress.

- Use of the word 'employees' in relation to learning and development creates a negative impression in those organisations where planned learning is approached on a partnership basis, and terms such as 'associates' or 'colleagues' have replaced that older terminology.

- The term 'HRD' more clearly points to the strategic role that the developmental process should play in organisations. An emphasis on HRD as part of a wider human resource management (HRM) response to strategic issues is a central theme in the literature. Pettigrew, Sparrow and Hendry (1988: 31) carefully distinguished between HRD, which they saw to be about 'having a conscious strategy, rather than being a response to external forces' and 'more narrowly conceived training issues'.

> Usually re-titled 'Human Resource Development', an organisation's investment in the learning of its people acts as a powerful signal of its intentions...to take a longer-term view.
>
> (Bratton and Gold, 1994: 226)

To improve performance in the workplace and develop the competencies needed to meet future challenges, HRD must be business-led *and* strategic. The HRD process will be business-led if it can justify itself in business terms. It will be strategic if, in addition to being responsive to current business needs, it is driven by longer-term goals and perspectives that give overall coherency and direction to its activities through time. Strategic HRD interventions must be 'built to last' and must be given time to prove their worth if they are to adequately support strategic business goals.

Vision is the picture that people hold in their minds about what kind of business and organisation theirs should be. Vision should be powerful and coherent across the organisation, yet should also be challenging and have sufficient ambiguity to encourage creative thinking.

The organisational *mission* is the articulation of vision in some concrete form that then becomes a guideline for strategy. The word *policy* can be synonymous with mission, although usually a firm's overall policy in each of its key areas of activity, including HRM, is more detailed than its mission statement. Sometimes people refer to an organisation's mission when what they actually mean is its vision. Sometimes a mission statement simply represents top management's view, and may be largely disregarded by many in the organisation. It is more important to have a clear and powerful vision than to have a mission statement. However, research indicates that where the mission statement has been arrived at by a consultative process and is agreed across the organisation as an incentive to action, it then has value.

Strategy is the route that has been chosen for a period of time and from a range of options in order to achieve business goals. It is a guide to action and therefore sets the framework within which policies – including those human resource (HR) policies that relate to the planned learning and development of people – can be agreed and implemented. Because strategy unfolds as a pattern of decisions and activity through time, the term 'strategic' can only be meaningfully applied to activities in which the organisation wishes to invest now for some future return. Strategy must be adaptive, since it may from time to time have to be amended or even abandoned as the organisation's environment or internal circumstances place new pressures on the business, or provide hitherto unforeseen opportunities.

Implementation concerns the execution of strategy. The capability to implement strategy is all-important, and too often much time is spent generating strategic options and choosing from them without due attention to the factors – especially the human factors – that may in reality make a particular option impossible to carry out.

Terminology

Briefly define what is meant by **each** of the following terms and explain their interaction:

HRD vision

HRD policy

HRD strategy

HRD IN A STRATEGIC FRAMEWORK

There are four sets of factors that significantly determine the extent to which the HRD process can become of strategic value to an organisation: the measures of performance that dominate the business; the values of the main stakeholders; the role and impact of HRD practitioners; and their strategic expertise and credibility.

Measures of organisational performance
There are many ways in which stakeholders measure the performance of an organisation, each with its own implications for HRD. Three of the most frequently used, either singly or in some combination, are:

• *financial performance*, as measured by return on assets (ROA), return on sales (ROS) and return on equity (ROE). These measures are to do with current profitability and the state of the end-of-year balance sheet. They incorporate measures of labour productivity ('defined as the ratio of sales over employment, in the firm, divided by the ratio of sales over employment in the industry', Patterson *et al*, 1997: 3) and of real profits per employee ('profits before tax, deflated by the producer price index of the industry to which the firm belongs and controlling for size of firm based on the number of employees', *ibid*).

- *strategic performance*, as measured by market-based measures such as market share, growth, diversification and product development. These measures are to do with taking a longer-term perspective, with growth of or share in existing businesses and with the future positioning of the business.

- *organisational effectiveness*, as assessed by stakeholder-based measures related to quality of products and employees, levels of employee morale, the quality of life in the workplace, and the organisation's fulfilment of its external social responsibilities.

Broadly speaking, organisations that are dominated by short-term financial measures of performance are unlikely to make any significant investment in HRD beyond job-related training and short-term competency development. It is in organisations measuring performance by strategic and/or organisational effectiveness measures that one can expect to find attitudes more supportive of investing in HRD over the longer term.

The distinction between financial and strategic measures can be a fine one. The crucial issue for HRD is the extent to which shareholders are concerned primarily with performance affecting the immediate bottom line, or with investment that will add value to the business through time. One popular measure that bridges gaps between financial and strategic categories is Economic Value Added (EVA). Hailed by Peter Drucker as a unique measure because its continuous increase will always bring good, it 'shines a light on all four ways wealth can be created in business' (Stewart, 1996: 2.5): cost-cutting, release of unproductive capital, reduction in cost of capital, and investment in value-added activity. The questions raised by applying such a measure are fundamental: what company-wide impact will this strategy or activity or innovation have, and what kind of value will it add? HR practitioners, in promoting their vision and strategy, must reflect on the kind of value released or created by HRD activity in the organisation in the past, and look forward to assess the value it is likely to achieve. More will be said about this in Chapter 6.

Values of the main stakeholders

If top management and other powerful internal and external stakeholders are unaware or unconvinced of the role that HRD can play in adding value, then they will not agree to an investment in it, regardless of the performance measures they favour. And without their commitment, line managers and other organisational members will not be supportive. The practical implications of this are explained in Chapter 6. Suffice to say here that unless powerful stakeholders have positive values about the contribution that the HRD process can make to the business, then it will probably be impossible for HRD to make a strategic contribution. It is here that the expertise and credibility of those carrying HRD responsibilities, and the outcomes that they achieve for the business, become so important.

Roles and impact of HRD practitioners

The formal roles of those holding HRD responsibilities, whether as the whole or as only part of their job, will be a significant factor here, but role alone is not enough; and there is a difficulty too. If top management is not committed to HRD, the function itself is unlikely to be given high status and position; but if it does not have high status, how can it influence top management? This is why the senior HRD spokesperson in the business needs to have a high level of business expertise, and it is where the impact of the HR spokesperson for HRD at the top organisational levels becomes critical. Here, there is cause for concern. It is no longer the case that HR people are not getting onto the board: a 1999 report by the Institute of Directors showed that HR representation at board level had jumped from 55 per cent to 72 per cent in only one year (Walsh, 1999). The problem lies in the continuing failure of HR professionals once at that level to prove the worth of the HR function for the business. The IoD's head of director development was quoted as saying that despite an improved skills and resource base for HR departments:

> we go in and see what has become 'institutionalised HR' – a department that doesn't know how to prove its value.
>
> (Walsh, 1999)

The real issue, then, is not one of 'being on the board'. It is one of contributing something meaningful when at board level. And that is the problem, also, in HRD. In the UK in the 1990s, although there was quite widespread developmental activity in relation to culture change, decentralisation, workforce competences and formal strategy planning skills, there was often little internal consistency in these initiatives (Storey, 1994) and this reduced their business impact. Such a scenario undermines the credibility of HRD as a strategic process. So too does a situation where HRD is not supported by wider HR policy and practice, and/or where employee resourcing is not strategically planned or closely aligned with business strategy (Keep and Mayhew, 1994).

These situations suggest a lack of collaboration between HR practitioners across the business, and lack of a business partnership between them and line managers. The difficulties are compounded when HRD is a stand-alone function in the business. Then, the HRD professional must in addition to his or her specialist tasks convince the organisation's management of the need for a framework of HR policy and action, must advise on what that framework might be, and must propose how best it can be implemented.

Performance measures and HRD in your organisation

What are the main measures of performance used in an organisation with which you are familiar, and how do they affect the focus of HRD policy and activity?

Here follows a case-study to explore the theme of barriers and facilitators to HRD in an organisation.

Case-study: Recruitment in a local authority

Identify the main HRD issues in the following case-study, and the barriers to effective HRD at Ensdale CC. What should management do in the future to keep people like Michael?

Ensdale County Council is operating in an increasingly difficult climate: it has to provide high-quality customer-focused services and achieve a variety of government-imposed standards, while having to cut costs and face increasing pressures on its scarce resources. It has an enthusiastic HR manager who, working with a small team of six (most with long service in the authority), has in the past year or so introduced a range of initiatives to 'change the face of HRM at Ensdale'. These include a reduced reliance on full-time staff and increased employment of part-time and temporary staff across the authority; contracting out a range of activities, including many training operations; the introduction of a 'performance management system'; and a drive for total quality management. The initiatives have not all proved durable, and many claim that they are piecemeal and too costly for the likely benefits.

A year ago a young graduate was recruited as personnel assistant – the previous one had left after a year, and a lot of effort went into producing an attractive recruitment brochure and a demanding selection procedure that would make clear that this was a professional and forward-looking department.

Michael came from outside the region; he had just left a new university with a good BA Honours in Business Studies. Throughout the selection process he was impressed by the emphasis on the need for commitment to continuous improvement and quality, and on scope to use initiative. He liked, too, the idea of working with the small HR team, although he did not actually meet any of them (except the HR manager) during the selection process.

The HR manager made it clear that Michael would be working with a supportive team where his learning needs would have a positive response. Michael agreed to enrol immediately on a part-time Institute of Personnel and Development course at a local college in order to 'start the process of continuous professional development', as his manager expressed it.

After nearly a year Michael had become frustrated and disappointed. Despite the new performance management system, his own appraisal by the HR manager was perfunctory. There was little clarification of forthcoming targets or meaningful feedback on work done. The manager was preoccupied with employee relations issues and – ironically – with organising appraisal skills training across the authority. There was no real opportunity for Michael to innovate, and he was constantly being given routine or awkward jobs that others in the 'team' preferred not to do. He found that the culture of the small department backward-looking, and it soon became clear to him why, over the past three years, turnover of new young HR recruits had been high. The only thing he enjoyed was his IPD course, where he was doing well and getting to know an increasing number of local personnel practitioners. It was at an IPD branch meeting that he heard of a vacancy in the personnel department of a local manufacturing organisation. The pay and conditions were little different from those he was currently receiving, but the firm's reputation as an employer was impressive. He knew through his IPD classes a couple of people who worked there, and so was able to get first-hand information on the excellence of the firm's HRD policies and the coherency of its HRM strategy and systems. He applied for the job and was successful. Once he was there, his real professional career began. For Michael it proved in every way a very lucky break.

Feedback notes
- The authority is operating in an increasingly tough environment to achieve goals that, being to do with both cost reduction and improved quality, are not easy to reconcile. The HR manager's vision is not being carried through effectively, and HRD has to operate within a weak strategic framework.

- Unless there is a better alignment of HRM with business and individual needs, others like Michael will continue to leave, or will be infected by the negative culture of the HR department and become demotivated and unproductive. Either way, the authority will keep losing valuable human resources and HRD will contribute little to the needs of either the organisation or individuals.

- In this case, there are five steps (shown in Table 2) that will be critical to establishing HRD within a strategic framework, and that will help to keep people like Michael in the future.

Table 2 Five steps to ensure that HRD operates within the strategic framework of the business

---

1   Relate investment in the development of people realistically to the vision, values and strategic goals of the organisation.

2   Ensure that there is a clear and internally consistent HR strategy, within which goals for HRD are established.

3   Formulate HRD strategy to meet those goals.

4   Agree on realistic, specific, measurable and well-costed HRD plans that are consistent with the wider framework of HRM and business strategy.

5   Establish mechanisms for monitoring, feedback and further relevant action.

STRATEGIC HRD

Six questions can help to identify the extent to which there is a strategic framework for HRD in an organisation:

1   Is strategic HRD happening?

2   What prevents its happening more widely?

3   When is it most likely to happen?

4   How to know when it is happening?

5   How to start linking HRD strategy to business goals?

6   Why work as 'business partners'?

1 Is strategic HRD happening?

Figure 2 (opposite) draws attention to the fact that HRD in an organisation is a means to an end, not an end in itself. Operating within the wider function of human resource (HR) policy in the organisation, it can either support or work against the vision and strategic goals of the business. It is helpful to think about human resource management (HRM) as a door. Open, it signifies the removal of human barriers to achieving those goals, and the encouragement and facilitation of required human performance. Closed, it signifies the reinforcement of those barriers, and a consequent likelihood of poor human performance and failure to realise potential.

Figure 3 (opposite) shows the HR context for HRD: the 'wheel' of HR policy and systems that should operate in close alignment in the workplace, and that defines the ways in which the organisation's workforce is planned, deployed and managed.

- *HR planning* determines how many people should be employed, how, when and where, and how they will be used. The context established here is the critical one within which HRD policy, strategy and plans must be formulated.

- *Recruitment and selection* are the processes through which people move into the organisation: this human material, if well chosen, will prove to have the abilities and wish to respond positively and fruitfully to developmental initiatives. Ineffective recruitment and selection will almost always defeat every attempt to instil skills and knowledge and unlock potential.

- *Leadership* provides the vision and values that drive HRD in an organisation.

- *Teamwork*, like leadership, will either provide continuing developmental opportunities that maximise the organisation's investment in people or will erect barriers that may lead to rapid depreciation in that most expensive of its resources.

- *Appraisal* is the process at the heart of development, but attempts to use it as also a major method of control may defeat its developmental objectives, as will be seen in Chapter 14.

- *Learning activities and opportunities* appropriate to the needs of individuals, groups and the organisation as a whole can be in part formally structured but should also permeate daily operations in the workplace so that a process of continuous development and improvement can take place. Continuous development, principally through the integration of learning and work, has as its major objective the achievement of operational goals and the steady growth in the ability to learn and reinforce or generate new knowledge at every organisational level. Whereas the main concern in training is to help people to acquire skills related to a particular task or tasks, continuous development is primarily concerned with uncovering and using potential, and in developing those core learning skills of observation and reflection, analysis, creativity, decision-making/problem-solving and evaluation (see Chapter 14).

Figure 2   HRM and the business

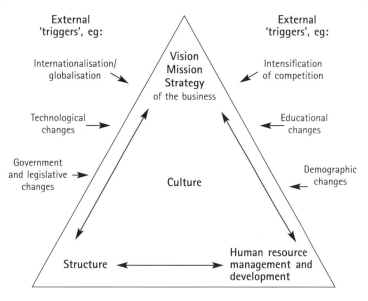

Figure 3   The wheel of HRM and the business

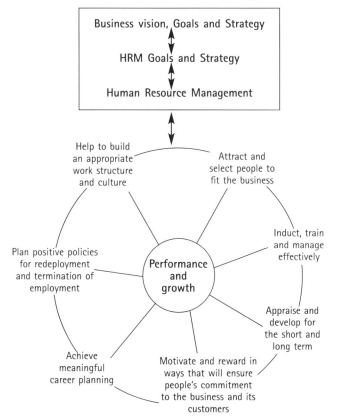

Based on Harrison, 1993a: 40

- *Incentive and reward systems* will either help to encourage people to develop or will be so irrelevant to the HRD process that individual and team motivation to develop will be low. Particular attention should be paid to measures that will protect employees against discrimination, and that will ensure their health and safety.

- *Career planning*, to recognise mutuality of interest and need between individual and organisation.

- *Disengagement policies and practices* should ensure that when people leave the organisation positive steps are taken to facilitate their continued development after that exit point is reached, rather than leaving them with little hope or positive expectations.

2 What prevents its happening more widely?

The main external factor inhibiting HRD from achieving a strategic role in many organisations is the lack of incentives for either individuals or organisations to invest in training, education and planned long-term development. For individuals in the UK, as we have already seen in Chapter 2, there has been far less incentive to invest in training than in many competitor countries, notably Germany, where increased wages and career prospects are linked to training and qualifications, and young people are not distracted by high-pay temptations. If there is a significant labour market for young people without many educational qualifications, and if young people are offered attractive rates of pay, then they (and many others, in or out of work) will see little point in investing in vocational education and training, because it will not bring them better jobs, pay or career development. Since the early 1990s the UK government has been attempting to change this situation, but there is much progress still to be made.

However, internal factors are more important here. It is in the fabric of the organisation that the biggest inhibitors to HRD are to be found. Failure to achieve a strategic impact by HRD can be due to a variety of factors: to weakness or absence of well-articulated corporate strategy, lack of integration of HRD with corporate strategy where it does exist, or lack of HRD's vertical integration with HR policy and with the firm's employment system. In the view of many commentators (see, for example, Hendry, 1995; Patterson *et al*, 1997), the most consistently significant factors are lack of top management support and commitment, and lack of competence and business credibility among HRD practitioners. Comments on these have already been made earlier in this chapter.

Training practitioners in the UK continue to see the integration of training into business strategy as a problematic issue (Darling, Darling and Elliott, 1999: x). Wide variations in the extent to which training strategy is integrated with corporate strategy have been reported (*ibid*: xi). However, this is not invariably the fault of those responsible for the HRD process at the strategic level. It is often to do with weaknesses in the strategic process itself. That process in turn – the capacity of an organisation to make effective corporate strategies – depends significantly on the quality of management and decision-making (Hendry, 1995: 96–8). The HRD process can help here – as will be seen in detail in Part 5 of this book – through effective management assessment and development processes, through improving information dissemination, and through developing the kinds of learning that improve the quality of strategic decision-making. However, where business strategy is driven by short-term and mainly financial considerations, or is incoherent or non-existent, there is little hope for HRD to become strategically focused. Instead, whoever is charged with responsibility for the function would do better to ensure that all their operational tasks are performed well than to pine for a strategic role. By HRD activity that achieves value-adding outcomes, by working in partnership with stakeholders, by benchmarking appropriate activities and processes, and by being knowledgeable about the business and its environment, HRD practitioners can build up their business credibility. When the organisational situation changes, favouring a generally more strategic approach, they should be poised to become strategic players.

3 When is it most likely to happen?

The reasons for investing in the development of people at work are never as simple as they seem, so any generalisation can mislead. However, there are three scenarios that raise a need for coherent, durable and business-focused developmental activity – in other words, scenarios that trigger a more strategic approach to HRD:

Costly capability gaps

These are likely to have been caused by reliance on *ad hoc* HRD activity. Lost opportunities in the market place and longer lead times when developing new projects are typical results of miscalculation related to the development of people (Prais *et al*, 1990). The ability to react rapidly to changing external scenarios and reap the benefits they offer can be enhanced by a more strategic approach to the recruitment, retention and development of the right people. Unfortunately, it may take a crisis on several fronts to produce an awareness of the need to invest in HRD. A timely search by HRD professionals for best practice outside the organisation can be helpful in reducing the possibility of such crises.

Changes in the competitive environment

These can lead to a need for new business goals, almost invariably calling for changes in performance, skills and organisational capacity. All of that has implications for the HRD process, and often points to the need for a more strategic HRD approach. The firm's human resource base is a vital source of its distinctive capabilities, defined as 'what the firm is able to perform with excellence compared to its competitors' (Nordhaug and Gronhaug, 1994: 95). However, those distinctive capabilities depend for their full effectiveness on the organisation's 'capacity to deploy resources, usually in combination, using organizational processes, to effect a desired end' (Amit and Schoemaker, 1993: 35). 'Capacity' is produced by organisational structure and culture, routines and procedures, budgetary controls and corrective actions, business processes and organisational networks.

Many HR practices make an impact on organisational capacity, particularly those that:

- affect the entire organisation

- are institutionalised within the organisation

- are recognised and have a visible impact on attitude and behaviour of employees in the organisation (Ulrich, 1987: 173).

Ulrich's six 'domains of HR practice' – development, together with organisation planning, staffing, rewards, appraisal and communications – are identified as critical precisely because they are the main 'policies, procedures, systems, and activities used to shape, monitor, and direct attention of people within the organization' (*ibid*: 173–6). However, it is the ability to ensure effective implementation of practice that matters most here. Top management's vision of the organisation and the way that this is communicated and reinforced, and management style and actions across the organisation, significantly determine workplace culture. They establish an organisational context that either supports or inhibits the effective implementation of groups of HR practices that can lead to improved business performance (Hendry, 1995; Patterson *et al*, 1997: 8–12, 18–19).

Terry and Purcell, reporting in 1997 on seven organisations restructuring in order to become more competitive, identified the most important tasks that helped to change organisational capacity in those organisations (Terry and Purcell, 1997). All had HRD implications if they were to be understood, accepted and competently introduced and embedded:

- communication process to explain the strategic purpose behind restructuring

- team structures and technology to spread knowledge across the organisation.

- competency frameworks to identify and foster behaviour needed

- career structures to provide life-skills and employability

- reward systems, often group-based

- systems for monitoring and measuring performance, including appraisal

- training interventions, especially for team leaders, to equip them with the skills needed to manage team members as well as products.

Changes in the external labour market and/or technical base of the organisation

Where an organisation can no longer recruit suitable personnel from the external labour market, it will have to rely more on its own HRD process to provide the skills it needs. Major changes in the technical base of the organisation call for organisational restructuring, reskilling of large sectors of the workforce, and changed patterns of management and decision-making. Both types of change require a more strategic approach to the development of people across the organisation.

4 How to know when it is happening?

When HRD is operating effectively within the strategic framework of the business it will be:

- *meaningful and durable* – relevant to the long-term direction of the business, and sustained over the long term

- *aligned* – tied closely to the organisation's vision and strategic goals

- *internally consistent* – supporting, and supported by, other HR policies

- *management-led* – with any HR staff playing a supportive role

- *expert* – characterised by skilful provision and management of appropriate learning and development processes

- *value-adding* – increasing the value of the organisation's human assets and of the returns that are achieved by the business.

In Chapters 6 and 7, ways of achieving these outcomes will be examined.

5 How to start linking HRD strategy to business goals?

Those carrying HRD responsibilities must work closely with the stakeholders in HRD – that is to say, with those who are resourcing its operations, those who are actively involved in its process whether as learners or as managers or colleagues of those learners, and those who are most affected by its outcomes. There should be a shared identification of the main strategic initiatives to which the organisation is committed, and agreement on the HRD goals, strategy and plans that will best support them. For example, if a company is de-layering and downsizing but also wants a responsive and adaptive workforce, then it will need training initiatives related to teambuilding and multiskilling. Those who will have to manage that changed work system and workplace culture must also be helped to acquire the necessary skills and understanding.

Here is an illustrative case-study, based on a real-life example.

Case-study: Wesdale Acute Hospitals NHS Trust

Wesdale Acute Hospitals NHS Trust is a major provider of health care, catering for the needs of around 300,000 people in its area. It has many stakeholders – patients, staff, the local Health Commission, Community Health Council, Community Healthcare and general practitioners. The Trust's philosophy is 'Partners in Quality – working together to deliver a sensitive, caring health service, changing to meet your individual needs – today and in the future'. Its current priorities are the building of a new District General Hospital (DGH) over the next five years and implementing an interim rationalisation plan related to that radical organisational change.

The Trust has four strategic goals, of which one is explicitly related to its people: 'valuing all those who work with and for us, and developing their capability and commitment through a wide range of individual and corporate training and development opportunities and programmes'. Triggered by the business goals and strategy put in place over recent years, the Trust must establish a strategic approach to training and development at three levels: corporate, business unit and operational.

At corporate level, the HR director to whom the HRD manager reports has a seat on the board and is responsible for HR policy. This, and a major HR agenda leading up to the opening of the new DGH, ensure that HRD goals and strategy are continually related to the goals of the Trust. As part of the Trust's Annual Plan, a training plan identifies a range of activities to be undertaken within the framework of overall corporate strategy and ensures evaluation of past activities as well as assessment of future investment needed.

At unit level, clinical directorates' business plans now include the training needed to support changes and developments in services. A multidisciplinary Training and Development Group has been established that oversees the implementation of a corporate approach to the delivery of all initiatives. The Group identifies HRD responses to organisational requirements identified in the Annual Plan.

At operational level, the Trust was recognised some years ago as an 'Investor in People' and has recently been re-accredited. It runs its own National Vocational Qualification (NVQ) programmes. There is a business-led framework for the HRD process that, in the devolved management structure, is the primary responsibility of line management. That process involves identification of training needs through annual appraisal, personal development plans for all staff, encouragement to achieve national occupational qualifications, monitoring of staff performance, and development and evaluation of training events. Together, these activities enable a 'bottom-up' as well as 'top-down' approach to be taken to developing HRD strategy in the Trust.

As Figure 4 (opposite) indicates, the Trust's HRD process is driven by the strategic direction of the Trust. Its outcomes also feed back into it, thereby aiming to improve the strategic as well as operational capability of the organisation.

Developing a strategic approach to HRD

At this point, identify ways in which HRD is becoming increasingly strategic at Wesdale Trust.

Feedback

- *All HRD activities are goal-driven* – they arise out of and feed back into HRD goals that in turn support the wider goals of the business.

- *HRD has real strategic status* – it is formally supported by corporate, unit level and operational management, and there is a real belief at those levels that it is supporting and also helping to drive business strategy.

Figure 4   Linking HRD to a Trust's strategic and business planning cycle

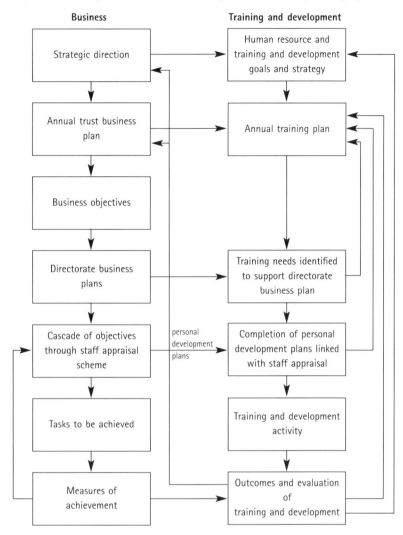

- *There is a clear HRD strategy* – and all HRD activities, including appraisal, training, continuous development, programmes to achieve multiskilling, total quality and culture change, are being brought increasingly into line with that strategy.

- *There is increasing consistency with other human resource policies* – whether related to recruitment and selection, recognition and rewards, or redundancy and redeployment, all support and are supported by HRD policies.

6 Why work as business partners?

It has already been made clear at various points in this chapter that it is only through the commitment of all the stakeholders in HRD to its goals and operations that HRD's strategic potential can be achieved. Without partnership, the clash of different interests will tend to place barriers in the way of effective implementation of HRD strategy. A partnership process should lead to:

- agreement on the HRD initiatives that will link up with different business priorities – and on a budget for those

- joint setting of milestones to mark each major stage in the implementation of those initiatives

- as each milestone is reached, sharing of information about outcomes related to the initiatives

- agreement on any changes needed in initiatives through time.

There will be further discussion of these points in Chapter 7.

To conclude this section: the strongest commitment to a strategic approach to HRD in the organisation will arise from commitment by stakeholders to HRD as an essential process related to the achievement of business targets and corporate goals. Regular monitoring of the performance and environment of the business should identify any triggers indicating a need for HRD to become more strategic in its focus and to produce initiatives that will produce real value for the organisation. It is a change in focus and direction for HRD, and a new prioritisation of its operations, that are the issues here: there does not have to be an immediate increase in its cost. Through time, of course, because of their widening scope and scale, HRD initiatives are likely to require a higher level of investment than hitherto if they are to achieve their pay-back.

Assessing HRD in its strategic framework

What does the application of the six questions just covered tell you about HRD in your organisation? What are the most significant findings revealed by your response, and why are they significant?

CONCLUSION

Having read this chapter and completed its reviews and self-checks, you should now:

- understand the meaning of 'strategic, business-led' HRD

- be able to identify the presence or absence of a strategic framework for HRD in an organisation

- understand the factors inhibiting or enhancing the ability of HRD to make a strategic impact on the business

- understand the concept of working as a 'business partner'.

To test yourself against these objectives, what five-minute answers would you give to the following questions? (Dates in brackets refer to the IPD qualifying examination paper in which a question appeared.)

- Explain how an ED function in an organisation can be business-led yet fail to be strategic. (May 1998)

- Identify and explain **three** areas of employee resourcing policy that directly influence people's development in an organisation. (November 1997)

- What are **four** of the signs that indicate that HRD is becoming strategic in an organisation?

USEFUL READING

HARRISON R. (1993) *Human Resource Management: Issues and strategies.* Wokingham, Addison Wesley. (Case-study on Thorn Lighting, pp375–80, and related feedback notes in Instructor's Manual.)

McGOLDRICK A. (ed.) (1996) *Cases in Human Resource Management.* London, Pitman.

6 'Adding value'

LEARNING OBJECTIVES

After reading this chapter you will:

* understand how the HRD process can 'add value' for the business

* be able to identify the critical features that relate to HRD's ability to make a significant impact on organisational performance and progress

* understand how to produce feasible and value-adding HRD goals and plans to meet critical business needs

* be able to explain how to assess the value of HRD's contribution to the business.

INTRODUCTION

The concept of HRD's 'adding value' is one that some do not find appealing. It smacks too much of a commercial approach, they feel. This is a mistaken understanding of the term's meaning. To add value, in an organisational context, is to add significantly and efficiently to the organisation's capability to achieve its goals – in other words, to make a difference where it matters most. In one case, adding value might be to do with increasing performance levels; in another, with stimulating creativity and innovation; in another, with enhancing ability to achieve better quality or better service. What is at issue here is that as a result of the efficient operation of an appropriately focused HRD process, the organisation is better able than it was before to deal with the challenges and threats that face it as it pursues its chosen path. The HRD process will then have achieved returns for the organisation that are over and above the cost of the HRD investment.

One approach here is that followed by the Audit Commission's 'Best Value' framework, which requires local authority services over five years from 2000 on to be examined against four criteria, summarised by Gorman (2000) as:

Challenge	Why is the service carried out at all?
Consult	What do customers think about our service and the level of performance?
Compare	How does our performance compare against the best of the public and private sector?

Compete   Can the service be delivered more effectively by alternative providers?

The personnel service is one of many that will be reviewed in this way, and as Gorman pointed out, 'Service reviews in other areas will inevitably lead to questions about the value added by personnel as a support function.' A similar approach can be found in van Adelsberg and Trolley (1999).

Yet helpful though such approaches are in ensuring a strategic approach to the HRD function, and one that delivers value for money (Spurling and Trolley, 2000), they do not quite grasp the essence of adding value. It is not enough to pare costs to the bone, to please clients, or to conform with good or best practice. There must in addition be the elements referred to at the start of this section, which can only be achieved by focusing on what matters most, and making a real difference there. So to add value, there must be an improvement to those capabilities of the organisation that will enable it to differentiate itself from other, similar organisations so that it can make progress in its environment.

In an article critical of HR professionals' 'obsession with best practice' that often leads to a lack of attention to the specific needs of their own organisations, the managing director of a strategic HR consultancy urged a focus on adding value if those professionals are to play a more central role in shaping business strategy and in improving performance (Green, 1999). He criticised HR professionals for a failure to sufficiently research the impact that specific interventions or tools can make to improved performance, for an inadequate focus on the key drivers of organisational performance, and for measuring inputs rather than outputs. The three final points that he made provide good advice to those who seek not only to provide 'value for money' in HRD activity, but to provide 'added value':

- *alignment* – pointing people in the right direction

- *engagement* – developing belief and commitment to the organisation's purpose and direction

- *measurement* – providing the data that demonstrate the improved results achieved.

In this chapter there is an explanation with illustrations of ways in which to ensure that the HRD process and function in an organisation achieves its value-adding potential. This is followed in Chapter 7 by an exploration of methods, techniques and processes to achieve well-focused, organisationally relevant and effective outcomes for the HRD function.

Adding value in your own organisation

Research the concept of the 'value chain' in a business. Then identify two or three ways in which the HRD process could 'add value' in your organisation – and also identify any barriers to its ability to add value.

VISION AND VALUES

Vision and values underlie crucial decisions relating to investment and the deployment of the organisation's resources, including its people. Later in Part 2 we will explore in detail ways in which HRD professionals can develop influence in their organisations and promote positive values about HRD at different organisational levels. In this chapter, main themes are introduced.

Having a written mission statement for HRD may or may not matter: it depends on the style of the organisation. More important is a strong and compelling sense of shared purpose: HRD needs its vision – but it must be consistent with the overall organisational vision, not exist in some separate dimension.

Case-study: My worst mistake

John Garnett, director of the Industrial Society from 1962 to 1986, admitted that his worst mistake was trying to sell ideas in relation to his own objectives rather than the objectives of the people to whom he was selling. He described how his passionate vision about the value of developing people's abilities and potential blinded him during his time as personnel manager of the plastics division of ICI to the equally important need to relate what he did to the objectives of the business. It led to the loss of his job because, he explained,

> My work, in the view of the board, was irrelevant and, more seriously, distracting. They were in the business of making profits in plastics, while I seemed to be in the business of developing people, which took their eyes off the main purpose.

Source: John Garnett, the *Independent on Sunday*, 8 March 1992

Unless the purpose of HRD is seen to be about 'the business', then HRD will fail to convince key stakeholders of its value. This could lead to the function's demise. Typical attitudes that reflect a confused vision about HRD and do it no service must be confronted at this stage. Let us look at a few examples:

• *HRD is inherently valuable.* Some will see the development of employees as a crucial task, and argue for a heavy investment in it while at the same time showing no real concern to put it in the context of specific business needs or to measure and evaluate its outcomes. Like John Garnett, they simply believe that developing potential is answering a central human need and is of such inherent value that it is bound to bring benefits to the organisation.

• *HRD is essential to keep up with the pack.* Others may argue that HRD must be worthwhile because 'the best companies do it'. Again there will be no emphasis on clarity of purpose, responsiveness to specific needs, or measurement of outcomes. Best practice is a useful tool for standard-setting in HRD – but only when HRD itself is relevant to the business.

• *HRD is worthwhile in no matter what form.* Others may believe that investing in HRD is justified by a particular organisation's general employment philosophy, and that any developmental activities, provided that they are well designed and stimulate people's 'growth', are worthwhile.

If the vision of HRD in an organisation rests on these kinds of assumptions, then HRD in practice will tend to be unsystematic, non-strategic and unconvincing to sceptical managers because they do not see its business relevance. The HRD process must be planned and managed to achieve high business credibility. This will produce and sustain positive values about HRD across the organisation and ensure support for HRD activity. To be able to add value, and thereby make a critical difference, the HRD process must have the involvement of stakeholders at all organisational levels, integrating HRD policy and business policy at each level:

At corporate level
HRD considerations must be integrated into corporate strategic decision-making, and there must be performance-linked HRD goals and strategy for the organisation. These in their turn should be an integral part of an overall performance management process.

At business-unit level
Here, there should be collaboratively produced plans to implement corporate HRD strategy, and to ensure that HRD activity adequately meets local needs. That activity should be supported by, and consistent with, the operation of the performance management process at local level.

At operational level
Here, there should be routines and processes to ensure competent performance, and a supportive learning environment that encourages people to take responsibility for their own learning and development in the workplace. The enhanced ability of individuals and of teams to learn, and to adapt to changing business needs, will make a real difference to the ability of the whole organisation to achieve its goals and make progress in its environment.

How is HRD valued and managed in your organisation?

Take each of the following statements and give it a mark of 0 to 3 according to the extent to which you agree or disagree with each:

*0 = Disagree   1 = Unsure/don't know   2 = Agree more than I disagree
3 = Strongly agree*

In this organisation the vision and goals for HRD
are set at the very top, and there is strong
commitment to HRD across the
organisation.   _____

In this organisation, HRD is seen to have a vital role to play in supporting and improving people's performance. Managers have been given the main role to play in relation to the training and development of their staff.   _____

In this organisation, all HRD plans are business-focused, well understood and effectively implemented in the workplace.   _____

In this organisation, all HRD plans to improve performance arise out of business goals and targets, and are regularly reviewed to take account of changes.   _____

In this organisation, HRD makes a major contribution to the overall performance management process. HRD activities are regularly shown to have added real value to the performance of individuals and teams.   _____

In this organisation, HRD operations and resources are well managed. Those with HRD responsibilities are fully competent and have high credibility in the workplace.   _____

In this organisation, HRD staff are always looking for better and innovative ways of designing and delivering training programmes and other learning experiences.   _____

In this organisation, all employees have a personal responsibility for the continuous improvement of their performance, and are expected to play an active part in identifying, and thinking of how best to meet, their own HRD needs.   _____

TOTAL   _____

A score above 15 indicates that HRD operations to improve performance in your organisation are strongly led by the needs of the business, well aligned with business goals, and well managed.

A total score between 12 and 15 indicates that improvements must be made if HRD is to make a powerful contribution to performance.

Anything below 12 indicates either that the present state of HRD gives rise to serious concern, or that there is inadequate information for any assessment to be made about its impact in the workplace: in either case urgent action is needed.

Source: Harrison, R. (1999). *The Training and Development Audit*. Cambridge, Cambridge Strategy Publications, p19. Reproduced by kind permission of the publisher.

Table 3 opposite will help to cast further light on your scores.

In Figure 5 (page 102) I have produced a model of training and development in the business that identifies the critical features relating

Table 3   **Matrix to identify training and development role and contribution to the business**

T&D activity	Alignment with business goals	T&D seen financially by management as	T&D formal responsibility of	Ownership of T&D felt mainly by	Focus and purpose of T&D mainly	Main mode of delivery
Peripheral to the business	Negligible	A cost to the business, one of the first that can be cut back in contingency	Specialist T&D/ personnel staff or some individual on full/part–time basis	Specialist staff of whoever holds formal T&D responsibility	No systematic focus, and *ad hoc* purposes	Formal and knowledge–based courses and/or picking up skills on the job from more experienced individuals
Business-led	Linked to current business goals and targets	An essential 'bottom-line' business cost	Specialist staff/ managers	Top and line managers, specialist staff, and to some extent workforce generally	Job-related, for individuals and teams, to improve current performance and prepare for specific changes in jobs, systems and workplace practices	Systematically designed internal learning events, and job-related external courses, skill and knowledge–based
Strategically focused	Linked to strategic goals at corporate and unit levels	A value-adding investment, essential to the future of the business	Member of board, specialists/ managers, teams and individuals	Shared by the parties	Continuous improvement of performance, and continuous development of organisation, teams and individuals. Purpose also to build a general climate of self-initiated learning and development	Planned and experiential learning to develop skills, knowledge and attitudes, and to aid development of learning skills

T&D = Training and Development
Source: Harrison R. (1999) *The Training and Development Audit.* Cambridge, Cambridge Strategy Publications, p8. Reproduced with kind permission of the publisher.

Figure 5 A model of training and development's impact on workplace performance

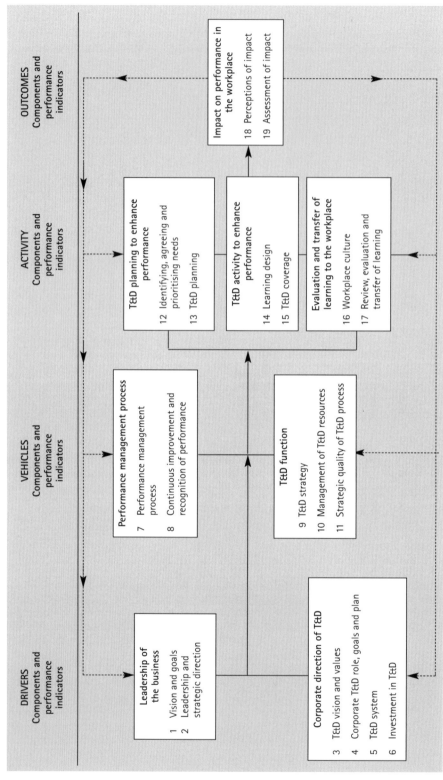

Source: Harrison R. (1999) *The Training and Development Audit*. Cambridge, Cambridge Strategy Publications. p9. Reproduced with kind permission of the publisher.

to HRD in an organisation. Its eight components, with 19 associated performance indicators, will enable you to understand the drivers, vehicles, activity and outcomes of HRD. The model is of course conditioned in its functioning by organisational context and external environment. Internal and external pressures, threats, opportunities and possibilities that provide the ultimate context for decision-making and action must be regularly scanned if intended outcomes of corporate plans and of HRD operations are actually to be achieved.

There is no 'one best way' of ensuring that HRD activity achieves added value for the business. HRD is organised in different ways from one enterprise to another, and different HRD cultures operate across organisations and countries. Not all the terminology and performance indicators used in this diagram will be equally relevant in every organisational context. They should be interpreted in each particular situation as common sense dictates.

INTEGRATING HRD WITH OVERALL HUMAN RESOURCE STRATEGY

We have already seen, in Chapter 5, the importance of focus, fit and integration so that HRD becomes part of a bundle of carefully chosen HR practices that help to improve organisational and business performance. I have picked out a case-study concerning the early stages of turnaround at Cummins Engine Co., Darlington. Much has been written about the company, and an extended version of this case-study appears elsewhere (Harrison, 1996). We shall also learn about some of its current HRD practices in the next chapter. The purpose here is to show how HR strategy and practice can provide a supportive context within which the HRD process can achieve its full potential to make a critical difference to the organisation's ability to attain its goals.

Case-study: Cummins Engine Co. Ltd, Darlington, UK, 1979–90
Business context

Cummins Engine Company Inc. is the world's largest independent manufacturer of diesel engines. Cummins Engine Co. Ltd is the UK subsidiary of the company, and has three manufacturing locations, one of which is at Darlington, in the northeast of England. In 1979 the workforce at Darlington numbered around 3,000.

By 1984 the company worldwide was suffering from overcapacity and new competition in a stagnant market, especially from Japan. In the previous year the chairman, whose vision of the company was long-term – a company watchword was, and remains, 'We're in it for the long haul' – had announced a new strategy to achieve enhanced standards of excellence by investing heavily during the 1980s in order to achieve long-term growth in the 1990s and beyond. The strategy was to be driven by restructuring, high investment in new technology, research and engineering, immediate price-cutting and a compensatory 30 per cent cost-reduction target, all to be achieved by mid-1986. At the Darlington works urgent requirements were to drive down costs and, within 18 months, to introduce sophisticated new technology at one of the sites. The need to negotiate changes with two major unions presented only one of the many challenges faced by the plant's management at that time.

HR strategy at Darlington, 1984

In 1984 Darlington's HR strategy had to be closely aligned with the new UK-wide HR strategy. There were three measures to achieve the overall goals of a flexible, efficient and high-quality workforce:

1) continuous reduction in unit labour costs

2) the elimination of demarcation barriers, improved rewards for people, and complete harmonisation in terms of pay, terms and conditions of service

3) new forms of work organisation to improve the workflow processes.

This strategy in turn involved three priorities for HRD policy to tackle:

• *To achieve a lean, high-quality and efficient workforce.* Reducing materials costs would make the most impact on the Cummins world-wide target of 30 per cent reduction in costs, since they accounted for 80 per cent of turnover, whereas labour costs accounted for only 20 per cent. The need was therefore to make the labour force more efficient rather than to reduce it (although some downsizing was essential). All unit labour costs had consequently to be reduced, especially those related to production time, turnover and absenteeism, time-keeping, working methods and procedures, accidents, materials wastage, quality, and inefficiencies due to demarcation.

• *To ensure that the workforce had the skills needed to operate the new technology.* A new product, the 'B' series engine, was to be introduced at the Darlington site. Its smooth and fast installation was essential in order to achieve full operational efficiency quickly.

• *To develop a workforce with high added value.* With a target of growth in the 1990s it was essential straight away to start to improve the skills base of the workforce and employees' ability to learn fast, and be flexible and adaptive. The aim was to reduce costs and to add value to the human resource.

HRD goals and strategy

The next step, therefore, was to establish clear HRD goals within the framework of these priorities. The three HRD goals were:

• to help people acquire and apply the new competencies needed to operate more efficiently, and to adapt to the new culture aimed at meeting the challenges of change

• to encourage and enable people to work effectively in teams

• to develop managers, especially supervisors, who could manage teams effectively.

HRD strategy flowed from those three goals. Its components were:

- *building an enhanced quality of basic skills in the workplace.* Relevant training was to be provided for those with the capacity and desire to acquire the skills needed to operate the new technology. For those who were unable or did not wish to do so there were opportunities for early retirement; this also helped to reduce headcount in a relatively painless way.

- *training for all, geared to business needs.* Everyone was to have the opportunity to learn one new skill every year over the following few years. Each employee could achieve up to six skill module increments, and each module was worth 6.6 per cent of salary – a pay progression that supplemented annual pay negotiations.

- *teamworking.* The aim was to develop during the 1980s a new breed of supervisors who would operate quite differently from the way they had before, and who, given initial training, would adapt quickly. This has proved to be one of the most challenging areas of HRD activity for the company. It is still involved in developing fully effective teamworking to support the extraordinary rate of increased productivity and advancement made at Darlington during the 1990s.

HRD goals and strategy at Cummins in the 1980s had three defining characteristics:

- They derived from the clear definition and measurement of 'productivity' in different sectors of the workforce, and agreement with key parties on which needs would best be met by developing people and which by other kinds of HR policies.

- They were carefully aligned with overall HR strategy and corporate objectives, and they were consistent with wider HR activity – most crucially, policies to achieve integrated pay systems and harmonisation of the entire workforce (Pottinger, 1989).

- Experienced HR practitioners with a fundamental grasp of the business and its environment, as well as expertise in HRD, worked as business partners with managers, unions and workforce. They operated on the basis of sound and comprehensive data and of learning from carefully monitored experience.

With acknowledgements to the company

HRD goals and strategy in your organisation

Use the same approach that has been outlined in the case-study to produce relevant HRD goals and strategy for an organisation with which you are familiar. Note any difficulties you encounter in using the approach. What are their implications for HRD in this organisation?

ADDING VALUE AT EACH ORGANISATIONAL LEVEL

Adding value at corporate level

Today, there is a preoccupation with ensuring that HRD aims and strategy are aligned with the business goals. At first sight this may seem a top-down and overly prescriptive approach for HRD, in conflict particularly with the principles of a 'learning organisation'. After all, those principles emphasise the need for a continuous natural emergence and resolution of learning needs as part of an ongoing cycle of interactive individual and organisational development. The conflict is apparent rather than real, however. A commitment to fostering learning that can help to produce adaptive, innovative people does not preclude a need to ensure also that learning gaps related to current and longer-term business goals are identified and matched by planned HRD activity.

As the Cummins case-study illustrated, the value-adding approach to developing HRD strategy focuses on prioritising HRD activity around business drivers, in the belief that activity related to these will produce the most significant returns for the organisation. Fundamental business drivers in any organisation are:

• current business strategy and plans

• operational priorities

• major changes in the organisation's business environment and technical base.

Other HRD requirements to be taken into account include those that are identified through performance appraisals and succession planning.

The value-adding process to determine corporate HRD goals and strategy is therefore 'top-down' *and* 'bottom-up'. It involves key decisions about HRD needs and strategy that are initiated at board level so that they can be made at the stage when business strategy and other plans derived from it are being formulated. HRD considerations should in this way influence as well as be influenced by strategic decision-making. The outcomes of those decisions are then communicated to business unit managers and, through them, down through the organisation. At each level, they set the framework within which HRD targets and plans specific to those levels are produced. Managers must decide on how best to ensure, through HRD activity, an adequate response to overall business goals and to the needs of the units in their local environments. They must also feed back to board level those emerging needs at their level that need a strategic response. This dynamic cycle of interaction between corporate and local needs must work effectively if the organisation as a whole is to progress. (There are other, less widely used approaches to establishing corporate HRD goals and strategy. Information about two of the most well-known – problem-centred and comprehensive – is given in Appendix 4.)

HRD information required by the board must be provided by whoever is formally responsible for HRD in the organisation. The information must be accurate and timely, and must be presented in a form that, when discussed in relation to business strategy, should lead to sound decisions about the direction HRD strategy should take and the goals it should serve. The HRD manager from his or her vantage-point may perceive needs that no one at board level can as yet see. If that is the case, he or she must work hard to catch the board's attention and influence its judgement. Convincing the board – either directly or through an intermediary such as the personnel/HR director – is vital, since only the board can authorise HRD strategy and resource its implementation.

One important way in which planned learning and developmental processes can add value at corporate level (and indeed at any level at which strategic decisions have to be made) is to use them to improve the strategic process. The aim here is to help strategists to improve the quality of their decision-making and of their teamwork so that they can plan and think for the longer term rather than just for the present, and take effective, durable action on key strategic issues. They should be able to produce and continuously communicate a relevant vision of the organisation, generate challenging goals, and choose and implement the strategies that will best support them. This goes to the heart of what I call the 'strategic capability' of the organisation. However, enhancing strategic capability is a complex task, and it is not one that every person in an HRD role will be able to perform. It brings into play issues of power, politics and collective learning that not all will have the knowledge or the influence to deal with. The task has been identified here, but will not be pursued further at this point. It is explored fully in Part 5 of this book.

Adding value at unit level
Within the framework of corporate goals and strategy for HRD, plans covering each main unit or sector of the business can then be drawn up. Those plans should operate on a rolling basis, and be flexible enough to respond quickly to emerging needs. Line managers and HRD professionals (where they are employed) must collaborate to ensure their effective implementation. Major direct and indirect costs (such as lost opportunity time, lost production time, reduced quality and wastage during learning time, the cost of training and trainers, and so on) must be identified, as must those benefits that will outweigh the costs and bring added value for the business.

A company's annual report should contain a section within the business plan completed by every business unit about that unit's human resources and their performance and productivity levels. This should be matched with information about the unit's investment in HRD. This identification of HRD plans in the annual report gives clear recognition of HRD as crucial to business success.

Adding value at individual level
It is particularly important that plans for individuals working in the business units are agreed and valued by those individuals. There are often tensions here. Some will arise because manager and individual disagree over what training and further development are needed, and why. Some will arise because certain developmental objectives urged

by the manager as essential in relation to business needs will not seem equally important to the individual, or because the parties disagree on priorities for objectives. All these tensions have to be resolved if HRD at unit level is to respond to business needs while also having the commitment of individuals. They will be discussed in more detail in Chapter 14.

This rather detailed explanation of how to achieve a business-focused approach to the operation of the HRD process must not be read to mean that the approach is bureaucratic or mechanical. The reverse must be the case. It must be the product of a partnership, working continuously to adapt HRD activity to critical needs, and also to anticipate the areas where HRD can most productively be used to make a difference to organisational ability to achieve its goals and move forward in its environment. At unit level, the approach can be summarised in five steps, shown in Table 4.

Table 4   Five steps in producing HRD plans at unit level

1   Focus on corporate goals and the unit's business targets for the coming period, related to those goals.

2   Identify group and individual gaps in skills, knowledge and attitudes in the division or unit that it is essential to close in order to meet targets, and express these in terms of standards to be achieved.

3   Agree on HRD plans to meet the standards.

4   Set specific objectives for every component of the plans.

5   Monitor HRD at regular milestones and adjust as necessary.

Delivering and adding value through the HRD process

Read more on how to link training and development to 'the business', drawing especially on reading listed at the end of this chapter. Then produce some recommendations on how to improve the planning and delivery of HRD at local level in your own organisation (or one with which you are familiar).

ASSESSING THE VALUE

Problems of measurement

In determining how to assess the value of what HRD achieves for the organisation, it is worth recalling some of the realities of organisational change:

• *Many organisations are in the process of radical and continuous change.* These changes are frequently perceived to be driven purposively by HR strategy. HR in this sense is taken to mean an approach that seeks to align an organisation's systems, structures, knowledge and skills with business strategies in order to improve organisational effectiveness.

• *These changes are usually associated with changes in organisations' environments.* Research indicates that such claims made for the impact of HR strategy are in reality often misplaced. The changes in question are more often the unexpected results of a trial-and-error reaction to environmental pressures than the planned outcome of any rational analysis of that environment and the formulation of HR strategy to deal with it.

• *The changes occur on a number of levels.* Such levels are structural, cultural, to do with job design, pay systems, competencies, and the composition and deployment of the workforce. Tracking their start and finish is difficult, as is the estimation of how far and in exactly what ways the introduction of change in one part of the HR system has affected other areas. Again, then, the extent to which HR strategy has produced the changes, and exactly how or at what level it may have done it, is often quite unclear.

• *These changes occur at different points in time.* Agreeing on where to start and at what point to finish the measurement of HR outcomes is therefore a critical decision. Too soon, and measurement may be vulnerable to the argument that the outcomes have had no chance to become established. Too late, and so many other variables could have been responsible for producing those outcomes that there can now be no certainty as to their true cause.

• *These changes are perceived in different ways across the organisation.* For example, what may at the time have been intended as a radical HRD initiative, and subsequently be genuinely perceived as such by senior management or HRD staff, can be viewed quite differently by others in the organisation – and indeed may have gone virtually unnoticed by some.

• *There is often a difference between espoused and actual HR goals and strategy.* Thus the so-called 'flexible workforce' can in reality be constituted by a low-cost, easily manipulated, vulnerable workforce. 'Empowerment' can conceal the fact that the locus of decision-making remains essentially unchanged, that management style is still authoritarian, and that resource control remains centralised at the top.

For all these reasons it is therefore often hard, if not impossible, to be certain about the specific outcomes of HR or HRD strategy. As the last point makes clear, there can also be doubt about the nature of the outcomes actually sought by management. Such uncertainties are increased by the diverse ways in which outcomes can be measured and by the matter of who does the measuring.

> The hope that HRM can easily be linked to the competitive performance of a firm is illusory. The disarray of the competitive process is mirrored by the fragility and impermanence of many HRM instruments.
>
> (Whipp, 1992: 52)

Although it is important to set standards and targets, to monitor progress and to assess the outcomes of HRD strategy and initiatives, those activities will thus always be inexact, usually time-consuming and expensive in time and expertise. The critical issue will be the nature of the true driving forces behind HRD strategy. It is those driving forces that in reality will do most to determine whether or not formal HR aims are achieved, and are believed across the organisation to have been achieved.

It is the process of HRD in the business rather than the formally prescribed strategy for HRD that therefore becomes crucial to the setting and measuring of outcomes. In order to assess the impact of HRD outcomes, that process must be collaborative and goal-focused. It should ensure that:

• there is a clear vision of the initial state of affairs, and of how that state of affairs will have changed once the HRD process has achieved its intended outcomes

• there is a clear definition of the goals that the HRD process must achieve in order to produce that changed state of affairs (For example, a goal to do with 'improving managerial effectiveness' is too imprecise. In what ways is it necessary for managers to improve? How must they have changed once training and development has taken place? What will they know and be able to do, and how will they behave then, as distinct from now?)

• there is a clear idea of the HRD path that will be followed to achieve those goals – of the planned learning initiatives and processes that will be introduced and followed through

• there is agreement on the kind of workplace environment needed in order for that path to be feasible, and for learners to both acquire and be able to apply new skills and knowledge (For example, technology-driven learning will be ineffective in a workplace where there are no skills to use it, no infrastructure to support it, and no willingness on management's side to exploit its full potential. For more on that topic, see Chapter 12.)

• there is clarity and agreement about what measures to apply in order to decide if the goals have been reached.

'Value for money' or 'added value'?
'Value for money' is usually interpreted as a pay-back approach: an attempt to measure in financial or analogous terms a return on training investment (Lee, 1996). A typical 'value for money' exercise would involve measuring the impact of training outcomes on variables like turnover, profit, increase in sales, conversion of leads to sales – what accountants call the 'direct return' achieved. One example, provided by practice in the insurance company Frizzell Financial Services, was described by Lee in his article. Another was recounted by Armstrong (1987: 33–4) describing practice at Book Club Associates in the late 1980s. There, all training and development programmes aimed to improve output and minimise costs, and were designed to support productivity drives. Their specific objectives were easy to define because the company's performance management programmes included the specification of clear performance standards against which

people's performance was formally appraised. That kind of approach to establishing pay-back involves:

- *measuring identifiable costs (outflows) of training, direct and indirect.* This means identifying the basic annual cost of running the training function and the costs of running particular training activities.

- *measuring identifiable benefits (inflows) to the firm in financial terms (or those that can easily be equated with money).* Performance measures can be categorised, starting with the most easily quantifiable and going on to more difficult qualitative indicators (Robinson and Robinson, 1989).

- *comparing costs and benefits to give a cost-benefit ratio or rate of return for capital employed.* This involves assessing whether other types of HRD intervention would be more cost-beneficial than the one currently being considered – on-the-job learning rather than a formal course, for example. Cost-benefit analysis is concerned with establishing the costs of an activity and then comparing these with the benefits it is likely to confer. It should take into account efficiency as well as effectiveness in establishing the benefits. To test ourselves on this, consider the following case.

Weighing up the training options

A training manager has a choice of improving supervisory performance in her organisation by sending supervisors away on an accredited national supervisory training programme, run at the local college, or producing an in-house programme with the help of her very capable training officers, who are experienced in this type of training. What criteria should she use to help her decide which option to choose?

Feedback notes
The following list shows at least six major issues that should be considered when weighing up training alternatives, together with a sample of the kind of questions to be raised under each heading.

- *Budgeting* – Would each option be affordable in terms of training budgets?

- *Training policy and strategy* – Which of the options would be most consistent with the organisation's overall HRD strategy?

- *Training needs* – Have supervisory training needs been carefully analysed? Is there any conflict here between individual and departmental or organisational needs? Which alternative would best meet the balance of needs?

- *Training benefits and evaluation* – Which of the options is most likely to help job performance, motivation and commitment of the supervisors, and carry other benefits for the organisation? What information can be obtained about the value of each option, by reference both to past initiatives in the organisation and to external best practice?

- *Transfer of learning* – How will transfer of learning be ensured if the supervisors attend the external course? Would there be better transfer if they attended an internal course?

- *Other options* – Are there any other ways in which the same kind and level of results offered could be achieved, but at less cost? What about team-briefings, quality circles, project groups? What would be the costs of doing nothing? Would that lead to reduced motivation of the supervisors, to lack of development of their ability and potential, to longer learning time for new techniques, or to poorer-quality work, and higher rates of absenteeism or sickness?

If cost-benefit analysis is to reveal the extent to which not only value has been (or will be) achieved for money expended, but value has been (or will be) added to the business, then it must involve more than merely financial calculations. There must be discussion not only of quantitative data but also of qualitative outcomes and methods of measurement. There must be a consideration of strategies to do with 'growing people' as much as of strategies to do with 'training for competency'. The crucial issue is to assess what kind of investment is needed in order to produce outcomes that will make a critical difference to the organisation's ability to move forward in its environment.

Here is another case-study, this time set in the National Health Service (NHS), to demonstrate how, by focusing on the extent to which an organisation has achieved additional capability to achieve its goals with the introduction of a strategic HRD initiative, the true value of the HRD investment can be assessed. This is a real-life case-study. It refers to an evaluation that I was asked to carry out, over a period of months in the late 1980s, into the effectiveness of an organisation-wide management development programme to improve managerial capability and ease the path of technological change.

Case-study: Management development at a prescription pricing authority

The programme concerned took place over four years. It was designed in-house, by the authority's personnel department, and delivered using both internal and external resources. Its purpose was to develop managers in a regional prescription pricing authority in the National Health Service (NHS) to manage effectively in a new organisational structure and culture, spearheaded by a new chief executive officer. Another aspect of the fundamental organisational change process taking place throughout this period was the introduction of new technology across all offices of the authority, so managers had to develop the knowledge, and the technical and social skills, to cope with the implications of that also.

After the collection of a wealth of financial and non-financial data relating to the programme, I was able to establish that it had cost the prescription pricing authority £47,400 over four years to put 210 officers through this Management of Change programme and to provide some of those officers with the skills needed to facilitate the job-related training of a further 1,730 clerical officers. Some of that cost had been met by central NHS funding, some by the authority itself.

I was also able to establish – by desk review, by a questionnaire survey, and by follow-up face-to-face discussions with staff drawn from each staff sector covered by the survey, some of whom had taken part in the training, some of whom had not – that the programme had achieved outcomes that appeared to me to amply justify not only the expenditure on the programme to that point, but also an application for further national funding to expand the programme's scope to cover more junior levels of staff in the authority.

The evaluation report that I produced for the PPA was detailed, but concluded with the following summary:

> At a time of major changes to a traditional, rigid organisation, whose managerial and supervisory staff had an average length of service of 25–35 years, the programme was widely seen – by participants, and also by those who had been unable to take part, for whatever reason – as having made a significant contribution to the successful and rapid introduction of those changes, including the installation of new technology across the authority. During this time of fundamental change, there had been virtually no reduction in productivity. There was a positive approach to industrial relations issues, and an increased motivation, commitment, and interest apparent in the significant majority of officers who went through the programme. All the evidence points to the conclusion that without the programme such a positive state of affairs would not have been achievable.

To ensure objectivity here, it was important to identify any factors apart from training that had contributed to those favourable outcomes: alterations in top management and the consequent change to a more flexible, team-centred, open style and culture at the top of the organisation, which was gradually making itself felt throughout the authority's structure; changes in roles and job content due to computerisation; a greater recognition of, and focus on, individual rates of productivity because of new control systems; more delegated responsibility with the innovations in budgetary systems. The impact of all these factors was considerable. To offset them, however, there was the threatening nature of change as perceived by long-serving staff who had worked for many years without any major alterations in their jobs or workplace environment; the specialised nature of many people's jobs, which would make it hard for older staff, in particular, to get jobs outside the authority should that become necessary; and the poor financial rewards available for most staff.

Seen in this context of some real improvements, but also of many perceived threats, uncertainties and disincentives, the programme was generally experienced as a constructive, motivating and energising initiative. It helped newly promoted staff to establish themselves with more certainty in their managerial or supervisory roles. It helped longer-serving staff to sit back, away from their daily and pressurised routine, and reflectively evaluate their own performance and approach to work, while learning from tutors and colleagues in a supportive and team-centred atmosphere. Comments by one supervisor represented the views of many about what the programme had achieved at her level:

> All aspects of the course are in my mind daily. The week flies by, and I look forward to any further training.

What was most interesting about these comments was that they came from an officer working in a division of the authority that had a persistently poor industrial relations record, and that her reactions to the programme were echoed by both the administrative assistants in that division. Since the programme, weekly team meetings had been introduced in that division, at the initiative of those staff.

The conclusion drawn from the evaluation study was that the results of the management development programme had produced returns that were over and above the costs of the investment that had been made in it, and that further investment would enable the full benefit of that 'added value' to be spread more widely across the authority. In the event, further funding was obtained from the NHS at centre, and the programme was extended in line with the report's recommendations.

Focusing on the future

As the case-study and discussion thus far have shown, 'adding value' is not only about assessing the costs and benefits of past initiatives to establish if 'it was worth it'. It is also about what Lee (1996: 31) called 'pay-forward': the idea that investment in training must regarded as primarily future-oriented, to do with enhancing the capability of the whole organisation to move forward. In the case of the prescription pricing authority, evaluation showed that the costs of the programme had been offset by sufficient benefits to justify that past investment. More importantly, though, evaluation demonstrated the ongoing value of that investment, and the barriers to the authority's future progress that a major training programme had done so much to remove. Evaluation in that case was not only about pay-back. It was very much about pay-forward.

This approach to assessing the value of the HRD investment does not, of course, mean that there is no need to measure outcomes of the HRD function in some detail, or to evaluate the design and delivery of specific learning events. Such evaluation must be carried out by HRD staff as a necessary part of their ongoing quality assurance process, and will be discussed in Chapters 7 and 17.

ENSURING THE CONTRIBUTION

At this point, we can suggest four leading questions to ask about an HRD function that seeks to make a value-adding contribution to the organisation:

- Is there a good fit between the vision and strategy of HRD and wider human resource and organisational vision and goals?

- Is HRD activity focused on areas that will make a critical difference to the organisation's ability to achieve its goals and move forward in its environment?

- Does the way the function is organised enhance its ability to make that difference?

- Are those who carry HRD responsibilities expert in their tasks and deeply knowledgeable about the business?

To ensure that HRD priorities are correctly identified, and that appropriate strategies and interventions are produced and are effectively implemented, a partnership approach is essential (see, for example, Harrison 1992a). It is illustrated in Table 5.

Table 5 **HRD as a partnership process**

1 Establish and maintain informed, proactive and collaborative relationships with the key parties in the organisation, especially at corporate and business unit levels.

2 Ensure understanding of key issues and commitment to action at the top level.

3 Move around the organisation regularly, identifying HRD needs and establishing a proactive HRD presence in the business.

4 Carry out continuous data-gathering and planning with line management and other key parties.

5 Continuously align and prioritise HRD policy and plans with business strategy, ensuring consistency with HR policy and practice.

6 Identify the ways in which HRD initiatives will produce value for the business.

7 Work with management to ensure ongoing monitoring and feedback of results, and relevant action arising from that feedback.

8 Be a credible business partner. Keep fully informed about the business, identifying any internal or external changes that have important implications for the HRD process.

In the following chapter we shall see in detail how this partnership process can operate.

CONCLUSION

Having read this chapter and completed its reviews and self-checks, you should now

- understand how the HRD process can 'add value' for the business

- be able to identify the critical features that relate to HRD's ability to make a significant impact on organisational performance and progress

- understand how to produce feasible and value-adding HRD goals and plans to meet critical business needs

- be able to explain how to assess the value of HRD's contribution to the business.

To test yourself against these objectives, what five-minute answers would you give to the following questions? (Dates in brackets refer to the IPD qualifying examination paper in which a question appeared.)

- Justify criteria to use in order to decide whether or not a proposed Employee Development (ED) initiative is likely to add value for the organisation? (May 1999)

- What is the difference between giving value for money and 'adding value', when these terms are applied to HRD?

- Identify ED's main stakeholders in any organisation, and explain some ways in which you think that their commitment to an organisation's ED goals can be obtained. (November 1999)

USEFUL READING

MAYO A. (1998) *Creating a Training and Development Strategy.* London, Institute of Personnel and Development.

WALTON J. (1999a) 'Outsourcing: what stays in and what goes out', in J. Walton, *Strategic Human Resource Development.* Harlow, Financial Times and Prentice Hall, pp279–99 (for its discussion of value chain analysis).

7 Setting and achieving outcomes

LEARNING OBJECTIVES

After reading this chapter you will:

- understand key principles associated with the setting and achievement of HRD standards and outcomes
- understand uses and methods of benchmarking and setting standards
- understand how to audit the outcomes of HRD in the organisation.

THE WORKPLACE ENVIRONMENT

Where HRD's value to the business is accepted, it will be one of a number of processes expected to contribute directly to corporate goals and also to support other functions in their similar endeavour. For HRD initiatives to achieve their intended outcomes, however, there must be an employment system and a workplace environment that will release the effort and commitment needed from individuals and teams across the organisation. There must also be processes and procedures that encourage and aid the standard-setting process and stimulate continuous improvement of performance.

Standard-setting and continuous improvement of performance can be stimulated and supported by:

- regular team briefing, and emphasis on teamworking and flexibility of work and skills
- shop-floor-located continuous improvement teams
- accessible training rooms which also act as informal break-away areas for discussing quality issues and continuous improvement projects
- emphasis in the workplace on setting business-focused targets
- performance indicators and benchmarks used as business measures
- value analysis teams drawn from across the organisation, to improve quality, reduce costs and ensure that products and services remain competitive
- learning networks involving customers, suppliers, producers and other key stakeholders.

Organisational culture and systems that demonstrate recognition for, and practical commitment to, HRD as a business process with benefits also for the individual:

- regular, voluntary appraisal of training needs of teams and individuals, from which development plans ensue

- high-quality job-related training and personal development

- facilities for open learning, and encouragement and support for individuals to take the initiative in their development

- good basic pay, and harmonised terms and conditions of work

- no financial incentives or reward schemes except those tied to the acquisition of qualifications and additional relevant skills

- high standards of health, safety and counselling services (usually off-site and always confidential and optional for the individual)

- accessibility of all company information to all company employees – contributing to the business requires understanding of the business; employees as business partners must be trusted to use access with discretion.

It is important to 'take the temperature' of the workplace environment regularly. Some organisations use a 'health of the business' survey for this purpose. One example is an internal questionnaire focused on four areas to do with sharing the vision, integrating the effort, sustaining a healthy community and making intelligent decisions. Each area is broken down into a series of descriptive statements, with ratings listed against each statement. Surveys can be carried out every year and the results then compared with previous norms in the company, external norms in comparable businesses (Cranfield holds manufacturing norms that offer competitive benchmarks) and UK norms. The results must be communicated quickly to aid discussion and action-planning.

SETTING STANDARDS AND ACHIEVING OUTCOMES FOR HRD

One question to which those carrying HRD responsibilities in an organisation must always know the answer is: will the expected outcomes of HRD prove relevant to key business needs?

Key stages in establishing and achieving HRD outcomes are:

- allocating responsibilities for delivery of strategy

- drawing up action plans in order to implement strategy

- setting targets and standards, the means for measuring them, and the timing and levels of responsibility for implementing the plans

- continued oversight, monitoring and adaptability to ensure that there is minimal drift between strategy and its implementation across the organisation

- continuous communication of interim progress and problems, and shared decisions about any amendments to plans needed to meet unexpected contingencies.

In the following review, try to assess how well-informed your own training and development function and its practitioners are about the business and its environment, and how well-equipped they are to set standards (intended outcomes) that are relevant to the needs of the business and informed by external and internal best practice.

Assessing the quality of HRD service in my organisation

Does your training and development function collaborate in joint ventures with employee development (ED) functions in other organisations to develop and offer value-added services? _____

Does your training and development function have its own business plans for developing its capability and performance, and are these plans related to the challenges facing your client businesses? _____

Does your training and development function use regular structured feedback and benchmarking in order to assess its performance? _____

Does it work to an explicit set of ethics and values that have been agreed at the highest level? _____

As an HR professional, are you clear about who your customers, suppliers and business partners are, and do you understand the people and organisational implications of the challenges they are facing? _____

Are you clear about the purpose of your job and the processes that you are responsible for managing? _____

Do you create and pursue your own development plan? _____

Do you assess your own performance with regard to: _____

- meeting standards _____
- satisfying your customers _____
- your contribution to your customers' performance _____
- finding more cost-effective ways to improve your contribution? _____

With acknowledgements to Fonda and Rowland, 1995

Let us look more closely at benchmarking and best practice.

Benchmarking, best practice and milestones

These are techniques associated with quality management, and can be defined in general terms as a continuous search for and implementation of best practices that lead to superior performance.

Benchmarking involves finding a particular standard, whether internal or external, and using that as a continuous marker for a particular strategy, process or initiative. There are three major types of benchmarking:

- *Internal benchmarking* looks at and compares similar processes within an organisation to achieve internal best practice. For HR, an example might be the selection, induction or appraisal process. The exercise of ascertaining how this is carried out in different parts of the organisation offers two benefits: the highlighting of inconsistencies and the identification of internal best practice that can then be used as a marker across the organisation.

- *Competitive benchmarking* is where organisations in the same sector – for example, a hospital trust and a community healthcare trust – agree to work together to compare best practice in key areas. For example, two areas might be the matter of privacy and dignity, and the publication and distribution of patient information.

- *Functional benchmarking* takes place where a particular process is identified and then compared to best practice outside the organisation. An organisation that wishes to improve its measurements of customer satisfaction may thus take two or three external organisations of different types as comparators, and finally select one to use for benchmarking.

Benchmarking as a process is divided into four stages:

- preliminary planning

- analysis, in which the gap between current performance and desired performance is identified as a result of benchmarking research

- action, in which changes are implemented and measured

- review and recycling stages in order to achieve continuous improvement.

Rationale for benchmarking

Why might it be helpful for your organisation to benchmark some of its HRD practices and processes – and which practices and processes would you recommend for the purpose?

To conclude: benchmarking is not merely copying, or picking up handy hints. It is about planning comparisons in order to decide how to enhance performance. Organisations agree to being benchmarked because they acquire insight and information from the process too, and because it gives them a higher profile in the competitive environment.

Best practice involves gathering information across the academic and practitioner field to formulate general principles that will help to determine how best to carry out a particular process or initiative. Although internal and competitive benchmarking are likely to produce improvement, it is the search for best practice and new ideas that is most likely to change an organisation's collective mindset, and so lead to transformation. This is illustrated in the following case-study.

Case-study: English Nature's use of benchmarking and best practice

English Nature, the Government's adviser on nature and conservation, aspires to be a learning organisation, and so decided to benchmark approaches to training with a wide range of companies in order to achieve that transformation. The account produced by S. Dolan, its training manager, illustrates the many ways in which examining practice in other organisations can help an HRD department to set standards, decide on particular practical approaches and monitor progress.

Twelve companies across all sectors were visited because they had adopted innovative approaches to learning and business development. Their beliefs, strategies and a range of key features were analysed and compared with those noted in the 'learning organisation' literature that had already been studied at English Nature. Common traits soon became evident, and it emerged that in a number of respects English Nature already had the elements needed. The company introduced many initiatives to develop the rest, at the heart of which was a range of programmes to strengthen the links between learning and action across the organisation. Company personnel also continued to develop external learning networks with other organisations in conservation and business.

Source: Dolan, 1995

Milestones should be set to enable progress towards the achievement of planned outcomes to be monitored and discussed at crucial points. Here is another case-study to illustrate how they can be used.

Case-study: HRM strategic milestones in a British investment bank

During 1990–91 County NatWest, an investment bank, asked all its business units, including its personnel department, to establish strategic milestones for a five-year period, against which, by specified target dates, their performance would be measured. This forced the personnel department into considering its contribution to the organisation at the strategic level in the context of the bank's overall five-year business plan.

The requirement to produce strategic milestones as an input to the business plan 'marked an important watershed in defining the contribution of personnel to the business at a strategic level. It forced the department to reflect on the nature of that contribution.' Eighteen separate strategic milestones were duly authorised by the senior management of the bank. The milestones were consistent one with the other, and overall addressed issues that consultation within business units and across the three personnel teams had shown to be critical to business success.

Each milestone was then assigned to a designated individual and was incorporated into their own targets of performance. Quarterly reviews on progress, involving the whole department, were subsequently held to ensure that the milestones were on target.

Source: Riley and Sloman, 1991

Here is a case-study to demonstrate practical ways of setting and measuring the achievement of HRD standards.

Case-study: Standards and indicators at Cummins Engine Co. Ltd, Darlington, UK

In Chapter 6 we looked at an historical case-study about HR strategy in the 1980s at Cummins Engine Co., Darlington, a US-owned manufacturing company with locations across the world. The case now goes forward to 1997, by which time 'customer-led quality' was the vision that drove Cummins' new production system, providing the focus for goals, standards, performance and recognition.

At the Darlington plant in 1997 human resource management and development (HRMD) was identified as one of seven 'functional excellence' functions. HRMD was regarded as a core function in the business because the company believed that it was only by a continuous and focused investment in attracting, developing and retaining high-calibre people that it could achieve the human capability it needed to maintain its world-class competitive edge.

In 1997, the HRMD function operated in relation to 11 policy areas where standards of performance were set and maintained:

- leadership
- environment
- health, safety and security
- administration
- staffing
- performance management
- training and development
- organisational design
- compensation and benefits
- employee relations
- community.

Standards to be achieved in each of these policy areas were expressed in terms of performance indicators with points allocated to each. Every year the HRMD function was rated by its internal and external customers against those indicators. A score was achieved in this way for the department's performance in each of the 11 policy areas. To take an example: 'Performance management' had seven performance indicators, which together carried a total possible score of 10.

The plant had five business goals to do with customer-led quality, and HR staff had to make a contribution each year to those goals. They also had to take lead responsibility for the goal related to 'Developing outstanding people'. Contribution was achieved through projects managed by HR staff that also formed the basis for their appraisal as individuals. In 1996, for example, the training and development manager had a number of projects, each with its targets, timescale and methods of measurement, which together constituted her personal responsibility for helping towards 'Developing outstanding people'.

With acknowledgements to the company.

At companies like this, benchmarking, best practice, standards, performance indicators, targets and milestones are all used to establish outcomes and measure performance of an HR/HRD function in relation to its key policy areas and to assess its overall contribution to the business. The process used across all such companies is similar. It is one whereby HR staff and their business partners regularly agree together on which HR outcomes to target. Thereafter, the presumption in the company is that if those outcomes are clearly materialising, and if the function and its staff have the confidence and respect of management and workforce, then HRD is justifying its investment. It is only a failure of outcomes to materialise, or poor ratings on the annual customer survey of the HRMD function, that would lead to a special exercise to assess the value of that investment.

Analysing standards and performance indicators in an HRD function

Consider an organisation known to you which has a specialist HRD/training function or section. What are the main standards of performance that provide the framework for HRD? What are the performance indicators by which HRD staff's performance is assessed? How far do these standards and performance indicators seem to result in HRD's making a business-focused contribution?

AUDITING HRD

The audit

Auditing is a way of assessing the nature and outcomes of HRD activity at particular points in time. It has been described as 'a process that produces an official accounting and verification, most often conducted by third-party evaluators. Auditing typically relies on samples of information that are critical to the organisation and its decision-makers' (Murphy and Swanson, 1988).

The aim of an audit is to supply a snapshot of the current situation across the organisation in order to compare what is happening with what should be happening, and to identify any action needed. Audits enable trends to be identified. They form part of a strategy to ensure continuous improvement of a function or of an area of operations in an organisation.

Who should carry out the audit?

Most audits are carried out by a team, and for the auditing of HRD in the workplace, a small team of HRD staff, line managers and an external consultant offers the best balance of internal expertise and organisational insights, and external credibility, objectivity and knowledge of best practice. Additional contributions can be invited on an *ad hoc* basis, but for ease and speed of operations the core team should not exceed six members (Harrison R., 1999: 13). In the smaller organisation, an audit will probably be carried out by only one or two people, who may or may not be employees of the organisation.

How should the audit be constructed?

Every audit must have its own focus and framework. Options for the focus of an HRD audit include:

- the effectiveness and efficiency of HRD staff as a service to the business

- the effectiveness and efficiency of line managers as HRD managers

- the contribution of HRD to specific business goals, such as those to do with quality and performance

- the contribution of particular HRD activities or programmes

- the skills, flexibility and culture of the workforce.

Once the focus has been decided on, a framework for the audit must be produced, and decisions must be made on the areas of questioning that will produce the most relevant information. The focus of the well-known US-based Malcolm Baldridge National Quality Award is on quality in the business. Looking at human resource management and development, it requires information to be gathered about five components, or standards, each of which is defined and to each of which performance indicators are attached. One of these areas is 'Employee development'. The others are:

- HRM strategy and the implementation process

- Employee involvement

- Employee performance and recognition

- Employee well-being and morale.

The European Foundation for Quality Management's 'Business Excellence' self-assessment model is based on best practice and regularly updated. It uses nine criteria, five of them 'enablers' and four 'results'. The model is based on the premise that excellence depends on partnerships, resource and processes. It is a helpful one to use when seeking to place human resource practice in its business context. However, the Investors in People (IIP) standard provides the most familiar audit framework in Britain for assessing links between training and development and the business. It is currently under review, but at the time of writing the standard covers four areas and has 23 performance indicators. IIP has been criticised for not being sufficiently concerned with the outcomes of HRD activity, as distinct from the inputs and operations that it involves, but its value as an audit is still considerable. Of course, its use involves working with external advisers and assessors, and so it is more costly than self-assessment audits.

In Chapter 6, I introduced an original framework, or model, of HRD that I devised in 1999 as part of a self-assessment process to audit the impact of training and development in the organisation. I am reintroducing it at this point as Figure 5 (by kind permission of

Figure 5 A model of training and development's impact on workplace performance

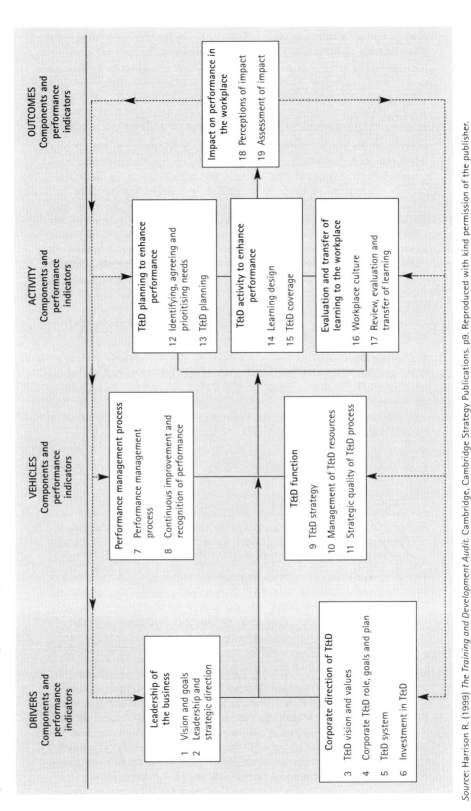

Source: Harrison R. (1999) *The Training and Development Audit.* Cambridge, Cambridge Strategy Publications. p9. Reproduced with kind permission of the publisher.

Cambridge Strategy Publications) in order to illustrate the practicalities of auditing.

The framework identifies four critical areas of HRD – its drivers, vehicles, activity and outcomes. Related to these, it focuses on eight components, with 19 associated performance indicators. Once information has been gathered on these indicators, the auditors will be able to assess the effectiveness of HRD as a process and set of operations to improve the performance of individuals and groups across the organisation.

What comes next?

When the decisions have been made on who is to carry out the audit, and an appropriate audit instrument has been chosen or devised, then a six-step process has to be tackled.

Ensuring commitment

The first priority must be to ensure that top management and all senior managers are fully committed to the audit, to communicating its main findings to employees, and to taking action related to those findings. Then, all employees must have a clear understanding of the audit's purpose and intended outcomes, and be convinced that the audit has the full backing of all levels of management.

Planning the audit

This involves decisions on what data to collect, from whom, using what methods, and over what period of time. It also involves assessing all the resources needed to carry out and support the audit process, and gaining authority for those resources. A proper budget must be established and maintained.

Table 6 shows those in the organisation who should be approached in order to gain relevant information for the audit envisaged in Figure 5.

My own audit, like most, involves a mixture of methods in order to produce information of good quality. It falls into three parts:

- *Part I*: a diagnostic survey to identify current perceptions across the organisation about the role, organisation and impact of HRD in the organisation.

- *Part II*: seven more audit steps to obtain information from all levels of management and from HRD specialist personnel about the drivers, vehicles and activity shown in Figure 6. Those components are explained in the audit instrument by reference to their 19 performance indicators, and for each indicator a best-practice profile is provided. Indicators and profile act as guides to the kind of information needed by the auditors.

- *Part III* involves the integration of the Part I data from all employees, and the Part II data from managers and HR specialists, in order to identify any gaps between what management intends HRD to achieve, the reality as perceived by the workforce, and any gaps that have to be closed if HRD is to make a powerful contribution to the business, and if the quality of HRD practice is to continuously improve. Conclusions are then reached.

Table 6 Rationale for involvement in the audit process

Involvement of	Rationale for involvement	Information to supply about
Top and senior management	Responsible for corporate vision and goals, and for overall direction and resourcing of T&D. Their active involvement is needed in order to ensure commitment of all management.	Corporation vision, leadership and direction. Business environment, corporate strategy. Performance management process. T&D function, plans and process. Internal image and impact of T&D.
Middle management	Responsibilities for T&D of their staff. Their active support is needed in order to ensure commitment of teams and individuals to T&D. They implement T&D strategy and control the structure within which it operates.	Corporate vision, leadership and direction. Business unit environment and strategy. Performance management process. T&D goals, strategy and plans. Image, coverage and impact of T&D activity at unit and operational levels.
Team leaders/ supervisors	They see the operation of T&D at operational levels and identify important performance-related needs. They must be committed to T&D activity intended to improve performance.	Corporate vision and goals. Workplace environment and performance management process. T&D activity and its impact in workplace.
Specialist staff	Where they are employed, they play a leading role in the planning, provision and evaluation of T&D, and operate the T&D systems.	Corporate and functional T&D role and goals. T&D function and process. Type, image and impact of T&D activity across the organisation.
Main body of employees	Their understanding of the role that T&D does and should play in the business, and of the purpose and relevance of T&D activity, together with the credibility they attach to T&D staff, all have a direct impact on their motivation to learn the skills, knowledge and attitudes needed for effective performance and development of future-related capabilities.	Type, image and impact of T&D activity across the organisation.
External individuals, agencies and institutions	Their view of T&D in the organisation can help to attract external resources and build external image. Some will be involved in strategic T&D alliances with the organisation.	External image of T&D activity. Best practice and benchmarks.

Source: Harrison R. (1999) *The Training and Development Audit.* Cambridge, Cambridge Strategy Publications. p16. Reproduced with kind permission of the publisher.

Piloting the survey

All audits of this kind involve a diagnostic survey to reveal the initial state of play. It is important to pilot the survey on a small group of people before carrying it out across the organisation. This will reveal any design weaknesses or other problems likely to be encountered in the administration of the survey. These can then be put right before proceeding further.

Collecting and analysing data

For every audit step it will be important to obtain views and perceptions from a variety of sources. To supplement data obtained by questionnaires and/or face-to-face discussions (either individually or in focus groups), desk reviews must also be carried out. They involve the examination of current and historical documentation relating to HRD systems, processes, procedures, policies and operations. Desk reviews 'aid verification of policies, procedures and outcomes; the identification of trends; and assessment of the likelihood of those trends continuing or changing in the future' (Harrison R., 1999: 33).

Establishing findings and conclusions

Comparisons should be made throughout the audit process between what people say or think is happening and what various kinds of written information – taken together – indicate to be the 'reality'. Historical data recording past intent, actions and their outcomes will supply the necessary backdrop to current trends and events. Auditors must always assess carefully the credibility that can be placed on all their sources of information.

At the conclusion of each step, and once the data have been carefully recorded to aid final analysis, the auditor/s should record their responses to three generalised questions about the component that has been examined (*ibid*: 34):

- How long have the present standards relating to the component covered in this audit step been in place, and how long are they likely to remain?

- What are the most helpful aspects of the current situation relating to this component?

- What are the least helpful aspects of the current situation relating to this component?

Producing the audit report

Any report should commence with a brief introduction to the organisation and its environment, the HRD framework used for the audit, and an explanation of the audit process and information sources used.

In the body of the report on my own audit, there should be coverage of each of the drivers, vehicles and activity areas shown in Figure 6. For each of these components there should be a brief narrative assessing it by reference to its associated performance indicators. The purpose of the narrative is to 'provide concise, well-evidenced commentary on such issues as:

- the main actions being taken in the organisation in relation to the component

- any examples of good or best practice in the organisation, and any areas of concern to the auditors

- any significant gaps between espoused intentions, the situation as it is perceived to exist by various parties, and the situation that is needed if best practice is to be achieved

- reference to the appendices where a master list of documents and examples of noteworthy initiatives supporting this component can be provided' (*ibid*: 79).

The report's recommendations should identify actions needed now, actions to take in the short term to enhance HRD's contribution to workplace performance, and longer-term actions to ensure continuous improvement.

Auditing can lead to valuable outcomes that go beyond those which formed its initial frame of reference. The following are typical:

- the identification of HRD areas that need further research

- the development of a relevant language and of concepts across the organisation for discussing HRD problems and opportunities

- the reorganisation of HRD roles and functions

- the development of a greater awareness of the scarcity of human resources and problems of developing and conserving them, which then begins to inform the 'political debate' about HRD and business strategy

- a more strategically aware HRD team ('team' refers to those who hold formal responsibility for HRD in the organisation).

Planning an audit of HRD in an organisation

Draft a plan for an audit of HRD in your organisation, or a part of it with which you are particularly familiar. Give reasons for the audit, and explain the benefits that it should achieve for the organisation. Choose any purpose and framework for the audit that you wish, but be sure to justify them.

PRINCIPLES TO AID ASSESSMENT OF HRD OUTCOMES

We can conclude from this chapter, and from recalling many issues that have emerged throughout the book thus far, that in order to set and achieve outcomes for HRD that are of value for the organisation and its people, it is essential to work with the stakeholders of HRD in the organisation and

- agree on the key business goals that HRD activity must support

- agree on the particular HRD initiatives that will most efficiently and effectively give such support – and agree on a budget to resource them

- agree on ways of measuring the outcomes of those initiatives

- have workable plans in place for the implementation and monitoring of those initiatives

- use good practice surveys, targets, performance indicators, surveys and milestones in order to establish clear outcomes and monitor progress towards achieving them

- share information through time about progress towards outcomes

- agree on any amendments needed to plans, especially those caused by changes in the business or its environment, and by unforeseen problems in the implementation of the plans themselves.

When measuring HRD outcomes, remember that

- evaluation should be related to outcomes originally agreed between the parties

- measurement will not of itself achieve credibility for HRD – it is measurement of a kind agreed at the start between the stakeholders that is essential

- you should seek broad and flexible indicators and measures that will capture the essence of HRD activity without interfering overmuch in operations by imposing excessive and time-consuming checks and balances

- for hard objectives, use quantitative measures; for softer objectives, use a range of techniques such as behaviourally anchored rating-scales, surveys and benchmarking to ensure cross-checks on value and outcomes

- measurement and evaluation should be simple, focused on the future rather than the past, and efficient – 'measure everything that matters' is not a natural law: it is a dangerous obsession.

If the stakeholders' (and especially management's) active involvement in the HRD process is achieved at every stage, then HRD has every chance of becoming taken for granted as an essential part of business activity instead of being required to prove its worth at every step and responding by 'drowning in a sea of quantitative and qualitative measures' (Lorenz, 1994).

CONCLUSION

Having read this chapter and completed its reviews and self-checks, you should now:

- understand key principles associated with the setting and achievement of HRD standards and outcomes

- understand the uses and methods of benchmarking and setting standards

- understand how to audit the outcomes of HRD in the organisation.

To test yourself against these objectives, what five-minute answers would you give to the following questions? (Dates in brackets refer to the IPD qualifying examination paper in which a question appeared.)

- As an Employee Development (ED) manager, explain **four** steps that you would always take to ensure that all planned learning events for which you are responsible are managed in a cost-efficient and cost-effective manner, and why you would give these steps priority. (November 1997)

- You have been asked to produce a check-list for assessing the quality of the ED function's service in an organisation. Identify and justify **four** items that should appear on such a check-list. (November 1998)

- On being appointed to the post of Training Manager in an organisation – the previous occupant having moved to another firm – what immediate steps would you take on discovering that a considerable amount of money has been wasted annually on irrelevant training? (November 1999)

USEFUL READING

FONDA N. *and* BUCKTON K. (1995) *Reviewing the Personnel Function: A toolkit for development.* London, Institute of Personnel and Development. (Contains specially designed assessment tools to address key personnel and HRD issues, and builds on the frameworks of the Personnel Standards Lead Body and Management Charter Initiative.)

HARRISON R. (1999) *The Training and Development Audit: An eight-step audit to measure, assess and enhance the performance of your organisation's training and development.* Cambridge, Cambridge Strategy Publications.

INDUSTRIAL SOCIETY *Managing Best Practice.* (Monthly reports on achieving excellence in the key areas of managing people.) Available by subscription or as single copies: 0121 410 3040.

8 Handling the politics

LEARNING OBJECTIVES

After reading this chapter you will:

- understand what is meant by 'the politics of human resource development (HRD)'

- know how to analyse the context of an organisation by reference to its primary culture, structure and power sources

- be able to diagnose the main political issues in a challenging training and development situation, and outline a strategy for dealing with them.

THE POLITICS OF HRD

Politics, or 'the art of achieving the possible', is what HRD is often about, and politics is one of the enduring facets of human and organisational existence. Perhaps it is for this reason that it has not been necessary to alter much of substance in this chapter since earlier versions appeared in my 1988 and 1992 IPM textbooks.

In Chapter 2 we saw how national vocational education and training (NVET) in the UK was for decades the creature of political activity that, at government level, preoccupied with other concerns. HRD at organisational level often mirrors that wider situation as it so often becomes subordinated to matters thought to be more pressing. The negative image is made worse in organisations where no strong case is made for HRD and there is scant attempt to convince powerful parties it is worth significant investment.

There are predictable reasons for this failure to make an impact. Specialist training functions are quite often headed by managers with little formal status in the organisation. Sometimes, too, training managers (regardless of position) operate in ways that fail to gain them credibility in the eyes of those whose support they need: line managers, unions, the workforce, the board. Or there may be a lack of supportive employee resource systems to ensure the effective implementation of theoretically valuable HRD initiatives.

If HRD is to make its optimum contribution to organisational goals, those responsible for the function at different levels must examine their own role, position, resources, skills and organisational context, and identify what it is possible and necessary to achieve. Then an appropriate strategy must be adopted. In this sense the management of HRD is like a military activity, with a set of goals, an overall strategy for achieving them, and short-term tactics to meet different contingencies. Political skill is crucial to success, not just for the specialist but for all those in the organisation who have a major responsibility for the development of people.

Gaining support

To be accepted as a crucial business process, HRD must be well aligned with:

* *business strategy* – Identification and communication of the HRD implications of business strategy, and the proposal of feasible plans to meet them, is essential in order to obtain management's support for HRD. Changes in strategy often trigger a range of needs to which the skilled HRD practitioner must be able to respond quickly. Examples include needs for a multiskilled workforce, for new skills related to technological innovation, for downsizing, redeployment and new patterns of working, and so on.

* *internal values* – HRD practitioners must work ceaselessly to achieve credibility and impact in their operations in order to create positive values about HRD across the organisation. Without that, there will be no commitment to the process. In Chapter 6 we looked at the importance of the concepts of 'adding value' through 'business partnership' in this respect.

* *external catalysts* – There are many ways in which, looking outwards, HRD practitioners can draw attention to external issues, trends and standards that can become catalysts for higher levels of support for HRD within the organisation – for example, skills shortages in the market and their implications for the organisation's internal labour market, data obtained from benchmarking and best-practice exercises, or the desirability of committing to well-known standards such as Investors in People to gain a higher external profile.

Real, lasting support for HRD activities, however, comes with one thing only – success. Choosing the areas of priority where HRD will be seen to add the most value, then succeeding in those areas and ensuring awareness of that success, is essential in the politics of HRD.

But first, what about failure? We all make mistakes, and denying them is neither honest nor, usually, convincing. How does the politician deal with failure?

Explaining failure

How do you deal with your failure in a particular task or area of work when it has to be discussed with your manager, or with a powerful colleague, or admitted to those who work for you? Identify three or four methods typical to you of how you deal, in such discussions, with your failures.

Feedback notes

You have probably mentioned at least one of the following type of responses. There are so many ways of coping with failure that this is by no means an exhaustive list – it outlines just a few of the most common methods:

- I admit the failure, and try to show that I have learned from it and that it will not happen again.

- I try to cover up, blaming other people, events, problems.

- I minimise the seriousness of the failure, and try to show that there were compensating successes.

- I attempt to convince others that it was not actually failure at all but part of a plan, and that the true benefits are shortly/in the longer term going to emerge. I deflect attention to the plan and its benefits so that it, rather than my failure, becomes the focus of discussion.

As can be seen by watching the behaviour of politicians, political success is, sadly, more often than not a matter of practising the last three tactics rather than the first. Politics is the art of the achieving the possible, and of surviving. Strategies for both achieving and surviving are essential. To be seen to fail too often and too badly is the one sure way of never achieving anything. However, it is important to remember that tactics must fit the individual and the situation. Sometimes the organisational climate is such that honest admission of failure, together with convincing evidence that it will not happen again, is the most effective way of responding. Sometimes dealing with failure is not so easy. Only the individual can decide how to operate in harsher political systems – but honesty is, of course, central to the professional ethics of human resource (HR) practitioners, and compromising personal and professional values is not the hallmark of the respected HR manager or specialist. At the end of this chapter we shall tackle a case-study which will require you to look in some detail at this difficult area of dealing with failure.

THE POLITICAL CONTEXT OF HRD

So far we have discussed politics in a general way and have reached the conclusion that the essence of politics in training is to get support, to be – and to be seen to be – successful, and to know how to survive failure. But we have also observed that politics are rooted in the particular situation. Success in politics is about understanding the context in which you have to operate, and adapting to it.

You will probably have met at least one manager who came to his or her present job with an excellent record of success, but who since arrival has somehow failed to repeat that success. On analysis, some factor or factors in the two situations or 'contexts' will be different, and inability to identify and respond to that difference can be disastrous. So now we need to consider the particular context of training – its specific situation. We shall examine three key aspects of context: culture, structure and power.

There are, of course, many other factors that the manager must consider when drawing up plans for training and development. There are also many more complex and insightful ways of analysing the political reality of organisational life (Silverman, 1970; Pfeffer, 1981) and the different meanings that people attach to it (Morgan, 1986). However, in this chapter use is made only of the simplest possible approach compatible with developing a practical understanding of organisational politics. It is in the culture, structure and power system of the organisation that politics are embedded. If, therefore, we are unable to analyse these three aspects, we shall have no chance of success in handling the politics of HRD.

Organisational cultures and structures

First, cultures and structures. Try to give your own definitions of these terms. If you are familiar with organisation theory, that should not be difficult, but if you are not, have a guess anyway. Think about phrases like 'the culture of our country' or 'the structure of the family' because they contain some clues.

Culture and structure

What, in general terms, is meant by the 'culture' of an organisation?
What, in general terms, is meant by the 'structure' of an organisation?

Feedback notes

If you have responded with anything similar to the following, then you are clearly familiar with what we are going to discuss. If you have not, then hopefully your queries will be answered in the next few pages. You should also read Torrington, Hall, Haylor and Miles (1991: Chapters 8 and 9) for a fuller exposition of organisational structure and culture.

- The *culture* of an organisation refers to the set of norms, practices, ideas and beliefs about 'how things ought to be done' in the organisation or in a particular part of it. Sometimes the word 'climate' is used instead; it carries the same kind of meaning.

- The *structure* of an organisation refers to the network of roles and relationships whereby activities are allocated to different levels, parts and people of the organisation. It concerns the way the organisation is designed, or 'shaped'. We can envisage structure as the 'skeleton' of an organisation. In its more detailed sense structure also encompasses the systems and procedures that regulate and shape activity in the organisation.

The culture of the organisation is critical to the achievement of its mission and goals. Much has been written about organisational culture and its consequences (Hofstede, 1980, 1984; Peters and Waterman, 1982; Deal and Kennedy, 1982), but one comment is useful to note at this point (Payne, 1991: 27):

A corporation that can create a strong culture has employees who believe in its products, its customers and its processes. They sell it willingly because it is part of their own identity.

Organisational structure too has long been a focus of research and an acknowledged primary influence on organisational behaviour and performance. Child (1984) wrote in clear and practical terms about how to analyse structure and select what is appropriate for the particular organisation. Mintzberg (1983) developed one of the widest-known models for the analysis of structure. Drucker (1988) provided a critique of the whole area.

Culture and structure do not exist in isolation from one another but are tightly interrelated. Roger Harrison developed in 1972 the first version of a widely used and much-adapted 'culture-structure' model. Commenting on it, Handy (1985) observed that every organisation has its own distinctive culture which both gives rise to and in turn arises from (among other things) its particular structure. Many organisations, especially larger ones, contain more than one culture and structure, so that a differentiated system prevails. These writers identified at least four main types of culture to be found among and often within organisations, each associated with a particular structure.

Subsequently Handy has moved away from this straightforward set of concepts to raise complex questions about the kinds of structure that an increasing number of organisations may have to design, given the discontinuous types of change now facing them in their turbulent environments (as in Handy, 1989). None the less Harrison's original four-fold model and Handy's initial comments on it still provide a useful introductory guide to understanding our own organisations. The model (amended in one crucial respect) is summarised here.

The power culture and web structure

This is the culture of centralised power. It is most often found in small entrepreneurial firms, and at the top of large, bureaucratic organisations. Control is exercised by one person, or by a small set of people, from whom rays of power and influence spread out, connected by functional or specialist strings. The structure to which such a culture gives rise is therefore web-like.

Essentially, such organisations, or parts of them, are political. Decisions are taken largely on the outcome of the balance of power rather than according to set procedures or on purely 'rational' grounds. People who succeed in this kind of organisation are those who want and can handle power, the politically skilled risk-takers rather than people concerned with security. Such organisations, since all key decisions in them are made only by one or a few people, move fast and react quickly to threats: they 'think on their feet'. Success equals getting the results desired by the point of central power; means tend to count for relatively little. Organisational life is highly competitive, and survival even at the centre is difficult. In the end, the quality of those at the centre is their key to success, and when a key figure goes or is displaced, the balance of power in the system may change radically.

Those concerned with, or responsible for, HRD in such a system have to produce the kinds of success desired by the central power source, and to relate training objectives and plans to needs recognised as important by that source – by no means an easy task.

The role culture and pyramid structure

This is the culture of bureaucracy, sustained by the belief that an organisation should have its purpose and overall plan defined at the top, and then rest for its strength on a clearly defined hierarchy of functions or specialisms. Co-ordination of the descending levels of departments is carried out at the top by a narrow band of senior management, advised by specialist functions. Rules and procedures govern every role and position in this pyramid, or temple, or hierarchy. They also govern communications and the conduct of disputes. Precedents dominate decision-making, and the whole organisation tends to be security-oriented, with a tendency to rigidity rather than to innovation. Role cultures and structures are slow to see and accept the need to change. Change itself is usually a lengthy and difficult process, with job descriptions, rules, established working practices and routines all capable of pulling people back to the past rather than forward into the future. At the same time, the role structure is probably the most widely used way of organising large numbers of people around a common goal, not only in work organisations but in states and religions. One has only to think of mid-twentieth-century China, Germany or the Soviet Union to realise the enduring organisational power of the bureaucratic model, as well as the dangers inherent in its misuse.

The formal position allocated to whoever carries special responsibility for HRD in such a system will be the major initial source of power. The higher the position, the more the possibility of influencing events. However, even if formal position is fairly low or peripheral, all is not lost – knowing ways round and through the rules, the files and 'the system' can often secure the achievement of desired ends.

The greatest danger is that in this departmentalised and inward-looking world open-minded, objective and 'professional' vision can become 'departmentalised' too. How many managers have you met who have become absorbed in the goals and interests of their little empire, rather than striving for the benefit of the whole? But given the type of culture that prevails, is such behaviour surprising?

The human investment culture and network structure

Handy (1985) used the term 'task culture' to describe an organisation in which people come together because there is a job or project to be done, irrespective of personal power or of formal position. Later he used the term 'shamrock' and other variants on this theme, but the emphasis remained on the team rather than the individual. The culture so described was one of teams brought together to work on projects as they come in, and which are then disbanded, so that new teams are formed as new projects arise. The structure could be pictured as a net with some of its strands thicker and more permanent than the rest. Much of the power lies at the permanent knots of that net.

There are many organisations that have this form of matrix structure. In the strategic management literature, however, researchers like Miles and Snow (1995) have taken the concept further, claiming that the evolution of network organisations is forcing a new view of human resources and that a new, spherical structure typifies many businesses today. These are de-layered systems that have to be highly flexible and responsive to market forces. They 'array themselves on an industry value chain according to their core competences' (Miles and Snow, 1995: 5) and use strategic alliances and outsourcing to this end. Firms with a spherical structure 'rotate competent, self-managing teams and other resources around a common knowledge base', and can be linked together in a multifirm network, as the authors illustrated in their paper (Miles and Snow, 1995: 6). The keys to success for such a structure are knowledge as a key intangible asset and expert people who can operate with minimal supervision, interacting continuously and in complex ways with others inside and outside the business. Keywords are partnership, co-operation and collaboration, trust and mutual interdependence.

Success for the individual is achieved by expertise and networking, and by acquiring, retaining and transforming knowledge. Speed of reaction, flexibility, sensitivity and creativity are often more important than depth of expertise. Life may be challenging and stimulating, but few find it easy because it requires constant effort to keep up to date in expertise, to move through a maze of networks, to accept the need for continuing co-operation and trust in working with others, and to remain committed to the matter in hand no matter how stressful the pressures it generates. As Miles and Snow (1995: 11) observed, the work demands effective 'relationship management' skills and working with partners in a continuous self-development process. Management in such a structure is about building people's strengths and investing in their long-term development; about acting as the partner of individual employees and supporting the work of self-managing teams; and about managing the changing knowledge base of the organisation. More on the concepts behind this thinking can be found in Part 5 of this book.

When resources become constrained in this kind of system, the norms of the culture become challenged. Often there is a shift towards either a power or a role culture, and sometimes this can lead to a permanent change and to a new structure. Specialist skills, not specialist functions, are the need in such structures, and over the past few years, as organisational shapes have gradually changed, many training managers have lost their roles, even their jobs, through lack of planning against such a contingency.

The person culture and galaxy structure
This is not so much a type of organisation (although some professional partnerships operate on this basis) but more a way of describing those clusters of individuals to be found in most organisations who see their job and the resources available to them mainly as a means of serving their own interests. Often these

cultures exist where there is one person who has a unique contribution to make on the basis of specialist skills or knowledge, thus becoming the 'star' around whom everything and everyone tend to revolve.

Anyone trying to promote the development of people in such a situation can find it a hard task. Often 'star' individuals not only need development themselves but are also exercising a stifling effect on the development of others. Because they have unique and valued skills, they can usually get other jobs without too much difficulty, and the threat of moving on is one they will often use. Or they may have protected tenure, again adding to their power base. In either case, they will probably fail to acknowledge any expertise as greater or more compelling than their own. Appealing to that expertise may, however, prove to be one way of persuading them to develop others. Few can resist the flattering plea to help those less gifted than themselves by passing on the benefit of their wisdom and experience.

A different way of looking at person cultures is to see them as

---

The structure and culture of my organisation

Consider an organisation with which you are familiar, or a division of it, and analyse its primary structure and culture. The questionnaire originally designed by Harrison (1972) and subsequently amended by many, including Handy (1985), offers a straightforward and effective way of achieving practical insights into organisational culture and structure.

Start your analysis with a brief explanation of the 'organisation' and whether your chosen frame of reference is the whole organisation or a particular part of it. Explain, too, how far your organisation, or your chosen part of it, is considered to be 'successful', and any major problems and/or opportunities it faces in operating. Thereafter pay particular attention to the following points, illustrating your analysis with practical examples and explanations wherever possible:

- the kind of culture and structure you think top management intends and believes to exist, and the kind of culture and structure you feel actually exists

- how far the culture and structure promote or hinder the achievement of organisational goals at various levels

- the kind of people who 'get on' in the system, and the reasons for their success

- the kind of people who are unsuccessful in the system, and the reasons for their failure

- how far people's needs, aspirations and development are matters of real concern to the organisation

- the pressures and opportunities facing HRD because of the culture and structure of the organisation.

dominated by a belief in people's potential, and therefore characterised by a focus on the development of people and on delegating to individuals as much responsibility for decision-making and resources as is feasible. The skill of management in such a culture is to hold in continual balance this belief, with its concern for appreciating and responding to individual needs and aspirations and continuously developing abilities and potential, with the responsibility of ensuring that work targets and commitment to organisational goals are also achieved.

Feedback notes

There are no set answers to this exercise: the results are bound to be different for each person who attempts it. However, if you are a student tackling the analysis wholly or partly as a class exercise, your tutor could split the class up into groups so that in each group members can exchange information arising from their analyses. A plenary session thereafter can obtain from each group what are judged to be the most interesting outcomes from those discussions. The sorts of issue that can be examined include:

• Where people come from the same, or similar, organisations, are their perceptions of the culture and structure in which they work the same, or different? Why? For example, someone employed in a rigid bureaucracy may none the less work in an HR department organised as a task structure. Its management culture may favour teamwork, participative decision-making and achieving a dynamic, pro-active role for HR in the organisation. In that case the individual's perception of 'the organisation' will be very different from that of a colleague working in a more bureaucratised area.

• What about personnel and training staff? Do they have influential roles in their organisation? If not, why not? If they are influential, what explains this?

• How has political skill, or lack of it, affected the performance and credibility of personnel and training staff?

• How far is the development of people in the different organisations a major responsibility of the personnel department; and/or of a training specialist or function; or primarily the responsibility of line management?

• What sorts of attitudes and policies are there about HRD in the various organisations, and how do these relate to the cultures and structures of those organisations?

In this section we have been looking at different kinds of cultures and structures between and within organisations, and we have seen that one easy and useful way to classify them is by using a four-fold system. There are at least four main types of culture, each with its typical associated structure. It is essential for anyone seeking to promote the development of people in an organisation to identify the primary culture and structure to which they must relate, and to adapt their strategy accordingly. Culture and structure are two of the three factors relating to the political context of HRD. The third factor is *power*.

Power in organisations

> Power is a property that exists in any organisation...Politics is the way power is put into action.
>
> (Torrington and Weightman, 1985)

It is essential for anyone trying to promote the development of people in an organisation to understand the bases of organisational power and how to acquire and use it in order to achieve objectives. There are innumerable studies of power in organisations. One of the most compelling is the social action analysis contained in Silverman's complex but fascinating book (1970). French and Raven (1959), Pfeffer (1981) and Handy (1985) also offer absorbing discussions. There are many power sources in an organisation. It is important to identify the type of power possessed by oneself and by others. Knowing how to use and relate to different types of power is an essential political skill. Now try the following exercise.

Types of power in organisations

Here are six types of power commonly wielded in organisations. Attempt a brief explanation of each:

- physical power

- resource power

- position, or legal, power

- expert power

- personal power

- negative power.

Feedback notes

- *Physical power* means the power that derives from physical strength or appearance. Often someone's mere presence in a workplace is enough to galvanise people into action.

- *Resource power* derives from control of resources valued by those you wish to influence. The resources can be anything – money, promotion, a bigger carpet in the office. What matters is that they are wanted, valued. Many of those who are responsible for developing others have few direct resources of their own, and so one of their first tasks must be to discover who holds the resources that they can use.

- *Position power*. The formal position that someone occupies, and the status that goes with it, is an important source of power, especially in a 'role' culture.

- *Expert power* in one's field is, as we have seen, highly valued in human investment cultures, although less reliable as a power source in a role culture (where the 'expert' can quite quickly be cut down to size by rules and procedures, time-lags, and the many convoluted decision-making mechanisms).

- *Personal power* is seen at its most obvious in power cultures, where it is often used to reinforce all the other power sources of the person or group at the centre. However, it is an important quality for a training practitioner to possess if working in a task culture, where interactions are often difficult and sensitive to manage. When confronted with a person culture, some other holder of personal power may offer the only hope of influencing the 'stars' when they are causing problems in the system.

- *Negative power* is the power, possessed by us all, to refuse to expend our energy and effort and commitment on a particular task, or in a particular cause. Sometimes the results are not as we had hoped. Unless we are in a job, or have a skill, that is vital and is difficult to replace, then withdrawal of effort even by a large number of people may have no real impact. However, HRD depends for its success on securing the full commitment and enthusiasm of everyone – from the manager who provides or withholds crucial information about the learning needs of staff, to the individual required to learn but not necessarily motivated to do so. Inability to understand and deal with the exercise of negative power is a major weakness in anyone responsible for developing learning in the organisation.

So far in this chapter we have looked at three aspects of organisational life that relate centrally to the politics of HRD: the culture, structure and power system of the organisation. We have recognised that to be successful in HRD a high level of political skill may be required, and that the ability to analyse and understand organisational politics is an important element of that skill. Now here is a case to put some of these ideas to the test. Please read it carefully before tackling the questions. It can be used as a self-review or (if you are a student) as coursework or a class activity.

The management training problem

You are a training officer, aged 26, who has worked for the past three years in the HR department of a large private-sector service organisation in the Midlands. Previously, you worked as a training officer in a local authority, where most of your work involved administration of a Modern Apprenticeship scheme. You have a degree in business studies, and in your present post you are responsible for the administration of various management and supervisory programmes and for organising short courses, mainly of a technical nature.

You have no formal personnel or training qualifications, although you would like to acquire some. There are several other personnel staff, one of whom is a training officer specialising in technical training.

Your boss, the HR director, is Roger Mason, CIPD-qualified, and considered by top management to be effective. He has been with the organisation for 10 years, and before that had 15 years' experience in a variety of firms. He is not so highly regarded by the other staff in the organisation, who see the personnel function as a very bureaucratic department, too absorbed in paperwork and procedures. Currently Mason is heavily involved in drawing up an equal opportunities policy for the organisation. He has always tended to 'manage by exception', which translates in his case into 'start to worry only when things go wrong'. Staff are reluctant to ask him, or each other, for help because they are afraid that this may be construed as a sign of incompetence on their part. Most stick rigidly to their job descriptions. You do not much like working in the department but are hoping that once you have a little more experience you will get another post and move on. You intend to specialise in training.

Just after you joined the organisation Mason told you to 'do something about educating our junior and middle managers'. He said that top management felt the performance of these groups, and of supervisors below them, was not always as good as it might be (although he gave you no specific evidence on this score). Furthermore, the younger people at least, many of whom were in technical functions, would be moving up in the next few years, and it had been decided that they needed a greater awareness of what general management involved. He wanted some courses organised, although nothing too expensive.

Although you know little about management training, it never the less seemed to you that education should be an important part of employees' development. It broadened their minds and gave them new knowledge and ideas. You therefore suggested that about six managers at various levels and from different departments in the organisation should be sent on a two-year part-time Diploma of Management Studies (DMS) course at the local university each year.

Mason liked the idea, particularly as it did not involve his department in anything more than calling for nominees and organising their attendance. Subsequently, 16 managers have gone on the DMS, at the rate of around five a year. All were chosen by Mason from nominations made by the superior officers of the staff concerned. He did not explain to you the criteria for nominations or selection. Mason has just been asked by top management for some information about the management programme to go into the annual report. Last week he came to you in a panic, asking you to provide the information for him in two weeks' time.

You have now talked to everyone who has been through a DMS or is still studying for it. It is popular with the staff from departments like management services and sales and marketing, all of whom tend to be in their twenties or thirties, with degrees or equivalent qualifications. They find the content intellectually stimulating, and some are able to apply newly learnt techniques to their jobs, although the majority find that there is no real support for or interest in this within their departments. However, the remark made by one of them to you typifies the general feelings of this group:

> I won't be here for ever, so I'll be able to use the learning in the next job I get. In the meantime, it's certainly made me more aware of the deficiencies of this place – especially how out-of-date my boss is! Pity you couldn't persuade him to do one of these courses!

The nine staff from this group who have gone through the DMS or who are currently studying for it have all done well in coursework and final examinations, and have particularly enjoyed the project work.

Unfortunately, the seven staff from technical departments are neither so satisfied nor so successful. Their average age is mid-thirties to mid-forties, and all have technical qualifications, one a degree. Some of them have managerial responsibilities; others do not. All find the course hard, some because so much of the content is outside their experience completely and the others because, to quote one:

> We've been doing our jobs perfectly well up to now. Why are we being pushed onto these college courses? We're not going to get more pay or promotion, and there's nothing new in any of it except that organisational behaviour stuff – and that's just common sense, anyway.

One of the technical staff dropped out after two months, and although three others passed the examinations last year, one did not, and has to resit this year. Most feel that the DMS is pointless for them. It does not help them with their daily problems, and they resent the fact that while 'whiz-kids from sales and marketing have got it made', they themselves cannot even get cover when they are away each week, and they already have such a mass of work to do that piling up 'all this homework business' is just an impossible burden.

You have had a preliminary chat with Mason about these reactions, and he is rather concerned, especially about the technical people and their managers, with whom he has never had particularly good relationships. He has asked you to see him tomorrow to discuss the situation, and to decide what should be reported about the programme. Your discussion will need to be handled with considerable political skill.

Why? What are the main 'political' issues? Outline how you propose to deal with the discussion, and what you hope and intend to get out of it.

Feedback notes

The training officer will have to explain the failures in the programme to his or her HR director not only in a way that will leave the training officer's credibility intact but in a way that will help the director in turn to present a positive rather than a negative picture in his annual report.

- *Clarify the outcomes sought* from the discussion. The training officer's major concern should be that, in future, needs for training are accurately assessed, training objectives and plans are agreed and understood, and training has the commitment of all the interested parties. The design of courses should motivate and help learners to gain results that are of value to the organisation and to the individual. He or she will also want to leave the meeting with the active support of the HR director. Aiming for these outcomes will give focus to what are the priorities.

- *Put failure into context* and look for successes. The benefits from the programme so far (and there are quite a number) need to be identified, and failures put into context. The programme has, after all, run for three years, so some failures are inevitable. Furthermore, major activities such as this not infrequently uncover problems that were probably always there, and could have come to the surface at any time. For example, the gaps between older and younger staff, and between different specialists and generalists, involve essentially organisational issues which must be viewed in that wider context. What rewards does the organisation offer its older managers and supervisors for the effort required of them in going through a tough examination course, for example? How far does its salary and career structure support such initiatives? What explanation was offered to staff initially about their enrolment on the DMS? Why is there inadequate support for many of the staff when they try to put their new learning into practice? (For a discussion of such problems, see Fairbairn, 1991.)

- *Develop support for training.* Having looked at the successes of the programme, and emphasised the need for a wider perspective on some of the problems which have come to light during the three years, the training officer can then suggest that joint planning and design between training, managerial and supervisory staff would be a positive way forward. Other, more work-related, developmental initiatives may be relevant now, rather than just concentrating on educational courses, and the ideas of the staff and their managers will be essential here. Such work-based activities would also be relevant and motivating for older staff and those in technical positions. Involving their managers in discussions would also be a way of getting those managers more interested in the whole idea of developing their staff, and thus of reducing the problems of learning transfer that some staff experienced when they tried to apply learning from the DMS course to their jobs.

- *Consider culture, structure and power factors.* The situation described in this case-study is very common in a large bureaucratic organisation with a culture that does not encourage a systematic or creative approach to HRD, or stress its relationship to business needs. Of course the training officer should have queried the need for the focus on managerial training and development in the first place: what was the evidence that there were deficiencies here? Or that training was the best response to those deficiencies? And of course he or she should have looked at other ways of responding to the HR director's instructions – what about training and development through work-based activities rather than, or as well as, an educational programme? There should have been careful monitoring of the selection and progress of staff on the DMS, together with evaluation at the end of each course, and, later, when staff got back into their jobs. And what about pre-course briefing and post-course debriefing for the staff?

- *Be focused.* So there are many things the training officer should have done, but obviously inexperience and a junior position in the HR department help to explain the failure to do them. No doubt by now he or she is well aware of personal deficiencies. For the discussion, however, it is essential to avoid too much breast-beating, or the training officer may be made a scapegoat by the HR director rather than achieving anything constructive. The aim instead should be to agree with the director on establishing positive links between training and line management staff, and on developing simple but effective procedures for the diagnosis of learning needs, and for selection and monitoring of staff on training and educational programmes. The training officer should also point to the value of trying to take a wider perspective on HRD in the organisation.

Since our interest here is related to political issues, don't worry if you missed some of the more specialised points that I have covered in the feedback notes – it is the general political stance that it is important to consider. To summarise:

• Be clear about the outcomes you seek.

• Reflect on culture, structure and power factors.

• Put failure into context and identify successes.

• Have a clear vision of the place HRD should have in the organisation.

• Get support for HRD initiatives, and make sure they have a clear, relevant focus.

CONCLUSION

Having read this chapter and completed its reviews and self-checks, you should now:

• understand what is meant by 'the politics of human resource development (HRD)'

• know how to analyse the context of an organisation by reference to its primary culture, structure and power sources

• be able to diagnose the main political issues in a challenging training and development situation, and outline a strategy for dealing with them.

To test yourself against these objectives, what five-minute answers would you give to the following questions? (Dates in brackets refer to the IPD qualifying examination paper in which a question appeared.)

• What advice would you give to a business whose employee development philosophy embraces the concept of commitment to the individual as well as to the organisation yet which faces a period of downsizing? (Specimen paper, 1996)

• List and comment briefly on **four** sources of power in an organisation that ED professionals need to be aware of in order to operate effectively at the political level. (November 1997)

• Identify **three** areas of employee development work where 'political skills' need to be exercised, and describe what actions a newly qualified human resource practitioner could take to develop those skills in himself/herself. (May 1998)

USEFUL READING

ANTHONY P. (1994) *Managing Culture*. Buckingham, Open University Press.

DEAL T. E. *and* KENNEDY A. A. (1982) *Corporate Cultures: The rites and rituals of organizational life*. Reading, MA, Addison Wesley.

JOHNSTON R. (1996) 'Power and influence and the HRD function', in J. Stewart and J. McGoldrick (eds), *Human Resource Development: Perspectives, strategies and practice*. London, Pitman. pp180–95.

MILES R. *and* SNOW C. (1995) 'The new network firm: a spherical structure built on a human investment philosophy'. *Organizational Dynamics*. Vol. 23, 4. pp5–18.

9 Establishing roles and standards

LEARNING OBJECTIVES

After reading this chapter you will:

- be able to identify different types of training and development roles in an organisation, and advise on the expertise and commitment they require

- be fully acquainted with training and development occupational and professional standards and their implications for training and development roles and practice

- be able to identify aids and barriers to the development of influential training and development roles in an organisation.

INTRODUCTION

What do we mean by 'role'? The dictionary definition is '*Role*: an actor's part ... a person's or thing's characteristic or expected function' (Allen, 1990). This is a useful way of thinking about 'role' because of the emphasis on playing a part, on interacting in a particular way with others, as well as on functions to be performed. It also highlights the concept of dynamism: every actor differs in his or her interpretation of a given part, and makes of it something unique, as well as fulfilling its formal requirements. These related ideas of a given and a developed element are emphasised in much of the published research about training roles.

CLASSIFYING TRAINING AND DEVELOPMENT ROLES

The change in the conceptual and practical base of HRD over the past few years has been considerable. Let us look now at two approaches to the classification of training and development roles and then produce a typology ('classification system') of our own.

A contemporary typology

This is the outcome of research sponsored by the (then) Institute of Personnel and Development (IPD) in the late 1990s into the changing role of the trainer (Darling, Darling and Elliott, 1999). (The IPD became the CIPD, or Chartered Institute of Personnel and Development, in July 2000.) The report on the research is of considerable value to anyone who seeks an in-depth understanding of current training/HRD roles. In brief, it revealed that the four main activities in which training personnel now appear to be involved most commonly are:

- *development activities*, including training, needs analysis, coaching and evaluation – tasks which are now carried out by a variety of personnel, sometimes working in conjunction, sometimes on their own: internal HRD specialists, line managers, training providers, consultants, and so on

- *delivering training*

- *administration*, particularly subcontracting – now greatly on the increase

- *managing demand and marketing* the training function internally.

The researchers found that the forces that have contributed to this range of roles include:

- an increase in outsourcing, particularly of the delivery of training

- an increase in consultancy/advisory activities

- an increased emphasis on the role and responsibilities of line managers as developers of people

- an increase in the use of work-based developmental approaches

- greater interest in the strategic contribution of training.

They also found that those in training roles fall into a four-fold typology (Darling, Darling and Elliott, 1999: ix):

- those working as managers or equivalent in training organisations such as TECs/LECS and NTOs (see Chapter 2)

- those providing a service function in organisations

- external providers and consultants

- line managers.

Classifying HRD roles in your organisation

Use the four-fold typology outlined above to identify HRD roles in your own organisation. What does your analysis suggest to you about HRD's present purpose and scope in the organisation?

The national standards typology

In 1995 the Employment Occupational Standards Council (EOSC) – a body formed by the merger in 1994 of the employer-led Training and Development Lead Body (TDLB), the Personnel Standards Lead Body and the Trade Union Sector Development Body – published T&D Standards at Levels 3 and 4, following these with Level 5 Standards in 1996 (there are no T&D Standards at Levels 1 and 2). The standards provide the basis for vocational qualifications for those in training and development roles. At each level of the standards, qualification involves the completion of a number of core units plus a number of optional units.

Levels 3, 4 and 5 of the T&D Standards relate to four types of role. In the accompanying literature, careful distinctions are made between the term 'Training and Development' and the term 'Human Resource Development', as can be seen below (EOSC, 1996: 6–8):

- *Level 3: Training and Development* – for those who deliver training and development programmes and those who carry the responsibility for their design and evaluation

- *Level 4: Human Resource Development* – for those who have management responsibility for training and development, and who are involved in identifying organisational training and development needs, and planning the implementation of training and development objectives. They will also be responsible for the improvement of a range of training and development programmes

- *Level 4: Learning Development* – for those involved in the delivery of learning programmes and more concerned with the facilitation of a broader range of learning opportunities than the direct instructional training which characterises Level 3

- *Level 5: Training and Development Strategy* – for those with a strategic responsibility in HRD who may either be employed at a senior level in an organisation or be a consultant at a strategic level. These standards encompass, *inter alia*, training and development within the wider context of an organisation and its human resource (HR) policies, developing organisational culture and values, and complying with professional and ethical requirements, as well as evaluating and developing own practice.

A typology of HRD roles

Taking the role implications of these Standards into account, and recalling the classification system that emerged more recently from the IPD-sponsored research, we can now produce a typology of our own in Table 7 below.

The typology is not entirely satisfactory. This is because the Lead Body Standards are based on the concept of training and development

Table 7 **A typology of HRD roles**

Role	Lead Body Levels at which role is practised	Focus of role
Strategic change agent	4	HRD strategy and organisational change
Consultant	3, 4, 5	HRD advice, planning, organisation and assessment in order to ensure added value for the business
Manager	4, 5	Management of the T&D/HRD function
Trainer/learning facilitator	3	Design, delivery and evaluation of training and learning processes and events in the workplace
Administrator	3	Support for HRD operations

as a set of discrete functional tasks and competencies that operate at different organisational levels, whereas in reality the practice of HRD involves continually interacting learning and developmental processes that often cross functional boundaries and organisational levels. Also, many HRD practitioners have to carry more demanding responsibilities than their titles and organisational level alone reveal. In Table 7, for example, the role of change agent might have to be attempted by a middle-level practitioner. In some organisations, too, even the larger ones, the person in overall charge of HRD in the business may be located at Level 4 yet may be fulfilling elements of all the roles in Table 7 as he or she strives to ensure an effective contribution for HRD to that business.

The consultant role

The consultant role deserves special comment at this point. The HRD consultant, whether internally based or bought in by the organisation, is there to provide a service for customers, and must work alongside them in order to ensure that the service is relevant and of high quality. Consultants need to be 'professional', to be clear about targets, costs, activities to be carried out, and about ways of establishing what outcomes have been achieved. (For practical techniques to help internal consultants improve their effectiveness, see Thomas and Elbeik, 1996, and, for a useful article on the skills such a role requires, see Linklater and Atkins, 1995.) They must form business partnerships and ensure that the projects for which they are responsible are delivered on time, efficiently and to specification.

HRD practitioners who are only internal consultants need to remember that they have no clear strategic role, and that potentially they are in competition with external consultants. Competition may sharpen their efforts, but it also means that they and their operations can be outsourced. Outsourcing should be viewed as a healthy challenge that can bring benefits to HR personnel as well as to their organisations, but many see it as a threat. In a world of downsizing and concern for added value, the internal consultancy concept is capable of creative interpretation that should send out warning-signs to 'career trainers', especially those who are passive in their roles. The following example shows both sides of the internal consultancy coin.

Case-study: Changing training roles at Barclays Bank, 1997

In 1997 Barclays Bank 'embarked on a fundamental shift in its approach to training' by identifying skilled managers to develop as trainers 'more akin to business consultants than simple deliverers of training packages'. Their role involved carrying out business output analyses on units and making recommendations on staff training needs, staffing levels and workloads. They had to develop competency-based performance criteria within departments. They were themselves required to gain national occupational qualifications and were offered a range of professional and higher educational qualification opportunities also.

The move, typifying a direction being considered by many banks following downsizing and increased exposure in the competitive market place, was a response to the results of a company-wide survey showing that employees want more opportunities to develop their skills. It was also seen by the company as a way of giving units and branches more flexible resources. The bank's central training unit welcomed the innovation as one that enabled the unit to adopt a proactive position, working with the managers as a team of internal consultants to market themselves alongside external suppliers. Some commentators, on the other hand, queried whether such a move might ultimately point to the demise of internal career trainers.

Source: Welch, 1997: 7.

TRAINING AND DEVELOPMENT STANDARDS

Turning now to HRD standards, we shall examine the Lead Body Standards in more detail, and then look at the CIPD's standards for employee development. Both sets of standards have implications for HRD roles.

National occupational standards

Uses of national occupational standards for training and development

In the information below you will find a summarised explanation of the national occupational standards for training and development. Identify some of the uses to which the standards can be put in an organisation.

The training and development role in the Standards is presented as having a dual purpose: the development of human potential to assist both organisations and individuals to achieve their objectives. In producing the Standards, the systematic training cycle was used to define five functional areas of competence related to this purpose. Appendix 5 gives a detailed explanation of the relationship between that cycle and the areas, but in outline those areas are:

A Identify training and development needs   (*Identify*)
B Plan and design training and development   (*Plan and design*)
C Deliver training and development   (*Deliver*)
D Review progress and assess achievement   (*Evaluate*)
   and
E Continuously improve the effectiveness of training and development.

These functional areas are subdivided into 14 sub-areas (see Appendix 5), each of which contains a number of Units of Competence. These are, in turn, composed of two or more Elements of Competence which include associated performance criteria (the national standards). Range statements then describe the range of contexts and applications in which a competent person would be expected to achieve the element. An evidence specification is attached to each standard.

Some training and development activity requires competence in other occupational areas also, including roles such as training manager, training administrator and training centre manager. Standards for other Lead Bodies can be added to the training and development standards for such roles.

Feedback notes

Occupational standards in training and development can be used:

- to clarify what is involved in the exercise of HRD roles at different levels

- as a basis for job descriptions of HRD staff

- as a guide to recruitment and selection of HRD staff

- as an aid to organisational and individual development, career-planning and progression

- as a benchmark to ensure best practice

- to aid evaluation of the effectiveness of HRD both at individual and at organisational level and as a basis for appraisal

- to encourage greater flexibility and responsiveness to changing demands on organisations and individuals.

The standards offer a national basis for HRD activity. Adherence to these standards would improve levels of competence in the field and enable managers and practitioners to examine critically what they do and how they do it. By specifying a core series of units, a common base of competence and knowledge can be achieved. By allowing optional units, flexibility in and adaptability to individual work roles are facilitated. There are, however, limits to the value of the standards. While they should improve competence, they cannot ensure that HRD practitioners, whatever their level in the organisation, will make a fully effective contribution to the business.

These limitations to the value of the occupational standards stem from three factors: their functionalist basis, their rational approach, and their training-oriented language.

The functional basis of the standards

The functional analysis approach used to identify standards has resulted in training and development's being defined in terms of a logical sequence of five functions which change in scope but not in essence as they move through Levels 3 to 5. This framework contrasts sharply with the role analysis approach used in the first section of this chapter. Analysis of roles actually held by practitioners enables the different kinds of relationships between those practitioners and their organisations to be captured and understood. Since the type of training and development tasks carried out by practitioners varies greatly according to work settings and cultures, these are not the main focus of attention in role analysis, whereas with functional analysis they are all that is considered.

The rational approach they embody

Functional analysis involves an atomistic approach to identifying standards. Sloman's (1994) criticism of the systematic training model underpinning the work of the Lead Bodies is relevant here: the orderly and sequential tasks that it – and functional analysis – imply do not adequately represent the messy and complex world of practice. Each training or developmental intervention must fit well with wider HR policies and systems or it will not take root. A culture favourable to learning and development, as distinct from simply training, has to be established in the workplace. The practitioner also needs to exercise many interpersonal, intellectual and creative skills in attempting to build up status and credibility and achieve managerial commitment to HRD. Those skills cannot be developed prescriptively, although an attempt is made to describe their nature in, for example, the Level 5 standards relating to 'Managing relationships with colleagues and customers'.

The training-oriented language of the standards

Although the revised standards now make a distinction between training and development and between operational and strategic activity, the basic language is still that of training and of formal learning events. In reality, at the highest level the development role should involve helping to build and manage the knowledge base of the firm so that the organisation can become a learning system capable of generating new strategic assets and of ensuring people's full contribution to organisational transformation and progress. Such complex matters to do with the management and development of the firm's knowledge base do not yield to functional analysis, yet they must be a central preoccupation of the HRD process in the many organisations that are operating in increasingly turbulent environments (see Chapter 22).

At the time of writing (early 2000), these national occupational standards are under review, as are those that follow in the next section: the Chartered Institute of Personnel and Development's professional standards.

(C)IPD professional standards

In 1996 the IPD – formed in 1994 from the merger between the Institute of Personnel Management (IPM) and the Institute of Training and Development (ITD) (and from July 2000, as stated earlier, the Chartered Institute of Personnel and Development or CIPD) – produced professional standards relevant for all personnel and development practitioners working in the field, and for those studying to achieve professional qualification. The IPD's purpose in this was to establish and promote standards incorporating technical, behavioural and ethical guidelines for the whole profession. Thirty sets of standards currently exist across the whole spectrum of personnel and development. They take core managerial as well as generalist and specialist responsibilities of personnel professionals into account. There is a clear basis for comparability between these and national occupational standards, since the professional standards have been mapped against National Vocational Qualifications (NVQs) and Scottish Vocational Qualifications (SVQs) and can contribute to their acquisition (and *vice versa*). The CIPD is currently reviewing its standards in an extensive consultation process. The revised standards are expected to be put in place in mid-2001 and will become the basis for national professional qualifying examinations and competency assessment 18 months later.

In the *Professional Standards* book (IPD, 1999 edition), each set of standards is shown with its rationale, the learning outcomes that those seeking assessment against the standards must achieve in order to demonstrate competence, and the areas where they must demonstrate knowledge and understanding. To guide those preparing for assessment, each set of standards has a section on 'Indicative content', offering a detailed explanation of the skills and knowledge base of those standards.

Professional standards for the 'Employee development' field can be found in:

- the standards incorporated into the CIPD Certificate in Training Practice – devised to cover those skills required by proficient trainers whether specialists or line managers, and underpinning the Level 3 NVQ in training and development

- the Core Personnel and Development (P&D) Standards against which all students seeking CIPD qualification through the Professional Qualification Scheme must be assessed

- the Employee Development Generalist and Specialist Standards, which map Levels 4 and 5 of the national occupational standards.

The CIPD's professional standards recognise vital non-functional professional and workplace dimensions in a more meaningful way than functional analysis can provide. These dimensions are to do with professionalism and ethics, the commitment of line management, and integration, and can be outlined as follows:

Professionalism and ethics

What is the essence of 'professionalism'? One compelling definition (Jenkins, 1999) is this:

> To give advice on the basis of a body of training and experience, and to stand by the integrity of that advice irrespective of financial reward.

Issues of professionalism and ethics imbue all the standards, instead of being expressed in any separate form. This emphasises the need for them to be an integral part of all professional practice. As Marchington and Wilkinson (1996: 60–86) described, the ethical issues and dilemmas faced by HR professionals tend to increase as they rise in the organisation. The need to be informed and to take a stance on the ethical dimensions of HRD may not always be in the forefront of the busy practitioner's mind. Ethical behaviour is, however, one of the hallmarks of the professional. The inclusion of ethics in both the occupational and the professional standards is therefore a vital contribution to HRD practice and progress. The key elements of 'professionalism' for personnel and development practitioners are highlighted in the CIPD's standards and in other information sources freely available to its students and members (see Useful Reading list at the end of this chapter). They relate to the need for those practitioners to endeavour at all times to enhance the standing and good name of the profession, with particular reference to:

- *accuracy* – They must maintain high standards of accuracy in the information and advice they provide to employers and employees.

- *confidentiality* – They must respect their employer's legitimate needs for confidentiality and ensure that all personnel information (including information about current, past and prospective employees) remains private.

• *counselling* – With the relevant skills, they must be prepared to act as counsellors to individual employees, pensioners and dependants, or to refer them, where appropriate, to other professionals or helping agencies.

• *developing others* – They must encourage self-development and seek to achieve the fullest possible development of employees in the service of present and future organisation needs.

• *equal opportunities* – They must promote fair, non-discriminatory employment practices.

• *fair dealing* – They must maintain fair and reasonable standards in their treatment of individuals.

• *self-development* – They must seek continuously to improve their performance and update their skills and knowledge.

As in any profession, codes of practice or conduct are only a beginning. What is essential is to find ways of ensuring that they are enacted in the real-life setting, guiding the professional in the exercise of their everyday work. Those carrying HRD responsibilities must therefore develop an awareness of the meaning and importance of ethics in their field, ensuring that their operations always have an ethical core, and are founded on relationships based on mutual respect. (See endnote, page 166.)

The commitment of line management
Another theme running through the CIPD standards is the need to obtain the commitment of line management colleagues by convincing them of the importance of professional activity in personnel and development. Without that commitment there cannot be full relevance and impact of HR policies and actions in the organisation.

Integration
In requiring all those wishing to qualify as professionals to achieve the Core P&D Standards, the CIPD is emphasising the need for vertical integration across human resource (HR) and business activity in the organisation. These Standards focus on the links between personnel and development, broader business strategies and the organisational context. In so doing they aim to improve the understanding and competence of HR professionals in taking a wide-ranging and informed view of the business issues and the context to which HR policies and practice must always relate.

The professional qualification structure involves another kind of integration – the horizontal. Core P&D Standards provide the spine for the key generalist standards on employee resourcing, development, relations and reward, thus addressing the issue of the need for internal consistency and coherence across all HR areas. Each of those sets of standards focuses on the generalist skill and competences that are crucial to effective practice in the workplace. Applying the same principle of horizontal 'fit' to the specific fields that derive from each main HR process, each set of generalist standards has attached to it an evolving 'string' of specialist standards. For employee development there are currently six, each consistent with the former ITD approach and with national occupational standards. Candidates can obtain professional status by choosing four specialist electives, or by going across various areas of HR activity in order to emerge with a more generalised grounding in personnel and development work.

The CIPD is an awarding body for vocational qualifications and for assessor/verifier awards in personnel and development. As such, it has more than 30 licensed external verifiers all with high levels of generic and occupational competence. One of its roles is to approve centres that wish to provide programmes for these qualifications. In 1997 alone there were some 160 centres, involving 15,000 candidates undertaking competency-based programmes with the CIPD's Awarding Body. With regular increases in this number, the influence of the CIPD over professional standards and the quality of NVQ provision and verification is expanding significantly.

HRD work: the professional perspective

Identify an area of HRD work in your organisation or one with which you are familiar that to your mind raises issues – particularly ethical – that as a professional you believe must be very carefully considered. Analyse what those issues are, and what stance the HR professional should take in relation to them.

Feedback notes
There are many possibilities here, so the three examples that follow are necessarily selective.

- You may be involved in training ethnic groups where careful attention must be paid to cultural and linguistic differences and to differences in body language, since all of these differences can produce severe stress for some unless they are dealt with skilfully and with due respect to the participants.

- You may be a member or facilitator of an action-learning set in which confidentiality of process is a fundamental prerequisite if the openness and mutual supportiveness essential to action-learning's success is to be achieved for all participants.

- You may be designing an outdoor development programme as your response to a client's request for a stimulating management development experience for participants. You know that you can produce a programme that incorporates exciting features which will give participants a great sense of personal achievement and should produce excellent evaluations – hence lucrative repeat business for you – when they return to their organisation. You also know that such a programme will not in reality lead to learning outcomes that are superior to those achievable through other training approaches you could propose. However, it will produce considerably higher profit margins for your consultancy business.

Comparing the national occupational and professional standards

At this point we can compare the CIPD's professional standards in Employee Development (ED) with the national occupational standards already examined.

- The occupational standards have been developed across a narrower area and go into greater (even minute) detail in the performance criteria and range statements than the professional standards.

- The professional standards have been developed across a broader area than the occupational standards, leaving more flexibility for application in the particular organisational context. They are used to define professional ED competence and also as bases for educational and developmental programmes. They therefore place great emphasis on knowledge and understanding relating to ED as well as on competence in ED tasks.

- The CIPD standards are not derived from functional analysis – although there is recognition of the need for functional skills and knowledge – but from agreement with stakeholders on outcomes to be achieved in each major area of training and development. They also emphasise context: the context of the workplace and its practices; of the business and its needs; of the competitive national and international environment; and of the professional standards and ethics that should influence the values, behaviour and work of practitioners in whatever organisation they are currently located. They can thus be argued to relate more closely to the real world of HRD, more accurately reflecting the scope, responsibilities and complexity of the HRD process in organisations.

FACTORS THAT INFLUENCE HRD ROLES IN THE ORGANISATION

Going back to the start of this chapter – when actors play a part, it is the interplay of their given role and the way they develop it in combination with their own personality that explains the uniqueness of their performance. Relating this concept to training, we can say that formal and informal factors influence the parts, or roles, that people play, and so also influence training and development roles in a particular organisational context.

Factors that influence training and development roles

Use our typology of roles on page 150 to identify the kind of role occupied by whoever holds the main formal responsibility for employee development in your own organisation, or in some organisation with which you are familiar. (It may, for example, be a personnel director or manager, or a training manager, or a designated line manager.) Identify the main influences on that role, and the way in which it has developed through time.

Feedback notes

What follows not only gives feedback on the work you have just completed but also expands on and concludes our discussion of factors influencing training responsibilities and roles. The comments are therefore quite lengthy, but they include some of the most important influences.

- *The external environment of the organisation.* This refers to the outer world of the organisation and the opportunities and constraints, and threats and challenges that it presents. HRD policy in an organisation that is fighting for survival in an increasingly competitive market will have no choice but to be business-led, and the more HRD initiatives can be shown to make their desired impact on business performance, the more likely it is that there will be an increase in significant HRD roles at the upper organisational levels.

  One example of the potentially productive consequences for HR professionals of events unfolding in the external environment can be found, somewhat unexpectedly, perhaps, in the Social Chapter legislation. In a survey in 1999 reported by Welch (1999), nine out of 10 HR directors of the UK's highest-earning firms believed that the controversial European Union Social Chapter not only safeguards employees' rights but also provides a valuable platform for personnel professionals to influence business strategy. There are HRD-related issues here. As a regular stream of court cases lost to the employer demonstrate, it is essential to ensure that the practical implications of the Social Chapter are understood at all organisational levels – for example, in relation to part-time working, parental leave, and to the Working Time Directive. There are skills to be developed too, especially in large firms where there is a need to operate uniform methods of consultation and information-sharing along works council lines. Those in HRD roles should be taking the lead in identifying the kind of training and development initiatives that will ease understanding, acceptance and effective implementation of this crucial legislation. Those roles could gain significantly in influence as the result of this kind of proactive and business-focused thinking.

  External agencies can help those in HRD roles in an organisation to develop valuable initiatives, thereby increasing the profile of those roles as well as helping the business. They can do this by providing funding, sponsoring learning, giving advice and granting access to useful networks (see Mackinnon, 1995 for helpful advice here). An organisation's commitment to achieving external best practice or quality standards like the Investors in People (IIP) standard also has a significant effect on the profile and status of training and development internally.

- *Business goals and strategy.* As we have seen in Chapters 5 and 6, the direction and type of business goals and strategy fundamentally determine HRD policy and plans, and therefore also the HRD roles and responsibilities appropriate to the particular organisation.

- *Organisational structure and culture.* The corporate philosophy about people, the values and styles of leadership and management, and the social system in the workplace will act either as enablers or inhibitors of HRD policies and strategies. The primary culture of an organisation is closely related to its structure, since it is structure that determines formal roles, responsibilities and tasks, as well as the systems, procedures and routines by which people work. Type of structure is a significant influence on choice of HRD goals and strategy, and one very important factor here is the place and operation of the personnel function in the organisation. This leads us into the next contextual factor: that of employee resourcing (ER).

• *The employee resourcing context.* The size, behavioural patterns, performance, occupational structure and learning needs of the workforce employed or utilised by the organisation will all influence the training and development roles and the tasks to be performed. However, it is ER strategy and practice that define the ways in which the organisation's workforce is planned, deployed and managed, hence the importance of the ER context in which the HRD process has to operate.

• *Technology.* This refers to the way in which work and work processes are organised, the type of technology used and the technology available for training and development. An important finding of the IPD-sponsored research referred to earlier in this chapter was that technology is an issue of growing concern to training practitioners, who often have problems with its resource and utilisation and sometimes are resistant to expending limited resources on initiatives like intranets. The researchers observed that 'Learning resource centres have had a mixed reception and some of our respondents emphasised the continued need for support for individuals in using open-learning technology' (Darling, Darling and Elliott, 1999: x). There is a detailed discussion of the impact of new technology on the HRD/training function in Chapter 12.

To produce this list I have made use of the model of the organisation as a system shown in Figure 6.

This demonstrates in simple form how environment, goal and tasks, structure and culture, technology and employment system interact and influence the roles, both formally ascribed and informally developed, of those responsible for HRD in the business. The passive or inept HR practitioner has little chance of improving the role of HRD in the organisation and may indeed find that as a consequence of repeated failure to seize opportunities and to prove the value of training and

Figure 6 **The organisation as a system**

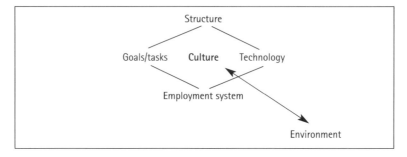

development, the role becomes further reduced. The influential line manager who shows colleagues and team how little he or she values HRD will foster a climate of scepticism that will be hard to change.

ACHIEVING MORE INFLUENTIAL HRD ROLES IN THE ORGANISATION

What can be done to ensure that influential HRD roles are more widespread in organisations? The responsibilities and expertise involved in managing HRD at the three main levels of the business will be discussed more fully in Chapter 10, but an outline is relevant at this point.

Corporate level

Since the organisational vision, and the working environment in which employees live, are created and sustained above all by top management, there should be a leading HRD role at that level. Let us look at an example.

Case-study: Kwik-Fit, 1990

Webster (1990) discussed the philosophy and systems for continuous development and improvement of its workforce at Kwik-Fit, a company distinguished both by its high standards of quality and customer service and by its policy of integrated and continuous development of the whole workforce. He described the ways in which, as human values spread through an organisation, they can produce an environment in which 'the vision takes root and flourishes'. He commented that this needs to be a purposive, not an accidental, process, since it is values and vision that give the organisation direction.

He saw in Tom Farmer, then CEO at Kwik-Fit, an awareness of the impact of every action he took as CEO in either producing healthy growth in the workforce or inhibiting it. It is at the top of the organisation that action must be taken to 'review the systems, the organisation structure, the physical layout and the human resource policies ... with the specific purpose of creating through them the environment in which people may thrive'.

Source: Webster, 1990: 44–7

In this case, the CEO in his role as HRD change agent ensured that across the organisation there was a conviction that investment in the development of people would provide a real pay-off for the business. The role of any corporate-level spokesperson for HRD – whether it is a CEO or a human resource professional – is to ensure that there is this conviction. To be able to do this, the spokesperson must be knowledgeable about the implications of alternative proposed corporate strategies for employee resourcing and development, and give a persuasive assessment as to where the balance of advantage lies between one strategy and another. They must also take full account of HR policy and practice in the organisation, since unless HRD initiatives are supported by that policy and practice, they are likely to prove impossible or damagingly expensive to implement.

There are harsh realities for the HR spokesperson to face at the corporate level, and they often emerge too at strategic business unit/divisional levels. They can be illustrated by a brief reference to the tensions than can arise when trying to apply the so-called 'systematic' approach to determine corporate HRD goals.

Rationality and power

The traditional 'systematic training cycle' process was used to formulate the initial attempt to produce Lead Body Standards for training and development. The cycle involves a circular process of identifying and analysing training needs, planning and designing training, delivering training events, monitoring and evaluating their outcomes and effectiveness, and feeding the results of that evaluation into ongoing identification of needs. The cycle lies at the heart of the 'comprehensive approach' described in Appendix 4. Systematisation, however, was not enough in that case. The first attempt at the Standards proved so controversial on wider consultation in the field that they were effectively abandoned, and the laborious process of formulation had then to start all over again. Systematisation relies on logic – but not everyone's logic is the same, or carries the same weight in politically charged situations.

Some thought at the time that HR strategy-making would become increasingly systematised as the Lead Body Standards as a whole achieved more visibility and influence (Marchington and Wilkinson, 1996: 182–4). But in the matters of setting HR goals and priorities for the business and passing final judgement on the success of any HR strategy, the ultimate say lies with top management, not with HR professionals, no matter how senior. It is therefore upon the exercise of top management's power that the direction of HRD strategy depends, and that power may not always be expressed in the detached way implicit in the systematic training cycle process, or be driven by the same logic. When there is disagreement at the higher reaches of management about HRD needs and priorities, the HRD spokesperson will have to marshal arguments and evidence with considerable political skill: the presentation of systematically obtained information will not be enough. At board level, the language of functional logic has little chance when it is at odds with the dominant language and logic of the business. That baseline is unlikely to alter, and it leads to the need to reflect a little further on the kind of skills that are required by HRD professionals at the higher levels of the organisation.

Achieving external consistency

From research in the Netherlands Kessels (1993) has demonstrated that if corporate training interventions are to achieve a real impact in their organisations they must from the outset achieve what he called 'external consistency'. That is to say, they must be perceived as valuable by the key actors, who should be actively involved in the identification of needs and in the general operation of the interventions. This is especially true of high-level and costly developmental programmes that seek to enhance the effectiveness of strategic managers (Harrison and Miller, 1999). It highlights what Kessels described as the 'relational' aspects of HRD and reinforces the view of those who regard training as a negotiated process in which political, rather than purely rational, analytical skills are of primary importance.

In all these respects, the present record of HRD practitioners in the UK, as in the USA, appears to be unimpressive. To select one out of a variety of criticisms that are reported at not infrequent intervals: on 23 April 1999, BBC Radio 2 News highlighted the Police Federation's announcement that police force training specialists had been producing training strategies for the force at least 50 per cent of which had proved to be irrelevant and counter-productive. Their strategic planning competence in their own field was perceived as so low, and its consequences so damaging for their organisations, that it was exposed in an item of national news. If HRD practitioners cannot produce HRD strategies, they will certainly command no credibility in the wider strategic arena. For whatever combination of reasons, it is the case that in many organisations HRD is still given little specialist weight at board level. Personnel directors could be expected to play a key role in promoting the strategic value of HRD. Recent research has, however, revealed doubt about the extent to which some of them are 'tuned into' training (Darling, Darling and Elliott, 1999: xi).

In the USA the same trends are apparent. HRD academics have sought evidence of links between HRD and the strategic planning process, but in 1998, summarising much of their work, Conine and Criswell could find few signs of success. They drew attention to the 'notable absence' of HRD executives from the strategic process, although they could offer 'numerous' well-authenticated reasons for linking HRD into strategic formulation and for a stronger leadership role for HRD (Conine and Criswell, 1998: 6.1, p2). They emphasised the crucial importance of commitment from top management, of credibility of HRD professionals, and of the need for those professionals to be actively involved in, and knowledgeable about, business operations if HRD is to be strategy-linked (*ibid*: 6). In a similar survey in the UK, training and development practitioners echoed those views (Darling, Darling and Elliott, 1999: xi).

The real issue here, however, goes wider. It lies in the continuing failure of the wider HR function within which HRD is located to convincingly prove its importance to the bottom line. This has been mentioned before in this book, and was referred to in some detail at the start of Chapter 6. So what are the critical skills needed by HR professionals – including those with HRD responsibilities – to ensure that more of them in future are given and convincingly discharge roles at strategic levels of the business? Hendry (1995) stressed sensitivity to changing needs, stage of growth and strategic orientation of the business. He believed that such sensitivity may best be attained by developing a deep knowledge of the business, its attributes and its environment rather than by trying to adhere slavishly to various theoretical models of HR in the business. The American academic and consultant, Mark Huselid (whose research was discussed in Chapter 1, page 16), reinforces these points. He believes that if HR specialists do not have the professional personnel capabilities and the business competence needed, then they should not make crucial HR strategy decisions – let alone, presumably, play a part in the strategy arena more widely (Guest, 1998). Ulrich, another HR expert in the USA, agrees with Huselid and lists the key competences that HR specialists need (in order of priority) as personal credibility, ability to manage change and culture, knowledge of HR practices, and understanding of the business (MacLachlan, 1999).

Unit level

Line managers carry the fundamental responsibility for ensuring that people are enabled to perform their jobs effectively and efficiently, and to enjoy continuous learning opportunities through which their abilities and potential can be developed. This responsibility means that managers, whether alone or with the help of specialist staff, must:

- create a work environment, policy and systems at their management level that encourage and support the acquisition of the skills, knowledge and attitudes people need in order to perform well in their jobs

- regularly review work targets, appraise performance and assess potential in order to help people to improve in their jobs and develop in ways that will be beneficial to the organisation, as well as motivating to themselves

- regularly monitor and evaluate the results of formal and informal learning in the workplace.

At this level professional HRD staff should have a managerial orientation, working closely with line managers to help in the production of HRD policies and plans that will boost the performance of units. They will be helped in this by mastering the functional competencies related to the tasks they have to perform, but it is their mastery of the human processes involved in their work that will enable them to make their best contribution to the business and to individuals' learning and growth. In Chapter 10, a case-study will illustrate how line managers can effectively perform their HRD role, and in Chapter 14, guidelines will be given for developing a climate conducive to continuous learning and development in the workplace.

Operational/individual level

HRD managers and professionals at this level need in essence the same skills as at business-unit level. They have a particular responsibility here for helping to establish and maintain a climate within which HRD can take root in the workplace.

As members of an operational team, individuals each have a responsibility to consider what their own learning needs are in relation to their daily work, forthcoming changes and their career aspirations. Self-directed learning and self-development are increasingly important for everyone – not just to improve performance but to enhance employability security. Furthermore, if the organisation does not take the initiative in offering opportunities for individual development, these may be the only ways in which people can realise their potential.

The argument that individuals must take an active role in articulating their needs and in making a positive contribution to the decisions on how needs may be met is familiar enough: only in this way can planning, execution and evaluation of their development become a genuinely two-way process. Only thus can individuals hope to influence those who carry developmental roles (especially, of course, their own managers at whatever level) and so put pressure on managers to aim for a marriage rather than a divorce of individual and organisational training and development goals.

Unfortunately, there are often no incentives for individuals to press for training, since the rewards, material or otherwise, in most organisations, whether the individual is in or out of work, are so few. Moreover, as Paul Victor, personnel manager of Rolls-Royce observed, references to 'empowered individuals' often mask a very different reality, in which true power remains at the higher levels and an invitation to 'take the initiative in your development' is no more than 'an abrogation of responsibility' by management (Victor, 1995: 23). He believed that vague mission statements about achieving world-class status are meaningless as a guide to developmental action for the individual. What is needed is 'a clear picture of the business, its mission, strategy and objectives...translated into meaningful terms for different departments, groups and individuals' (*ibid*).

At every level of the organisation HRD roles and responsibilities should be shared and should have a strong professional and ethical framework. Without that framework the practice of HRD lacks true professionalism, since it will not be imbued with those enduring values that link HRD in the particular organisation with HRD in the wider professional world.

Aiming for a strategic role

A training officer in mid-career aims ultimately to become a HRD professional operating at corporate level. She has just completed a learning styles inventory and has scored high as an activitist and pragmatist, but low as a reflector and theorist. Looking at these scores and reflecting on her career goals, what practical advice would you give her, and why? (If you are unfamiliar with LSIs, or need to quickly refresh your memory, read (eg) Marchington and Wilkinson 1996: 165–8 before doing this self-check.)

CONCLUSION

Having read this chapter and completed its reviews and self-checks, you should now:

• be able to identify different types of training and development roles in an organisation, and advise on the expertise and commitment they require

• be fully acquainted with training and development occupational and professional standards and their implications for training and development roles and practice

• be able to identify aids and barriers to the development of influential training and development roles in an organisation.

To test yourself against these objectives, what five-minute answers would you give to the following questions? (Dates in brackets refer to the IPD qualifying examination paper in which a question appeared.)

- Outline a typology of training roles, briefly explaining each role. (May 1997)

- What are the **five** areas of competence identified in the National Training and Development Occupational Standards, and why are they described as 'functional'? (November 1997)

- The IPD's Professional Standards for the ED Generalist module identify a need to 'operate as professional personnel practitioners in a variety of situations'. What do you think the word 'professional' means here, and how can such professionalism be acquired? (May 1999)

USEFUL READING

GILLEY J. W. *and* EGGLAND S. A. (1989) *Principles of Human Resource Development*. New York, Addison Wesley. Chapter 5.

HAMLIN B. *and* DAVIES G. (1996) 'The trainer as change agent: issues for practice', in J. Stewart and J. McGoldrick (eds), *Human Resource Development: Perspectives, strategies and practice*. London, Pitman, pp199–219.

The CIPD publishes regular information about professional standards and practice through a variety of easily accessible information sources. Its website on professional practice (see www.cipd.co.uk) lists all its free information sources, and enables downloading of the relevant publications, namely:

- *Key Facts* papers on different aspects of human resource management and development that are issued free, and at regular intervals, in the CIPD's twice-monthly professional journal, *People Management*.

- *Position papers, surveys and reports*, which clarify the CIPD's official position on a wide range of current issues. These are available through the Institute's library information service.

ENDNOTE

In 1999 the American Academy of Human Resource Development published *HRD Standards on Ethics and Integrity*, a detailed and uniquely important 17-page document, which can be obtained from the President of the AHRD; the e-mail address is office@ahrd.org

10 Organising the function

LEARNING OBJECTIVES

After reading this chapter you will:

- understand the scope of the human resource development (HRD) manager's role

- understand different ways in which the HRD function can be organised

- be able to draw up an action plan to organise HRD staff and develop their abilities and potential both as individuals and as members of a professional team.

THE MANAGERIAL ROLE AND ITS SCOPE

A conventional definition of a training manager role would be one that relates this to a specialist training section or department. This, however, would be a mistake. The trend for HRD responsibilities to be located with line managers means that if there is a specialist HRD function in the organisation, then it must be managed as a resource base and enabler, a business partner in all stages of the developmental process. With the growth of part-time and temporary work, there is also a need for the HRD or training manager to identify and respond to the learning needs of those more 'flexible' workers without whom the operations of many organisations could not be carried out.

Any trends to outsource training and development operations and to extend the organisational learning network across the boundary of the organisation to encompass stakeholders such as suppliers, customers, distributors, purchasers, franchisees and volunteers, carry important implications for HRD managers. They present a need to manage a function whose scope may have to be expanded to cover at least partially many who are not the direct employees of the organisation (Walton, 1999).

Putting training and development operations in context
When deciding how best to manage training and developmental operations for the business, the HRD manager must not only take careful account of the culture, structure and technology of the organisation, but must also identify those stakeholders inside and outside the system who have a potentially important part to play in the organisation's learning network. You can test this out in a case study.

The new HRD manager

You have been appointed as an organisation's first HRD manager (any organisation of your choice). You have the responsibility for advising on developmental policy and planning for the organisation (you may assume that your manager is a member of the top management team, and you may decide whether he or she is personnel director, managing director, or other). You will also have to draw up training and development plans for various sectors of the organisation. Finally, you will have to establish and hold responsibility for a central training budget (you may decide whether or not, in this exercise, there are also training budgets at divisional/unit levels of the organisation).

It is your first day, a Monday morning, and you are sitting in your small office, empty of everything except a desk, a chair, a telephone and a filing cabinet. Tomorrow you will meet with your manager to discuss how to plan and organise training and development in the organisation. What sorts of issues and questions will you raise with him or her at that meeting?

Feedback notes

There are innumerable issues and questions that you could list. They include the following:

Organisational environment

• What is the current and projected future position of the business in relation to its environment?

• What are the forces for change inside and outside the business? Where are the main pressure points and what, if any, responses are being planned in relation to these?

• Is there an organisational policy and strategy for HRD? If so, what are the priorities? If not, why not?

• What education and training links already exist with people and institutions outside the organisation?

• If there are such links, what use is made of them, why, and with what results?

Business goals and strategy

• What are the current business goals and longer-term strategic objectives that HRD is meant to serve?

• At what levels does HRD operate in the business? Is there:

– no systematic approach to HRD? If so, why, and what impact has this failure had on the skills base of the organisation and its human potential for the future?

– isolated tactical training at operational level? If so, does this produce adequate pay-backs for the organisation? What evidence is there here?

– focused HRD at the business-unit level? Is HRD making a direct contribution to the achievement of business targets at this level? Is it helping to meet present and future skills needs? What kind of relationship exists between training staff and business-unit managers?

– strategic HRD at the corporate level? Is HRD linked to key business drivers? Is there a coherent and durable strategy focused on clear HRD goals that underpin corporate goals? Who is the spokesperson for HRD at this level, and does he or she take a reactive or proactive stance in relation to HRD strategy? What are perceived to be the priorities for HRD? Why?

Organisational structure, routines and culture
* What is the primary structure of the organisation – power, role, network or person structure? Is the organisation decentralised/multi-site/part of a conglomerate/large, medium-sized or small?

* What are the intended links between HRD and other business functions in the organisation?

* How is the employee resource (ER) function currently organised? Is there internal consistency and coherency between ER processes? Where does HRD 'fit' in relation to the wider ER function?

* Are you to be given a free hand in planning and managing HRD? What is the nature of your authority and discretion here? Are you able to recruit any staff to help you?

* What formal and informal procedures related to training and development tasks, learning activities and experiences currently exist in the organisation? To what extent will you be able to change current training and development systems and procedures?

* When staff are sent on training programmes or other external learning events, what is the nature and extent of your responsibility for those staff?

* What is the general climate of opinion – the dominating values and beliefs – about HRD and learning in the organisation? Which managers and other key personnel in the organisation support and understand the language of HRD? Who have no interest in HRD, or are likely to oppose various initiatives and have the power to thwart them?

* Is HRD generally perceived as a crucial function in the organisation? What criteria are used to judge its contribution?

* Will there be any problems in involving line managers in discussions about individual, team and organisational learning needs and how best to respond to them?

The employment system
* What is the size of the workforce, its pattern and its occupational structure?

* Is there any attempt to build an internal labour market? (See Chapter 7 if you have forgotten that phrase.) If so, which occupational/professional groups are encompassed?

- What are perceived to be the critical training and development needs of different sectors of the workforce? Does training and development respond to the learning needs of all stakeholder groups, or only to those of the direct employees of the business? If only the needs of direct employees are considered, what other groups should come under the umbrella of HRD in the business?

- What are the incentives and rewards for people in relation to training and development?

- How, generally, is the function of HRD perceived in different sectors of the workforce and by other key stakeholders? Positively or negatively? Reasons?

Technology
- What are the main systems and processes of work organisation in the workplace? What are their implications for training and longer-term development?

- Is new technology to be introduced into the workplace? What are its managerial and skills-based implications?

- What kind of training and learning technology exists, or is available? How far, if at all, is new technology applied to training and learning processes? Is there a learning resource centre?

The list is long but becomes manageable if the questions are grouped under major headings, leading to reflection and analysis of their implications. The headings relate to the simple model initiated through concepts of structure and culture in Chapter 8, and developed further when conceiving the organisation as a system in Chapter 9.

Politics, of course, will go far to determine the support given to the HRD manager as he or she explores what needs really exist, and how they can best be met. One critical factor in this case-study will be the personality, attitudes and values of the new manager's own manager and his or her reactions to the new recruit. In their first meeting the training manager must not only try to establish the facts about training needs. He or she must also begin to build up a mental picture of the organisation, getting the 'feel' of it and identifying constraints and opportunities.

Organising the HRD function
Stredl and Rothwell (1987: 291) listed four questions relevant to the task of organising a training function:

- How much authority will be delegated, and to whom and about what?

- How many positions will report to the training manager?

- How will jobs be grouped?

- How will tasks, duties and responsibilities be divided?

Let us look at three scenarios placing different kinds of demands on the HRD manager: the decentralised function, the line-managed function, and the outsourced function.

The decentralised function

In organisations where there is a generalised push to decentralisation, HRD may be particularly vulnerable and, ultimately, could be stripped of its strategic influence. Decentralisation is a feature of public-sector organisations as well as of those in the private sector. One example is the hiving-off of many Civil Service and local authority functions to agencies of outside contractors. By the early 1990s local government decentralisation had already resulted in between 60 and 80 authorities' de-layering management at the expense of the personnel function, pushing personnel off the top management team and 'absorbing' it lower down. The financial problems of authorities can make human resource (HR) functions increasingly vulnerable, to the point that they become marginalised. That, in turn, can have a direct impact on the organisation and influence of HRD, which usually operates under the wider HR umbrella in local authorities (see also Kessler, 1990). Furthermore, in any organisation where decentralisation is increasing, it is not uncommon to find that centralisation is increasing also – of the policy, strategy and control function. The key question then becomes, who holds the strategic HR role in that situation? Take the following case of London Underground in the 1990s as an example:

Case-study: London Underground's plans to decentralise the personnel function

In January 1992 it was announced that London Underground intended to keep a small central personnel department, retaining responsibility for questions of corporate policy and standards, employee relations and management development. Thereafter most of the function would be devolved to the nine underground lines run as business units and having their own personnel managers and support staff. Those personnel staff were to be given wider responsibilities 'to enable them to act more like factory personnel managers'.

At the same time there was to be 'a massive increase in training linked to the introduction of multi-skilling and flexible rostering'. In the past there had been a high frequency of last-minute withdrawals from training programmes for operational reasons, with adverse effects on the cost and impact of training. Personnel Director Roger Straker expected that, when the new proposals had been carried out, training would be better organised and given a higher priority.

Source: Personnel Management (1992: 1–5)

Such optimism about the retention of a strategic role for HR can be misplaced. The trend towards this kind of decentralisation poses strategic and organisational challenges for the management of people generally, and for HRD as a key HR process: those of 'tight–loose fit', discussed in Legge (1995: 132–5).

Basically those challenges are about how to strike a balance between a strong and unifying corporate business strategy and culture, and the special needs of divisions and units. If HR strategy has to be differentiated from unit to unit to meet the needs of the units' different business strategies, then the result may be that every unit will pursue its own personnel policies at the expense of any overall integrative HR strategy. This, indeed, is exactly what appears to have happened at Shell UK, which 'had to rethink its approach to decentralisation after finding it led to worsening performance' (Pickard, 1992: 1). It found that pushing decision-making down to business units diluted the traditional corporate culture, and resulted in the units being 'given more independence, [becoming] too cut off from each other and from the expertise at the centre' (*ibid*). Shell's decision was to make business units more accountable to each other and more guided by a primary company culture while also retaining the basic decentralised structure.

The decision about whether or not to decentralise HRD will usually be out of the hands of the HRD manager. It is still important, however, for HRD managers to understand the context in which they have to function and its implications for them as managers. Typical approaches to decentralisation include:

- organising most of the specialist staff to work permanently in or with the units, retaining only a small core staff at headquarters to make and co-ordinate HRD policy and strategy (as at London Underground)

- having a small specialist function working collaboratively with line managers who themselves have been trained and developed to carry an increasing range of development functions – a model examined closely in the next section

- contracting the function out, whether in whole or in part (discussed below).

Good boundary management skills must be developed in HRD staff working in a decentralised organisation who are either permanently seconded to business units or who need to work collaboratively with those units from the base of a central training function. They will need to have:

- a wide-ranging knowledge of 'the business' to give them credibility in the units, and to enable them to fully understand units' training and development needs

- skills, motivation and professional commitment to ensure that they neither identify so closely with business units as to 'view the central function as an influence to be kept at bay' (Fowler, 1992); nor identify so closely with the central function as to lose credibility at unit level and become inflexible in their approach.

The line-managed function

Here we are looking at a situation typical in a decentralised organisation: responsibility for HRD held substantially by line managers. There is still likely to be a specialist HRD function. However, its role will usually be one of ensuring overall strategic direction and of oversight and monitoring of implementation. Let us look at a practical example. Company X, described next, is a case-study that draws on the ways in which training and development are organised in many benchmarking companies.

Case-study: Company X, Part 1: handing over HRD to the line
Vision and mission

Company X is a UK-owned company operating across the world. It has a long history of investment in the development of its workforce, and has a creative capability that has led over the years to a stream of innovative products.

HRD purpose and strategy

There is a core of common training across the company, and small teams of expert specialists work within each strategic business unit in order to help managers implement that training and also to identify and respond to local needs. A training and development policy is built into corporate business strategy, and sets the strategic goals and direction for HRD in the company.

Organisational and policy integration of HRD at different levels of the business

At corporate level there is a coherent HR strategy owned by the board. A small headquarters HR team is responsible for maintaining the strategic direction of HR across the organisation. At this level an HRD director advises on the scope, overall policy and long-term strategic goals for HRD in the company. A corporate HRD budget is focused on meeting company-wide needs. In these ways there is what Mabey and Salaman (1995: 169) called 'organisational integration' of HRD into the business.

HRD leadership and commitment

At Company X, leadership must be in deed as well as in word. There are high-priority in-house training programmes for the most senior staff which reinforce the cultural, strategic and organisational developments needed. Strong leadership and commitment are expected from the chief executive of each business unit in and to the following areas of the company's training policy:

- a focus on customer-led quality, on understanding and responding to customer needs

- effective development of the company's people at all levels of the organisation – corporate, business unit and operational

- a competency-based approach to training for excellent performance, and equality of access to this training by every employee

- rewards for those employees who achieve relevant vocational qualifications

- a substantial investment in familiarising every employee with the company's and the units' strategic objectives, and in ensuring that each individual has performance targets and longer-term development to enable them to help those objectives to be achieved

- planned change will include a provision for appropriate and timely training of the staff involved.

Each strategic operating unit is responsible for its training policy and arrangements. These must be in line with group policy, but must also respond to the unit's local needs. Specialist training and development staff work within business units, helping managers to produce and implement a set of policies at unit level that will help to ensure a high-quality, committed workforce. Each unit has its own training and development budget, and support is given to the training policy through other HR policies. Most important of all, the company has a world-wide framework for performance management which includes performance development as a key component. In all these ways there is 'policy integration' of HRD into the business and a coherency with wider HR strategy (Mabey and Salaman, 1995).

Line management responsibility for HRD

It is upon the success of the line managers' HRD role that the effective implementation of training strategy across the business primarily depends. Line managers' development responsibilities are clarified in a *Group Training Manual* which is issued throughout the world-wide group. Responsibilities include:

- ensuring that employees are equipped with the necessary knowledge, understanding and skills to do their current jobs competently

- determining training and development needs, both present and future, setting priorities, allocating resources and reviewing results

- ensuring that training activity is reinforced as an aspect of the process of managing performance

- providing a work environment in which individuals can take responsibility for their own training and development.

Each manager must have documented plans, reviews, reports, records and performance evaluations as evidence that the principles of HRD and the company-wide performance management system are actively implemented at this level.

Individuals' responsibility for self-development

Individuals must take significant responsibility for their own development throughout their careers in the company by:

- learning and applying the knowledge, understanding and skills necessary for the performance of their jobs

- working with their managers to identify current and future learning, training and development needs and opportunities.

Now let us review this study in order to summarise learning thus far:

HRD at Company X

In what ways can Company X be said to exemplify good practice in its approach to the management of the HRD function across the organisation?

Feedback notes

HRD at Company X carries the hallmarks of a well-managed function because it has:

- a clear HRD vision and strategy that is in line with overall business goals and strategy

- strategic objectives that are carried through into detailed, practical plans for implementation of the policies that serve those objectives

- a form of organisational structure and company-wide procedures that ensure that the policies are carried out with the commitment and expertise of all who have been assigned training and development roles and responsibilities

- a system of training, guidance, monitoring, appraisal and rewards related to performance in those roles

- good management and utilisation of training and development resources.

The outsourced function

For the new HRD manager there are three points to consider in relation to outsourcing:

- Should any training and development activities be outsourced?

- Might the whole function in future be outsourced?

- Would the HRD function and its staff benefit from outsourcing?

In relation to the first point, the key issues are to do with cost-efficiency, added value and retention of control. Often an external party can provide training and development operations at a lower cost than is possible internally. Provided that the HRD manager can be assured that the organisation will retain control over targets and standards, and has good evidence that value will accrue to the organisation by outsourcing – whether on an occasional or permanent basis – then there can be many benefits. Three noted by Hardingham (1996: 45–6) arise from an effective partnership between internal and external practitioners:

- 'The combination of internal clout and external credibility is a winning card to play in designing and delivering the most challenging types of training' – that is, training of major importance to the organisation, but which also involves major tensions, difficulties or fundamental behavioural changes.

- External training designers and deliverers can represent a source of best practice for internal HRD practitioners.

- The internal practitioners' own approach and values can be transformed through partnership with external agents. This, in turn, can help to change values within the organisation.

In relation to the second point, the training manager must continually keep in mind the fact that there are now a number of question marks around the role of the traditional training and development practitioner (Roy Harrison, 1996). Curnow (1995) argued powerfully that HR professionals and management consultants need to develop strengths in each other's mainstream competencies as the former increasingly carry an internal consultancy role, and the latter are having to behave more like personnel directors in their formulation of policy changes and proposals as part of corporate change programmes.

The issue of rediscovering a significant role for training staff was one of the most important to emerge at the 1996 Conference of the American Society of Training and Development. There was an awareness of the implications for directive trainers of the learner-centred approaches necessitated by the drive to develop 'learning organisations'; of the tendency to hand over HRD to line managers, especially in downsized and de-layered organisations; of the powerful and efficient learning routes now available with the advance of information that need little support from a specialist function; and of the dissatisfaction expressed by many chief executives in the USA about the returns being offered to them by their training professionals – one study indicated that 70 per cent of the $300 billon annual investment in training in the USA was failing to produce any measurable improvement in job performance.

The kinds of question that the HRD manager needs to confront objectively include the following:

• What if there were no HRD function in this organisation? Where and how does it add value?

• If it is essential to the business, does it need to be carried out internally or could it be outsourced – in whole or in part?

• Should it be market-tested (a process involving tendering of certain operations to external agencies)?

• Is it sufficiently large to be made into an agency and floated out of the organisation?

Nuclear Electric management development manager Paul Rann's creative use of a network of associate tutors to address management training needs at a time of cost reduction and closure of the company's management training centre demonstrates the value that can be achieved by unusual, creative forms of partial outsourcing (Poulteney, 1997). Contracting out or conversion into an agency can in reality offer opportunities rather than threats for HRD staff. Another example is that of Northumbria Water (NW), the privatised water company located in the northeast of England, where training and development operations were reorganised on an agency basis in the late 1980s, around the time of privatisation. HRD specialists were able to choose either to work in the agency or to stay in the parent organisation, where they would be developed for any new roles it might be more appropriate for them to take on. In its early years the agency was assured of a full workload from NW, but thereafter was expected to achieve commercial viability in its own right. The agency, CPCR, rapidly became a successful business and achieved full autonomy, with NW only one of its many clients. It continues to thrive. Meanwhile, HRD remains a core function of NW's business, but is mainly in the hands of line managers. The HR department provides an umbrella of company goals and policy, and supporting administrative and personnel systems. It also provides training of managers for their HRD roles and monitors HRD across the company.

The possibility of most, if not all, of an organisation's learning delivery being outsourced in the future is one that the HRD manager should keep clearly in mind. Leigh (1996) argued that most organisations would benefit from handing their entire training function over to external suppliers and predicted that in many cases full outsourcing is now inevitable. Roy Harrison (1996) speculated that in order to survive 'the training designer will become a performance technologist and the training manager will be a performance improvement manager, separate from the HR function'.

What is essential is that a core strategic developmental role should remain at the heart of the business; if that too is contracted out, HRD will cease to be an organisational player. It is helpful at this point to reflect on outsourcing by considering your own organisation:

Outsourcing training and development operations

Consider your own organisation, or one with which you are familiar. Are any training and development operations outsourced currently? What benefits or deficits do you think this has brought for the organisation? In your view, should any, or further, outsourcing take place?

MANAGING SPECIALIST HRD STAFF

Unless specialist staff are supported in the organisation, are committed and expert in their jobs, and are flexible in skills and outlook, the whole function can soon decline into the role of 'passive provider'. There are seven key aspects to the management of such staff:

- employee resource planning
- job analysis
- recruitment and selection
- induction and basic training
- appraisal
- continuous development
- career development.

Employee resource (ER) planning

There must be an ER plan for the function, no matter how small in size it may be. It is essential for the training manager to work out the kind, number and level of staff currently required; and to identify what is likely to be needed through time in the light of the organisation's predicted needs for training and development. An informed assessment of the current staffing situation can then be carried out;

new work and responsibilities can be allocated; and job and career development plans for training staff can be formulated.

Job analysis

There must be analysis of training and development roles and tasks in the organisation, and identification of the skills, knowledge and attitudes they require. These tasks need to be informed by:

- *national occupational standards in training and development.* These standards provide the basis for vocational qualifications for those with training and development responsibility, whether they are line managers or specialists. They also play an important part in providing a wider framework for those personnel than that provided simply by the context of the particular organisation in which they work at any one point in time. Furthermore, since those personnel will, increasingly, be encouraging other employees to acquire National Vocational Qualifications (NVQs), it is essential that they take the lead in this by themselves going through the whole process and achieving occupational and verification qualifications.

- *CIPD professional standards related to employee development.* It is important that HRD practitioners see and present themselves as members of a professional community, working to recognised professional standards. We have seen in Chapter 9 the importance of those standards and the mindset about employee development in the business that they aim to develop.

- *analysis of the roles and responsibilities to be carried by HRD staff in the particular organisation, and of their organisational context* (Chapters 8 and 9). Ensuring that those staff fully understand the rationale for their roles, how those roles may be developed as their expertise in them grows, and how they can manage their roles in the particular organisation in which they work are all tasks for the HRD manager to perform as he or she builds and develops the HRD team.

Recruitment and selection

Job descriptions and personnel specifications will aid the recruitment and selection processes. They will also provide valuable information to help in the planning of training and development and allocation of work to staff. It should be remembered that with some appointments it will be more important for the person to make the job rather than the reverse, and this will determine how tight or loose the job description and personnel specification should be.

Attention needs to be given to who carries out recruitment, short-listing and selection. Many poor-quality training appointments are made because of lack of skill at this stage, or because those who have had the major say in selection have understood little about HRD jobs and the kinds of competency and motivation they require. It is as important to recruit staff with the disposition to operate in the culture of the particular workplace as those with the functional skills to do so. Ability means nothing if there is not the will to exercise it.

Induction and basic training

There must be proper induction of all new staff in order to explain the different contexts in which they will have to operate, and the work and organisation of the HRD function. Basic training may also need to be provided. For many positions it will be advisable to have a probationary period, during which new staff can be regularly appraised and receive coaching, guidance and other forms of support and development. Mentors for new members of staff can be invaluable counsellors, friends and facilitators of learning during this important period. It is as important for the job-holder to be given this period to learn what the job and the organisation is really like as it is for the organisation to be sure that the selection decision was a wise one. More detail on these processes is given in Chapter 14.

Appraisal

Appraisal should lead to three outcomes:

- *feedback on performance*. Remember that the training manager will not be aware of all the detail of how staff perform in their jobs, and the appraisal interview is therefore an important source of feedback for the manager as well as for appraisees.

- *work-planning*. This should focus on taking stock of work over a period of time and drawing up work objectives and plans for the forthcoming period.

- *diagnosis of training and development needs and action related to them*. This will lead to the implementation of plans to respond to training and development needs and expectations of staff.

These appraisal sessions must be genuine developmental and motivating experiences, otherwise none of the outcomes can be achieved (see Chapter 14). Again, occupational and professional standards can provide guidelines for appraisal discussions and assessments.

Retraining and continuous development

Retraining is an important aspect of the development of HRD personnel when the management and orientation of the function are changing, often quite dramatically. A focus on the 'learning organisation', for example, creates a need in many training staff to learn how to take on a more strategic role in the development of their organisation. That role will call for new and complex skills, as well as different ways of looking at the world. In a stimulating article, Alan Phillips (1995) described how he took groups of National Health Service (NHS) trainers through a programme called 'Trainers as Leaders' to give them the confidence and basic competence needed to cope effectively with a changing scenario in the NHS, where development was fast emerging as a strategic activity. Instead of their 'conventional role, where they were often at the organisational margin' these trainers were increasingly being drawn 'into the organisational mainstream', and many needed help in adjusting quickly to its demands and making the most of the opportunities it offered (Phillips, 1995: 32). Such stories are useful examples not only of the importance of regular checks on HRD staff's retraining needs (which in this case emerged at annual appraisal, but which ideally should not be left so long to become evident), but also on the ways in which external consultants can provide valued expertise and experience in unfamiliar territory.

All personnel, including the HRD manager, should be actively committed to self-development on a continuous basis. There may be little time, money or opportunity for the formalised training and development of HRD staff, and self-development will therefore be the only way to ensure regular diagnosis of their learning needs and updating or changing of skills, knowledge and attitudes through time. Self-development is also important because staff, through becoming committed to the process, will gain valuable insights into the relationship between the understanding and practice of learning styles and skills and the developmental process. Finally, continuous learning and self-development are essential to improving the employability security of HR professionals. These themes will be discussed in detail in Chapter 19, but it should be noted here that the CIPD's Continuous Professional Development pack is an essential tool for the HRD practitioner.

Career development

There must be a strong focus on career-planning and development for staff (see Chapter 19). Attention must be given not only to those who are likely to be moving up but also to those who may not be able to move from their present job or organisational level. Williams made an observation in 1984 that remains relevant today. He noted that the 'upward and onward' view of careers:

> does not square with what organisations are able to offer today; promotion is for a still smaller minority than in the past. There needs, therefore, to be a shift away from the advancement-orientated view of careers, and an increased emphasis on career development at the same organisational level or within the present job.
>
> Williams, 1984: 32

Davies and Deighan (1986) argued in a memorable article that it is as important to be concerned for the development of the 'solid citizens' and apparent 'dead wood' in a department as it is to have plans for the 'learners' and the 'high fliers' – more so, perhaps, since the solid citizens and the dead wood may be the people who constitute the majority, and in any event will have a strong influence on newcomers to the department. Unless ways are found to stimulate and regenerate these personnel, they may increasingly pull down the whole department. The requirement that every member of the department should have personal development plans will aid the processes of self-development and career development, and will give impetus to 'growing' a learning culture in the training and development department.

Since achieving vocational qualifications is an important part of the career development of HRD staff, their manager must consider the kind of workplace experience and formal education and training that will help them to progress towards those qualifications.

ORGANISING AND DEVELOPING LINE MANAGERS WITH HRD RESPONSIBILITIES

In relation to the organisation and development of line managers who have specific training and development roles to perform, the same basic principles apply as we have already noted for specialist staff. The nature of their roles, and of the tasks, competencies, personal skills, knowledge and attitudes that they require must be identified to establish necessary guidelines. Let us return to Company X in the second part of that case study:

Case-study: Company X, Part 2: Developing managers as trainers and developers

At Company X, HRD is a key area of every manager's job; managers are appraised and rewarded for their performance in this as in other key areas of responsibility. Appraisal and rewards are essential, because busy managers will not take their HRD roles seriously unless they perceive that these are regarded by the company as a key area of business activity.

Equipping line managers with HRD skills

Corporate HRD policy has four objectives to ensure that line managers are well equipped to carry out their HRD roles:

- to raise line managers' awareness of their responsibility for staff training and development

- to enable line managers to own training and development

- to develop line managers' skills in leading and managing people for performance

- to enable line managers to respond flexibly and effectively to an ever-changing business environment.

At Company X managers have proved to be excellent trainers, hundreds becoming certified trainers with NVQs at Level 3. A wide range of procedures, initiatives and formal programmes has been established in order to ensure that they take their training and development roles seriously and are equipped to perform them to a high standard. Some of the approaches used are:

- appointing line managers in key functions or departments to overview training and development

- running workshops about current major business topics with line managers and encouraging advocates among them for training and development implications of emerging plans

- selecting influential middle managers and training and developing them to achieve NVQs in training and development at Levels 3 and 4

- encouraging committed managers to raise the profile of training and development as part of the core responsibilities of line management through the agenda of management meetings

- establishing a mentoring system and training managers as mentors

- creating more flexible and accessible methods for delivering training and learning

- requiring all managers to have personal development plans, and ensuring that their staff have such plans also.

Continuous learning and improvement

All managers in the company must ensure that the focus of planned learning is on the job, where it can directly feed into the individual's development, the achievement of business targets and the longer-term growth of the organisation. They must record what they do in that respect, linking the components of:

- strategic business objectives

- the individual's business role

- performance-planning

- performance development

- personal assessment

- performance-related recognition and reward.

Managers are encouraged to achieve NVQs at Level 4 related to 'learning development' as a way of achieving added personal value in the work they do to develop a culture of continuous learning and development in the workplace.

Measures like these ensure that at Company X managers have the skills and the attitudes needed to promote effective development of people. Managers who are well trained themselves are the ones most likely to take training seriously and ensure their own staff are also trained and continuously developed in their work performance.

LEADERSHIP AND TEAMWORK

Unless those holding development responsibilities, in whatever capacity, have skilled leadership and can act as an effective team, their basic abilities and commitment, and their impact on the organisation, will suffer. The training manager has two issues to consider:

- *leadership style.* What should be his or her leadership style – tight or loose, authoritarian or participative, task-centred or person-centred?

- *teamwork.* How should HRD specialist and line management staff be organised in relation to their HRD responsibilities and to the training manager? As a close-knit team or a loosely knit collection of individuals, or somewhere between the two?

If there is a devolved structure for the training department, with central staff transferred out to or already working in units, then there is a danger of professional isolation for those personnel. There is also a possibility that they will become so closely involved with the units in which they are working that they will lose their identity as members of the HRD team. Fowler (1992: 23) observed that the leader in that situation must act as 'head of profession', retaining functional responsibility for staff's professional and career development, and holding regular meetings with them.

Careful thought must be given to the leader's own preferred style and characteristics. It is pointless trying to be 'authoritarian' if this runs quite counter to your personality and to others' fixed perceptions of the kind of person you are. This has to be balanced against the preferred leadership style of the group, and their own personal, occupational and professional characteristics, which may call strongly for one style rather than another. The matter of 'fit' is so important as to be a critical factor at selection stage. However, 'fit' must be seen in a wider perspective: adapting to the preferences and expectations of a group is not productive if the group's behaviour and performance is at odds with what is needed in the organisation, or if currently they are prejudicing the effectiveness and credibility of HRD in the organisation.

Now here is a task based on a real-life case: I have called the firm 'Vitex' – not its real name, but one given to ensure anonymity:

Case-study: Vitex Ltd

After reading this case-study, please answer the following questions on the role of HRD manager:

1   *How will you decide what kind of leadership style to use in your department?*

2   *Do you see individualised work or 'teamwork' as relevant to your new department? Give reasons for your reply.*

3   *What is the first action you will take in relation to establishing leadership and work processes in the department?*

(A variant on this would be to organise this task as a group role-playing exercise instead, using the questions as the starting-point for a meeting between the new HRD manager and his or her staff.)

Vitex is a well-known engineering firm in southeast England. Ten years ago it had a workforce of 2,000 and was extremely successful, operating in many home and overseas markets. Its training department consisted of a training manager, three specialist training officers, two instructors responsible for apprentice and commercial training, a clerk and a secretary. Training tasks tended to be predictable and repetitive, and members of the 'team' operated mainly as individuals. Training policy and the annual company training plan were established by the training manager working in partnership with the personnel director; thereafter work was allocated to the appropriate people, with monitoring to ensure the training budget was not exceeded. There was little real evaluation of training and no in-depth diagnosis of needs. It was assumed that the future would be very like the past and present, and so training itself was mainly a matter of sending people on external courses, or doing some internal, job-related training if this seemed necessary. Training staff tended to work on an individualised basis, the three training officers working within different business units.

Vitex, up against very severe competition in its markets, is now a much smaller firm, with a workforce of around 800 working on three sites all within five or so miles of each other. It makes maximum use of new technology and has established a reputation for innovation and high-quality products. As part of the general move towards 'slimming down' and rationalisation, the size of the training department has been reduced to a training manager, a training officer and a secretary/administrative assistant. There is no apprenticeship programme, and the previous training manager was moved three months ago into production management (where he had earlier experience). The training officer, a man in his forties without any professional qualifications but a good record as a training administrator and instructor, is one of the original three training officers. His colleagues have been redeployed in other service departments. There is a new secretary, a pleasant and efficient woman of 30, who was moved from the sales department to training a year ago.

You have just been recruited as the new HRD manager, with a brief to make the function much more business-led. Your role is a mix of HRD manager, internal consultant and strategic change agent. Top management fully supports training but has made it clear that from now on the function must provide tailor-made answers to real organisational needs that have been expertly diagnosed. External resources can be used where the expense can be justified by the results likely to be achieved. Each business unit now holds its own training and development budget, with managers responsible for deciding on training needs in their units. The now-styled HRD department has only a small central budget to meet organisation-wide needs and special contingencies.

Feedback notes
- You can use our simple systems framework developed in Chapter 9 (page 160) in order to decide on the most appropriate kind of leadership style:

  - *environment* – The organisational environment of the leader, the group and the task is team-based and operating in an uncertain, competitive external environment. This should push the HRD department towards a flexible structure, with values that relate to helping achieve the 'mission' of Vitex, and provide expertise that will meet organisational needs.

  - *structure and culture* – Although the training department may have had a bureaucratic structure and culture in the past, these are no longer appropriate. Leadership that will develop an entrepreneurial department is clearly needed, and there must be business partnership with line managers as well as with the personnel function (about which no details were given in the case-study).

  - *goals, strategy and tasks* – At Vitex, the goal is for HRD to provide tailor-made services to meet organisational needs, so training and development tasks may change rapidly through time, and are unlikely to be routine or highly specialised. This emphasises the need for effective teamwork in the HRD department.

- *people* – The leader's own preferred style and characteristics have to be considered, as do the preferred leadership style of the group, and their own personal and professional characteristics, which may make one style more appropriate than any other. A problem may arise with the 40-year-old training officer, who has worked in a situation where the norm was administrative tasks rather than creative and diagnostic work. He is not used to operating as a member of a close-knit professional team. Particular attention must be paid to his training and development. The secretary's expectations and perceptions of the new situation should also be explored.

- *technology* – The HRD manager should assess if value can be added by incorporating new technology into training and learning processes. There must be clear justification and cost-benefit analysis, but the HRD function must become knowledgeable about innovative approaches to learning, and may be well advised to use and learn from external consultants to design and pilot certain learning systems. Those consultants, too, will have to be carefully selected, managed and monitored, and drawn into a partnership with internal training staff.

- All the evidence points to the need for the leader to build a cohesive, flexible team, whose members can contribute to the overall goal of the training department, pooling knowledge and skills instead of working on an individualised and specialist basis. In this context, the contribution of the secretary, and the image she gives of the department, is crucial. If she proves capable and willing, her role and type of work could themselves change through time from being purely secretarial to incorporating other types of responsibility. A number of personnel and training officers start off as secretaries, and her routes for development (like NVQs, or gaining part or full membership of the CIPD) should be integrated into a career plan. The training officer, too, has valuable experience and skills to offer: giving him an early assignment of collecting information from external sources on new learning systems and on funding sources to pilot new training technology initiatives would test his skills, explore his potential, give him the chance to work on something of real importance and expand his knowledge as well as his network of external contacts.

In initial team meetings with staff, the HRD manager will need to strike a balance between on the one hand pursuing a collaborative approach and on the other demonstrating leadership that has a clear, appropriate and powerful vision for the department, as well as a strategy to ensure that that vision can be realised at the practical level. The extent to which inputs from staff can or should influence the determination of organisational training and development policy and/or strategy is something that only the leader can determine.

CONCLUSION

Having read this chapter and completed its reviews and self-checks, you should now:

*   understand the scope of the human resource development (HRD) manager's role

*   understand different ways in which the HRD function can be organised

*   be able to draw up an action plan to organise HRD staff and develop their abilities and potential both as individuals and as members of a professional team.

To test yourself against these objectives, what five-minute answers would you give to the following questions? (Dates in brackets refer to the IPD qualifying examination paper in which a question appeared.)

---

*   Identify **three** of the employee development responsibilities you would expect to be held by managers in an organisation where there is no specialist employee development function but a strong commitment by top management to effective performance management and to the continuous development of its workforce. (May 1997)

*   If, as a line manager, you are told that, regardless of any specialist training and development function, you have the basic responsibility for the development of your staff, what would you see as the main activities you would have to carry out in order to fulfil that responsibility – and why? (November 1997)

*   A small organisation (around 200 employees) advertises for a T&D manager post and refers to the need for applicants with team management skills and 'the ability to lead, train and motivate staff'. Identify and briefly explain the kind of role and key tasks that such a post is likely to involve. (November 1998)

USEFUL READING

FOWLER A. (1998) *The IPD Guide on Outsourcing*. London, Institute of Personnel and Development.

MERRICK N. (1999) 'Premier division'. *People Management*. Vol. 5, 16. pp38–41. (An account of the first local authority to outsource most of its personnel function, and the positive results achieved for HR.)

11 Managing finance, marketing and records

LEARNING OBJECTIVES

After reading this chapter you will:

- be able to advise on how to cost the activities of a training function
- understand how to establish and manage a training budget
- understand what is involved in establishing a training record system
- understand the main issues related to marketing HRD in an organisation.

MANAGING TRAINING AND DEVELOPMENT RESOURCES

The human resource development (HRD) manager's resource base will need skilful management if it is to be cost-efficient, add value and remain continuously relevant to a changing business situation and to the emergent needs of the workforce. Those new to HRD usually find the costing aspect one of hardest to grasp. With their needs particularly in mind, I have tried in this chapter to provide the kind of basic practical information that is needed by anyone who is seeking clarity on the basics of costing and budgeting applied to training and development operations in the business.

There are two main categories of training and development resources: the tangible and the intangible.

Tangible resources
- personnel available within and outside the organisation

- physical resources – accommodation, equipment, training materials, etc – available within the organisation and through external sources

- finance available within the organisation for the training and development of the workforce, whether allocated to a central training budget or to departmental training budgets, and finance available from external sources.

Intangible resources
One of the most important intangible resources is time. The time available to carry out any activities in training, including the management and development of training resources, will have a

crucial effect on training policy and strategy, on managerial strategy and effectiveness, and on day-to-day training and management.

Other intangible resources include assets such as the past image and reputation of training within the organisation; the learning capability and disposition of the workforce; external learning networks that can offer a potential source of knowledge and expertise to improve learning in the organisation; and natural learning opportunities available in the organisation in the normal course of work. These intangible learning resources should be identified and used to the benefit of job performance and the development of human potential in the business. We shall discuss them further in Part 4; in Part 5 they become a major focus of attention.

In order to be able to manage these resources effectively, the HRD manager must:

- observe and reflect on the present situation – he or she must look at the current training budget (or, if none is available, some equivalent figures that show the costs of running the training function and carrying out training activities) to establish what is done and what it costs, and must identify the other tangible and intangible training resources available – materials, equipment, accommodation, personnel – and consider how they are currently being used

- analyse this information by reference to key contextual factors in order to establish whether the department's resources are being used rationally to meet key HRD needs

- be creative and think of alternative, more efficient or effective, ways of using resources

- make decisions, choosing the most feasible, cost-efficient and cost-effective action

- monitor and evaluate, choosing those methods that are both simple and effective enough for the purpose, and agreeing well in advance who is to carry out these processes, and when.

Good resource management thus requires the use of those core learning skills defined by Kolb, Rubin and McIntyre (1974) in their learning cycle: observation and reflection, analysis, creativity, decision-making and problem-solving, and evaluation.

The management of resources requires the development of measures of activity, and at this point material presented in my two previous texts published by the (then) IPD will be reproduced with few changes. What was relevant then, after all, remains so now: a straightforward approach that will provide the basic information needed and can be rapidly mastered and applied to a wide variety of situations. There are, of course, many financial management techniques that can be applied to the training investment, and in that regard consultancy-oriented texts like those of Moorby (1991: 68–93) and Bentley (1990: 32–42) are helpful for both the student and the practitioner.

MANAGING THE BUDGET

The first place where one expects to find a categorisation of training and development activities and their costs is in the budget. Budgeting can take any of three main forms: there may be a budget for the HRD department; money for training and development may be held in unit/departmental budgets for which line managers are responsible; or, as in our Company X case-study, there may be both a corporate training budget and unit budgets.

Whoever has budgetary responsibility, it is essential that resources and activities should be costed and managed in such a way that full value for money is obtained. It is also important that where, at first sight, priority needs cannot be met within current budgets, a sound case is put forward for obtaining more money or for meeting needs by the use of changed approaches.

Presentation of the budget

The type of format to be used in the presentation of financial information about training depends on four factors:

- *why the information is needed* – This will determine what information is to be collected, and what focus to give the costings.

- *for whom the information is needed* – This will determine the way the information is expressed and the specific format to be used. If financial information is needed by the accounts department, this should follow the format and language used in their accounting system. If data on costs and benefits of one training solution compared to another are needed by busy line managers to help them decide which solution to choose, then the data must be expressed in language that is immediately comprehensible to the managers.

- *when the information is needed and what is available* – If a request comes in today for information needed tomorrow, then it may prove impossible to obtain all the data theoretically desirable. The format must be tailored to match whatever data can be produced in time so that the overall presentation makes its proper impact even if it cannot fully cover the ground.

- *the availability of time and expertise* – Extending the previous point, budgeting is a time-consuming activity involving a variety of skills. It is essential to put the task into perspective, calculating how much time and expertise should be devoted to it given its importance relative to other HRD tasks.

The main headings to use for a budget depend on who it is being produced for, and why. For an organisation's annual ED budget, the headings would typically be to do with:

- personnel, overhead and administration costs

- costs incurred through the provision, monitoring and evaluation of training and development activity, including provision to support employees' attending external education, training and development events.

Headings like these will then be broken down into sub-headings that identify and cost the main categories of training and development activity across all divisions or departments of the organisation, and across different occupational groups.

When producing a budget to use for internal purposes *within* the HRD department, some prefer to identify two main categories of costs: direct – to do with the variable costs associated with the provision of training and learning events; and indirect – to do with the fixed costs of running the department. We will look at what is involved here in the following section.

Producing a training budget

Study the paper presentation of *either* an organisation's annual training budget *or* of its HRD departmental budget, looking carefully at format and content. How comprehensive is the information that has been produced, and to what extent does it clearly identify all critical costs?

A basic approach to costing

In order to draw up a budget, there must be a clear grasp of how to cost training and development activity. Three pieces of information are essential to identify here:

• the overall annual running cost of training operations

• how to recover that cost

• how to identify and compare the costs involved in training and development alternatives.

In relation to these, two terms are fundamental:

• *trainer day* costs – This refers to the daily costs involved in the basic running of a training function.

• *training day* costs – This refers to the total costs involved in running a training function and in carrying out its specific training activities.

Finally, there are the three areas of tangible costs: personnel, overheads and administration.

Calculating the annual running costs of training operations

Table 8 deals with the basic costs of running a specialist training department. It does not include capital expenditure or the costs of providing training services (except in relation to administration costs where, in order to get an acceptable figure, we have to consider the sort of demands likely to be made, given the training envisaged). In our next examples the provision costs will be calculated separately.

Personnel and overhead costs are fixed (that is to say, the organisation must pay them, whether or not training activities are carried out), but administration costs are variable, because they depend on what kind

Table 8 Basic annual running costs of a training department (with acknowledgements to Alan Rutter, University of Northumbria Business School)

	Cost (£)
Personnel (two training officers and a secretary)	
Training staff salaries plus, say, 25 per cent for employment costs (pension, NI and other payments)	40,000
Support staff (administrative and clerical) plus 25 per cent	12,000
Overheads	
Annual rent and rates (or some approximate calculation of these) related to training accommodation (one training room; two offices); to heating, lighting and cleaning; and to other maintenance costs of training accommodation	6,000
Administration	
Estimate/actual:	
telephone and postal costs	
printing, photocopying etc costs	
computer costs (eg cost of computer time, software)	4,000
Total basic annual running costs	£62,000

of training activities take place or are envisaged. If a forecasting exercise is being carried out, then administration costs can be estimated in one of three ways:

- If there is no annual training plan, but the pattern of past activity has been quite similar to that of the activity proposed, a reliable enough figure can be reached by taking an average of total administration costs incurred during, say, the last two years' training activities and adding on an amount for inflation.

- If there is an annual training plan, the training manager can look at the administration costs actually incurred by the activities involved in last year's plan and, knowing the kind of activities planned for the forthcoming year, assess how much more or less the related administration costs are likely to be. Again, an inflation cost will have to be built in.

- If there is no specialist training department, or any training overheads, and there is no relationship between past and planned provision, the basic annual running costs of the training role and function can be calculated by reference to two areas of tangible costs:

  - *personnel costs* – the number of days each manager is likely to be spending in carrying out training and training-related activities for others, expressed as a proportion of their annual salary and employment costs. (A more sophisticated calculation would include lost opportunity costs – the estimated cost to the organisation of deploying line managers on training work when

Table 9 Cost of a trainer day (with acknowledgements to Alan Rutter)

	Cost £
Days actually worked by the two training staff (ie once holidays etc have been taken) = 240 each = total of *480 days*	
Annual running cost of the training dept (see Table 8)	62,000
So cost of each day the training staff are actually working	62,000 ÷ 480
Cost of one trainer day (to nearest £)	£129.00

they could have been doing something else. It would also include provision for the continuous professional development of training staff.

- *administration costs* – the identifiable administration costs that will be incurred by work on training and training-related activities, expressed in annual terms.

Recovering running costs

First, we need to find out the cost of a trainer day in the organisation. Table 9 continues with the example we have just used, adding further information. (This same approach can, of course, be used to calculate the 'trainer day' costs of anyone who carries out training/development activities, whether or not they are training staff.)

This simple calculation of the trainer day cost tells us that if it is required to recover the annual cost of running its training department (£62,000), this particular organisation, given the provision of training for 480 days a year (ie 240 days by each of the two training staff), must charge £129 a day for that training.

We can now see how the basic running costs of a training department or function can be expressed as a trainer day cost, calculated as follows:

$$\frac{\text{Annual running cost of the training function}}{\text{Number of days each staff member involved in training work}} = \text{trainer day cost}$$

But if it is necessary for a training department to recover its identifiable costs on a rigorous financial basis, how can it be done? A case-study can provide an illustration at this point.

Case-study: Mintech Ltd: Part 1 (In collaboration with Alan Rutter, University of Northumbria Business School)

Mintech Ltd has a training department employing two training officers (Mike and John) and a secretary.

The basic annual running cost of the department = £62,000

Number of days worked by the two officers:

	Mike: 250 + John: 250	= 500
Trainer day cost	£62,000 ÷ 500	= £124

The department is involved in two sorts of training activity, the direct costs of which are shown below:

Training people	*Assisting people to attend external training*
The trainers keep a record of the number of days they spend on face-to-face training of people:	The trainers keep a record of the number of days they spend on work connected with external courses, ranging from analysis of needs through to evaluation of results:
Mike: 30 days	Mike: 220 days
John: 20 days	John: 230 days
Total: 50 trainer days	*Total: 450 trainer days*
Cost: 50 × £124 = £6,200	*Cost: 450 × £124 = £55,800*
The trainers add up the number of days that staff spend participating in these courses = 300	The trainers add up the number of days that staff spend participating in these courses = 3,000
Amount to be recovered for internal training activities:	Amount to be recovered for external training activities:
£6,200 for 300 training days	£55,800 for 3,000 training days
Total cost of internal training day = £21	*Total cost of external training day = £19*
But:	
Additional costs (fees, travel, subsistence, accommodation, course materials, per person)	*Additional costs* (fees, travel, subsistence, accommodation, course materials, per person)
per day = £5	per day = £200

To recover its costs of £21 per person for everyone who undergoes internal training, and £19 per person for everyone who attends external training, as well as covering the additional costs involved, Mintech's training department can do one of two things:

If it has its own budget, it must include in the budget estimate enough to cover a cost of £21 per day for every member of the organisation who will be attending internal training courses, and a cost of £19 per day for every member of the organisation who will be attending external training courses. It must then add to the estimate the additional costs of fees, travel, subsistence, accommodation and course materials involved in the training events concerned

or

If there is no central training budget, but each department has its own budget from which training costs must be met, it must 'charge' departments £21 per day for every member of staff who will be attending internal training courses, and £19 per day for every member of staff who will be attending external training courses and add on the additional costs of fees, travel, subsistence, accommodation and course materials involved in the training events concerned.

The Mintech case-study shows us that in order to calculate how to recover the costs involved in running a training department and in carrying out its training activities, the training day cost must be calculated as follows:

$$\frac{\text{Trainer day cost}}{\text{Number of training days}} = \text{trainer day cost}$$

Note that the number of training days is simply arrived at by adding up all the days it has taken to train people throughout the organisation, in one case internally, in the other case externally. So if 100 people each went on three days' external training in a year, then the total number of external training days would come to 300.

Costing training

Briefly explain the use of the trainer day cost and of the training day cost in relation to running a training function.

Feedback notes
• The trainer day cost can be used to calculate the basic cost of running the training function.

• The training day cost can be used to calculate the charge to be made by the function for training, if its running costs are to be recovered on a strict financial basis.

We have now seen how to provide two of the three crucial pieces of information that every manager of an HRD function should possess: the overall costs of running the function, and how to recover that cost.

Identifying and comparing costs involved in training alternatives

Using the same Mintech case-study, we can look at a typical situation facing many personnel and training officers: staff requests to go on education or training courses. We shall see how, by comparing the costs of internal and external supervisory training, a sound decision can be reached by someone who is concerned to achieve both relevant training and good management of resources. If you tackled the task on 'Weighing up the training options' in Chapter 6 (page 111), you will find this is a virtually identical exercise but it contains detail that it was not relevant to put in at that earlier stage of your learning about cost-benefit analysis.

Case-study: Mintech Ltd: Part 2

Three supervisors from different departments have applied to the training department to go on a day-release supervisory studies course at the local college. It lasts for a year, involves absence of half a day plus an evening (same day) over three terms, and ends with an examination leading to a national supervisory skills qualification. Mike, one of the two training officers, first identifies the costs involved in sending the three supervisors away on the day-release course. To help him do this calculation, he uses the 'training day cost' identified in the Mintech case-study, Part 1.

Option A

Sending supervisors on external training course leading to national supervisory qualification:

	Cost (£)
Fees (£1,000 per person per year) £1,000 × 3	3,000
Travel and subsistence (£5 per person per day at college):	
£5 × 3 × 30 days	450
Materials (books and other items used by trainees on	
the course) £60 × 3	180
Administrative overhead cost External	
training day cost × number of days	
× number of trainees	
(£19, already calculated, × 30 × 3)	1,710
Total cost of sending three people on course	**£5,340**

Mike could have made out a more complicated list that would have included indirect as well as direct costs. The indirect costs incurred by attending the external course would include: lost opportunity costs, reduction in output or quality of service of their staff due to less effective staff management during the periods of their absence, lost salary and related employment cost, due to the supervisors' reduction in hours worked 'on the job' during the period of the course, and so on. In practice such costs are rarely taken into account unless direct costs are occasioned by the supervisors' absence (for example, overtime payments due to their work having to be done by others). Of course, if Mike had needed to make a particularly powerful case against sending people away on an external course, he would have done well to draw attention to these 'hidden' costs!

The next step is for Mike to think carefully about the external course. His calculations show that sending three supervisors on the course will be an expensive undertaking, and it may not be possible to offer the same opportunity, in the current year, to any further supervisory applicants. So what are the other options? (At this point you may like to take over and do some creative thinking to generate a list of alternatives. For the purposes of this exercise I am developing only one other option, but in fact several are possible.)

One such option is for job-related training needs of all Mintech's 16 supervisors to be identified through appraisal interviews and other methods, and for the training department to organise internal courses to meet common needs, leaving needs specific to each individual to be met in some other way.

Mike discusses this idea with his colleagues and they agree that three one-week courses run by the training department in its conference room would cover the necessary material well, and would be a real benefit to at least 12, instead of only three, supervisors. The department has a good reputation within the company for running tailor-made programmes, and so it is unlikely that this would be viewed as inferior by the supervisors. Admittedly it would not lead to National Vocational Qualifications (NVQs), because the company is not yet tied into the NVQ system, but should that become an important consideration in the future, then this particular option can be reconsidered then. What will the option cost at this point?

Option B

Internal supervisory training course run by training staff

There would be three one-week courses, each led by one tutor and involving a total membership of 12 supervisors, four attending each course.

	Cost (£)
Fees	N/A
Subsistence Mid-morning and mid-afternoon refreshments for four participants and one trainer, @ £1.50 per head per day × 3 one-week courses	112.50
Materials (£50 per trainee plus 3 trainers' copies)	750.00
Administrative overhead cost Internal training day cost (£21, previously calculated, × 5 × 12)	1,260.00
Total cost of training 12 supervisors internally	**£2,122.50**

Mike was interested to note the cost per trainee involved in each of the options: £1,780 for Option A, but only £176.88 for Option B. He realised that in Option B he had not included the cost of identifying training needs of the supervisors, designing the one-week programmes for them and producing the necessary training materials. This was because he was confident that they could be substantially offset by repeat runs of the programmes for further groups of supervisors.

Summary

Through the various examples so far examined we have discovered how to extract three crucial pieces of information noted at the start of this chapter:

• the basic annual cost of running training operations

• how to recover the running cost on a strict financial basis

• how to identify and compare costs involved in training alternatives.

There is one more activity that we have to carry out in order to ensure that cost-effective decisions are made in relation to the use of training resources: cost–benefit analysis. We have already looked at this in

Chapters 6 and 7, when we examined a variety of ways by which the value and outcomes of training and development can be assessed and measured.

The running costs of a training department

Take a training department in your own organisation, or some other with which you are familiar. Using the methods described thus far, produce a calculation of the approximate annual running costs of that department, and then identify how far those costs are recovered by the department's training operations. Produce any recommendations for action that you may feel necessary on completion of the exercise.

A STRATEGY FOR MANAGING TRAINING RESOURCES

What have we learned about the management of resources thus far? That HRD operations, if they are to be cost-efficient, require:

- *accurate costing* – The costs of learning activities must be estimated as accurately as possible, and expressed in a way that is meaningful to the managers of the organisation concerned.

- *relevance to organisational training needs* – Decisions about expenditure on training activities must be consistent with decisions about the overall HRD policy and strategy of the organisation, and must meet real training needs and priorities.

- *consistency with other employee resource (ER) policies and processes* – Decisions about learning activities must also be consistent with other ER policies and processes, for example employee resource planning and utilisation, staff appraisal, promotion and career development planning, and financial and other reward strategies.

- *evaluation of options* – Alternative ways of using resources and of achieving learning objectives must always be considered and costed before final decisions are made.

- *comparisons of costs* – Compare the costs and benefits of the options (including that of doing nothing). Make a decision which strikes the best balance between being cost-beneficial, generally feasible and politically sensitive.

- *monitoring and evaluation* – All learning events must be controlled, and their value as well as their validity must be assessed. Ways of measuring outcomes have been explored in detail in Chapters 6 and 7.

MARKETING HRD

The marketing process
The HRD manager has another important area of activity: the marketing of HRD in the organisation. We have seen earlier in this book the significant role that HRD practitioners possess as 'internal consultants' – and the increasing threat of outsourcing that faces many

training and development departments unable to convince their organisations that they are worth continued investment in the services they offer. Such considerations underline the need for ensuring that the HRD function offers real value to the business, and for effective marketing of that function.

Marketing in this sense means 'that HRD practitioners will aim all their efforts at satisfying their clients' (Gilley and Eggland, 1989: 242). It is not to do with glossy brochures or expensive selling efforts. It is to do with finding out the kind of service or product that best meets the needs of internal customers as well as of those outside the organisation for whom planned learning events provided or initiated by the company also have significant value.

As Price (1966) argued, marketing does not assume that there is one way to strategic success. It enables the development of the right kind of products for a particular organisation. Marketing is therefore an integral part of the collaborative relationship that must exist between HRD professionals and their organisation if the function is to be taken seriously. To quote again from Gilley and Eggland's illuminating chapter (1989: 243), it is a matter of those professionals becoming 'skilled at understanding, planning and managing exchanges' so that value is offered to and received by the parties.

Little attention has been paid in the past in British academic texts to the concept of marketing as part of developing a strategic approach to HRD. Now, however, that has changed. It has become commonplace to talk of the firm's value chain, of functional departments needing to serve internal as well as external customers, of the need for vision and goals to drive every area of business activity. Now it is easier to see the meaning of 'marketing' in relation to HRD. In Part 3 of this book we shall see how to formulate and agree on purpose and strategy for learning events and how to involve stakeholders actively in the design, delivery and evaluation of those events. The subject is raised here to ensure that marketing the HRD function overall is understood by the HRD manager and team to be one of their central tasks. Using rather different language, we are reiterating what has been continuously emphasised in the book thus far – that once HRD's true value is understood and it achieves strategic integration at various levels of the organisation, it can realise its potential to be a key business function and a fundamental process to stimulate change, innovation and growth.

Marketing HRD in the organisation

How are training and development marketed in your organisation (or one with which you are familiar)? Use Table 5 in Chapter 6 (page 115) to help you analyse the effectiveness of that marketing, and to identify any changes you think should be made.

We have seen in Chapters 6 and 7 that the strongest commitment to training and development in the organisation will arise from a shared awareness among stakeholders that HRD can produce real value for the business as well as for individuals. Spending time on developing that awareness will be more productive than mechanical and time-consuming attempts to 'prove that HRD was worth it'. This is not to deny that training and development resources and activities should always be costed and managed effectively. HRD personnel must, of course, be able to speak as convincingly about the costs and benefits of what they do as any other manager in the business, and must be able to show that resources are being well deployed and well managed. However, they must spend as much time on developing an HRD process that will actively involve stakeholders and create a climate of awareness of the centrality of HRD to the business.

THE IMPORTANCE OF THE HRD RECORD SYSTEM

Marketing HRD depends to a significant extent on having and maintaining a record system that provides an accurate, up-to-date and comprehensive database. However, records are important for far more than marketing purposes alone, as the following two cases show.

Case-study: The Southall train crash

In its report into the 1997 rail crash in Southall in which seven people lost their lives, the Health and Safety Commission extensively criticised the training function. One of the most disturbing deficiencies that the report highlighted was a failure to maintain and pass on drivers' records, so that key performance errors which training should have remedied were not always identified. Another was a 'surprising' absence of any unified record system. One of the recommendations is that Railtrack and the Association of Train Operating Companies set up a national qualification and accreditation system for drivers. This would enable centrally held records to be made available to the current employer (Cooper, 2000).

Case-study: The police force's new database

The National Police Training body (NPT) announced early in 2000, in the wake of the Macpherson report into the Stephen Lawrence murder investigation, that it was setting up a database to ensure that there is a central outlet 'for the extensive reserves of knowledge and information held by the UK's regional police forces' (Pawsey, 2000). The database will enable quick access to information about best practice. More importantly, it will enable those with HRD responsibilities in the police force to provide the most relevant and effective training for all personnel.

The database will focus on equal opportunities and performance management issues, since these are critical areas for the police force. By concentrating attention on them the record system will be able to provide added value and help the police to become more competitive with the private sector. The establishment of the new record system was timed to coincide with the introduction of mandatory audit of police services in April 2000, and was the result of 'a wide-ranging shake-up of training methods' (*ibid*).

> **The value of a training and development record system**
>
> What benefits for the organisation can flow from a good record system?

Feedback note
* The database contained in a good record system will aid the identification of training needs, supply evidence of HRD activity, provide details of when, where, why, for whom and for what purposes that activity has been undertaken, and provide a centralised source of up-to-date knowledge, experience, practices and ideas.

In this section I shall restrict discussion to an outline of the needs that a record system must serve, and implications for the manager to consider.

What the record system must ensure is that:

* *activities can be identified and monitored* – It should be possible at any time to check on how far, in what ways, at what cost, and with what results training and planned development activities are being carried out in every part of the organisation. The more collaborative the approach to training is, the easier it will be to obtain and record that information. Records must also be comprehensive, up-to-date and accurate.

* *training needs, learner profiles and the consequent training and development of individuals, are recorded* – Personal records need to be kept showing the numbers and identities of those who are trained and developed through time, the reasons for that training and development, and the learning outcomes. They must also facilitate monitoring to ensure non-discrimination.

* *knowledge is accessible for dissemination across the organisation* – Knowledge, good practice, ideas and experiences arising from training and learning processes can be recorded on a centralised database, where they should be centrally accessible to stimulate continuous improvement, creativity and innovation

* *the law relating to employment is being observed* – It must be possible at any time to identify how far, and in what ways, the law relating to employment is being observed. In the context of HRD this means that records must pay particular attention to areas of training activity related to dismissal, redundancy, discrimination, health and safety, data protection, and Social Chapter legislation. In all of these areas failure to ensure that employees have the right knowledge and skills can mean that employers as well as employees become liable for breaches of the relevant legislation. Up-to-date information must be available to show exactly what steps have been taken to prevent discrimination in the workplace. The records must show that all employees, no matter what type of contract they hold with the organisation, have equal opportunity for access to training and development relevant to their jobs and their future employment prospects in the organisation. We shall examine some of the implications of this in Chapter 18, when we look at ways in which

such access can be facilitated for minority groups and disadvantaged individuals.

• *the record system itself adheres to the law* – The record system must adhere to legal requirements in the way in which it is designed and operated, and in its accessibility. For training and development activity, fundamental legislation is contained in the Data Protection Act 1984 and also in the less widely known European Union Data Protection Directive 1995 (Aiken, 1996).

Employees have the right to access all their files, whether in manual or computerised systems. Employers must also have instructions listing the purposes for which information is collected, clarifying access and security arrangements and guaranteeing that no additional use will be made of the information without first obtaining the consent of the person in overall charge of employee records.

• *the record system is cost-beneficial* – The record system should be as simple as possible, using sophisticated methods and processes only when the ensuing benefits can be shown fully to justify the human, physical and financial resources and costs. Particular attention must be paid to such questions as how detailed particular records should be, for how long records should be kept, who should keep records, and how often records should be updated.

• *HRD records are consistent with other HR records* – Training and development records should have a positive relationship with records maintained in any other areas of human resource management in the organisation (a highly relevant factor in the Southall case reported above). They should whenever possible therefore be drawn up using a format and technology that complement rather than confuse other HR record-keeping and data analysis.

• *confidentiality is observed* – Particular attention must be paid to confidentiality and accordingly to what information goes on record, to who should have access to various records, and to how access can be protected.

These, then, are eight key factors to take into account when establishing a record system. A record system, together with the budget, is an invaluable aid to the control of resources. However, like the budget, the criteria for determining what goes into records depend on four factors:

• why the information is needed

• for whom it is needed

• when it is needed and what information is available

• what time and expertise can be devoted to this task, given other demands on the HRD function.

CONCLUSION

Having read this chapter and completed its reviews and self-checks, you should now:

- be able to advise on how to cost the activities of a training function

- understand how to establish and manage a training budget

- understand the main issues related to marketing HRD in an organisation

- understand what is involved in establishing a training record system.

To test yourself against these objectives, what five-minute answers would you give to the following questions? (Dates in brackets refer to the IPD qualifying examination paper in which a question appeared.)

- What are some of the considerations that should influence the establishment of a training record system? (May 1997)

- You, the training manager in an organisation, have been asked by your personnel director to draft a pro-forma for an annual training and development budget for the organisation. What headings will you use, and why? (May 1998)

- Explain why there is now so much interest in how to 'market the Employee Development function', and outline what 'marketing' means in this context. (November 1998)

USEFUL READING

GILLEY J. W. *and* EGGLAND S. A. (1989a) 'Marketing and positioning the HRD program within the organization'. *Principles of Human Resource Development*. Wokingham, Addison Wesley and University Associates Inc. pp.243–65.

12 Harnessing new technology

LEARNING OBJECTIVES

After reading this chapter you will:

- understand what is meant by 'e-learning' and its importance in the knowledge economy

- be able to explain why harnessing new technology to the learning and knowledge processes is increasingly essential for organisations

- understand the tasks and challenges that it involves for HRD practitioners

- know how to find sources of information on new technology applied to training and learning.

THE TECHNOLOGY REVOLUTION AND E-LEARNING

Consider these four scenarios:

Scenario 1: The formation of AOL Time Warner
In January 2000 the world's biggest Internet service provider, America Online, merged with the old US information giant Warner Communications. All the superlatives applied. It was the world's largest corporate takeover, creating the world's largest on-line media company and its fourth-largest corporation.

Imagine this: AOL's 150 million customers were now potentially able to 'download any of the 5,700 films made by Warner Bros, listen to the latest track from the Red Hot Chilli Peppers, or watch the latest episode of *ER*, or flick through the celebrity gossip in *People* magazine' (Martinson, 2000). And Time Warner's customers? They could access 'the world's largest on-line and e-commerce platform' (*ibid*).

New AOL Time Warner was at a stroke poised to lead the transformation of 'economic growth, human understanding and creative expression, made possible by the digital revolution' (Gerald Levin, CEO of the new company, quoted in Murphy, 2000).

Scenario 2: Harnessing new technology to education
On 7 March 2000 the UK Prime Minister announced in a speech that he was committing the country to a goal of universal access to the Internet by 2005. 'It set a new agenda to take Britain ... into the information age.' By 2002 all schools in Britain were to be linked to the Internet (Michael Wills, Learning and Technology Minister, 2000).

Meanwhile, David Blunkett, Minister for Education and Employment, was announcing the arrival of Universitas 21, sponsored by the Department for Education and Employment, and linking Massachusetts Institute of Technology, Cambridge University, and the Institute of Enterprise. What would the link do? It would enable the institutions involved to:

> share resourcing, facilitate staff and student mobility and use new technology to spread excellence ... [By such means, Government intends to] harness globalisation as a force for progressive change. ... In a knowledge economy, expansion in high-quality higher education is critical to social justice.
>
> (Blunkett, 2000a)

Blunkett also announced that the Higher Education Funding Council was now calling for bids from consortia of universities and private companies to create 'e-universities' which, alongside learndirect (the University for Industry – see page 53), will ensure that the UK is 'at the cutting edge of global developments in virtual learning' (*ibid*).

Such alliances already exist. On the day of Blunkett's clarion-call for a new age of e-learning, the universities of Leeds, Sheffield, Southampton and York made public their plans to link up with the universities of California at San Diego, Pennsylvania State, Washington, and Wisconsin-Madison. This 'Worldwide Universities Network' will share research and teaching facilities, and use new technology to give students access to long-distance learning and teaching (Smithers, 2000).

Scenario 3: learndirect – e-learning for you and me
The UfI (which adopted 'learndirect' as its public name in November 1999 in order to boost its high-street image) offers on-line training packages, accessible to all, backed up by paper-based induction courses to help individuals to learn how to use the packages. The training is supported by on-line and face-to-face mentoring and group discussions over the Internet. The aim is that through learndirect anyone, anywhere, using a computer, will be able to identify courses to meet their interests, enrol, pay for courses, receive learning materials and support – all electronically. Delivery methods will include interactive digital TV, video, CD-ROM and Internet. You don't yet own a computer? Then go to one of the UfI's 250 learndirect centres around Britain and use one of theirs ...

Scenario 4: In the near future ...
You are watching a factual programme on the BBC. Your interest is aroused and you switch to interactive on-line packages that provide you with more information about the subject matter. You want to learn even more. You link into tailor-made, on-line short courses, their content built around research that was carried out to develop the programme that originally sparked off your interest. The course gains you accreditation from a British university (Ewington, 2000).

Or you are on another kind of learning journey. You are watching a programme on dinosaurs. You bookmark the parts that particularly intrigue you. Afterwards, you click on your bookmarks and gain access to more information:

> It might explain the scientific discoveries that allowed us to create the lives of dinosaurs.... If you then want to go over to your PC, you could build a dinosaur skeleton from its bones.
>
> (Head of Science at BBC, quoted in Ewington, 2000: 56–7)

Now consider this scenario:

Trainers and new technology

> We have made a real mess of technology-based training by allowing the technologist to define and develop the methodology for training, while trainers appear to have run away from it.
> (Ralph Houston, joint UK MD of training consultancy Fielden-Cegos, quoted by Rana, 1999f)

In 1999, research by the International Data Corporation predicted that technology-based training would increase by more than 50 per cent by 2002, and would become the largest delivery vehicle for corporate training (Rana, 1999g). It was also estimated that there were 1,600 'corporate universities' around the world, many perhaps merely 'the repackaging of existing training under a new label' (Carnall, 1999: 54) but some the generators of best practice 'in which companies are attempting to convert knowledge into profits, and to achieve genuine integration of learning with both corporate and business development' (*ibid*).

In the same year, an IPD report revealed that few trainers disputed the importance of information technology 'but many are reluctant to really get to grips with its potential' (Darling, Darling and Elliott, 1999: 28). While most shared the view that 'the new role for trainers may lie in organising different training solutions, and in facilitating or moderating rather than actually delivering face-to-face training', an emphasis on IT as a major influence on this role was 'expressed less strongly' (*ibid*).

In 2000 the (then) IPD's second annual survey revealed a sharp increase among companies in the use of new technology as a training tool. By now, more trainers acknowledged a need to acquire new training technology skills. However, it remains a common criticism that in the field of new technology, trainers are failing to take any lead and some do indeed appear to have 'run away'.

---

e-learning

What do you think 'e-learning' means, and why is it important for those with training and development roles to get to grips with its practical implications?

Feedback notes

E-learning means learning via technology. It is a global phenomenon, central to many industries, especially the financial services sector. The spread of e-learning is inevitable. No HRD practitioner can afford to ignore it. The following points were made by a world expert in the field (Masie, 1999):

• There is likely to be increasing alignment of e-learning and e-commerce: 'Information collected on the World-Wide Web about product knowledge, for example, can be accessed in the same way for someone else to learn from' (*ibid*: 32).

- Web technologies reduce decision-making time and time spent on communicating and implementing decisions. They are a vital business tool.

- 'Organisations train on-line for competitive advantage: to deliver knowledge to all of their employees between 1 and 10 per cent faster or better – or both' (ibid: 34). Especially for multinationals, speed is of the essence. Their competitive environment is fast-moving: new knowledge is needed to produce new developments, and that new knowledge must be generated by increasingly rapid learning of employees. Effective e-learning is fast learning.

- Likewise, new knowledge must brought into the organisation as soon as it is available; it must then be rapidly disseminated across the organisation to stimulate the creativity and innovation needed to produce new strategic assets for the organisation. New technology enables the rapid acquisition and sharing of new knowledge.

- Allied to the need for speedier learning and knowledge processes in organisations is the need for more efficient learning. E-learning can deliver exactly what the learner needs, at the time when he or she needs it, and in the form that he or she prefers.

- On-line training networks offer organisations an efficient way of gathering information about learners in order to produce skills profiles of individuals and jobs:

  > This information ... can be used to determine an organisation's knowledge bank or intellectual capital.... The world of learning will increasingly be influenced by the parallel universe of knowledge management.
  >
  > (ibid)

The last point is worth expanding on. The Internet and intranets can enable the tracking of learners and the use they make of training courses, capturing information about their prior knowledge and how they interact with on-line material (Hills, 2000). Websites 'can also combine learning material with competency profiles and personal learning plans', enabling information to be recorded for analysis and accreditation (ibid). Computer-based assessment (CBA) is another facility, allowing instant scoring and feedback of results to learners (ibid). Many are sceptical about the use of CBA, especially where the purpose is not to test learners on accuracy related to facts, or on choice of a 'right' response, but to assess their ability to think for themselves, to use not only their knowledge but also practical wisdom and experience to generate their own solutions to problems where there are no black and white answers. None the less, used in an appropriate context – for example, to test ongoing (formative) rather than final (summative) learning – there is no doubt about the aid that CBA can offer to learners and to those administering the learning process.

Warnings to employers and trainers of the dangers of failing to harness new technology to learning appear regularly. Rana (1999g) referred to a number of reports, developments and predictions all pointing to the same critical issue: 'Employers that fail to ensure their training providers are able to cope with rapid changes in delivery will find their competitiveness reduced.' KnowledgePool was launched in August 1999 by ICL in order to maintain its lead in the IT training sector. By amalgamating its six European training businesses, it established a new company that provides training services 'ranging from multisite programmes tailored for global companies to distance-learning for individuals via the Internet, intranet or CD-ROM' (*ibid*). By 2001 IBM expected to deliver half of its internal training on-line, not to completely replace traditional learning but to integrate it with new learning technology.

What all these scenarios demonstrate is that in the knowledge economy, rapid learning and the fast development of knowledge are essential and can be integrated ... but what *exactly* does that mean?

THE KNOWLEDGE ECONOMY

The knowledge economy is a way of describing a world in which economic growth is increasingly dependent on the rapid generation and application of knowledge – a world in which 'knowledge' has become the key to wealth. In this world, the 'knowledge worker' is a leading figure. What is a knowledge worker? Peter Drucker (1993) claims to be the originator of the term, and his views have been summarised thus:

> Wealth creation in contemporary society is increasingly dependent on the application of new knowledge to existing knowledge and, therefore, on the contribution of specialist 'knowledge workers'.... [These are] individuals who have high levels of education and specialist skills combined with the ability to apply these skills to identify and solve problems.
>
> (Scarbrough, Swan and Preston, 1999: 6)

The importance of knowledge workers has come about because of 'the emergence of a globalised, post-industrial economy in which knowledge displaces capital as the motor of competitive performance' (*ibid*: 7). The whole issue of knowledge-productive organisations – organisations whose unique base of tacit and explicit knowledge and its effective utilisation enables them to compete and advance successfully in their environments – will be treated in more detail in Part 5 of this book. What is more to the point here is the relationship between e-learning and today's increasingly knowledge-driven economy: the kind of economy dominated by conglomerates like AOL Time Warner.

A vital issue in the knowledge economy is how to 'manage' knowledge as well as knowledge workers. Knowledge management is a complex concept that has been defined as a way of describing:

> any process or practice of creating, acquiring, capturing, sharing and using knowledge, wherever it resides, to enhance learning and performance in organisations.
>
> (*ibid*: 1)

Knowledge management thus focuses on 'the ways in which firms facing highly turbulent environments can mobilise their knowledge base (or knowledge assets) in order to ensure continuous innovation' (*ibid*: 2).

In the knowledge economy, 'the future of e-learning will blur the distinctions between training programmes, knowledge databases, and performance support' (Masie, 1999: 34). Why is this? It is because, as technology-based learning becomes an integral part of training, the learning and knowledge processes will increasingly merge, just as in Scenario 4 at the start of this chapter. Reflect on the person who started by watching a television programme and ended by building a dinosaur ... In their professional practice, trainers and other facilitators of learning cannot ignore the fact that more and more individuals will wish and be able to learn by the easily accessible and immediate routes and methods that e-learning offers. The many who will be using those routes in their leisure time will come to expect similar approaches and facilities at their place of work.

Let us consider this more closely, though. It is not simply a matter of people's becoming more familiar with e-learning, and more able to learn for themselves. People now increasingly work in automated workplaces. They carry out tasks that are facilitated by electronic means. These workplaces, dominated by computer-based information technology, can provide an environment for thinking and problem-solving. The worker's role can then become transformed, so that it is

> not only to push buttons to control processes, but also to use the information generated by the technology to 'push the business' – to redefine process variables, to improve quality, and to reduce costs.
>
> (Schuck, 1996: 199)

In such an environment there is the potential for all employees to become knowledge workers, since their intelligence can be developed to exceed the intelligence of the software with which they interact. The interaction then becomes not only one whereby employees learn. It becomes one that produces new knowledge – the knowledge of the employee.

When new technology is applied to training, there should therefore no longer be two distinct roles – one of 'trainer', one of 'student' – which are never interchanged (Schuck, 1996: 200). Learning can and should be a 'collective activity in which the focus is on asking questions and engaging in dialogue by all who are involved in that activity' (*ibid*). This clarifies the real distinction between traditional training methods and technology-based learning. Traditional training methods teach people *what* to think rather than *how* to think. They stimulate the learning process, but e-learning not only can do that: it can also fuel the development of knowledge. In the act of e-learning, there is the potential for the learner to generate and apply new knowledge.

This returns us to the issue of the workplace environment. It must be conducive to the installation of e-learning systems: there must be the capital expenditure, the human expertise and the operational infrastructure to support it. But, just as important, the culture in the workplace must be such as to facilitate all e-learning's potential outcomes. If the workplace is of the traditional kind, where the role of some is to think, to make decisions and to pass on instructions, and the role of others is to perform the tasks that those instructions involve, then the true potential of e-learning cannot be realised. It is pointless for an individual to participate in a learning process through which they develop not just operational competence but also 'the intellective skill required for original, independent problem-solving' (Schuck, 1996: 205), only to return to a workplace where that skill cannot be used, and where their potential role as knowledge worker is not recognised. In such a workplace, new technology can be harnessed to training, but its use, essentially, will be restricted to speeding up traditional learning and instructional methods, making them more accurate, quicker and more accessible. Its most powerful potential will not be utilised.

As Schuck observes, technology-based learning has the power to develop smart people, once its 'informating quality' is recognised.

> In the informated environment, on-line, interactive learning is necessary if people are to create new meanings out of the information generated by computer technology.

(ibid: 212)

Here is a case-study showing how the power of e-learning has been harnessed across an educational institution.

Case-study: Thames Valley University: the 'whole organisation' approach to learning technology

Cost-cutting and changing attitudes and expectations in students, together with rapid technological advance, have all had an explosive effect on most educational institutions. The development of multimedia products is becoming widespread, and the implications of the global Internet network in particular cannot sensibly be ignored. As Lymer pointed out, the World-Wide Web is 'not just a tool to provide access to existing data in more flexible, user-friendly, timely ways' but is changing the way new information is generated by offering users 'a new medium through which to exchange ideas, formulate proposals and generate solutions in ways not previously possible' (Lymer, 1996: 9–10).

Thames Valley University (TVU), chosen in 1997 by the (then) Institute of Personnel and Development as a key provider of learning materials for its professional qualification flexible learning scheme, is in the forefront of innovation both in educational and in learning technology. TVU has not just expanded its open learning operations, using the term to mean 'any scheme of education or training that seeks systematically to remove barriers to learning whether [of] time, place or space' (Nicholls, 1997). It has transformed itself into a 'flexible learning environment' (Nicholls, 1997) which enables its 27,000 students – 65 per cent of whom are part-time and therefore not eligible for state subsidies – to obtain an affordable, fully accessible and self-paced education.

Transformation is the appropriate term. The whole university has been radically reorganised, with 40 per cent of its campuses turned into technologically sophisticated learning resource centres. At the Ealing centre, for example, each of its 12 floors houses books, videos and CD-ROMs relating to a different subject group, and each contains study and seminar areas, and teaching and learning support facilities, including a shop where computers can be purchased or hired.

The most significant change at TVU has been its 'strategic approach to printed resources', comprising free course folders and books for all students, made possible by economies of scale and by a reduction of course modules from eight to six. 'Everything at TVU is a heavily managed process designed to give the student as much support as possible while encouraging self-directed learning' (Nicholls, 1997a).

A case such as that at TVU demonstrates how new technology applied to learning can flourish, given the right conditions. It demonstrates the added value to be achieved when a creative approach to learning is allied to the vision and strategy of the organisation: that which benefits the learners can also become a unique source of competitive capability for the business.

Source: Nicholls, 1997, 1997a

THE TASK OF HRD PRACTITIONERS

Tasks and concerns of the practitioners

Of course, not all organisations have automated workplaces. But in those that do not, there is still an increasing drive to harness new technology to the learning process. Much of the pressure to use IT and on-line learning products comes from a desire and a need to reduce the amount of time learners spend away from the workplace. This is inevitable when organisations, and therefore their employees, need to be able to change faster if they are to survive and make progress in their business environment.

So one way and another – whether to help produce new knowledge workers, or to continue to perform their more familiar role of developing the competence of individuals and teams – trainers have no choice. They must begin to integrate on-line learning into their curriculum. They cannot remain solitary inhabitants of an old island that is now being submerged under the waves of technological advance. They need 'to understand the strengths and weaknesses of new technologies and be able to identify when and where they can offer cost-effective solutions' (Cannell, 1999).

Concerns of practitioners

Imagine that you are a trainer in an organisation where little use has so far been made of new technology in training courses or other planned learning initiatives. Management is urging you to jump onto the technological bandwagon. You have done quite a lot of thinking and research on the applications of new technology to learning, but you still have some concerns. What might these be?

Feedback notes

You are right to express a need for caution before moving into what can be a very expensive investment. Your concerns probably include the following:

- On-line training must be focused on the learner, or it risks failure. On-line packages and support systems will not work unless they are carefully tailored to the organisation's specific needs, to the individuals' learning styles, capabilities and expectations, and to the workplace environment. This is what Ralph Houston meant when he referred to the danger of leaving it to the technologist to define and develop the methodology of training (page 205). Multimedia education also works 'only if it mimics the human learning process. It must induce failure and allow explanation' (Schank, 1999: 57). So a learning package or process, delivered electronically, must be capable of 'allowing many choices and stimulating realistic responses to all of these' (*ibid*).

- It is essential to ensure that e-learning material is of high quality, and that the infrastructure to support new technology-based learning is effective and efficient.

- There must also be a way 'of motivating and rewarding the learner through human contact' – unless well organised, e-learning can be an isolating process (Hills, 2000).

- New technology is expensive in terms of capital investment, specialist expertise needed, and the costs to the organisation if its introduction does not bring the benefits expected. There are certain situations in which it is unlikely to be as effective as more traditional methods. These include:

  - when other, cheaper and equally effective modes are available

  - when learners dislike computer-based training

  - where lead-time is short and software has to be custom-made yet may only be used infrequently by learners

  - where senior decision-makers and line managers are not committed to its use

  - where trainers fear its introduction and do not have the skills that it requires

  - where support of IT professionals is not available and there is no appropriate infrastructure for the technology (Cannell, 1998: 2,3,6,7)

  - where there is evidence to show that the cost of installing and training for technology-based training and learning is unlikely to be offset by the outcomes that it will produce for the business.

The IPD produced an excellent short guide for those interested or involved in new technology applied to learning (Cannell, 1998). In it, the point is made that trainers 'need to be able to work with IT specialists to develop solutions that make the best use of available technology and which can be married to more traditional learning approaches' (*ibid*: 1). It is that integrative approach that is so important in any technology-based approach to learning – the avoidance of exclusive use of either traditional or the IT-based modes and methods, but rather the bringing together of the two in imaginative, stimulating and cost-effective ways. The real issue for trainers and developers is not (as they often think it is) how far new technology is more, or less, effective than traditional approaches. It is motivation:

> While technology can create or remove barriers to learning, it cannot by itself create the motivation to learn. So there is a need to plan learning and development in an integrated way.
>
> (Carnall, 1999: 54)

Harnessing new technology to learning: some practicalities

Benefiting from technology-based learning

From your reading thus far, and from your own reflections and research, in what learning situations do you think it most likely that technology-based learning will bring returns over and above its costs for an organisation?

Feedback notes

Cannell (1998) suggests the following:

- situations in which the learning content will not change much through time

- courses which are significantly knowledge-based

- where training need is long-term and will repeat itself regularly through time

- where the learners are geographically scattered – ie over many sites, often up and down the country or across the world

- unusual, expensive or dangerous situations where simulation is vital in order to learn in a safe environment how to deal with the problems involved. For example, the Health and Safety Commission's report on the Southall train crash of 1987 made clear the need for simulated training to improve drivers' reactions and performance in confused signalling conditions and when confronting potential crash situations.

E-learning depends for its success on those factors that distinguish any effective learning situation (Schank, 1999: 57):

- having a clear goal

- helping learners to play a role in realistic situations during which they can accomplish the goal

- providing access to the knowledge needed to achieve the goal

• providing instruction from experts when needed.

It also depends on the extent to which individuals' needs are taken into account when implementing new ways of learning. As already noted, e-learning can be a lonely process, although it does not have to be. 'People tend to see using technology for training as a solitary experience which takes place away from the real job' (Hills and Francis, 1999: 48). Not only do they often dislike that image, but it also makes them feel that e-learning does not relate sufficiently to what goes on in the workplace. Human interaction is a source of great satisfaction in the workplace. People also need to believe in the relevance of what they learn. So e-learning must be organised in ways that take account of those needs.

The responsibilities of those who have to harness new technology to learning should now be clear. They must study best practice, calculate costs, weigh them against the anticipated benefits, and pay particular attention then to the following:

• the setting of clear, relevant training and learning objectives

• the identification of typical learners and the careful consideration of how best and most feasibly to meet their needs and take account of their learning styles, skills and preferences

• ensuring that any technology-based training packages or learning processes are well tailored to specific needs

• the understanding of new learning models, and the acquisition of the skills to use them by the trainers/learning facilitators as well as by the learners

• the piloting of any new e-learning processes and on-line training packages and services before making a final decision to invest in them on a bigger scale.

In a study of Lloyds TSB's 450 learning centres across the UK, Hills and Francis found some regions to be significantly better than others in achieving enthusiasm among employees for computer-based training. The main reasons for this emerged as the role of local training administrators and the involvement of managers, both as users themselves and as developers of people. They were supportive, proactive and imaginative in their approach to learners and the learning experience (Hills and Francis, 1999).

Creating awareness and stimulating interest

Motivating employees

'Ultimately, every conscientious, ambitious employee should want to get onto a computer-based technology course' (Masie, 1999: 35). Why? And as a training manager, what would you do to stimulate an enthusiasm for e-learning among employees in your organisation?

Feedback notes

You will have given many responses to this question. No doubt you will have stressed the need to publicise the successes of e-learning in organisations similar to your own, to raise awareness by involving people across the workforce in best practice and perhaps benchmarking processes, and to run pilots before introducing CBT in training and learning events. Here are some other points:

- The perceived value should be promoted in terms of the investment it has taken to produce the course, and so the high value that the organisation is placing on learners' developing their skills (Masie, 1999: 35).

- There should be an explanation of the opportunities given by electronically based courses to communicate with others, creating a network of learners (*ibid*).

- There must be relevant evaluation of initiatives, to discover not so much 'Did the learners achieve their learning objectives?' but rather 'Did the business achieve the change it wanted?' (*ibid*: 36).

- Remember that 'learning only becomes truly effective in a social environment' (Hills and Francis, 1999: 49). CBT can bring people together, if colleagues are encouraged and helped to coach each other and work together to improve performance. HR professionals can stimulate this activity, and people's interest and confidence will be further increased when they know that senior managers are using computers for their own learning (*ibid*).

GETTING STARTED: INFORMATION AND SERVICES

There are many sources of information to help those with HRD responsibilities make decisions about how to harness and use new technology in the most appropriate and cost-efficient ways. Here are some of the most widely used. Each will take you into further information sources.

Sources of immediate knowledge for those seeking self-development

- BBC Online, Europe's most popular website: www.bbc.co.uk/education/home

- Open University: www/open.ac.uk

- University for Industry: www.ufiltd.co.uk

Information sources for trainers/learning facilitators

- Technologies for Training, a DfEE-backed national consortium: www.tft.co.uk. It helps on all facets of IT-based training, and sends out e-mails on new developments. It plans to link into more than 350 information points and demonstration centres across the country.

- A classroom of the future website has been set up on the National Grid for Learning: www.futureclass.ngfl.gov.uk

Sources of services (Masie, 1999)

- Learning Service Providers (LSPs) offer learning delivery systems customised to an organisation's needs. They will distribute the systems to organisations' staff and will monitor their use. Training can thus become a variable expense for the organisation, not a capital expense tied to a single system. This can therefore break the stranglehold of the IT department over on-line learning plans of trainers, reducing the organisation's requirements for IT resource.

• Publicly accessible systems such as learndirect. Some offer access to learning materials, some to catalogues of learning materials that can be searched, purchased and downloaded by the user.

Now, see how familiar you are with the following. If you do not know all the answers, you will need to do some research – electronically or by traditional methods!

What are the following, and what might be their uses for training and other learning processes?

Flat-screen monitors	Business television
Electronic whiteboards	Computer-assisted assessment
Wireless networks	Computer-based training
Plasma displays	Computer-mediated communication
Video conferencing	Virtual reality
Broadband connections	Computer conferencing
Network computers	Computer-mediated learning
Interactive keypads	Extranet
Portable computing	Interactive video
WAP-enabled mobile phones	Integrated Services Digital Network
(*Answers*: Cole, 2000: 10, 11)	(*Answers*: Cannell, 1998: vi–x)

To conclude, here is a case-study that brings together a number of themes explored in this chapter.

Case-study: Training in the call-centre industry

There are an estimated 203,000 call-centre employees around Britain. The figure is likely to rise to 270,000 by 2003, thereby exceeding the combined workforce of coal mining, steel and vehicle production. Almost two-fifths of these employees work at the heart of the knowledge economy, in financial services and insurance (Brown, 2000). They provide the human infrastructure for the knowledge workers who dominate those industries. Their jobs are pressured, fast-moving and rapidly changing. They may spend 80 per cent of their time on the phone and 'sales teams have systems which can start dialling the next number when a call is nearly over' (Brown, 2000). There are big challenges for those in charge of planning and delivering training in the call-centre industry, as a glance at the nature of that industry makes clear.

As the call-centre industry grows it is embracing Internet technology (Warman, 2000). Call-centres link customers to information sources direct, whether by telephone (the most familiar aspect to the public), by postal communication, by e-mail or by other web-related communications. It is the latter mode that is increasing most rapidly.

Many companies are establishing websites without understanding the implications. Warman (2000) referred to a survey of call-centres carried out for Merchants Limited, one of Europe's largest call-centre and customer management organisations. It surveyed 269 companies in the UK and overseas. Growth in call-centre companies' setting up a website was about 15 per cent a year, and by 2000 had covered about 90 per cent of large companies and 75 per cent of small. For many, the learning curve was steep. As soon as a company goes live as a 24-hour operation, e-mails are immediately generated. In the survey, e-mail was used by 61 per cent for inbound communications, and by 44 per cent for outbound, but many companies were not ready to deal with this escalation from 29 per cent and 19 per cent respectively in 1999. This kind of problem becomes acute when, as is often the case, 'technical staff add "call me" buttons to websites without talking to the operatives first' (chairman of the Call-Centre Management Association, quoted in Warman, 2000).

Call-centres have been widely criticised for employing 'armies of sweating tele-workers' (Brown, 2000), and although this description cannot be applied to all, it is the case that many are inadequately trained and poorly prepared to handle their stressful jobs. In the worst cases, new workers are thrown in with just a few days' training. Unsurprisingly, some companies lose a third of their employees every year. In training-aware companies, however, training is well-designed, with the use of multimedia software and the capacity for learners to practise at their own pace. Soon, it is predicted, call-centres will become a focal point for customer interaction – with interactive TV – and that has big training implications.

> In training staff the focus will move from the transaction to the agent as an adviser to the customer. To that end, work is under way to design NVQ programmes for the call-centre industry.
>
> (Warman, 2000)

CONCLUSION

Having read this chapter and completed its reviews and self-checks, you should now:

- understand what is meant by 'e-learning' and its importance in the knowledge economy

- be able to explain why harnessing new technology to the learning and knowledge processes is increasingly essential for organisations

- understand the tasks and challenges that it involves for HRD practitioners

- know how to find sources of information on new technology applied to training and learning.

To test yourself against these objectives, what five-minute answers would you give to the following questions? (Dates in brackets refer to the IPD qualifying examination paper in which a question appeared.)

If an organisation decides to introduce 'open learning' for its sales force, what might this involve in terms of design and delivery of training? (Specimen paper, 1996)

Select **two** of the following modes or methods of learning. For each, identify a type of learner **or** a type of learning situation for which it would be particularly well suited, and explain why you think it would be well suited.

- interactive training via tele-conferencing

- an organisation's learning resource centre with out-of-hours access

- CD-ROM training packages

- virtual reality training methods. (May 1999)

How might technology-based learning be used in a small firm, and how might funding be obtained to support its introduction?

USEFUL READING

CANNELL M. (1998) *The IPD Guide on Training Technology*. London, Institute of Personnel and Development.

CARNALL C. (1999) 'Positive e-valuation'. *People Management*. Vol. 5, 17. pp54–7. (Examples of how to integrate IT into corporate development programmes.)

CHARTERED INSTITUTE OF PERSONNEL AND DEVELOPMENT *Training and Development in Britain: Annual survey reports*. Available by sending an A4 SAE to Mike Cannell, Training and Development Policy Adviser, CIPD, CIPD House, Camp Road, London, SW19 4UX.

HUNT M. *and* CLARKE A. (1997) *A Guide to the Cost-Effectiveness of Technology-Based Training*. Coventry, National Council for Educational Technology and Department for Education and Employment.

MEISTER J. (1998) *Corporate Universities*. London, McGraw-Hill.

TUCKER B. (ed.) (1997) *Handbook of Technology-Based Training*. Aldershot, Gower.

WALTON J. (1999b) 'Working in the virtual organisation', in J. Walton, *Strategic Human Resource Development*. Harlow, Financial Times and Prentice Hall. pp.536–57.

In addition to the information sources referred to throughout this chapter, local public libraries, universities and other learning centres, journals and the press all offer information and advice on new technology and its educational, training and learning applications.

To give only a few examples: Cambridge University has a virtual classroom open to all (www.english.cam.ac.uk/vclass/virtclas.htm). www.uhi.ac.uk is a pioneering university for northwest Scotland. Coventry University has 2,600 course modules on-line for distance-learning. *The Sunday Times* publishes an insert in its weekly edition of *Culture* called 'Doors', keeping readers up to date with developments in new technology. The Saturday *Telegraph*, the *Guardian Education* and the *Independent* all provide similar regular features and inserts.

13 Training and development in the smaller organisation

LEARNING OBJECTIVES

After reading this chapter you will:

- be familiar with the context in which human resource management (HRM), training and development are undertaken in the smaller organisation

- understand the main issues related to the practice and provision of training and development in the smaller organisation

- be able to identify an appropriate approach to training and development for a smaller organisation, and know how to fit training and development initiatives to the small firm situation.

SMALLER ENTERPRISES

Small to medium-sized enterprises (SMEs) are those independent organisations that employ a workforce of up to around 500 people. Some argue that there is a case for also including in this category divisions and establishments of large groups that employ no more than 500 people, are in most respects autonomous, and operate in an insecure environment. SME definitions vary, but all involve dimensions of workforce size, ownership and annual turnover. The Department of Trade and Industry uses the following classification system:

- *micro*: up to nine people

- *small*: 10 to 99 people

- *medium*: 100 to 499 people.

Annual turnover can range from £500,000 for the smaller firms to around £33 million for medium-sized enterprises.

To impart a perspective on the scale of small-firm employment and its impact on the economy, Becket (1996) – generalising from a wide range of research findings – observed that

- in 1993 there were 3.6 million active SMEs in the UK, of which 2.6 million were sole traders (including those self-employed) or partnerships without employees

- 96 per cent of all companies in Britain employ fewer than 20 people, and that 91 per cent have fewer than 10

- around one-third of all jobs are in firms with fewer than 20 employees, and half of all jobs are in firms with fewer than 100

- 3,000 of the UK's largest businesses account for 37 per cent of jobs and 43 per cent of total turnover, whereas 80 per cent of VAT revenue is collected from 1 per cent of businesses

- small companies account for 23 per cent of gross domestic product (GDP), and in 1995 SMEs grew by 9 per cent, compared with 2 per cent for all GDP.

The nature and extent of SMEs' contribution to the economy has been much debated. Britain had a far greater increase in self-employment in the 1980s than other developed countries, and created more new businesses than most of its international competitors, yet by the 1990s there was little evidence that there had been any impact on total employment (Batchelor, 1992).

Whatever the arguments, the established smaller firm clearly has a role to play in promoting economic growth, in widening society's entrepreneurial base and exploiting new market opportunities, and, in recession, in absorbing capable unemployed people – especially executives – who have suffered from the downsizing and de-layering of larger organisations.

MANAGING AND DEVELOPING PEOPLE IN THE SMALLER ORGANISATION

Unique context

Most of the literature concerning HRM in the UK derives from its observation in larger organisations, but there is no evidence that the conclusions reached in that context apply to managing people in smaller organisations (see Ritchie, 1993). Managerial issues, problems and feasible solutions in SMEs tend to be very different from those facing large firms. Keasey and Watson (1993: 195–200) explained some of the reasons:

- Costs – not least the cost of time spent dealing with paperwork – are a major preoccupation. Relatively high transaction costs typify the smaller firm, which has to deal with a complex set of regulatory requirements and negotiation, financing, monitory and bonding activities.

- Major uncertainties surround SMEs' continued viability and survival:

  - They have a limited customer and product base and are vulnerable in the market, especially when they operate in areas in which competition is fierce or are struggling for a new market where there are many obstacles to entry.

  - Capabilities of owner–managers vary widely and directly affect the firm's chances of survival. Some will have little knowledge of basic management practice. Many see no need to acquire any, priding themselves on 'gut feel' for the business they are in. (The term 'owner–manager' is used in this chapter as shorthand for those who run small firms as a single owner, a partnership, a franchisee, or similar.)

- Opportunities for growth may be passed over, the owner–manager often fearing that they will threaten his or her desire for independence and for doing a good job. Many small firm owner–managers do not have substantial growth as their goal: survival and stability constitute the focus of their financial strategy, and loss of control is seen as the greatest threat posed by growth.
- Face-to-face conflict is endemic in smaller firms because the owner–manager is so intimately involved in managing employee relations and carries a high burden of financial risk.

These factors, in their complex interaction, exert unique pressures on areas of HRM such as recruitment, rewards, training and employee relations. They differentially affect the way each SME is structured, its decision-making processes, how much the owner–manager is paid and the extent of profit retention.

Management in the smaller organisation

Consider any smaller organisation with which you are familiar – perhaps a business or a charitable undertaking, a professional partnership or a franchise. Analyse the organisation with reference to the factors just listed, and comment on the ways in which they appear to influence management style and systems in the organisation, and the kind of problems it typically experiences.

Employment relationships

Employment relationships in the smaller firm are therefore not simple. Not all small-firm employees share the aspirations and outlook of the owner, so that the concept of employee protection through collective organisation can be highly relevant in some cases. Conditions in SMEs can be harsh and exploitative, far from the 'small is beautiful' image (Ritchie, 1993). None the less, the exercise of managerial control tends to be easier in the smaller than in the larger organisation, even if it is not necessarily more effective. Marlow and Patton identified common characteristics of small owner–manager firms that are relevant here (1992: 8, 9):

- SMEs are less likely to have a union presence, and owner–managers are unlikely to consider trade union issues relevant to their organisation. This gives the owner considerable power over the contractual relationship, work conditions and the management of performance.

- In the formative years especially, management style and tactics will exercise a dominating influence on the culture of the firm. Every employee will be directly exposed to the owner's managerial style and will know it well.

- Whatever their conditions of employment and work, employees will tend to identify strongly with the owner's strategies and business goals because their jobs and security are so directly tied up in them. Goal conflict, and the need for bargaining to resolve it, however, is likely to develop once ownership spreads to more than one or two individuals, and once salaried managers are introduced.

• Recruitment and selection techniques will be biased towards identifying individuals who 'fit' the culture rather than those who possess formal professional managerial qualifications.

• SMEs are flexible and small enough to change their management practices and training initiatives as the organisation fluctuates in size. The necessity for and results of such change can also become quickly apparent.

In summary, management and development in the smaller as compared with the larger organisation operate in a context of more flexible labour, more individualised employment relationships, a clearer and shared perception of the primary goal, and a greater awareness of the need for change.

HRM as a planned activity in SMEs

There are two ways of viewing HRM in smaller organisations. One is to see its practice as a conscious attempt to manage people in ways that will help the firm to achieve competitive edge. The other is to see it as little more random activity, arising as the unplanned consequence both of lack of management skill to introduce formal HR systems and emerging from the particular pattern of management–labour relations in the smaller firm (Marlow and Patton, 1992: 9).

There is little evidence of a planned or strategic approach to HRM in SMEs in the UK. This is despite the fact that HRM practice and philosophy directly affect the predominantly informal and continuous processes of strategy-making and implementation in smaller organisations (Pettigrew, Arthur and Hendry, 1990). In 1990 Price Waterhouse looked at SMEs throughout Europe and concluded that although management and production skill shortages are critical barriers to growth, British SMEs are less likely to have employment management strategies or training schemes to overcome these barriers. It seems that HRM in smaller UK organisations is not widely held to 'matter' in any formal, strategic sense, even though the effective management and development of people is such a key determinant of their survival.

This apparent failure to take HRM seriously in smaller businesses is not, on reflection, surprising. Managers will always focus their attention on those factors that they see as most likely to bring success, and only rarely do management skills and the administration of the employment relationship come under scrutiny here. Financial factors are the most frequently quoted in studies of SME failure, and the widest-used measures of success relate to increased sales, employment growth and crude profit levels (Kelmar, 1990). HRM factors receive little attention, despite their potential value: 'Effective and efficient use of human resources can make the relatively small differences which allow some firms to make step function increases in performance while others struggle to make marginal gains' (Marlow and Patton, 1992: 4).

Many owner–managers in the UK will also have had little if any formalised management/HR education or training, and so are often unaware of HRM's true meaning or possible relevance for their organisations. In a study of how best to implement Investors in People (IIP) programmes in smaller organisations, Harrison and Lord (1992: 6) observed that owner–managers 'are unlikely to be able to relate their fragmented and unfocused experience of managing people to the formal systems and procedures' involved in such programmes. Also, they are preoccupied in the early growth years of the business and in transition and terminal stages with coping with urgent and demanding financial and market pressures, and so:

> are unlikely to have the time, knowledge or experience to make appropriate policies [or] to make the shift from task to people orientation. They have a strong need to appreciate the relevance of any initiative that may eat into their business time.

Subsequently efforts have been made by Training and Enterprise Councils/Local Enterprise Councils to reduce IIP's bureaucratic aspects and make the process more adaptive to the needs and culture of smaller organisations.

Understanding employee resourcing and development in SMEs

Hendry *et al* (1991) showed that to understand a smaller firm's employee resourcing practices it is necessary to:

• understand the history of the firm

• examine its survival and growth strategies

• identify its strategies to obtain skills, and the factors influencing those strategies

• examine its approach to training and development.

***

HR consultancy for the smaller organisation

You are a consultant advising a small enterprise on its business strategy (choose any kind of small organisation you wish for this exercise, but preferably one with which you are familiar since this will make the task more convincing). In discussion with the owner–manager you have quickly reached the point where you realise that you must convince him or her of the need for a more effective use of the enterprise's people. Your reasons are to do with business growth, complexity and change, and with the associated need to move into longer-term planning in order to advance in a competitive market. What should you do, and how should you do it, to help the owner–manager understand the issues and appreciate the need to develop some kind of planned approach towards the recruitment, retention and development of the kind of people the business now needs?

***

Feedback notes
• Your aim is to raise the awareness of the small-firm owner–manager of the cost, value and potential of the human resource employed in

the business. To do this you can use a series of apparently simple but revealing questions that focus consistently on cost and pay-back.

• Avoid any appearance of lecturing the owner–manager on 'the importance of personnel–HR management'. Speaking the language of the business is essential, but the real challenge will lie in applying it in a way that ensures that key HR issues emerge naturally as the dialogue unfolds. I once had to involve a small group of owner–managers on a business growth course in a discussion of this kind. Each of them came from an entirely different kind of business, and each had a quite different personal profile, history and approach to the management of his or her organisation. Their scepticism about 'HRM' was evident. At first they gave fairly dismissive responses to questions. As I probed more deeply, however, they had to think things through more carefully. Gradually they became more involved and before long were engaged in heated discussion. Later, all volunteered that they had not thought in this way about their people before – and that they now realised that there were some pressing issues that they needed to take seriously. The kinds of questions they were asked were straightforward. They included:

  • What is the current turnover of the business, and how far has it increased or declined since last year? What is the target for next year?

  • What are the main areas of cost – for example, what is your total salaries and wages bill?

  • How much of your own time do you spend directly on people matters? What is that in terms of a proportion of your salary?

  • What return do you get on your employee investment? Cost per unit of labour? Productivity per unit of labour? Do you know? If not, why not?

  • If the business had to be closed down tomorrow, could you afford to do that – or would the cost of disengaging the workforce make that impossible? Could you 'sell' your workforce – would anyone else want to buy it?

  • What kind of people do you have working for the business? Why? How did they come to be there? Should they be there?

  • What kind of culture and structure does the firm have? Does it encourage and facilitate people's commitment and good performance? How do you know?

  • What is the age, sex and occupational structure of the workforce? Do you know? Is there anything to be concerned about here?

  • How are people 'inducted' into the organisation? Does the process familiarise them with the culture of the organisation as well as with their job?

  • What do you do about training people, giving them feedback on performance and helping them to be as productive as possible? Are the processes effective? What is their cost-benefit?

- What do you do to retain people? Pay? Education and career development? Job design and organisation of work? Culture of the business? Anything planned at all? Do you keep the people you want, and for positive reasons?

- Have you got the people you need for the future? How do you know?

- What about management style, both of individuals and teams? Any concerns here? Any controls?

- What about discipline and grievances? Any consistent procedures? Are they fair and open? Do they work?

- What about communications? Do people get the information they need to do their work and to remain committed to the firm? Do they get it in a timely and clear fashion? Do they understand and accept it?

TRAINING IN THE SMALLER ORGANISATION

Training practice

Training should be a key issue for any smaller firm once it has survived the initial start-up period. Four of the factors that, interacting together, form the most powerful context for training in the SME are its size, its sector, the stage reached in its life cycle and its skill supply strategy (Hendry *et al*, 1991).

Size

Increasing size usually brings a more complex occupational structure into the firm, and it is that structure that has a direct impact on training needs and practice. Larger firms tend to employ staff in all recognised skill categories, indicating that they have a high proportion of clearly defined jobs, whereas about 70 per cent of micro firms do not employ any workers in most recognised skill categories (Cambridge University Small Business Research Centre, 1992: 53). Such firms are also less likely to need or to undertake formal training, and tend to have a low regard for the standards and quality of external training – often through ignorance. Larger firms tend to do more internal training because they see it as flexible and relevant to their needs. They also tend to recruit significantly from national labour markets, whereas smaller firms are more dependent on their local market (Pettigrew, Arthur and Hendry, 1990: 16).

Sector

Recruitment and training needs differ significantly across sectors. For example, most SMEs (except micro firms) in manufacturing and service sectors have problems in recruiting the skills mix needed to maximise their competitive potential, even at times of high unemployment. Such needs become complex for SMEs at times of technological change and when they try to survive in increasingly segmented markets (Cambridge University Small Business Research Centre, 1992: 53). There is thus an emphasis on internal training in firms in these sectors. Even here, however, easy conclusions cannot be drawn – service firms, for example, tend to recruit more trained staff (*ibid*: 54).

Looking at subsectorial differences, it is skills in the technological and science areas that have grown most, especially in manufacturing firms. This directly affects the recruitment and training strategies of such firms, although much depends on the availability of skills within and outside the individual firm.

The stage reached in the firm's life cycle

HR needs in most SMEs change as the firm itself moves from start-up, through growth, to either a period of stability or further growth, or to failure and close-down.

In start-up ventures the need is often – although not always – to have labour flexibility and loosely defined tasks. Recruitment takes place in that context, and training will tend to be informal and on-the-job, restricted to teaching or showing people how to reach required performance levels (Hendry *et al*, 1991: 84). During the period of initial growth, as in the start-up period, other pressures make it inevitable that any except the most obviously necessary training will tend to receive little attention. In these two periods the factors most likely to influence the ways in which people are attracted, retained, rewarded or disengaged are the values and style of the entrepreneur and an interacting range of product market structure and industry structure factors. In so far as HRM processes are recognised as being important, most attention will be paid to recruitment, pay and termination.

As the firm becomes more mature, often undergoing change of ownership, organisational structure and managerial style, the need to develop people for the future is likely to become more apparent. At that point the opportunity emerges for training and development to make a strategic contribution to the business. However, there is a problem here. At the time, it may be impossible to establish what stage of development a firm is entering or leaving – such stages are easier to perceive in retrospect. Also, progress through stages of the life cycle is by no means necessarily a linear process. A deliberate choice may be taken not to grow the firm beyond a certain size or to 'go for growth'. An owner–manager may decide to close the firm down prematurely, or for no apparent reason let it be acquired at some stage. A poll commissioned in 1996 for *The Sunday Times* (Oldfield, 1996) indicated that as many as a quarter of owner–managers would like to sell their business. Most of the firms were not in financial difficulty. Quite simply, and for various personal reasons, most owner–managers wanted to 'retire'. In the smaller firm the quirks of human behaviour are more visible than in the larger, and often have a more direct and immediate impact on the management and development of people.

Skill supply strategy

All firms have some kind of skill supply strategy, no matter how intuitive or disorganised. Keasey and Watson (1993: 211) observed that although in the early days the entrepreneur is likely to favour the internal market, new managerial skills and new levels of sophistication in existing skills are needed as growth occurs. They found that in responding to such pressures there appear to be three types of skill supply strategy:

- The owner may himself or herself develop new skills or implement new procedures.

- There may be internal promotion and development.

- New people may be recruited from outside.

Provision of training

The way in which training is organised and provided in the smaller organisation is, again, to do with a number of interacting factors such as:

- the value attached to training

- the extent and type of training done

- the pace of change affecting skills within the organisation

- the extent to which an enterprise has a significant proportion of key and/or genuinely unique jobs, leading to an emphasis on firm-specific skills

- an emphasis on personal qualities and recruitment from unconventional sources

- the cost of training compared to its likely immediate benefits, and the organisation's relationship with external providers.

It is important to clarify what is meant by 'training provision' in the smaller enterprise. It means that training activity is actually taking place, no matter how or by whom it is being provided. Abbott (1994) found in his research into 350 owner-managed firms employing a maximum of 25 people that a number of constraining factors, including lack of financial resources and time, made the provision of training extremely difficult. This did not, however, necessarily mean that training was either absent or low. He found that in some sectors where there appeared at first sight to be uniformly low levels of training, firms tended to make less use of public provision and rely more on informal training. Some owners, however, did not think that such a way of acquiring or developing skills was 'training' and so did not enter it as such in their official returns on training provision.

In assessing the provision of training in smaller organisations, some commentators tend to regard 'high' (planned, strategic) training as superior to 'low' (informal, fragmented) training. This is misleading. It is not that 'high' is better than 'low', but that these two forms of training are different. The critical issue is whether the training carried out, be it high or low, will most effectively raise the skill base of the labour force.

There is a good deal of informal training in SMEs, and it makes a vital contribution to the business (Jones and Goss, 1991: 25). The sector of the firm is important here: in a sector such as the free house, restaurant and wine bar informal training is widely prevalent for various obvious reasons to do with the nature of the job, the small workforces and the wide geographical dispersion of the sites. Such training can be extremely effective and efficient.

There is another aspect of informal training. It is to do with the nature of the critical skills needed in smaller businesses and how they are acquired. 'Tacit' skills are crucial in small firms (Manwaring and Wood, 1985: 172–3). These are skills that are not taught or acquired by formal processes. They are largely instinctive, part of the individual's repertoire of natural talent or skills mastered so long ago that they have now become habitual and are practised without the need to think about them. They are typified in the way in which someone develops their unique 'knack' of tackling a job and always does it to a high standard of performance and quality. The worker may not be able to explain quite what the key is to this consistent success, but as others watch, copy and listen to him or her as he or she works, they too can begin to achieve similar outcomes.

We shall say more about tacit skills and their value in the final chapter of this book. Suffice it to stress here that for a small firm, tacit skills can represent vital strategic assets. This is because their derivation is obscure, they are hard to copy, and they explain much of the high performance and excellent results that are achieved by the business. Where they are unique to the people of the particular organisation and are valuable in the market, they give competitive advantage. Their development in the smaller firm in many informal and complex ways illustrates powerfully that the informal development of people in the smaller firm is often superior to a formal approach to training. This is especially true where informal processes help to spread, yet also obscure the true nature of, tacit skills in the workforce. Once a skill becomes explicit, and systematically based training can be provided for it, the skill can be poached or copied by other organisations. Loss of valuable tacit skills represents a loss of strategic assets. Hendry and his colleagues found that there was a high proportion of genuinely unique jobs in many smaller firms, and noted the 'desire of SMEs to hang onto and keep hidden specific skills and competences developed within the firm' (Hendry *et al*, 1991: 84).

Here is a case-study to review and consolidate learning thus far. It draws on many real-life small business scenarios.

Case-study: Triggers to training and development in the small firm

What has triggered Rob Jones's adoption of an increasingly planned approach to training and development in this case, and what are the key T&D issues facing him?

Rob Jones, now 47, is the owner–manager of a small manufacturing firm which he founded eight years ago. It has secured a solid place in the market and is now expanding as demand for the product increases. Turnover has increased from £1 million in the early years to nearly £5 million in the current year.

Rob has a team of three key people who, with him, carry the responsibility for the management of the firm. All are around his age and were recruited at start-up. They are hardworking and dedicated to the success of the firm, but are not yet agreed on future strategy. Rob and Mark, the production manager, see an international future as the ultimate goal to go for. On the other hand, Bill, the finance manager, is concerned about the implications of that and feels that an expansion within the national market, clearly targeted, would be desirable: it should generate sufficient profit and investment revenue without ultimately leading to the likelihood of merger or takeover. Tony (sales and marketing) is keen to expand the customer base, but has concerns about the fast-growing firm's ability to maintain its quality, delivery and sales standards. The team is shortly to go away for a three-day hotel break in order to hammer out their future goals and strategy – a technique used regularly, but in this case they have a particularly challenging task because of the growing complexity of the business and of the strategic choices it faces.

Rob set up the firm after working for some years as a marketing executive in a multinational firm. In a major restructuring and de-layering exercise, he was one of several to take a golden handshake. Having benefited from a good university education, he is a believer in the educational system and therefore invested some of his severance pay in a 'small business growth course' at a local university business school. He formed many useful academic and small-business contacts while on the course, and at its end he established his own firm, which has prospered.

Rob has always believed that management development in a small firm must mainly be achieved by natural learning processes: their relevancy, low cost and direct relationship to the work situation bring unique benefits. He also believes that the structure of the firm, like the jobs within it, will directly affect flexibility, quality and commitment. The flat, matrix structure he and his small team have carefully developed has so far produced the flexible labour force and adaptable culture that the firm has needed to ensure its survival and growth.

There are three watchwords in the firm: quality, service and best-in-class. Managers and team leaders attend external learning events regularly in order to keep up to date and to develop strong networks; Rob's business school and other external links are productive here.

Rob sees 'development' as getting and keeping a high-calibre management group and workforce team, and enhancing their capabilities for the future. Training means, for him, a combination of informal on-the-job learning and skills-based formal interventions. He uses a management consultant with whom the firm has worked since start-up to help him either provide or buy in the necessary expertise here. As issues of management succession, organisational restructuring and skills change bite deeper, Rob realises the need for a longer-term and planned approach to training and development, and is wondering quite how this can be achieved.

Rob has always spent a large proportion of his time on people-related activities – about 75 per cent, he estimates. Now, with the business entering the most complex and highly pressured stage of its existence, he has major decisions to make – not only about future direction and investment in the business, but about the management and development of an increasingly diversified workforce. He can see that the influx of people at different levels, not least the managerial level, bringing with them different histories and work experiences, has implications for skill and pay levels and for expectations, culture and behaviour in the workplace. He is unsure at this stage whether to continue to rely on consultants for advice in these areas, or whether to buy in some kind of HR person.

Feedback notes

* In the study, major issues related to training and development include the need for the owner–manager to adopt a more coherent approach to developing employees – especially current and potential managers – as the firm grows and enters a more complex stage of development; the values of the owner concerning training and development; and the organisational restructuring and requirement for new skills that a changed business strategy will make likely.

* Hendry *et al* (1991) found in their research that although the growth of formal business planning in the firm did not tend of itself to act as a trigger, often – like Rob – the managing director had a view of where the company should be in the future and would broadly support educational initiatives in line with that. It is in this way that a focus on development rather than just on immediate training can emerge. Harrison and Lord (1992: 10) found that training and development activities in small firms became more managerially oriented and time-consuming with growth, many being 'related to new staff or potential "stars" who were identified to take the weight from the owner–manager in terms of administrative help or staff training'.

Hendry *et al* (1991) identified a number of common triggers for a more formalised and systematic approach to training in the smaller enterprise. Their interactions tend to be unique to the particular firm, but there is value in identifying them at this point, since several can be found in the case-study.

* *The skill supply strategy of the firm* – Inability to achieve the kind of skill supply it needs often directs a firm's attention to the value of a longer-term, planned and systematic approach to training within the firm. The extent to which this trigger operates, and the way in which it does, will be influenced by several interacting factors: the competitive environment, the firm's existing or proposed technology, the type of external labour market from which it can draw its labour, typical pay rates and training costs in its sector, the vulnerability of its labour market to government intervention of various kinds, and the firm's size and stage of development.

* *The acquisition of new technology* – The introduction of new technology may in some firms lead to a drive for training or retraining, but in others to a drive for recruitment, or to a reorganisation of the workforce – everything depends on the specifics of the situation.

* *Customer relations* – Attempts to improve quality systematically can

lead to formal training initiatives, but they can also, or alternatively, generate a changed environment in which HRD becomes naturally built into changed ways of working – project teams, worker involvement and participation, improved work systems, re-education in the workplace, and so on. Such attempts can also prompt the workforce to raise developmental issues such as personal career advancement, demands for a job-grading structure and clearer pay progression.

- *Growth* – Growth, like the acquisition of new technology, affects different firms in different ways. With rapid growth, and especially with pressure of production, training may be influenced adversely or positively. Adverse effects will occur, for example, if management has a short-term perspective with no forward planning or vision. Too much will then be likely to happen at once for there to be the clarity of thought that will produce ordered training and longer-term development strategy. 'A strategic vision – backed by market projections but not necessarily embodied in a formal plan – is therefore an important underpinning' (Hendry *et al*, 1991: 69).

- *Management culture related to training* – The values and perceptions of whoever owns or controls the SME have a dominating influence on all aspects of the business. Often those stakeholders may be ignorant as to how training and development can contribute to performance and growth. On the other hand, if they are convinced of the need for a planned, systematic investment, then that conviction will become a major trigger for HRD.

- *Workforce expectations and desire for betterment* – Although these are strongly affected by management's stance towards training, employee attitudes can be ambivalent. Their own background and qualifications will be as important as those of top managers in setting the climate for training in the firm (*ibid*: 70).

- *Systematisation of pay in relation to skill* – The introduction by a firm of a pay structure that defines skill requirements and specifies how these can be acquired through training and education is a powerful trigger for a more systematic and formal approach to training in that organisation.

- *A recognised structure of skills and vocational qualifications for the whole workforce* – Such a structure will have the same kind of effect as the pay structure, and should help to ensure that the potential of everyone in the firm is realised, rather than promoting a situation in which some appear to be advancing more than others. Over time it should produce a positive and committed culture related to training and development in the firm.

- *The advent of a large cohort of new recruits* – The sudden recruitment of a relatively large cohort into a smaller firm can radically disrupt planned training and distort patterns of growth. For SMEs it is particularly important to provide a 'natural life-cycle of training which matches the cohort progression of employees' (*ibid*: 82).

- *Costs of training* – Constrained resources, especially of finance, can inhibit training in the smaller firm. Another constraint is the difficulty of releasing people for off-the-job training. What will matter most is the cost of formalised training balanced against the extent to which it can give demonstrably short-term results to offset those costs (Cambridge University Small Business Research Centre, 1992: 54).

EXTERNAL SUPPORT FOR TRAINING IN SMEs

Government agencies are often perceived much less favourably in terms of standards and quality than further education institutions, but smaller firms do give considerable support to external vocational education. Awareness of group training schemes and facilities, external funding, and cheap but good-quality external educational provision can all help to minimise formal training costs. However, many government initiatives in the past have been launched and delivered without real evaluation (Jennings, Richardson and Beaver, 1992: 10) and in consequence many smaller organisations have little certainty that external training provision will meet their needs. This is a pity, given the help that various forms of external aid can give to promoting valuable training and development in the smaller organisation. Renewed efforts are now being made to spread awareness of important initiatives.

Amongst these, a new programme from Investors in People was produced in 1997, with help from Scottish Enterprise, the Confederation of British Industry and the Federation of Small Businesses. The aim was to make the package practical, allowing businesses to gauge how well they are doing compared with similar enterprises. It was aimed at the bottom end of the size scale, with eight elements instead of the 23 that, at that time, larger organisations had to be measured against for IIP accreditation. This represented a real advance in thinking, making IIP more attractive, meaningful and accessible for smaller organisations whatever their type and sector.

In July 1999, the Department for Trade and Industry issued its consultative Green Paper on the new Small Business Service. That Service is to be introduced in 2001 to allow small firms to be given higher priority and greater influence within government. It is intended that it will offer improved coherence and quality of support to that provided by Business Links, introduced in 1992 as a nationwide network of business advice centres to act as one-stop shops concentrating their activities on helping mature small firms. (Equivalent services in Scotland currently are Business Shops, in Wales, Business Connect, and in Northern Ireland, the Economic Development Network for Northern Ireland.)

The Business Link system will be retained, and still act as a one-stop shop, delivering all the government support services on offer to small firms and thereby achieving more accessible and coherent provision than in the past. The Green Paper was another clear signal of Government intent to improve and to make more coherent the services offered to small firms.

Externally provided information and expertise can often clarify misapprehensions that many smaller organisations have about the cost and value of training and development. The most common reasons why such organisations do not make a more significant investment in training and development are:

- scepticism about value, often coming from history – 'a bad training experience can be damaging to training provision' (Kirby, 1990) and repetition of such experiences reinforces the scepticism

- a perception of inability to pay, of lack of time, and of the likelihood of lost opportunity costs

- failure to recognise skills shortages and areas of lack of managerial capability

- lack of awareness of sources of external provision and expertise – Harrison and Lord (1992), in their study of the impact of IIP on a sample of small firms, found that very few owner–managers or their customers had significant awareness of the standard. Those that did often confused it with other standards such as BS 5750 and feared becoming ensnarled in more bureaucratic procedures. Likewise, although there is a national framework of occupational standards and qualifications for owner–managers, similar kinds of ignorance and confusion explain why many small organisations do not go down the NVQ route.

Various external parties can help to reduce such problems. Sometimes government will introduce initiatives such as IIP and the Small Business Service. Sometimes an external consultant known for being experienced in the small enterprise field is contracted to help the small organisation. Through such interventions, outcomes like the following can often be achieved.

- *The organisation can be helped to identify a particular area of need with a clear impact not only on the current bottom line but on future capability* – The provider should work closely with key parties in the firm to provide a cost-efficient learning experience targeted to achieve one or two clear objectives, and should agree at the start on measures to indicate the success of the initiative. A progression of such carefully planned and targeted learning initiatives should slowly begin to change the culture to one that sees 'value' (rather than 'cost') in planned learning (rather than 'training') in the firm. This was the aim of the 1997 IIP programme for small businesses.

- *The use of benchmarking and good practice* can reduce scepticism, promote interest and stimulate change.

- *Training costs can be reduced* – A good consultant can help the smaller firm to become more aware of funding sources and of provision, in line with its needs and its purse. Even where a particular initiative is genuinely too costly, the consultant can help to explore ways to facilitate that learning relatively cheaply – by mentoring and work-shadowing, for example, instead of formal induction; by project teams rather than expensive outdoor development programmes; by regular team briefings rather than externally provided 'teambuilding' courses. Ineffective consultants are, of course, key barriers to systematising training provision and many lack experience and understanding of SMEs (Jennings, Richardson and Beaver, 1992: 26). Using the local network to find out about consultants and their track record is crucial because 'Small businesses ... find it hard to select the right training of the right quality in a market oversupplied with consultants and private providers of training' (Wood, 1992: 8).

• *External and intra-organisational learning networks can be developed –* They provide access to many sources of HRD aid for the firm and also stimulate interest and boost confidence. There are now many easily accessible websites, also, that act as a gateway to all kinds of information for small firms – some of these are listed at the end of this chapter.

External support for training in the smaller organisation

From your reading on training and development in smaller organisations thus far, and from your own knowledge of SMEs in your locality, what can be done by outside individuals and agencies to stimulate an SME's awareness of training and development activity that can add value for the organisation at affordable cost?

OUTCOMES OF TRAINING AND DEVELOPMENT IN THE SMALLER ENTERPRISE

There is little evidence in smaller organisations of training in training needs analysis or training plans (Harrison and Lord, 1992: 10). Failure to document either needs or plans can give the impression either that no training is being done or that any that is taking place must be unplanned and therefore invalid. As noted earlier, such conclusions can easily be mistaken. Pettigrew, Arthur and Hendry (1990: 25) showed that the outcomes of HRM and training in SMEs can be evaluated:

• in terms of impact on current performance goals, as indicated by a range of measures (performance will be the dominating criterion at an early stage of the firm's life cycle)

• in terms of development, as indicated by impact on prospective medium-term outcomes associated with planned changes in products or services, or adjustments to environmental forces

• in terms of learning related to prospective long-term outcomes that are impossible to specify but can be assured only by the growth of strategic capabilities 'so that the firm can cope with crisis or make the big strategic leap forward which unexpected opportunities may present'.

It is important to achieve strategic awareness and thinking across the workforce in smaller organisations, and forms of development and work experience that can enhance those abilities are therefore of particular value.

Training and development pose particular challenges in the smaller firm, but an effective approach to those challenges can offer a better model of alignment of HRD with business needs and of consistency with other areas of HR practice than is to be found in many large-scale businesses. In the smaller firm, for the development of people to survive, let alone succeed, it has no choice but to become an integral part of the everyday operations and processes of the firm. For the HRD practitioner to be effective – whether as internal or external consultant – he or she must have a comprehensive grasp of the business and its competitive environment, must speak in the language that stakeholders understand, and must be expert at managing the training and development infrastructure of the firm. Such skills are essential to the effectiveness of any HR professional or manager, yet are often found wanting in larger organisations.

Finally, many smaller organisations come close to being what can be recognised as 'learning organisations'. They are fast-reactive, well-informed about their external and internal environments, and foster a climate of continuous learning leading to the development of knowledge that is used to innovate and advance. They operate like this not necessarily because there has been any conscious decision to do so, or even an awareness that this is what is happening, but simply because it is in this way that those organisations thrive and manage to attract and retain high-calibre people.

CONCLUSION

Having read this chapter and completed its reviews and self-checks, you should now:

- be familiar with the context in which human resource management (HRM), training and development are undertaken in the smaller organisation

- understand the main issues related to the practice and provision of training and development in the smaller organisation

- be able to identify an appropriate approach to training and development for a smaller organisation, and know how to fit training and development initiatives to the small firm situation.

To test yourself against these objectives, what five-minute answers would you give to the questions on the next page? (Dates in brackets refer to the IPD qualifying examination paper in which a question appeared.)

- You are a human resource consultant, asked by the owner-manager of a small but growing firm to advise her on how best to organise training and development in the firm. What three or four contextual factors will you examine before giving her your advice – and why?

- A general practitioners' (GP) practice is recruiting a practice manager for the first time. The job-holder will be responsible, among other managerial tasks, for employee development related to the practice's 10 reception, nursing and GP staff. What purpose and core tasks would you expect the practice manager's ED responsibility to entail, and why? (May 1999)

- Explain the main steps that you would recommend the owner–manager of a small, rapidly growing firm to take in order to provide it with high-calibre managers for the future. (November 1999)

USEFUL READING

HARRISON R. (1993a) 'Strategic human resource management at HMH Sheetmetal Fabrications Ltd, 1993', in R. Harrison (ed.), *Human Resource Management: Issues and strategies*. Wokingham, Addison Wesley, pp335–9.

HENDRY C., ARTHUR M. B. *and* JONES A. M. (1995) *Strategy through People: Adaptation and learning in the small-medium enterprise*. London, Routledge.

HILL R. *and* STEWART J. (1999) 'Human resource development in small organizations'. *Human Resource Development International*. Vol. 2, 2. pp103–23.

WALTON J. (1999c) 'Small and medium-sized enterprises and human resource development', in J. Walton, *Strategic Human Resource Development*. Harlow, Financial Times and Prentice Hall. pp324–51.

There are many websites that offer helpful information for smaller organisations, including the following:

- Until 2001, Training and Enterprise Councils or their equivalent bodies in Scotland and Northern Ireland (www.tec.co.uk); thereafter, by the Small Business Service or its equivalent in Scotland, Wales and Northern Ireland (see www.businesslink.co.uk; www.scotnet.co.uk/sb/bsu.htm; www.cbc.org.uk; and www.ednet.ni.com)

- The Enterprise Zone, run by the DTI, provides links to wide-ranging functional information for smaller enterprises, including human resources (www.enterprisezone.org.uk)

- Information about training can be found through learndirect's drop-in centres, and through www.ufiltd.co.uk

Part 3

DEVELOPING PERFORMANCE IN THE WORKPLACE

14 Developing individuals' performance

LEARNING OBJECTIVES

After reading this chapter you will:

- have a framework for identifying and understanding people's learning needs at work and the relationship of those needs to the demands of the organisation's performance management process (PMP)

- understand the importance of an effective balance between managing and developing people in the PMP

- be able to explain an integrated organisational programme for induction and basic skills training, appraisal and improvement of performance, and continuous learning and development.

Please note that throughout this chapter the term 'individual needs' may be taken to refer also to group/team needs.

PERFORMANCE MANAGEMENT AND DEVELOPMENT: INTRODUCTION

Performance management has been defined as a continuous process in which:

> organisations clarify the level of performance required to meet their strategic objectives, convert them into unit and individual objectives and manage them continually ... [so] that they remain relevant and consistent with overall strategic objectives.
>
> (Lockett, 1992: 14)

The performance management process (PMP) should be driven by the vision, corporate goals and strategy. The first essential, therefore, is that top management produces and communicates a powerful and cohering vision of the organisation, and ensures that goals and plans to support it are relevant and understood by all employees. Lockett (1992: 37–46) described the performance management cycle as involving seven stages: establishing the performance contract, clarifying performance requirements, agreeing on support requirements, reviewing performance, and taking actions related to meeting, exceeding or failing to meet the performance contract. In the context of employee development, the key elements of a PMP are those to do with:

• setting targets and establishing desired performance levels

• appraising and improving performance

• ensuring continuous learning and development

• giving recognition and rewards.

In this chapter, we look at how to manage the learning process in ways that will improve individual performance and help individuals to continuously develop. For those wishing to obtain detailed guidance on organisational and individual training needs analysis, specialist texts such as Boydell and Leary (1996), Hardingham (1996a) and the Bees (1994) are recommended. Approaches to job training analysis will be discussed in Chapter 15.

THE LEARNING PROCESS

> Learning is a relatively permanent change in behaviour that occurs as a result of practice or experience.
>
> (Bass and Vaughan, 1967: 8)

This well-known working definition treats 'learning' as a noun – as a state to be achieved. It emphasises the importance of experience and reinforcement in achieving 'relatively permanent change in behaviour'. Interestingly, it does not refer to changed ways of perceiving, thinking and knowing (in the sense of understanding, making sense of the world). Later in their book, of course, the authors did have much to say about those outcomes. I am drawing attention to them here in order to emphasise the need to see learning not just as behavioural change but also as knowledge. Management must foster the kind of individual and collective learning that not only produces changed behaviour but that also adds to the store of valuable knowledge which the organisation possesses and on which its long-term future depends.

The word 'learning' can of course also be used as a verb, indicating a dynamic process. HRD practitioners must understand this process if they are to help their organisations to achieve those 'relatively permanent change[s] in behaviour' necessary to business survival and organisational progress. There are many theories about the learning process (see Marchington and Wilkinson, 1996: 161–8 for a helpful summary). I have chosen only two to discuss here because, taken together, they have much of value to tell us about how learning can be managed in an organisational context.

The experiential cycle

Learning can be viewed as a circular process, as in Figure 7. Individuals tend to learn more rapidly at some stages of the process than others, influenced in part by their natural learning styles. Honey and Mumford (1992), for example, identified Activist, Reflector, Theorist and Pragmatist styles (see Marchington and Wilkinson, 1996:

Figure 7 The experiential cycle of learning (based on Kolb, Rubin and McIntyre, 1974)

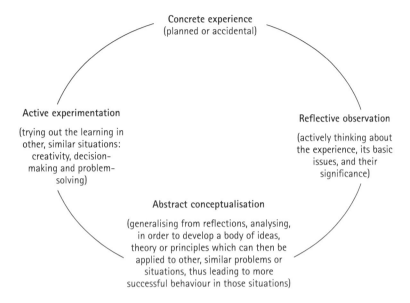

Concrete experience
(planned or accidental)

Active experimentation

(trying out the learning in
other, similar situations:
creativity, decision-
making and problem-
solving)

Reflective observation

(actively thinking about
the experience, its basic
issues, and their
significance)

Abstract conceptualisation

(generalising from reflections, analysing,
in order to develop a body of ideas,
theory or principles which can then be
applied to other, similar problems or
situations, thus leading to more
successful behaviour in those situations)

165–8 for a critique of the Honey and Mumford and other learning style inventories).

Learning from my own experience

When was the last time you felt that you really learnt something? Take yourself back to that occasion, reflect on it, and try relating it stage by stage to the experiential learning process.

As your response to the above question will probably show, the learning process is not so easily explained as this particular theory of learning implies, but the theory does give helpful insights. Applied to an organisational situation, it can enable us to see where learning is being inhibited because people are struggling with experiences, tasks or demands that are simply too difficult for them at this stage. Perhaps, if provided in simulated form in a training programme, the experiences are felt to be artificial or irrelevant. Perhaps the learners lack time, encouragement or ability to reflect on and therefore learn from experience (whether it is a work project, part of a structured training or educational programme, or an unexpected event). Perhaps they lack the skills to produce accurate diagnoses of situations or the generation and testing of new responses.

Whoever is responsible for the learning process, be it the individual directing his or her own learning or the manager of a learning event, they must ensure the right kind of stimulation, practice and feedback at crucial stages of learning. If they can 'manage' a variety of everyday work situations in ways that will foster the key skills involved in the learning cycle, then those skills can be continuously applied to an ever-widening range of organisational issues. Not only individual but organisational performance will then be enhanced.

Stimulus-response theory

Our second theory about learning explains the mastery of the learning process in terms of four key factors (see Bass and Vaughan, 1967; Stammers and Patrick, 1975; and Gagne, 1977 for an extension of this simple framework): Drive, Stimulus, Response and Reinforcement.

- *Drive.* For learning to occur there must be a basic need that makes someone want to learn, and that acts as the continued spur to that activity: in other words, there must be a drive, or motivation, to learn.

- *Stimulus.* A stimulus means a message that makes an impact on our senses because it relates to one or more of our primary or secondary drives. For learning to be effective, people must become actively involved in the learning situation. Methods of learning must, by stimulating various senses, make a sufficient impact to ensure that people learn in that situation.

- *Response and reinforcement.* In every learning situation the learner must acquire appropriate responses – skills, knowledge, attitudes – that will lead to improved performance or to some other kind of needed development. These responses must be reinforced by practice, experience and feedback until they are fully learnt. Unproductive responses must be corrected before they become habitual.

This may seem an oversimplified and mechanistic explanation of human learning. It recalls the so-called 'law of effect' in classical conditioning theory, and pictures come to mind of the dog, cat or pigeon being 'trained' to perform in desired ways by a process of instruction, reward and punishment. It seems at odds with Kolb's naturalistic concept. In reality, however, both learning theories discussed thus far point to the importance of five factors when making decisions about organisational and individual learning needs, and how best to respond to them:

- *Stimulation.* The learning process can be activated only by some state of arousal in the individual or the organisation. This will happen naturally if a particular situation makes a direct impact on already strongly felt needs. On the other hand, arousal may have to be stimulated deliberately in order for desired learning to take place.

  Take the example of a training course that management are convinced is essential for a group of employees, but for which those employees see no need. How can the group become convinced of the importance of that training? Exhortations or commands will not be enough: people can be driven into a training room but, once there, they cannot be forced to learn. Management must communicate a clear purpose for the training, and demonstrate that the specific outcomes it promises will bring mutual benefits.

  If that communication does not convince, and the group comes unwillingly to training, then (and this should in any event be the case) the learning experience itself must be so designed as to quickly arouse and sustain the learners' attention. Soon, they will come to see for themselves the importance of learning, whatever new knowledge, skills or attitudes are at issue.

Individuals cannot be made to learn, but learning will occur once they can identify with its purpose, undergo a relevant learning experience and are in the hands of skilled trainers or facilitators.

- *Purpose and planning.* Being clear about the purpose of learning, and planning for it to occur, are essential components of the organisational learning process. Kolb, Rubin and McIntyre (1974) believed that learning should be an explicit organisational objective, 'pursued as consciously and deliberately as profit or productivity'. They stressed that there must be 'a climate seeing the value of such an approach...developed in the organisation'.

  The definition of the purpose of a learning event, and the setting of objectives to achieve it, may be the responsibility of the individual learner, the manager of a group at work or a human resource (HR) specialist. The purpose may be generalised or specific; it may be corporate and long-term – for example, the purpose of developing a 'learning organisation'; or it may be to do with an individual or team achieving immediate targets. Establishing purpose and planning for learning to occur will not necessarily lead to formal training or developmental events; nor will there be an inevitable need for 'trainers' or 'tutors'. The importance of agreeing at corporate level on the purpose of a learning event, and of planning organisational learning strategies, is that top management is thereby required to stop and reflect on what it is trying to achieve.

- *Learning processes and strategies.* Learning processes must help employees to move through the key stages of their organisational life – entry, mastery of the job, continuous improvement and development, and preparation for exit. Learning strategies must be those best suited to purpose. Often, integrating learning with work – the 'experiential' approach – will be appropriate and cost-effective. However, there will also be times when it is relevant to provide a more formalised learning approach.

- *Reinforcement of learning.* There must be regular practice and feedback if learners are to acquire new learning quickly and confidently and test it out in their practical situations. Kolb's theory emphasises this when it shows the stage of experimentation leading into further experience, which then generates the possibility of review, analysis and modification or repetition of the new learning.

- *Review at organisational and individual levels.* Learning should be reviewed at organisational as well as at individual levels so that only the most relevant learning strategies are developed and subsequently reinforced across the organisation as well as in the particular workplace. Appraisal is an important, although of course not sufficient, way of ensuring feedback and review of experience.

Now try to apply these ideas to your own organisation (or one with which you are familiar):

Developing motivation to learn in the workplace

Consider your own organisation. Identify an area where there is *either* a clear, but unmet, need for guided learning *or* where there is real enthusiasm for learning by managers and their staff. Use our five-factor framework to analyse reasons for the situation you have identified.

If there is lack of enthusiasm for learning, what action would you recommend?

Learning approaches and types
Types of learning
Learning that aids individual performance has been classified into three types: instrumental, dialogic and self-reflective (Mezirow, 1985).

• *Instrumental learning.* This means learning how to do the job better once the basic standard of performance has been attained. A key strategy to achieve instrumental learning, once initial formal training has been given (and quite often in place of that formal training), is learning on the job. This can involve an interaction of formal and informal processes and can be highly effective, provided that there is someone to encourage learners in the course of their daily tasks to identify problems, formulate appropriate action, try it out, observe the effects and learn from them. That 'someone' may be a trained member of the workteam. For example, at McDonald's, new entrants go through a three-hour induction and are then partnered with a 'buddy' who comes from a 'training squad' of specially trained employees belonging to their workteam. 'In a typical restaurant employing a crew of 50, about five will be members of the training squad' (Cannell, 1997). The on-the-job learning for which 'buddies' are responsible is rigorously organised and very effective. On the other hand, the 'someone' may be a high-performing member of a workgroup who has proven training skills and the disposition to foster job-related learning in others.

Managers need to be good at helping – or training and encouraging others to help – new recruits to learn from their mistakes as well as successes, and to focus on continuous improvement of work processes rather than simply on the achievement of task targets. They also need to set the recruits new challenges from time to time in order to stretch their abilities. Such managers should be recognised for their achievement in developing powerful on-the-job learning systems in the workplace. Those systems are of unique importance to the organisation when they ensure that knowledge and skills are transferred from the experienced to the inexperienced, from the highly skilled to those building up their understanding and ability to do a job or task.

• *Dialogic learning.* Dialogic learning involves interacting with others in ways that will produce a growing knowledge and understanding of the culture of the organisation, and of how it typically achieves its goals. The value of dialogic learning is that it can help to acclimatise individuals so that they can more quickly make sense of the organisational world they have entered and develop the confidence to operate competently in the workplace.

Dialogic learning is therefore important at the stage when newcomers enter the organisation, or when people are promoted into parts of the organisation with which they are unfamiliar. Mentoring is one of the most powerful ways of ensuring dialogic learning.

• *Self-reflective learning.* This is the kind of learning that leads individuals to redefine their current perspective in order to develop new patterns of understanding, thinking and behaving. It is needed when people have to operate in roles or situations that are very different from those to which they have become accustomed in the past. Because self-reflective learning involves challenging, and breaking out of, old mindsets it requires unlearning as well as new learning. As Argyris (1982) pointed out, that is possible only in an environment that 'enables and empowers individuals to be responsible, productive and creative' and to see error as a positive learning vehicle, as well as 'acknowledging uncertainty and spanning information boundaries'.

Educational and training programmes have an obvious part to play in generating self-reflective learning. So too have work-based learning processes like quality circles, briefing groups, benchmarking and best-practice exercises, secondments, new project work and action-learning sets, because such processes all expose people to new ways of thinking and new situations, making them question familiar prescriptions, operations and routines.

Single- and double-loop learning

It will have become apparent that instrumental and dialogic learning involve a different approach from that required by self-reflective learning. The difference is to do with the stance of the learner – in the first two cases seeking continuously to improve skills, behaviour or attitudes so that they fall in line with existing standards and norms, and in the third case taking a questioning, proactive approach in a situation where standards and norms may themselves need to be challenged.

This introduces one of the best-known – yet quite often poorly understood – ways of classifying approaches to learning: the concept of single- and double-loop learning. Chris Argyris first formulated the concept (1977) and developed it with Donald Schon in 1978. In essence it distinguishes the approach that simply tackles 'surface symptoms of a problem' (single-loop learning) from the approach that is concerned to 'question why the problem arose in the first place and ... tackle its root causes' (double-loop learning) (Pickard, 1997: 34).

Not all researchers in the field of individual and organisational learning believe that the concept of single- and double-loop learning adequately explains the different types of learning outcome in question. Some see it as too simplistic, ignoring the possibility of discontinuous, non-linear learning to explain the sudden leaps in understanding that result in people breaking out of customary ways of thinking and perceiving. However, the concept is undeniably powerful and well researched, and it has influenced generations of scholars and practitioners.

DEVELOPING INDIVIDUALS' PERFORMANCE

Understanding performance

Performance is the outcome of the interaction between an individual's needs, perception of the results required and rewards being offered, and the amount of effort, energy and expertise that the individual has or wishes to apply to the task in hand. Handy (1985) called the outcome of this process the 'motivation calculus'. He explained that performance can be understood by reference to four factors, which revolve around the learner, their manager and their workplace: needs, results, rewards and 'E' factors. We can see links here with the learning theory discussed earlier in this chapter.

- *Needs.* How far, in individuals' minds, do their jobs or tasks relate in any positive way to the needs that those individuals bring to work? What we should try to discover is not all their needs, but those which influence them at work. If a particular task or job relates to those needs only in a minor way, then clearly we cannot expect more than minimal performance from the job-holder.

  We must be careful about the labels we attach to people. An individual may be regarded as 'ambitious' – but ambition can take many forms. Trying to motivate such an individual to take on extra work by dangling the carrot of 'enhanced chances of promotion' will be ineffective if in fact he or she is driven by the need not for the increased responsibilities or high level of skill that promotion would involve but for some form of professional or work group status. Taking on another task when already expending maximum effort on an existing workload could mean a reduction in that individual's overall effectiveness, and a consequent loss of status. Or perhaps he or she has a need for personal power which is already being satisfied through influence exercised over members of the workgroup.

- *Results.* How far do individuals appreciate what is wanted from them? Do they fully understand what their jobs involve, the results they are supposed to achieve, and the opportunities, constraints and challenges that surround those jobs? Have they had any opportunity to set work targets jointly with their managers, rather than simply have these imposed on them? There is much evidence to show that joint formulation of work plans and targets leads manager and job-holder to share a common view of the job, and to increased motivation and commitment in the job-holder. Do individuals know when they are achieving good results, and why? Do managers help them by acting as good role models, reinforcing effective performance and discouraging poor performance?

- *Rewards.* Does the task or job offer valued rewards to the individual? Rewards can take many different forms: not just money and position (which may have less impact than managers believe, or may not be within their power to offer) but also status and praise – non-financial recognition. It is essential to talk and listen to employees about *all* the rewards that they value, instead of simply acting on assumptions.

It is important, furthermore, to understand how people view the promise of rewards. Promises are often treated with scepticism because they have been made before but, for whatever reason, not been fulfilled.

- *'E' factors*. How far do individuals see it as worthwhile to expend *e*ffort, *e*nergy, *e*xcitement and *e*xpertise in the task, given the results that are required, the rewards it appears to offer them, and the workloads they already carry? And what level of those 'E' factors do those individuals actually possess? Are assessments about this accurate, or is either less or more expected of job-holders than they are actually able to give?

It is the interaction that takes place between needs, results, rewards and 'E' factors that explains the performance of individuals but, for every individual, that interaction is unique. Over time, the records of a poorly performing member of staff may show high levels of absenteeism, sickness and notes of continued refusals to take on new tasks. These records may cause unfavourable judgements to be made about him or her, so that training or development is considered inappropriate. In such cases the individual has been written off. Yet, with more insights into the factors that lie behind performance, quite a different picture may emerge. That picture may lead to an awareness that changes need to be made in the ways in which staff recruitment, work allocation, leadership functions or appraisal are carried out in a department. Once again, as so often before in this book, we see the importance of the organisation's total employee resourcing system in framing the particular activities related to the management and development of people in the workplace.

In the workplace, there are four major influences on performance:

- *the learner,* who needs the right level of competence, motivation, understanding, support and incentives in order to perform effectively

- *the learner's workgroup*, whose members will exercise a strong positive or negative influence on the attitudes, behaviour and performance of each new recruit

- *the learner's manager*, who needs to act as an effective role model, coach, stimulus and communicator related to performance

- *the organisation*, which may produce barriers to effective performance if there is no powerful, cohering vision; ineffective structure, culture or work systems; unsupportive ER policy and systems; or inappropriate leadership and management style.

Learning difficulties in the workplace can arise in relation to:

- *task performance*, where they are connected with difficulty in carrying out one or more specific tasks related to the job

- *task management*, where they are connected with difficulty in general planning, problem-solving and decision-making in the job

- *boundary management*, where they are connected with difficulty in operating confidently and effectively in the role and job by reference to the social and political environment in which the job-holder must operate

- *motivation*, connected typically with mistaken expectations about the job, or its level and content, or with unsatisfactory training, support and rewards, or with poor supervision and feedback on performance.

Any HRD professionals working in or for an organisation should build up close informal as well as formal interactions with managers and other personnel in the organisation, in order to acquire insights into the issues that lie behind performance. They should ask probing but diplomatically phrased questions to determine causes of poor performance, and to discover whether performance could be improved by training, development or some other process. It is essential to understand the relationship between individuals, their managers, their workplace environment and the organisation's performance management process - and to be able to identify any problems and advise on how they might be tackled.

Poor performance in the workplace

Identify an area of your organisation (or one with which you are familiar) where there are problems in performance – perhaps involving one or two individuals, or perhaps characterising everyone who works in that area. Use our four-factor model to explore possible causes of that poor performance, and to identify some ways in which it might be tackled.

Tensions between controlling and developing people

Central to performance management is a drive to control: to control the targets that are set for people; to control their performance by rewarding the achievement of targets; and to control their training by focusing it on closing gaps between standards sought and standards achieved. The increasing popularity of competency-based frameworks in performance management systems must be treated with caution in this context. An obsessive preoccupation with competencies and an inexpert approach to competency-based analysis can be costly and counter-productive (Healy, 1995; Sparrow, 1996), narrowing the focus of performance management to exclude the development of more generalised abilities needed to survive in an unpredictable future.

On the other hand, a robust competency framework focuses attention on key areas for performance in the organisation, and on what is needed to ensure adequate or superior performance levels in those areas. In Chapter 15 we shall look at ways of analysing competencies, and Chapter 20 will show their importance in management education and development. Competency-based analysis can be a cost-beneficial process when it is well integrated into the PMS.

Many competency frameworks aim to produce not only the kinds of performance but also the values and styles of behaviour that top management see to be essential to good performance There is nothing inherently threatening to the individual in working for an organisation that seeks or demands compliance to certain norms of behaviour – such, after all, is human life in social institutions. What matters is that the parties involved should agree what constitutes desirable norms, and how they will be measured and rewarded. What is demotivating for employees is an excessive focus on control, and abuse of the power to control.

Evidence emerged in the late 1990s that indicated a more developmental approach to performance management in UK-based organisations. An IPD survey reported by Armstrong and Baron (1998) revealed significant differences between the findings of this and past, comparably based, IPD surveys. In many of the organisations surveyed, the emphasis had switched markedly from rigid, formal systems and procedures to more processual approaches, and to a concern to find what was fit for the purpose. Whereas earlier IPD surveys had revealed a neglect of developmental aspects of PMSs, 'the philosophy of planned personal development as part of the overall process has now become firmly embedded in the policies and practices of a large proportion of the organisations covered' (*ibid*: 387). Consistent with this was a notable shift from a directive to a supportive approach to the management and development of performance in 'best practice' organisations. Development was more tailored to purpose, being achieved through a variety of modes: 'coaching, counselling, guidance, training, redesigning roles or redefining team responsibilities' (*ibid*).

Managing and developing people in your organisation

Describe the main elements of the performance management process in your own organisation. Assess how far – if at all – there is effective integration between the reward-driven and development-driven integration strategies, and what explains the situation you have identified. (You may find it helpful to do some more reading around the subject - see 'Useful reading' at the end of this chapter.)

A CORPORATE LEARNING PROGRAMME TO DEVELOP INDIVIDUALS' PERFORMANCE

In this part of the chapter, we shall use as our discussion framework three of the four developmental elements of a PMP and their associated organisational learning strategies to which we referred on page 238. The relationship is indicated in Table 10 (overleaf).

Evaluation of the many types of reward system that can be used to support the fourth developmental element – giving recognition and

Table 10 The performance management process and a corporate learning programme

Developmental elements of PMP	Organisational learning strategies
Setting targets and establishing desired performance levels	Induction and basic skills training
Managing performance	Work review and performance appraisal
Developing for the future	Personal development planning

rewards – can be found in specialist texts, such as Armstrong (1996) and Armstrong and Baron (1998).

Induction

Although the HRD manager may be involved in aspects of the selection process, we shall take as our practical starting-point the entry of a newcomer into an organisation (or the movement of an employee into a new job in some part of the organisation hitherto unfamiliar to him or her).

The purpose of induction should be not only to introduce newcomers to their job and workplace, to its main systems and procedures, and to the business goals and environment; it should also help them to understand and adapt to the vision of the organisation and its implicit values and norms. In other words, induction should facilitate dialogic learning.

Induction also needs to promote self-reflective learning. It is through self-reflection that individuals learn more about their own values and belief systems (and where those may need to change), achieve greater self-assurance and self-esteem, and are helped to function confidently and in new ways in the organisation they have just joined (or in the organisational unit or role to which they have just moved internally). Such learning should continue through the formative stages of the newcomer's job/role occupancy.

Many organisations arrange induction programmes for groups of new recruits rather than on an individualised basis. They include a carefully balanced range of activities and experiences through which dialogic and self-reflective learning can be promoted. Outdoor development courses are often used in this context, focusing on acclimatisation to company culture, and also on fostering skills relating to teamworking, problem-solving, creativity and holistic personal development. Many induction programmes culminate in individuals being helped to produce personal development objectives and plans which will contribute to their work performance and personal growth.

Mentors can be chosen to act as coaches, guides and counsellors during the induction process and thereafter. They can facilitate not only dialogic and self-reflective but also instrumental learning, because, in the atmosphere of trust and friendship that effective mentoring creates the new recruit feels able to admit openly to any performance problems, to reflect on and learn from them, and steadily to improve.

To summarise: induction should be concerned with providing

essential organisational and job-related knowledge, and with the promotion of dialogic and self-reflective learning. It should be planned so that it leads into a process of instrumental learning and then of continuous development.

Producing an induction programme

Take a particular group of new recruits in your own organisation (or one with which you are familiar) and design a programme for their induction. You will need to give a rationale for the programme and an indication of its structure, content, objectives and time-scale. You will also need to note the sources of information you have had to explore in designing your programme.

Feedback notes
- First, there has to be an overall purpose for induction. Fowler (1996) suggested that induction should aim to reduce low-quality work, high error rates and overlong learning periods. The purpose for your induction programme could perhaps be along lines proposed by Fowler: to enable new employees quickly to become fully integrated members of their working groups and to prevent a high incidence of early leavers by helping the newcomers to adjust to their new jobs and organisational environments.

- Consideration must be given to the kinds of learning to be achieved – dialogic, instrumental and self-reflective – and how they are to be ensured; also to the likely learning styles and skills of the new recruits and how best to respond to these in designing their induction process. Decisions must be made on how to achieve a balance between individual and group training, on what information to impart over what timescales, on the duration, content and learning methods to be used, and on the roles to be taken during induction by line managers, HR staff and other personnel.

- Important sources of information will include:

  - *exit interview records* or other data indicating reasons for early departure from the organisation. Do these hold any implications for induction?

  - *views of recent recruits.* If they went through an induction programme, what did they get out of it, both positive and negative, and have they any views on whether or not it should now have different aims, design, content or operation? If they did not have any kind of planned induction, what do they think should be offered to newcomers?

  - *views of managers* for whom the recruits will be working, or who may need to be involved in the induction process for other reasons. What do they think induction should achieve, and what programme would they find meaningful?

  - *internal and external best practice.* There may be approaches to induction in different parts of the organisation that are innovative, successful and could be adapted to suit the needs of this programme. Likewise contacts with external organisations and reading the literature to find best practice will help to ensure quality.

- *any up-to-date job descriptions and personnel specifications* for new recruits. These will offer important information about the recruits' main areas of work, about the organisational environment and culture that they will enter, and about the kinds of personal profile required by different jobs and roles. This information will also be important when planning basic training for new recruits.

Basic training

Objectives and programmes for basic training should be set out in an organisation's employee development policy. However, if that policy has only just been established, or if no such policy has yet been agreed, how can needs of potential learners be identified?

- *Define the objectives of basic training.* Objectives might be to attract and retain the calibre of people needed by the organisation; to provide training that is standards-based and related to National Vocational Qualifications (NVQs); to establish a cost-effective way of reinforcing company culture as well as ensuring good standards of job performance; and to build a base for flexibility of skills.

- *Audit existing learning and performance.* In looking at the ways in which employees currently acquire basic skills, be aware that sensitive political issues may be involved in proposing new training approaches related to the acquisition of new skills. Therefore the process of the audit as well as its operational design and implementation is important if outcomes are to be achieved to which all parties will be committed.

- *Produce a business case.* Draw up and achieve agreement on integrated proposals for induction, basic training and education, and continuous development for all learners, making sure that they are focused on business needs, and convince that they will be feasible and cost-effective.

A short case-study is useful at this point.

Case-study: Basic training at SmithKline Beecham

At SmithKline Beecham in 1995 the company sought to achieve all four of the basic training objectives suggested above through achieving multiskilling of operators and craftsmen on a site where there were still strong traditional demarcation lines. The divide was particularly marked between these two groups, and working practices were deeply entrenched.

Given the importance of a partnership approach, working parties made up of white- and blue-collar workers set about identifying situations where it would be sensible for an operator to carry out basic engineering tasks. Outsiders, including a senior union official, were brought in to talk about multiskilling elsewhere in order to give insights into best practice and to show the positive outcomes of the process.

There were inevitable difficulties as current ways of learning were examined in order to identify how best to organise the training for new skills. However, helped especially by winning a substantial grant from the European Commission under the Force programme (later superseded by the Leonardo programme), which required employers to forge links with transnational partners, mindsets began to change. The internal and external partnership approach helped to build trust, and eventually a powerful basic skills training programme using a mix of national occupational standards and internal standards was developed.

Source: Arkin, 1995

Basic training needs to be available not only to enable new recruits to move confidently and competently into their new posts but also to support them throughout the early stages of job occupancy. It is at these stages that performance problems are most likely to occur but, provided that newcomers have the ability to achieve good job performance (ie that there has not been a selection error), such problems are not likely to endure and indeed can become valuable learning vehicles.

This emphasises the need for regular monitoring and support during probationary periods. It is essential to identify any problems as they arise in order to ensure that they are corrected before becoming ingrained and habitual. Monitoring and support are also important. Where new recruits are left to learn by trial and error on their own, neither they nor the organisation can judge their real capabilities. The result can be low morale, lack of confidence and increased labour turnover.

Newcomers to a job or role should also be helped to formulate personal development plans at an early stage and should have the support of their managers and mentors (the two should be different) to pursue the plans through time. Clear, measurable targets for job performance also need to be agreed between the individual and the manager, giving an objective and reliable basis for the regular discussion, feedback and planning of work.

Approaches that can enhance the quality of basic training and probationary periods include – again – mentors to provide support and guidance; short training events; special assignments and projects; coaching by managers or other relevant parties in the organisation; access to flexible learning packages; and visits to other organisations or departments and educational events to achieve a higher level of professional knowledge or a broadening of business awareness.

Much of the information needed to enable a good basic skills training programme to be drawn up cannot be obtained until details about the individual recruit are known. It is important that, whatever strategy for learning is chosen, it should be adaptable to individual learning styles, as well as being capable of developing skills, knowledge and attitudes that the personnel specification shows are unlikely to be present in new recruits, and yet are vital to effective performance in the job or role.

Basic training in your organisation

Use our three-point 'basic training' check-list to assess basic training in an area of your own organisation, and to produce any recommendations needed to improve that training. You may find it helpful before starting this review to look through some past editions of *People Management* and similar professional journals to find informative articles.

Appraising and improving performance
The appraisal of performance

Four factors have a direct influence on the appraisal process: the wider employee resourcing (ER) and organisational context; the relationship between the parties; the nature of the appraisal scheme; and appraisal methods used.

- *The wider ER and organisational context.* We have already seen (on page 238) that the appraisal process must be understood and managed within its wider organisational context. For example, it is fruitless to try to introduce a developmental appraisal process into an organisation that has a rigid, divisive role structure, and a culture and a controlling management style that discourage openness, the use of initiative and the development of individuals' potential.

- *The relationship between the parties.* The relationship between the parties is the single most powerful influence on the conduct and outcomes of an appraisal discussion, and constitutes one of the major areas of difficulty related to it. If the appraiser–appraisee relationship is not open and supportive, it is most unlikely that a formalised appraisal system can make it so.

- *The nature of the appraisal scheme.* Much has been written elsewhere about the characteristics of effective appraisal schemes. Suffice it to say here that, for a scheme to be developmental, it must have: objectives and an approach to appraisal that reflect that aim; the full commitment of management and staff; the opportunity for mutual learning and understanding; and a process that emphasises review, diagnosis and future-oriented action-planning as well as planning to improve current performance.

- *Appraisal methods.* Some methods used within the appraisal process are more likely to produce valid information than others. A popular appraisal method is 360-degree appraisal: it reduces reliance on the limited number of sources otherwise involved in reviewing the individual's performance. Another helpful method is that of the 'balanced scorecard', which takes account of external as well as internal feedback. In the late 1990s the Halifax Building Society introduced it as a major lever in radical restructuring and the development of a new business culture. HR professionals need to be well informed on such innovative developments which, however, are not without pitfalls. Although the views of peers, customers, functional bosses and other parties will all carry weight, those of the line manager are still likely to be the most powerful in determining the outcomes of appraisal in most organisations and for most individuals.

Here is a case-study to illustrate the need for a conducive organisational context if appraisal is to be an effective development process.

Case-study: Tackling the improvement of formal appraisal in an organisation

Appendix 6 presents a seven-step approach to appraisal which you may find helpful to apply in your own organisation or in one with which you are familiar, if formal appraisal there is in need of some improvement. I devised the approach during a consultancy assignment for a unit of a large organisation with an appraisal scheme that allowed units flexibility in applying the scheme to their own context and needs.

Formal appraisal in the unit concerned had an unhappy history of failure to achieve improvements in the management of performance or development of its people. Its operational weaknesses had been compounded over recent years by a lack of any clear, effective HR strategy or systems to support developmental appraisal, and by a business strategy for the unit that, although convincing at design stage, repeatedly ran into problems of implementation. The unit had long had an uneasy relationship with the wider organisation, which regarded it as something of a maverick, performing strongly in relation to some targets but poorly in relation to others, with a generally capable and committed workforce but unreliable in its direction and management.

The new approach to appraisal was welcomed by staff during a series of workshops attended by mixed appraiser/appraisee groups across the unit. In conjunction with the workshops, it was seen by most to lend clarity to a confused process, and to identify ways in which appraisees could gain more control and exercise more initiative in relation to the annual formal appraisal process.

In the event, although the appraisal discussions themselves appeared to proceed more effectively and to receive more commitment from staff, and although top management resourced the whole training and appraisal process generously and was actively involved in it, the outcomes of the process proved little different from those in the past. This was unsurprising, since the original barriers to the success of appraisal in the unit, although identified and discussed with management on this occasion and apparently taken seriously at the time, subsequently remained. The expectations created by the improvements to the appraisal process were frustrated, and led to a further decline in staff morale. During the following year organisational and strategic changes occurred in the unit that increased rather than reduced those barriers.

Retrospectively the consultancy assignment can be seen, perhaps, as a wasted exercise. Sadly, appraisal, like the HRD process of which it is simply one element, cannot resolve deep-rooted problems related to business strategy, organisational effectiveness and HRM policy. At best it can expose them, but at worst it will be destroyed by them.

The development discussion

The discussion of developmental needs, whether or not within the context of formal appraisal, makes many demands on managers anxious both to ensure high standards of performance in their units and to help individuals develop over the longer term – and on the training analyst who needs to understand performance problems in order to produce relevant training and development initiatives. Some common problems are disagreement on learning needs, failure to agree priorities and claims of discriminatory treatment.

Disagreement on learning needs

- Some managers may not admit to failings in their performance and become hostile and defensive at any attempt to discuss them. Some, lacking self-confidence, may have too low an opinion of their performance and potential.

- Some may have too high an opinion of their performance and potential and be overconfident and resentful, seeing no need for training or development.

- Some managers may not be skilled or confident enough to deal with these forms of behaviour.

- Some may not know enough about the detail of what the individual actually does in his or her job, or about technical aspects of it, to feel able to give a view on the performance of the individual, or to identify developmental needs accurately.

Failure to agree priorities

- A manager, for example, may think that an individual needs interpersonal skills development, whereas the individual may think that this relates to only a very minor problem, and sees other training or development as much more important. A manager may want to focus all effort on training to reduce current gaps in performance, whereas the individual may be trying to achieve some discussion also of how his or her longer-term development in the company can be enhanced and where he or she is likely to be going in the company, ultimately.

Claims of discriminatory treatment

- The individual may not be able to appreciate why he or she is being denied opportunities for development that someone else enjoys. If the manager cannot give convincing reasons, then clearly the individual has a justifiable grievance. This could lead to a case for discrimination being taken to an employment tribunal (on grounds of failure to be given certain kinds of training or development that would give access to job or career opportunities in the organisation).

Tackling problems in the appraisal discussion

When faced with any of the above problems, how would you tackle them?

Feedback notes

Such problems cannot always be resolved, but useful aids to reducing their potential for wrecking the appraisal discussion include:

* training to tackle common problems and to build up those task and process skills essential for productive discussion of performance and development needs; Haringey Council's Housing Services, for example, trained all its housing managers over four years from 1990 in the skills of performance managers, with a particular emphasis on developing skills related to correcting poor performance constructively (Harris, 1995)

* special emphasis on training appraisers in the avoidance of discrimination in appraisal and its outcomes; records must be maintained to show patterns of training and development across a workforce, procedures used to identify needs and provide related learning opportunities, and the outcomes of such action

* the availability of ongoing guidance and counselling to help appraisers and others involved in the monitoring and improvement of individuals' performance try out their new skills and improve with practice

* the avoidance of an appraisal scheme design that incorporates ratings or rankings, where the aim of appraisal is to improve performance and develop potential

* the use of individual performance objectives that help individuals to understand their priorities and how their work fits in with the objectives of the organisation

* the appropriate use of competencies within an appraisal scheme; approached with a sense of proportion, discussion of competencies needed in the job can help individuals to understand their performance better, and to identify areas of strength even in a generally weak performance.

* (in some organisations) an appeals procedure related to the appraisal scheme. However, such a procedure may make appraisal a divisive process instead of a vehicle for joint problem-solving, planning and learning.

In any discussion of performance, a strategy of self-appraisal can be valuable in reducing interpersonal tensions because it gives the early initiative in the discussion to the job-holders, enabling *their* viewpoint on *their* performance and needs to be clearly expressed and to be the main driving force behind the opening up of the discussion. The appraiser must focus on listening, because the need is to learn and understand, not to judge. Once immediate needs have been agreed, there should be a discussion as to what kind of longer-term perspective the job-holder has on his or her work and career, and the kind of developmental actions that might bring the best advantage to individual and organisation in the coming period.

All action that is agreed should be recorded, noting:

* a clear distinction between job-related training and development on

the one hand and on the other learning experiences to support the individual's longer-term personal development plan (an aspect of career planning to be covered in detail in Chapter 19)

- the recommended training and development plan for the individual for the coming period

- timings for key elements of the plan

- resources needed for the plan

- the first date for appraiser and appraisee to meet in order to discuss progress with the plan.

Continuous development

In organisational life, everyday experience is the most fundamental influence on people's learning. This experience consists not simply of the work that people do, but of the way they interact with others in the organisation, and the behaviour, attitudes and values of those others. It consists, therefore, of people's entire work environment. If people are to learn continuously and to take advantage of the rich resources offered by the organisation as a learning system, they must be able to cope with the demands that change places on them and must have a mastery of the learning process. How can this learning ability be fostered? How, for example, can those responsible for employee development in a large organisation, with several thousand people in its workforce, hope to ensure continuous development for those individuals?

Continuous learning and development at Company X

Go back to Chapter 10 and read again the two-part case-study about Company X (pages 173–4, 181–2). Then identify the ways in which a climate conducive to continuous learning and development has been achieved, and how the commitment of line managers to supporting such learning is ensured in that company.

Feedback notes

The case-study produces a store of relevant information which we can summarise by recalling that, at Company X, the development of people is viewed by management as a fundamental business process, enabled and encouraged by:

- a clear HRD vision and strategy that is in line with overall business goals and strategy

- strategic HRD objectives that are carried through into detailed, practical plans for implementation of the policies that serve those objectives

- a form of organisational structure and company-wide procedures that ensure that the policies are carried out with the commitment and expertise of all who have been assigned training and development roles and responsibilities

- a system of training, guidance, monitoring, appraisal and rewards related to performance in those roles

- good management and utilisation of training and development resources.

We shall look again at self-development in Chapter 19, where we shall discuss methods that the individual can use, and the tasks of the HR professional in promoting self-development in his or her organisation. Suffice it to say here that continuous improvement and development of performance should be achieved mainly through day-to-day management actions and through an appraisal process that leads to the identification of developmental needs and to personal development plans.

As in all areas of HRD, *process* is what matters most here. There needs to be a collaborative approach between managers, any HR professionals, and individuals towards the management, review and development of performance. There must also be a conducive workplace environment, where weaknesses in performance can be admitted to, discussed and then tackled in a positive way. Good performance must also be recognised and built upon.

PULLING IT ALL TOGETHER

To review all the learning points in this chapter, here is a final task:

Auditing performance management and development

Imagine that you are have the task of planning an audit of the performance management process in your organisation. What 'Best practice' criteria would you propose in order to assess 'The performance management process' and 'Continuous improvement and recognition of performance'? Identify around six criteria under each of those headings.

Feedback notes
(The following is an extract from Harrison, 1999, pages 48–9, published by kind permission of Cambridge Strategy Publications)

Best-practice profile for the performance management process (PMP)

- There is a distinctive, well-communicated and well-understood process for the management of performance in this organisation.

- It is based on the philosophy that everyone shares the responsibility for the effective management and development of performance, and that all are jointly accountable for results that will help to achieve the organisation's goals and purpose.

- The PMP ensures clarity about the purpose of every job, role and function in the organisation. There are clearly defined, well understood standards of performance for every job, and the competence levels and values associated with those standards are well communicated and understood.

- The selection process ensures that people with appropriate aptitudes and values are placed in appropriate positions.

- There is a sound balance achieved in the PMP between the focus on performance needed to ensure achievement of work targets and the focus on development needed to ensure continuous improvement and adaptability.

- The effectiveness of the PMP is regularly evaluated, using such methods as questionnaires following review meetings, periodic attitude surveys and focus groups.

Best-practice profile for continuous improvement and recognition of performance

- Regular appraisal of individuals and of teams results in an accurate assessment of their performance, and in identification of their training and development (T&D) needs.

- Appraisers and appraisees jointly set targets, review performance and produce work plans. Together, they agree on how best to meet T&D needs.

- Personal development plans that are the outcome of the PMP are regularly monitored to ensure their effective implementation.

- The PMP ensures effective differentiation of performance levels achieved by individuals and teams.

- Effective performance of individuals and of teams is recognised and rewarded in ways that ensure a shared commitment to achieving the organisation's purpose and aims.

- The PMP ensures guidance and support when performance falls below required standards.

CONCLUSION

Having read this chapter and completed its reviews and self-checks, you should now:

- have a framework for identifying and understanding people's learning needs at work and the relationship of those needs to the demands of the organisation's performance management process (PMP)

- understand the importance of an effective balance between managing and developing people in the PMP

- be able to explain an integrated organisational programme for induction and basic skills training, appraisal and improvement of performance, and continuous learning and development.

To test yourself against these objectives, what five-minute answers would you give to the following questions? (Dates in brackets refer to the IPD qualifying examination paper in which a question appeared.)

- What can be done to achieve developmental appraisal in an organisation where appraisal in the past has been a token exercise with few, if any, meaningful outcomes? (Specimen paper, 1996)

- Explain and justify the response you, as training manager, would give to a manager who wants a group of his or her poorly performing staff to 'go on a training course to get up to scratch'. (November 1998)

- In organisation 'X', the form identifying an individual's training and development (T&D) plan produced as a result of an annual appraisal process has two sections. One section is to do with T&D related to his or her job in the coming year, and the other is to do with that individual's ongoing 'personal and professional development' (PPD). Outline and justify the kind of information that should be included in the PPD section. (May 1999)

USEFUL READING

ARMSTRONG M. *and* BARON A. (1998). *Performance Management: The new realities*. London, Institute of Personnel and Development.

FOWLER A. (1996) *Employee Induction: A good start*. 3rd edn. London, Institute of Personnel and Development.

HARRISON R. (1999) *The Training and Development Audit: An eight-step audit to measure, assess and enhance the performance of your organisation's training and development*. Cambridge, Cambridge Strategy Publications.

HONEY P. *and* MUMFORD A. (1992) *A Manual of Learning Styles*. 3rd edn. Maidenhead, Honey.

15 Learning design and delivery: Stage 1

LEARNING OBJECTIVES

After reading this chapter you will:

- have been introduced to an eight-stage approach to the planning, design and delivery of learning events

- in relation to the first stage, be able to identify and explain an appropriate framework and techniques for job training analysis to suit the particular situation

- be able to produce a job training specification and a training proposal to aid the development of competent performance.

INTRODUCING AN EIGHT-STAGE APPROACH TO LEARNING DESIGN AND DELIVERY

In Chapter 14 we saw that it is not necessary to have formalised training or planned learning events for valuable learning to be achieved. However, planned learning events usually form the core component of an organisation's overall human resource development (HRD) programme. It is with such events that this and the next three chapters are concerned. In these chapters the term 'learning event' will be used to indicate any learning activity that is formally designed in order to achieve specified learning objectives.

Table 11 (overleaf) shows the eight stages involved in the inception, design and delivery of a learning event. The first stage is covered in Chapter 14 and this chapter; in Chapter 16 we shall examine Stages 2 to 4; and, in Chapter 17, Stages 5 to 8.

STAGE 1: ESTABLISHING NEEDS

Job training analysis

In Chapter 6 we looked at the analysis of organisational learning needs within the strategic, business-led framework of HRD established in Chapter 5. In Chapter 14 we examined the analysis of individuals' learning needs, in relation to the performance management process and the longer-term goals of organisation and individuals. More detailed information and guidance on the analysis of organisational, group and individual needs can be found in the specialist texts noted in those chapters and in their reading lists.

However, it is also necessary to identify any important learning needs

Table 11 Eight stages in the inception, design and delivery of planned learning events

1 Establish needs.
2 Agree on the overall purpose and objectives for the learning event.
3 Identify the profile of the intended learning population.
4 Select strategy, and agree on direction and management of the learning event.
5 Select learners and produce detailed specification for the learning event.
6 Confirm strategy and design event.
7 Deliver event.
8 Monitor and evaluate event.

embedded in jobs: that is to say, the demands made by a job in terms of type and level of skills, knowledge and attitudes. This information can be obtained through job training analysis, which can be summarised as:

> the process of identifying the purpose of a job and its component parts, and specifying what must be learnt in order for there to be effective work performance. A key outcome of job training analysis is usually a job training specification which enables learning objectives to be established and appropriate training to be designed.

All jobs comprise three broad components: skills, knowledge and attitudes.

- *Skills.* Skills may be, for example, manual, diagnostic, interpersonal or decision-making. They include any component of the job that involves 'doing' something.

- *Knowledge.* Knowledge may be, for example, technical, procedural or concerned with company organisation. In the context of this chapter it relates to that which enables sense to be made of a job in order to ensure its competent performance. It is knowledge that endows meaning. It has been defined as 'a person's range of information' or sum of what he or she knows and understands (Allen, 1990). We shall be returning to the full organisational implications of that definition in the final chapter of this book.

- *Attitudes.* It may be important in a job that certain attitudes and types of behaviour are demonstrated at all times, for example courtesy and sensitivity in dealing with customers or clients; flexibility and co-operation when working in a close-knit team; or calmness and patience in coping with various tensions. The training analyst must note any attitudes that are critical to job performance.

Each of these components has implications for learning design and methods. A programme focused on the development of skills will be very different in its design and operation from a programme where the central focus is the promotion of certain attitudes or of particular areas of knowledge that the job-holder needs to acquire. With different combinations of these components occurring from one job to the next, it is essential to choose an appropriate analytical approach and techniques. We will now look at job training analysis (JTA) in some detail.

THE JOB TRAINING ANALYSIS PROCESS

JTA is a long-established process, described in many texts. In my case, I was particularly influenced by a framework first developed in a rather different form by Reid and Barrington (1997: 297–301). My own version follows here:

1 Initial investigation

Any request for training should always be met first with investigatory questions like the following:

Is training really the answer?

For example, poor performance may be due to ineffective supervision, lack of financial or other incentives, or lack of innate ability. If any of these is the primary cause, then training is not going to improve performance, and job training analysis is pointless.

Is training the most cost-beneficial answer?

There may be other ways that knowledge, skills or attitudes may be developed without the expense of formal training. Would careful integration of work and learning be more cost-beneficial? Or would buying in the skills or some other non-training solution be more appropriate?

Are there sufficient incentives for training to succeed?

Fairbairn (1991) pointed out that training will not be effective unless people want it; and they will only want it if they see that the skills, knowledge and attitudes it is promoting are important in their job, and recognised in their workplace. There must therefore be an analysis of how far the task or job is valued in the organisation, and how far effective performance in it will be supported and rewarded in ways that are meaningful to the job-holders.

This is particularly relevant when organisations are attempting to achieve multiskilling. For example, at Cummins Engine, Darlington (the company used as a case-study in Chapters 6 and 7), in the late 1980s and early 1990s employees were offered financial rewards for going through a series of modular skills training courses related to different areas of skill. That rebounded to some extent, because the message it appeared to convey was that training, rather than the outcomes resulting from it, was what was valued: training had become an end in itself. As a result, Cummins had to find ways of shifting the emphasis from rewarding people for undergoing training to rewarding them for the more skilled performance that was the outcome of training (see Harrison, 1996, for a full account of how HRD helped to ensure productivity and lay the foundations for long-term growth at Cummins during the 1980s).

Is analysis necessary?

Perhaps reliable and up-to-date information already exists about the job. Perhaps there is already a job training specification, either internally or externally produced.

Is the job likely to change?

If so, a new analysis will be needed when the change takes place, and that consideration has a bearing on the analytical approach to be chosen now. If change is likely, then why, how often, and over what period of time? Or is this a stable job, which will not alter much through time and will therefore repay the expense of detailed analysis now? Is it a job that many people do, or is it fairly unique?

Should the person be adapted to the job, or the job to the person?

With certain jobs – for example, those at the top level of the organisation, those that are very specialised or those involving a high degree of innovative talent – it may be more important for the person to make the job than the job make the person. The job-holder's vision of how the role should be translated into reality, and the identity they give to the job, may matter far more than any predetermined specification. In such a situation selection and reward, not training, are the critical processes.

2 Selecting the analyst

In most organisations it is specialist staff, whether internal or external, who carry out job training analysis. However, it is the line manager and the person who actually does the job who know most about the job, so whoever carries out the analysis must be acceptable to those parties. A related point is that much of a sensitive nature can be uncovered during the process of job training analysis: motivation, discipline and supervision problems; misunderstandings caused by ill-defined responsibilities; and conflict and inefficiency arising from inappropriate organisation structures or cultures. The training analyst, having identified these issues, must know how to draw them to the attention of those who can deal with them, and must influence those parties to take action. Until that happens training cannot be effective.

3 Gaining co-operation

Before the job training analysis process starts, everyone involved in, and likely to be significantly affected by, the activity must be given a clear explanation of its purpose, how it will be carried out, by whom, over what period of time, and with what probable outcomes. If the analysis is likely to have outcomes tied to pay awards and/or gradings, then there must be an appeals procedure. Willing co-operation of all the parties is essential to the success of job training analysis.

4 Selecting analytical approach and techniques

Information obtained in steps one to three will enable the analyst to decide which approach and techniques to choose (these will be explained in the next section).

5 Carrying out the analysis

Here the analyst needs to consider two factors: the sources of information to use and the depth of analysis required.

Sources of information

Written sources are liable to be produced on differing bases, and may be out of date, or not comprehensive. Care must therefore be taken when referring to technical manuals or to records of various kinds. Records should reveal essential information such as whether the job is one where there have been many problems in performance, or whether good standards of performance are the norm; and whether there are any trends in labour turnover, absenteeism, sickness or lateness that could relate to difficulties experienced in the job. Job descriptions will be particularly useful, but will need careful checking to ensure they are up to date, accurate and comprehensive.

Oral sources of information – eg the job-holder, the job-holder's manager, co-workers – are all liable to be biased, and may sometimes contradict one another in their perception both of the content and characteristics of the job and – very important – in its order of priorities. Such sources may be deliberately or unintentionally misleading. Handling them will require considerable interpersonal and political skill.

Depth of analysis

In any method of job training analysis, it is vital to decide how much detail is needed about a task and the skills, knowledge and attitudes required to do it. Annett, Duncan, Stammers and Gray (1979) suggested that every task in a job should continue to be broken down and described until the point is reached where the remainder of the task can be readily learnt without training and does not in any case require flawless performance. As we shall see when looking at the different approaches, this principle will not always work in practice.

The analyst must also look for any problems in the workplace – either social or work-related – that could impede transfer of training by making it difficult for the trainee to apply learning acquired in a training programme.

6 Producing the job training specification

When the process of analysing the job is finished and the information has been carefully checked, the analyst will in most cases have to produce a job training specification, agreed as accurate by the parties involved.

> **The job training specification**
>
> What is a job training specification, and what does it specify?

Feedback notes

- The job training specification describes in overall terms the job for which training is to be given, or the key problem areas in a job which training will enable learners to tackle.

- It then specifies the kinds and levels of knowledge, skill and, where relevant, attitudes needed for effective performance, together with the standards that will operate in the job and the criteria for measuring achievement of standards.

To understand how to produce a job training specification, we need to look more closely at job training analysis approaches, since each approach tends to call for a particular format of job training specification.

JOB TRAINING ANALYSIS APPROACHES

There are many approaches to job training analysis. Some useful sources of information about them are shown at the end of this chapter. Outstanding in the field, as are so many US texts on HRD, is Mills, Pace and Peterson (1988).

For this section I have selected four of the commonest job training analysis approaches:

* comprehensive analysis

* key task analysis

* problem-centred analysis

* competency-based analysis.

Comprehensive analysis

This involves a detailed examination of every aspect of the job until each task has been fully described in terms of its knowledge, skills and (if relevant) attitudes. The task must also be described by reference to its objectives, its frequency of performance, its standards of performance, and ways of measuring that performance.

Clearly this is an extremely time-consuming analytical approach and requires much skill. The first question to ask, therefore, is 'In which circumstances is it to be recommended?'

Here are some criteria:

* *when tasks are unfamiliar to learners, difficult, all more or less equally important, and must be learnt quickly and to standard.* In such a situation there is a need for a thorough approach that will cover the full scope of the job

* *when change is unlikely* and new recruits are fairly frequent. If these conditions apply, the expense involved in comprehensive analysis will soon be offset by the number of times training resulting from it can be carried out before it is necessary to do any fresh analysis. New recruits may be frequent because this is a category of job held by large numbers of people in the workplace, or perhaps because there are unavoidably high levels of turnover

* *when the job is closely prescribed.* If little or nothing can be left to the initiative of the job-holders, then it is essential that they learn the correct ways of performing virtually all tasks in the job

* *when resources are adequate.* There must be the resources available (time, skill, numbers of staff) to carry out this detailed, complex and time-consuming approach.

What is involved in comprehensive analysis? Two key tasks:

Producing a job description

This is a broad statement of the purpose, scope, responsibilities and tasks that constitute a particular job. The job description should contain:

* the title of the job

- its overall purpose, preferably expressed in a sentence summarising the purpose as far as the organisation is concerned

- the name of the department/division/unit in which the job-holder works

- the title of the person/s to whom the job-holder is responsible directly and (if different) ultimately

- brief details of any other key relationships, for example with staff in another department/division/unit, and/or with people or institutions outside the organisation

- an indication of any major resources for which the job-holder is accountable (finance, physical resources, personnel)

- an indication as to whether the job-holder works mainly on his or her own, is part of a fixed team, or is expected to move through various teams according to task needs

- a list of major tasks and priorities

- brief details of any difficulties commonly experienced in the job which need attention in training.

Producing a job training specification

For every task of the job, divided as necessary into sub-tasks or elements, the job training specification should show the skill, knowledge and (if relevant) attitudes required; the standards of performance to be reached; and how performance will be measured. The way the specification is laid out and the kind of information it contains will depend on the analytical techniques used. However, the specification is a guide to action (because it leads to the design of a training programme) and must therefore have a simple, easily understood format and be clearly expressed.

Key task analysis

This approach takes only the crucial tasks within a job – ie those tasks in which performance of a certain kind is critical to competency in the job overall. Comprehensive analysis is used most commonly for jobs consisting of simple, usually manual, repetitive and unchanging tasks. On the other hand, those jobs involving more complex skills such as observation and reflection, analysis, creativity, decision-making and problem-solving, and evaluation need a clear overview of the job, together with a focus on what is most essential for successful performance. For such jobs the key task approach is often the most appropriate.

Once again, a brief job description needs to be produced in exactly the same format as in comprehensive analysis. However, the job training specification must this time be selective, covering only those tasks crucial to competent job performance.

Key task analysis is appropriate for any type of job where the following conditions apply:

- *Tasks are varied, and not all are critical.* The job should consist of a large number of different tasks, not all of which are critical for competent performance. It is assumed that the job-holder requires training only in those tasks that are crucial (key) to effective performance in the job.

• *The job is changing in emphasis or in content*, so that priority tasks, standards and identification of skills and knowledge may have to be identified and analysed regularly.

Problem-centred analysis

This approach focuses on defining problem/s that require a training solution. The analysis seeks to identify the nature and causes of each problem and the skills, knowledge and attitudes (if relevant) needed to cope successfully with it. The analytical process actively involves job-holders in considering what kind of training they would find most effective.

Warr and Bird (1968) did pioneering work on this approach with their 'training by exception' technique. They developed it when their attempts to use, first, comprehensive and then key task analysis to identify supervisory training needs failed because of the diversity of supervisory tasks and the amount of time needed to analyse them.

The problem-centred approach is most appropriately used when:

• *training is urgent*, but analytical resources limited

• *the job-holder's work is satisfactory* except in one or two 'problem' areas

• *involvement of learners* in analysis is important.

It is a relevant approach to use in conjunction with key task analysis when designing training for people new to jobs for which they already have most of the skills and knowledge required, but where they must get to grips quickly with any problematic areas. The two approaches also work well together when it is important to ensure that the job-holders have a clear understanding of key tasks and difficulties commonly associated with them.

With the problem-centred approach there is no one way of gathering and collating the information. Whichever methods are used must ensure that the perspectives on the problems of job-holder/s, their supervisors, managers and any other key parties are obtained. This approach does not involve drawing up a job description or a job training specification because its outcome is simply a description of the problems and how they can be tackled in training. Problem-centred analysis will reveal:

• *common training needs*. Needs will emerge that are common to all or most of the group. These can form the basis of a core training programme or other kind of learning event.

• *individualised training needs*. There will also be needs specific to individuals that will have to be met using personal learning plans.

• *training/learning strategies suggested by job-holders*. These will be the learning approaches and methods that job-holders are confident will best help them to overcome identified problems.

• *learners' commitment*. Because of the methodology it involves, the approach is likely to obtain the commitment of those who will be participants in the ensuing planned learning events. They have to take a leading role in the diagnosis and analysis of their problems and needs and in suggesting training solutions, and so the objectives and relevance of the learning events do not need to be explained to them. From the start of the analytical process they begin to 'own' those events, and the drive to learn is a natural outcome.

Competency-based analysis

This approach involves identifying what is needed to produce effective performance in a role, job or function. Like the problem-centred approach, it is both job- and person-related, and tends to be used in an organisation when:

• *there is a need to develop clearly defined standards of performance relating to one or more occupational groups.* This is usually because lack of such standards is impeding attempts to measure and improve performance and to establish clear guidelines for selection, training, development, rewards, and succession and career-planning.

and/or when

• *there is a need to relate training within the organisation to national vocational training standards and qualifications.* Competencies identified in a particular organisation as necessary to performance of jobs at different levels can be related to lists of competencies required at each of four or five levels in order to achieve National Vocational Qualifications (NVQs) across different occupations. Appropriate training, development and assessment in the workplace can then enable individuals to acquire NVQs at the necessary level.

and/or when

• *the main concern is to identify the core behavioural attributes* needed in order to perform effectively across a job sector (usually, but not necessarily, management) and the extent to which those attributes are, or are not, possessed by all job-holders in that sector.

Woodruffe (1991) observed that the word 'competency' carries two different meanings:

• Used in a job-related sense, it refers to areas of work at which a person is competent. Here, he recommended use of an alternative term: *areas of competence.*

• Used in a person-related sense, it refers to dimensions of behaviour that lie behind competent performance. Here, he recommended use of the term *competency.*

For a thorough explanation of competencies and the applications to which competency frameworks have been put, you are recommended to read Whiddett and Hollyforde (1999). Other useful texts and articles are shown at the end of the chapter. Here, the aim is simply to provide an introduction to the field.

We have already outlined the concept and practical applicability of a competency framework (Chapter 9, pages 157–8 and Chapter 14, pages 246–7). Many organisations now base training and development programmes on definitions of 'competencies' relating to a particular group or sector in the organisation.

Competency-based analysis results in the production of:

- a statement of the role or purpose of the general category of job being studied (ie managerial jobs, or managerial jobs at a particular level) in the organisation

- a breakdown of that role into its discrete areas of competence

- statements of the competencies needed to perform satisfactorily in each of those areas

- criteria for measuring competency in each area.

To review what has been covered so far in this chapter on job training analysis:

Job training analysis

Outline four job training analysis approaches and identify the kinds of situation most appropriate for the use of each. Then take one type of job in your organisation where a different approach to job training analysis would lead to more effective training; explain why.

In this part of the chapter we have looked at four job training analysis approaches. Now let us examine some of the techniques with which they are associated.

JOB TRAINING ANALYSIS TECHNIQUES

Again, this section simply outlines a range of techniques described in more detail in specialist texts. Widely known techniques that need no coverage here include:

- activity analysis (Miller, 1962)

- manual skills analysis (Seymour, 1966; Gentles, 1969). This is one of the best-known techniques. However, it is very time-consuming and requires a high degree of specialist skill. The obvious danger with such a costly technique is that one change to an operating method may well lead to the whole analytical process having to be repeated

- critical incidents analysis (Flanagan, 1954)

- faults analysis, and stages and key points analysis (Reid and Barrington, 1999, 209–12)

However, there are three sets of techniques that, because they are particularly valuable in relation to complex jobs/roles, will be discussed at this point. They are those involved in role analysis, interpersonal and interactive skills analysis, and competency-based analysis.

Role analysis

In managerial jobs especially, it is vital to be clear about the role, or roles, that the job-holder must carry. As was demonstrated at the start of Chapter 9, training for anyone who is moving into a training manager's job will benefit from being based on role analysis, because of the importance of role issues in training management.

The technique involved derives from the behavioural sciences, notably from the work of the industrial psychologist McGregor (1960), who emphasised how important it was to build up a shared perception of the manager's role among members of that manager's role set. French and Bell (1978) summarised the various procedures to be carried out. Basically they require job-holder, manager and (usually) one or more other members of the role set (ie those people with whom the role-holder regularly interacts) each to produce a list of the duties and behaviour that they perceive necessary if the job-holder is to be effective. A role description is then produced from joint discussion of the different lists. It contains the key features of the job.

Machin (1981) showed how an 'expectations' approach can highlight any disagreements within the role set about the role being analysed. Use of the approach can generate open discussion in order to produce full understanding of the role, the resolution of most disagreement and a job description which has the assent of the parties. If, despite this, conflicting perceptions and expectations remain, then the analyst must bring these to the attention of management. If the conflict is not tackled it will impede job performance, create wider organisational problems and produce situations for which training is not an effective remedy.

Interpersonal and interactive skills analysis

A wide range of jobs, especially supervisory, managerial, professional and technical, make heavy demands on the job-holder in terms of their requirements for skill in dealing with face-to-face situations and in achieving the effective interaction of people and tasks in a work cycle. Such skills are difficult to analyse, but there are a number of well-established techniques available. These include Rackham, Honey and Colbert's (1971) techniques for analysing interactive skills; transactional analysis, described fully by Carby and Thakur (1977); and diagnostic techniques and instruments related to developing leadership and teamwork skills produced by researchers and trainers like Belbin (1981), Leigh and Maynard (1996), and Wright and Taylor (1994).

Competency-based analysis

There are many techniques that can be used here, including behavioural event interviewing (Boyatzis, 1982), a complex technique for which special training is required. To give a flavour of what is involved in this kind of analysis, let us carry out a task based on analysing two case-studies. They are repeated from my 1992 text and, in the sense of management development's having moved on since then in both organisations, they are out of date. However, both remain valid when used to illustrate in a quite striking way two different approaches to competency-based analysis.

Case-study: Competency-based management development

What strategy lay behind the use by BP and Manchester Airport plc of a competency-based approach to management development? What is the main difference between the approaches they used?

British Petroleum (Source: Greatrex and Phillips, 1989)

In the late 1980s BP carried out much work on management competencies in order to ensure effective management performance, and training and development to cope with the major changes that were then taking place in the company. Because of new directions in its business strategy, its culture had to become more market-oriented and client-centred, and its managers had to be more entrepreneurial in their approach to the business. There was also a need for a less hierarchical management structure, devolved accountability, and a more open and flexible management style throughout BP.

There was a concern to avoid reliance on any universal list of competencies. Instead, analysis was organisation-specific, identifying those competencies needed in order to manage effectively in the BP environment.

By 1989 a rigorous process of analysis had produced a list of 11 core areas of competency, grouped into four clusters of behaviours that differentiated high-performers from the rest. BP had always placed a high value on assessment centres as a way of diagnosing training and development needs and highlighting potential. It now incorporated competency assessment into its assessment boards, and individual managers were assessed and ranked in relation to the 11 competency areas using a five-point behaviourally defined scale to identify the extent to which they possessed each individual attribute. From this process of analysis and diagnosis, development programmes for individuals were in due course drawn up.

BP derived its competencies from its vision and values and then used them in many of its personnel initiatives and in its culture change. The approach proved particularly valuable as an aid for training, personal and career development, and for the self-development of managers.

Manchester Airport plc (Source: Jackson, 1989)

A competency-based approach to management development was also used by Manchester Airport in the late 1980s in order to achieve a systematic approach to the selection, training and development of senior managers at a time of fast growth and major changes when the airport had just (1986) become a public limited company (plc).

The first stage in the design of a programme was to develop a template for superior performance at senior management level. In 1988 the directors met to agree the attributes that the company expected from its managers at this level. They were based on 15 of the defined (US) McBer list of managerial competencies, which have been found quite widely to predict success in performing managerial jobs. The role of the group had to be examined, since it was clear that, in assessing what was needed for future performance, reliance could not be placed on past types of competency.

The profile that emerged identified clusters of behaviours associated with the three core competencies needed by all senior managers at Manchester Airport plc, whatever their specific jobs:

- *understanding what needs to be done* – critical reasoning; strategic visioning; business know-how
- *getting the job done* – achievement drive; proactivity; confidence; control; flexibility; concern for effectiveness; direction
- *taking people with you* – motivation; interpersonal skills; concern for impact; persuasion; influence.

This profile was checked against job analysis information already in existence at the airport to ensure its validity. It was also agreed that the new criteria for successful performance of the job would be used for subsequent selection and promotion decisions within the group. Performance review and reward decisions would be based on the criteria agreed as underpinning superior performance (Jackson, 1989: 4).

All managers then had to go through a two-day assessment centre; they were assessed by the directors (who had received special training) and the consultants, who had helped internal personnel staff design the whole project. Each manager was rated against every attribute. Attributes associated with core competencies were defined in behavioural terms at four levels, from 'Low' to 'Outstanding'. Thus, for example:

Attribute involved in 'Getting the job done': Direction.

Definition: being able to tell others what they must do and confront performance problems; to plan, organise, schedule, delegate and follow up.

Low: unable to confront others about performance problems, to enforce rules, or to insist that subordinates comply with directives. No experience or is unwilling to delegate to subordinates the responsibility for doing anything other than less significant tasks.

Outstanding: confronts staff when they fail to meet standards. Has contingency plans for all objectives. Sets demanding objectives for staff. Demonstrates the ability to organise large numbers of people.

After the assessment process individual profiles were drawn up, summarising the assessed level for each competence. Written reports were produced, and each manager had feedback sessions first with a consultant, then with personnel and top management staff. Personal Improvement Plans were produced by each individual and were incorporated in annual targets for the forthcoming year.

Jackson detailed the positive results of the project, and concluded that the model for superior performance was confirmed by the evidence.

Feedback notes
- In both examples the strategy was the same: to define the core competencies needed by all managers in the specific organisational context in which they have to operate (whether or not they break them down into different levels within the management sector, as was

done at Manchester Airport); and to use those competencies both as criteria for assessment of individuals in order to define training and development needs and as aids to improving work performance.

- The difference lies in the ways competencies were identified. At BP, analysis of the performance of the company's managers led to identification of clusters of attributes associated with the core competencies perceived to underpin effective work performance. Analysis thus started with examining prevailing patterns of behaviour and led ultimately to the identification of core competencies needed by all BP managers.

- We are not told here what technique was used to identify core competencies, but it could well have been Boyatzis' (1982) Behavioural Event Interviewing. This technique involves taking a range of job-holders currently working in the organisation. Usually they are chosen by senior managers, although sometimes the views of peers and subordinates may also inform that choice. The aim is to select a mix of those agreed to be excellent in their performance and those who are rated as adequate but no more than that.

- The next stage is to interview the job-holders, using interviewers specially trained for this purpose who have no knowledge of the performance ratings of the job-holders. Each individual is asked to describe a number of events in which they played a key part, and is then probed to establish exactly what he or she did in each event; why; the thought processes that shaped behaviour at the time; and the outcome of the event.

- There is then a complex and lengthy process of analysing the data from these interviews, with a number of cross-checks used to ensure uniformity of standards and techniques and objectivity of analysis. The analysis leads to the production of a 'competency profile' of each individual which is then compared with previously obtained rankings of their job performance (see above). In this way, the characteristics and behaviour patterns unique to those who are high-achievers emerge, and core competencies required for excellent performance can thus be identified and described in appropriate behavioural terms.

- A similar process, but aimed at identifying the characteristics of effective (rather than, or as well as, excellent) performance, can be devised by widening the sample group to include some who are generally agreed to be less than satisfactory in their job performance.

- At Manchester, that BP process was reversed. Core competencies were defined first, using a universal model (McBer's). They were then checked against definitions of management jobs in the company and felt to be valid. Next, analysis was carried out to define the clusters of attributes needed to reach a satisfactory standard in each of those core competencies. Finally, individuals were assessed to find how much or little of each attribute they possessed, and development plans were produced after discussing and agreeing with managers that these were indeed attributes they recognised as necessary to effective performance in their jobs. Checks were made to ensure that the universal model had been used in a way that fully met the particular needs of the airport's senior managers.

Performance analysis

Analysing a job-holder's performance can be classed as a technique in the sense that it should reveal any problems being experienced or likely to be experienced in reaching required performance standards; typical faults encountered in the work and how to deal with them; and other valuable information.

Where performance analysis is not an intrinsic part of an analytical technique it should always be carried out in addition. There has already been discussion about how to tackle the analysis of performance in Chapter 14. More detailed discussion can be found in the usual specialist texts.

PRODUCING A TRAINING PROPOSAL

In this chapter we have so far reviewed four approaches to job training analysis, and a variety of analytical techniques that can be used singly or in various combinations, as appropriate. Now, it is important to understand how to incorporate key information from analysis into a training proposal for submission to management – in other words, how to make a business case for a proposed learning event.

Training proposals

A proposal should be as brief as possible (see an example in Gilley and Eggland, 1989: 211–12), and it must be expressed in 'business' language. It should cover the following:

- the aim of the training/development event – why it is needed, what it will cost

- the outcomes that the event should achieve, and their relevance and value to the organisation

- the learners who will be involved, by reference to number, types and levels of jobs in the organisation, and any other relevant information

- the timescale proposed for the event

- how and by whom the event will be monitored and evaluated

- a brief outline of the proposed event, showing design, main content areas, learning strategy and key personnel who will be involved in its delivery

- any training of those personnel that may be needed (for example, any competency assessment for NVQ purposes to be done will require expertise for which training will be essential).

Information needed

Job training specifications supply crucial information needed in order to produce a training proposal, because they contain the following:

- a description in overall terms of the job for which training is to be given, or the key problem areas in a job which training will enable learners to tackle

- a specification and prioritisation of the kinds and levels of knowledge, skill and, where relevant, attitudes needed for effective performance

- a statement of the standards that will operate in the job and the criteria for measuring achievement of standards.

In addition, information about the following will help in the production of a training proposal:

Previous programmes

Have programmes been run for this job before? If so, are there any evaluations, formal or informal?

Job changes

Have there been any changes in the job – its purpose, key tasks, etc – since the job training specification and personnel specification (if any) were drawn up? If so, do those changes have training or development implications?

Training standards to be attained, and the type of learners who will be involved

What type of learners will be involved in this training event, and what are the standards to be achieved? For example, if this is to be a basic skills training course for new recruits, then will it need to take those new recruits up to an above-average or only to an essential level of performance?

A good personnel specification should list qualities/ competencies needed to perform a job at two levels, not one: 'desirable' and 'essential'. This will enable differentiation at selection stage between applicants likely to perform the job to a high standard immediately, and those likely to be able to perform to only an adequate level. The basic skills training course must take those different performance levels of new recruits into account.

Timing of the training programme

When and for how long is the event to run? How will its timing relate to work schedules of the departments concerned, and to the timescale for achieving the performance goals with which the event is concerned?

Here is an exercise that requires you to integrate learning and knowledge from both this and the previous chapter in order to feel confident you understand the first stage of our eight-stage approach to the planning and delivery of learning events. In the next chapter we shall move on to Stages 2 and 3.

Producing a training and development proposal

Using the seven headings noted at the start of this section on training proposals, produce a proposal for a learning event that will meet needs related to a job in your own organisation or one with which you are familiar. The job should be one for which either a job training specification is available, or for which you yourself, as part of this activity, can produce one.

CONCLUSION

Having read this chapter and completed its reviews and self-checks, you should now:

- have been introduced to an eight-stage approach to the planning, design and delivery of learning events

- in relation to the first stage, be able to identify and explain an appropriate framework and techniques for job training analysis to suit the particular situation

- be able to produce a job training specification and a training proposal to aid the development of competent performance.

To test yourself against these objectives, what five-minute answers would you give to the following questions? (Dates in brackets refer to the IPD qualifying examination paper in which a question appeared.)

- Identify **three** different approaches to job training analysis and the kinds of situation for which **one of those three** approaches would be best suited. (May 1997)

- When designing a training programme to prepare a small group of employees who have been selected for promotion and in two months will move up into supervisory posts in different parts of their organisation, what approach to job training analysis should be used, and why? (May 1998)

- As training manager, you are preparing to submit to management a written proposal for a new basic skills training course relating to a particular type of job in the organisation. List and justify essential points that you must cover in that proposal. (November 1998)

USEFUL READING

BEE F. *and* BEE R. (1994) *Training Needs Analysis and Evaluation.* London, Institute of Personnel and Development.

BOYDELL T. *and* LEARY M. (1996) *Identifying Training Needs.* London, Institute of Personnel and Development.

BRITTAIN S. *and* RYDER P. (1999) 'Get complex'. *People Management.* Vol.5, 23. pp48–51. (Challenges conventional wisdom on competencies.)

COOPER C. L. (ed.) (1981) *Improving Interpersonal Relations: Some approaches to interpersonal skills training.* Aldershot, Gower.

HACKETT P. (1997) *Introduction to Training.* London, Institute of Personnel and Development.

THOMAS K. *and* MELLON T. (1995) *Planning for Training and Development: A guide to analysing needs.* London, Save the Children. (For those working in the voluntary sector on the identification of training needs, production of development plans and budgets, and training evaluation.)

WHIDDETT S. *and* HOLLYFORDE S. (1999) *The Competencies Handbook.* London, Institute of Personnel and Development. (Gives a comprehensive and practical introduction to the competency field.)

16 Learning design and delivery: Stages 2 to 4

LEARNING OBJECTIVES

After reading this chapter you will:

- understand the importance of clear and appropriate purpose and objectives for a learning event

- know how to produce a profile of a learning population and relate this to a choice of learning strategies

- understand the practical issues affecting choice of learning strategies

- be able to draw up purpose, behavioural objectives and strategy for a learning event.

THE EIGHT-STAGE APPROACH TO PLANNING AND DELIVERING LEARNING EVENTS (CONT.)

Let us look again (Table 11) at the eight-stage approach introduced in Chapter 15. Summarising Stage 1, we have seen in Chapters 14 and 15 that learning needs can be identified in a number of ways, relating both to a current situation and to future contingencies. Once needs have been agreed and prioritised, there must be confirmation that some form of learning event is required to meet those needs.

In this chapter we shall look at the next three stages of the approach – agreeing on the purpose of the learning event, identifying the profile of the learners, and planning the event.

STAGE 2: ESTABLISHING PURPOSE AND OBJECTIVES

The purpose of a learning event answers the question why the event is taking place, whereas its objectives define what attitudinal, behavioural

Table 11 **Eight stages in the inception, design and delivery of planned learning events**

1   Establish needs.
2   Agree on the overall purpose and objectives for the learning event.
3   Identify the profile of the intended learning population.
4   Select strategy, and agree on direction and management of the learning event.
5   Select learners and produce detailed specification for the learning event.
6   Confirm strategy and design event.
7   Deliver event.
8   Monitor and evaluate event.

or performance outcomes are to be achieved. It is essential to define the purpose and objectives of a planned learning event clearly, since these provide the context of the event. If there are errors at this stage, expensive resources are going to be wasted in carrying out irrelevant activities.

The interrelationship between purpose and objectives

Ideally, the designer of the learning event should have been involved in formulating the learning objectives, in line with an overall purpose that has already been agreed with a 'client' in the organisation. In reality, the designer may have to work to objectives that have already been established by someone else. This can pose many problems if, even when it seems clear that objectives should be changed or modified in some way, such change seems impossible. Here is a case-study based on a real-life situation. Certain specifics have been changed in order to ensure the anonymity of the institution.

Case-study: 'X' University and the course review

The business school of X University had just gone through the external teaching review process, and one of its programmes – a two-year part-time post-experience management course – had been singled out for critical comment. The programme has been running for many years, but in the last five has undergone a significant change of emphasis. Key points made were:

1 The programme had in the past carried a clear educational purpose which had been reflected in its formalised and theoretically focused methods of assessment. Five years ago, however, the business school decided that, in order to reflect national trends, there had to be a change in focus to the development of managerial competencies (although it decided not to deliver a competency-based programme tied to national occupational standards – the focus was on competencies in the more generalised sense).

2 Consistent with this overall purpose, the learning objectives had become skills-oriented. However, the dominating method of assessment remained the formal examination. All subjects were assessed in that way, and the format of each paper remained what it had long been: a three-hour, closed-book paper, with a choice of four out of 10 or 12 questions.

3 Students who did well in the examinations, and in the programme overall, were consistently those with a proven record of high academic attainment, whether accompanied by practical competence or not. Those without such a record, however competent they were known to be in the workplace and however well they did in the practical activities and assignments on the course, achieved notably less well. Such students in fact made up the bulk of those who failed the programme – usually about 15 per cent.

4 The skills-oriented objectives of the programme called for a resource level that the course leader, struggling with the large classes that she was obliged to recruit and with inadequate staffing ratios, could rarely obtain. Access to film, closed-circuit television, video,

computers and library facilities was difficult because of the heavy demand on those resources made by other programmes. Technical support was also patchy and unreliable.

5 Students recruited on to the programme differed widely in the skills and knowledge that they possessed related to the course content. This was unsurprising in such a large part-time programme, where the selection process was not very discriminating. They also entered the programme with widely varying levels and types of learning skills and styles. Several had no ongoing experience of one or more of the core modules, and practical activities during class time provided the only medium through which they could be helped to 'acquire' such experience. Visits to external organisations were rare because of the large numbers of students and timetabling problems. Good outside speakers were highly valued, but those charging fees were little used because of their cost; the performance of voluntary speakers, on the other hand, was variable.

The review concluded that the examination failure rate was understandable in the circumstances but unacceptable, and noted the declining rate of recruitment on to the course, coupled with decline in the quality of recruits. The business school was advised to reconsider the overall purpose of the programme, its learning objectives and its assessment methods; and to revise the cost and activity base of the programme in order to generate more resources if it could find no other way to resolve its resource problems.

The business school responded to the review by confirming the purpose and most of the overall objectives of the course, and by altering the structure and methods of assessment accordingly. A new emphasis was placed on assessing competencies at final as well as interim stages mainly through the vehicle of work-based projects. Resourcing, however, remained a taxing problem not only in relation to this programme but more generally in the business school and the university.

In this case-study, note the influence exercised by the overall purpose and the learning objectives of the management programme. Discrepancies there started off a chain of difficulties which led, in the end, to unsatisfactory outcomes of the whole complex learning event. If, five years ago, the course leader and her colleagues had looked more critically at the educational and practical implications of running the kind of revised programme the business school wanted them to deliver – in other words, if at the start of the change process they had queried the programme's overall purpose and objectives – then at least some of the problems would have been avoided and the resource issue would have been highlighted at a time when it could have been properly considered.

Note, too, how little is said in the study about contextual factors that would, in real life, be important to examine in order to decide whether or not the programme itself should be continued. Perhaps it has outlived its purpose, and consideration needs to be given to other ways of improving the business school's ability to achieve its business goals. What is the nature of those goals, and the business and human resource (HR) strategies to achieve them? What role does the school play in the wider university? What is the position of the university itself in what will undoubtedly have become a dynamic competitive environment?

The main lesson to be learnt from such case-studies is that the designer of a learning event should always challenge its purpose or objectives if they seem inappropriate in some important way, given the nature of the event, its planned outcomes, the context in which it must operate and the place it occupies in the organisation's overall programme for developing its people.

Levels of objectives

Except in very simple learning situations, it is helpful to formulate learning objectives at two levels: final and intermediate.

Final behavioural objectives

Sometimes known as 'ultimate' or 'criterion' or 'overall' objectives, these, however they are titled, explain the kind of outcomes that the learner should have achieved once the learning event is completed.

Intermediate behavioural objectives

Sometimes known as 'interim' or 'specific' objectives, these, however they are titled, explain the kind of outcomes that the learner should have achieved at key stages of the learning process.

You may have noted the use of the phrase 'behavioural objectives' in the above definitions; also the reference to 'outcomes'. This is because the clearest guide to design can be obtained not so much by stating what the learning event aims to do in general terms but in closely specifying what the learner should be capable of by the end of parts or the whole of the event.

To illustrate this point, consider the difference between two ways of defining one of the objectives of this chapter:

Example 1

One of the aims of this chapter is to explain the term 'learning objectives'.

Example 2

After reading this chapter and completing the various checks it contains, you should be able to understand what is meant by 'learning objectives' in order to be able to draw up objectives related to a learning event.

From the reader's point of view, Example 1 says what the chapter aims to do, but only in a very generalised way, with no explanation of intended outcomes. On the other hand, Example 2 gives concise information on 'what'. It should therefore act as a stimulus to readers by explaining what they will be able to do by the end of the chapter (provided, of course, that the learning outcome is something they want to achieve).

From my own point of view, if I had been given the kind of generalised brief set out in Example 1 it would have been hard to decide what to put into the chapter. However, with Example 2 it is clear that providing a simple explanation of 'learning objectives' will not be enough. I realise that I shall have to help the reader to understand the meaning of the term 'learning objectives', and then to make practical use of the concept. So I shall have to build in a variety of practical illustrations (like this one), exercises, and review activities, as well as theory.

Expressing objectives in behavioural terms identifies not only what the learning event aims to do, but what sort of skills, knowledge or attitudes the learner should acquire and the kind of content and methods of learning that will be appropriate. Objectives should also indicate the conditions in which learners will ultimately carry out the learning, and the standards they will need to reach.

Behavioural objectives

What is meant by 'behavioural objectives', and how should they be expressed? Draw up some behavioural objectives for a training course of your choice.

Feedback notes
- Behavioural objectives give a clear focus to the learning event and to its design by explaining the outcomes they will help the learners to achieve.

- The most helpful objectives are those that describe not only the kinds of behaviour to be achieved at the end of the learning event but also the conditions under which that behaviour is expected to occur and the standards to be reached in that behaviour.

Your behavioural objectives should therefore meet these two criteria.

STAGE 3: IDENTIFYING THE PROFILE OF THE LEARNERS

Once needs, overall purpose and ultimate objectives of the learning event have been agreed, the type of learners to be involved should be identified. At this stage, little may be known about individuals – selection for the learning event will probably come at a later stage. What will be known is the sort of numbers likely to be involved, the levels of the organisation from which they will be drawn (some, of course, may come from outside the organisation, perhaps from suppliers or purchasers) and the kinds of learning strategies likely to be most relevant for them.

Information should at this stage be sought on four aspects of the learning population. Subsequently, when individuals have been selected for the learning event, this information will need to be expanded and the design of the event adjusted as necessary:

- numbers and location

- jobs and competencies

- learning styles and skills

- attitudes and motivation.

Numbers and location of learners

Small numbers should enable quite individualised learning. However, the location of the learners will be important: a small number spread over different, and widely dispersed, physical locations indicates at first sight a need for some form of distance learning, with occasional workshops to bring the group together (see, for example, the sales training programme proposed by Hugman in Harrison, 1992a). On the other hand, it may be important that, although widely dispersed in a physical sense, these learners form a cohesive group and establish a strong team identity through the vehicle of the learning event. That suggests a different approach to learning design. If it is a small group from a single workplace, the best strategy may be to arrange the event around their work location, or in proximity to it. Alternatively, it may be desirable to take them away from the work environment and focus their attention on wider issues. That could argue for one or more external residential events.

Numbers and location of the learners must, therefore, be viewed in the context of the purpose and objectives of the learning event in order to help decide on an appropriate learning strategy.

Jobs and competencies of the learners

At this early stage, it is important to acquire as much information as possible on the kind of jobs held by the learners and their general level of competence in them. Once individual learners have been selected, a more detailed analysis will need to be carried out.

Learning styles and skills

We looked briefly at learning styles on page 239. We noted Honey and Mumford's (1992) four-fold categorisation system, but it should be remembered that people can usually develop learning skills in more than one mode, and that some learners can move easily between the four modes, able to learn equally well in any of them.

While little may be known at this stage about specific individuals, nonetheless the type of jobs held by the proposed learning population, together with their overall age and ability range, their length and type of experience, and other similar information will give useful insights into the type of learning styles and skills they may possess. This information will indicate those learning situations and methods most likely to promote stimulating and effective learning for them.

In selecting a learning strategy – and later in designing the detail of learning events – it is important to consider not only how the event can build on the learners' primary learning styles and learning skills, but also to what extent the event should itself seek to change those styles and skills. Honey and Mumford's work, for example, has indicated that trainers as a profession tend to be activists rather than reflectors or theorists. If this is the case (and getting a particular learning group to complete the LSI questionnaire and send it to the designer some time before the learning event begins should give some helpful indicators), then any event seeking to train trainers should aim to redress that imbalance by involving learning experiences that promote styles and skills in all four modes, rather than simply encourage continued dependence on and preference for only the activist approach to learning.

When a learning event calls for learning styles and skills of quite a high order, and the type of learners envisaged are unlikely to have reached the required level, then a 'study skills' input can serve a useful purpose before the main event begins. Useful too are 'access' or 'foundation' courses which introduce the main topics at a lower level than will be experienced in the main learning event, thus building a grounding of skills that will make entry to that event easier and progress more effective.

Attitudes and motivation

Even at this early stage enough will probably be known about key behavioural aspects of the intended learning population (rates of absenteeism and turnover, performance levels, reactions to earlier learning events and any conflict patterns) to assess their likely motivation related to proposed learning events being organised for them. Little useful learning can occur if the individual does not want to learn, so it is important to assess the probable needs and expectations learners will bring to the learning event and to take these consciously into account when choosing an overall learning strategy.

Motivation can be considered under two headings (Gagne, 1977): social motivation and motivation related to task mastery.

Social motivation

This relates to the social situation in which the learners are placed: their social needs, characteristics, problems and types of relationship with each other and with the training staff. All these factors will affect their motivation during the learning event. Take as an example the design of a course in a new and difficult area of skills for a group of people who may come from different departments, levels or even organisations. If they are brought together into a cohesive group from the start, sharing expectations and concerns, this will help to build up an atmosphere of social supportiveness that will stand them in good stead as they try to master the various learning tasks.

Many organisations, including educational institutions, hold outdoor development periods towards the start of training or educational programmes. The aim is to bind participants into a close-knit group, motivated to tackle a long-term learning experience as a team rather than as a heterogeneous collection of individuals; and to develop appropriate learning styles and skills. Outdoor development periods can also be used at key stages during a long learning event as a way of consolidating and progressing learning in major areas. In a sense they can act as strategic milestones in an extended developmental programme.

Another approach, often used in conjunction with outdoor development work, is to help individuals to develop personal learning goals and plans that relate to the learning event as well as to outcomes that they value at a personal level. Skilfully done, such an exercise improves the individual's motivation to learn because relevance of the learning to their needs is clearly established.

Motivation related to task mastery

Here the issue is raised of what drives different learners to succeed. Some may seem spurred on by a need to 'win', achieving most in a competitive learning situation; others may be stimulated by any opportunity to learn something new – a 'curiosity' motive. While classifying learners in such ways may prove to have considerable practical value in some design situations (see, for example, Otto and Glaser, 1972) generalised assumptions must be avoided. As we saw in Chapter 14 (see page 244), performance is the final outcome of a complex interaction between needs, results, rewards and 'E' factors. Design of any learning event must pay careful attention to that concept of the motivation calculus.

In Chapter 17, where there is another look at motivation at the more individualised level, you will find practical guidelines to help the designer and trainer in the task of achieving and sustaining learner motivation, and of stimulating learners to master their tasks (pages 305–8).

When selecting a learning strategy, three points about motivation should be considered. Depending on their relevance to the particular case there may have to be considerable flexibility built into the learning system, so that adjustments to planned content, delivery and focus of certain components can be made just before, or even during, the learning event.

- *unpredictability.* Motivation will vary, often significantly, from one group of learners to the next, even with types of learning events that have often been run before.

- *individual differences.* There can be significant individual differences in motivation and expectations within a group of learners.

- *dynamism.* Motivation is dynamic, often changing during the course of a learning event.

There must be careful monitoring of learning events. Time must be spent before, at the start of, during and at the end of key events in diagnosing the needs and expectations of the learners and in responding to them. This requires close collaboration between designer and trainer (if the two processes are carried out by different parties) from the outset and during monitoring stages so that any motivational problems that do arise can be carefully analysed, and the style, pace or content of the learning event adjusted accordingly.

Let us end this section by tackling a real-life consultancy assignment (although minor details have been changed to ensure anonymity of the client organisation). The main purpose of this task is to reinforce the learning we have covered in this section. This is the equivalent of a major case-study, so expect it to take you some time to complete. Because the assignment itself is about appraisal, you may find it helpful to read Chapter 14 again before starting, and to refer to its contents as you tackle the assignment.

Case-study: The retail store's appraisal project: Part 1

You are a management consultant, and you have just been invited to visit the local branch of a national retail store in order to discuss the possibility of carrying out training in appraisal skills for about 15 managers and supervisors. The work is to be done in the next two months.

You arrive at 9.00 am and are met by the personnel officer (PO), a CIPD-qualified woman of about 55, well liked by employees, and a long-serving member of the store. She tells you that the managing director (MD) with whom you are both going to spend the morning is new to the job, having been appointed six months ago from a senior management position in another chain of stores. He is 38, a high-flier with an impressive record of success behind him. He is already establishing himself as a man of action: open, committed to increasing the store's turnover and full of ideas about how that can be done. Once he makes a decision he puts it into practice at once. He needs to make a major impact on the store, with results in 18 months at the latest.

Throughout the subsequent discussion the PO says very little, since the aim of that discussion is for the MD and yourself to analyse the proposed assignment and arrive at some shared conclusions.

You start off by asking the MD to explain what the assignment is about. He replies that he wants you to 'train all the managers and supervisors (about 15) in appraisal so that I can find out what their performance really is, get a few standardised disciplinary procedures sorted out, diagnose training and development needs, assess potential, and get the managers working together as a team'. He wants the training done within the next two months.

He explains that the store, a long-established one, is profitable but that its turnover has declined in the last five years, and competition is increasingly severe. It has had a paternalistic role culture for some years, which has stifled the drive and initiative of its managers and supervisors, most of them long-serving employees in their forties and fifties. A few have become complacent because profits (due to cost increases and customer loyalty) are still good.

At the time the new MD arrived there were some redundancies (approved although not initiated by him) at all levels of the store, and a makeshift appraisal scheme was used to determine who should go. This caused quite a lot of trouble and has led to a belief in some quarters that the MD himself is a hatchet-man, with a list of those he intends to get rid of in the next year or so. This is, in fact, a mistaken belief. The MD is genuinely determined to build up a high-calibre, committed and enthusiastic team of people who will regain the store's hold on the market. He has already reduced the management hierarchy from five to three levels and, having given early retirement on advantageous terms to three directors, has reorganised their jobs and brought in two new directors in their early thirties who work closely with him, and are fully committed to his way of doing things. His style is open and positive. He sets high standards and rewards those who achieve, while seeking to understand reasons for poor performance before passing any judgements. His views on appraisal can be summed up in the phrase: 'I may not know much about the detail of appraisal, but I know what I want it to achieve for me.'

He says that he wants to start off with closed appraisals, because he thinks anything else at this stage would be 'too threatening'. By closed appraisals he means that each appraiser should produce a written report on his or her staff. Those reports may or may not be followed up by an appraisal discussion with the staff concerned, but in any event, staff will not be able to see them. The reports will then 'be pushed through the system', to enable him to see what sort of skills and potential exist in his workforce and what kind of performance is being achieved, as well as examining needs for training and development. The MD adds that he does not want a complicated ranking system on the reports, just something simple and understandable.

The MD wants to be involved in the training. He himself is appraised by the chief executive of the chain of stores, and appraises his two directors. He intends the appraisal system to stop at supervisory level, with supervisors appraised but not, at this stage, appraising levels below them.

You have broken off the discussion for lunch, and are due to resume in a couple of hours' time. What issues will you then raise with the MD, and what will you try to achieve during your discussion with him, in order to reach agreement on the task that you will help the organisation to carry out?

Feedback notes
The initial discussion between the consultant (myself), the MD and, later on, the PO took in reality almost a day. However, at the end of that time the crucial issues had been straightened out, leaving the way clear for agreed action to take place. Obviously, you will have all sorts of ideas about how to tackle the discussion, and all I can usefully do, therefore, is to tell you the major issues that any similar discussion needs to confront, and how they were actually dealt with in this case. The notes that follow are longer than usual, in order to help you through a complex consultancy task.

The overall purpose of the learning
The first issue to clarify is the true reasons for the consultancy assignment. At present there is no clear overall purpose, and there is also an inconsistency in objectives. Many questions relating to the initial need for training must therefore be asked. There is also a confusion in terms: the MD refers at one point to 'appraisal' and at another to 'assessment' as if they are the same activity, whereas to the consultant they are quite different activities, the former related to examining current work performance, the latter to diagnosis of potential. Terms must be defined at the outset and a common language developed if any lasting agreement is to be reached between the parties.

• What is the MD really after? He mentions the need to find out people's abilities and performance, but also a need to develop fair disciplinary procedures. He refers to a need to discover people's potential, but also wants to find out their training and development requirements. He talks about a major need for teamwork, but then refers to closed appraisals. These are mutually contradictory needs.

Too many of the results he wants to achieve from appraisal will appear threatening to his managers and supervisors, and will almost certainly result in their opposition to appraisal and any training related to it.

- Discussion of this issue did, in fact, lead to agreement that what he most wanted was to introduce appraisal as an aid to reviewing work performance, helping work-planning, and diagnosing training and development needs. If this could be achieved as a first step, then establishing effective disciplinary procedures, sorting out how to perform assessments of potential, and so on could be tackled at a later date. By that time there should be more confidence in appraisal related to current work and to training and development, and the appraisal scheme would have had the chance to get over any teething problems and be working well. This part of the discussion also looked at what was meant by the terms 'appraisal' and 'assessment'. The MD realised he had been using the terms indiscriminately. Once the distinction between them had been clarified and agreed, many other things became clearer, and a shared frame of reference and language began to develop between us.

The learning objectives

The next issue is the behavioural learning objectives. The MD has referred to 'appraisal skills training', but what, specifically, are to be the outcomes of any training that takes place? Initially his one answer, that his managers should be able to operate a closed system of appraisal, presupposes three things: that there is an appraisal scheme already in existence, to which training can be related; that it has the support of his managers and supervisors, so that they will welcome training; and that closed appraisal is consistent with his overall purpose of using appraisal as an aid to reviewing work performance, helping work-planning, and diagnosing training and development needs.

Discussion of this issue took a long time, but in the end significant progress was made. It emerged that:

- there was no appraisal scheme worthy of note; the one used for selection for redundancies was agreed to be unsuitable from every point of view

- before skills training could take place, an appraisal scheme would have to be designed

- closed appraisal, especially at this particular time, would be viewed with great suspicion. It would be wiser to involve the managers and supervisors in the design of an appraisal scheme, opening up the entire design as well as the operational process from the start. Such an approach would also be consistent with the MD's other major need – to bind his managers and supervisors together into a close-knit managerial working team: the design task could start to build up that relationship

- if the objectives of the appraisal scheme were simply to do with work review and planning and the diagnosis of training and development needs, then no rating or ranking system related to performance was needed. Furthermore, dispensing with it would further reduce fears of the managers and supervisors that there was some ulterior motive behind the exercise.

Profile of the learning population

The third issue is the learners. What are their characteristics and situations in relation to the consultancy assignment? It is vital to get as much information about them at this early stage as possible, in order that the whole of the learning task facing the consultant is clearly understood.

- Discussions on this issue confirmed that the managers and supervisors were mainly in the 40–50 age range. Most had been with the store since their youth. In terms of learning styles and skills, they had no management training or education, although they had whatever technical and professional qualifications were needed. They would tend to be activists in the learning situation, distrustful of theories and simulated situations unless very clearly relevant to their work situation.

- Over the last 10 years, with a rather old-fashioned, complacent and authoritarian leadership of the store, some managers had become disillusioned and pessimistic about their futures. Others felt that they had received little support from senior management in their attempts to perform well, and this had bred a lack of confidence as well as confusion and some stagnation. Although the MD had a high opinion of the managers' real levels of ability and potential, it was essential to restore their original enthusiasm. Also, one or two seemed to see no need to work harder or differently from the way in which they worked at present: what therefore would be the incentive for them to do any of the things desired by the MD?

- The MD believed that motivation would improve as they began to realise the possibilities that lay before them: a market which they could start to win back; and the opportunity to become a small, high-calibre and high-achieving professional team, with rewards for those who proved their worth in meeting challenging standards. It was also evident that he was determined that appraisal would be introduced: he was fully committed to it. Also, his two directors would be positive in their support for the initiative. This should do much to convert any apathy, suspicion or apprehension into willingness to experiment. It would engender a commitment to make appraisal work, once there was a belief that this was not just one more 'flavour of the month' technique but a strategy offering real benefits.

- In terms of relevant skills and knowledge, few of the managers (including, said the MD, himself) knew anything much about appraisal.

The agreement reached with the MD

The final issue was to establish, after all this discussion, what the learning strategy should actually be and how it should be implemented. The following agreement was reached:

- The consultancy assignment would proceed in stages, with both consultant and client able to withdraw at the end of any stage if that seemed necessary or desirable.

- Stage 1 would consist of initial information-gathering by the consultant to determine whether the kind of diagnoses made in this initial discussion were valid, or whether other needs and problems existed which called for a review of the tentative conclusions reached at this stage.

- If the diagnoses did prove to be valid, the consultant would run a workshop for all 15 managers and supervisors, with the aim of working with them to design a simple appraisal scheme for the store. Initially it would be a pilot scheme, covering only managers and supervisors. If subsequent evaluation proved positive, it would then be extended to the rest of the store. Recommendations for a scheme would be presented to the MD at the conclusion of the workshop, in order that he could present a report on them to the board of directors.

- Stage 2 would consist of appraisal skills training, to develop those skills needed to introduce and operate the pilot scheme. The details of that stage (which again would fall into the two components of initial information-gathering and a workshop) would be determined once a decision had been made on whether the consultant was to go ahead and carry out that stage.

- Stage 3 would take place once a pilot scheme had been introduced and was under way. It would consist of a review day on which consultant, management team (which included those titled 'supervisors'), MD and personnel officer would come together to review the scheme's operation and agree on any further action needed.

Thus agreement between consultant (myself) and client (the MD) was reached by a process of jointly identifying the real learning needs and agreeing on:

- the overall purpose and objectives of learning

- the profile of the learning population

- a learning strategy.

Note how important it was for me to do what was advised early on in this chapter: challenge learning objectives I was asked by the client to achieve, if those objectives seemed inappropriate or ambiguous.

STAGE 4: ESTABLISHING STRATEGY, DIRECTION AND MANAGEMENT

Choosing a learning strategy

As we saw in Chapter 5, strategy is the route to be followed in order to realise vision and overall purpose. In the case of a learning event, strategy must therefore relate to its overall purpose and general objectives. Learning strategy involves looking at alternative ways in which purpose and objectives for learning can best be achieved and then choosing the kind of events and delivery pattern which seem most likely to achieve the purpose.

In the case-study the agreed learning strategy was to help the learners to design their own appraisal scheme, using the consultant as a facilitator; and then to provide skills training to ensure effective operation of the scheme. In order to enhance teamwork and develop the learners as managers, the strategy included taking the whole management group away on two residential workshops, rather than organising learning events for some or all of them within the workplace itself.

A good fit must be achieved between learning strategy and the resources available for learning together with the organisational climate in the workplace. Let us look briefly at those two factors.

Resources
We have already dealt with learning resources in Chapter 11. They involve internal and external, tangible and intangible resources. Particular attention must be given to deciding whether to use external providers and how such provision should be managed (see Hackett, 1997). Alternative learning strategies must be analysed in relation to their likely cost, the time they will involve, and the extent to which they will utilise and relate to learning in the workplace.

Organisational culture and climate
It is important to reflect on the climate of the organisation, and especially of that part of it from which learners will be drawn, in relation to different options for learning strategy. There must be a conducive workplace culture, as well as policies, procedures, roles and skills, if continuous development through the integration of learning and daily work is to be an effective learning strategy. An organisation planning to move into the delivery of learning through computerised learning systems and distance learning packages will not only have to set up the administrative machinery to make that strategy possible, but will have to prepare people – both learners and their managers – who have thought of learning only in terms of conventional training or educational programmes to see the benefit of these approaches, and how they can best be organised and the learning from them effectively transferred to the workplace.

The climate in the workplace, too, needs to be one that will support learners who come from a learning event with new knowledge, skills and, perhaps, changed attitudes. Cultures are slow to change, and those who have 'been away' on a learning event may find invisible and possibly impenetrable barriers awaiting them on their return. New learning must be fertilised if it is to take root, but too often that process does not occur because no one in the organisation has seen the need to prepare the ground.

Direction and management of the learning event
Different strategies will make different demands on expertise, so careful thought must be given to how the learning strategy and event will be directed and managed. Who and how many will be needed to carry out the work involved in design, direction and control, administration, delivery and evaluation? If the learning strategy to be

pursued is one of training courses, then internal or external specialists will have to provide these, and will need careful selection, briefing and management. If the strategy includes an educational programme using day or block release, there will have to be effective liaison with the educational institution concerned. Any requirement to assess workplace competencies and then use those for accreditation purposes will need extensive preparation, including training of workplace assessors. If there are to be elements of work-related learning, or a strategy of continuous development, then relevant experiences and how best to organise them must be agreed with the managers concerned, and it will probably be advisable to establish mentor roles. Agreement must also be reached on how, at what stages, and by whom monitoring and evaluation of the learning event will be carried out (see Chapter 17).

What matters most is that design and content are agreed between the key parties to be fully relevant to the purpose and objectives of the programme and to the type of learners concerned; that they are feasible and cost-efficient; and that ways of transferring learning to the workplace are agreed and put in place before the programme begins.

To demonstrate the importance of these issues of learning strategy, and the direction and management of the learning event, we can conclude our case-study.

Case-study: The retail store's appraisal project: Part 2

Once the overall purpose and learning objectives had been agreed in outline, the MD, PO and consultant (myself) spent considerable time together deciding how to carry out the first stage of the project. Here, the discussion revolved around resources. The following points emerged:

Direction and management of the project

The management of the project was agreed without difficulty: the MD would approve the overall parameters of each stage of the project, leaving the PO and myself to work on the detail relating to staffing, materials and physical accommodation.

I would determine the detailed behavioural objectives, both final and intermediate, of each workshop, and would be responsible for its design and delivery. I would return six or so months later to carry out a one-day review (Stage 3 of the project) with the workshop members, and the PO would arrange pre-workshop and post-workshop briefing/debriefing sessions for all workshop members and their managers, with special reference to following up action agreed in the workshop. The PO would also organise longer-term evaluation a year after the entire project had ended.

Staffing posed problems. It needed more than one person to run a workshop, whether the Stage 1 workshop (designing an appraisal scheme) or the Stage 2 workshop (developing appraisal skills). The Stage 1 workshop required one more tutor, while the Stage 2 workshop, if carried out, would require four. It was decided that the PO would act as co-tutor on the first workshop, thus reducing costs and increasing internal training expertise. It was agreed to leave the matter of staffing of Stage 2 until a decision had been made about whether or not that stage would, in fact, go ahead.

Another resourcing problem was that for the Stage 1 workshop (on the assumption that one would be needed), there would have to be either

> *Option 1*: one workshop for all the course members, with consultant and PO there throughout the two or three days;

or

> *Option 2*: two workshops, with half the membership attending one, half attending the other, staffed by consultant and PO throughout on both occasions.

The direct cost of running the first option was less than the cost of running the second, because the first involved only one set of consultancy fees and only one sustained period of absence for the PO instead of two. However, difficulties of releasing all 15 store staff at the same time, together with obvious indirect costs incurred if these key people were all to be away from their departments for three days during a week, might make the second option necessary. Checking of dates when consultant and course members would all be available at one time also made it clear that Option 1 could not take place within the two-month period initially desired by the MD.

On the other hand, Option 2 would take longer to carry out than Option 1, and this again brought us up against the time factor. It would also split up the learning group, when keeping them together in order to build them up as a work team was an important objective. Finally, if Option 1 could be carried out over a Sunday plus Bank Holiday period when the store was closed, all managers could attend.

Physical resources
Materials and equipment needed for the workshops were available – and these constituted a relatively cheap part of the programme. Accommodation proved more difficult: the store had conference accommodation, although of limited size, and at first the MD felt that, to reduce costs, all workshops should be held there. We then discussed the psychological advantages of taking the whole management and supervisory team of 15 away from the store to a local hotel for the duration of the workshops. The relationship between consultant and course members, so important to cement quickly given the demanding task they jointly faced, should benefit greatly from such a location, and the social, as well as task mastery, motivation of the course members should receive a strong and continued boost. Equally important, managers and supervisors would be together as a team for a sustained period, away from their usual work situation, and this would be a very positive way of starting to develop the managerial team identity that the MD saw as so crucial. This strategy was subsequently agreed by the MD.

Finance
A maximum budget for the entire three-stage consultancy project was

agreed, based on tentative costings I had produced. The budget was tight but not inflexible: it did, for example, allow for the possibility of some increase in initial costings over the period of the three stages. However, financial considerations posed problems related to staffing the workshops, as already explained.

Organisational climate

After discussion, it was agreed that it would be sensible to proceed more slowly than originally hoped in order to give time for a positive climate about appraisal to be developed in the store. The MD also decided that the objective of building up a strong managerial team from the start was more important than his wish for the whole project to be concluded quickly. It was therefore decided that Option 1 would be followed (one workshop, involving all 15 people, at a Bank Holiday weekend), with a relaxation of his initial timescale, so that Stages 1 and 2 would be spread over a five-month instead of a two-month period. This timescale would have the final and important advantage of allowing time for a considered decision to be reached after the end of Stage 1 on whether to proceed to Stage 2, rather than a rushed and possibly invalid decision.

I hope that this case-study has helped to reinforce understanding of how to produce, implement and manage learning strategy and the event to which it relates. Here is a final task to test out learning from this chapter.

Planning a learning event

Produce a handout for distribution to *either* training practitioners attending a course on distance learning methods *or* line managers attending a course on 'on-the-job coaching'. The handout should summarise the overall purpose of the course, its learning objectives and strategy, and how it will be directed and managed.

CONCLUSION

Having read this chapter and completed its reviews and self-checks, you should now:

• understand the importance of clear and appropriate purpose and objectives for a learning event

• know how to produce a profile of a learning population and relate this to a choice of learning strategies

• understand the practical issues affecting choice of learning strategies

• be able to draw up purpose, behavioural objectives and strategy for a learning event.

To test yourself against these objectives, what five-minute answers would you give to the following questions? (Dates in brackets refer to the IPD qualifying examination paper in which a question appeared.)

- What are the key stages in the inception, design and delivery of planned learning events? (May 1997)

- When a reputable consultancy firm delivers a short course that, as soon as it starts, produces complaints by participants that the consultants do not understand the organisation and are 'way out' in their approach, what should the organisation's training manager do, and why? (May 1998)

- When drawing up the profile of a group of learners for whom you are designing a programme, what are the main types of information you will need, and why?

USEFUL READING

BASS B. M. *and* VAUGHAN J. A. (1967) *Training in Industry: The management of learning.* London, Tavistock Publications.

BEE F. *and* BEE R. (1994) *Training Needs Analysis and Evaluation.* London, Institute of Personnel and Development.

GILLEY J. W. *and* EGGLAND S. A. (1989) *Principles of Human Resource Development.* Maidenhead, Addison Wesley.

HACKETT P. (1997) *Introduction to Training.* London, Institute of Personnel and Development.

HARDINGHAM A. (1996a) *Designing Training.* London, Institute of Personnel and Development.

ROBINSON D. G. *and* ROBINSON J. C. (1989) *Training for Impact.* London, Jossey-Bass.

17 Learning design and delivery: Stages 5 to 8

LEARNING OBJECTIVES

After reading this chapter you will:

• understand the issues involved in the selection of learners

• be able to apply principles of learning to the design and delivery of a learning event

• know how to evaluate learning events appropriately.

THE EIGHT-STAGE APPROACH, STAGE 5: SELECTING LEARNERS

In this chapter we conclude our analysis of the eight stages involved in the design of learning events by looking at Stages 5 to 8. These involve the selection of learners and the design, delivery and evaluation of learning events.

Selecting the learners

When it comes to the actual selection, the choice of whom to take into a learning event will often be out of the hands of those planning and designing that event. However, if the criteria for selection are within their control, they should then focus their attention on the overall purpose and objectives of the event, identifying the people for whom the learning outcomes will clearly be of most benefit and who have appropriate competencies, attitudes and learner characteristics.

Mistakes in selection are frequently made. The danger is probably greatest with externally provided courses, because when places are hard to fill the temptation is strong for the provider to accept people whose needs or abilities do not absolutely match the course profile. A menu-driven approach to the provision of learning events will tend to lead to an insufficiently discriminating selection process. Organisations quickly become wary of internal as well as external providers who try to 'sell' off-the-shelf products rather than respond flexibly and appropriately to specific learning needs.

Trainability tests

Useful information about the extent to which potential learners are in fact 'trainable' can be obtained from trainability tests – originally pioneered for manual workers by Sylvia Downs at the Industrial Training Research Unit at Cambridge.

The trainability test comprises the detailed instruction of a job applicant in a piece of work which is part of the job being applied for. The applicant then has to perform the task without further assistance, while under scrutiny from the instructor. He or she is rated according to the number and type of errors made while performing the operation. Such tests:

• are designed to include parts of the training that trainees find difficult, as well as elements of the job itself

• involve a structured learning period

• include the use of detailed error check-lists written in behavioural terms (Downs, 1984).

The focus is thus on how the individual learns the task, and a key criterion for selection becomes trainability. There are four factors that must be considered before a decision is made to use such tests:

• *cost* – A trainability test is a specialised instrument. Each job has to have its own test, so the expense can be high.

• *design and validation* – Tests need to be carefully designed and validated, so those who administer them must be fully trained – another high-cost element.

• *time* – Trainability testing is very time-consuming and therefore, again, expensive.

• *insurance* – There must be special insurance against accidents for non-employees who take the tests.

Trainability tests have proved to be a major aid to selection and training in a wide range of manual jobs, especially in the clothing industry. As to their applicability to non-manual jobs, work has been done in developing trainability tests for supervisory and managerial positions, and in this connection Task Observation – while not amounting to full trainability testing – can provide useful information about existing levels of ability in certain key tasks. The individual is asked to perform a typical activity which is an important part of the total job, and their existing level of competence is then assessed. Work-sampling of this kind, taken to its logical conclusion, leads to the comprehensive and structured methodology of assessment and development centres. Such centres (see Chapter 19) can provide another useful, if expensive, method of selecting for entry to learning events.

Specifying the learning required

This takes us back to Chapters 14 to 16. The knowledge, skills and attitudes required in the job and needed by the learners must be identified and analysed so that a specification can be produced of the gaps that the learning event should fill. Learning purpose, objectives and strategy can then be formulated.

Here is an example of the planning of a lengthy learning event, to demonstrate key points made in the previous chapter and in this one so far. It was used in my 1992 text but contains updated material, since the programme did not finish until 1994 and further research based on the data it generated has subsequently taken place.

Case-study: Planning and designing a management development programme for clinical directors

Throughout the first eight months of 1991 the then Northern Regional Health Authority (NRHA) and Durham University Business School (DUBS) worked together to plan, design and jointly manage a three-year management development programme for 24 clinical directors (CDs) in the region. The programme was funded by the National Health Service's Management Executive (ME), so decisions about overall purpose, ultimate objectives, learning strategy and the outline structure of the programme had to be made at the stage when funding was being sought – in the event, a year before the programme itself began.

Overall purpose

The purpose of the programme, which was evaluated by two external bodies as well as by the NRHA and DUBS, was to help senior clinicians in, or preparing to take on, CD roles to effectively fulfil the managerial demands of that role in order, ultimately, to ensure high standards of patient care. There were 24 participants, split into three cohorts of eight over the 1991–94 period to enable an individualised learning system to drive the cycle of three staggered repeat programmes. Figure 8 shows the configuration of learning events characterising each programme and their timescale, using the first run of the programme as the reference-point.

Analysis of learning needs

Once funding had been obtained to run the programme (early in 1991), eight months were spent by NRHA and DUBS programme designers expanding a base of initial information on learner- and job-related needs in order to produce a sound specification for the programme. The CD role was a new one within the radically changed NHS structure introduced in April 1991. It was sparsely documented at any level, and proved to be different in its interpretation and operation across virtually every organisation in which it existed. The initial eight participants, too (selected in mid-1991 for entry that September to the first of the series of three programmes) were very heterogeneous in their professional, managerial and personal characteristics. Lengthy interviews were held by NRHA and DUBS staff with each of them and with their managers during that summer, to identify needs and expectations of these key parties in relation to the programme. This exercise was repeated with each cohort, and adjustments to their programmes made accordingly.

A problem-centred approach and role analysis proved the best methods to identify and analyse learning needs, but the needs identified during this period were so diverse that it proved difficult to agree on how to interpret findings and to classify and prioritise the needs. There were three sets to reconcile:

Organisational needs derived from the overriding concern of the ME to improve the quality of patient care by ensuring effective management

Figure 8 The Clinical Directors' Programme – first cohort

NRHA–DUBS Clinical Directors' Programme: Intake 1 (1991–93)

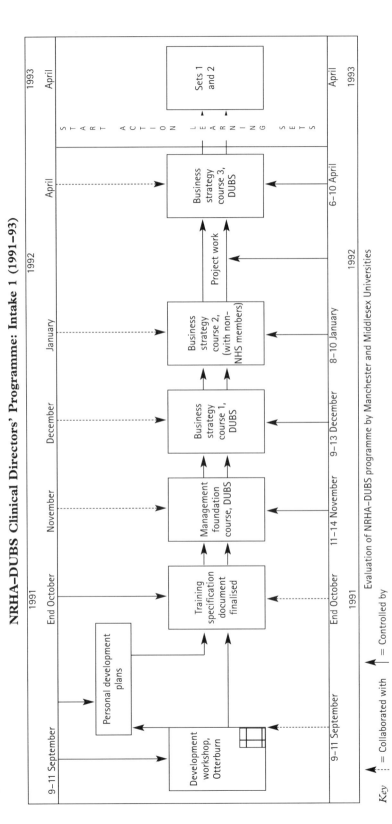

Evaluation of NRHA–DUBS programme by Manchester and Middlesex Universities

Key   ◀┈┈┈ = Collaborated with   ◀─── │ = Controlled by

in the reorganised NHS. They also derived from needs expressed by the NRHA client and the participants' organisations – the NHS units who nominated them for the programme and gave them the time and other support to attend. These needs set the focus and direction of the programme, and helped to generate its overall purpose and objectives.

Group needs were derived from those areas of skill, knowledge and competency that all programme participants – and their organisations – saw as essential in a programme to enable them to learn quickly how to become not only managers but, in most cases, managers who had a significant strategic role at business-unit level in their local organisations.

Individual needs were identified both in the interviews and in the diagnostic workshop held as the first stage of the learning event (see below). They were expressed in personal development plans (PDPs) that were followed up by NRHA and NHS mentors throughout the programme. These helped to drive the programme and achieve objectives related to the provision of a tailor-made sequence of learning events that would help each individual to understand fully the new role and perform confidently and competently. They thus helped to ensure instrumental, dialogic and self-reflective learning (see pages 242–3).

The core NRHA/DUBS team that identified and analysed these needs was initially composed of four. In mid-1991 it expanded to include two external management consultants recruited by DUBS for their particular NHS-related expertise, to help in the initial design process and to lead the delivery of the programme. During this period the school's programme staff therefore had to guide both design work and a complex process of human interactions, ensuring an effective two-way flow of information and ideas. They acted as a bridge between the NRHA and the DUBS group as all strove to make sense of a mass of often incomplete data and to develop shared perceptions and language about the programme.

There were tensions during the period, relating to matters of interpretation and focus and to the relative roles to be played by the NRHA and DUBS in the selection of learners, the organisation of the diagnostic workshop, and the monitoring and evaluation of the ongoing programme. However, the agreement to take the overall purpose and objectives of the programme as the base reference-point in all discussions enabled differing views eventually to be reconciled and workable compromises to be reached. By August 1991 a draft job training specification had been produced, and an agreed plan for the first programme was almost ready for delivery in September.

Programme design and delivery

At this point flexibility was crucial, since a three-day personal development diagnostic workshop organised for the first cohort of CDs by the NRHA staff was to take place a few weeks before the formal programme started. It incorporated teambuilding through an outdoor development period; analysis of a previously completed computerised assessment questionnaire about the CDs' managerial competencies and needs as identified by themselves and a sample of their managers, subordinates and peers; and work on personal learning goals and plans. The insights obtained from this exercise had to be incorporated into the final programme plan.

Every programme component had its own stated purpose and three or four clearly defined final learning objectives. Within each formal module, interim objectives were established for each session. These interim and final objectives became the criteria against which the learners were asked by the programme planners to evaluate the modules. From start to end of each programme continuous fine-tuning took place in order to adapt the programme to emerging needs. The growing cohesiveness of the core team facilitated this process: working increasingly closely together, its members developed over the first year a shared language and philosophy about the programme that facilitated joint action on any problems in delivery.

At the conclusion of the formal components, each programme moved for a six- to eight-month period into action-learning (AL, see Figure 8) sets, each comprising four clinicians with an experienced set adviser. To design this component, the planning team had once more been expanded to incorporate two international AL experts contracted by DUBS. Again, the planning process was initially hampered by differences in views between the experts and both groups in the core team about how best to integrate the formal and action-learning components of the programme. And again, it was the overall purpose and ultimate objectives of the programme, together with the shared commitment of the parties to achieving them, that helped to resolve differences and drove that essential period forward.

See also Harrison and Miller, 1993; Harrison, Miller and Gibson, 1993; Harrison, 1996a; Kessels and Harrison, 1998; Harrison and Miller, 1999.

In this study, the focus has been not only on the overall purpose, objectives, learner population and learning strategy chosen for a complex learning event, but also on its planning, management and design process. Further comment on the latter follows under the next heading.

STAGE 6: CONFIRMING STRATEGY AND DESIGNING THE LEARNING EVENT

Confirming strategy

Once the participants in a learning event have been selected, it is essential to confirm or modify the learning strategy and design initially proposed. Although in most cases confirmation will be all that is called for, from time to time the more detailed information gained when examining the needs of the participants may indicate a requirement to change strategy or design, sometimes radically. Occasionally, the information may even indicate that the objectives or purpose set for the learning event are misconceived. Ignoring such indicators may put at risk the viability of the whole event.

Designing the learning event

Designing the learning event requires first that each component carries clear behavioural objectives aligned with its overall purpose and final objectives. This approach, linking needs, purpose, objectives and outcomes, exemplifies the operation of what is known as the systematic training cycle. An explanation of that cycle was given in Chapter 9 (Appendix 5) when describing the work of the national Lead Bodies in producing occupational standards.

Achieving external and internal consistency

However, linking key design elements to achieve a systematic approach to the design of a training programme is not of itself sufficient to obtain the confidence of key parties in a programme's outcomes and assure its success. Our case-study has demonstrated the importance of involving key actors from the earliest stages in programme planning and delivery so that their perceptions about the event become and remain mutually compatible. Kessels described this as a process that generates 'external consistency' – shared expectations and orientation of the key parties involved in a learning event so that an increasingly close fit is achieved between the event itself and the external environment in which its learning must take root (Kessels and Harrison, 1998).

Kessels' research (*ibid*) provided strong evidence to indicate that although internal consistency is important in determining the success of planned learning events, external consistency has the most decisive impact. Even in programmes shown in his study to have achieved a high degree of internal consistency, lack of strong involvement of stakeholders led to reduction in desired impact – and sometimes to failure of the event.

As will be seen later in this chapter, there is little doubting the impact achieved by the NRHA/DUBS clinical directors' programme – but it was the process of involving the parties from the start, as much as the systematic approach to the tasks of programme design, that appears to explain the unanimity with which the different parties judged it to have been successful once completed. The importance of process in HRD has been stressed throughout this book. Here again it is process that is being emphasised as crucial to effective performance in roles related to training and the facilitation of learning.

Choosing content, media and methods

We can distinguish between media and methods thus:

• Media of learning are the routes, or channels, through which learning is transmitted to the learner.

• Methods of learning are the ways in which that learning is transmitted.

'Training technology' refers to the technical aids available to promote the acquisition of skills in a learning event. 'Learning technology', on the other hand, has a broader meaning: it refers to the way in which learning media and methods are incorporated into the design and delivery of a learning event. It can often leave much to be desired. Events can be expensively produced and persuasively designed, yet be delivered using such inappropriate media and methods that they are ineffective. The more HRD staff become skilled in the technology of

Table 12 Some media and methods of learning

Media	Methods
Oral (spoken word)	Talk, lecture, discussion, seminar
Printed (written word)	Handouts, books, distance-learning texts
Radio, TV, electronically based learning media	Wide variety of methods, didactic and interactive
On the job	Learning from a supervisor or co-worker
	Learning by trial and error
	Using a training manual or a self-administered training package
	Coaching; job rotation
Off the job	Any learning event organised away from the workplace, including mentoring and other internally based processes
Vestibule	Simulated work situation, in a training room or centre, or other premises near the workplace.

learning, the less their organisations will have to bear the consequences of such expensive mistakes.

The opposite danger, of course, is to become so immersed in the pursuit of new training technology that the fundamentals which make for a successful learning event are forgotten. Table 12 shows some major media together with examples of the kind of methods most frequently associated with them. Clearly, one learning event may use several media as well as a number of different methods.

For a full discussion of media and methods there are regular articles in personnel and training journals. One of the clearest discussions remains that in Gagne's book (1977), which not only offers excellent practical advice about the design of learning events but illuminates it at the scholarly level, with his discussion of the psychology of learning. In what follows I draw significantly on his ideas.

It is important to be clear that there is no single best medium or method, whether in relation to a particular kind of learning objective, learner or learning event. Certain media and methods may enjoy current popularity. For example, as we have seen in Chapter 12, e-learning media and methods are in vogue because of their increasing availability, speed, diminishing cost, the stimulation they offer the learner, and the fact that they are adaptable to the learner's needs in terms of time, place, pace and feedback.

Yet whatever the popularity at a particular point in time, there is no evidence to support a generalised superiority of any one medium or method, so other criteria for choice in the specific learning situation must be found. A simple three-point checklist can act as an adequate

---

Designing a one-day workshop on time management

The workshop will have up to 20 members. It is to be held in a company's training centre, and the learning objective is that course members should, by the end of the day, know and be able to apply about six methods of time management in the organisation of their daily workload. What considerations will guide your choice of media and methods?

---

guide to the designer. We shall illustrate its use in a task that I have retained from my 1992 IPM text because the popularity of time management courses remains undimmed!

Feedback notes

Here is a three-point checklist to use when choosing media and methods.

- *Consider the purpose and objectives of the learning event and the characteristics of the learners.* Clear learning objectives will indicate to the designer the typical situations to which the learner will have to respond after completing the learning event, and the behavioural outcomes that the event must help the learner to achieve. Types of situations and outcomes will help to suggest relevant media and methods. Factors like the biographical and occupational characteristics of the learners, the geographical location and the size of the learning group need to be analysed when choosing media and methods. Learning styles and skills will have a particularly strong influence on the ways in which learners are likely to adapt to different approaches because, being usually formed at an early age, it is unlikely that they can quickly change. Initially, therefore, the choice of media and methods should be capable of adaptation to existing styles and skills. For example, many learners may find distance-learning hard to cope with but can learn quite effectively in a face-to-face learning medium. Those who do not learn well when lectures predominate may respond better to group and practical work of various kinds. Those who cannot review their own learning processes can be helped to do so by using a learning styles inventory, and by reflective discussion with a trainer or mentor.

- *Consider the principles of learning and their practical application.* Which approaches are likely to achieve most stimulation and retention of learning? In a one-day workshop there will be a need for a judicious mix of tutor-led talk, printed materials that can reinforce key points and act as a permanent record, and interactive events. When considering whether to use methods such as case-studies or an in-tray exercise, prior information from the learners or with previous participants in a similar event can aid choice. For example, a pre-workshop check may reveal that for certain tasks in-tray exercises may be more productive than case-studies because the latter are likely to be viewed by these learners as too artificial and difficult to absorb. An in-tray exercise may offer more readily transferable learning, more stimulation and quicker mastery. So at this second stage we have narrowed the field of choice further by considering how best to respond to key principles of learning.

• *Consider practical issues.* We must look at what is most feasible by reference to our total budget and to the learning environment. Remember here the importance of the organisational climate. For example, some senior managers may not see the value of external courses as a way of developing their line managers, while others may see such courses as an essential part of the developmental process, and fully support them as a learning route for their staff. Information on past effectiveness of certain media and methods in organisational learning events should also be checked, as should best practice in similar learning events elsewhere.

As this checklist shows, most learning events need a combination of different media and methods, and must be flexible enough to enable changes to be made if learning problems develop. In today's world, training and development professionals need to be highly knowledgeable about the wide choice of media and methods, and creative as well as cost-conscious in selecting those best suited to the purpose and most likely to bring additional value to the learning situation.

Applying principles of learning to the design and delivery of learning events

We have just discussed the importance of considering basic principles of learning when choosing media and methods. We can now expand that discussion by examining how principles of learning themselves should inform the design and delivery of a learning event.

In providing a set of eight guidelines, I am again drawing significantly on Gagne's (1977) ideas.

1 Design an appropriate structure and culture
In this context, 'structure' means the framework of a learning event – the way it is shaped and the type of interactions planned to occur within it. 'Structure' also refers to how tightly or loosely controlled the event should be. For example, where active participation is particularly desirable in a programme, how structured or unstructured should that programme be?

'Culture' is about the learning climate established for the event – about the style and pattern of relationships between the parties and the values they will be encouraged to share in the learning situation.

2 Stimulate the learners
This involves ensuring that the purpose and objectives of the event are perceived by the learners to relate directly to their needs. To guarantee continued stimulation throughout the learning event, choose media and methods that will actively involve them (using the three-point checklist we have just developed). Key points in learning must stand out and become memorable – in other words, they must achieve 'perceptual distinctiveness'. It is the beginning and end of a learning event that make most impact, so it is important that the essence of what is to be learned is outlined at the start, and that at the end

learning is summarised in a way that takes the learners back to that starting-point. This closes the learning loop.

3 Help understanding

Choose content that strikes a chord with the learners, and regularly check on their understanding of it as the event unfolds. Be ready to go back to difficult points and to vary the learning pace and approach in order to ensure a better grasp of the material and concepts.

4 Incorporate appropriate learning activities

Activities in which the learners are involved during the event must involve situations or the use of skills and knowledge that are relevant to their real-life environment and roles, that carry the learning process forward, and that build expertise and confidence. Remember three aspects of motivation noted in Chapter 16: unpredictability, individual differences and dynamism (page 285). Be ready to adapt the learning situation to emergent learning needs.

5 Build on existing learning

Initially (until a strong positive relationship has been established between learners and those guiding the learning event) it is helpful not to fight against what learners think, feel or are sure they know. Instead, aim to make past learning and current mindsets an aid to the learning process. If brought to the surface in a non-judgemental way, they can be tested naturally by problems and activities built into the learning event. Unlearning and relearning are complex processes and can be painful, yet they are essential to the acquisition of much new learning. The skill lies in creating an atmosphere where entrenched learning and views can become clear and then be treated in such a way as, in time, to become integrated with new learning or – where irrelevant – gradually fall away. Sometimes the tensions between old and new learning are too great to resolve. Such a breakdown in the learning process indicates possible faults in the original diagnosis of needs, or in the purpose set for the event, or in the choice of learners.

6 Guide the learners

There must be regular feedback and guidance on learning progress. The instructor or facilitator will need technical competence to carry out instructional functions, and also interpersonal skills to ensure a supportive relationship with the learners as they struggle with areas of difficulty.

7 Ensure that learning is retained

There are two major issues to consider here – practice and rewards.

Practice reinforces learning until the point is reached when the behavioural patterns become habitual. But how much practice, and what distribution of it? The concept of learning curves is useful here. A learning curve means the average amount of time it takes to achieve mastery of what is to be learned. Curves vary greatly from task to task and person to person, being related to the difficulty of the task, the characteristics of the learners, and the duration and spacing of practice.

We can rarely provide the ideal amount and spacing of practice that each learner requires. We must therefore select the most critical and/or the most difficult learning tasks and give those priority. Thus, for example, throughout this book I have built in tasks and examples around issues that are critical to the mastery of human resource development (HRD) theory and practice, and also around those which usually cause significant difficulty. The tasks and examples are also designed and spaced to stimulate and maintain interest in what would otherwise soon become a mass of indigestible material!

Training designers should record learning curves in relation to typical learning events in which they will be involved. However, careful monitoring of the learning process will always remain necessary since learning curves can at best only be generalised predictors.

Quite simple rewards such as a smile or a word of praise may be enough to reinforce effective behaviour in the learning situation. It is also important to explore with the learner why learning has proved successful, since sometimes correct responses are achieved only by chance.

Punishment of incorrect responses is less predictable in its consequences. A critical comment, a harsh word, a misplaced joke may frighten or shame the learner into renewed effort, but equally may inhibit further learning. In an extreme case the learner may simply give up. Usually, failure is in itself punishment enough. To correct it, careful demonstration by the trainer, followed by repeated practice by the learner, may be effective; or a repetition of the initial instruction session, using slightly different methods – or a supportive discussion of precisely what the learner has found to be an obstacle, and how he or she may be helped to overcome that obstacle. There are many ways in which initial failures can be overcome, provided always that the basic ability to learn is there.

Where the ability or motivation to learn is lacking, there has probably been a selection error which may prove impossible to resolve. Always, therefore, ensure provision for the counselling and guidance of learners. Exit points and processes from a learning event when it is clear that effective learning is not going to be possible also need to be established.

8 Ensure transfer of learning

There are two points at which transfer of learning needs to be effective: transfer of learning into a learning event, and from it upon its completion. Past learning will transfer positively into the event if that learning can be used in the new situation. It will transfer negatively if it seems to the learner impossible to apply or if it contradicts what is being taught in the new situation (we have already noted some ways of dealing with negative learning).

The same principles hold true for the transfer of learning from the learning event into the workplace situation. Successful transfer at that point will depend on how far:

- the event has been appropriate to the learners' needs in their work situation

- its learning tasks have been within the capability of the learners and been mastered by them

- it has achieved stimulation and relevancy of learning throughout its duration

- participants will be enabled and encouraged to use their new learning in the workplace.

The process of achieving external consistency (page 302) is one that leads to the achievement of these aims. It does so by committing the external parties so powerfully to the learning event that their support for the transference of its outcomes is thereby ensured. (Illuminating case-studies on transfer of learning are contained in Marchington and Wilkinson, 1996, Chapter 10.)

Preparing a talk

You have been asked to speak for an hour and a half to a local meeting of your IPD branch on 'How to decide on training methods'. Prepare an outline of the talk, including its purpose and main objectives, and explain how its design incorporates key principles of learning. (For advice, see Fowler, 1995.)

STAGE 7: DELIVERING THE EVENT

In delivering as well as in designing a learning event, the political, interactive and managerial processes involved will be as critical as technical expertise in ensuring the achievement of desired outcomes. Delivery should pose few problems if the event itself is agreed by the parties concerned to be an appropriate response to needs; if learning strategy, learners and those delivering the learning event have been well chosen; if the event has been effectively designed; and if the planning and managerial processes are of good quality. Flexibility will be crucial. Going back to our case-study, fine-tuning of focus and delivery had to continue throughout the clinical directors' programme. Subsequent evaluations confirmed that this adaptability to emergent needs had been central to the programme's ability to achieve its desired outcomes.

STAGE 8: MONITORING AND EVALUATING THE EVENT

In contrast to the discussion of assessment and measurement in Chapters 6 and 7, the purpose here is to move to the micro level and provide a simple, practical approach to the evaluation of specific learning events. The section does not encompass a review of key literature on evaluation or cover techniques in any detail. For that kind of discussion the reader is referred to specialist texts, particularly Kearns and Miller (1996) and Bramley (1996). Kearns and Miller provide particular value because they also show the importance of assessing the future impact of investing in planned learning activities, and explain how this can be done.

Five key questions about evaluation

Evaluation looks at the total value of a learning event, not just at whether and how far it has achieved its learning objectives. It thereby puts the event in its wider context and provides information essential to future planning. Faced with an evaluation task, there are five crucial questions to answer:

- *Why* evaluate?

- *What* to evaluate?

- *Who* should evaluate?

- *When* to evaluate?

- *How* to evaluate?

1 Why evaluate?

There are many reasons why evaluation might be required in a specific situation. Perhaps cost has to be justified, or effects on learners, or impact on job performance, or outcomes relevant to the profitability, performance, flexibility or survival of the organisation as a whole. Each kind of aim involves the evaluator in a different set of activities, and will provide the frame of reference for the four remaining questions.

2 What to evaluate?

A four-fold framework is helpful here, drawn from models provided by Warr, Bird and Rackham (1970) and Hamblin (1974), whose texts give practical guidance on evaluation techniques and procedures. The dimensions to be evaluated are those of the so-called CIRO approach, namely the:

- *Context* within which the learning event has taken place: organisational, analytical and diagnostic

- *Inputs* to the learning event: tangible and intangible, internal and external resources; the learning system designed for the event; and the recruitment to the event

- *Reactions* to the learning event: those of the learners and other relevant parties

- *Outcomes* of the learning event, both at its end and over the longer term.

Under question 5 we shall look at how to evaluate each of these four dimensions.

3 Who should evaluate?

Depending on the answers to the first two questions, there will be a range of possibilities here. Trainers, line managers, the personnel function, top management, external consultants, all will have particular skills to offer. However, because each will bring their own viewpoints and aims to the task, none can be relied upon to be free of bias. It is here that it becomes so important to understand the evaluation task and its purpose: failure to ensure a good choice of evaluator will make the organisation very vulnerable to manipulation. Evaluation is a sensitive and technically difficult matter whose outcomes can be only as reliable and valid as the process that produces them.

The choice of evaluators should be determined by five criteria:

- *objectivity* – What, if any, connection have potential evaluators had with the design, running and outcomes of the learning event? Are they likely to cover up any weaknesses or strengths in the event – or to exaggerate them?

- *expertise* – Have they carried out evaluation before? For whom? With what results? Does their explanation of how they will approach the task convince you of their knowledge, skill and professionalism?

- *interpersonal skills* – What sort of relationship do they have, or can they be expected to form, with those whose views they need to obtain? Are they likely to receive trust and co-operation? What sort of relationship have they established with you, and what does that tell you about their interpersonal skills?

- *credibility* – This will depend partly on the factors already examined above but also, and crucially, on the understanding they demonstrate of the organisation and its environment.

- *cost* – If you are considering using consultants, will the fee be worth the result? What will happen when they leave? Will they have trained your staff to take over from them, especially in implementing any further stages of a lengthy project? Could anyone else do the job more cheaply but as well? Could your own staff do the job – and could they be spared to do it?

4 When to evaluate?

There are several choices possible here.

- If the purpose of evaluation is to find out how valid the learning event was in helping the learners to reach identified standards by its end, then monitoring standards reached *before* and *at the end of* the learning event may be sufficient. However, it would be advisable to evaluate at least once again, at a later date, in order to assess how far learning has been retained and its ultimate impact.

- If the cost-efficiency of the inputs is to be evaluated, evaluation using reactions of the learners *during* and *at the end of* the event, and pre- and post-tests of the learning they have acquired in relation to the objectives of the learning event will probably prove sufficient.

- If the cost-effectiveness of a programme needs to be evaluated in order to decide whether the organisation should invest again in such a programme, it may prove necessary to evaluate by reference to job performance *in the short-term*, and the *longer-term* impact on both job performance and overall organisational trends in, perhaps, profitability, morale and flexibility.

Timing must also take practical considerations into account. To evaluate in depth using sophisticated methods at five different points in time, for example, would be very costly. This may not be possible or justifiable given the benefits likely to accrue from the exercise. On the other hand, a simple form of monitoring carried out at fairly regular intervals will be cheap. Given all the advantages of information, control and good planning that it offers, it will usually repay the repetitive effort it requires.

5 How to evaluate?
This depends on what is being evaluated and when evaluation is needed. The CIRO approach already explained in this section offers a basic framework for evaluation. Use it to evaluate:

Context of the learning event
This involves examining how accurately needs were initially diagnosed, why this particular kind of learning event was decided on as a solution, and whether the right kind of learning objectives were set.

Look, therefore, at how and by whom the information that gave rise to the diagnosis of the need for the learning event was collected, and at what process they used. Then examine how that information was analysed, what learning needs emerged from it, and what measure of agreement there was between key parties on the kinds of skills, knowledge and attitudes to be acquired.

Next examine how learning objectives were set; how well they related to the overall purpose of the event and the needs it was intended to serve; how far they took into account the organisational context within which the learning would have to take place and any constraints or advantages offered by the organisational culture and structure in relation to the learning event; what standards were established; and how the achievement of standards was to be measured.

Inputs to the learning event
Here the concern is to discover how well the learning event was planned, managed, designed and delivered by establishing how cost-efficient, cost-effective and feasible and well-chosen its major inputs were.

It is necessary to identify and, within reasonable limits, cost the resources used to meet learning needs (time, money, staff and expertise, physical accommodation, materials, and the natural learning resources in the organisation); to assess the cost and appropriateness of the chosen learning system, media, methods and content; and to establish how far selection choices for entry to the event were appropriate, so that the right learners were chosen for the event.

Reactions to the learning event
This involves discovering the learners' feelings – their immediate reactions – about the event. Establishing what people feel, as distinct (often) from what outcomes have actually been achieved, is important because those views and feelings will influence others, including future potential participants, as well as explaining any motivational problems or successes during the event. It also involves discovering the reactions of other parties directly involved in or with the learning event, and comparing them with the reactions it was hoped the event would achieve.

If the main concern is with assessing perceptions and feelings about what learning has been achieved, then reactions should be sought mainly from participants and from their tutors. If, on the other hand, there is a particular concern to find out how people felt about course content, methods and delivery, the views of the learners, deliverers and any observers will be the most significant.

It may be important to test reactions after every session of an event, or after every key element, or – in a modular programme – at the end of every module. Evaluation of reactions must suit the needs of the exercise. Hamblin (1974) recommended the use of session assessments on training courses, where each session can be looked at in terms of any aspects in which the evaluator is interested: enjoyment, length of time given to discussion, level of presentation, informational content, relevance, length of the session; or to monitor the progress of a practical activity, perhaps with a view to establishing typical learning curves of different types of learners.

Outcomes of the learning event

This involves attempting to establish what actually happened as a result of a learning event – its outcomes, which should be measured at any or all of the following levels, depending again on the object of the evaluation exercise:

• *the learner level* – This involves recalling not only the reactions of the learners to the learning event, since they themselves are a type of outcome (as described above), but also establishing changes in the learners' knowledge, skills and attitudes at the completion of the training that can be objectively ascertained (for example, by tests) and comparing them with levels of knowledge, skills and attitudes identified at the start of the programme (by techniques such as appraisal, tests, repertory grids, etc).

• *the workplace level* – This involves identifying changes that subsequently take place in the learner's job behaviour. These can be measured by appraisal, observation, discussion with the learners' managers/peers/customers/clients, and performance records, as well as by the reactions (see above) of the learners themselves, and how far these are in line with the views of others about that performance. (Research quoted by Warr *et al*, 1970 indicated that there is usually quite a close correlation between those two sets of views.)

• *the team/department/unit level* – This involves identifying changes that take place in part or all of a team, department or unit as a result of a learning event, using the kind of techniques described in relation to evaluating outcomes at the workplace level.

• *the organisational level* – This involves identifying changes that take place in the organisation as a whole after the completion of the training programme and that appear strongly related to that programme.

These last two kinds of outcome are the most difficult to evaluate, yet – with careful thought – meaningful evaluation even here should be possible. It will, however, depend on the setting of clear objectives for the learning event, and on prior agreement on how achievement of those objectives will be measured. At departmental level the sort of changes that could be involved include alterations in departmental output, costs, scrap rates, absenteeism, turnover, or accident frequency; improvement in productivity rates, labour costs, absenteeism and turnover rates; or the effectiveness in some other way of the total organisation. At organisational level they could be about change in the culture of the organisation, more flexibility and reduced levels of conflict in relation to the introduction of change, and enhanced ability to attract and retain valued workers.

Depending on when evaluation is to be carried out, the methods used could include one or more of the following:

- *pre-course, interim and post-course assessment* – Put the participants through an assessment process before the learning event in order to establish their present standards of performance and typical attitudes and work behaviour. Put them through a similar process during and after the programme in order to measure changes.

- *pre-course, interim and post-course opinions (semi-structured or unstructured) about performance* – Obtain general views about their behaviour and performance from various parties, including external people (as relevant), both before the learning event and when they are back in the workplace. Ask for *specific* examples of changed performance, behaviour and attitudes rather than unsubstantiated views.

- *pre-course and post-course ratings of performance* – Obtain the views of peers and colleagues in deciding how far the learning event has achieved its objectives with the managers concerned, using behavioural rating scales and other structured evidence of specific behaviour and performance.

We can go back to our clinical directors' programme to see how evaluation was carried out there.

Case-study: The clinical directors' programme: Part 2

Because of its strategic importance in the region, the programme was subjected to evaluation by two universities outside the region on behalf of the Northern Regional Health Authority (NRHA) and the Management Executive (ME). It was also monitored continuously by the programme staff at the NRHA and at Durham University Business School (DUBS). The latter used daily reaction sheets for the critical first module – the Management Foundation Course – to test perceptions of and reactions to the achievement of module objectives, and to its delivery and content. Subsequently, they distributed questionnaires only at the end of each module, testing reactions to each main component. This elicited essential information while avoiding what otherwise could have been an excess of questioning in view of evaluation exercises also being conducted at regional and national level.

Finally, DUBS organised a detailed evaluation exercise near the end of the programme in September 1993 and a longer-term evaluation in February 1995, both linked to review seminars. On each of these occasions evaluative data were obtained not only in the form of opinions from the key parties but also in the form of specific examples provided by the clinical director participants (CDs) and their managers of changes in knowledge, attitudes, behaviour and performance.

The information obtained demonstrated clearly that the stakeholders had a shared perception of the purpose and objectives set for the programme, and that for the overwhelming majority both purpose and objectives were valuable and had been satisfactorily achieved. Caution must, of course, be exercised at this point. Distortions can be caused by biases of evaluators, by timing, by the design of questionnaires, and by concerns over who would see the evaluations and to what use they would put the data. That said, however, evidence of the programme's perceived effectiveness was wide-ranging and came from multiple sources through time.

Of particular significance was the impact of the longer-term evaluation exercise in relation to assessing the value of the action-learning (AL) component (Harrison, 1996a). In longer-term evaluation questionnaires, four CDs cited AL as one of the most valuable elements of the programme. The strategic role of these clinicians had steadily expanded since the conclusion of the programme. For three of them it had been fully supported by their organisational context where they received encouragement, support and, often, further training and development to fully practise that role in line with their new learning. For the fourth, the organisational context had been less favourable but by February 1995 it was at last changing in a positive way.

Of the eight other CDs who by then were also in markedly more strategic roles, but who had made no comment on AL, four rated the programme's formal modules highly, although their learning had not subsequently been supported by their organisational contexts; and one saw the programme's unique value in its 'focused, small-group, safe environment to explore and experience issues away from work'. Three had been critical of AL in their earlier evaluations. Both of the clinicians who were not by then in more strategic roles failed to mention AL in their long-term evaluations.

This information indicates the critical importance of a supportive and developmental organisational context in ensuring the long-term positive impact of an AL period. It demonstrates the unique value of obtaining evaluations at some stage after the completion of a learning event. Had the evaluation process stopped on completion of the CD programme, perceptions of the value and impact of the AL component would have been quite different, and the planners would have been reluctant to use AL again in a similar programme, given its high cost in relation to the benefits evident at that point.

Finally, here is a task to integrate learning from this section.

Evaluating a management development programme

You are a training manager planning a six-month management development programme involving a mix of off-the-job formal modules and work-related projects, visits to external organisations and other experiential learning approaches. What are the five or six activities that you must carry out in order to evaluate the programme for the purposes both of validation and future planning?

Feedback notes

Here is a six-point guide to evaluating a learning event effectively and efficiently:

1   *Plan the evaluation in advance of the programme* – As you plan it you are likely to realise that adjustments need to be made to aspects of programme-planning in order to ensure that effective evaluation can be carried out.

2   *Ensure external consistency* by involving the learners' managers and other stakeholders in deciding on an evaluation process, and in monitoring and evaluating the programme. This will help to create the shared perceptions about the programme that will generate commitment to transfer its learning to the workplace and provide full support for the learners to practise their new learning over the long-term. Identify timescale, resources and arrangements for managing the exercise when agreeing on who should evaluate.

3   *Identify strategic milestones for the programme,* working backwards from the timing of its completion – when its final objectives should have been achieved – to its inception. (If you need to check on the meaning of 'strategic milestones', see page 121) Carrying out a check on progress at each milestone will enable information to be shared with key parties. They can then become involved in decisions about any adjustments that may be needed to the programme or its organisational context in order that the next milestone can be met.

4   *Identify targets and performance indicators within the programme* in order to decide how the achievement of outcomes related to each milestone is to be measured. If they do not enable meaningful evaluation to be done, change them.

5   *Monitor the development of learning,* ideally from a point before the learning event begins to some point subsequent to completion. Job training analysis and personal development diagnosis and planning as carried out in our case-study (Part 1) will supply useful reference-points as, of course, will the specified learning objectives.

6   *Ensure feedback of results* to the key parties in order to influence the planning of future events. The results of effective evaluation can go far beyond validation of a particular programme. Bee and Farmer (1995) described how a study that started life as a simple training evaluation task became an exercise in helping the management of change at London Underground.

CONCLUSION

Having read this chapter and completed its reviews and self-checks, you should now:

- understand the issues involved in the selection of learners

- be able to apply principles of learning to the design and delivery of a learning event

- know how to evaluate learning events appropriately.

To test yourself against these objectives, what five-minute answers would you give to the following questions? (Dates in brackets refer to the IPD qualifying examination paper in which a question appeared.)

- Outline and justify the guidelines you would suggest to someone preparing a talk that must attract and maintain the interest of the audience throughout. (November 1997)

- What are the main topics that you would include, and why, in a three-day course on 'Managing a training and development department', to be run by a consultancy firm for up to 15 newly qualified human resource (HR) professionals from a wide range of organisations? (May 1999)

- Outline and justify how to evaluate the course outlined in the previous question. (May 1999)

USEFUL READING

BEE F. (2000) 'How to evaluate training'. *People Management.* Vol.6, 6. pp42–3. (Brief, clear, practical guidelines.)

BEE F. *and* BEE R. (1998) *Training Needs Analysis and Evaluation.* London, Institute of Personnel and Development.

GAGNE R. M. (1977) *The Conditions of Learning.* New York, Holt Saunders.

GOUGH J. (1996) *Developing Learning Materials.* London, Institute of Personnel and Development.

HARDINGHAM A. (1996a) *Designing Training.* London, Institute of Personnel and Development.

SIDDONS S. (1997) *Delivering Training.* London, Institute of Personnel and Development.

18 Specialised training and development

LEARNING OBJECTIVES

After reading this chapter you will:

• understand why the design and delivery of special types of training and development programmes involve the same principles as those that relate to planned learning events in general

• know how to plan training and development programmes and processes to respond to the needs of different occupational groups, and to special needs and contingencies.

INTRODUCTION

There are many triggers to the design and delivery of special HRD initiatives. These include requirements for:

• the training of specific occupational groups such as clerical and administrative staff, apprentices, supervisors and team leaders

• the training of non-full-time employees, such as part-time and temporary employees and voluntary workers

• the training of those with special needs, such as ethnic minorities, the unemployed, or those returning to work after a career break

• training to respond to new legislation

• HRD initiatives to respond to business-led triggers such as a drive for customer care or total quality, a forthcoming downsizing or de-layering programme, or the introduction of new tasks, patterns of work organisation or new technology.

In all such cases the same planning and design principles apply that have been examined in Chapters 14 to 17. They were introduced in Table 11 in Chapter 15 (repeated overleaf).

Practical issues
Ignoring the basic principles of learning planning and design shown in Table 11 will inevitably result in failure. Sometimes that failure can have the gravest implications, not just in the organisation but beyond its boundaries. Take this as an example:

Table 11 Eight stages in the inception, design and delivery of planned learning events

1 Establish needs.
2 Agree on the overall purpose and objectives for the learning event.
3 Identify the profile of the intended learning population.
4 Select strategy, and agree on direction and management of the learning event.
5 Select learners and produce detailed specification for the learning event.
6 Confirm strategy and design event.
7 Deliver event.
8 Monitor and evaluate event.

Case-study: Metropolitan Police criticised for failures in training to erase racism

In 2000, a 'damning report' was published by Her Majesty's Inspectorate of Constabulary on the Metropolitan Police's efforts to erase racism (Cooper, 2000a). The race awareness training introduced since the Macpherson report on the Stephen Lawrence murder investigation was found to be particularly inadequate. The study, however, also criticised the Met's previous record of training, on the grounds that 'from 1989 to 1998 it wasted £780,000 on training community race relations trainers whom it then failed to use' (*ibid*). Why was there failure on such a scale?

In part it appeared to be because senior personnel chiefs had not been able to exercise enough influence in the decision and delegation process; this, in turn, was evidently because they lacked the necessary organisational weight and credibility to do so. In part, it was because of failure in the most fundamental elements of training design planning:

- confusion as to where the responsibility lay for training at a senior level

- lack of clarity on overall training strategy and how it fitted with wider HR functions

- lack of understanding as to who would be trained to what standard, and when

- lack of rigorous training needs analysis

- lack of effective and long-term evaluation strategy.

Source: Cooper (2000a)

Particularly important issues to clarify in the planning and design processes for special HRD initiatives are:

At which levels and across which sectors in the organisation do the needs exist?

Needs may exist at one or all of the following levels: corporate, business-unit or operational. They may be specific to one group (for example, team leaders) or may relate to many or all employees (for example, initiatives to do with equal opportunities, health and safety, total quality or customer care).

Are there any occupational standards, special legislation or specific issues that must be taken into account when training and developing the learners involved?
Examples would include health and safety legislation applying to this particular group of learners, professional or occupational codes and standards of practice that must be embodied in their training, findings from national reports that have identified issues requiring a special focus in their training, and so on.

How can the stakeholders become fully involved in the development and delivery of the learning initiatives so that their support is achieved throughout?
Without the commitment of those whose support is essential – particularly managers and team leaders who have to ensure transfer of training to the workplace – the initiatives will fail.

At what stages in the performance management process should the learning events related to these needs be provided (see Chapter 14)?
Should they be provided in relation to

- induction and basic training (and therefore be aimed at newcomers or those newly promoted)?

- improving current performance (and therefore be aimed at existing job-holders)?

- continuous development and career planning (and therefore be aimed at all employees)?

How should the needs be analysed?
Various approaches and techniques have been outlined in Chapters 14 and 15. However, with a special contingency, auditing is particularly useful (see Chapter 7). It will identify perceptions of key parties about learning needs, reveal learning outcomes required, and generate valuable ideas about learning design, content and methods.

Could the learning events lead to National Vocational Qualifications (NVQs) or other qualifications?
If so, this will enhance employability security for the learners and should provide an additional stimulus for the event.

In this chapter you will find areas of special need that are widely encountered in organisations – teamwork, equality in the workplace, and the learning and development of non-employees. Examples of good practice help to demonstrate general principles of planning and design.

TEAM DEVELOPMENT

Teamworking is one of the most familiar outcomes of downsizing, de-layering and decentralisation. There are many examples available to illustrate ways in which training can be organised, but not all of them focus equally on the needs of leaders and of members.

Team leaders as first-line managers are critical to organisational and team success. They carry the responsibility for organising and managing people, ensuring the quality and profitability of products or services, improving safety, cost control and other functions which require them to possess a considerable knowledge of the commercial, economic and customer-care aspects of a business. They also need mastery of many interpersonal skills and processes. Research has made it clear that the competencies and attitudes needed to perform well in team leader roles are specific to the particular organisational context (Warr and Bird, 1968). Careful analysis is therefore required to ensure the relevance of the purpose, design and outcomes of initiatives to develop team leaders.

Many team training programmes ignore the needs of those who come to team leader roles with experience of supervising sections or individuals but who have no understanding of the processes involved in managing flexible and autonomous teams and no awareness of how different the roles of team leader and of the traditional hierarchical supervisor are. In the following case-study, this mistake appears to have been avoided.

Case-study: Developing teamworking at Yardley Cosmetics
By the late 1990s, Yardley's manufacturing site in Basildon employed around 650 people, mainly women. Yardley had been taken over by the US group Wasserstein Perella in 1990, and a radical programme of strategic change and organisational restructuring then commenced. The need was to improve customer service in a company that had been a traditional functional hierarchy, with poor communication across the business and little control over sourcing and supply of materials for its large range of products.

Steve Reddington, the new business director, came from Unilever to Yardley in 1990 with experience in co-ordinating a total quality programme. Initial changes were to do with breaking down functional barriers by setting up cross-functional management teams. The concept of internal customers and suppliers was developed, and clear and interrelated targets were set for all managers in the supply chain.

A 'common-sense' approach to teamworking was a natural consequence of the new order, but some formalisation rapidly became necessary. As production controllers were replaced by production managers, so supervisors were replaced by team leaders 'whose role was to help people achieve their goals and work as members of their own team' (Arkin, 1995a: 31). Triggered by the need to focus on customer service and quality in order to improve competitive edge, it was decided to invest in employee development, particularly via a new training centre with a training co-ordinator. A major need was team development – an area that had received little attention in the years before the take-over. The context for this training was that of the three production units: cosmetics, fragrances and body-care. A carefully integrated plan to select, train and develop teams and their leaders was established.

- A project team was set up to identify the skills and attributes needed by team leaders and members in their new work environment.

- Training consultants then designed a programme to improve team communication and problem-solving skills while also focusing on understanding the teamworking concept so that people would be thinking, as well as working, together.

- As the first stage of the programme, current supervisors and other employees went through an assessment centre in order to identify those to be given team leader positions. Not all supervisors made the transition, while some employees who had previously held only operator positions were found to have the necessary potential.

- Presentations were held on-site to explain the team training programme, and then four half-day modules were organised first for workers in the cosmetics production unit. They were also attended by the training co-ordinator and a training adviser who would later deliver the same programme to those working in the two other production units.

- In parallel, modules were delivered that focused on 'helping team leaders think of themselves as coaches rather than supervisors' (Arkin, 1995a: 31).

Meanwhile the company was moving into another key stage of restructuring – the creation of integrated business units. Purchasing and planning departments were disbanded and those working in them were brought into the manufacturing units which, in turn, took responsibility for all aspects of production. Each unit was given clear goals and had to operate as a competitive unit benchmarked against other companies. At this point it became clear that team leaders would need further training, especially in running team briefings, in order to give the teamworking initiative sustained impetus within the new business-unit context.

Source: Arkin, 1995a

Analysis of this case-study reveals that:

- *External factors can trigger off a more strategic approach to employee development throughout an organisation.* In this case, the initial triggers were to do with a more competitive environment and consequent changes in business strategy. The investment in employee development, especially by setting up a training centre, was a mark of the company's determination to ensure that over the long term, as well as immediately, training would be a major lever to the achievement of the new business goals.

The speed with which the first stage of training was organised in response to those triggers clearly owed much to the working partnership between external and internal training consultants. As we saw in Chapter 10, external consultants can bring benefit to the organisation in many ways, especially when changes in mindsets as well as in skills are needed, and when internal HRD staff must acquire new skills quickly.

- *New initiatives in training and development must be aligned with business strategy.* In this case, changes in business strategy led to organisational restructuring as well as new customer service and quality goals. Training became essential in order to achieve the goals and to ensure that employees operated effectively in the new structure. Alignment of HRD with business goals gave the necessary commitment at all levels to that learning process.

- *Planning, design and evaluation of learning events should be done on a continuous basis.* It is easy to see how the eight stages involved in planning, designing and delivering a learning event were followed in this case-study. What should also be noted is the way in which the company ensured that as business and organisational changes continued, the focus of training changed to take account of them.

- *The identification of the key skills, knowledge and attitudes of the learners is crucial in determining what they need to learn.* Identification of the level of competence and motivation already possessed by the learners in relation to that which they need to reach in their new work environment should be a starting-point in the design process. It enables a clear focus to be established and standards of performance and behaviour to be put in place. In this case-study, the identification and analysis of learning needs in the roles and jobs concerned (by the project team) was paralleled by the assessment of those selected to occupy those roles and carry out those jobs (through the medium of the assessment centre).

It is in that combination of leader and members that the power of the team as a group lies. In this case-study there was a focus both on developing team skills within a team and on helping team leaders to function effectively in their new roles.

There are many accounts of team training in professional journals, and these should be scanned in order to develop insights into good current practice. Such a review is also important in order to check how, in different organisational contexts, team training is integrated within the performance management process and how it is aligned with human resource practice in the workplace.

DEVELOPMENT RELATED TO ACHIEVING EQUALITY IN THE WORKPLACE

The role of HRD in achieving equality in the workplace

Inequality at work occurs when a person or group is treated in an unjustifiably less favourable way than another is, or would be, treated in the same sort of situation. It is essential to ensure that every effort is made to prevent discrimination occurring in the organisation and to achieve full equality of treatment and opportunity for all employees.

At present the law offers protection for people against discrimination on grounds of sex, marriage, race, disability, and ethnic or national origins (for a fuller account, see Marchington and Wilkinson, 1996: 76–85). However, there are other forms of discrimination, particularly those related to age, religion (it is only in Northern Ireland that discrimination on grounds of religion is forbidden by law) and sexual orientation.

Discrimination related to age and disability are particularly widespread in Britain, and effective training initiatives are particularly necessary here. The Disability Discrimination Act 1995 encourages supported employment across a wider range of occupations and locations than hitherto by allowing profit-making firms as well as voluntary bodies to operate schemes to support people with learning disabilities in employment (see especially the Next Step Project described by Arkin, 1995b).

What is the role for HRD in relation to equality at work? First, to ensure that the employer operates within the law. Next, to help ensure the kind of good practice that will help the organisation to attract, retain and develop a fully effective workforce. To achieve equality in the workplace the employer must:

- ensure that there is no unlawful discrimination

- develop good employment practices for all employees equally

- identify groups who are underrepresented in certain jobs and take any necessary action to remedy this

- have, by effective monitoring, a defence against complaints of racial discrimination by individuals

- eliminate overt discrimination and employment practices that are discriminatory in the ways they operate

- provide special training for employees who would otherwise be unable to enjoy the full benefits of an equal opportunities policy (CRE, 1983).

This indicates that HRD should focus on three areas of need related to: the raising of awareness and development of good practice, the avoidance of unlawful discrimination, and positive action across the organisation.

General awareness and practice in the organisation
Training and guidance should be available for everyone who makes policies and procedures, administers or is in any way actively involved in human resource management and development in the workplace, in order to ensure that all practical steps are taken to avoid discrimination. Such personnel include supervisory and managerial staff, HR specialists and reception staff. The key HR processes are those to do with

- HR planning

- recruitment and selection

- basic pay, terms and conditions of work

- appraisal, training and development

- career development, promotion and transfers

- benefits and rewards

- health, safety and welfare

- termination of employment.

Such training and guidance must ensure that managers and others understand what direct and indirect discrimination means, and know how to identify any discriminatory attitudes that may affect decision-making. They must understand the importance of recording ways in which applications for positions, training and rewards are handled, as well as the decisions made in those cases. Without such records to demonstrate that all reasonable practical steps have been taken to avoid discrimination occurring, it will be difficult to disprove claims of unlawful treatment.

There must also be knowledge of the law related to providing access to opportunities for training, promotion and other forms of reward or development. For example, if it is a condition of a management development programme that all participants must spend six months on a course in another area or region, and there is no convincing justification for this (because there is a good course run locally or the learning could be achieved by some other medium), then the condition could be held to be unlawful because it discriminates against married women with children who would always find such a condition more difficult to comply with than other types of employee would.

Problems of communication and understanding often cause or increase discriminatory attitudes and behaviour at work. Training to raise awareness of how these problems can arise, and of the special needs of minority groups in the workplace, can make a significant contribution to reducing these problems.

All organisations should have an equal opportunities policy. Guidance must be given so that it is fully understood at every level and so that the roles and responsibilities it involves are clear and are carried out competently.

Avoiding unlawful discrimination in HRD
Information about training, educational and other developmental opportunities, and how to apply for them, must be made known to all eligible employees. They must not be communicated in ways that could exclude or disproportionately reduce the numbers of applicants from a particular minority or racial group or sex.

There must be no direct or indirect discrimination in selecting people for training and development, and checks must be made regularly to see whether people from a particular group or sex do not apply for employment or promotion; are not recruited or promoted at all; or are appointed, but in significantly lower proportions than their rate of application. If any of these problems is occurring, the training manager must find out whether a major cause lies in a lack of appropriate training or qualifications among these individuals. If it does, and if the reason is that training or other forms of development were not as accessible for them as for other employees, or that the design or 'language' of the learning methods involved posed particular problems for them, changes must be made.

Positive action in training
Although it is not lawful to discriminate against some groups in order to improve the position of others previously disadvantaged, this does

not preclude positive action to help those in the latter category. For example, where in the previous 12-month period there have been no or proportionately few employees of a particular sex or racial group in certain jobs, areas, or level of work, then:

- employers may provide access to training facilities that will help to fit them for such work or responsibilities

- employers may encourage them to apply for training or education, whether it is provided internally or externally

- the training manager may design training schemes for school-leavers designed to reach members of such groups; and may arrange training for promotion or skills training for those who lack particular expertise but show potential (supervisory training may include language training).

It is also lawful to give access to relevant training when minority groups have special needs in respect of education or training. For example, if the workforce includes employees whose English is limited, the training manager should ensure that communications are helped by training in English and communication skills, training for managers and team leaders in the background and culture of ethnic minority groups, and even by providing, where possible, interpretation and translation facilities for grievance and other procedures and terms of employment.

Women's management training regularly attracts interest as more evidence is uncovered to reveal continuing bias against women who strive for promotion in male-dominated sectors or organisations. However, women in non-managerial jobs have career development needs too, and Arkin (1991) described an award-winning personal and career development programme for such women, Springboard, pioneered at the BBC and still a widely used initiative.

Case-study: The Springboard programme
What does the case-study emphasise, related to the planning, design and delivery of programmes catering for special groups and needs?

Springboard evolved from a 'Women's development programme' launched by the BBC in 1989 that won the Lady Platt Award for the best equal opportunities training initiative.

That programme arose out of a perceived need that, while the BBC had done much to open up opportunities for women managers, it was essential to widen these initiatives, extending personal and career development opportunities to women (between 8,000 and 9,000) employed in non-managerial positions at the BBC. Better utilisation and motivation of such a huge organisational resource was clearly in the interests of the business as well as being of benefit to those individuals.

Consideration of the kinds of learning media and methods to be used indicated at first sight that distance-learning would be the most appropriate medium, given the extremely large size of the learning population. However, analysis of the profile of that population highlighted the importance to the learners of support and encouragement from other women, and this led to the decision to design a programme which involved a good deal of face-to-face learning. Its components were:

- three one-day workshops held over three months

- a workbook involving about three hours' work a week for participants, and involving a range of self-assessment and personal learning plan activities

- the formation of formal and informal networks

- a mentoring system in the workplace

- the involvement of senior women in the organisation.

The programme, designed by the BBC's management training unit working with Biographic Management consultancy, became so highly regarded that it was renamed Springboard and tailored for the use of other organisations, including Grand Metropolitan Foods, Europe, which incorporated it within a much larger initiative called the 'Learning Edge', designed to create a learning environment in which all employees could develop their full potential.

Source: Arkin (1991)

Feedback notes

Analysis of the study shows how carefully the programme was tailored to the needs of the organisation as well as of the individuals concerned. Particular points to note here are that:

- *learning media and methods must be appropriate, efficient and flexible*, given the needs and situation of the learners. Choice was determined by an analysis of the purpose and objectives of the programme and of the profile of the large learning population involved, of the need to encourage, motivate and stimulate the wide variety of learners, and of the practicalities of the situation. This resulted in a programme that offered a well-integrated range of media and methods that were relatively cheap and highly effective. The costs of designing and reproducing the workbook would have very quickly been offset by the numbers of people using it. It provided an ideal way of helping learners to prepare for practical sessions, reflect on learning, and transfer it continuously to their own individual situations. Thus the choice of media and methods echoes the principles discussed in Chapter 17 (pages 302–4).

- *external recognition of a new programme can lead to its extension to similar groups in other organisations* – We can see the value that external recognition (the Lady Platt Award) can bring to a programme. The extension of Springboard has helped many more women than the BBC group for which it was originally intended.

- *new HRD initiatives must be integrated into wider HRD strategy and plans* – This is the significance of Grand Metropolitan's reaction – a new programme designed to meet the needs of a special group became an integral part of overall HRD strategy in the organisation.

Unless this happens, new initiatives can lose their impact and die once the needs of a particular set of individuals have been met.

Training and development initiatives that facilitate re-entry after periods of absence from employment can also make a significant contribution to the business, as well as meeting individual needs. Without such schemes, for example, many women who take maternity leave do not or cannot return to their organisations. Particular organisational benefits of such initiatives include:

- improved returns on the training of staff, and the retention of skills and talents that might otherwise be lost

- saving in recruitment and relocation costs

- a pool of trained, committed ex-employees available to cover peaks in workload, holidays, long-term absence and maternity leave

- increased employability security for individuals.

THE LEARNING AND DEVELOPMENT OF NON-EMPLOYEES

Part-time and temporary workers

We have already noted earlier in this book the short-sightedness of focusing all of an organisation's HRD investment on full-time employees. The contribution of part-time and temporary workers, for example, can be crucial to the success and growth of the business. Research by the Policy Studies Institute (1993) indicated that flexible workers are an underperforming resource, and failure to integrate part-time and temporary workers into the organisation's HRD system subsequently gave rise to concern at government level (White, 1996). Here is a case-study showing how innovative HRD policies can help to build up a flexible workforce in which temporary workers play a leading role.

Case-study: Developing a flexible workforce at Beeton Rumford

By the late 1990s the Earl's Court Olympia catering company Beeton Rumford employed around 200 temporary workers. It was unusual in the catering trade in its promise of a good benefits package and equal commitment to the development of all its workers, not only those occupying full-time positions. The determination of the managing director, Richard Tate, to have an integrated workforce was so great that he banned the term 'casual'. He first developed his philosophy in an earlier career with Trust House Forte.

At Beeton Rumford the role of temporary employees was crucial but had in the past been undervalued. After 1991 the aim had been to ensure that through focused recruitment aimed at attracting and retaining high-calibre staff, and through eradicating from the company the casual ethos, temporary staff would be recognised by themselves and others as the backbone of the organisation, supported by rather than supporting full-time staff. After 1991 the company had been restructured from a functional to a customer-focused business, and a separate staff department had been established to recruit, train and manage temporary personnel.

At first, a large and relatively unproductive effort went into improving the status and training of temporary staff. Operational managers found it hard to support such a change in focus, given the stop-start nature of the business. Despite their efforts, the sizable pool of expensively recruited and trained temporary talent would disappear at the end of every catering event.

Further ER policy change took place, and this brought the improvements sought. Now, temporary staff were no longer laid off at 24 hours' notice but were treated as full-time in terms of the focus of their jobs, being given information about events scheduled over the coming year in order to aid their own planning activity. At the heart of the development strategy was a six-tier career structure based on core competencies, with appraisals carried out during each exhibition.

Source: Pickard (1995)

In the mid-1990s Beeton Rumford provided a model of good practice in how to respond to changing business needs and labour market patterns in ways appropriate to the organisation's business context. Often, however, such workers have less access than permanent full-time workers to four key areas of HRD practice:

- upskilling through training, growth in the job and increased responsibility

- performance management processes that combine appraisal reviews, target-setting, performance feedback and merit pay

- increasing personal discretion in tasks

- decentralised decision-making.

White (1996) noted that although the lowest skill categories of part-time and temporary workers fared worst, part-timers in management were particularly excluded from PMSs, and temporary workers (expecting less than one year's employment) suffered disproportionately in every area except that of initial training. Contract workers, on the other hand, did well – 'the healthier picture for this group indicates that it is possible to adapt development systems to meet the needs of flexible workers' (*ibid*).

Access to HRD by part-time and temporary workers

Take an organisation with which you are familiar where part-time and/or temporary workers are employed in significant numbers. What (if any) access do they have to the four key areas of HRD practice that are identified above? If their situation needs improvement, what steps would you recommend to achieve that?

Crossing organisational boundaries

Extending the scope of HRD beyond an organisation's boundaries is important for two reasons. First, it ensures that those on whom the organisation depends for the ultimate quality of its products and services are trained to the same standards as its own employees and understand its business processes and systems – the training rationale.

Second, external stakeholders have skills, knowledge, networks and ways of perceiving and understanding the business environment and the organisation that can enhance organisational learning and knowledge. Developing learning networks across organisational boundaries can therefore improve an organisation's strategic progress – the learning rationale. To achieve this, however, the process of learning involved must be 'focused, continuous and systematic ... aligned with satisfying the needs of the organisation and its stakeholders' (Batchelor, Donnelly and Morris, 1995: 1).

The customer–supplier relationship is a case in point. Supplier development programmes tend to be driven by the training rationale. Most focus on issues of task, process and skill development. However, a few, driven by a different rationale, seek to achieve a proactive learning partnership where people from inside and outside the organisation work together to improve their strategic thinking and creativity. The aim is a relationship where the organisation responds to the learning needs of the stakeholder in ways that produce double-loop learning – the kind of learning that involves questioning why certain problems occur in the first place and identifying underlying causes instead of only their surface symptoms. This contrasts with single-loop learning, where the aim is simply to reduce or eliminate a problem by training to improve performance (the training rationale). It is when double-loop learning occurs that things begin to change and new, more appropriate, ways of thinking and behaving develop.

Argyris (1996) explained the value of double-loop learning by reference to what he called 'skilled incompetency': the way in which skilful actions of individuals and groups can become counterproductive if they lead to defensive routines which, spreading across a workplace or entire organisation, produce a culture that avoids confrontation. In such a culture basic assumptions that people hold about work, organisational goals, and the business vision and environment cannot be tested. Fundamentally important issues can thus become undiscussable. Nothing will then change until 'something occurs that blows things open' (Argyris, 1996: 87).

Research shows, however, that in order to overturn what has now become embedded in the culture of an organisation nothing less than trauma is usually required – a threat to the organisation's survival, and/or the bringing in of new blood at the top. Argyris himself used the example of ultimate catastrophe: the 1986 Space Shuttle disaster. Only then 'were the mixed messages and defensive routines used during the decision to launch exposed. The disaster made it legitimate for outsiders to require insiders to discuss the undiscussable.'

Finally, it is appropriate at this point to mention one category of non-employee rarely given prominence either in research or the generalist literature of HRD: the voluntary worker. Increasingly these personnel offer knowledge, skills, commitment and a network of contacts that are of unique value to the business. Think, for example, of the reliance that the National Health Service places on volunteers in areas of hospital and community care work. The management committees of housing association trusts too rely heavily on voluntary members who work with chief executives in developing and maintaining the strategic direction of those associations. In charitable bodies, likewise, voluntary staff carry a heavy burden of responsibility.

While the personal orientation of volunteers is by definition different from that of other non-employees, their loyalty to the cause of the organisation is as great or greater, and their contribution is essential. Competition for volunteers is intensifying as, for a variety of reasons, their supply diminishes (Welch, 1997a) and essential services are scaled down when recruitment efforts fail. Adapting an organisation's HRD policies to meet volunteers' special learning needs can therefore now be seen not as an optional but as a necessary element in recruitment and retention strategy.

KEY PRINCIPLES WHEN ORGANISING SPECIAL HRD INITIATIVES

Designing learning initiatives to meet special needs

The case-studies contained in this chapter have been chosen as examples of good practice in areas of training and development need that are common across many organisations. Reviewing the material in this chapter, and assessing the case-studies for their wider implications, what six or seven key principles can you identify in relation to responding to the learning needs of special groups and contingencies?

Feedback notes
- Particular learning events should be analysed in the context of the needs of the business and its strategic goals. This should secure management's commitment to such events and ensure that the investment made in them produces due value for the business.

- Each new HRD initiative should be fully integrated within and be supported by the framework of wider HRD and HR policy and practice in the workplace.

- The success of learning initiatives to meet special needs can produce an ever-widening impact on the HR function. It can also lead to the identification of other important learning needs within the organisation. External recognition of effective and imaginative initiatives can trigger their extension within and beyond the organisation.

- The identification of key competencies needed in the job and the person is central to the planning and effective outcomes of such learning events, and their evaluation should influence any subsequent planning and design.

- Learning media and methods must be appropriate, efficient and flexible, adaptable to the needs of the particular learners.

- Where possible, training should lead to vocational qualifications, in order to enhance employability security and the motivation of learners.

• The scope of special learning and development initiatives should cover 'flexible' workers and extend across organisational boundaries to respond to the needs and interests of key stakeholders who, although not employed by the organisation, have a vital contribution to make to its success.

CONCLUSION

Having read this chapter and completed its reviews and self-checks, you should now:

• understand why the basic steps involved in the inception, design and delivery of training and development related to special training and development needs are the same as those for any planned learning event

• know how to plan HRD initiatives to respond to special and emergent needs.

To test yourself against these objectives, what five-minute answers would you give to the following questions? (Dates in brackets refer to the IPD qualifying examination paper in which a question appeared.)

• What might be the reasons for failure to achieve hoped-for levels of teamwork in an organisation despite much teamwork training and a de-layered organisation structure? (Specimen paper, 1996)

• You want to provide a flexible learning induction programme for the use of new recruits to your geographically dispersed sales force. What general principles would you bear in mind when designing the programme?

• What are some of the most typical triggers to the design and delivery of special HRD initiatives?

USEFUL READING

BELBIN R. M. (1964) *Training the Adult Worker*. London, HMSO.

CHARTERED INSTITUTE OF PERSONNEL AND DEVELOPMENT (CIPD). From its creation in July 2000 the CIPD will be producing a series of publications under the headings *Briefing Papers*, *Research* and *Surveys*, available either through Plymbridge distributors (01752 202 301) or the Institute's library, that examine contemporary employment issues.

INSTITUTE OF PERSONNEL AND DEVELOPMENT (IPD). The IPD published between 1994 and 2000 a range of *Guides* and *Key Facts* on employment issues, available either through Plymbridge distributors (01752 202 301) or the Institute's library. See also the Chartered Institute of Personnel and Development (above).

MABEY C. *and* ILES P. (EDS) (1994). *Managing Learning*. London, the Open University and Routledge. (See Parts IV and V, on 'Developing team effectiveness' and 'Managing diversity'.)

MERRICK N. (2000) 'Thrills and skills'. *People Management*. Vol. 6, 1. pp44–6. (Account of national training award-winning team training programme for an ailing company of financial advisers.)

ROBERTS C. (2000) 'The only way is up'. *People Management*. Vol.6, 1. p25. (Account of how challenges have been overcome in making positive-action training work for ethnic minority women in the National Health Service.)

Part 4

BUILDING FOR THE FUTURE

19 Developing careers

LEARNING OBJECTIVES

After reading this chapter you will:
- understand the importance of a strategic approach to career development in the organisation and the typical triggers for such an approach

- be able to explain how to establish a career development process based on mutuality and the psychological contract between employer and employee

- be able to identify and explain some major methods of assessing potential to aid career development

- as an HR professional, be able to advise others on continuous self-development, and raise awareness of its importance.

CAREER DEVELOPMENT

Mutuality and the psychological contract

Career development has been defined as 'an organised, planned effort comprised of structured activities or processes that result in a mutual career plotting effort between employees and the organisation' (Gilley and Eggland, 1989: 48).

Traditionally, the concept of 'career' has been one of upward movement involving:

- entry criteria linked to educational attainment or vocational training

- a planned structure of job experiences and promotional steps

- progressive status and/or salary

- membership of an external professional or occupational body with its own codes and culture. (Sparrow and Hiltrop, 1994: 427).

The relationship that binds individual and organisation is two-fold. There is a legal contract that specifies duties, terms and conditions, and material rewards; it clarifies the legal obligations of the parties. There is also a psychological contract consisting of felt and perceived expectations, wants and rights. It is this contract that provides the framework for the continuing relationship between the parties. If the organisation wishes to change the legal contract of employment, it can do so only on the basis of renegotiation and a new agreement between the parties. In the same way, if the basis of the psychological contract changes during the individual's career with the organisation, then that too should be acknowledged as cause for the parties jointly to identify the key issues raised by the changed situation, what each party wants in that new situation, and a renegotiation of what each will offer to the other.

Although the traditional concept of 'career' may not have changed as radically as is sometimes assumed, it is shifting. Organisations are now less able to guarantee lifetime job security and, in many waves of de-layering, have produced flatter structures. The concept of the 'portfolio career' is increasingly common, and in the knowledge economy (see Chapter 12) many organisations find it more difficult to attract and retain valued knowledge workers. The phrase 'the talent war' is not an uncommon one to indicate the problems here. Such trends lead to a greater emphasis on 'career' in the sense of job occupancy carrying with it coherent induction, training and development, increased employability security by the accrual of experience and qualifications valued in the external labour market, and continuous development through responding to more challenge, problem-solving and decision-making responsibilities at every organisational level.

Career tracks are in consequence more focused on mutuality of interest and need rather than on planned upward movement. Schein (1978: vii) observed over two decades ago that career development marks the point at which the shifting needs of an organisation's people confront the shifting nature of its work, going to the heart of the psychological contract joining the two parties, employer and employee. The challenge it embodies is one of matching the needs of the organisation with those of the people who work for it, and to do so from entry into the organisation, through each career transition-point thereafter, until exit, in order to achieve a mutually beneficial relationship over time.

The double reference to 'mutuality' in the above paragraph is deliberate. Unless mutuality is embedded in career development systems, the commitment of the individual to any career planning process will be lost: there will be a crisis of credibility and a negative impact on organisational as well as individual learning and growth.

Triggers for a more planned approach to career development

Taking your own organisation, or one with which you are familiar, identify any major change that has triggered a need for a more planned approach to the management and development of careers there. You can focus on particular occupational or professional groups, or on the whole workforce.

Feedback notes

In your response you will probably have listed one or more of the following triggers, since these are the most typical across organisations today:

- *a policy of continuous internal promotion and growth* in order to attract and retain scarce skills and ensure continuity of supply. The rigours as well as the organisational benefits of the strategy of recruiting high-calibre employees and then investing heavily in their internal development and promotion have been well documented (see, for example, White and Trevor, 1983 and Wickens, 1987). However, where external supply is weak or unreliable, and the need to obtain and retain scarce skills is high, 'growing our own' may be the only feasible policy for the organisation and will, in turn, require a planned approach to career development for those individuals or groups of employees concerned.

- *affirmative action programmes*, such as the Civil Service's and the National Health Service's in relation to female employees. Their implications mean that long-term career progression patterns have to be identified and career paths clearly established in the organisation.

- *a radical shift in the organisation's path*, involving a change of culture that will be aided by investing in a durable career development programme. A typical example would be the need, following downsizing, to develop the remaining employees into a flexible workforce and therefore to negotiate a new psychological contract focused on a career development system that can gain their commitment to the changed situation.

The common factor linking such triggers is an imbalance – due to external or internal changes – that has developed in the psychological contract between the individual and the organisation, and a consequent need to review and renegotiate that relationship. The following study provides a case in point.

Case-study: SCO's approach to career development

SCO, a computer software company founded in the USA, was typical in the late 1990s of many young, fast-growing firms whose rapid rise depended on a judicious mix of acquisition strategy and restructuring in order to develop new skills and products. Career development in such firms is inevitably an uncertain process. Yet the type of employees needed – with rare and high-level technical skills – have to be attracted and then motivated to stay long enough to make an impact on the firm's growth that repays the investment in recruiting them.

Macaulay and Harding's (1996) account of SCO's approach to employee development identified the starting-point as the recognition by the company of the need to change traditional employee expectations about career development to one more consistent with what it was possible and appropriate for the company to offer. Internal surveys and focus groups revealed widespread employee discontent with the gap between expectations and reality: 'loyalty no longer guaranteed security or promotion' (Macaulay and Harding, 1996: 34). Employees were also critical of the HR department which, they felt, did not offer the expected level of support or expertise in relation to personal development.

A 'best practice' review of other world-class organisations showed the need for a career development system that was closely aligned with the company's vision and direction, that attracted, motivated and rewarded high-performing people, and that communicated well. This led SCO to develop a plan of action focusing on four parameters:

• building a learning culture through emphasising self-development and career management driven by the individual

• improved feedback and communication

• a more effective performance management system (PMS)

• increasing the ability of individuals to bring about change.

The authors explained the kind of practical interventions involved in this plan: the production and distribution to all employees of a self-development guide containing a variety of inventories and activities, and stressing the joint nature of development in the company; career management workshops; project teams for specific business issues, incorporating technical problem-solving workshops; lunchtime training sessions on key company issues; a move towards total quality and continuous improvement; workshops on managing transition; and a review of the PMS.

The account made it clear that these interventions have not been trouble-free, and that the company is only at the start of a complex process requiring management's sustained commitment to invest heavily in time and effort over the long term if the desired rewards are to be achieved. The company sees no alternative, however, if it is to survive and grow in its turbulent and highly competitive market environment.

Source: Macaulay and Harding, 1996

SHIFTING CAREER PATTERNS

The final paragraph of our case-study is arguably its most important. Schein (1978) differentiated between the concept of the 'internal career' – meaning the individual's pursuit of an occupational path during his or her lifetime – and that of the 'external career' – meaning the developmental path established by the organisation for employees during their time with that organisation. There is also another kind of differentiation: between those types of career paths that involve repeated movement for the individual between the external and the internal labour market, whether primary or secondary (see pages 61–2) and those that offer meaningful progression within a single organisation for most of an individual's employed life. In today's economy, the latter is becoming less common than the former.

The career development issues facing organisations and individuals today have no easy solutions. Few firms may now feel able to offer long-term internal career paths to their employees. Some cannot offer any meaningful career paths at all; others may still be able to offer them for certain employees, but not all. For those individuals whose career paths involve the need for, or inevitability of, regular movement between external and internal labour markets, the consistent pursuit of self-development and opportunities for continuous learning is essential in order to ensure high employability security.

A report of research by the Institute for Employment Studies in the mid-1990s (Hirsch, Jackson and Jackson, 1995) made it clear that people need help in managing their careers. It is not enough for companies to allocate major resources to self-development. There must be a strategy for careers that tackles career management in an integrative way. It is also essential that line managers ensure the effective implementation of that strategy. In those organisations that can no longer offer long-term job security, open recognition of mutuality of interest seems more likely to generate high performance and adaptability than appeals to loyalty and commitment. Such organisations must produce strategies to build up and retain valuable skills and experience while at the same time giving support to individuals at critical transition points in their working lives. Without such a purposive approach by organisations to career development, 'employability security' could prove to be just one more fashionable term disguising a very different situation for many in the internal and external labour markets. Furthermore, the organisations themselves would not reap the benefit of individuals' learning that, better supported and stimulated, should bring organisational benefits.

Here is a historical example of a company that attempted to provide a motivating career development process from which all the stakeholders could benefit.

Case-study: Career development at BP during the 1990s
When Robert Horton became chairman of BP in 1990 he published the following statement about BP's mission.

BP vision, values and themes
BP is a family of businesses principally in oil and gas exploration and production, refining and marketing, chemicals and nutrition. In everything we do we are committed to creating wealth, always with integrity, to reward the stakeholders in BP – our shareholders, our employees, our customers and suppliers and the community.

We believe in continually developing a style and climate which liberates the talents, enthusiasm and commitment of all our people. We can then respond positively to the increasing pace of change in a rapid and flexible way to achieve real competitive advantage. With our bold, innovative strategic agenda BP will be the world's most successful oil company in the 1990s and beyond.

(Harrison, 1992: 452)

As part of the process of developing a new culture and structure at BP, Horton promised vigorous promotion of career development and the recognition of both individual contribution and collective teamwork. Employees would be encouraged to strike a balance between their responsibilities to BP and to their home life. There was to be a particular focus on personal development, with the hope that every employee would agree a personal development plan with their manager.

The issuing of his statement coincided with the unveiling of Project 1990, announcing the radical restructuring of the group, with de-layering and decentralisation of authority. Job cutbacks were followed swiftly by programmes right across the group aimed directly at changing attitudes and behaviour (Butler, 1990).

In 1996 Hirsh and Jackson provided further information about career development at BP. They gave an illuminating insight into the problems that so often occur as companies attempt to implement and sustain career development strategies at times of complex business and organisational change.

Their article showed that the change process at BP did not go smoothly. There were tensions between the old corporately managed hierarchic career and the newer concepts of teamworking and empowerment, and fears for job security made it harder for those newer concepts to take root. By 1996 the focus in career development had moved from highlighting the need for self-management of careers to emphasising the need for partnership: a joint approach by individuals and the company to managing careers. Personal development planning remained a central concept, but initially it tended to founder for lack of sufficient assistance to individuals – sometimes because of failure in some parts of the devolved structure to put appropriate systems in place, sometimes because of a tendency to try *ad hoc* initiatives which were not sustained.

As is so often the case, the main focus of attention tended to be with the high-potential, fast-track managers, linking in to corporate succession planning. The needs and expectations of others in the workforce were felt by some employees to have been relatively neglected in that process.

Despite these setbacks, the authors saw positive signs for the future lying in three factors: the 'clear and honest communication about what has been happening to the business' that had 'helped staff to adjust their ideas about careers' (Hirsh and Jackson, 1996: 25); the realisation by the company that career management is a long-term process and must be tackled as such; and the company's determination to ensure that changes were handled at local more than at corporate level, and that business-unit managers understood, accepted and carried out the responsibilities they held for the career development of all their staff.

Sources: Harrison, 1992; Hirsch and Jackson, 1996

Such cases show how difficult it can be for companies to implement and sustain their plans for career development. They also demonstrate the importance of longitudinal research in order to establish 'what is really going on here' and the ultimate outcomes of various HRD initiatives. The need for such research has already been emphasised at various points in this book.

Four processes to ensure mutuality in career development
The 1995 IES research into career development already mentioned (page 337) identified three major areas where reality of organisational practice falls far short of espoused intent. Organisations repeatedly fail to achieve:

• an appropriate and honest message

• workable career development processes

• a real intention to deliver.

Looking at these gaps and reflecting on the concept of mutuality, we can see the importance of four processes in any organisation's approach to career development (Herriot and Pemberton, 1995):

- informing
- negotiating
- monitoring
- renegotiating and/or exiting.

Informing

The provision of information should be a continuous process, starting at recruitment. Its aim is to keep organisation and individual informed about what each expects of the other now and in the future. Vehicles for such information-sharing include the induction process, mentoring, appraisal discussions, employee satisfaction surveys and personal development plans.

Negotiating

This process should occur whenever employees' wants and needs significantly alter. Such a change may occur because of some altered personal circumstance on the individual's side, or on the organisation's side because of necessary changes in business goals and strategy, workplace environment or human resource (HR) policies.

Monitoring

There is a need for continuous checking to ensure that new skills and knowledge are being developed to meet emergent organisational, team and individual needs.

We saw in Chapter 5 how at an acute hospital's National Health Service Trust, line management carries primary responsibility for identifying the ongoing training needs of staff through annual appraisal, personal development plans, monitoring of staff performance, and development and evaluation of training events. Together, these processes are intended to ensure that a 'bottom-up' as well as 'top-down' approach is taken to developing HRD strategy in the Trust. In 1995–97 many unanticipated changes took place within the Trust. These were triggered by the need – arbitrarily imposed by government policy – to move away from public-sector funding towards a private-sector financial initiative in order to enable the building of the new district general hospital in 1999 to proceed. They were exacerbated by acute financial problems caused in part by pressures similar in kind to those being experienced at that time in a growing number of NHS Trusts in the UK. As cost reductions intensified, the timetable for planned organisational restructuring had to be shortened, and this in turn had a strong negative impact on employees' perceptions relating to their job security and their changing duties and responsibilities. The process of renegotiation at all levels became continuous, not only to take into account issues related to contracts of employment but also to ensure that the Trust responded in practical and convincing ways to the changed wants and expectations of a workforce, and to its reduced ability to offer employment security to all its personnel.

Renegotiating and/or exiting

There should be planned exit routes at each career transition-point for the different occupational groups in the organisation, so that organisation and individuals are enabled to adjust the psychological as well as the legal contract in the least damaging way to the parties when the situation requires. Disengagement of individuals, whether at the planned retirement date or before it, whether because of poor organisational or individual performance or disappointed career expectations, whether arising from the wish of the employee or the need of the business, should be achieved with fairness, with mutual respect, and be aided by supportive and consistent ER processes.

For the organisation, the concern must be to retain for as long as possible those who embody the organisation's strategic and competitive capability – that is to say, those whose skills, knowledge and disposition make them of crucial value to the continued progress of the organisation. The concern must also be to maintain a reputation and image in the labour market of being a fair employer, with a genuine concern for employees.

BUILDING AN EFFECTIVE CAREER MANAGEMENT SYSTEM

Six critical success factors

It is commonly in the area of succession planning that organisations tend to focus most of their career development effort. However, a career management system should be wider than that in its scope. Six factors will be critical to its success:

- It must embody a transparent process owned by line managers.

- It must be a process that can evolve through time and is integrated with existing HR systems, ensuring fair operation of the internal labour market.

- It must comprise a system, based on full information about people's career expectations and about the needs of the organisation, that ensures that the business has committed people in the right roles at the right time, with their capability for the future identified, developed and safeguarded.

- There must be measurement of standards to show whether the system works.

- There must be clear communication about development processes and responsibilities to all employees, and provision for all employees of relevant and full information about career paths.

• There must be support for employees in planning their development.

Such a system need not involve radical change, although it is essential to ensure that it takes fully into account structural and cultural factors. In this connection, Mayo (1994) observed that career management is made more difficult when an organisation has to operate in a rapidly changing and unpredictable world and in situations where there are structural trends such as flatter organisations, decentralised profit centres and elimination of central overheads. None the less, as his many examples powerfully demonstrated, given strong direction from the top and wider integration of career development policy with business and human resource (HR) policy, much can be achieved.

The importance of integration

The career management system must be integrated in a number of ways and at three organisational levels.

Strategic integration

For career management to be a strategic activity rather than simply responding in *ad hoc* ways to each changing situation, it needs to be pursued at corporate, unit and operational levels of the organisation (Hall, 1984: 176–81). The process of career development will secure the full commitment of the organisation only when it is seen by line managers as well as top management as a business-led activity. It must therefore also be a jointly managed process to ensure its wider organisational integration.

• *At corporate level* it must be part of business strategy and planning, where it should be the direct responsibility of senior management, not of personnel specialists. Only in this way can there be full commitment to developing objectives and a policy for career development throughout the organisation, and means to ensure that policy is implemented. At this level the framework for career development is set by the decisions made about work to be done, the structure required for the organisation, the roles needed within the structure and the goals to be achieved across the organisation.

• *At unit level* managers must be stimulated to take responsibility for managing the career development of their people. This responsibility needs to be made into a key result area on which they are appraised, trained and rewarded. The skills they need to acquire are those related to job design, career coaching and counselling, mentoring, succession planning, the giving of feedback and the assessment of potential. They, working in partnership with the HR function (if there is one), can enhance career development by arranging job movements, including inter-unit co-operative arrangements such as transfers, secondments, special projects and other assignments.

- *At operational level* there should be a process of joint career planning that involves individual and manager (or some other person or body responsible for career development in the organisation) in exchanging information about wants and expectations and in negotiating ways in which the individual's career can be progressed to meet their and the organisation's needs.

HR integration

In his classic text on career development Schein (1978: 191) showed how the HR system can act as the repository of those key processes whereby the aims and interests of organisation and individual are matched. Some central integrative body (often a career or personnel development committee) needs to develop company-wide policy, systems and procedures for career development. Evaluation of career development activity can then reveal whether the system is achieving its success criteria, and whether chosen development programmes and other activities are providing the most mutually beneficial growth paths for individuals and for the organisation. This is particularly important when the organisation is undergoing fundamental restructuring leading to new pay systems and the identification of new competencies.

Organisational integration

Some of the most intractable problems in developing career paths in an organisation lie in the need to achieve consistency and coherency in career management systems from one occupational or professional group to the next. In organisations like the NHS and the Civil Service the complexity of the occupational structure makes internal integration in this sense very difficult. Each group has its own historical patterns of recruitment, training, pay, and terms and conditions of service; often it has its own negotiating rights.

There are also important issues about the need to ensure full access to career paths for minority groups in the organisation, whether in full-time or part-time positions; and about how to manage career breaks not only for women wishing to leave temporarily to have children (Hirsh, 1985) but – of increasing relevance given today's demographics – for those who have responsibility for the care of elderly family members. Few European companies have thought much about eldercare policies (Goodhart, 1994a), in this respect comparing poorly with large US companies. Goodhart noted exceptions: Ford and Daimler-Benz, which offer up to 12 months and flexible working time to carers; the BBC, which has a support group for employees caring for older relatives; and a growing number of the big clearing banks. However, in general, Continental European companies are significantly more progressive in career break policies, seeing more clearly the stress factors related to attempting to combine a full-time career with childbearing or eldercare, and the adverse affects on productivity and performance likely to result from them.

Finally, how to integrate international career development into a company's career management system is a field of study in its own right. The literature is growing (see especially Sparrow and Hiltrop, 1994) as penetration of international markets increases. In leading European organisations career development has become the major challenge in human resource management (HRM) (Evans, 1992), international careers becoming a common feature for so many senior, and even middle, managers.

In this chapter there is no space to consider such issues in more detail. Readers are instead referred to specialist texts in order to obtain relevant knowledge and to be able to relate theory to practice in their own organisations.

Without carefully planned integration, all that will result from joint action planning at unit or individual levels of the organisation is a proliferation of initiatives without any overall coherency or purpose, bringing frustrated expectations as action fails to materialise. Schein (1978: 198) quoted the example of a manager and employee agreeing that a functional move would be to the individual's benefit – but failing to set up any process or resource to evaluate the wider benefits such a move might bring, or to ensure that it could be implemented, monitored and evaluated. The HR function or its equivalent must carry out those wider, integrating roles.

The management of careers in the organisation
From discussion thus far it can be seen that five different kinds of planning are needed for a career management system to achieve its aims in an organisation. They are shown in Table 13. That table makes it clear that the HR planners, HRD staff, management and the individual all have roles to play in ensuring that the needs and aspirations of the individual are linked productively to those of the organisation in a continuous cycle of activity. For this process to be effective it must be simple, visible and well communicated. All employees should have a meaningful career path during their time with the organisation. For some, that path will not involve upward movement, but it will be meaningful it if offers them work that is consistent with their abilities and potential, and if it offers recognition of the value of that work to the organisation.

Now try to integrate the learning in this chapter so far through a short assignment.

Table 13 Integrating organisational and career development (developed from an original framework suggested in Schein, 1978: 201)

HR planning	HR activity	Learning strategies	Career transition points
For staffing	Job analysis, job design. Audit of skills. Deploying personnel to build up a cohesive internal labour market.	Induction and basic skills training.	Entry to organisation.
For performance management and development	Establishing desired performance levels. Improving performance. Facilitating continuous development. Establishing reward systems. Assessment of potential. Planned approach to career development.	Coaching, mentoring and continuous feedback. Performance review and appraisal. Continuous learning and self-development. Promotions, job movement and access to continuing education and training opportunities.	Progress within particular areas of work. Mid-career with the organisation.
For change	New internal skills audit. Re-analysis of patterns of skill supply in external labour market. New balancing of skills and capabilities to adapt to changed internal and external situation. Achievement of consistency with wider HR policies and systems to facilitate and support change.	Retraining of individuals, teams, management sectors. Organisation development programmes to achieve cultural change and the development of new organisational and individual capabilities.	Changes in psychological contract with the organisation.
For levelling off and dis-engagement	Career counselling, joint planning, job redesign, disengagement counselling and planning.	Using experience and wisdom of those nearing final stages of their career with the organisation.	Later career with the organisation.
For replacement and restaffing	Policies to ensure retention of strategic capability of the organisation at corporate, unit and individual levels. Integrative approach to disengagement and new recruitment.	Supportive disengagement strategies and timely phasing in of new internal and external recruits.	End of career with the organisation. Retirement or return to the external labour market.

Career paths in your own organisation

Identify the career paths open to one or two occupational groups in your own organisation. Analyse how far those paths are integrated into an overall planned career management system, and assess the extent to which that system meets the six critical success factors noted earlier in this chapter. What are the main actions needed to improve the planning and/or operation of the system?

Before answering this question you may find it helpful to read Schein, 1978, Chapter 14, and the account of Xenova biopharmaceutical company's development of a dual career path system that recognised both the scientific and managerial skills of its employees (Garmonsway and Wellin, 1995).

The career life cycle

Let us now consider the practical implications of Hall's (1984) concept of career development across the life cycle of employees. The concept encompasses the stages shown in the right-hand column of Table 13.

Entry to the organisation

At this point individuals need information about themselves and their career opportunities. They should be involved in self-assessment activities, in drawing up personal development plans to initiate a long-term process of self-directed career planning, and have opportunities for a variety of developmental experiences. (We have already discussed this stage in Chapter 14 under 'induction and basic training'.)

Progress within particular areas of work

This stage too has been discussed in Chapter 14. Established employees who are steadily progressing in particular jobs or areas of work need interesting, challenging tasks and supervision that gives autonomy and support while making clear its high expectations of what the individual can achieve. There should be career coaching, counselling and planning, mentoring, job design, appraisal, feedback and development planning, in order to manage employees' career paths effectively at this stage. Training in such skills will therefore need to be provided at unit level, together with the kinds of monitoring, incentives and rewards to help develop positive attitudes in managers at this level. Linking individual career plans to work objectives is another way of ensuring that those plans are aligned with the needs of the business as well as of the individual.

Mid-career and change

These are particularly difficult stages to manage (see Lewis and McLaverty, 1991). It is essential not only to facilitate the continued development of the high-fliers, but also to help those unable to move up, on or out to see that they still have 'careers' in the sense of meaningful work, challenges and opportunities for stimulation and achievement. The stimulation and growth of those who have reached their job ceiling can be enhanced by such developmental strategies as job rotation, cross-functional moves, job redesign, recognition and rewards for job performance, and temporary assignments outside of the company, including eg consultancy opportunities. It is also important to keep more mobile employees informed about corporate career opportunities and high-level technical or professional positions available elsewhere in the company, since these openings are often not adequately publicised.

Later career

As employees move towards the end of their career with the company, either as a natural process or as a result of downsizing or de-layering, their careers still need careful management. It is particularly important that the effects of low morale and stress caused by preoccupation with the forthcoming termination of employment do not quickly spread through a workforce. Advance warning of downsizing and redundancy decisions, counselling for those who have to leave and also for the survivors, help with job searches and pre-retirement programmes, and a phased approach to disengagement (including the opportunity for secondments and for a protracted period of part-time work before, and possibly after, departure) – these are some of the many ways in which disengagement can become a more positive, even developmental, process than is too often the case.

The career development process should be built around key transition points in people's careers – 'moments of opportunity' where it is important to develop a set of shared values and renegotiate, if necessary, the psychological contract between organisation and individual in order to promote mutually beneficial career planning. At each key point there must be the provision of accurate and up-to-date information to help that planning process. There must also be a framework that provides guidelines on blending on-the-job development and other developmental tools with more formal development experiences at each career phase. The tools to be used for different developmental purposes must be identified.

End of career with the organisation

It is the final stage of employment in the organisation that is often the most difficult to manage. In the past in the UK, Inland Revenue rules have discouraged gradual retirement, even though such a strategy can mitigate most of the negative aspects of early retirement for the organisation and the individual. By 1997, however, changes were in hand opening up a range of possibilities for phased, partial or part-time retirement in the UK as in so many EU member countries. Imaginative planning can minimise organisational and personal disruption, help individuals to manage disengagement effectively, and ensure that those vital to the organisation's continued strategic capability are retained and remain committed to their work and roles (Reday-Mulvey and Taylor, 1996).

However, the issue of retirement is more complex than this. It has been estimated that by the year 2030 in the 18 Western European member-states of the Organisation for Economic Co-operation and Development (OECD), the size of the over-65 age group will have risen to 70 million, compared with 50 million in 1990 (Willman, 1994). Over the same period the number of people of working age is likely to have fallen to fewer than three for every person aged 65, compared with five in 1994. These trends are similar across all leading world economies, but are much less marked in newly industrialised countries. The economic impact will be radical, but so complex as to be impossible to predict with any accuracy. The most likely outcome, however, will be a marked shift in competitive advantage from the old to the newly industrialised countries.

As Willman (1994) observed, once the flow of young people into organisations begins to diminish so will there be an increasing need to hold on to older workers and to attract back into employment those currently not in the labour market. Consumers too will be ageing, and so products and services will have to meet their distinctive needs. Retirement policies, once relatively simple and attracting little of management's attention (except in those organisations that advertised their status as benevolent employers sensitive to all employees' needs) will have to carry a heavier burden of bottom-line responsibility. They will have the potential to make a direct negative or positive impact on a company's ability to remain competitive.

Positive policies for disengagement, as for retention, should aim to help individuals to understand that the most important focus for them is that of their long-term career path, rather than simply their career within a particular organisation. They must also help the survivors of reorganisation to retain their morale and career orientation at a time when both will be weakened yet when the organisation must continue to function effectively. The need for such help should not be underestimated. Finally, they can be beneficial to the external image of the organisation, thus improving its chances of continuing to attract high-calibre recruits and of sustaining proactive links with local communities.

ASSESSMENT RELATED TO CAREER DEVELOPMENT

At the heart of any career management system there must be a process of assessment in order to establish the needs and identify the potential of individuals.

Such assessment can be done in a variety of ways – through systems established by the organisation and/or by processes initiated by the individual. In the former category, the appraisal process has an important role to play in identifying the career development objectives and proposed plans of an individual and in offering a vehicle for manager and individual to agree on appropriate action. (This has already been discussed in Chapter 14.) However, the formal appraisal discussion is not an adequate or appropriate occasion for comprehensive assessment of potential. Let us therefore now look at assessment and development centres.

Assessment and development centre methodologies

An assessment centre is a systematic approach to identifying precisely what is required for success in a particular job and then labelling these requirements in terms of a short-list of tightly defined criteria. Leadership, integrity, tenacity and team-building skill are typical criteria which might be included for a management position.

(Stevens, 1985)

An assessment centre typically combines a series of exercises. As they tackle these, participants are observed by a trained team – usually, but not always, of company managers – who subsequently pool and discuss their information in order to reach as objective an assessment as possible of each individual. The aim is to ensure the identification of those who most closely fit the requirements of the job, and to build up a list of individuals' training and development needs.

Dulewicz (1991) noted many problems commonly associated with this methodology: poor design of exercises, inexpert assessors, lack of commitment of managers to ensuring transfer of learning to the workplace, and lack of long-term monitoring. He recommended the appointment of a mentor for each participant and concluded that the critical factor was always the commitment of the individual, and how much the participant does to develop himself or herself.

Such accounts, while demonstrating some of the difficulties involved in the use of assessment centre technology, also provide evidence of their advantages, which typically include:

- *improved decision-making* – Decisions relating to the selection, transfer, promotion and to training needs of staff are based on substantially more 'facts' than in the past.

- *improved feedback* – Assessment centre methodology offers an increased opportunity for meaningful feedback related to performance and potential, and this is especially valuable in relation to career and other counselling services.

You may have noticed that although our heading for this section included reference to development centres, we have so far only discussed the use of assessment centres. What, if any, is the difference between the two? Well, to many writers there is no difference. Stevens (1985) saw centres not only as a way of assessing potential but also as a way of helping to diagnose people's training needs. However, it is important to differentiate between development and assessment centres.

In both types of centre, groups of participants take part in a variety of job simulations, tests and exercises with observers who assess their performance against a number of pre-determined, job-related dimensions. If the collected data are used to diagnose individual training needs, facilitate self-development or provide part of an organisational development audit, then the most appropriate description would be *development centre* (Rodger and Mabey, 1987). If, however, the data are used primarily to feed into decisions about promotion or some other form of employee redeployment, then the term *assessment centre* is more relevant.

It is essential that employees understand the purpose of each, and do not confuse the two. Bower (1991: 53) told how Rover's assessment centres, used primarily for selection during the 1980s, brought only mixed success. Their decision to shift from assessment to development centres using competence-based criteria proved more successful because it gave 'greater visibility and credibility to the process, and ... spin-off benefits in performance appraisal, training objectives and for succession and development planning purposes' (*ibid*).

Development centres can offer a particularly valuable opportunity for the individual to clarify career anchors, notably by bringing personal values and motivation to the surface. Schein (1978: 127) used the concept of career anchors to highlight the importance of the individual's self-perceived talents, motives and values in determining career choice path. He identified five types of anchor: technical functional competence, managerial competence, security, autonomy and creativity. Each reflects a different type of underlying motive, need, values and perceived as well as discovered talents in the individual. Each is determined in part by experience and opportunity, and in part by latent talents and motives. A career anchor is thus significantly affected by those four processes to which attention has been drawn earlier in this chapter: informing, negotiating, monitoring and renegotiating. It may change or be reinforced at each of the main transition-points through which the individual's career in the organisation passes between entry and exit.

Here is a task concerning methods by which to help employees gain career insights.

Case-study: Career planning at Allied Domecq Spirits and Wine
Why do you think that participants in the workshops at Allied Domecq in the mid-1990s viewed them so favourably?

John Refausse, HR director (customer services and development) at Allied Domecq Spirits and Wine, described a career planning workshop introduced in 1995 as part of a much wider programme of organisational change following some years of re-engineering and far-reaching strategic change in an international company formed by the acquisition of Allied Lyons – the mainly UK-based firm – and the Domecq group. Flatter management structures, significant job changes and movement into new markets all meant that there was a mismatch between organisational needs and expectations and those of individuals. In a climate of uncertainty for the business as well as for its workforce it was seen in the mid-1990s to be essential to help people adjust to the changes and become less focused on job security, more capable of planning their own future careers.

The workshop was piloted in 1995 for senior middle managers who confronted such uncertainties. Its aims were to help them 'take stock of their own achievements, identify the factors that had contributed to their past successes and understand how they matched up against the core competencies of the business' (Refausse, 1996: 34).

Development centre methodology enabled participants to generate and handle a wealth of information that clarified their career anchors and helped them to assess these, and produce development plans and statements of their career aspirations. The workshop enabled individuals to gain insights into their fundamental motivation and talents, and into the past career choices they had made. This in turn 'helped them to look at their current roles and consider how these might be made to fit their aspirations and needs more closely' (*ibid*: 35).

Refausse described motivational outcomes for most of the eight participants. Two negotiated major career moves shortly afterwards: one, managing director of a wine subsidiary, achieved greater autonomy from her line manager; another applied successfully for promotion from a specialist to a general managerial post, having discovered during the workshop a 'creative professional' career anchor that he had never previously identified or considered.

Source: Refausse, 1996

Feedback notes
Accounts of innovative and apparently successful development centres abound. To assess their true value, however, they need to be followed up through time, and the views of participants as well as of observers and organisation must be obtained. Iles and Mabey (1993), commenting on a range of empirical studies, found that some career development practices tended to be much better regarded by recipients than others, and that development centres, psychometric

tests with feedback, and career review with superiors were particularly well viewed. The reasons were revealing:

- focus on the future as much as on the past and present

- promotion of reflection and insight as well as measurement of skills or competencies

- two-way, collaborative processes

- overt, with participants able to see clear evidence for assessments

- realistic, not only on account of the methodology used but also because managers were involved as assessors and because of the focus on the actual career criteria and activities used in the organisation.

Allied Domecq also achieved those three essentials identified on page 340:

- an appropriate and honest message

- workable career development processes

- a real intention to deliver.

Many of the 'third generation' centres set up purely to develop people and therefore avoiding any focus on assessment for other purposes had run into difficulty by the late 1990s on grounds of affordability. As Woodruffe (1997: 32) observed, there was a growing concern in some organisations to move away from that sole focus on development and to use the information generated by a centre also to 'influence their decisions about participants' careers and to decide on the further development that an individual will be offered'. This hybrid approach, which for participants may raise fears of assessment and selection for promotion and therefore of a divisive element, is the more likely in organisations whose approach to performance management tends towards the control rather than development end of the spectrum – as we saw in Chapter 14. Woodruffe's article provided helpful advice on how to mitigate the most demotivating effects of such hybrids when they are unavoidable.

Principles underpinning the assessment of potential to aid development

From the discussion in this section of the chapter, identify six principles that should underpin assessment and development centre methodologies.

Feedback notes
- *Place the methodology in context* – The use of development centres must be placed in a firm context of major training and development

programmes so that they are seen to be a positive aid, not a threat, to all who go through them.

- *Involve management* – Line management must be involved from the start in the development and operation of assessment/development centre methodology.

- *Ensure that there is expertise* – There must be a high level of skill in the design and operation of assessment and development centres and in the handling of feedback to participants. Dulewicz's article (1991) shows the damage that can be caused if this expertise is lacking.

- *Ensure openness, honesty and confidentiality* – Trust and commitment of the parties can only be assured if there is clarity and agreement about the true purpose – or purposes – of a centre, about who will have access to the information produced by the assessment processes, and about how that information will be used.

- *Achieve action* – The methodology must lead to action although, as Rodger and Mabey (1987) observed, 'for a whole host of reasons development activities may not happen immediately'.

- *Evaluate* – The results achieved by the use of such methodology must be evaluated, including analysis of the effects its introduction has had on personnel at various levels in the organisation.

SELF-ASSESSMENT AND SELF-DEVELOPMENT

Self-assessment

Assessment of learning needs can be carried out by individuals alone, using self-assessment to determine their strengths and weaknesses, formulate appropriate ways of meeting the needs thereby revealed, and plan for ongoing monitoring and evaluation of their performance. Pedler, Burgoyne and Boydell (1978) recommended four stages in the process:

- *self-assessment* – This must be preceded by careful analysis on the part of individuals of their work and life situation.

- *diagnosis* – Analysis must lead to the identification of individuals' learning needs, and to their prioritisation.

- *action-planning* – This must cover the identification of objectives, and of aids and hindrances to action; the determination of resources (including people) needed to carry out the action plan; and an agreed timescale.

- *monitoring and review* – Monitoring and review procedures must be determined, and a timescale established for those processes to take place.

Self-assessment involves individuals in rating themselves in each area of skill in their job, and/or in each area of occupational competence. Questionnaires to facilitate the process can be completed by individuals working alone or with someone else. Tackling self-assessment with the help of another has the secondary advantage of developing diagnostic and counselling skills in that partner who, in the process of questioning, also has to practise and learn more about those skills of observation, listening, discussion and appraisal that are vital to the good coach. Mutual learning and benefit can thus emerge from the exercise.

In self-assessment it is essential to identify organisational barriers as well as aids to learning and development, and to plan how best to circumvent or overcome those barriers. We should also remember that development can take place not only at but away from work, and not only through formalised activities but in a wide range of informal ways. Belonging to activity and interest groups outside work can help to develop skills, knowledge and attitudes highly relevant to individuals' career aspirations and can expand their CVs.

Self-development

Taking responsibility for one's own development and career is not an easy matter. It requires an informed and objective assessment of the kind of skills and experience that will be relevant for the individual for the future, together with access to opportunities to develop those skills and acquire that experience. Where the future is impossible to predict, it will be difficult for the individual to find a focus for self-development in which he or she can feel confidence.

Many organisations now provide resources and facilities to aid self-development. These include personal and career development workshops and seminars to encourage individuals to take responsibility for their careers, and resource centres giving access to a variety of opportunities for self-directed and self-paced learning at the company's expense, although in the employee's time. Such centres can offer occupational guides, educational references, computerised self-assessment questionnaires or other diagnostic instruments to help people consider their career interests, values and competence, together with computerised educational and training programmes (see, for example, Dorrell, 1993). Some organisations provide access to career and counselling services of local colleges and universities and to their vocational and non-vocational courses.

Tasks for the HR professional

It is easy to produce a list of 'what to do about self-development' guidelines. I am about to do so myself! However, not all HR professionals practise self-development, even though the professional body (the Chartered Institute of Personnel and Development) has produced a Continuous Professional Development pack and has built into its professional qualification the need for continuous updating.

Many professionals' very livelihood depends on keeping up to date, on looking ahead, on constantly sharpening their learning skills. In the profession of personnel/human resource management, such urgent spurs to continuous learning and development may not seem evident at first sight. Yet they are certainly there. In today's organisational world, the urge to downsize, de-layer and outsource seems as yet undiminished, oblivious often to rational argument (since research does not demonstrate the expected benefits, and has identified many inherent dangers). In that world, simply continuing to do what has been done for so long – no matter how expertly – will not suffice, certainly not in an area (HRM) that is often struggling for credibility and advancement. Those who survive and flourish in the field will be those who have a convincing vision of human resource management and development and who can provide clear, practical processes and policies to meet unfolding needs. They will have to have an up-to-date understanding of trends and best practice in their field. They will also have to be well-informed about the business environment. They will need to convince that they can operate credibly in it. Without continuous learning and self-development, these kinds of capability cannot be achieved.

If we reflect like this on the dangers inherent in neglecting our own professional self-development, then it is easier to produce guidelines about how best to stimulate others in that process:

- *Become an effective learner* – HR practitioners who are trying to help people become effective learners must themselves have an adequate mastery of each of the major learning styles and skills. They can rate themselves by using Honey and Mumford's learning inventory (1992), or Kolb, Rubin and McIntyre (1974), which offers an interesting alternative. Illuminating comparisons can be drawn from the two sets of scores. It is then essential to develop a plan of action for self-improvement.

- *Promote self-directed learning* – In many organisations individuals now have to draw up personal development plans and review these with their managers formally at appraisal and regularly during the year. In training appraisers and appraisees, the HRD practitioner has the opportunity to explain why self-directed learning matters and how it can be achieved. He or she can also raise awareness by publicising simple guidelines on self-development in such discussion (see, for example, Forrest, 1993).

Simply urging people to develop themselves is not likely to have much success. Honey and Mumford have produced a 'Learning Environment Questionnaire' (1996) which can encourage managers to look at their own behaviour and practise and diagnose which of the four roles needed to create a learning climate in the workplace they possess or should develop: the Role Model, the Provider, the System Builder or the Champion. HR professionals can also advise their organisations on the affordability, feasibility and benefits of a learning resource centre, where that is an appropriate investment (Malone, 1997).

• *Promote awareness about continuous learning and development* – HR staff can have informal discussions with managers and other key personnel in the organisation – over coffee or lunch, after meetings, during talks about people's learning needs. In a variety of informal, as well as more formal, ways they can build up an awareness in the organisation about what continuous development means, and about its relationship to flexibility and to enhancing people's motivation through improving their employability security.

• *Design events to develop learning styles and skills* – If training and other planned learning events are to be accessible to all who need them, they should be designed in such a way as not only to avoid discriminatory barriers but also to accommodate whenever necessary a range of learning styles, rather than appealing to only one type of learner – the activist, or the reflector, for example. On the other hand, such events must also help learners to acquire or develop those styles most suited to the tasks they have to carry out. A training managers' course, for example, should promote all four types of learning style in order to produce at the end of the day people who are not predominately activists but who have a balance of skills across the four categories, thus enabling them to function effectively in the different situations in which training experts have to operate.

• *Seek to identify and reduce organisational barriers to the development of appropriate learning styles and skills* – HR professionals should likewise promote an awareness of the value the organisation can derive from recognising and encouraging a diversity of learning approaches.

For example, the preferred mode of learning in a particular organisation may be by initial basic skills training and then simply by unsupervised trial and error through time. This may be because there is no understanding of other ways in which people could develop their performance. Trial and error may appear a cheap way of learning to perform to adequate levels. In reality, however, it is likely to involve significant indirect costs caused, typically, by high turnover of new recruits, high rates of wastage, poor quality, lost production time during the extended learning period, and many demotivated, underperforming workers. Indirect costs over the longer term are likely to accrue through lack of innovative skills and flexible attitudes, and a tendency for closed mindsets. Approached with the right degree of social and political sensitivity, it should be possible to help key parties to view the organisation's or unit's preferred mode of learning more critically, and to see the value of trying to vary customary approaches to learning and development.

• *Influence assessors and appraisers to consider learning styles when examining performance, and in the selection process* – HR professionals should seek to influence those involved in all forms of assessment and appraisal processes including selection, transfer, promotion and disengagement from employment (an easier task if there is a call for appraisal training in the organisation, and/or if personnel and training are closely integrated functions). Criteria should be developed that relate to the learning, problem-solving and decision-making styles and skills needed, and these criteria should help to guide judgements. In this way not only should assessments and decisions become more valid but, in the process of discussing this extra dimension, there should be an improvement in managers' understanding of how central a part learning style and skills play in people's behaviour and performance at work.

CONCLUSION

Having read this chapter and completed its reviews and self-checks, you should now:

• understand the importance of a strategic approach to career development in the organisation and the typical triggers for such an approach

• be able to explain how to establish a career development process based on mutuality and the psychological contract between employer and employee

• be able to identify and explain some major methods of assessing potential to aid career development

• as an HR professional, be able to advise others on continuous self-development, and raise awareness of its importance.

To test yourself against these objectives, what five-minute answers would you give to the following questions? (Dates in brackets refer to the IPD qualifying examination paper in which a question appeared.)

• Briefly define what is meant by 'career development' and identify **three** typical triggers in organisations to a more systematic approach to the planned management and development of careers. (May 1998)

• Explain and justify **three** ways in which an employee development manager can promote continuous professional development of personnel and development specialists in an organisation. (November 1998)

• A manager has asked what you mean by a need to 'manage the workplace as a continuous learning system' and wants to know why she should take on such a responsibility. Outline and justify your reply. (November 1999)

USEFUL READING

GILLEY J. W. *and* EGGLAND S. A. (1989) *Principles of Human Resource Development*. Maidenhead, Addison Wesley. pp47–73.

HALL D. (1984) 'Human resource development and organizational effectiveness', in C. J. Fombrun, N. M. Tichy and M. A. Devanna (eds), *Strategic Human Resource Management*. New York, Wiley. pp159–81.

HERRIOT P. (1992) *The Career Management Challenge: Balancing individual and organizational needs*. London, Sage.

INDUSTRIAL SOCIETY (1997) 'Self-managed learning'. *Managing Best Practice*. No. 40. October. (Published monthly by the Industrial Society and available from the Communications Department, 020–7479 2127.)

INSTITUTE FOR EMPLOYMENT STUDIES (1996) *Strategies for Career Development: Promise, practice and pretence*. IES Report, No 305. London, Institute for Employment Studies.

JACKSON T. (2000) *Career Development*. London, Institute of Personnel and Development.

MEGGINSON D. *and* WHITAKER V. (1996) *Cultivating Self-Development*. London, Institute of Personnel and Development.

WOODRUFFE C. (2000) *Development and Assessment Centres*. 3rd edn. London, Institute of Personnel and Development.

20 Developing managers

LEARNING OBJECTIVES

After reading this chapter you will:

• understand what the management development process (MDP) involves and the need to link management development to organisational goals and strategy

• be able to explain the characteristics of an effective MDP, and how to manage the MDP

• be able to advise on the generalised design of a management development programme

• understand how to integrate succession planning within the MDP.

INTRODUCTION TO THE MANAGEMENT DEVELOPMENT PROCESS

Managers are major decision-makers in any organisation. For that reason alone, an effective management development process (MDP) is crucial to organisational success. Its generalised purpose can be described as one of increasing the organisation's present and future capability in attaining its goals (French, 1987: 379).

The development of managers takes on an additional dimension in those organisations – of whatever size, type or sector – that have to operate in an increasingly globalised and technology-driven environment. Such organisations must be able to rapidly set and achieve new productivity, quality and effectiveness standards, develop and implement new strategies, change and sustain new corporate cultures. For all organisations, the MDP is, therefore, a potentially powerful 'strategic tool' (Osbaldeston and Barham, 1992).

Who are 'managers'?
Using the International Labour Office's classification, Brewster and Tyson (1991: 218) defined managerial and professional staff as those who:

• are salaried members of an organisation

• have achieved a higher level of education and training or recognised experience in a scientific, technical or administrative field

- perform functions of a primarily intellectual character involving a high degree of judgement and initiative

- may hold delegated authority to plan, manage, control and co-ordinate the work of other organisational members

- do not occupy positions as first-line supervisors, foremen or top-level executives.

In many organisations today, however, this classification system is losing validity. Brewster and Tyson pointed to the blurring effects of technology on the lines of distinction between managerial tasks and the work of other occupations. There are also the effects of de-layering and decentralisation, which involve devolution of problem-solving and decision-making. Decentralisation often results in 'supervisors' having to take on team management roles, while an increasing number of those occupying traditional middle management positions may find themselves in charge of semi-autonomous business units. Professionals, too, are frequently having to assume more managerial responsibilities (as seen in the case of those clinical directors in the National Health Service described in Chapter 17). The meaning and parameters of 'management' are therefore expanding and changing.

Of fundamental importance in explaining these 'blurring effects' is 'the relentless drive to add value ... [that] is having a radical impact on the nature of everyone's work, from front-line staff to top management' (Guile and Fonda, 1998: xi).

> Companies and public services are seen less and less as hierarchies of 'command and control' and more and more as chains and networks of processes that must be managed to this end.
>
> *(ibid)*

With this new emphasis on partnership rather than control, and on processes that will add value, there is a related focus on management behaviours. The 1998 Institute of Personnel and Development report on 'Performance Management through Capability', for example, highlighted 20 behaviours perceived to be essential to develop in future-oriented managers (Guile and Fonda, 1998). Managers still have to manage – but how they should manage, with whom they should collaborate as they manage, and how they should behave in order to achieve desired outcomes, are now vital questions for anyone involved in planning their development.

There is another important implication behind the blurring in the meaning of 'management' in many of today's organisations. It is that it may be necessary to extend the scope of the management development process so that it takes in every employee, and involves the total process of learning, continuous improvement and change in the organisation (Wille, 1990). Such a learning environment characterises some small enterprises. It should ensure a broadening of mindsets and a continuous supply of leaders and managers who best 'fit' the organisation and its environment, vision and strategy through time. The point needs careful reflection. It will not be pursued here, but will receive attention in Part 5 of this book.

Agendas for the management development process

An organisation's MDP can have many agendas. Mabey and Salaman (1995: 147–8), drawing on work by Lees (1992: 89–105), showed how varied they can be and how each carries its own characteristics, assumptions and typical outcomes. Of the agendas they identified, three can cause problems for the MDP that seeks to improve management effectiveness across an organisation:

- *functional performance*, typified by the Lead Body Standards framework for management competencies, and focused on improvement in the performance of managers' functional tasks. A rational, systematic, task-oriented approach typifies programmes in this kind of MDP. As will be seen later in the chapter, this agenda may not produce managers who are effective – simply managers who can perform certain functional tasks competently.

- *political reinforcement*, where those in charge of the MDP are mainly concerned that however it is designed and whoever it involves, the process should sustain the current political order in the organisation. Management development methods are selected accordingly, and are unlikely to include any that will lead to challenges to the status quo, or to radically new managerial thinking and behaviour.

- *compensation*, where management development is offered as a reward to secure 'loyalty' and commitment to the organisation rather than as a process to improve effectiveness and develop future-oriented skills and values.

Reflect on these agendas as you read through the rest of this chapter.

Tasks involved in the management development process

Essentially, the MDP involves three tasks:

- the analysis of present and future management needs

- an assessment of the existing and potential capability of managers against those needs

- producing and implementing policy, strategy and plans to meet those needs.

These tasks involve decisions about individuals' career routes, about management succession, and about organisational performance. The decisions can be complex, depending on how far the focus of the MDP is only on the micro or is also on the macro level.

If it is mainly on the micro level, it is perhaps more accurate to refer to it as *manager development*. The aim here is to improve the performance and develop the potential of individual managers (singly or in groups) in order to remedy specific performance gaps, and to ensure that they are competent in their jobs and are well prepared for future responsibilities.

If it also operates at a macro level, then it is essentially to do with making decisions about how to develop management as a whole, across the organisation. It is indeed about *management development*. The aim here is one of building a shared culture across the whole management group and enhancing management capability throughout the organization in order to improve the organization's capability to survive and prosper.

(Brodie and Bennet, 1979)

Management development in your organisation

- What is your organisation's management development policy, and what agenda does that policy seem to serve in reality?

- How far does the MDP in your organisation focus on 'manager development' and how far on 'management development'?

MANAGEMENT DEVELOPMENT DESIGN

For those whose responsibility it is to advise on, or implement, management development design in an organisation, there are some testing issues to resolve. Here are some of the most common.

The challenge of organisational reality

Management development design is often dominated by a highly systematic approach, leading to blocks of training and development aiming to 'teach' managers (and potential managers) their roles and tasks in an orderly, sequential fashion and to help them acquire sets of functional skills.

But organisational life is not ordered or predictable. As will be seen in the discussion shortly on competency-based frameworks, simply learning how to perform specific functional tasks is not enough. The MDP should help managers to prepare for uncertainty and turbulence. Managers have to operate at the heart of complex webs of social interaction. They have to continuously adapt to changing internal and external pressures and opportunities. They have to think and operate across many internal boundaries, and often across external boundaries too. The MDP must ensure that managers have the adaptability and flexibility of skills and disposition to move through what are often rapidly changing managerial roles and organisational circumstances.

Organisational values

Lippitt (1983: 37–8) warned that management development must be centrally concerned with organisational values and with attitudinal change.

One aspect of that concern is the attitudes of those being developed. Dogmatic attitudes in managers mean that they are unlikely to be able to function effectively in a changing world because they cannot accept that they themselves need to change. Management development that does not focus on attitudes can, unwittingly, simply ensure the perpetuation of old attitudes to the detriment of new learning.

The other aspect of that concern is the values of those in the organisation who most influence organisational culture. When designing management development programmes it is essential to plan the kind of workplace that will be conducive to the acquisition, retention and full utilisation over the longer term of learning, knowledge and values that participants acquire. How many graduate trainees, for example, quickly leave the organisation they have joined because, despite promises of fast-track advancement and the stimulus of innovative management development programmes, the reality of life in that organisation increasingly contradicts the expectations that the MDP has encouraged them to hold? How many managers, eager to put into practice new ideas and new ways of managing and behaving, are unable to do so because there is no support for such changes among their colleagues and superiors? There must be a real willingness in the organisation to accept the challenges that can result from a powerful MDP, or the management development investment will not realise its potential value.

> The most meaningful aspect of personal change resulting from a management development process is the examination and alteration of attitudes within the organisation. Reinforcement will need to be related to meaningful renewal systems.
>
> (Lippitt, 1983: 38)

The points raised above introduce in their turn other issues. For example: in order to ensure that the organisation has an adequate supply of managers whose attitudes and values are future-oriented, who are adaptive to change, and who are receptive to new ideas, what balance should there be between investing in internal management development and buying in from outside? And at what point and organisational level should any buying in start?

If 'renewal' is not desired by those who hold the most powerful positions in the organisation, it can only indicate that the true agenda for the MDP is a political one: the process is not intended to produce fundamental changes in the status quo.

Training, education and learning: achieving a balance
Mabey and Salaman (1995: 140) distinguished between training and learning. Most of the reports on management development focus on the former, yet it is the process and outcomes of learning rather than the specific thrust of training that will make the most fundamental impact on managerial capability. As we saw in Chapter 13, even though in many smaller organisations there may be few signs of a systematic, formalised approach to training, much productive learning goes on none the less. Mumford, Robinson and Stradling's 1987 report on the development of directors concluded that the possession of a management qualification is of little relevance – what promotes the most effective learning is experience and role models. Most of the directors studied had not attributed their success to any formal development processes, which explained the emphasis of the report on the value of self-development in a greatly diversified range of roles over a variety of organisational settings.

That is one view, and a widely held one. Work-based learning can be stimulated in many ways. Currently the most popular methods and processes include development through project work, self-development, action-learning, coaching and mentoring. A balanced mix of these in the MDP can prove effective, relatively cheap and beneficial to the organisation as well as to participants in the MDP. Such methods can also provide a powerful bridge between externally based programmes and work-based learning (see the clinical directors' long-term programme, in Chapter 17), ensuring effective two-way transfer of learning and experience between work role and job and programme.

However, no single approach to development is likely to be able to guarantee managerial effectiveness through time. Careful consideration must certainly be given to the kind of work-based experiential learning that can achieve improved performance and strengthen the ties between managers and the organisation. But it is equally important to consider the benefits to be gained from in-house or external training and educational programmes that can broaden current and potential managers' vision, challenge their views of the business, and expand their intellectual capacity.

Where managers are poorly educated, this can lead to low levels of ability to cope with new technologies, to manage and develop people, and to think and act strategically in order to achieve sustained organisational progress. To look briefly at some of the most obvious differences between the UK and competitor countries here, most well-educated Germans do not join a large company until 27 years of age because they tend to have followed an apprenticeship after school and then pursued a degree and often a higher degree in subjects such as engineering, law or economics. In Japan and in Britain, the average age for joining such a company is 22, but in Japan, the potential manager will study law or engineering at a top university, and, after entry to a large firm, will go through a 'rigorous process of job rotation, private study and classroom learning which can last for up to 15 years' before being promoted to the first level of management (Handy, 1987).

In France, the route to management in a larger organisation is either through business or engineering at one of the Grandes Ecoles, or through some other educational pathway leading to the same kind of functional qualifications as in Japan and Germany. In France, too, the law requires all firms to spend 1.1 per cent of the wage bill on continuing education and training, and corporations with more than about 2,000 employees spend three times that amount, about one third going on management training. Such investment is common across most of mainland Europe and the USA, but not in the UK.

In the UK during the 1970s and 1980s the low participation rate in management education came under critical fire, with the publication of a stream of reports pointing to the urgent need for improvement if our economy was to become more competitive. One message emerging from these reports was that those who are uneducated, untrained and undeveloped themselves are unlikely to be committed to the education, training and development of others – so in every organisation, a low level of management education threatened the future supply of educated managers also.

During the 1990s the situation in the UK changed. Managers became steadily better qualified, and the Master of Business Administration (MBA) award achieved high and sustained growth. Business studies is now one of the most popular undergraduate programmes. However, the UK still lags considerably behind France, Germany, Japan and the USA in terms of basic educational attainment, while emerging industrial countries invest heavily in their education systems in order to produce capable leaders and workforces for the future.

Management education – for whom?

Management education programmes can do much to inform and broaden the mind. For what types of current and potential managers do you think such programmes have most relevance?

Feedback notes

No MDP should rely exclusively on educational programmes. However, they can offer particular value as part of the MDP for four types of individual or groups:

- young potential managers who have yet to decide where they want to specialise and what kind of managerial role will best suit their disposition as well as their abilities

- managers involved in structural and role change in their organisation – they need help in developing new abilities, understanding and social skills to perform effectively in that new situation

- managers who are so focused on their customary ways of thinking, behaving and performing that they are blocking the development both of themselves and of their teams – they need the challenges that powerful educational programmes can provide if the barriers they are unwittingly creating are to be demolished

- managers who are being prepared for more strategic roles in their organisations and need an interplay of on-the-job development and demanding intellectual activity in order to help them in that transition (as in the clinical directors' programme, Chapter 17).

It is important to achieve a balanced perspective on management education. The real question to ask is not 'Why do we not have enough qualified managers?' It is 'Will qualification make our managers more effective?' (Chambers, 1990). The Japanese and the Germans virtually ignore the Master of Business Administration route to management development, yet as a sector their managers are highly regarded. In both those countries recruits have a high standard of educational attainment by the time they enter employment; the same tends not to be true of the average new recruit to employment in the UK. The case for the educated employee is therefore clear; the case for the management-educated manager rather less so.

The next section takes one approach to management development – the competency-based approach – and examines it in more detail. The reason for this special treatment is that competency frameworks are widely used, but are also expensive to design, install and monitor. If they are not well conceived or adequately evaluated through time, they can prove an expensive mistake for the organisation.

COMPETENCY FRAMEWORKS FOR MANAGEMENT DEVELOPMENT

Key features

A competency framework provides a template against which teams as well as individuals should be developed, since no individual will have more than a few of the competencies needed for superior organisational performance. It provides a clear set of performance criteria both at organisational and at individual levels, and identifies the expected outcomes of achieving those criteria.

Management competencies are the set of character features, knowledge and skills, attitudes, motives and traits that comprise the profile of a manager and enable him or her to perform effectively in the managerial role.

Functionally based frameworks

These have been popularised in the UK through the work of the Management Charter Initiative (MCI). The MCI was established in the late 1980s with the aim of improving the performance of UK organisations by increasing the standard and accessibility of management education and development. Supported by the Confederation of British Industry, the British Institute of Management, the Foundation of Management Education and the Department for Education and Employment, it led to the establishment of national professional management qualifications at three levels – certificate, diploma and degree/master's level – existing qualification courses such as the Diploma of Management Studies and MBA being integrated into a national, hierarchical structure.

The MCI competency framework is derived from functional analysis (see Chapter 9 for an explanation of this method). The national standards relating to this framework are expressed as a ladder of qualifications to complement the continuous development of managers in the workplace. They are popular with many organisations for their value in aiding staff recruitment and appraisal as well as training and development, and in enabling first-level management trainees to get a national certificate qualification.

National Management Standards were finalised in 1997, at a time when the (then) Institute of Personnel and Development (IPD) was reviewing its own professional management standards. (The IPD became the CIPD – or Chartered Institute of Personnel and Development – in July 2000.) Those were subsequently aligned with the national standards to achieve broad consistency. They too emerged from a national consultative process, but were conceived more pragmatically and take more account of the need for managers to have higher-level holistic, integrative and political skills as well as functional competence (see Chapter 9 for fuller discussion of the approach used by the CIPD to develop its professional, including management, standards). CIPD management standards do not really fall under the heading of 'competency-based frameworks': they are better viewed as a set of generalised performance indicators for those entering or preparing to enter first-level management positions.

The MCI competency-based framework fits well within the performance management culture common in so many private and public sector organisations in the UK today. The aim is to improve the capability of managers by applying standardised criteria to the description of their roles and tasks and appraising their performance against clearly defined, measurable behavioural and task targets.

This approach to competency-based management development seems most relevant for those working in relatively stable, hierarchical structures with a range of positions through which managers can systematically develop and progress along specified career pathways. Programmes can be run at different management levels and career stages, and can aim to develop both core and role-specific competences.

However, the model has also been applied in some organisations to less obviously relevant contexts such as newly decentralised units where middle managers face radically changed roles and tasks. In such contexts, a future-oriented thrust is often attempted by including a development centre component from which every participant leaves with a development programme specifying 'present competency levels, appropriate developmental priorities, learning targets, and a timetable of training and development methods' (Colloff and Goodge, 1990: 52).

Generic frameworks
This type of competency framework derives mainly from work on generic management competences carried out by the American Management Association in the 1970s (Cave and McKeown, 1993: 123). Boyatzis (1991) distinguished between threshold and superior management competencies, in order to differentiate between what is needed for adequate and for superior performance. He also distinguished between surface and core elements of competency in the individual. Core motives and traits that influence competency are seen as the least amenable to development, being embedded in the individual's personality. Surface, or explicit, skills and knowledge are seen as the most amenable, and so can form a basis for developmental activity.

Concerns about competency frameworks
The competency-based approach to management development, whether based on generic or functional frameworks, has many critics. Their concerns are that it is an insufficiently discriminating approach to analysing and meeting managerial needs, except in that minority of cases where the managerial role can be adequately described by reference to a number of discrete components that remain relatively

constant and standardised through time. Let us look at some of the concerns in more detail.

The manager's world

Managerial work across all levels ... is characterized by pace, brevity, variety and fragmentation ... It is hectic and fragmented, requiring the ability to shift continuously from relationship to relationship, from topic to topic, from problem to problem.

(Partridge, 1989: 205)

Even first-level and middle managers use a range of skills that cannot easily be categorised. Many of those skills are, and must be, integrated in their practice, and this may lead to a synergetic effect – that is to say, one where the outcome of management action is greater than the sum of its parts. Such skills have been styled as 'overarching competences' (Burgoyne, 1989). They include skills to do with analysis, synthesis, balance and perspective (Johnston and Sampson, 1993: 218) that are not amenable to functional analysis.

Mintzberg (1973) found managerial roles to be highly variable, involving the often simultaneous pursuit of a variety of objectives in changing ways according to the judgement of the individual manager in the particular situation. This explains why managers are usually allowed very wide discretion, enabling the individual to choose how best to operate, what tasks to tackle and how, at any one point in time.

The development of managers and of the management sector in an organisation needs to be related closely to the organisational context in which they work. This is the main reason why many argue for the MDP to be based on the ongoing management process in the organisation rather than on often irrelevant educational and training programmes however they are accessed.

That context is pressured and can be highly politicised. Research shows that management is not an objective and consistently rational activity. Instead, it involves constantly trying to find 'a way through contradictory demands in a world of uncertainty' (Edwards, 1990). Political skills and creative ability, as well as purely functional skills, are crucial in enabling managers to cut through these complexities in order to produce the results for which they are responsible.

The changeability of managers' roles and jobs

Competition between companies and countries is no longer dominated by access to capital, equipment, systems or location. It is the capability of people to generate, share and deploy knowledge for value-added purposes which makes the difference.

(Sir Geoffrey Holland, in a Foreword to Guile and Fonda, 1998: vii)

This IPD report in 1998 amplified on those fundamental changes to show that 'the new corporate capabilities of organisations and the individual capabilities of people will need to be managed as a single process'. The authors identified 20 capabilities that managers needed to operate in roles and jobs that, for many, continue to change dramatically. Can functionally based competency frameworks adequately cope with such a rapid pace of change?

Strategically focused competency frameworks

A distinguishing feature in many competency frameworks is the attempt to formalise and link both individual and organisational competencies to strategic priorities and to human resource systems (Alvarez, 1996). Organisational competencies are those unique and core capabilities embedded in an organisation that enable that organisation to innovate and advance.

One example of a strategically focused competency framework was that of British Petroleum (BP) in the 1990s, described by Sparrow and Hiltrop (1994: 417–19). It embodied 67 essential behaviours related to four organisational culture dimensions, and involved a lengthy and apparently successful process of cross-national, cross-cultural implementation. It was part of a strategy to radically change the structure, culture and strategic performance of the organisation world-wide, as has already been described in Chapter 19 (pages 338–9), and was supported by extensive changes to BP's HR policies and systems.

A fundamental concern here is whether a competency framework is likely to reinforce *any* given strategy, regardless of its quality. Alvarez (1996) expressed the fear that such frameworks could dangerously narrow managerial perspectives, inhibiting the intellectual independence needed to question given strategy in the light of an ever-changing environment. Certainly, a competency framework is likely to develop from, and become part of, the dominant logic of an organisation, defined as 'the way in which managers conceptualise the business and make critical allocation decisions' (Prahalad and Bettis, 1986: 490).

Looking at the managers themselves, those operating at strategic levels or with strategic tasks to perform as part of their managerial roles do need to develop some functional competencies related to their strategic tasks. For example, for many managers at unit level, formal planning and the specific techniques and skills it requires are still central to their work. However, taking the higher-level capacities that managers involved in the strategy arena need, there is continuing debate about how far abilities such as those to do with judgement, intuition, mental elasticity, abstract thinking and tolerance of risk and ambiguity can be viewed in the same light as more measurable 'competencies' (Mintzberg, 1994 and 1994a). It seems logical to conclude that a reliance on functional frameworks when planning the development of strategic managers will mean that 'the integrated work of managing still gets lost in the process of describing it' (Mintzberg, 1994a: 11).

Balancing the arguments

What conclusions can be drawn about the appropriateness of applying a competency framework to an organisation's MDP? To simplify, perhaps the following:

• In the short term, and in the more stable organisations, a competency-based approach to management development can produce excellent results, enabling the linking of performance criteria, development activity and performance outcomes at individual and organisational levels.

- However, competencies should always be analysed in the context of the particular organisation and agreed as meaningful and relevant by the key parties involved in and affected by the MDP.

- There is evidence to show that a competency-based approach can also be of value when the business is moving into changed conditions, provided that there is a high degree of certainty and agreement on the kind of future-oriented qualities and skills needed by those who will have to cope with those conditions.

- Where it is clear that tomorrow's environment will be radically different from today's, with complex, unfamiliar problems and no certainty as to the exact nature and interrelationship of the competencies needed to deal with it – in other words, when that environment is turbulent – then an alternative framework for the MDP should be considered.

Designing a strategically focused management development programme

You are now invited to produce a design for a management development programme aimed at a strategic management level – not the board, and not senior executives, but senior middle managers. You may feel a need, before tackling it, to do more research into management development methods. In performing the task, you will need to integrate your skills and understanding related both to the MDP (covered in this chapter) and to learning design (covered in Part 3 of this book).

As you tackle the assignment you should become better able to appreciate what is involved in deciding on and organising a demanding management development programme.

Designing a management development programme

You are an HRD consultant to the company described below. Read through the account and then produce a design for a management development programme that meets the brief you have been given (see paragraph three).

Business and organisational context

You are advising one of the country's leading companies in the supply of a diverse range of electronic, analytical and computational products and services. It has always been characterised by high innovation and quality, and by its positive values related to developing its workforce. The company now faces globalised competition and a fast-changing business environment. This means that its managers at all levels must quickly become more strategic and outward-looking in their values and thinking, and develop skills to match. They must be able to respond quickly and appropriately to the big competitive issues that confront the company. With key markets on the decline, new technology needing heavy investment, major competition from small, fast-growth companies and low-cost foreign companies, and costs rising rapidly within the company, these managers now have to become much more entrepreneurial.

The managers come mainly from a technical background, and fewer than 40 per cent have any formal business education. Most have worked for years in the company, and until recently – because of the company's long-standing success and high profit ratios – have paid little attention to costs. Managers are also used to the autonomy and local cultures of the company's functional matrix management system. Many tend to pay more attention to local needs of their units than to the wider business scenario.

The management development programme

Working with a national business school whose reputation for high-quality effective business programmes is excellent, you have been asked by the company's top management to design a company-wide management development programme. It is to be aimed at senior middle managers, aged 30 to 40, with 10 years' or more service in the company, a technical background and education, and responsibility for 20 to 50 people. Promotion is increasingly unavailable, so it is important that this programme is seen not as a promotion ticket but as a way of improving managerial competence in current roles.

Key criteria for the programme:

- It must be business-focused, cost-efficient, have the involvement of senior company executives, and reflect corporate issues.

- It must have a national, not a local, focus.

- It must be capable of being delivered by each of the company's regional training teams, and within their resources.

- It must emphasise managers' responsibility for self-development and stimulate them to an active commitment in this respect.

- Teamwork must be a key feature, so that participants learn from and support each other in the learning processes and develop project management and team skills.

- The programme must focus on making the target population more effective in their current roles as well as on developing future-oriented skills and values.

Feedback notes

This is an example of a programme that is part of a management development process whose agenda is to build up a management sector that will make the organisation more effective now and for the longer term. Here are some generalised ideas relating to its design:

- The programme must focus on strategic business issues that the company faces. One measure of the success of the programme will be how far it enhances managers' ability to understand and deal effectively with those issues.

- Methods must involve learning from and through experience, in order to increase competence and test it on real issues. Methods could include live project work, practical assignments, the use of benchmarking and best practice to suggest improvements to business strategy at corporate and unit levels, SWOT analysis and business planning, and the development of a wide variety of strategic options in order to enhance the quality of strategic choice.

- Knowledge and techniques needed to tackle strategic issues can be provided in part by theoretical inputs, in part by help in various forms (not only talks, but also mentoring, coaching, secondments, and so on) from skilled senior executives in the company, and in part by external educationalists. Teamwork can be achieved by group-based projects supported by informal networking systems extending beyond the programme back into the various workplaces of the participants – action learning is a particularly powerful process for this purpose.

- There must be the active involvement of regional training staff during the programme. This can be achieved through a rotation of such staff in the delivery of the programme, as well as through their involvement in programme design.

- You and the business school must work collaboratively with the company, not impose ivory-tower attitudes or content on the programme. Business school staff will need to form part of the core planning team (say, two, together with the management development manager and a rotating regional training manager). They can then partner managers on the programme and respond to participants' need for 'a blend of internal knowledge and external wisdom which participants can exploit, particularly in developing their projects' (Carter and Lumsdon, 1988).

- Such a programme was organised at Hewlett Packard in the 1980s, although in that case the task was even more demanding: to develop the company's European managers (Carter and Lumsdon, 1988). The whole programme centred on groups of managers carrying out project work related to the 10 most important strategic issues facing Hewlett Packard Europe. Top management took a leading role in identifying and explaining the issues, agreeing the projects, evaluating them, and being committed to their implementation. The programme helped managers by training them in various skills. Through the learning strategies it involved, it also broadened their knowledge and began to change the culture of the whole management group concerned.

This kind of programme must make a powerful link between management development and competitive advantage. It must develop managers in ways that improve their abilities to generate strategic options, choose strategies that fit the company's situation, make strategic decisions, and ensure their effective implementation across the company. It must also help managers to develop the ways of thinking and behaving, and the dispositions, that are needed in order to be effective in strategic roles. Where obstacles emerge there, the company's top management must look again at their strategic management selection process.

THE CHARACTERISTICS OF AN EFFECTIVE MANAGEMENT DEVELOPMENT PROCESS

As with the human resource development process more widely, the MDP differs across organisations. Sadler and Barham (1988) identified six characteristics that make a MDP effective, no matter what management development methods are used. Osbaldeston and Barham (1992) expanded on them:

- a clear MDP mission, linked to the organisation's business strategy

- specific programme objectives that relate to the external challenges that the organisation is facing

- a focus also on major internal organisational issues

- programmes tailored to organisational and individual needs

- the systematic assessment of management development needs, aims and outputs

- a professional, business-led approach to the MDP.

To enable you, if you wish, to reflect at this point on the MDP in your own organisation, and to identify how far the process seems to be 'fragmented, formalised or focused' (Sadler and Barham, 1998), you will find a questionnaire in Appendix 7.

SUCCESSION PLANNING AND THE MANAGEMENT DEVELOPMENT PROCESS

As we saw earlier, planning for the future is one of the three main tasks of any MDP. Gratton and Syrett (1990) emphasised that systems for management succession planning should be tailored to the needs of business strategy in the organisation, and should take account of any changes in organisational structure. They also noted that despite the importance of building the needs of the individual into succession programmes if key personnel are to be retained and committed, many companies still focus succession planning on career structures that have been imposed on participants instead of being planned with them. The concept of mutuality, discussed in Chapter 19, therefore goes to the heart of succession planning for managers.

The traditional model
Conventionally, succession planning has been based on a model of identifying needs related to the business plan, identifying high-fliers at an early stage and grooming them over an extended timescale for positions at the top of the organisation. Development has usually been a matter of initial formal training followed by specialisation until a late stage, when those still left in the race have been rotated through various functions in order to become 'generalists'. Assessments, often using incomplete, unreliable and subjective information, result in a diminishing number of the original cohort continuing to climb steadily up the ladder, others falling from it at various points into permanent positions in the structure. Wastage, in this model, can come arbitrarily, and may mean that some of the most valued people leave

the organisation unpredictably, with consequent gaps at stages where they may prove difficult or impossible to fill.

This traditional model assumes that there is a long-term business plan, that it is accessible to those responsible for HRD, that it is sufficiently detailed to enable succession planning needs to be identified from it, and that the longer-term future of the organisation can be forecast and is not likely to be radically different from the past. The model also presupposes a stable, hierarchical structure of positions through which people are developed and progress along specified career pathways that remain in place through time. Finally, it assumes the exercise of centralised rather than localised control over the whole process, with ownership of career development by the centre rather than by individuals.

Succession planning in turbulent environments

The traditional model may cope with some change, but it is not relevant for an organisation that operates in a turbulent environment in which threats and opportunities are likely to be complex, unfamiliar and unpredictable. Furthermore, in decentralised organisations the kind of managers and competencies needed will change. Managing strategic business units requires a profound knowledge and understanding of the business and its environment, as well as entrepreneurial skills that can come only from multifunctional experience and adaptability to rapidly changing situations. In such an organisation, succession planning and management development policy based on competencies defined by reference to the current roles and tasks of those in senior positions cannot be a valid approach to succession planning. An attempt to identify and put in place a specific successor to every key position will also be unrealistic and unjustifiably costly.

Here is a case-study that first appeared in my 1992 IPM text. In one sense it may seem only of historical interest now. However, in another it is highly relevant to our discussion because it still represents a model of good practice. It demonstrates important principles about how to organise management development in a business that has grown very fast and needs an adaptive MDP.

Case-study: Organising the MDP at United Biscuits (UB) in the early 1990s

Context

By the early 1990s UB had moved rapidly from being a small, centralised organisation dominated by a paternalistic leader (Sir Hector Laing) to a large, divisionalised organisation in which managing directors had a high level of autonomy.

The central personnel group carried out at that time a review of perceptions related to management development across the company, and from this it was clear that there was widespread agreement on the need for management succession to be achieved through a continued strategy of cross-divisional or cross-functional moves. The group therefore decided to involve the divisional managing directors actively in responsibility for management development.

A management executive was set up consisting of the managing directors (one of whom was selected to be the chairman and also became the next chief executive of UB), the personnel director and management development director. The executive produced a business-led mission for employee development (including management development) and a strategy focused on ensuring that the best people were available, and on high individual performance levels.

Mission

To generate and drive training and development activities enabling all individuals to achieve the standards of performance demanded by the business.

Strategy

All employees were to receive the necessary training and development to do their job and prepare them for their next roles. Management development would be achieved through a UB development programme with three components: management essentials, experienced manager development, and high potential managers' development.

The respective roles of centre and divisions in management development were then identified. The centre was to have responsibility for all management development policy and practice, and would have to agree all senior appointments. Divisions were to implement company-wide practices.

Components of the MDP

The 'management essentials' component targeted direct-entry graduates, other external recruits and managers promoted from within (typically aged under 30). The aim was to give them job knowledge and skills, ensure that they were knowledgeable about all the key business functions of UB and achieved required standards of performance, and equip them with skills and knowledge related to managing people. This component lasted about two years, ending with a diagnostic career development workshop leading to the identification of ongoing development needs and planning related to their subsequent careers.

The 'manager development' component targeted all other established managers (about 98 per cent of the sector). It focused on needs tightly related to the individual's job performance and on self-development activities that had to be recorded by the individual as they occurred. Because of their developmental responsibilities, all UB managers were trained and developed in how to appraise, identify training needs, coach and develop, and use work-related experiences to help people learn.

The 'high potential managers' development' component was managed through appraisal, audit and divisional reviews, co-ordinated and driven by the Management Development Executive. All individuals were evaluated annually using a dossier of their learning and development activities. All had to attend three centrally organised programmes – in business management, managing change, and strategy.

Results after two years
There were quite severe initial tensions caused by the apparent loss of autonomy by personnel directors working in the divisions. However, the relationship between them and the new executive soon became more effective and the executive, meeting every two months, had after two years demonstrated a strong commitment to the MDP. It introduced a new and more business-focused appraisal scheme, changed the remuneration system and identified strengths, weaknesses and future needs of functions in the business. HR-planning and succession planning were now reviewed annually. Assessments and career development movements of individuals were continuously monitored, and divisional priorities and plans for management development were agreed at executive level.

Working to a common purpose with shared responsibility for auditing and agreed standards for training and development activity gradually produced a system the management of which was carried out by a strong team of divisional management development and training managers.

Source: Doyle and Norman, 1991.

MANAGING THE MDP

Note in the case-study not only the flexible, non-traditional approach to management succession, but also the way in which the MDP was managed. Two points are important here.

- The development of managers, one of the most powerful sectors in any organisation, is a political process, needing effective collaboration between the key parties if it is to succeed. As we saw in the case of the clinical directors' programme in Chapter 17, and in the strategic programme task you tackled earlier in this chapter, external consistency is crucial to the success of formal management development initiatives.

- If longer-term outcomes are to be achieved, the MDP must be integrated with wider employee resourcing policy and practice in order to achieve consistency across the processes of planning, recruitment, selection, appraisal, rewards and development. This argues for the human resource (HR) function to have a central involvement in planning and managing the MDP. However, the more important point here is that the MDP must have the full commitment of management at every level; its planning and management must not be dominated by specialists.

When the organisation is decentralised, it is essential to actively involve the units as well as the centre in planning, operating and evaluating the MDP. The case-study illustrates the need to ensure that while the management development is 'owned' by units it is also well integrated across the whole organisation. The danger of loosening central control is that divisions/units will take too much power into their own hands, and end by doing things their own way according to their own cultures. The danger of putting central control into the hands of a personnel function is that its specialists may hold insufficient power, and be seen as 'outside' the real management system of the organisation.

Managing the MDP in an organisation

Looking back through this section and the United Biscuits case-study, what do you see to be three essential requirements for the successful management of the MDP?

Feedback notes

When managing the MDP, three essential requirements are that:

- *Management development must be owned by managers* and achieve strong external consistency. Managers, any human resource (HR) practitioners and other key stakeholders should work as business partners in this, and be clear as to their respective roles and responsibilities.

- *The MDP must have a vision and strategy* that are understood and supported by the managers involved in its operation. The process must be driven by business needs as well as respond to individual needs. It must enable the continuous identification, assessment and development of potential and be grounded in an agreement between managers and HR specialists as to its purpose and management.

- *Managers must be trained* in the processes involved in training and developing others, and must have a shared commitment to implementing the MDP across the organisation. HR specialists need a thorough knowledge of the business, its goals and strategy in order to advise on the design, delivery and evaluation of management development strategy and programmes.

CONCLUSION

Having read this chapter and completed its reviews and self-checks, you should now:

- understand what the management development process (MDP) involves and the need to link management development to organisational goals and strategy

- be able to explain the characteristics of an effective MDP, and how to manage the MDP

- be able to advise on the generalised design of a management development programme

- understand how to integrate succession planning within the MDP.

To test yourself against these objectives, what five-minute answers would you give to the following questions? (Dates in brackets refer to the IPD qualifying examination paper in which a question appeared.)

- Advise on an evaluation system for a major and long-term management development initiative in your organisation. (Specimen paper, 1996)

- The six members of the top management group in an organisation do not work well together as a corporate team, and strategic direction is suffering in consequence. Identify **three** possible causes of this failure, and against each suggest a training or other developmental approach to tackle the problem. (May 1998)

- You have been told that management development in your organisation is poorly managed. What criteria would you use to decide if this is really the case?

USEFUL READING

GUILE D. *and* FONDA N. (1998) *Performance Management through Capability*. London, Institute of Personnel and Development.

MINTZBERG H. (1994) 'Rounding out the manager's job'. *Sloane Management Review*. Vol. 36, 1. pp11–26.

MUMFORD A. (1997) *Management Development: Strategies for action*. 3rd edn. London, Institute of Personnel and Development.

STEWART R. (1984) 'The nature of management? A problem for management education'. *Journal of Management Studies*. Vol. 21, 3. pp323–30.

WHIDDETT S. *and* HOLLYFORDE S. (1999) *The Competencies Handbook*. London, Institute of Personnel and Development.

Part 5

ENHANCING STRATEGIC PROGRESS

21 Building strategic capability

LEARNING OBJECTIVES

After reading this chapter, you will:

- understand what is meant by 'strategic capability', and its relationship to the strategic progress of the organisation

- understand HRD's potential to play a role in enhancing the strategic capability of an organisation

- appreciate some of the ways in which the management development process can contribute to building strategic capability.

INTRODUCTION

Throughout the book, themes of challenge, business partnership, professional development and the importance of coherence in the HRD process have been pursued. Theories, frameworks and prescriptions have jostled for place in an attempt to express both the intellectual rigour involved in the study of HRD and the imperative for it to achieve outcomes that will substantiate its claim as a strategic lever for the business. A central theme has been the importance of aligning HRD with business goals in order to enhance organisational as well as individual performance and progress. Now, in this final part, the treatment broadens to encompass issues of collective learning, knowledge development, strategic progress and organisational transformation.

In these last two chapters, the aim is to discuss and reflect, and to examine practice. There are few self-checks: the emphasis is on illustration. There are no final review questions – the complexity of the issues, and their unresolved state in theory and in practice, argue against any quick responses to the puzzles that they generate. However, at the end of this chapter an assignment to extend learning is suggested.

This chapter introduces aspects of strategic progress. It then explores ways in which the management development process can help to build 'strategic capability'.

STRATEGIC PROGRESS

Case-study: The case of BTR

> BTR's extraordinary downfall is a story of how a winning strategy in the fragmented markets and corporate inefficiency of the 1970s and 1980s produced an unmanageable empire up against increasingly strong competitors in the 1990s. It is also the story of how management failed to adapt as engineering and manufacturing turned upside around the world.
>
> (Potter, 1998: 33)

BTR, built on the base of the tiny Birmingham Tyre and Rubber Company in 1963, reached its peak as an industrial conglomerate some years ago, being one of the 10 largest corporations in Britain and retaining a premium rating from the stock market. By the 1990s its strategic direction was beginning to drift. It was announced in November 1998 that it was to merge with Siebe, another UK manufacturing giant. In reality, the merger was widely viewed as a takeover by Siebe. How could such a reversal have occurred?

In 1993 BTR's founding father, Sir Owen Green, had retired. He was succeeded by Norman Ireland, former finance director. It was a curious and unsuccessful appointment. The world was changing rapidly. Advances in information technology and crumbling capital barriers allowed manufacturing to go global (Potter, 1998) and by 1994 BTR's margins were beginning to slide. The real problem, however, was at the top, where Ireland and Alan Jackson, who had been appointed chief executive in 1991, continued to be dominated by the old BTR mindset – cyclical acquisitions, cost-cutting, adding value at the margins, and then seeking bids to move through the cycle once again. By the early 1990s that prescription was fast becoming inappropriate (*ibid*). The fashion was for focus and specialisation, for re-engineering. Also, in the low-growth environment of the time the risks involved in contested takeovers did not seem to make sense – yet still Jackson concentrated on sticking to that old BTR knitting.

Lorenz (1995) observed BTR's new vulnerability to the turbulent climate, doubly worrying as its top men retired and its traditional stock of home-grown replacements ran out. For three decades BTR had nurtured its own top management and resisted even the appointment of external non-executive directors. After September 1994, however, its performance had slowed down and become erratic, for two reasons: 'It is facing a seismic shift in its business environment; and the people who must lead BTR's response to this fundamental change will be men with no previous connection with the company' (*ibid*). But by the time Ian Strachan took over as CE at the end of 1995, it was really too late. By 1998, Siebe – the UK's most highly rated engineering stock – sought out BTR because of its process controls and power-drives businesses. These would enable Siebe to sell more systems rather than get stuck in the increasingly unproductive components-manufacturing end of the business. Commentators feared that it might have taken on too much. BTR was the bigger enterprise of the two, and it might be too complex for its partner to understand and to manage. There might not be the organisational capacity or the effectiveness of strategic direction to make the new conglomerate work. It might then founder (Potter, 1998).

The case of BTR, presented even in this outline form, can be viewed as illustrating the rapidity with which the strategic direction of an organisation can founder. Such stories raise questions about how that risk can be reduced, when turbulence – in the sense of profound commotion, disturbance – in such firms' environment is increasing. In an article published in 1994, Prahalad and Hamel identified many ways in which firms' competitive space was changing. Causes included deregulation; structural changes brought about by technology and customer expectations; excess capacity inviting radical restructuring; mergers, acquisitions and alliances; the impact of environmental concerns; reduction in protectionism leading to exposure of inefficiencies; technological discontinuities spawning new industries; the emergence of trading blocks that are changing the basis and patterns of trade; and global competition, even in local businesses.

There is also the growing power of external stakeholders. Shareholder activism is well established already in the USA and is growing fast in the UK where, by January 1999, six fund managers between them controlled £200 billion in British shares (Waples, 1999). During that month alone, they used their power to initiate a whole series of high-profile takeovers, mergers and boardroom sackings in order to enhance shareholder value. In the public sector, too, there are new monitors, agencies, targets and league-tables.

The rapidity and complexity of all these changes are calling into question the strategic approaches and tools of the past. There can be no reliance on traditional prescriptions or on detailed long-term planning in a world of such unpredictability. Strategic decision-makers must have the wisdom needed to guide their organisations forward when an *absence* of formal strategy – by a curious quirk of logic – may offer the best way forward, through the challenge that the consequent combination of threats, possibilities and ambiguity presents to everyone in the business. Workforces must be increasingly able to adapt to whatever new challenges emerge. They must have flexible skills and mindsets. They must understand the fundamental *vision* of the organisation and must be strongly committed to aiding the realisation of that vision no matter what changes in directions and fortunes that may involve.

Such reflections suggest the possibility of a new role for HRD in the business – one to do with strategic learning, strategic direction, and the development of strategically focused capabilities. But what, exactly, might that role be, and what tasks might it involve?

Turbulence and strategic progress

First, let us look more closely at the issue of 'turbulence'. It has been explained by Ansoff and Sullivan (1993) by reference to four variables:

- the complexity of events in the environment

- familiarity of the successive events

- the rapidity with which the events evolve after they are first perceived

- the visibly impending nature of the consequence of these events.

The greater the levels of turbulence, the more profound the implications for the direction of the organisation. At the stable end of the environmental spectrum, the past can act as a good guide for the present, and strategic decision-makers will need formal strategic planning skills together with competence in financial and human resource management and a focus on continuous improvement. At the unstable end, however, there must be increasing reliance on entrepreneurial skills, on collective learning and on adaptability. Change will be discontinuous. The past will no longer be an adequate guide to the future. In fact, it may act as a distorter, and there will be an ever greater danger of the organisation's becoming trapped in its customary ways of thinking and doing.

To fully grasp the challenges facing HRD in today's business world, we must understand not only the external environmental turbulence with which all organisations must increasingly contend. We must also recall the ambiguities from which HRD itself suffers.

Human resource development – a process in turmoil?

At the start of this book, I introduced a definition of HRD by an American academic:

> the identification of needed skills and active management of learning for the long-range future in relation to explicit corporate and business strategies.
>
> (Hall, 1984: 159)

This definition is used again here because of its stress on a managerial investment in learning in the workplace that will produce its greatest returns over the longer term, thus helping to build a future for the organisation. The pressure to provide learning and developmental initiatives that will produce an immediate bottom-line payoff has become an acute preoccupation of those with HRD responsibilities. Managerial awareness of the need for investment in work-based learning and development that will fuel future progress is not common. One way and another, the task envisaged for the HRD process here is a challenging one.

Through the years there have been regular exhortations from academics and consultants to 'link HRD to business strategy' (Wissema, Brand and Van der Pol, 1981; Hendry and Pettigrew, 1986; Ulrich, 1987; Storey and Sisson, 1990; Ready, Vicere and White, 1994). Yet, as was seen in Chapter 1, there is still little evidence in the UK to show that this is happening, despite considerable anecdotal data to indicate that training is increasingly being used to develop skills needed to support organisational culture change, devolved decision-making and more participative structures. The problem is not always to do with a non-strategic approach to HRD. It can often be because an organisation lacks well-articulated corporate strategy. Without that, it is not possible to achieve strategically focused HRD policy.

Academics can help here by producing business-focused theoretical constructs of which the operational implications are clearly expressed and have been well tested. The conceptual framework that I am now going to present is only in its initial stages of design, but it represents an attempt to provide a construct that has both academic and practical value.

A NEW CONCEPTUAL FRAMEWORK

The key capabilities of an organisation
Let us look now at the contribution that HRD can make to the long-term future of an organisation by taking as our reference point the organisation's key capabilities.

Capabilities refer to 'the capacity for a team of resources to perform some task or activity' (Grant, 1991). In the literature of business strategy and competitive performance, the so-called 'resource-based view of the firm' highlights organisational resources and capabilities as critical in explaining variations in the ability to become and remain profitable (Penrose, 1959; Wernerfelt, 1984; Barney, 1991; Rumelt, 1991; Peteraf, 1993; Schendel, 1994).

A capability must be 'valuable' if it is to be a differentiator of firm performance in the competitive environment. It must enable the firm to exploit opportunities and reduce threats in its business environment, and so must have a number of characteristics:

• It must meet or create a market need.

• It must have uniqueness (scarcity value).

• It must – therefore – be hard to copy (so it must be difficult to understand in terms of its basic components and how they interact).

• It must be so deeply embedded in the organisation, and in such complex ways, that there is little possibility it can be transferred to any other organisation (therefore making it easy for competitors to poach).

Although there is no consensus on how to classify capabilities, a study of the literature suggests the existence of three generic types that together have a significant influence on the performance of the firm – resource-based, organisational, and strategic. The impact they actually achieve will be mediated, as indicated in Figure 9, by the outcomes of policy decisions in the business and by the firm's strategic position in its industry at any given time – its 'positional capability', which, arising from the interaction of a range of external factors that produce a munificent or hostile environment for the organisation, broadly decides its potential for growth and

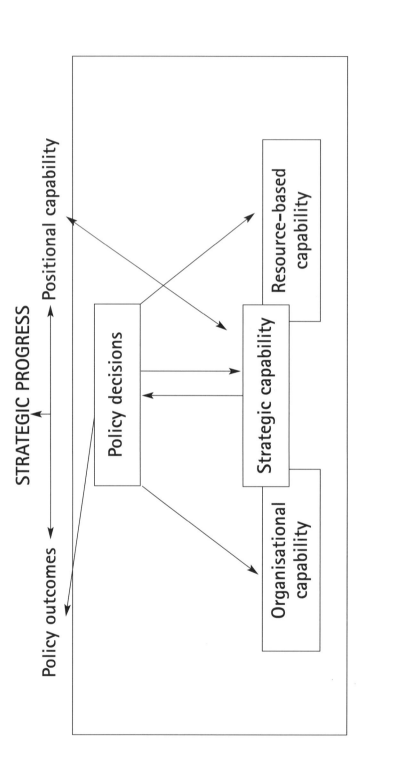

Figure 9 The key capabilities of the organisation and its strategic progress

profitability (Porter, 1980, 1985; Coyne, 1986; Hamel and Prahalad, 1993).

In this chapter the focus is not on the outcomes of policy decisions or on how the firm should deal with external factors in order to improve its competitive position. It is on how to develop those internal capabilities that are the source of the organisation's present and future strategic assets.

Resource-based capability
This capability can be described loosely as what the firm 'knows and can do', vested primarily in the legacy of knowledge, strategic assets, networks and reputation conferred by its past human resources, and the knowledge and skills of its current workforce (Badarraco, 1991; Hall, 1993; Markides and Williamson, 1994).

The task for HRD in relation to resource-based capability is one with which few managers or HR practitioners are not familiar. It is to help to build up the levels and kinds of educational and knowledge base, and the human competence, motivation and commitment that the business needs to achieve its goals. This is part of HRD's value-adding function and we have spent much time exploring it in previous chapters. To give just three examples here, those with HRD responsibilities can

- raise awareness in the organisation of the ways in which the development of people can add value for the business and for individuals, and achieve commitment to the development process

- aid the recruitment, selection and performance management processes by organising induction, training and development that will motivate learners, achieve competent performance and build commitment to organisational goals and values

- advise on organisational competency-based and other skills frameworks to aid recruitment, selection, performance, promotion and continuous development.

Much more can be done. Take the problems created by acquisitions. It was estimated by Crozier in 1998 that since the mid-1980s in the UK fewer than 25 per cent of deals had generated economic value for the buyer. He attributed much of the failure here to the ineffective human resource planning and activity that so often accompanied or followed in the wake of acquisitions. Management turnover, for example, was typically between 39 per cent and 54 per cent. Too often, as also in redundancy situations, the competent people on whom much of the firm's future depends leave, and those who stay fall prey to loss of focus, reduced commitment and ultimately loss of performance with its consequent adverse impact on productivity. The same scenario has been identified in research in the USA. Cannella and Hambrick (1993), for example, found that when established leaders in an organisation left, or were forced out, after an acquisition, there was usually a significant, and sometimes a terminal, decline in subsequent firm performance. This was because they took with them a unique knowledge of the particular firm and also because the high internal status they had possessed there was lost, leaving a vacuum in leadership. As Crozier observed, when a company's intellectual capital and competitive knowledge base departs with the executives who possess it, the cost is incalculable. The need for effective reward systems is clear here. There is also a role for those with HRD responsibilities in relation to effective career and management development processes and in performing an awareness-raising task. For example, executive development programmes can be a powerful vehicle for debate and learning about such issues (see also Schweiger and Weber, 1989).

Organisational capability

Resources cannot be deployed and utilised to their maximum potential unless they are supported by an appropriate organisational system (Nelson and Winter, 1982; Wheelwright and Clark, 1992; Baud and Scanlan, 1995; Miles and Snow, 1995). 'Organisational capability' involves building and adapting to changing needs the structure, the business processes, and the routines and procedures that will enable resources (including people) to be deployed, combined and recombined through time in strategically productive ways. It is about having networks of stable contacts between internal and external parties that form the firm's 'strategic architecture' (Baud and Scanlan, 1995: 112–13). It also involves developing an organisational culture that can be a unique source of competitive advantage because it enables rapid learning, unlearning and relearning throughout the organisation. If resource-based capability is about 'can do', organisational capability is about enabling powerful resources to become fully productive not only to meet current performance requirements but also in relation to whatever future the firm may face or seek to achieve.

Those with HRD responsibilities can help to enhance organisational capability by providing training and learning experiences through which people can acquire the skills they need in changed or changing organisational roles, structure and working environment. They can produce and help to implement developmental strategies and plans to aid redeployment and re-skilling, and to facilitate disengagement. The tasks for HRD are therefore about helping to ensure that

- the organisation's purpose and driving goals are understood and communicated to everyone, and are embedded in the HRD process so that they inform performance and development at all levels

- there are the skills to design and use management systems and business processes that will enable decision-making to be pushed down to the levels where quick responses can be made to competitive forces – and the awareness that this is a crucial task

- there is effective team leadership, teamwork and project management, and that those who take on cross-functional roles, in which influence and persuasion are more relevant than the exercise of direct control and authority, have the skills to operate in those roles

- there is the development and application of learning skills, and that managers and team leaders appreciate and accept the importance of building a workplace environment conducive to continuous learning and improvement

- there are roles and networks to ensure effective operational and learning relationships with internal and external customers, clients and suppliers

- there are learning and developmental processes to ensure that new knowledge is reflected on, absorbed and shared with wider organisational audiences.

These tasks are challenging. We saw in Chapter 14 the tensions that can accompany efforts to achieve a balance between the control often thought necessary by management to achieve desired levels of workplace performance, and future-oriented developmental initiatives. None the less, the tasks are central to the enhancement of organisational capability.

Continuous learning

How can the workplace be managed so that it becomes a continuous learning system?

Feedback notes

Managing the workplace as a continuous learning system involves understanding, resourcing and mobilising opportunities for continuous job-related and developmental learning that exist naturally in employees' everyday work and human interactions. Managers should accept the responsibility this involves, and should themselves be given policy guidelines, training and resources for the purpose, because

- this will establish a partnership approach to learning

- a continuous learning system in the workplace ensures that valuable learning occurs informally and efficiently, as part of the daily work routine

- this brings benefits to the business – it also motivates employees by increasing their confidence in their ability to learn, and in their ability to play an active part in the whole learning process.

Strategic capability

In Chapter 1 (page 18) I introduced the concept of strategic capability in this way:

> Strategic capability provides the vision, the rich and sustained learning and knowledge development, the integrity of purpose and the continuous direction and scope to the activities of the firm that are needed to secure long-term survival. It is based on a profound understanding of the competitive environment, of the resource base, capacity and potential of the organisation, of the strategy process, and of the values that engender commitment from stakeholders to corporate goals.

Strategic capability significantly determines the extent to which the organisation achieves the best possible fit between its unique assets and the position it occupies in its environment. It is also to do with

- choosing and communicating the most appropriate vision, long-term goals and objectives for an enterprise

- building a quality of life in the organisation that will generate the sustained commitment of internal and external stakeholders to the organisation's corporate goals (Harrison and Smith, 2000)

- determining and managing the courses of action and the allocation of resources necessary for achieving strategic goals (Chandler, 1962; Grant, 1991: 17; Barney, 1991).

- selecting and ensuring the development of strategic assets that ensure continued progress of the business.

Stalk, Evans and Schulman (1992: 58) attributed the US retail firm Wal-Mart's extraordinary success in the 1980s to a strategic vision, a set of business decisions and a competitive capability that in a short space of time took the company from nowhere to a dominating position not only in the USA but throughout the world. They concluded that the strategic choices that managers make will increasingly determine organisations' fates. Yet, as their article itself demonstrated in its detail, the effectiveness of the strategy process is dependent on the quality of its interaction with organisational and as well as with human capability. An organisation's workforce may be well-developed, high-performing, adaptive and creative. Its organisational capability may be strong. However, it is hard to envisage how those advantages can work to the full benefit of the organisation unless there are a clear focus for activity, decisions about an appropriate route to follow, goals to act as stimuli and to give purpose, and the flexibility of systems as well as people to change direction as need be in turbulent conditions.

To summarise. Strategic capability is in part an organisational attribute. In that sense it draws on the organisation's business processes and routines, its networks and structure. It is in part a human attribute. In that sense it draws on the knowledge, the abilities and the behavioural patterns of people in the organisation.

To enhance the quality of strategic capability as an *organisational attribute,* those with HRD responsibilities can help to

- raise awareness of the variety of strategy process modes that can be used in an organisation in order to ensure that as strategic issues are being identified, strategic options are being considered and strategic routes are being chosen, there is sufficiently broad-based knowledge and experience informing the debate, and that established ways of thinking and decision-making are regularly challenged so that innovation can occur. There is much research to demonstrate the need for attention to improving the quality of the strategy process (for example, Hart and Banbury, 1994; Floyd and Woolridge, 1994).

- raise awareness of the need to introduce informational processes to do with environmental scanning, scenario-building, the identification of strategic issues, and the generation and analysis of wide-ranging strategic options

- design learning processes and programmes that will help to build and maintain an organisational culture that focuses on strategic thinking and goal-directed behaviour.

To enhance the quality of strategic capability as a *human attribute,* those with HRD responsibilities can help with:

- competency development to ensure at all levels effective use of the organisation's strategic processes and routines

- training and development strategies to assess and continuously improve the cognitive abilities of strategic managers and teams – especially at middle management level where strategic orientation may be critical for organisational performance yet where many feel ill-equipped to deal with their newly acquired strategic roles

- initiatives and processes that will improve skills related to the implementation of strategy – for example, the ability to set and monitor clear, measurable, time-bound and appropriate objectives and targets at unit, team and individual levels

- the review and continuous improvement of appraisal, assessment and development processes underpinning management succession

- mentoring, coaching and career development processes to retain and realise the potential of those who are central to the future strategic capability of the firm

- the stimulation of the search for strategically valuable knowledge throughout the organisation through work-based learning processes such as innovatory projects to meet new strategic challenges (see Starkey, 1996 for many real-life examples across different types and sizes of organisation).

THE KNOWLEDGE-PRODUCTIVE ORGANISATION

The learning process and knowledge productivity

That last reference, to the search for knowledge, introduces the concept of knowledge productivity. What is a 'knowledge-productive' organisation? It is

> an organisation where there is an approach to the processes of work and learning at all levels, collectively as well as individually, that will lead to the expansion of existing knowledge and the generation of new knowledge.
>
> (Kessels, 1996)

To be knowledge-productive, learning is not enough. There must also be unlearning and relearning. 'Relearning' refers to the need to transfer old learning to new contexts, and to make the necessary adjustments that this process involves. Its significance in relation to all types of change situation is clear and in consequence it receives much attention in major organisational change programmes. Yet in the achievement of such change – and in relation to the development of strategic capability – 'unlearning' is arguably of even greater importance. The process involves the removal of any barriers to relearning and to new learning that are presented by previously acquired knowledge, skills, attitudes and cognitions. Little concern is shown for this vital process in practitioner texts (it is revealing, too, to find no definition of the term in the latest edition of the *Oxford Companion to the Mind*, and no reference to it in an otherwise admirable discussion there of learning and learning theory) (Gregory, 1998: 430–2), and this both reflects and helps to explain the lack of attention it so often attracts in the field. In the scholarly literature of strategy and of organisational learning, however, it has received increasing comment in recent years. The concept of the dominant logic has a particular significance here. It illuminates the danger of ways of thinking and behaving that have become so deeply embedded in individual and collective mindsets that they can, quite literally, prevent even the awareness that change is needed, let alone the willingness to learn how to achieve that change.

It was in an article focusing on corporate management of diversified businesses that Prahalad and Bettis first proposed their concept of the 'dominant logic'. It was mentioned first in this book in Chapter 20 as being:

> *a mindset or a world view or conceptualisation of the business and the administrative tools to accomplish goals and make decisions in that business* and stored as a shared cognitive map among the dominant managerial coalition in the organisation, 'expressed as a learned, problem-solving behaviour'.
>
> (Prahalad and Bettis, 1986: 491; italics my own)

One of the paradoxes raised by the dominant logic is that the more successful a business becomes, the less likely is it that it will be able to achieve the unlearning needed to produce a different logic when internal or external changes may require it. A case in point is that of Marks & Spencer (M&S) in recent years. An outline of that story follows. It illustrates the need for a planned interaction between the three capabilities that have just been outlined. It also demonstrates the difficulties involved in becoming and remaining a 'knowledge-productive' organisation in a rapidly changing business environment.

Case-study: Marks & Spencer

Until December 1998 M&S was a bell-wether of the British economy, and arguably the biggest retailer in Europe. Its reputation for quality and value was second to none. M&S invests heavily in its resource-based capability. Its business-focused HRD strategy is implemented largely through expert line-managed in-store learning and development. Its organisational capability, too, is impressive. There are famously close links with suppliers, and stores are strategically located across the UK, with an increasing number abroad. There is a network of business routines, systems and processes to ensure the effective and efficient transformation of inputs into high-value-adding outputs.

The group's corporate culture, however, was described as an impregnable fortress buttressed by consistently rising profits – 'those who question the Company Way tend not to stay' (Weaver, 1988). Under Lord Rayner in the 1980s, an evangelistic glow acted 'like a nuclear furnace in firing the engines of expansion' (*ibid*), but by 1998 increasing concerns were being expressed by business commentators about the extent to which corporate decision-makers were shielded from external criticism. M&S's stranglehold on clothing was by then being broken by changing high-street design trends and shifts in customer purchase patterns. At the same time there were aspirations to be a multinational mega-group that spanned countries and market sectors but uncertainty as to how exactly to handle that change of strategic direction. The investment needed ate into the group's profit base.

By late 1998, after a bitter and public boardroom battle, the posts of CEO and chair of the company were separated for the first time. Sir Richard Greenbury – a feared autocrat since in 1991 becoming the first non-family CEO and chair in the company's history – had to agree to become non-executive chair and to retire in July 2000, a year earlier than he had intended. However, he managed to ensure that Peter Salsbury, a man very much in the company image and his chosen successor, became CEO.

When it was announced in January 1999 that the previous year's profit level would be halved, M&S shares plunged. With M&S, of course, all things are relative. Its profits were still high, and the decline was attributed internally to excessive winter overstocking. Organisational capability was tackled by establishing three new business units and a new post of marketing director. But the board remained unwieldy, key faces were too familiar, and there was no liberation of young talent. The search for a new chairman appeared for some time to be deadlocked and the appointment of Woolworth's marketing director 'failed to impress the market' (Rush, 1999: 3).

By December 1999 shares were at their lowest level since August 1992, and morale at the company's head office was 'terrible', many believing that it had been a mistake for the non-executive directors to allow Sir Richard Greenbury to stay on (Rankine, 1999: 27). Rumours of mergers and takeovers began to spread, and at the time of writing (early 2000), two disturbing questions remain unanswered. How, initially, was it possible for such major strategic miscalculations to be made? And why has the decline continued?

One reading of the situation is that whatever its resource-based and organisational capability, lack of strategic capability in latter years was a direct contributor to the undermining of M&S's market position. The evidence indicates that over a number of years there was a steady deterioration in the quality of the organisation's strategic direction, finally perceived and tackled too late. Certainly, the case suggests that problems were encountered when new learning was needed but that the learning process was consistently blocked by failure to shed old values and ways of thinking. For too long, it appears, the old dominant logic continued to hold sway at M&S, preventing the unlearning and relearning that are essential in order to produce radical strategic change. What has come under particular criticism at M&S is the failure to listen until too late in the day to those lower down the hierarchy (for one of the problems here was indeed a rigid, hierarchical structure) who had important information, suggestions and views to offer that had a bearing on strategic issues facing the firm. In organisations operating in conditions of increasing turbulence, it is no longer possible for the chief executive to 'learn for the organisation'. There must be an integration of strategic thinking at all levels for this kind of company to make continued progress.

Lessons for HRD practitioners
The conceptual framework suggested in this chapter rests on the assumption that the quality of interaction between an organisation's three core capabilities can help to explain and influence strategic progress through time, and that HRD processes and activity can enhance the value of those capabilities. For those who carry responsibility for HRD in their business, this suggests two things:

- the need for a profound understanding of the organisation in which they operate, of its environment, and of the learning and developmental needs, capabilities and potential of those who work in and for that organisation

- the need for a clear grasp of where to focus their efforts and investment in HRD – and what kind of efforts those should be – in order to ensure that HRD adds strategic value.

The real question that suggests itself is not, therefore, 'How can HRD be more closely aligned with business goals and strategy?' It is: *What links can be forged between HRD and strategic capability in order that the organisation not only can survive but also, when need be, can take a major leap forward in its environment?*

LINKING MANAGEMENT DEVELOPMENT AND STRATEGIC CAPABILITY

> By and large in most organisations ... MTD is bolted on and not actually integrated into the business strategy. It raises all sorts of difficulties.
> (Quoted in Brown, Peccei, Sandberg and Welchman, 1989: 75)

When management development is integrated with corporate strategy, it has the potential to improve strategic capability. For that to occur, it needs to be consistent with the goals of that strategy and should ideally be incorporated into corporate strategy (Sisson and Storey, 1988; Brown *et al* 1989; Cave and McKeown, 1993). Even where that is not possible to fully attain – and it is important to be pragmatic in the HRD field – a management development process will achieve much to enhance strategic capability if, through its various components, it helps current and potential strategic managers at all levels to achieve:

- clearer strategic vision in order to improve their strategic decision-making

- strategic thinking both in themselves and in the teams that they manage

- a sharper focus on what is strategically important

- improved understanding of the rapidly changing business environment

- improved linking of strategy to operational implementation.

Another task for the MDP is to develop the skills related to managing individuals working in innovative organisations – those with a need to generate quite new assets and strategies. There are tensions here. Innovative organisations operate in a pressured world. They are more complex and demanding, more uncertain in their work patterns and routines than the traditional, hierarchical type of organisation. As more people learn how to initiate ideas, activities and projects that create work for still others, and are encouraged by the organisation to do so, there is a danger of losing the balance between operational and creative activity to the point that neither is satisfactorily being achieved. 'Empowered' employees working in such organisations are not easily managed. Too often they become disillusioned and cynical as fear of losing authority and control causes management to retrench, as once-effective teams become split by rivalries, and as strategic coherence breaks down. There is also reduced employment security in such organisations, and increased stress levels where not all can pursue the ideas and assignments that bring the most attractive rewards.

Understanding that such patterns of behaviour are likely to develop is the first step towards ensuring that they will not be inevitable. Through the MDP, managers working in such organisations need to become equipped with the knowledge and skills to achieve a balance in their teams between routine and innovatory activity, and to be able to foster creativity without endangering the performance of operational tasks.

To make any impact on strategic capability, the MDP must encompass a critical mass. Who should be developed in order to provide this? A growing body of research suggests that across most of today's more decentralised organisations it is the management team, broadly defined, rather than the chief executive, that most affects the quality and outcomes of strategy-making (Ghoshal and Bartlett, 1994; Hedlund, 1994). The MDP in such organisations therefore needs to focus on the development of middle as well as senior managers. Their strategic role can have a direct impact on the performance of the organisation, especially in those de-layered structures where innovation and market-sensitivity are essential to innovation and the advancement of the business in its competitive environment (Floyd and Wooldridge, 1994). This includes those working in quasi-market sectors such as the Civil Service, local authorities and the National Health Service. Many would go further, as we saw in Chapter 20, in the belief that scope of management development should take in every employee and focus on the total process of learning, continuous improvement and change in the organisation.

Management development and the knowledge base of the organisation

The relationship between managerial learning and the organisation's collective learning ability is a crucial one to consider when planning how to enhance strategic capability through the MDP. To explain what we mean by collective learning, it is necessary to consider the knowledge process – a more detailed treatment will be given in Chapter 22: this is by way of an introduction.

Imagine the organisation as a continuous 'stream of knowledge' (von Krogh, Roos and Slocum, 1994: 54). Imagine then the ways in which different approaches to the development of managers in the organisation can affect that stream of knowledge. They can change its shape and course, give it new outlets, or increase its force so that it can refresh and revitalise the sometimes barren territory of strategic decision-making. Finally, imagine knowledge as the firm's powerhouse, within which are stored the mental maps, the values and ideas, the customary ways of thinking, that generate in organisational members a shared way of looking at and making sense of their organisational worlds and the environment around it.

By using our imagination in these ways we can begin to grasp the planned connections that should be made between the MDP, the current knowledge base of the organisation, collective learning and the strategic process. Whether the MDP's potential is realised depends not only on management development strategy and methods, and on the motivation and learning ability of participants. It also depends on the extent to which the organisation is structured and managed in ways that encourage, absorb and make full use of learning, knowledge development and innovation.

If the MDP is to enhance strategic capability, it must use approaches and methods that stimulate learning and result in the development of knowledge that can then be shared and utilised in ways beneficial to the business. As has already been seen, it must help managers to unlearn ways of thinking and behaving that are no longer appropriate given the organisation's changed or changing environment, and it must enable them to reorganise and apply in different ways – 'relearn' – much of the learning they already possess. These concepts can be illustrated by recalling the clinical directors' programme in Chapter 17. There, new information had to be absorbed; old ways of thinking and behaving that were inconsistent with becoming a strategic manager had to be challenged so that they could be unlearned; yet at the same time, in order to be able to occupy both the professional role they still held and the new managerial role they now occupied, the clinical directors had to reorganise old knowledge, skills and values so that they could cope adequately with the demands of both roles – relearning as well as learning had to be achieved. (For an expansion on the role of the programme in enhancing strategic capability, see Harrison and Miller, 1999.)

Design features
We saw in the last chapter that it is often argued that the only effective form of development for strategic managers is organisation-based and grounded in their ongoing tasks. There is concern about the limited ability of formal programmes to achieve the fundamental shifts in mindsets needed by strategic managers who are new to their role or who are moving to a higher level.

The knowledge base of an organisation and its strategic capability can change as new insights, skills and ideas are applied to the analysis of strategic issues and to decisions about how best to respond to them. New approaches can be reinforced, and sometimes activated, by changes in business processes. Unlearning and relearning can take root when supported by organisational systems. A well-known example of this occurred in Shell, in its 1984 strategic development programme. It was recounted by de Geus (1996) and is summarised below.

Case-study: Shell – breaking the dominant logic

In 1984, as part of a strategic development programme, Shell's international planners were given a scenario that talked about $15 a barrel of oil, when the current price was $28. The aim of forcing these senior managers throughout the company to consider such an apparently absurd scenario was that they should begin to think about their world in a different way – as a world of $15 oil. In response, the managers asked to be told when the price would fall, how far it would go on falling, and how long the fall would last. The reply was that the future was unknowable, and that they must take one sample scenario – price-fall at the end of 1985. It is April 1986 and the price is $15. They must respond to three questions. What do you think your government will do? What do you think your competition will do? And what will you do? Although the case was 'only a game', it started off serious work throughout Shell in exploring the question 'What will we do if it happens?' In early January 1986 the price of oil was $27. By April it had fallen to the unprecedented level of $10. The game had become reality, and broadening the scope of scenario-planning then proved its value: it had significantly accelerated managers' strategic knowledge and understanding.

In order to accelerate institutional learning, Shell changed its planning rules in the mid-1980s. The announcement came without warning – strategic planning from now on must be carried out in the first half of the calendar year (there was already a business planning cycle that dealt with capital budgets in the second half). In the first year of the changed planning cycle the results were mostly just a rehash of the previous year's business plans, but in the second year the plans were fresher and in each subsequent year their quality continued to improve. So intervention in the planning systems of the firm may also be needed to produce a fast change in collective learning.

The MDP can, in such ways, incorporate both formalised and experiential approaches in order to ensure unlearning and relearning, as well as new learning. What is essential is to be continually aware of the impact an MDP can have on the importing, development, transformation and use of knowledge in an organisation. With the ability to generate new knowledge should come the creativity that produces innovation and progress for the organisation.

CONCLUSION

Having read this chapter, you should now:

* understand what is meant in the chapter by 'strategic capability', and its relationship to the strategic progress of the organisation

* understand HRD's potential to play a role in enhancing the strategic capability of an organisation

* appreciate some of the ways in which the management development process can contribute to building strategic capability.

Assignment

Choose an organisation with which you are familiar, and where you will be given good access – it may be your own, but need not be. Your task is to assess, by whatever means and approach you choose, what would be the most useful and feasible ways in which HRD could begin to enhance some aspect of strategic capability in that organisation, or in a major division, unit or section of it (choose whatever context in this respect is most practical and possible for you).

The assignment should be tackled in five steps: preliminary reading; decisions on methodology; gathering data; an analysis of findings and diagnosis of issues; the production of conclusions and recommendations.

USEFUL READING

Bates D. L. *and* Dillard J. E. Jnr (1993) 'Generating strategic thinking through multi-level teams'. *Long Range Planning*. Vol. 26, 5. pp103–10.

Ghoshal S. *and* Bartlett C. A. (1994) 'Linking organizational context and managerial action: the dimensions of quality of management'. *Strategic Management Journal*. Summer Special Issue. Vol. 15. pp91–112.

Guile D. *and* Fonda N. (1998) *Performance Management through Capability*. London, Institute of Personnel and Development.

Hambrick D. C. (1987). 'The top management team: key to strategic success'. *California Management Review*. Fall. pp88–108.

Semler R. (1996) 'The brave new world of Semco manufacturing', *Probono*, pp8–10, in K. Starkey (ed.), *How Organizations Learn*. London, International Thomson Business Press.

Stalk G., Evans P. *and* Shulman L. E. (1992) 'Competing on capabilities: the new rules of corporate strategy'. *Harvard Business Review*. March–April. pp57–69.

Ulrich D. (1987) 'Organizational capability as a competitive advantage: human resource professionals as strategic partners'. *Human Resource Planning*. Part 4. pp169–84.

Zabriskie N. B. *and* Huellmantel A. B. (1991) 'Developing strategic thinking in senior management'. *Long Range Planning*. Vol. 24, 6. pp25–32.

22 Managing the knowledge-productive organisation

LEARNING OBJECTIVES

After reading this chapter you will:

- understand the difference between organisational survival and advancement
- appreciate ways in which HRD can link to collective learning and the development and sharing of knowledge in an organisation
- understand the relationship between 'knowledge productivity' and an organisation's ability to move forward in its environment.

INTRODUCTION

In this last chapter, the focus moves to a vital issue for many organisations – how to develop the ability not only to survive but also to advance in order to remain profitable. 'Profitability' in this wide sense involves the generation of a rate of economic return sufficient to satisfy current stakeholders and to enable investment that will secure the organisation's future. It is essential for those with HRD responsibilities to be able to understand and carry out their role in contributing to this 'profitability'. This is true whether they work in the private or public sector, and in for-profit or not-for-profit organisations.

One case-study links the main themes of the chapter – that of strategic change at Hydro Polymers, Aycliffe, UK. It is supplemented by a small number of tasks to reinforce learning, but in this chapter, as in Chapter 21, the concern is primarily to express a viewpoint and encourage reflection, debate and creativity in fields where it would be naïve to pretend that any secure prescriptions can yet – or perhaps ever – be offered.

SURVIVAL AND ADVANCEMENT

Many companies do not survive for long, and some may not wish to do so. A third of the Fortune 500 industrials listed in 1970 had vanished by 1983. On the other hand, a small group had lasted for more than 70 years, some 'sticking to their knitting' but doing it increasingly well, others from time to time completely changing direction in order to remain profitable. The latter type have somehow developed the human and organisational capacity for sustained profitability. They consistently achieve the confidence of shareholders even when, every now and then, short-term results may flag. They also manage to innovate radically at key stages in their existence in order to leapfrog over their rivals and secure durable advantage. They survive, but they also advance (a distinction explained particularly clearly in von Krogh, Roos and Slocum, 1994: 64).

Let us look first, then, at the qualities that appear to be needed if an organisation is to be able not just to survive but also at certain stages to transform itself in order to make progress in its environment.

Capacity for change

There must be enough stability in the organisation to ensure that current operations can be performed consistently and well, and to ensure that it can alter its portfolio of products or services and its operational effectiveness in line with a need for improved achievement of its strategic goals.

However, there must also be the capacity to experiment, learn and innovate so that change of a kind that completely 'reinvents' corporate character, the behaviour and direction of the business and makes possible the generation of a quite different type of strategic asset is possible (Lorenz, 1992). Let us at this point define what is meant by 'strategic assets'. 'Strategic assets are those unique, hard-to-copy, durable products, services or processes that are valued in the external market and so become the firm's source of competitive advantage' (Amit and Schoemaker, 1993).

This kind of 'transformational' change (to use a term that tends to be applied indiscriminately to a good deal of change that is in reality nothing of the kind) enables the organisation to expand in its environment. IBM achieved this after a traumatic decline in the late 1980s in its customary markets. Shell's history is full of moves from survival mode to expansion and back again, and the information given about the company's approach to improving strategic planning in Chapter 21 helps to explain the way of thinking that has enabled it to do that, even if it does not reveal the answer to the real conundrum – where and how did that way of thinking itself emerge?

The capability to advance needs key decision-makers in the organisation who can think in lateral ways about the company, what it should be doing and where it should be going. Capacity to advance requires an organisational structure, material and financial resources, and a workforce with the skills and adaptability to be able to generate and absorb the necessary changes in direction and work with them. Only by having both capability and capacity can an organisation conceive and implement plans for new patterns of provision of services (as in a hospital trust) or a quite different type of product (as when Marks & Spencer and Virgin entered the personal pension field) or a radically new process.

Adaptive and generative learning

Surviving as an organisation through time without any major change of direction requires what is called adaptive learning (Senge, 1990). This is perhaps simply another way of describing the 'single-loop learning' approach explained in Chapter 14 (page 243). It means that individuals and groups, acting on feedback, adjust their behaviour continuously in relation to fixed goals, norms and assumptions so that the organisation becomes increasingly efficient and effective at achieving its current goals. Behaviour itself does not fundamentally change but steadily improves in relation to required performance standards.

Creativity and the innovation arising from it, however, require generative learning (Senge, 1990). Here, the very goals, norms and assumptions of the organisation itself must be open to questioning and the possibility of fundamental change. Whether generative learning arises out of adaptive learning, is a quite different process or involves a combination of several kinds of learning – single-loop, double-loop, even triple-loop (Swieringa and Wierdsma, 1992) – is immaterial at this point. What is important is that generative learning can produce three types of transformation in the true sense of that word. Each significantly alters the behaviour of most people in the organisation, as Blumenthal and Haspeslagh (1992) explained:

- *Radical operational improvement* is focused on the complete redesign of business processes and related changes to structure, skills and behaviour across the organisation. 'Business process re-engineering' typifies attempts, often unsuccessful, to achieve this type of transformational change.

- *Strategic transformation* occurs when fundamental changes in strategy result in equally fundamental changes in structure, processes, people and culture. The 1991 reorganisation of the National Health Service (referred to in Chapter 17, where it formed the external context for the clinical directors' programme) was an attempt to achieve this kind of transformation by introducing management and organisational structures new to the NHS and by creating the artificial internal market.

- *Genetic re-engineering* is achieved when top executives apply a holistic management approach which results in the constant renewal of the organisation by anticipating and responding appropriately whenever major changes in the market occur. This kind of transformation was sought by Hydro Polymers, as the case-study in this chapter will show. It is achieved not by a sudden, one-off and usually traumatic change process. It is the result, continuing through the long term, of a series of systemic changes which achieve a 'mesh of the formal and the flexible' (Lorenz, 1992) by tackling formal and informal aspects of the organisation in an integrated and consistent way through time. It involves creating many new structures, processes and behaviours across the organisation which are so profound and wide-ranging in their nature and effects that they can be loosely termed 'genetic' to distinguish them from changes that are more narrowly focused and less durable.

OD: process and interventions
Organisation development (OD) can usefully be mentioned at this point, although it is a specialist subject to be studied in its own right (see especially Beckhard, 1969 and Cummings and Huse, 1989). OD

is a process to improve organisational health and effectiveness, distinguished by its planned and system-wide application of behavioural science knowledge and practices to improve the organisation's ability to assess and solve its problems. Its focus is on the organisation's strategies, structures and processes and on the interpersonal and intergroup problems that inhibit problem-solving and threaten quality of life and productivity in the organisation.

OD can therefore help to facilitate any or all of the three kinds of transformational change that have been identified above – and indeed OD programmes and the appointment of specialist regional OD staff were a significant feature of the 1991 NHS reforms. However, its focus on personal and social needs rather than on technical and rational aspects of the organisation means that any OD intervention would need to be part of a wider strategy if such change is to be fully achieved and sustainable.

Change in organisations

Regarding your own organisation, or one with which you are familiar, identify a major change that is taking place, or has occurred. What type of change is it – continuous or radical? Try to find some information on the methods and processes used to produce the learning that helped to facilitate that change – or that explains it.

LEARNING AND 'TRANSFORMATION'

At this point it is relevant to consider at a more theoretical level the kinds of learning and knowledge that are likely to expand an organisation's capacity for discontinuous change and therefore for radical transformation, when that is needed.

The 'Learning Organisation'

Although the field of organisational learning is not new – indeed one at least of its major academics, Chris Argyris, was famous in management circles as far back as the 1950s – in the past decade it has attracted a resurgence of interest. There are two main triggers here: the high profile achieved by Japanese companies and management techniques and a consequent desire by competitors to understand the source of their ability to learn fast and effectively in the pursuit of innovation; and a growing preoccupation in the strategic management literature with the 'central evolutionary and transformational processes' through which organisations can renew themselves and with the kind of learning that can produce the knowledge that generates new strategic assets (Chakravarthy and Doz, 1992).

This interest has consistently focused itself on the 'learning organisation' – a well-developed subject in some senses, yet in others a curiously unsatisfactory one. It is well developed in terms of the sheer size of its academic and practitioner literature. It is unsatisfactory in terms of the failure thus far of that literature to achieve entirely convincing outcomes either at intellectual or practical levels. Let us look at some of the areas of uncertainty.

Conceptual ambiguities

One of the most widely quoted definitions of the learning organisation is that of Pedler, Burgoyne and Boydell (1991): 'an organisation which facilitates the learning of all its members and continuously transforms itself'.

As Coopey (1995) observed, this is not a definition that lends itself easily to practical implementation or measurement. It typifies the difference in stance between what Argyris and Schon in their masterly text (1996: 180) described as the 'practice-oriented, prescriptive literature of the "learning organization"...and the predominantly skeptical scholarly literature of "organizational learning"'. Too often, for example, it is assumed that the terms 'the learning organisation' and 'organisational learning' are synonymous. They are not. Another false assumption is that organisational learning is the sum of the learning of individuals and groups across the organisation. It is not – many studies (see, for example, Argyris and Schon, 1996) have confirmed that without effective processes and systems linking individual and organisational learning, the one has no necessary counterpart in the other.

Adler and Cole (1993) reported particularly powerful evidence on this point. They compared data on two car manufacturing plants: the Toyota–GM NUMMI plant in California, representing the 'lean production' model favoured in recent years, and Volvo's Uddevalla plant in Sweden, set up to demonstrate and reap the benefit of 'human-centred' ways of organising the labour-intensive production of standardised products typified in the research of earlier US organisational psychologists like Hertzberg (see Chapter 1). They concluded that 'although elements of the Uddevalla approach do indeed promise a higher potential for individual learning, NUMMI is the more effective model for encouraging organizational learning' (ibid: 86). They found that it created both world-class performance and a highly motivating work environment even though its work organisation followed the 'democratic Taylorism' model. At Uddevalla, management had provided a wide range of personal learning opportunities for its employees, focusing especially on team autonomy and decision decentralisation, in the belief that an increase in individual learning would automatically lead to an increase in collective organisational learning. In fact, the researchers came to the conclusion that 'this emphasis on individual learning had no counterpart in organizational learning' (ibid: 92). They found that NUMMI's combination of technical–economic and quality-of-worklife strengths made its production system 'the most appropriate type for relatively repetitive, labour-intensive activities' (ibid).

A further concern is the philosophical base of the learning organisation concept. Coopey (1995) argued convincingly that the notion of a learning organisation tends largely to ignore issues of who controls that organisation and the uses to which new learning will be put. In his view, the extent to which the 'learning organisation' offers a genuinely new approach to management and the organisation of people and their work is questionable. To indicate why, he asked the question, 'Who decides that this will become a learning organisation?' He added the supplementary questions, 'Why? And who then is most likely to control and gain increased power from the new learning that such an organisation will presumably achieve?' Too often, he proposed, the answers are likely to be 'management' rather than all organisational members collectively. For him, the traditional scientific management approach still dominates in Western organisations. Others fear the same:

> Even where organisations espouse an ED approach, all too often sufficient amounts of the machine ideal remain in place, and hidden from view, to present an effective and powerful barrier to organisational learning.
>
> (Bratton and Gold, 1994: 228)

A sense of proportion must be retained here. In organisations like Hydro Polymers one does not see any espoused attempt to become 'a learning organisation' or any signs of calculated exploitation of people's improved learning ability. What is evident instead is a genuine determination to develop a culture and system where people are encouraged to think as widely as they can in order to stimulate individual growth and ensure the company's long-term survival.

Still, the possession of knowledge does bring issues of power into play, and we can perhaps see the real nub of the matter here by considering the approach of 'action learning'. It has been hailed as 'a model of the learning organisation' (Morris, 1991). Whatever doubts there may be about that comparison (see Harrison, 1996), action learning is widely believed to lead to a radical questioning process that develops an openness to new experiences – 'shaking the cage' of entrenched attitudes and mindsets. However, on the evidence it is questionable how far that cage can actually be shaken beyond limits guarded by the organisation's senior levels. One commentator foresaw difficulties for members or facilitators of action learning sets when the questioning and proposed action began to challenge corporate norms and the dominating managerial logic: 'As action learning is by definition on-line there may be a limit to how much experimentation one is willing to undertake when real risks are at stake' (Raelin, 1994: 305). In a similar way there are unresolved issues about the uses to which a 'learning organisation' can be put by those who retain their old power base in that organisation.

However, like the concept of action learning so too the notion of the 'learning organisation' remains persuasive because of its rationality, human attractiveness and presumed potential to aid organisational effectiveness and advancement (see, for example, Senge, 1990; Mills and Friesen, 1992). The emphasis is on openness, support, a climate of trust and challenge, learning from reflection and experience, and a focus on a commitment to the learning that can resolve hitherto intractable organisational problems.

Practical ambiguities

Here again, though, the operational reality of the 'learning organisation', like action learning, is more complex. That reality at the formal level must be about developing the business processes and developmental approaches that will mesh together in ways conducive to learning and the production and utilisation of organisationally useful knowledge. At the more informal level it must also be about creating a 'rich landscape' (Kessels, 1996) of learning and development possibilities. In such a landscape people must be able to wander relatively free of managerial constraint, so that intuitions and spontaneous insights as well as more rationally based learning can, with reflection, debate and experimentation, produce a wealth of valuable knowledge. Such a skilful balance between formal systems and informal features presupposes an approach to the knowledge development and human relationships in an organisation that does not fit easily with the lack of expertise and awareness about HRD and learning that organisational research repeatedly shows to prevail.

There is a dissonance, too, between the rational and prescriptive framework of guidelines, questionnaire surveys and self-checks that typify the practitioner-oriented literature of the 'learning organisation' and the uncertainties that actually surround the processes of individual and collective learning. A rational model of the 'learning organisation' will undoubtedly encourage adaptive learning, but it is questionable whether the generative learning that leads to radical innovation and change is of the same order and therefore is equally likely to emerge. This point has been made earlier and it is a complex one (see Swieringa and Wierdsma, 1992; Argyris and Schon, 1996). Suffice it to observe here that commentators such as Tosey (1993: 188), influenced by the seminal work of Bateson (1973, 1979), see radical change in mindsets 'emerging spontaneously rather than by being caused in a direct, linear way' and as being embedded in the workings of emotions and personality as much as, if not more than, in reasoning.

Although it is limiting to view strategic change as an entirely rationally based activity, well-known UK exponents of the learning organisation such as Morris (1991) and Pedler and Boutall (1992) do appear to regard such change as essentially to do with rational and purposive activity. Reg Revans (1971), himself another influential name in the field not just of 'action learning' but also of learning organisations, when stressing the importance of companies' being committed to learning put his emphasis on the finding of better ways of tackling existing problems and of rationally reorganising work. It may well be that the kind of 'learning organisation' most typically encountered in the practitioner-oriented literature would in reality be more likely to reinforce than challenge dominant managerial logics. That matters little where what is needed is continuous learning of a kind that will lead to an improved ability in 'doing the knitting'. It is a dangerous weakness if what is needed is the discontinuous learning that produces transformational change.

Recently, there has been a 'reformulation' of the learning organisation model, accompanied by a robust rejection by some of the originators of popular theory that the concept or the practice is in decline (Burgoyne, 1999, 1999a). Unipart University has been used as a model of this new approach to the 'learning organisation' (Miller and Stewart, 1999), defined as one in which:

- 'learning and business strategy are closely linked

- the organisation consciously learns from business opportunities and threats

- individuals groups and the whole organisation are not only learning, but continually learning how to learn

- information systems and technology serve to support learning rather than to control it

- there are well-developed processes for defining, creating, capturing, sharing and acting on knowledge

- these various systems and dimensions are balanced and managed as a whole' (*ibid*: 43).

Yet this renewed attempt to reduce to guides, workbooks and prescriptions complex theoretical territory, where there is still no consensus on the fundamental concepts and issues, does not ultimately convince. For those like Critten (1999), for whom Burgoyne's proposal that the learning organisation formula needs to follow a similar trajectory to total quality management 'puts it right back into another box', it is now time to let the whole concept go.

Conclusion

In summary, much is written on 'learning organisations' but there are inconsistencies and areas of ambiguity. It has yet to become clear quite how such organisations come into existence, whether in fact they do so, what is or could be their specific impact on organisational capabilities, and how they can be managed. It is unclear whether they can ever represent more than an ideal state to which all should aspire.

Evaluating 'learning organisation' theory

Read the two articles just referred to – by Burgoyne (1999) and by Miller and Stewart (1999) – and then read Critten's letter. How far do you agree or disagree with the points made by Critten – and why?

MANAGING LEARNING AND KNOWLEDGE DEVELOPMENT

At this point, it is relevant to consider the knowledge process: how knowledge, as an outcome of learning, can be developed in an organisation, and the implications for organisational learning and knowledge productivity.

The knowledge process
The development of knowledge is repeatedly claimed to be an essential determinant of organisational profitability (Senge, 1990; Huber, 1991; Nonaka, 1994; McGrath, MacMillan and

Venkataraman, 1995: 264). It is, however, less easy to determine how that can be done, since knowledge develops in different ways in individuals and in organisations according to processes and variables that are only imperfectly understood.

It is helpful first to gain some simple insights into the knowledge-development process by distinguishing between data, information and knowledge itself.

Knowledge has been defined as 'a person's range of information' or the sum of what they know and understand (Allen, 1990). This draws attention to knowledge as the end result of some process to do with collecting or unconsciously absorbing pieces of information, and processing them internally in ways unique to each individual – because of the intervention in that process of factors such as intellectual capacity, previous knowledge, experience and values, customary ways of perceiving and treating information, and a range of social and emotional variables. Ultimately, either old knowledge is confirmed or new knowledge emerges.

Information has indeed been defined as 'items of knowledge' (Allen, 1990). The possession of new information therefore can lead to challenging the existing knowledge that others possess and (as already described) adding to or changing the knowledge we ourselves hold. Yet the availability of new information does not inevitably change people's current knowledge. First, information may be disregarded, discounted, or simply not noticed. Second, the way in which various pieces of information are put together and construed will make a difference to the kind of knowledge people actually gain. Three committees – as an example – will almost certainly arrive at rather different conclusions on any matter put before them (a form of 'knowledge'), even though they may be given identical information on which to base their decision. This is partly because their membership profiles are significantly different by reference to their values, levels and kinds of intelligence, perspectives, existing knowledge and customary ways of making sense of the kind of information now before them. If each committee has to make a decision on an issue about which its members feel strongly, the powerful emotions that will also then come into play will tend to result in even wider differences in conclusions and decisions.

Data have been defined as 'known facts or things used as the basis for inference or reckoning' (Allen, 1990). Information is formed as the result of a process of selecting and assembling data in a particular pattern. Two researchers, each using the same database, can come to very different conclusions depending on which data they select or reject, and on their own mindsets, perceptions, expectations and wants related to that data.

Another term to explain is 'knowledge connectivity'. By that is meant those processes, routines and systems that ensure transfer of information and knowledge from individuals and small groups to the organisation as a whole in order to achieve collective learning (von Krogh, Roos and Slocum, 1994). Ways of transferring knowledge into and across the organisation so that it influences strategic decisions must be planned, because neither individual nor group learning necessarily leads to organisational learning.

In providing all these definitions I have of course greatly simplified – and therefore inevitably distorted – a profoundly complicated and little-understood process. The development and management of knowledge is a subject that has long exercised minds in a number of fields – organisation theory, systems thinking, human resource management and development, the psychology of learning, philosophy and anthropology to name only the most obvious. No consensus has been reached on how knowledge does in fact form, grow and change; or on the exact nature of the process linking data, information and knowledge; or on the relationship between individual, group and collective learning and how it can or does affect the knowledge base of an organisation, its competitive capability, its performance or its advancement.

Knowledge management

It is essential at this stage, when we are considering how to develop strategically valuable knowledge, to consider also how that knowledge should be managed. To do so requires a distinction to be made between explicit knowledge and that which is tacit.

Explicit knowledge is that which has been articulated and 'codified' – for example, in procedures, protocols, guidelines, checklists, reports, memoranda, files and training courses – or, as we shall see below, expressed in patents and other legally protected formulae. Because it is or can be articulated, it can easily be observed, learned, copied or poached. When strategically valuable knowledge is explicit, it is therefore vulnerable.

Tacit knowledge has the highest potential value for an organisation seeking competitive advantage because it is embedded deep in the individual or collective subconscious, expressing itself in habitual or intuitive ways of doing things that are exercised without conscious thought or effort (Nonaka, 1991: 102). This kind of knowledge is hard to understand, to copy or to poach, and is therefore more likely than explicit knowledge to be the source of the organisation's most distinctive competencies.

When tacit and new explicit knowledge interact or are made to do so, tacit knowledge can expand. Innovation occurs as expanded tacit knowledge becomes embodied in new products, services and strategies. There are many examples to illustrate the role of tacit knowledge in developing an innovative organisation. These are better read directly in the text or articles in which they first appeared than reproduced in edited form here. Although the theory of tacit knowledge is often thought to derive from the work of Nonaka and therefore to be Japanese in origin, in fact it stems mainly from the writings of the Hungarian-born social philosopher Michael Polanyi (1958, 1966), who spent much of his working life in England. However, of all the academics now writing in the field it is Nonaka who has become the leading exponent, producing some of the most compelling illustrative case-studies (1991, 1994; Nonaka and

Takeuchi, 1995) in order to explore the ways in which 'knowledge-creating companies' develop.

The management of knowledge is a complex area of research and in this section only generalised guidelines can be suggested. What should by now be clear, however, is that the way in which knowledge is managed in an organisation should largely be determined by its type and uniqueness. As Hall (1996) pointed out, some codified, explicit knowledge is of such value to the organisation that it has to be managed as a legal entity, often with property rights (for example, patents, copyright and licences). Other codified knowledge may be so sensitive that access to it has to be restricted. Other codified knowledge again may be related to particular jobs, positions, tasks or functions, and so may call for training in order that it can result in improved efficiency or effectiveness.

Tacit, implicit knowledge, on the other hand, 'will be enhanced most effectively by a process of socialisation' (Hall, 1996: 6) – and this is where the culture of an organisation has particular significance. If the climate in the workplace encourages and facilitates teamwork, informal meetings and discussions, exchanges of views and observations of internal 'best practice', then, as Nonaka's (1991) account illustrates, it is likely to result in tacit knowledge's being shared widely among organisational members without its having to be made explicit. Explicit knowledge is mobile and therefore vulnerable. When uniquely valuable tacit knowledge is embedded in a number of people rather than a few, it is less likely to become explicit or vulnerable to poaching.

In a valuable book, Nancy Dixon (2000) proposed five types of transfer methods when managing knowledge, seeing the choice of method as needing to be determined by assessing three factors:

• whether the task in which the knowledge is used is routine or non-routine

• whether the knowledge related to it is tacit or explicit

• the degree of similarity between originator and receiver of the knowledge.

She described these transfer methods as:

• *serial transfer* – where a team performs a task and then repeats the task, but in a different context – an example of relearning, and a process in which tacit knowledge tends to be made explicit by the team concerned

• *near transfer* – where knowledge is transferred 'from one team to another doing a similar task, in a similar context, in a different location': typically, the knowledge is explicit and the task is routine

• *far transfer* – where 'knowledge about a non-routine task which affects a specific part of the operation is transferred between two teams' and will tend to involve more tacit than explicit knowledge – 'specialised, critical knowledge'

• *strategic transfer* – where 'very complex knowledge...is transferred between two teams that may be separated by both time and space', this transferred knowledge being both tacit and explicit and having an effect 'on large parts of the system'

• *expert transfer* – involving the transfer of explicit knowledge about a task that tends to be non-routine (Dixon, 2000a: 38–9).

Managing knowledge

Read Dixon's article (2000a). Then identify in your own organisation some examples of types of knowledge that need to be shared, and assess what kind of transfer method should be used for each type – using the article to help you to decide.

Managing the knowledge-productive organisation

Five principles can now be suggested about the knowledge process in organisations. They emerge from much of the research that has been done in the field – although, again, we must appreciate that there is no final consensus on any of these issues: to that extent I am being selective in the information that has most influenced my own thinking.

• *There is a need for a powerful and cohering vision of the organisation to be communicated and maintained* across the workforce in order to promote awareness of the need for strategic thinking at all levels. We call such a vision 'cohering' because it brings people, their knowledge and ideas together in a common search for whatever will drive the organisation forward. Such a vision will direct attention to the need to obtain from all sources information relevant to the advancement of the business, and to import, share and use that information in ways that will ensure its ultimate impact on the profitability of that business.

• *Organisations seeking to be innovative will probably benefit most from a vision that is relatively open-ended and ambiguous.* The ambiguity should encourage a search for a wide rather than a narrow range of strategic options, promote lateral thinking and orient the knowledge-creating activities of employees. 'Ambiguity can prove extremely useful as a source of alternative meanings . . . new knowledge is born in chaos' (Nonaka, 1991: 103). Such organisations will also need to ensure that their structures and business processes can support both operating and innovatory activity.

• *Within the framework of vision and goals, frequent dialogue and conversations are major facilitators of organisational learning* (Argyris, 1977: 115–24). In Shell, for example, de Geus (1996: 94) explained how planning is a crucial learning process 'because people change their own mental models and build up a joint model as they talk'. Talking, in formal and informal contexts, can help to create common ways of thinking and perceiving among employees and to develop a shared language and understanding – knowledge – about a range of major organisational issues and business processes.

There should therefore be networks, routines and processes within and between organisations that can encourage and enable organisational members to discuss their observations, make distinctions and causal associations, and exchange insights relating to information about and views on their organisation and its business environment. Such knowledge structures and connectors are essential to transfer tacit as well as explicit knowledge and to promote the development of new knowledge through time (Bohn, 1994: 62; von Krogh, Roos and Slocum, 1994: 61–4).

- *For new tacit and explicit knowledge to be developed, people should be continuously challenged to re-examine what they take for granted.* Such reflection 'is always necessary in the knowledge-creating company, but ... is especially essential during times of crisis or breakdown when a company's traditional categories of knowledge no longer work' (Nonaka, 1991: 103). Challenging behaviour like this requires a positive social climate of openness, support and trust, and time for experimentation, dynamism and humour (Nonaka, 1991; Nevis, diBella and Gould, 1995: 80–81; Boisot, Griffiths and Moles, 1995).

- *Any more prescriptive approach to learning and its outcomes may be counter-productive.* What is essential is a conducive learning climate, and a 'rich landscape' of educational and developmental opportunity available for organisational members, together with the organisational framework and business processes to ensure that information can flow into and through the organisation in ways that encourage the emergence of strategically valuable knowledge. Although there must be a sufficiently differentiated structure to support experimentation and innovation as well as operational activity, the emphasis should not be on management systems to control learning itself. Rather, there should be a search for 'new ways to encourage people to think creatively and feed their thoughts back into the organisation' (Russell and Parsons, 1996: 32) and help to ensure the skills needed to manage the projects that arise from that creativity.

With the right kinds of information and infrastructure, and with a powerful and shared vision of the business, the belief of such commentators is that people will organise themselves in ways that will ensure that their learning brings beneficial outcomes for the business and increases their own sense of self-worth.

Case-study: Hydro Polymers, Aycliffe, Co. Durham 1982–97 (with acknowledgements to the company and to Ennew and Ford, 1990)

History and context
Between 1946 and 1963 Bakelite Ltd, a US company well established in the UK, carried out chemical processing at a site in Newton Aycliffe, Co. Durham. After various changes in corporate structure, Norsk Hydro, Norway's largest industrial company, purchased the PVC Resin and Compound Facility at Aycliffe in 1982, merging vinyl production with their existing loss-making Vinatex plants at three other sites in the UK to form Norsk Hydro Polymers Ltd (NHPL).

In 1982 the Aycliffe plant was characterised by traditional restrictive working practices and attitudes, and a low-morale workforce. It compared badly in terms of both productivity and product quality with competitors, many of whom were already using sophisticated microprocessor production control techniques. In 1983 new strategic aims were announced for NHPL in order to enable it to improve its position in an increasingly competitive market. Flexible working practices and a larger investment programme were seen as essential to prevent further decline in performance.

In 1984 the company, at that time 90 per cent unionised, was restructured following a negotiated agreement on radical changes in working practices and payment systems. A Statement of Intent was issued, with goals of harmonisation of terms and conditions (including sick pay), improved flexibility in the workforce, a regular weekly wage for all and the removal of bonus schemes. Job losses were unavoidable but most were achieved by natural wastage and voluntary redundancy.

1985–97: the drive for education, training and competency

In 1985 a drive started to improve the educational and competency base of the company in order to enhance its capacity, as well as capability, for learning and change. A £6 million investment programme enabled its employees to commence training courses to broaden their skills and raise their level of educational attainment. The aim was training to standards and for competence.

Thereafter, the aim consistently remained to educate, not just train, the workforce in order to create a 'thinking' culture – explained by senior company personnel as one in which everyone thinks strategically, looking out into the environment for new challenges and ideas, and thinking for the future as well as for immediate improvements. People at Hydro Polymers are not paid to learn – there are no bonuses or special payments for attaining qualifications – but they are encouraged to do so both in the nature of the work that they do and in the opportunities offered for self-learning. Open learning is a major part of the culture, and there is access to the Open College, Open University (OU) and MBA courses (there are on-site tutorials for OU students). The mentoring process is an important one. Everyone has a self-development plan. The level of vocational qualification attainment is high.

The style at Hydro Polymers had fundamentally changed by 1997. It had become one of participative dialogue, not of the confrontational behaviour that in the early 1980s so divided management from the rest of the workforce. Close relationships were built too with suppliers and local firms, involving them in various training and team events. A project-based organisation structure facilitated and also reinforced this style. Figure 10 shows the structure of the continuous improvement process at Hydro Polymers, designed to achieve integration between training, steering of projects, project management, strategic planning, benchmarking and customer-surveying.

Figure 10 Continuous improvement process at Hydro Polymers, 1997 (with acknowledgements to Steve Cleary, total quality co-ordinator)

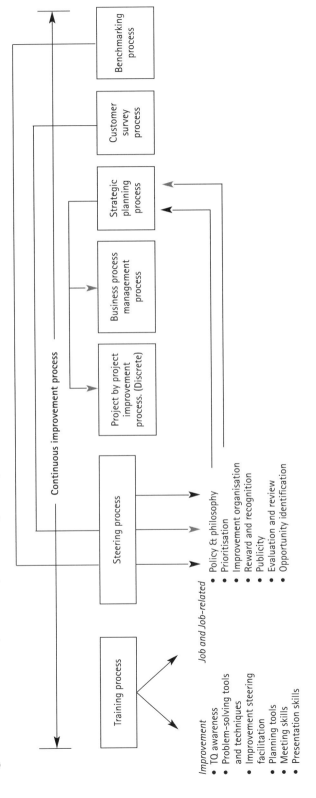

Case-study: Collective learning

The company relied on continuous improvement, accelerated learning and innovation to build a secure future for the business and its people. There was no suggestion scheme because it was thought to be divisive in a situation where the aim is to achieve teamwork, collective learning and shared commitment to new ideas. Financial rewards for new ideas were tried out for teams, and there is a small element of this still (mainly in the form of three annual prizes for teams who have produced the most outstanding projects, families also sharing in the awards), but it made far less impact than other forms of recognition now given regularly to successful projects. These included features in the company newsletter, presentation of projects to top management by those responsible for running them, Christmas hampers and gifts from Norway (more valued than the former annual bonus of, on average, £300, even though the cost was much less), and celebratory events in which the local community was involved.

The strategic role of middle management

Once the company's structure had been flattened, there could not be any 'ladder of success' (a term used by a senior executive), so there had to be other motivators. Money was not used for this purpose: basic pay was good, and attracted a high calibre of recruit to work for the company. The motivation was intended to be provided by the workplace environment. It was one in which people felt that they were fulfilling a valued role and that they were a crucial part of the company's outstanding success.

The supervisors had a key role. They drove the quality programme and they were the team leaders. Competent people at any level had the opportunity to take on new roles, and as a result of this many managers were now more involved in strategic planning for the two or three years ahead. Strategic planning at Hydro Polymers had acquired a specific meaning – about obtaining information from a wide variety of sources and generating a wide range of options, systematically analysing them, and doing all this with a longer- rather than shorter-term perspective.

1997: Outcomes

By 1997 the culture of training, learning and involvement seemed well embedded at Hydro Polymers. It had become accepted that the person doing the job was the one with most knowledge about it; all employees were able to be involved in what happened in their plant, the processes and the business; they all held responsibility for change and were trained to be aware of the need for quality throughout all their work.

By many quantifiable measures, striking improvements had continued to be made through the projects introduced across the business, saving more than £5 million in five years, helping the company to remain profitable and building security for employees. In 1995–96 alone, 57 new projects were introduced and 55 completed, with savings of £712,407 achieved. Business processes were understood and were being steadily improved on by the workforce. Hydro Polymers, like

Cummins Engine Co. at Darlington, was a company that was 'in it for the long haul'. Thus far it had not only survived – it had advanced.

It may be argued that project management of the kind that helped to lead this advance is likely to produce only continuous improvement, not the real innovation that generates discontinuous change – that is to say, change of a quite different kind from any experienced in the past (Chesbrough and Teece, 1996: 67). On the other hand, there is much evidence to indicate that the sustained and wide-ranging changes that took place at Hydro Polymers for over 13 years fall into the category of 'genetic re-engineering' – change of the fundamental kind most likely to develop capacity for radical innovation. The landscape of corporate learning in a company like this has become so rich and its key internal capabilities so well developed that the company's capacity to advance seems unarguable.

FOCUS FOR HRD

What role can HRD have to play in the territory of learning and knowledge that we have been surveying in this chapter? At the least, HRD professionals should be informed about the issues discussed here. They should be able to advise and propose on initiatives which, in straightforward and feasible ways, can help to develop, share and utilise learning and knowledge that will aid the organisation in its future progress. They should work with others active in the field of information dissemination and management – notably IT specialists – in order to ensure that learning is harnessed in appropriate ways to new technology (see Chapter 12) and that the potential benefits here are not undermined by lack of understanding, skills and confidence in the workforce.

There are three other focal points that can be suggested for HRD.

1 Focus on the key capabilities of the organisation
HRD staff can help the organisation to select, train and develop individuals and teams in order to improve the resource-based and organisational capabilities of the firm. They should also work with the organisation to generate the collective, organisational learning – and learning abilities – that will continuously improve the firm's strategic capability. They should develop a climate of awareness and a shared language in the organisation to describe strategic capability and to stimulate ideas about the ways in which it can be improved.

Table 14 below shows how HRD can be built into the business by focusing on the development of the organisation's key capabilities as we described them in Chapter 21.

2 Focus on flexibility and innovation
This will require a strong base of education and training, together with appropriate employee resource policies and systems related to selection, deployment, conditions and rewards, flexibility and disengagement. The Hydro Polymers study provides an example of this: the company was adamant that the accelerated achievement after 1990 had been made possible only by the new educational, competency and attitudinal base produced by the previous six years of

Table 14 Building HRD into the business

Strategic level	HRD's strategic focus is on:	HRD must:	Crucial processes for HRD:	HRD specialist/manager needs to:
1 Corporate	• formulating HRD mission, goals and strategy to achieve corporate goals • influencing and developing strategic and organisational capability	• 'fit' with wider HR strategy • be aligned with corporate strategy • help to secure appropriate balance between corporate goals for survival and for advancement • produce HRD strategy that is capable of implementation at Level 2	• collaboratively developing mission and goals for HRD • strategic planning and thinking • influencing key stakeholders	• have board-level position/access and skills • be pro-active as well as reactive • have deep knowledge of competitive environment • fully understand the value chain and strategic assets of the business • speak the language and logic of the business
2 Business unit/ managerial	• developing HRD policies and systems in line with strategic needs of the business unit • ensuring achievement of business targets • influencing and developing strategic, organisational and resource-based capability	• 'fit' with wider HR policies and systems • be aligned with business unit policy • have a clear plan within the overall business plan, with agreed evaluation measures • ensure feedback on policies to Level 1	• working with HR and business unit managers to produce policies and plans for acquisition, retention, growth/downsizing of workforce • developing key performance indicators • strategic thinking and business planning	• have strategic alliances with line managers and others • have collaborative relationships with other HR specialists • have deep knowledge of competitive environment of company and of business unit • fully understand how strategic assets can be developed • speak the language and logic of the business unit
3 Operational	• ensuring individual and team performance targets are met • improving acquisition, quality and motivation of people for the business.	• 'fit' between needs of the business and needs and aspirations of people • ensure HRD activities are expertly carried out and appropriately evaluated • ensure feedback of outcomes to Level 2.	• working with teams and individuals to implement business plans for training, appraisal, personal development planning to achieve targets and improve core competences and capabilities.	• have effective working relations with internal and external stakeholders • have effective and efficient systems and procedures • have deep knowledge of culture of the workforce • be expert and continuously self-developing.

steady investment in education, training and development of the workforce.

Strategic learning occurs when existing goals and processes are modified to match perceived changes in the external environment. Relying on natural learning processes in the organisation is not enough to ensure this will happen, since those processes tend to be myopic, concentrating on existing strategic goals and on tasks in hand. As we have already seen, they are also influenced by the dominant managerial logic in the organisation. It is rare for that logic to be questioned, let alone changed, without some traumatic event or intervention taking place, and any change must be backed up by the structure, systems and HR policies that ensure it stays in place and is maintained through time.

Again, our case-study provides an illustration of these points. It has shown how the new ownership of Hydro Polymers in 1982 led to a change in strategic direction – the 'traumatic event' that enabled the previous dominant managerial logic to be overturned; how a three-fold thrust of education and training, flexibility and technological innovation had to be established and then sustained in order to ensure the durability of that change in direction; and how further 'traumatic events' around 1990 in the external environment led to a dramatic acceleration in learning, capability and performance of the company.

3 Focus on the stimulation and sharing of knowledge
This involves helping people to develop the skills and knowledge to work in innovative ways over the long term, with the support of a structure differentiated enough to enable both operating and innovative activities to be pursued without the one unduly dominating the other. For example, a system of project management in which there is an allowance for some projects to be dropped if, after initial work and experimentation, they do not prove as useful or relevant as expected, can be part of the innovative structure of the organisation. However, it must run in parallel, or be effectively linked, with an operating structure that ensures that the daily work of the organisation is also performed effectively.

Applying the theory to organisational practice

- Read back through this chapter. Then also read 'System error' by Harry Scarbrough in *People Management*, 8 April 1999.

- Then consider your own organisation, or one with which you are familiar. Identify some ways in which you see knowledge being developed, shared and put to valuable use in the organisation. Analyse how this is being done, and relate your analysis back to the theory you have been learning thus far.

SOME GENERAL PRINCIPLES

To draw many threads together, I return to the Hydro Polymers case-study as an example that illustrates the practical meaning of the term 'a knowledge-productive organisation'.

- In 1982 the company just taken over by Norsk Hydro was a poorly performing business, characterised at the human level by backward-looking conflictual styles of behaviour and an ignorance of how to improve productivity and market position. There were no signs in the system of attempts to develop the knowledge base of the firm or its individuals, or even of an awareness that such development was important for the future of the company. The weak educational and competency base of the workforce and the many human and material barriers to flexible working and the sharing of skills, knowledge and ideas meant that there was little capacity, motivation or ability to do so in any case. It is therefore unsurprising that the company was barely surviving and could not advance.

- The new vision, strategic goals and drivers for change that were established by the new management in the company between 1982 and 1984 ensured – among much else – that it became essential for everyone in the organisation to become more informed about the business and its performance and growth. New knowledge was imported and disseminated through processes of selection, training, improved production technology and structural change.

- Developing the intellectual potential and the competency levels of employees while at the same time giving them clear goals, a compelling vision, full information about the business and its competitive position and systems and procedures for the generation and application of new ideas – all this, taken together, resulted in an upheaval and transformation in the firm's knowledge base from 1984 onwards.

- The main outcomes of that transformation in the short term were improvements across a wide range of performance indicators and a significant change in the culture of the workplace and in the style of behaviour and interactions at every level. Individuals acquired more marketable skills, experience and qualifications and became more motivated as their work and roles became more stimulating and responsible.

- In the longer term the changed knowledge base of the organisation, interacting with other changes, enabled the greatly accelerated pace of learning and improvement that followed the new challenges emerging in 1989–90. Those challenges themselves were responded to with confidence by the workforce, rather than with the introverted and negative forms of behaviour that had been prevalent in the company up to 1982.

An organisation whose climate and systems encourage and facilitate the development of knowledge that is strategically valuable has been called a 'knowledge-productive' organisation (Kessels, 1996: 10). The term focuses not so much on learning as a process but on the development by whatever means of knowledge that enables an organisation to survive and to advance as necessary in its environment. If top management begins to create the kind of changed climate and sense of purpose that was achieved at Hydro Polymers through its new strategic direction and three-fold thrust from 1984 onwards, it is likely that people will increasingly seek and use new knowledge in order to drive the business forward. This is because the development of knowledge has been signposted, facilitated and rewarded as an essential organisational task, resulting in the new ways of understanding business issues, new ideas and new solutions that will enable the organisation and its people to find a new and more hopeful future.

CONCLUSION

Having read this chapter and completed its reviews and self-checks, you should now:

- understand the difference between organisational survival and advancement

- appreciate ways in which HRD can link to collective learning and the development and sharing of knowledge in an organisation

- understand the relationship between 'knowledge productivity' and an organisation's ability to move forward in its environment.

In order to achieve the learning objectives of this chapter, the difference between organisational survival and advancement has been explained in the context of profitability – the ability of an enterprise to achieve a rate of economic return sufficient to satisfy key stakeholders and to enable investment for the long-term future. HRD's potential contribution to profitability has been identified by reference to the key capabilities of an organisation, and illustrated in a major real-life case-study.

Theories of the learning organisation, organisational learning and the growth of knowledge have been outlined and evaluated, and their practical implications discussed. Finally, principles have been suggested to underpin the management and development of learning and knowledge. They focus on the meaning and importance of knowledge productivity for organisations seeking to advance in their environment, and they bring together the key themes of this final chapter.

This book has involved a long journey across the corporate landscape of learning, development and knowledge. Sometimes that landscape has seemed barren, sometimes rich, and often the way ahead has seemed uncertain. Those harmonies so hopefully sought at the start remain not quite as nebulous, yet still they have not fully emerged. If that is a disappointment, it should also be a stimulus.

It is timely, then, to recall the quotation from Franklin Bobbitt that appeared in Chapter 1 (page 7). It must not become an epitaph for HRD practitioners and managers, for if it does, HRD itself has no likelihood of attaining strategic status, nor will it deserve to do so. It will have no useful or uniquely valuable outcomes either for the organisation or for those dependent on its survival and advancement for their own:

> We have aimed at a vague culture, an ill-defined discipline...an unparticularized social efficiency...

To read one's epitaph may prove a doubtful privilege, but it can stimulate transformational change, so the last message should after all be one of hope, like Vaughan the alchemist with whom this journey also started out, 'looking towards the west wind and hearing secret harmonies' ...

USEFUL READING

NONAKA I. *and* TAKEUCHI H. (1995) *The Knowledge-Creating Company.* Oxford, Oxford University Press.

SCARBROUGH H. *and* SWAN J. (eds) (1999) *Case Studies in Knowledge Management.* London, Institute of Personnel and Development.

References

ABBOTT B. (1994) 'Training strategies in small service sector firms: employer and employee perspectives'. *Human Resource Management Journal*. Vol. 4, 2. pp70–87.

ADLER P. S. *and* COLE R. E. (1993) 'Designed for learning: a tale of two auto plants'. *Sloan Management Review*. Vol. 34, 3. pp85–94.

AIKEN O. (1996) 'Be prepared for a data remember'. *People Management*. Vol. 2, 11. pp38–40.

AIKIN O. (1999) 'The right to learn'. *People Management*. Vol. 5, 13. p23.

ALLEN R. E. (1990) *The Concise Oxford Dictionary of Current English*. 8th edn. Oxford, Clarendon Press.

ALVAREZ J. L. (1996) 'Are we asking too much of managers?' *Financial Times*. 12 July. p13.

AMIT R. *and* SCHOEMAKER J. H. (1993) 'Strategic assets and organizational rent'. *Strategic Management Journal*. Vol. 14, 1. pp33–46.

ANNETT J., DUNCAN K. D., STAMMERS R. B. *and* GRAY M. J. (1979) *Task Analysis: Department of Employment and Productivity Training Information Paper, No. 6*. London, HMSO; reprinted Sheffield, Department of Employment.

ANSOFF H. I. *and* SULLIVAN P. A. (1993) 'Optimizing profitability in turbulent environments: a formula for strategic success'. *Long Range Planning*. Vol. 26, 5. pp11–23.

ANTHONY P. (1994) *Managing Culture*. Buckingham, Open University Press.

ARGYRIS C. (1957) *Personality and Organization*. New York, Harper and Row.

ARGYRIS C. (1977) 'Double loop learning in organizations'. *Harvard Business Review*. September–October. pp115–24.

ARGYRIS C. (1982) *Reasoning, Learning and Action*. San Francisco, CA, Jossey-Bass.

ARGYRIS C. (1996) 'Skilled incompetence', in K. Starkey (ed.), *How Organizations Learn*. London, International Thomson Business Press, pp82–91.

ARGYRIS C. *and* SCHON D. A. (1978) *Organizational Learning: A theory of Action Perspective*. Reading, MA, Addison Wesley.

ARGYRIS C. *and* SCHON D. A. (1996) *Organizational Learning II: Theory, method and practice*. New York, Addison Wesley.

ARKIN A. (1991) 'A springboard to equal opportunities'. *Personnel Management*. Vol. 23, 2. pp57–8.

ARKIN A. (1995) 'Breaking down skills barriers'. *People Management*. Vol. 1, 3. pp34–5.

ARKIN A. (1995a) 'More than just a cosmetic change'. *People Management*. Vol. 1, 8. pp30–31.

ARKIN A. (1995b) 'Training caters for special needs'. *People Management*. Vol. 1, 16. pp32–3.

ARMSTRONG M. (1987) 'Human resource management: a case of the emperor's new clothes?' *Personnel Management*. Vol. 19, 8. pp30–35.

ARMSTRONG M. (1996) *Employee Reward*. London, Institute of Personnel and Development.

ARMSTRONG M. *and* BARON A. (1998) *Performance Management: The new realities*. London: Institute of Personnel and Development.

AUTHERS J. (1994) 'Hard test at end of a crash course'. *Financial Times*. 24 August.

AUTHERS J. *and* WOOD L. (1993) 'Little knowledge is a dangerous thing'. *Financial Times*. 15 December.

BADARACCO J. L. (1991) *Knowledge Link: How firms compete through strategic alliances*. Boston, MA, Harvard Business School Press.

BALLS E. *and* GOODHART D. (1994) 'Can Europe compete? The high price of social cohesion'. *Financial Times*. 28 February. p11.

BARNEY J. (1991) 'Firm resources and sustained competitive advantage'. *Journal of Management*. Vol. 17. pp99–120.

BASS B. M. *and* VAUGHAN J. A. (1967) *Training in Industry: The management of learning*. London, Tavistock Publications.

BATCHELOR C. (1992) 'Management: the growing business'. *Financial Times*. 8 December. p9.

BATCHELOR J., DONNELLY R. *and* MORRIS D. (1995) 'Learning networks within supply chains'. *Working paper, Coventry Business School*. Coventry, Coventry University, Priory Street, Coventry, CVI 5FB.

BATES D. L. *and* DILLARD J. E. JNR (1993) 'Generating strategic thinking through multi-level teams'. *Long Range Planning*. Vol. 26, 5. pp103–10.

BATESON G. (1973) *Steps to an Ecology of Mind*. London, Paladin, Granada.

BATESON G. (1979) *Mind and Nature*. Glasgow, Fontana/Collins.

BAUD D. C. *and* SCANLAN G. (1995) 'Strategic control through core competencies'. *Long Range Planning*. Vol. 28, 2. pp102–14.

BEAUMONT G. (1996) 'Review of 100 NVQs and SVQs'. *A Report submitted to the Department for Education and Employment*. 25, Albion Road, Chesterfield, S40 IBR (Freepost SF10305), Beaumont.

BECKER G. (1975) *Human Capital: A theoretical and empirical analysis with special reference to education*. 2nd edn. New York, Columbia University Press.

BECKET M. (1996) 'Small business packs statistical punch'. *Daily Telegraph Business Monitor section*. 12 August. p27.

BECKHARD R. (1969) *Organization Development: Strategies and models*. Reading, Addison Wesley.

BEE F. (2000) 'How to evaluate training'. *People Management*. Vol. 6, 6. pp42–3.

BEE F. *and* BEE R. (1994) *Training Needs Analysis and Evaluation*. London, Institute of Personnel and Development.

BEE F. *and* FARMER P. (1995) 'HR projects on the right track'. *People Management*. Vol. 1, 16. pp28–30.

BELBIN R. M. (1964) *Training the Adult Worker*. London, HMSO.

BELBIN R. M. (1981) *Management Teams: Why they succeed or fail*. London, Heinemann.

BENTLEY T. (1990) *The Business of Training: Achieving success in changing world markets*. Maidenhead, McGraw-Hill.

BLUMENTHAL B. *and* HASPESLAGH P. (1992) 'Corporate transformation: amalgams and distinctions'. *Working Paper*. France, INSEAD: fax no. (France) 33–1–60724242.

BLUNKETT D. (2000) 'How partnerships can aid failing schools'. *Daily Telegraph*. 15 March. p22.

BLUNKETT D. (2000a) 'Digital dimensions'. *Guardian Higher Education Supplement*. 15 February. p1h.

BOBBITT F. (1918) *The Curriculum*. Cambridge, MA, The Riverside Press. Reprinted 1971. Boston, MA, Houghton Mifflin.

BOHN R. E. (1994) 'Measuring and managing technological knowledge'. *Sloan Management Review*. Vol. 36, 1. pp61–73.

BOISOT M., GRIFFITHS D. *and* MOLES V. (1995) 'The dilemma of competence: differentiation versus integration in the pursuit of learning'. *Paper Prepared for the Third International Workshop on Competence-Based Competition*. Ghent. November. pp16–18.

BOWER D. (1991) 'Case study: Rover', in V. Dulewicz, 'Improving assessment centres', *Personnel Management*, Vol. 23, 6, pp52–3.

BOYATZIS R. E. (1982) *The Competent Manager: A model for effective performance*. New York, Wiley.

BOYATZIS R. E. (1991) 'Building on competence: the effective use of managerial talent', in G. Salaman (ed.), *Human Resource Strategies*. London, Sage.

BOYDELL T. *and* LEARY M. (1996) *Identifying Training Needs*. London, Institute of Personnel and Development.

BRAMLEY P. (1996) *Evaluating Training*. London, Institute of Personnel and Development.

BRATTON J. *and* GOLD J. (1994) *Human Resource Management: Theory and practice*. London, Macmillan.

BREWSTER C. *and* TYSON S. (EDS) (1991) *International Comparisons in Human Resource Management*. London, Pitman.

BRITTAIN S. *and* RYDER P. (1999) 'Get complex'. *People Management*. Vol. 5, 23. pp48–51.

BRODIE M. *and* BENNETT R. (1979) 'Effective management and the audit of performance'. *Journal of General Management*. Vol. 4 (spring).

BROWN H., PECCEI R., SANDBERG S. *and* WELCHMAN R. (1989) 'Management training and development: in search of an integrated approach'. *Journal of General Management*. Vol. 15, 1. Autumn. pp69–82.

BROWN P. (2000) 'Trained to cope with anything'. *Times*. 22 February. p45.

BURACK E. H. (1991) 'Changing the company culture – the role of human resource development'. *Long Range Planning*. Vol. 24, 1. pp88–95.

BURGHES D. (1997) 'The uneven ground that devalues our A-levels'. *Sunday Times Education Courses Review*. 17 August: Section 7.

BURGOYNE J. (1989) *Management Development: Context and strategies*. Aldershot, Gower.

BURGOYNE J. (1999) 'Design of the times'. *People Management*. Vol. 5, 11. pp39–44.

BURGOYNE J. (1999a) *Develop Yourself, Your Career and Your Organisation*. London, Lemos and Crane.

BUTLER G. V. (1986) *Organization and Management: Theory and practice*. London, Prentice Hall International, in association with the Institute of Personnel Management.

BUTLER S. (1990) 'Cutting down and reshaping the core'. *Financial Times*. 20 March.

CAMBRIDGE UNIVERSITY SMALL BUSINESS RESEARCH CENTRE (1992) *The State of British Enterprise: Growth, innovation and competitive advantage in small and medium-sized firms*. Cambridge, Small Business Research Centre.

CANNELL M. (1997) 'Practice makes perfect'. *People Management*. Vol. 3, 5. pp26–33.

CANNELL M. (1998) *The IPD Guide on Training Technology*. London, Institute of Personnel and Development.

CANNELL M. (1999) 'Tradition before technology'. *People Management*. Vol. 5, 7. p35.

CANNELLA A. A. JNR and HAMBRICK D. C. (1993) 'Executive departure and acquisition performance'. *Strategic Management Journal*. Vol. 14. pp167–79.

CARBY K. and THAKUR M. (1977) *Transactional Analysis at Work. Information Report No. 23*. London, Institute of Personnel Management.

CARNALL C. (1999) 'Positive e-valuation'. *People Management*. Vol. 5, 17. pp54–7.

CARTER P. and LUMSDON C. (1988) 'How management development can improve business performance'. *Personnel Management*. Vol. 20, 10. pp49–52.

CATALANELLO R and REDDING J. (1989) 'Three strategic training roles'. *Training and Development Journal*. Vol. 43, 12. pp51–5.

CAVE E. and MCKEOWN P. (1993) 'Managerial effectiveness: the identification of need'. *Management Education and Development*. Vol. 24, 2. pp122–37.

CHAKRAVARTHY B. S. and DOZ Y. (1992) 'Strategy process research: focusing on corporate self-renewal'. *Strategic Management Journal, Summer Special Issue*. Vol. 13. pp5–14.

CHAMBERS C. (1990) 'Self reliant'. *Times Higher Education Supplement*. 6 April. p26.

CHANDLER A. (1962) *Strategy and Structure*. Cambridge, MA, MIT Press.

CHESBROUGH H. W. and TEECE D. J. (1996) 'When is virtual virtuous? Organizing for innovation'. *Harvard Business Review*. January–February. pp65–73.

CHILD J. (1984) *Organization: A guide to problems and practice*. 2nd edn. London, Harper and Row.

CLARE J. (1996) 'NVQs branded waste of £100m by watchdog'. *Daily Telegraph*. 5 October. p5.

CLARE J. (1996a) 'Dearing seeks to cut examination gap between schools and work'. *Daily Telegraph*. 28 March. p4.

CLARE J. (2000) 'School standards up but results gap is widening'. *Daily Telegraph*. 9 March. p1.

CLARE J. (2000a) 'Sponsors to take over bad schools'. *Daily Telegraph*. 15 March. p1.

CLARE J. (2000b) 'Any questions'. *Daily Telegraph Education Section*. 9 February. p20.

COLE G. (2000) 'Classroom of the future is switched-on'. *Daily Telegraph: Connected @telegraph.co.uk* 16 March. p11.

COLLOFF S and GOODGE P. (1990) 'The open track to elite status'. *Personnel Management*. Vol. 22, 11. pp50–53.

COMMISSION FOR RACIAL EQUALITY (1983) *Equal Opportunity in Employment: A guide for employers*. London, Commission for Racial Equality.

COMMISSION OF THE EC. (1989) *Education, Training, Youth*. Brussels, Task Force for Human Resources, Education, Training and Youth.

CONINE C. T. and CRISWELL B. P. (1998) 'The GEICO challenge session: a model for integrating human resource development and strategic planning', in R. Torraco (ed.), *Academy of Human Resource Development 1998 Conference Proceedings*. Baton Rouge, LA, AHRD, March, 6.1.

COOPER C. (2000) 'Southall rail crash report orders review of training'. *People Management*. Vol. 6, 5. p17.

COOPER C. (2000a) 'The Met fails inspection on race and recruitment'. *People Management*. Vol. 6, 2. p11.

COOPER C. L. (ED.) (1981) *Improving Interpersonal Relations: Some approaches to interpersonal skills training*. Aldershot, Gower.

COOPERS AND LYBRAND ASSOCIATES (1985) 'A challenge to complacency: changing attitudes to training'. *A Report to the Manpower Services Commission and the National Economic Development Office*. Sheffield, MSC.

COOPEY J. (1995) 'The learning organization, power, politics and ideology'. *Management Learning*. Vol. 26, 2. pp193–213.

COURT S. (1998) 'Lessons for life'. *Association of University Teachers' Bulletin*. April. pp6–7.

COYNE K. P. (1986) 'Sustainable competitive advantage – what it is and what it isn't'. *Business Horizons*. January–February. pp54–61.

CRITTEN P. (1999) 'To embrace the new, release the old'. *People Management*. Vol. 5, 12. p29 (letters page).

CROZIER A. (1998) 'Follow these rules – or takeovers could be bad for your wealth'. *Sunday Times Business*. 29 November. pp3–4.

CULLY M. (1998) 'The state we're in'. *People Management*. Vol. 4, 2. pp69–72.

CUMMINGS T. G. and HUSE E. F. (1989) *Organization Development and Change*. 4th edn. New York, West Publishing Co.

CURNOW B. (1995) 'Two worlds that need each other's expertise'. *People Management*. Vol. 1, 14. p25.

DAILY TELEGRAPH (2000) 'Blunkett's schooling'. *Daily Telegraph Editorial*. 15 March. p29.

DARLING J., DARLING P. *and* ELLIOTT J. (1999) *The Changing Role of the Trainer*. London, Institute of Personnel and Development.

DAVIES J. *and* DEIGHAN Y. (1986) 'The managerial menopause'. *Personnel Management*. Vol. 18, 3. pp28–33.

DE GEUS A. P. (1988) 'Planning as learning'. *Harvard Business Review*. March–April. pp62–9.

DE GEUS A. P. (1996) 'Planning as learning', in K. Starkey (ed.), *How Organizations Learn*. London, International Thomson Business Press, pp92–9.

DEAL T. E. *and* KENNEDY A. A. (1982) *Corporate Cultures: The rites and rituals of organizational life*. Reading, MA, Addison Wesley.

DEARING REPORT (1997) *Higher Education in the Learning Society*. Report of the National Committee of Inquiry into Higher Education.

DEPARTMENT FOR EDUCATION AND EMPLOYMENT (1998) *The Learning Age*. Green Paper. London, HMSO.

DEPARTMENT FOR EDUCATION AND EMPLOYMENT (1998a) *Lifelong Learning*. Green Paper. London, HMSO.

DEPARTMENT FOR EDUCATION AND EMPLOYMENT (1999) *Learning to Succeed*. White Paper. London, HMSO.

DEPARTMENT FOR EDUCATION AND EMPLOYMENT (1999a) *A Fresh Start: Improving literacy and numeracy*. London, DfEE. (Tel.0845 602 2260.)

DEPARTMENT OF EMPLOYMENT. (1988) *Employment News, No. 61*. Sheffield, DoE. June.

DIXON N. (2000) *Common Knowledge: How companies thrive by sharing what they know*. Boston, MA, Harvard Business School Press.

DIXON N. (2000a) 'The insight track'. *People Management*. Vol. 6, 4. pp34–9.

DOLAN S. (1995) 'A different use of natural resources'. *People Management*. Vol.1, 20. pp36–40.

DORRELL J. (1993) *Resource-Based Learning, Using Open and Flexible Learning Resources for Continuous Development*. Maidenhead, McGraw-Hill Training Series.

DOWNS S. (1984) 'Trainability testing'. *Personnel Management*. Vol. 26, 10. p79.

DOYLE M. *and* NORMAN R. (1991) 'Ensuring continuing commitment to management training and development by winning senior management support', in *Proceedings of the Institute of International Research in association with Sundridge Park Management Centre: Third Annual Forum on Developing Effective Business-led Management Training, London, 28 February–1 March*. London, IIR Ltd.

DRUCKER P. (1988) 'The coming of the new organisation'. *Harvard Business Review*. January–February. pp45–53.

DRUCKER P. (1993) *Post-Capitalist Society*. Oxford, Butterworth–Heinemann.

DULEWICZ V. (1991) 'Improving assessment centres'. *Personnel Management*. Vol. 23, 6. pp50–55.

EDWARDS P. (1990) 'Uncertain worlds'. *Times Higher Education Supplement*. 6 April.

EMPLOYMENT DEPARTMENT (1991) *Education and Training for the 21st Century*. White Paper. London, HMSO.

EMPLOYMENT DEPARTMENT GROUP (1991) *A Strategy for Skills. Guidance from the Secretary of State for Employment on Training, Vocational Education and Enterprise*. November. Sheffield, Employment Department.

EMPLOYMENT OCCUPATIONAL STANDARDS COUNCIL (1996) *A Briefing Note*. Rotherham, Cambertown Ltd.

ENNEW E. *and* FORD C. (1990) *The Management of Change: Reflections of change at Norsk Hydro Polymers Ltd, Newton Aycliffe, County Durham, 1984–1990*. London, Advisory Conciliation and Arbitration Service Work Research Unit.

EVANS P. (1992) 'Developing leaders and management development'. *European Management Journal*. Vol. 10, 1. pp1–9.

EWINGTON T. (2000) 'Teach yourself the lot'. *Sunday Times, Section 9: Culture* ('Doors'). 26 March. pp55–7.

FAIRBAIRN J. (1991) 'Plugging the gap in training needs analysis'. *Personnel Management*. Vol. 23, 2. pp43–5.

FLANAGAN J. C. (1954) 'The critical incident technique'. *Psychological Bulletin*. Vol. 51. pp327–58.

FLOUD R. (1999) 'The broader, the better'. *Guardian Further Education*. 16 November. pp3ff.

FLOYD S. W. *and* WOOLDRIDGE B. (1994) 'Dinosaurs or dynamos? Recognizing middle management's strategic role'. *Academy of Management Executive*. Vol. 8, 4. pp47–57.

FOMBRUN C., TICHY N. M. *and* DEVANNA M. A. (EDS) (1984) *Strategic Human Resource Management*. New York, Wiley.

FONDA N. (1989) 'Management development: the missing link in sustained business performance'. *Personnel Management*. Vol. 21, 12. pp50–3.

FONDA N. *and* BUCKTON K. (1995) *Reviewing the Personnel Function: A toolkit for development*. London, Institute of Personnel and Development.

FONDA N. *and* ROWLAND H. (1995) 'Take me to your (personnel) leader'. *People Management*. Vol. 1, 25. pp18–23.

FORREST A. (1993) *Fifty Ways to Personal Development*. London, Industrial Society. November.

FOWLER A. (1992) 'How to: structure a personnel department'. *Personnel Management Plus*. January. pp22–3.

FOWLER A. (1995) 'How to: decide on training methods'. *People Management*. Vol. 1, 25. pp36–7.

FOWLER A. (1996) *Employee Induction: A good start*. 3rd edn. London, Institute of Personnel and Development.

FOWLER A. (1997) 'How to: outsource personnel'. *People Management*. Vol. 3, 4. pp40–43.

FOWLER A. (1998) *The IPD Guide on Outsourcing*. London, Institute of Personnel and Development.

FOX S., TANTON M. *and* MCLEAY S. (1992) 'Human resource

management, corporate strategy and financial performance'. *Executive Summary of Research Project Undertaken for HM Government's Economic and Social Research Council's 'Competitiveness and Regeneration of British Industry' Initiative.* Lancaster University and University of Wales.

FRENCH J. R. P. *and* RAVEN B. H. (1959) 'The bases of social power', in D. Cartwright (ed.), *Studies in Social Power.* Ann Arbor, MI, University of Michigan Press.

FRENCH W. L. (1987) *The Personnel Management Process: Human resources administration and development.* 6th edn. Boston, MA, Houghton Mifflin.

FRENCH W. L. *and* BELL C. H. (1978) *Organisation Development: Behavioural science interventions for organisation improvement.* 2nd edn. London, Prentice Hall International.

GAGNE R. M. (1977) *The Conditions of Learning.* New York, Holt Saunders.

GALBRAITH J. R. *and* NATHANSON D. (1978) *Strategy Implementation.* St Paul, MN, West Publishing.

GARMONSWAY A. *and* WELLIN M. (1995) 'Creating the right natural chemistry'. *People Management.* Vol. 1, 19. pp36–9.

GARNETT J. (1992) 'My biggest mistake'. *Independent on Sunday.* 8 March.

GENTLES E. M. (1969) *Training the Operator.* London, Institute of Personnel Management.

GHOSHAL S. *and* BARTLETT C. A. (1994) 'Linking organizational context and managerial action: the dimension of quality of management'. *Strategic Management Journal, Special Summer Issue.* Vol. 15. pp91–112.

GILLEY J. W. *and* EGGLAND S. A. (1989) *Principles of Human Resource Development.* Maidenhead, Addison Wesley.

GILLEY J. W. *and* EGGLAND S. A. (1989a) 'Marketing and positioning the HRD program within the organization'. *Principles of Human Resource Development.* Wokingham, Addison Wesley and University Associates Inc. pp243–65.

GOLDSTEIN I. L. *and* GOLDSTEIN H. W. (1990) 'Training as an approach for organisations to the challenges of human resource issues in the year 2000'. *Journal of Organizational Change Management.* Vol. 3, 2. pp30–43.

GOODHART D. (1994) 'Can Europe compete? Convergence in the workforce'. *Financial Times.* 28 February. p11.

GOODHART D. (1994a) 'Fresh thinking needed on old labour problem'. *Financial Times.* 8 March. p14.

GORMAN T. (2000) 'C's the opportunity'. *People Management.* Vol. 6, 7. p57.

GOUGH J. (1996) *Developing Learning Materials.* London, Institute of Personnel and Development.

GRACIE S. (1999) 'Despairing firms do their own training'. *Sunday Times, Business*: 3. 19 December. p10.

GRAHAM G. (1994) 'Lack of training shuts out poor'. *Financial Times.* 14 March. p4.

GRANT R. M. (1991) *Contemporary Strategy Analysis: Concepts, techniques, applications.* Oxford, Blackwell.

GRATTON L. *and* SYRETT M. (1990) 'Heirs apparent: succession strategies for the future'. *Personnel Management.* Vol. 22, 1. pp34–8.

GRAVES D. (1998) 'Students shun traditional degrees in favour of vocational courses'. *Daily Telegraph.* 13 August. p4.

GREATREX J. *and* PHILLIPS P. (1989) 'Oiling the wheels of competence'. *Personnel Management.* Vol. 21, 8. pp36–9.

GREEN K. (1999) 'Offensive thinking'. *People Management.* Vol. 5, 8. p27.

GRIBBEN R. (1997) 'TECs prepare to adjust to the new order'. *Daily Telegraph Special Report: TECs 1.* 9 July. p35.

GUEST D. E. (1990) 'Human resource management and the American dream'. *Journal of Management Studies.* Vol. 27, 4. pp377–97.

GUEST D. E. (1998) 'Combine harvest'. *People Management.* Vol. 4, 21. pp64–6.

GUILE D. *and* FONDA N. (1998) *Performance Management through Capability.* London, Institute of Personnel and Development.

HACKETT P. (1997) *Introduction to Training.* London, Institute of Personnel and Development.

HALL D. T. (1984) 'Human resource development and organisational effectiveness', in D. Fombrun, N. M. Tichy and M. A. Devanna (eds), *Strategic Human Resource Management.* New York: Wiley, pp159–81.

HALL D. T. (1986) 'Dilemmas in linking succession planning to individual executive learning'. *Human Resource Management.* Vol. 25, 2. pp235–65.

HALL R. (1993) 'A framework linking intangible resources and capabilities to sustainable competitive advantage'. *Strategic Management Journal.* Vol. 14. pp607–18.

HALL R. (1996) 'Supply chain management – the challenges for the 21st century'. *Paper presented to the CIPS Conference at Durham University Business School.* 9 May. Durham University Business School, Mill Hill Lane, Durham City, DH1 3AY.

HAMBLIN A. C. (1974) *Evaluation and Control of Training.* Maidenhead, McGraw-Hill.

HAMBRICK D. C. (1987). 'The top management team: key to strategic success'. *California Management Review.* Fall. pp88–108.

HAMEL G. *and* PRAHALAD C. K. (1993) 'Strategy as stretch and leverage'. *Harvard Business Review.* Vol. 71, 2. pp75–84.

HAMLIN B. (1999) 'The national context', in J. Stewart, *Employee Development Practice.* London, Financial Times and Pitman Publishing, pp22–61.

HAMLIN B. *and* DAVIES G. (1996) 'The trainer as change agent: issues for practice', in J. Stewart and J. McGoldrick (eds), *Human Resource Development: Perspectives, strategies and practice.* London, Pitman, pp199–219.

HANDY C. B. (1985) *Understanding Organizations.* 3rd edn. Harmondsworth, Penguin.

HANDY C. B. (1987) 'The making of managers'. *A Report for the National Economic Development Council, the Manpower Services Commission, and the British Institute of Management on Management Education, Training and Development in the USA, West Germany,*

France, Japan and the UK. London, National Economic Development Office.

HANDY C. B. (1989) *The Age of Unreason.* London, Business Books.

HARDINGHAM A. (1996) 'Improve an inside job with an outside edge'. *People Management.* Vol. 2, 12. pp45–6.

HARDINGHAM A. (1996a) *Designing Training.* London, Institute of Personnel and Development.

HARRIS V. (1995) 'Moving ahead on cultural change'. *People Management.* Vol. 1, 6. pp30–33.

HARRISON J. *and* LORD P. (1992) 'Investors in People and the accreditation of training in SMEs', in *Proceedings of the 15th National Small Firms Policy and Research Conference.* Southampton, November. Northern Ireland Small Business Institute, United Kingdom Enterprise Management Research Association.

HARRISON R. (1992) *Employee Development.* London, Institute of Personnel and Development.

HARRISON R. (1992a) 'Employee development at Barratt', in D. Woodall and D. Winstanley (eds), *Case Studies in Personnel.* London, Institute of Personnel and Development, pp103–15.

HARRISON R. (ED.) (1993) *Human Resource Management: Issues and strategies.* Wokingham, Addison Wesley.

HARRISON R. (1993a) 'Strategic human resource management at HMH Sheetmetal Fabrications Ltd, 1993', in R. Harrison (ed.), *Human Resource Management: Issues and strategies.* Wokingham, Addison Wesley, pp335–9.

HARRISON R. (1996) 'Developing human resources for productivity'. Module 13 in J. Prokopenko and K. North (eds), *Productivity and Quality Management: A modular programme: part II.* Geneva, International Labour Office and Tokyo, Asian Productivity Association, pp1–53.

HARRISON R. (1996a) 'Action learning: route or barrier to the learning organization?' *Employee Counselling Today, The Journal of Workplace Learning.* Vol. 8, 6. pp27–38.

HARRISON R. (1999) *The Training and Development Audit: An eight-step audit to measure, assess and enhance the performance of your organisation's training and development.* Cambridge, Cambridge Strategy Publications.

HARRISON R. *and* MILLER S. (1993) 'Doctors in management: two into one won't go – or will it?' *Journal of Executive Development.* Vol. 6, 2. pp9–13.

HARRISON R. *and* MILLER S. (1999) 'The contribution of clinical directors to the strategic capability of the organisation'. *British Journal of Management.* Vol. 10, 1. pp23–39.

HARRISON R. *and* SMITH R. (2000) 'Practical judgement: its implications for knowledge development and strategic capability', in B. Hellgren and J. Lowstedt (eds), *Management in the Thought-Full Enterprise: A socio-cognitive approach to the organization of human resources.* Norway, Fagbokforlaget in association with Copenhagen Business School Press.

HARRISON R., MILLER S. *and* GIBSON A. (1993) 'Doctors in management, part II: getting into action'. *Journal of Executive Development.* Vol. 6, 4. pp3–7.

HARRISON ROGER (1972) 'How to describe your organization'. *Harvard Business Review*. September–October.

HARRISON ROY (1996) 'A role-over week for training as we know it'. *People Management*. Vol. 2, 11. pp47–8.

HARRISON ROY (1999) 'Faster track learning'. *People Management*. Vol. 5, 18. p69.

HART S. *and* BANBURY C. (1994) 'How strategy-making processes can make a difference'. *Strategic Management Journal*. Vol. 15. pp251–69.

HEALY M. (1995) 'Innovators beware!' *People Management*. Vol. 1, 6. pp24–5.

HEDLUND G. (1994) 'A model of knowledge management and the N-Form corporation'. *Strategic Management Journal, Special Summer Issue*. Vol. 15. pp73–90.

HENDRY C. (1994) 'The Single European Market and the HRM response', in P. A. Kirkbride (ed.), *Human Resource Management in Europe: Perspectives for the 1990s*. London, Routledge, pp93–113.

HENDRY C. (1995) *Human Resource Management: A strategic approach to employment*. London, Butterworth–Heinemann.

HENDRY C. *and* PETTIGREW A. (1986) 'The practice of strategic human resource management'. *Personnel Review*. Vol. 15, 5. pp3–8.

HENDRY C., ARTHUR M. B. *and* JONES A. M. (1995) *Strategy through People: Adaptation and learning in the small-medium enterprise*. London, Routledge.

HENDRY C., JONES A., ARTHUR M. B. *and* PETTIGREW A. M. (1991) 'Human resource development in small to medium sized enterprises'. *Research Paper No. 88*. Sheffield, Employment Department.

HER MAJESTY'S INSPECTORATE OF CONSTABULARY (2000) *Policing London: Winning consent*. Available from the Home Office on 020 7273 4000 or from www.homeoffice.gov/uk/hmic/hmic.htm.

HERRIOT P. (1992) *The Career Management Challenge: Balancing individual and organizational needs*. London, Sage.

HERRIOT P. *and* PEMBERTON C. (1995) 'A new deal for middle managers'. *People Management*. Vol. 1, 12. pp32–4.

HERTZBERG F. (1966) *Work and the Nature of Man*. London, Staples Press.

HETHERINGTON P. (2000) 'Nudge and fudge'. *Guardian*. 13 March. p17.

HEVEY D. (1997) 'The UK national (and Scottish) vocational qualification system: state of the art or in a state?' *International Journal of Training and Development*. Vol. 1, 4. pp242–58.

HILL R. *and* STEWART J. (1999) 'Human resource development in small organizations'. *Human Resource Development International*. Vol. 2, 2. pp103–23.

HILLS H. (2000) 'Not in the net yet'. *People Management*. Vol. 6, 5. p33.

HILLS H. *and* FRANCIS P. (1999) 'Interaction learning'. *People Management*. Vol. 5, 14. pp48–9.

HIRSH W. (1985) *Women, Career Breaks and Re-Entry*. London, Institute of Manpower Studies.

HIRSH W. *and* JACKSON C. (1996) 'Ticket to ride or no place to go?' *People Management.* Vol. 2, 13. pp20–25.

HIRSH W., JACKSON C. *and* JACKSON C. (1995) *Careers in Organisations – Issues for the future.* Institute for Employment Studies Report. London, IES.

HOFSTEDE G. (1980, 1984) *Culture's Consequences: International differences in work-related values.* Vol. 5. London, Sage.

HOMAN G. *and* SHAW S. (2000) 'Reframing the role of higher education in the process of lifelong learning – a UK perspective'. *Paper presented at the Conference on Convergence and Divergence in the European HRD Agenda: Comparing and Contrasting Research and Practice.* Kingston, Kingston University. 15 January.

HONEY P. *and* MUMFORD A. (1992) *A Manual of Learning Styles.* 3rd edn. Maidenhead, Honey.

HONEY P. *and* MUMFORD A. (1996) *Managing Your Learning Environment.* Maidenhead, Honey.

HUBER G. (1991) 'Organizational learning: the contributing processes and literatures'. *Organization Science.* Vol. 2. pp85–113.

HUNT M. *and* CLARKE A. (1997) *A Guide to the Cost-Effectiveness of Technology-Based Training.* Coventry, National Council for Educational Technology and Department for Education and Employment.

HUSELID M. A. (1995) 'The impact of human resource management: an agenda for the 1990s'. *International Journal of Human Resource Management.* Vol. 1, 1. pp17–43.

ILES P. *and* MABEY C. (1993) 'Managerial career development programmes: effectiveness, availability and acceptability'. *British Journal of Management.* Vol. 4, 3. pp103–11.

INCOMES DATA SERVICES (1993) *European Management Guides: Training and development.* London, Institute of Personnel Management.

INDUSTRIAL SOCIETY. *Managing Best Practice.* Monthly reports, available by subscription or as single copies: tel. 0121 410 3040.

INDUSTRIAL SOCIETY (1997) 'Self-managed learning'. *Managing Best Practice: The regular benchmark.* No. 40. October. London, The Industrial Society.

INSTITUTE FOR EMPLOYMENT STUDIES (1996) 'Strategies for Career Development: Promise, Practice and Pretence'. *IES Report, No 305.* London, IES.

INSTITUTE OF MANAGEMENT (1995) *Coming on Board.* London, IOM.

INSTITUTE OF MANPOWER STUDIES (1984) *Competence and Competition: Training and Education in the Federal Republic of Germany, the United States and Japan.* London, Manpower Services Commission/ National Economic Development Office.

INSTITUTE OF PERSONNEL AND DEVELOPMENT (1999) *IPD Professional Standards.* London, Institute of Personnel and Development.

INSTITUTE OF PERSONNEL AND DEVELOPMENT *Training and Development in Britain – Annual survey reports.* Available by sending an A4 SAE to Mike Cannell, Training and Development Policy Adviser, Chartered Institute of Personnel and Development, IPD House, Camp Road, London, SW19 4UX.

JACKSON L. (1989) 'Transforming managerial performance – a

competency approach', in *Proceedings of Institute of Personnel Management National Conference, Harrogate*, October. London, IPM.

JACKSON T. (2000) *Career Development*. London, Institute of Personnel and Development.

JAY J. (2000) 'Time for market disciplines in higher education'. *Sunday Times Business*. 2 February 27. p3.2.

JENKINS S. (1999) 'Whitehall farce'. *Times*. 17 December. p24.

JENNINGS P. L., RICHARDSON B. *and* BEAVER G. (1992) 'Improving the role of accreditation in the training and development of small business owner/managers', in *Proceedings of 15th National Small Firms' Policy and Research Conference*, Southampton, November, Northern Ireland Small Business Institute, United Kingdom Enterprise Management Research Association.

JOHNSON D. (2000) 'Scandal of our failing schools'. *Daily Telegraph*. 11 March. p22.

JOHNSON R. (1999) 'The real deal'. *People Management*. Vol. 5, 6. pp54–8.

JOHNSON R. (1999a) 'Macdonald puts forward a skills theory of devolution'. *People Management*. Vol. 5, 6. p20.

JOHNSTON R. (1996) 'Power and influence and the HRD function', in J. Stewart and J. McGoldrick (eds), *Human Resource Development: Perspectives, strategies and practice*. London, Pitman, pp180–95.

JONES R. A. *and* GOSS D. M. (1991) 'The role of training strategy in reducing skills shortages: some evidence from a survey of small firms'. *Personnel Review*. Vol. 20, 2. pp24–30.

JUDD J. (2000) 'Failing schools plan "is a sign of official panic"'. *Independent*. 16 March. p6.

KEARNS P. *and* MILLER T. (1996) *Measuring the Impact of Training and Development on the Bottom Line*. Technical Communications.

KEASEY K. *and* WATSON R. (1993*) Small Firm Management: Ownership, finance and performance*. Oxford, Blackwell.

KEEP E. (1986) 'Can Britain build a coherent vocational training system?' *Personnel Management*. Vol. 18, 8. pp28–31.

KEEP E. (1989) 'Corporate training policies: the vital component', in J. Storey (ed.), *New Perspectives in Human Resource Management*. London, Routledge, pp109–25.

KEEP E. (1989a) 'A training scandal?' in K. Sisson (ed.), *Personnel Management in Britain*. Oxford, Blackwell, pp177–202.

KEEP E. (1999) 'Missing links'. *People Management*. Vol. 5, 2. p35.

KEEP E. *and* MAYHEW K. (1994) *Scoping Paper for the 'What Makes Training Pay' Project*. London, Institute of Personnel and Development.

KELMAR J. (1990) 'Measurement of success and failure in small business – a dichotomous anachronism', in *Proceedings of 13th National Small Firms' Policy and Research Conference*, Harrogate, November, Northern Ireland Small Business Institute, United Kingdom Enterprise Management Research Association.

KESSELS J. (1993) *Towards Design Standards for Curriculum Consistency in Corporate Education*. Dissertation, Twente University. Hulshorst, Netherlands, Foundation for Corporate Education.

KESSELS J. (1996) 'Knowledge productivity and the corporate

curriculum', in J. F. Schreinemakers (ed.), *Knowledge Management: Organisation, competence and methodology: proceedings of the fourth international ISMICK Symposium, 21–22 October, Rotterdam, the Netherlands,* Wurzburg, ERGON-Verlag, pp168–74.

KESSELS J. *and* HARRISON R. (1998) 'External consistency: the key to management development?' *Management Learning.* Vol. 29, 1. pp37–68.

KESSLER I. (1990) 'Personnel management in local government: the new agenda'. *Personnel Management.* Vol. 22, 11. pp40–44.

KINGSTON P. (1999) 'Reaching the learners others cannot reach'. *Guardian Further Education.* 16 November. pp1f and 4f.

KIRBY D.A. (1990) 'Management education and small business development: an explanatory study of small firms'. *UK Journal of Small Business Management.* Vol. 28, 4. pp78–87.

KOLB D. A., RUBIN I. M. *and* MCINTYRE J. M. (1974) *Organizational Psychology: An experiential approach.* Englewood Cliffs, NJ, Prentice Hall.

LATCHFORD P. (1999) 'Past imperfect, future tense'. *People Management.* Vol. 5, 16. p31.

LEE R. (1996) 'The "pay-forward" view of training'. *People Management.* Vol. 2, 3. pp30–32.

LEES S. (1992) 'Ten faces of management development'. *Management Education and Development.* Vol. 23, 2. pp89–105.

LEGGE K. (1995) *Human Resource Management: Rhetorics and realities.* London, Macmillan.

LEIGH A. (1996) 'Why you should learn to rely on the experts'. *People Management.* Vol. 2, 20. p49.

LEIGH A. *and* MAYNARD M. (1996) *The Perfect Leader.* London, Arrow.

LEWIS J. *and* MCLAVERTY C. (1991) 'Facing up to the needs of the older manager'. *Personnel Management.* Vol. 23, 1. pp 32–5.

LIKERT R. (1961) *New Patterns of Management.* New York, McGraw-Hill.

LINKLATER J. *and* ATKINS H. (1995) 'Discovering what makes others tick'. *People Management.* Vol. 1, 18. pp 35–6.

LIPPITT G. (1983) 'Management development as the key to organisational renewal'. *Journal of Management Development.* Vol. 1, 2. pp36–9.

LOCKETT J. (1992) *Effective Performance Management: A strategic guide to getting the best from people.* London, Kogan Page.

LORENZ A. (1995) 'BTR breaks the mould'. *Management Today.* May. pp44–8.

LORENZ C. (1992) 'Different routes through the minefield of change'. *Financial Times.* 20 November. p14.

LORENZ C. (1994) 'Dissent in the measurement ranks'. *Financial Times.* 25 March. p16.

LYMER A. (1996) 'Educational impacts of the World Wide Web'. *Account.* Vol. 8, 1. pp9–10.

MABEY C. *and* ILES P. (EDS) (1994) *Managing Learning.* London, The Open University and Routledge.

MABEY C. *and* SALAMAN G. (1995) *Strategic Human Resource Management.* Oxford, Blackwell.

MACAULAY S. *and* HARDING N. (1996) 'Drawing up a new careers contract'. *People Management*. Vol. 2, 7. pp34–5.

MACDUFFIE J. P. (1995) 'Human resource bundles and manufacturing performance: flexible production systems in the world auto industry'. *Industrial Relations and Labor Review*. Vol. 48. pp197–221.

MACHIN J. (1981) 'Inter-manager communication: matching up to expectations?' *Personnel Management*. Vol. 13, 1, January. pp26–9.

MACKINNON I. (1995) 'How to approach your TEC for financial help and more'. *People Management*. Vol. 1, 1. p51.

MACKINNON I. (1999) 'On firm foundations'. *People Management*. Vol. 5, 15. p29.

MACLACHLAN R. (1999) 'High performers: National Conference'. *People Management*. Vol. 5, 22. pp15–24.

MALONE S. A. (1997) *How to Set up and Manage a Corporate Learning Centre*. Aldershot, Gower.

MANWARING T. *and* WOOD S. (1985) 'The ghost in the labour process: job redesign', in D. Knight (ed.), *Critical Perspectives on the Labour Process*. Aldershot, Gower.

MARCHINGTON M. *and* WILKINSON A. (1996) *Core Personnel and Development*. London, Institute of Personnel and Development.

MARKIDES C. C. *and* WILLIAMSON J. P. (1994) 'Related diversification, core competences and corporate performance'. *Strategic Management Journal, Summer Special Issue*. Vol. 15. pp149–65.

MARLOW S. *and* PATTON D. (1992) 'Employment relations, human resource management strategies and the smaller firm', in *Proceedings of 15th National Small Firms' Policy and Research Conference*, Southampton, November, Northern Ireland Small Business Institute, United Kingdom Enterprise Management Research Association.

MARRIS R. (1995) 'Worrying fortunes of the Anglo-Saxon underclass'. *Times*. 28 September. p29.

MARTINSON J. (2000) 'A media giant caught in the web'. *Guardian*. 11 January. p3.

MASIE E. (1999) 'Joined-up thinking'. *People Management*. Vol. 5, 23. pp32–6.

MAYO A. (1994) *Managing Careers*. London, Institute of Personnel and Development.

MAYO A. (1998) *Creating a Training and Development Strategy*. London, Institute of Personnel and Development.

MAYO E. (1933) *The Human Problems of an Industrial Civilisation*. New York, Macmillan.

MCGOLDRICK A. (ED.) (1996) *Cases in Human Resource Management*. London, Pitman.

MCGRATH R. G., MACMILLAN I. C. *and* VENKATARAMAN S. (1995) 'Defining and developing competence: a strategic process paradigm'. *Strategic Management Journal*. Vol. 16. pp251–75.

MCGREGOR D. (1960) *The Human Side of Enterprise*. Maidenhead, McGraw-Hill.

MEGGINSON D. *and* WHITAKER V. (1996) *Cultivating Self-Development*. London, Institute of Personnel and Development.

MERRICK N. (1999) 'Premier division'. *People Management.* Vol. 5, 16. pp38–41.

MERRICK N. (2000) 'Thrills and skills'. *People Management.* Vol. 6, 1. pp44–6.

MEZIROW J. A. (1985) 'A critical theory of self-directed learning', in S. Brookfield (ed.), *Self-Directed Learning: From theory to practice.* San Francisco, CA, Jossey-Bass.

MILES R. *and* SNOW C. (1995) 'The new network firm: a spherical structure built on a human investment philosophy'. *Organizational Dynamics.* Vol. 23, 4. pp5–18.

MILLER R. B. (1962) 'Task description and analysis', in R. M. Gagne (ed.), *Psychological Principles of System Development.* Eastbourne, Holt, Rhinehart and Winston.

MILLER R. *and* STEWART J. (1999) 'Opened university'. *People Management.* Vol. 5, 12. pp42–6.

MILLS D. Q. *and* FRIESEN B. (1992) 'The learning organisation'. *European Management Journal.* Vol. 10, 2. pp146–56.

MILLS G. E., WAYNE PACE R. *and* PETERSON B. D. (1988) *Analysis in Human Resource Training and Organization Development.* Wokingham, Addison Wesley.

MINTZBERG H. (1973) *The Nature of Managerial Work.* New York, Harper and Row.

MINTZBERG H. (1983) *Structure in Fives: Designing effective organizations.* Englewood Cliffs, NJ, Prentice Hall.

MINTZBERG H. (1994) *The Rise and Fall of Strategic Planning.* Hemel Hempstead, Prentice Hall.

MINTZBERG H. (1994a) 'Rounding out the manager's job'. *Sloan Management Review.* Vol. 36, 1. pp11–26.

MOORBY E. (1991) *How to Succeed in Employee Development: Moving from vision to results.* Maidenhead, McGraw-Hill.

MORGAN G. (1986) *Images of Organization.* London, Sage.

MORRIS J. (1991) 'Action learning: the long haul', in J. Prior (ed.), *Handbook of Training and Development.* Aldershot, Gower, pp611–28.

MOXON G. R. (1943) *The Functions of a Personnel Department.* London, Institute of Personnel Management.

MUMFORD A. (1997) *Management Development: Strategies for action.* 3rd edn. London, Institute of Personnel and Development.

MUMFORD A., ROBINSON G. *and* STRADLING D. (1987) *Developing Directors: The learning processes.* Sheffield, Manpower Services Commission.

MURPHY B. P. *and* SWANSON R. A. (1988) 'Auditing training and development'. *Journal of European Industrial Training.* Vol. 12, 2. pp13–16.

MURPHY P. (2000) '$350bn media merger heralds net revolution'. *Guardian.* 11 January. p1.

NADLER L. (1970) *Developing Human Resources.* Houston, Gulf.

NADLER L. (1980) *Corporate Human Resources Development: A management tool.* New York, Van Nostrand Reinhold.

NADLER L. (1992) 'HRD – where has it been, where is it going?' *Studies in Continuing Education.* Vol. 14, 2. pp104–14.

NATIONAL COMMISSION ON EDUCATION (1993) *Learning to Succeed – A radical look at education today and a strategy for the future*. London, Heinemann.

NELSON R. R. *and* WINTER S. G. (1982) An *Evolutionary Theory of Economic Change*. Cambridge, MA, Harvard University Press.

NEVIS E. C., DiBELLA A. J. *and* GOULD J. M. (1995) 'Understanding organizations as learning systems'. *Sloan Management Review*. Vol. 36, 2. pp73–85.

NICHOLLS A. (1997) 'Thames Valley: a new line on learning'. *Guardian Higher*. 21 January. piii.

NICHOLLS A. (1997a) 'Towards new horizons'. *Guardian Higher*. 21 January. pii.

NIVEN M. M. (1967) *Personnel Management, 1913–63: The growth of personnel management and the development of the Institute*. London, Institute of Personnel Management.

NOEL L., JAMES N. L. *and* DENNEHY R. F. (1991) 'Making HRD a force in strategic organisational change'. *Industrial and Commercial Training*. Vol. 23, 2. pp17–19.

NONAKA I. (1991) 'The knowledge-creating company'. *Harvard Business Review*. November–December. pp96–104.

NONAKA I. (1994) 'A dynamic theory of organizational knowledge creation'. *Organization Science*. Vol. 5, 1. pp14–37.

NONAKA I. *and* TAKEUCHI H. (1995) *The Knowledge-Creating Company*. Oxford, Oxford University Press.

NORDHAUG O. *and* GRONHAUG K. (1994) 'Competences as resources in firms'. *International Journal of Human Resource Management*. Vol. 5, 1. pp89–106.

OLDFIELD C. (1996) 'Quarter of small firms say they want to sell up'. *Sunday Times Business Section*. 15 December. p2.

O'LEARY J. (1997) 'Vocations and doubts'. *Times Education Section*. 6 June. p41.

OSBALDESTON M. *and* BARHAM K. (1992) 'Using management development for competitive advantage'. *Long Range Planning*. Vol. 25, 6. pp18–24.

OTTO C. P. *and* GLASER R. O. (1972) *The Management of Training*. London, Addison Wesley.

PARTRIDGE B. (1989) 'The problem of supervision', in K. Sisson (ed.), *Personnel Management in Britain*. Oxford, Blackwell, pp203–21.

PATERSON L. (2000) 'Hidden jobless must not be ignored'. *Times*. 16 February. p31.

PATTERSON M. G., WEST M. A., LAWTHOM R. *and* NICKELL S. (1997) *Impact of People Management Practices on Business Performance*. London, Institute of Personnel and Development.

PAWSEY V. (2000) 'Police pooling evidence to bolster training standards'. *People Management*. Vol. 6, 1. p12.

PAYNE R. (1991) 'Taking stock of corporate culture'. *Personnel Management*. Vol. 23, 7. pp26–9.

PEDLER M. *and* BOUTALL J. (1992) *Action Learning for Change: A resource book for managers and other professionals*. Eastwood Park, Avon, NHS Training Directorate.

PEDLER M., BURGOYNE J. *and* BOYDELL T. (1978) *Manager's Guide to Self-Development*. Maidenhead, McGraw-Hill.

PEDLER M., BURGOYNE J. *and* BOYDELL T. (1991) *The Learning*

Company: A strategy for sustainable development. Maidenhead, McGraw-Hill.

PENROSE E. T. (1959) *The Theory of the Growth of the Firm.* Oxford, Blackwell.

PEOPLE MANAGEMENT (1999) 'First learning accounts ready'. *People Management.* Vol. 5, 6. p16.

PERSONNEL MANAGEMENT (1992) 'London Underground to decentralise personnel function in wake of job cuts'. *Personnel Management.* Vol. 24, 1. p5.

PERSONNEL MANAGEMENT PLUS (1990) 'TVEI is being undermined by budget cuts, says opposition'. *PM Plus.* August. p5.

PETERAF M. A. (1993) 'The cornerstones of competitive advantage: a resource-based view'. *Strategic Management Journal.* Vol. 14. pp179–91.

PETERS T. J. and WATERMAN R. H. (1982) *In Search of Excellence.* New York, Harper and Row.

PETTIGREW A. M., SPARROW P. and HENDRY C. (1988) 'The forces that trigger training'. *Personnel Management.* Vol. 20, 12. pp28–32.

PETTIGREW A. M., ARTHUR M. B. and HENDRY C. (1990) 'Training and human resource management in small to medium sized enterprises: a critical review of the literature and a model for future research'. *Research Paper No. 56.* Sheffield, Employment Department.

PFEFFER J. (1981) *Power in Organizations.* Marshfield, MA, Pitman.

PHILLIPS A. (1995) 'Learning how to take the initiative'. *People Management.* Vol. 1, 17. pp32–5.

PICKARD J. (1992) 'Shell UK pulls responsibility back to centre'. *Personnel Management Plus.* April. p1.

PICKARD J. (1995) 'Food for thought'. *People Management.* Vol. 1, 20. pp30–31.

PICKARD J. (1997) 'A yearning for learning'. *People Management.* Vol. 3, 5. pp34–5.

POLANYI M. (1958) *Personal Knowledge.* Chicago, IL, University of Chicago Press.

POLANYI M. (1966) *The Tacit Dimension.* New York, Anchor Day Books.

POLICY STUDIES INSTITUTE (1993) *Employment in Britain Survey.* London, PSI Publishing.

PORTER M. E. (1980) *Competitive Strategy.* New York, Free Press.

PORTER M. E. (1985) *Competitive Advantage.* New York, Free Press.

POTTER B. (1998) 'The rise and fall of a corporate Goliath'. *Daily Telegraph Business News.* 28 November. p33.

POTTINGER J. (1989) 'Engineering change through pay'. *Personnel Management.* Vol. 21, 10. pp73–4.

POULTENEY J. (1997) 'Rapid reaction'. *People Management.* Vol. 3, 2. pp38–40.

PRAHALAD C. K. and BETTIS R. A. (1986) 'The dominant logic: a new linkage between diversity and performance'. *Strategic Management Journal.* Vol. 7. pp485–501.

PRAHALAD C. K. and HAMEL G. (1994) 'Strategy as a field of study: why search for a new paradigm?' *Strategic Management Journal.* Vol. 15. pp5–16.

PRAIS S. J. (1985) 'What can we learn from the German system of education and vocational training?', in G. D. N. Worswick (ed.), *Education and Economic Performance*. London, Gower, pp40–51.

PRAIS S. J *and* WAGNER K. (1981) 'Some practical aspects of human capital investment: training standards in five occupations in Britain and Germany'. *International Institute of Economic and Social Research Review*. November. pp46–65.

PRAIS S. J. *and* NATIONAL INSTITUTE OF ECONOMIC AND SOCIAL RESEARCH TEAM (1990) 'Productivity, education and training: Britain and other countries compared'. *National Institute Economic Review*. London, NIESR.

PRICE D. (1996) 'How marketing can sell your personnel product'. *People Management*. Vol. 2, 12. p21.

PUGH D. S. (1971) (ED.) *Organization Theory: Selected readings*. Harmondsworth, Penguin.

RACKHAM N., HONEY P. *and* COLBERT M. (1971) *Developing Interactive Skills*. Northampton, Wellens Publishing.

RAELIN J. A. (1994) 'Whither management education? Professional education, action learning and beyond'. *Management Learning*. Vol. 25, 2. p305.

RAINBIRD H. (1993) 'Vocational education and training', in M. Gold (ed.), *The Social Dimension: Employment policy in the European Community*. London, Macmillan, pp184–202.

RAINBIRD H. (1994) 'The changing role of the training function: a test for the integration of human resource and business strategies'. *Human Resource Management*. Vol. 5, 1. pp72–90.

RANA E. (1999) 'Firms take a dim view of New Deal'. *People Management*. Vol. 5, 11. p14.

RANA E. (1999a) 'NTOs debate radical plans for voluntary investment'. *People Management*. Vol. 5, 18. p17.

RANA E. (1999b) 'New Deal firms under fire for training deficiencies'. *People Management*. Vol. 5, 16. p18.

RANA E. (1999c) 'IIP's credibility questioned despite satisfaction poll'. *People Management*. Vol. 5, 20. p15.

RANA E. (1999d) 'Recipe for succession'. *People Management*. Vol. 5, 16. pp32–7.

RANA E. (1999e) 'Firms fear being sidelined in skills council overhaul'. *People Management*. Vol. 5, 21. p12.

RANA E. (1999f) 'E-learning "will fail" unless it is focused on the users'. *People Management*. Vol. 5, 24. p11.

RANA E. (1999g) 'Failure to embrace online learning will hit firms hard'. *People Management*. Vol. 5. p16.

RANA E. (2000) 'National Skills Task Force rules out universal levy'. *People Management*. Vol. 6, 2. p13.

RANA E. (2000a) 'IIP revamp aims to cut back on bureaucracy'. *People Management*. Vol. 6, 8. p14.

RANKINE K. (1999) 'M&S nervous as shares fall again'. *Daily Telegraph*. 25 September. p27.

READY D. A., VICERE A. A. *and* WHITE A. F. (1994) 'Linking executive education to strategic imperatives'. *Management Learning*. Vol. 25, 4. pp563–78.

REDAY-MULVEY G. *and* TAYLOR P. (1996) 'Why working lives must be extended'. *People Management.* Vol. 2, 10. pp24–9.

REFAUSSE J. (1996) 'Self-knowledge to lift career spirits'. *People Management.* Vol. 2, 10. pp34–5.

REID M. A. *and* BARRINGTON H. (1997) *Training Interventions: Managing employee development.* 5th edn. London, Institute of Personnel and Development.

REID M. A. *and* BARRINGTON H. (1999) *Training Interventions: Promoting learning opportunities.* 6th edn. London, Institute of Personnel and Development.

REVANS R. W. (1971) *Developing Effective Managers.* London, Longman.

RILEY K. *and* SLOMAN M. (1991) 'Milestones for the personnel department'. *Personnel Management.* Vol. 23, 8. pp34–7.

RITCHIE J. (1993) 'Strategies for human resource management: challenges in smaller and entrepreneurial organisations', in R. Harrison (ed.), *Human Resource Management: Issues and strategies.* Wokingham, Addison Wesley, pp111–35.

ROBERTS C. (2000) 'The only way is up'. *People Management.* Vol. 6, 1. p25.

ROBINSON D. G. *and* ROBINSON J. C. (1989) *Training for Impact.* London, Jossey-Bass.

RODGER D. *and* MABEY C. (1987) 'BT's leap forward from assessment centres'. *Personnel Management.* Vol. 19, 7. pp32–5.

RUMELT R. P. (1991) 'How much does industry matter?' *Strategic Management Journal.* Vol. 12, 3. pp167–85.

RUSH D. (1999) 'Baldock stays on in M&D chair'. *Sunday Times, Busine*ss. 26 September. p3.

RUSSELL C. *and* PARSONS E. (1996) 'Putting theory to the test at the OU'. *People Management.* Vol. 2, 1. pp30–32.

SADLER P. (1989) 'Management development', in K. Sisson (ed.), *Personnel Management in Britain.* Oxford, Blackwell, pp222–43.

SADLER P. *and* BARHAM K. (1988) 'From Franks to the future: 25 years of management training prescriptions'. *Personnel Management.* Vol. 20. pp48–51.

SAINT AUGUSTINE, *Confessions.* Tr. R. S. Pine-Coffin (1964). London, Penguin Classics.

SCARBROUGH H. (1999) 'System error'. *People Management.* Vol. 5, 7. pp68–74.

SCARBROUGH H. *and* SWAN J. (EDS) (1999) *Case Studies in Knowledge Management.* London, Institute of Personnel and Development.

SCARBROUGH H., SWAN J. *and* PRESTON J. (1999) *Knowledge Management: A literature review.* London, Institute of Personnel and Development.

SCHANK R. (1999) 'Courses of action'. *People Management.* Vol. 5, 20. pp54–7.

SCHEIN E. H. (1978) *Career Dynamics: Matching individual and organizational needs.* Reading, MA, Addison Wesley.

SCHENDEL D. (1994) 'Introduction to "Competitive organizational behaviour: toward an organizationally-based theory of competitive advantage"'. *Strategic Management Journal, Winter Special Issue.* Vol. 15. pp1–4.

SCHONFIELD D. (1999) 'Harmony at work – this year's model?' *People Management*. Vol. 5, 19. pp18–19.

SCHUCK G. (1996) 'Intelligent technology, intelligent workers: a new pedagogy for the high-tech workplace', in K. Starkey (ed.), *How Organizations Learn*. London, International Thomson Business Press, pp199–213.

SCHULTZ T. W. (1961) 'Investment in human capital'. *American Economic Review*. Vol. 51, 1. pp1–17.

SCHWEIGER D. *and* WEBER Y. (1999) 'Strategies for managing human resources during mergers and acquisitions: an empirical investigation'. *Human Resource Planning*. Vol. 12, 2. pp69–86.

SCOTT-CLARK C. *and* RAYMENT T (1995) 'Scandal of our dummy degrees'. *Sunday Times*. 3 September. pp12–13.

SEGALL A. (1996) 'OECD praises example of British jobs market'. *Daily Telegraph*. 22 May. p28.

SEMLER R. (1994) 'The brave new world of Semco manufacturing'. *Probono*. pp8–10.

SENGE P. M. (1990) *The Fifth Discipline: The art and practice of the learning organization*. New York, Doubleday.

SEYMOUR W. D. (1966) *Skills Analysis Training*. London, Pitman.

SIDDONS S. (1997) *Delivering Training*. London, Institute of Personnel and Development.

SILVERMAN D. (1970) *The Theory of Organizations*. London, Heinemann Educational Books.

SISSON K. (ED.) (1994) *Personnel Management: A comprehensive guide to theory and practice in Britain*. 2nd edn. Oxford, Blackwell.

SISSON K. *and* STOREY J. (1988) 'Developing effective managers: a review of the issues and an agenda for research'. *Personnel Review*. Vol. 17, 4. pp3–8.

SKINNER D. *and* MABEY C. (1995) 'How do organisations conceive, design and implement human resource strategies?' *Working Paper*. Open University Business School, Centre for Human Resource and Change Management.

SLOMAN M. (1994) 'Coming in from the cold: a new role for trainers', *Personnel Management*. Vol. 26, 1. pp24–7.

SMITH A. (1999) 'Get with the programme'. *People Management*. Vol. 5, 11. p33.

SMITH A. D. (1995) 'Europe has a multitude of systems and certificates'. *Guardian*. 30 May.

SMITH D. (1996) 'The training that just isn't working'. *Sunday Times*, 28 April. p8.

SMITH D. (2000) 'Why the New Deal isn't working'. *Sunday Times*, *News Review*. 16 April. p6.

SMITHERS R. (2000) 'Universities forge alliance for global teaching on net'. *Guardian*. 15 March. p5.

SPARROW P. (1996) 'Too good to be true'. *People Management*. Vol. 2, 24. pp22–7.

SPARROW P. *and* HILTROP J-M. (1994*)* *European Human Resource Management in Transition*. London, Prentice Hall.

SPURLING M. *and* TROLLEY E. (2000) 'How to make training strategic'. *People Management*. Vol. 6, 8. pp46–8.

STALK G., EVANS P. *and* SHULMAN L. E. (1992) 'Competing on

capabilities: the new rules of corporate strategy'. *Harvard Business Review*. March–April. pp57–69.

STAMMERS R. and PATRICK J. (1977) *The Psychology of Training*. London, Methuen.

STARKEY K. (ed.) (1996) *How Organizations Learn*. London, International Thomson Business Press.

STEAD V. and LEE M. (1996) 'Inter-cultural perspectives on HRD', in J. Stewart and J. McGoldrick (eds), *Human Resource Development: Perspectives, Strategies and Practice*, London, Pitman, pp47–70.

STEEDMAN H. (1987) 'Vocational training in France and Britain: office work', *Discussion Paper No. 14, National Institute of Economic and Social Research*. London, NIESR.

STEEDMAN H. (1990) 'Speaking practically, the French have it'. *Independent*. 5 September.

STEVENS C. (1985) 'Assessment centres: the British experience'. *Personnel Management*. Vol. 17, 7. pp28–31.

STEVENS J. and ASHTON D. (1999) 'Underperformance appraisal'. *People Management*. Vol. 5, 14. pp31–2.

STEWART B. (1996) 'Firms do better when EVA keeps the score'. *Sunday Times. Business Focus*. 8 December. 2.5.

STEWART R. (1984) 'The nature of management? A problem for management education'. *Journal of Management Studies*. Vol. 21, 3. pp323–30.

STOREY J. (1991) 'Do the Japanese make better managers?' *Personnel Management*. Vol. 23, 8. pp24–8.

STOREY J. (1992) *Developments in the Management of Human Resources*. Oxford, Blackwell.

STOREY J. (1994) 'How new-style management is taking hold'. *Personnel Management*. Vol. 26, 1. pp32–5.

STOREY J. and SISSON K. (1990) 'Limits to transformation: human resource management in the British context'. *Industrial Relations Journal*. Vol. 21, 1. pp60–65.

STOREY J., EDWARDS P and SISSON K. (1997) *Managers in the Making: Careers, development and control in corporate Britain and Japan*. London, Sage.

STOREY J., MABEY C. and THOMSON A. (1997) 'What a difference a decade makes'. *People Management*. Vol. 3, 12. pp28–30.

STREDL H. J. and ROTHWELL W. J. (1987) *The ASTD Reference Guide to Professional Training Roles and Competencies*. Amsherst, MA, HRD Press Inc.

SWIERINGA J. and WIERDSMA A. (1992) *Becoming a Learning Organization: Beyond the learning curve*. Wokingham, Addison Wesley.

SYRETT M. (1988) 'Taking licence with the future of management'. *Sunday Times*. 10 April.

TATE R. (1995) 'Food for thought'. *People Management*. Vol. 1, 20. p30.

TAYLOR F. W. (1947) *Scientific Management*. New York, Harper and Row.

TAYLOR R. (1994) 'Reconciling commitment and flexibility'. *Financial Times*. 1 June. p15.

TEECE D. J., PISANO G. *and* SHUEN A. (1994) 'Dynamic capabilities and strategic management'. *Working Paper.* Cambridge, MA, Harvard Business School.

TERRY M. *and* PURCELL J. (1997) 'Return to slender'. *People Management.* Vol. 3, 21. pp46, 47.

TESTER N. (1999) 'High on hope, low on detail'. *Guardian Further Education.* 16 November. pp2F, 3F.

THOMAS K. *and* MELLON T. (1995) *Planning for Training and Development: A guide to analysing needs.* London, Save the Children.

THOMAS M. *and* ELBEIK S. (1996) *Supercharge Your Management Role.* London, Butterworth–Heinemann.

THORNTON P. (2000) 'Manufacturing loses 122,000 jobs as unemployment falls to 20-year low'. *Independent.* 16 March. p20.

TIMES HIGHER EDUCATION SUPPLEMENT (1997) *The Dearing Report (Summary and views).* 24 July.

TORRINGTON D. *and* WEIGHTMAN J. (1985) *The Business of Management.* London, Prentice Hall.

TORRINGTON D., HALL L., HAYLOR I. *and* MYERS J. (1991) *Employee Resourcing.* London, Institute of Personnel and Development.

TOSEY P. (1993) 'Interfering with the interference: a systemic approach to change in organisations'. *Management Education and Development.* Vol. 24, 3. pp187–204.

TRADES UNION CONGRESS (1999) *Britain's Skills Gap.* Available from the TUC, tel. 020 7636 4030.

TRIST E. *and* BAMFORTH K. (1951) 'Some social and psychological consequences of the longwall method of coal-getting'. *Human Relations.* Vol. 4. pp3–38.

TUCKER B. (ED.) (1997) *Handbook of Technology-based Training.* Aldershot, Gower.

UCAS (1998) *A Statistical Bulletin of Subject Trend 1997 Entry.* Universities and Colleges Admissions Service.

ULRICH D. (1987) 'Organizational capability as a competitive advantage: human resource professionals as strategic partners'. *Human Resource Planning.* Part 4. pp169–84.

UNEMPLOYMENT UNIT AND YOUTHAID (1996) *Working Brief No. 52.* 409 Brixton Road, London, SW9 7DG.

VAN ADELSBERG D. *and* TROLLEY E. (1999) *Running Training Like a Business – Delivering unmistakable value.* San Francisco, CA, Berrett-Koehler. Distributed in the UK by McGraw-Hill.

VAN DER KLINK M. *and* MULDER M. (1995) 'Human resource development and staff flow policy in Europe', in A-W. Harzing and J. van Ruysseveldt (eds), *International Human Resource Management.* London, Sage, pp157–78.

VICTOR P. (1995) 'Companies cannot pass the buck on training'. *People Management.* Vol. 1, 18. p23.

VON KROGH G., ROOS J. *and* SLOCUM K. (1994) 'An essay on corporate epistemology'. *Strategic Management Journal, Summer Special Issue.* Vol. 15. pp53–71.

VROOM V. H. *and* DECI E. L. (eds) (1970) *Management and Motivation: Selected readings.* Harmondsworth, Penguin.

WALSH J. (1999) 'HR "slow to gain input at board level"'. *People Management.* Vol. 5, 15. p15.

WALTON J. (1996) 'The provision of learning support for non-employees', in J. Stewart and J. McGoldrick (eds), *Human Resource Development: Perspectives, strategies and practice*. London, Pitman, pp120–37.

WALTON J. (1999) *Strategic Human Resource Development*. Harlow, Financial Times and Prentice Hall.

WALTON J. (1999a) 'Outsourcing: What stays in and what goes out', in J. Walton, *Strategic Human Resource Development*. Harlow, Financial Times and Prentice Hall, pp279–99.

WALTON J. (1999b) 'Working in the virtual organisation', in J. Walton, *Strategic Human Resource Development*. Harlow, Financial Times and Prentice Hall, pp536–57.

WALTON J. (1999c) 'Small and medium-sized enterprises and human resource development', in J. Walton, *Strategic Human Resource Development*. Harlow, Financial Times and Prentice Hall, pp324–51.

WAPLES J. (1999) 'Revolting investors'. *Sunday Times Business Focus*. 31 January. p3.5.

WARMAN C. (2000) 'Face-to-face help', *Times*. 22 February. p45.

WARR P. B. *and* BIRD M. W. (1968) 'Identifying supervisory training needs'. *Training Information Paper No. 2*. London, HMSO.

WARR P., BIRD M. W. *and* RACKHAM N. (1970) *Evaluation of Management Training*. Aldershot, Gower.

WEAVER M. (1988) 'Inside the spending factory'. *Daily Telegraph*. 1 September.

WEBSTER B. (1990) 'Beyond the mechanics of HRD'. *Personnel Management*. Vol. 22, 3. pp44–7.

WEINBERGER L. A. (1998) 'Commonly held theories of human resource development'. *Human Resource Development International*. Vol. 1, 1. pp75–93.

WELCH J. (1997) 'Bank trainers take on "troubleshooter" role'. *People Management*. Vol. 3, 2. p7.

WELCH J. (1997a) 'Charities face battle to recruit volunteers'. *People Management*. Vol. 3, 5. p12.

WELCH J. (1999) 'Social chapter gives HR an opportunity to shine'. *People Management*. Vol. 5, 17. p13.

WERNERFELT B. (1984) 'A resource-based view of the firm'. *Strategic Management Journal*. Vol. 10. pp17–32.

WHEELWRIGHT S. C. *and* CLARK K. B. (1992) *Revolutionizing Product Development*. New York, Free Press.

WHIDDETT S. *and* HOLLYFORDE S. (1999) *The Competencies Handbook*. London, Institute of Personnel and Development.

WHIPP R. (1992) 'Human resource management, competition and strategy: some productive tensions', in P. Blyton and P. Turnbull (eds), *Re-Assessing Human Resource Management*. London, Sage, pp33–55.

WHITE M. (1996) 'Flexible response'. *People Management*. Vol. 2, 6. p33.

WHITE M. *and* TREVOR M. (1983) *Under Japanese Management*. London, Heinemann.

WHITEHEAD M. (1999) 'Task Force hints at return to seventies' training levy'. *People Management*. Vol. 5, 5. p17.

WHITEHEAD M. (1999a) 'Firms ignore staff needs in key areas of the economy'. *People Management*. Vol. 5, 3. p16.

WHITEHEAD M. (1999b) 'Compulsory training levy back on ministers' agenda'. *People Management*. Vol. 5, 4. p11.

WHITEHEAD M. (1999c) 'Blunkett drops TEC report in favour of wider review'. *People Management*. Vol. 5, 6. p11.

WHITEHEAD M. (1999d) 'Employers and colleges jostle over TEC review'. *People Management*. Vol. 5, 8. p14.

WHITFIELD M. (1995) 'High-flyer hazards'. *People Management*. Vol. 1, 24. p9.

WICKENS P. (1987) *The Road to Nissan*. London, Macmillan.

WILLE E. (1990) 'Should management development be just for managers?' *Personnel Management*. Vol. 22, 8. pp34–7.

WILLIAMS R. (1984) 'What's new in career development'. *Personnel Management*. Vol. 16, 3. pp32–3.

WILLMAN J. (1994) 'With a greyer picture of the future in mind'. *Financial Times*. 8 March. p14.

WILLS M. (2000) 'The new keys to learning'. *Daily Telegraph*. 16 March. p9.

WISSEMA J. G., BRAND A. F. *and* VAN DER POL H. W. (1981) 'The incorporation of management development in strategic management'. *Strategic Management Journal*. Vol. 2. pp361–77.

WOLF M. (1994) 'Can Europe compete? A relapse into Eurosclerosis'. *Financial Times*. 24 February. p21.

WOOD A. (1994) *North South Trade and Income Inequality*. Brighton, Institute for Development Studies.

WOOD L. (1992) 'Change starts at the top'. *Financial Times*. 25 August. p8.

WOODRUFFE C. (1991) 'Competent by any other name'. *Personnel Management*. Vol. 23, 9. pp30–33.

WOODRUFFE C. (1997) 'Going back a generation'. *People Management*. Vol. 3, 4. pp32–4.

WOODRUFFE C. (2000) *Development and Assessment Centres: Identifying and assessing competence*. 3rd edn. London, Institute of Personnel and Development.

WRIGHT P. L. *and* TAYLOR D. S. (1994) *Improving Leadership Performance: Interpersonal skills for effective leadership*. 2nd edn. London, Prentice Hall.

ZABRISKIE N. B. *and* HUELLMANTEL A. B. (1991) 'Developing strategic thinking in senior management'. *Long Range Planning*. Vol. 24, 6. pp25–32.

APPENDICES

APPENDIX 1

THE CHARTERED INSTITUTE OF PERSONNEL AND DEVELOPMENT'S PROFESSIONAL STANDARDS FOR EMPLOYEE DEVELOPMENT

Rationale

Employee Development (ED) focuses on the key generalist skills and competences required to manage and develop the potential of employees to the mutual benefit of employee and employer, in support of the organisation's overall business objectives.

The purpose of the 'generalist/specialist' module is to develop further the core module coverage with the aim of achieving basic professional competence in ED. The module is for those who wish to qualify, at least initially, as a 'generalist'. It is designed to provide sufficient knowledge, understanding and competence for individuals to operate as professional personnel practitioners in a variety of situations.

The module may either be followed as part of a 'generalist' route or alternatively it may be combined with other specialist ED modules to give input for the 'specialist' route to professional competence. It has been designed to be evolutionary in terms of the current CIPD Professional Qualification Scheme whilst being consistent with the former Institute of Training and Development approach and the emerging Personnel Standards Lead Body (PSLB) standards.

Learning outcomes

To be able to:

a) Identify an appropriate outline learning strategy from an organisation's business plan.

b) Prepare an ED policy statement and specify means for its continuous review.

c) Integrate the objectives of performance management with the learning strategy and ED policy.

d) Carry out a training needs analysis for a range of occupations and job levels.

e) Identify learning objectives to meet specific development needs.

f) Design training and development materials and select appropriate delivery methods and media.

g) Prepare and deliver a basic learning programme with an integral review process.

h) Identify the relative costs of alternative learning strategies. Prepare an annual budget for a variety of ED situations and analyse variations from budget. Determine corrective action for adverse variances.

i) Design approaches to assessment and evaluation for a range of development situations.

j) Identify the competencies required for a range of tasks and use these to identify development needs.

k) Specify the criteria required in the selection of training staff, conduct selection interview and identify the main elements of a suitable training and development programme.

l) Identify the main criteria used in specifying contract terms for the supply of training and/or education from an external source.

m) Design a policy for career and management development.

To understand and explain:

a) The nature of ED in a national and international context.

b) The nature of corporate learning strategy and its part in planned organisational change.

c) Identifying the current employee development contribution to the organisation's development, identifying the employee development strategic aim and gaining commitment.

d) The integration of ED with other areas of P&D with the business strategy.

e) The language of business and the need to be able to set ED in the context of the organisation.

f) How to identify the need for resources for training and to set up a training department, centre or contract with external suppliers.

g) A wide range of approaches to ED for all categories of employees.

h) The design test and use of technology-based approaches (including computer-based training, interactive video and multi-media) to learning.

i) How individuals can maintain their personal and professional development throughout their careers.

j) The identification and use of 'competencies' in the process of determining development and potential.

Indicative content

1 The Employee Development (ED) contribution

a) The nature of ED, its component parts and its role within a human resourcing policy; the integration of ED with business strategy.

b) Ethics and professionalism in ED.

c) ED in the national and international context; the impact of and lessons to be gained from different legal, political, social and value systems; the impact of global competition on ED strategies.

2 Development strategy and plans

a) Analysis and understanding of the organisation's strategy and goals; identification of the Learning Strategy and its contribution to corporate success.

b) Ways of identifying strategic choices and the management of change processes; the role of ED in change programmes.

c) The role of and alternative approaches to organisation development.

d) Characteristics of the 'learning organisation'.

e) How to manage the career development of individuals.

f) Approaches to ED strategy in a range of organisations, eg large and small companies, public and private sector organisations, non-profit-making organisations.

3 Performance management

a) The ED aspects of approaches to performance management.

b) Links with motivation, management styles and reward strategies.

c) The introduction and development of the skills necessary to implement performance management.

4 Training

a) The preparation of a training plan for a range of organisations.

b) Setting up, resourcing and managing a training function; the role of trainers as training deliverers, internal consultants, change agents and/or managers of learning resources.

c) The role of line management in ED; the manager as mentor or coach.

d) The identification of the costs and benefits of ED; the preparation of training and development budgets and their management and gaining commitment for the resources required.

e) The internal marketing of ED – preparing a marketing plan, 'branding' and monitoring customers' reactions.

f) The assessment and evaluation of the organisation's learning strategies and their contribution to the objectives of the organisation.

g) The development needs of ED staff; career patterns and learning events for developing skills; the management skills needs of ED practitioners.

h) The design, test and modification for use of Information Technology (IT) based development materials.

i) The 'competence' approach, the role of NCVQ and Awarding Bodies; the S/NVQ qualification structure and assessment of workplace competence.

5 Long-term individual development

a) The identification and implementation of career development and management development strategies – management/ graduate trainees, succession planning and the use of appraisal.

b) Continuing Professional Development (CPD) – the CIPD CPD statement, the implementation of CPD, identifying needs from training course to self-development; preparation of personal CPD plans.

6 Team development

a) The philosophy and content of a range of approaches, eg Belbin, Margerison and McCann, outdoor development.

b) Identifying the contribution and limitations of team development in improving performance.

c) The role of interpersonal skills training and leadership and assertiveness training in team development.

7 Equal opportunities and special training needs

a) Training and development in special areas: safety, induction, young people, the disabled, ethnic minorities, preparation for retirement.

b) Ensuring equal access to all ED activities.

APPENDIX 2

NATIONAL VOCATIONAL QUALIFICATIONS (NVQs)

An NVQ represents a statement of competence confirming that the individual can perform to a specified standard at one of five levels in a range of work-related activities, and has the related skills, knowledge and understanding that make that performance possible in a work setting. NVQs are awarded by various examining bodies whose courses incorporate standards laid down by the various industry Lead Bodies. Courses in England, Wales and Northern Ireland are accredited by the Qualifications and Curriculum Authority, set up in 1997. Those in Scotland are accredited by the Scottish Qualifications Authority. Certificates carry both the NVQ stamp and that of the examining bodies. (Further information can be found on the website www.qca.org.uk).

NVQs must by definition meet the needs of an occupational sector as a whole, not just those of an individual organisation. They must also prepare people for changing demands on occupations. Each qualification approved by the NCVQ is assigned to one of five levels within the NVQ framework from level one (semi-skilled) to level five (higher professionals). This framework provides comparability between different occupations and between vocational and academic qualifications. Some qualifications are easier to integrate into the NVQ system than others, because many professions have a highly structured system for gaining qualifications, some including competencies but some being more educationally based.

Credit accumulation and transfer (CAT)

CAT is a system that enables people to achieve a level of competence and associated NVQs through various methods of training and work experience, at various centres and over varying periods of time. The aim is that all qualifications should be designed in such a way that they can be offered on a modular basis and tested by judging someone's competence in the job. This is similar to the highly successful French vocational training and education schemes.

To this end every NVQ is made up of a number of units comprising groups of elements that state precisely in outcome terms what people are expected to do, together with the performance criteria that define the key characteristics of competent performance for each element.

Credits are then given for the acquisition of units. Using the CAT system a workplace supervisor with training responsibilities could gain one or perhaps two units of a training and development NVQ mainly through having his or her workplace performance assessed as meeting the standards laid down in those elements. Having been assessed as competent in those specific areas of activity, the supervisor could add to them subsequently at choice.

Each unit therefore builds up the credit balance of an individual's 'competence account'. Ways are being explored to express all existing qualifications in terms of units. Units certificated by different awarding bodies can then be accumulated and it should prove possible for units common to two or more qualifications to be transferred in order to avoid repetition in training and assessment.

Accreditation of prior learning (APL)

Since APL and performance in the workplace, or a realistic simulation of it, are central to the process of achieving an NVQ, assessment of workplace competence and of prior learning require close collaboration between colleges, training organisations and employers. The award of an NVQ depends upon a competent assessor being satisfied that a candidate has provided enough evidence of competence across all the elements/outcomes with their performance criteria and range, which make up the units in a particular qualification. This has clear implications for appraisal schemes and also for the identification of training needs and the design of training and development experiences that can both meet job-related needs and help in achieving NVQs.

APPENDIX 3

COMPARISON BETWEEN 1995 NATIONAL
EDUCATION AND TRAINING TARGETS FOR 2000,
AND 1998 NATIONAL LEARNING TARGETS FOR
2002

Foundation learning

By age 11 (1998 only)

80 per cent to reach level 4 in national tests in literacy, and 75 per cent in numeracy (1998)

By age 16 (1998 only)

50 per cent to reach GCSE Grade A to C equivalent
95 per cent to reach at least one GCSE

By age 19 (1995 and 1998)

85 per cent of young people to reach NVQ level 2 or equivalent (1998)

(75 per cent to achieve level 2 in core skills of communication, numeracy and information technology – 1995. Taken out in 1998.)

By age 21 (1995 and 1998)

60 per cent to reach NVQ level 3 or equivalent (1998)

(35 per cent to achieve NVQ level 3 in the core skills – 1995. Taken out in 1998.)

Lifetime learning (1995 and 1998)

50 per cent of workforce to reach NVQ level 3 or equivalent (1998)
(60 per cent, 1995)

24 per cent of workforce to reach NVQ level 4 or equivalent (1998)
(30 per cent, 1995)

45 per cent of medium-sized (50-plus employees) or large organisations and 10,000 small organisations (1998) to gain Investors in People standard *(70 per cent of 200-employee organisations and 35 per cent of those with more than 50 staff, 1995)*

(Sources: People Management, 31 May 1995, page 8, and National Advisory Council on Education and Training Targets)

APPENDIX 4

THE COMPREHENSIVE AND THE PROBLEM-CENTRED APPROACHES TO IDENTIFYING AND ANALYSING ORGANISATIONAL HRD NEEDS

These two approaches are based on the same general principles, but in their detailed operation they cater for different kinds of situation.

The *total, or comprehensive, approach* involves a systematic, full-scale analysis of all the organisation's training and development needs, identified by discussions with managers (and unions as relevant), by analysis of the corporate business plan, and by examination of any other sources of likely change affecting people in the organisation. Its product is an organisation-wide training plan containing unit and individual plans for the forthcoming year (a year is usually the planning period for this kind of approach). It can be relevant for organisations where the environment is relatively stable, and where longer-term training plans can feasibly be produced and pursued, although it is unlikely to be used unless there is a specialist personnel/training function. If you are following this approach you must ensure that you have the necessary time and other resources, and that it will justify such expenditure.

For organisations operating in an unpredictable environment, facing severe pressures, and/or (like many small to medium-sized firms) lacking the resources or expertise for the 'total' strategy, something more selective and immediate in its payback is needed. For them, the 'problem-centred' analytical approach may be the most appropriate.

The *'problem-centred' approach* focuses on urgent problems facing the organisation and requiring a training/development response. It places minimum reliance on paperwork. The assumption here is that the planning of training must be ongoing and focused on immediate needs, with long-term strategy at a minimum, there may be no formalised training plan other than papers that from time to time have to be drawn up for budgetary or external purposes. Training must respond quickly to any urgent needs, and so flexibility in the function and its operations is essential.

Both approaches are systematic; it is the timescale and scope of assessment and planning that are the major differentiating factors. Here is a step-by-step guide to their implementation.

THE TOTAL, OR COMPREHENSIVE, APPROACH

Step 1: Identify major needs

The first step is to study the organisation's business strategy and plan. Training/personnel staff should then discuss with every manager the training and development needs for their units. At this stage, they need to bring into the discussions implications of any impending organisational changes, new technology initiatives, new plant and machinery and new staff coming into the organisation. In establishing training needs they should be influenced by managers' interpretation of events as well as by areas of need identified in corporate strategy.

Step 2: Agree possible solutions

During this phase of the discussion, the degree to which training can contribute to meeting departmental needs must be assessed. Performance targets and outputs of the department must be examined, together with any other data that will give substance and objectivity to the discussions. Information about many training needs may come from the results of appraisal interviews. Where an appraisal system is not yet operative, information will come from such sources as managers' views and the views of any other key parties, performance records, career plans and potential reviews.

Problems perceived initially by managers to have a training and development solution may on analysis prove to be problems needing some other solution, and vice versa. It is therefore essential to be clear as to the real nature of a problem. If performance is poor, for example, it may be because of inadequate or non-existent training, but it could as easily be because of poor motivation, ineffective management or faulty equipment.

Thus in this second step the training manager (with help as needed) has detailed talks with line management to ensure that the departmental and individual needs they raise will be best and most cost-effectively tackled by some form of training or development. They will also need to jointly define and agree those needs and apply a prioritisation system that reflects overall objectives established in the organisation's corporate training policy.

Step 3: Select training options

At this point it is important to discuss options for training, with a view to the process being as cost-efficient as possible. Initially the possibility of on-the-job events to achieve the required learning should be discussed rather than looking at external courses of action as a priority. Such discussion can lead to a significant shift from a reliance on external courses to an emphasis on in-house training, much of it delivered by consultants. It can also lead to line managers, supervisors and other non-specialist training personnel in the organisation taking significant responsibility for design and delivery of training once they have acquired the necessary level of competency. Such a shift must obviously be accompanied by appropriate training and development of such external and internal personnel and by careful monitoring of processes and outcomes.

Step 4: Create training plan

Next, the training manager constructs the first draft of the annual training plan, which identifies each department's and each individual's training needs and the relevant courses of action agreed with the managers of those departments and individuals.

Step 5: Prioritise learning events

The budgeting process conducted by the training manager starts at this point, when, within the training plan, he or she classifies training needs and events on a scale (which could simply be an 'A' to 'E' rating system, A being 'essential training/development', E being 'desirable but not necessarily this year') according to priorities established in corporate training policy. This means that each training event is prioritised in accordance with corporate business needs, so that when finalised the training plan is geared to make an optimum contribution to the achievement of business objectives as well as to individual needs.

Step 6: Apply budgetary constraints

After training has been categorised, the training manager should then estimate the costs involved in the initial draft of the training plan, including the options that were discussed with managers. Costing should be done using current costs (an inflationary factor can be added later), examining both direct and indirect costs.

In an organisation where managers are required to submit departmental budgets for the coming financial year in, say, late January, total budget figures need to be allocated before the beginning of the financial year. This will enable managers to allocate resources appropriately according to their budget allocation, based on their January submissions. Once the training manager receives his or her budget allocation, adjustments to the plan are quite straightforward if it has been built up on a prioritised pyramid of costs, descending from 'essential' to 'can be deferred if necessary'. Reappraisal of the options available may result, for example, in the use of more internal training, or in dropping some training in the category that lists training agreed to carry lowest priority. In the latter event, subsequent reassessment of the original need should be carried out, to see whether or not training is still appropriate and needs to be done in the next budget year.

Step 7: Communicate results

Once the training plan has been fully costed and agreed by the board, a copy of the relevant sections should be given to each manager as an *aide-mémoire* and plan for each department. This then becomes an essential tool of reference for the review meetings the training manager holds with managers throughout the forthcoming year.

Step 8: Monitor and evaluate implementation

A continuous appraisal of progress and budgetary control should be maintained by the training department, using information supplied by management and those who go on training and development programmes. The task is not a difficult one when the training plan has been costed in relation to specific learning events and departments, with clear categories covering course fees, travel and related expenses, and fees paid to external consultants and trainers. Monitoring is vital for two reasons:

- It enables a tight control to be exercised over ongoing training, so that if at any point in time costs are exceeded appropriate action can be taken. If, on the other hand, it should happen that costs fall below estimate, then there is flexibility to either include any hitherto-deferred training or to carry out training to meet some unexpected contingency.

- It enables the training manager to build up a 'value for money' statement that can be included in the annual report on the training plan. This can include statements related to key parameters like:

  - outcomes of training, in relation to key needs it was intended to serve (using quantifiable and qualitative measures)

  - expenditure overall on training, compared with last year

  - number and cost of person days of training, compared with last year

  - number and cost of person days of training carried out externally and in-house, compared with last year.

THE PROBLEM-CENTRED APPROACH

Here is how the eight steps can be applied using the problem-centred approach. (Throughout, reference is made to 'the training manager' but this should be taken to mean anyone who carries the responsibility for formulating training policy and a training plan for the organisation.)

Step 1: Identify major needs
The training manager should identify with managers on a continuing basis the most urgent problems or challenges they face, for which it is felt that some form of training or development would be the best solution. Analysis itself is carried out in a similar way to that outlined in the comprehensive approach. At regular intervals (determined by the length of the business planning cycle) the training manager must check on any information available about business plans and likely future changes, to see if training is needed to feed into those.

Step 2: Agree possible solutions
Here, as with the 'total' approach, the training manager must analyse whether particular problems are not only relevant for training to tackle, but are problems to which training would be the most cost-effective and cost-efficient response. In making a decision consideration must be given, within the constraints of corporate policy and employee resource systems, to alternative options such as changing equipment, jobs, people or organisation structure.

With the problem-centred approach priorities are determined by the extent to which one problem, if resolved, would make a greater impact on immediate business performance than another. Areas of weakness that are currently impeding achievement of results crucial to the company's survival must therefore be tackled first. Longer-term issues such as succession planning needs must also be tackled on an ongoing basis in the light of their importance to ensuring continuity and calibre of uniquely valuable personnel.

Step 3: Select training options

Here, agreement must be reached on who is to be trained, how many, when and where they will need training, and how they will be trained. Training can be done in any cost-effective, feasible and agreed way, but must take place in or near the work environment wherever possible, both to reduce costs and to ensure immediate relevance and transferability of learning. Events selected under the problem-centred approach must be mainly concerned to achieve results in the shortest possible time, and in the most efficient manner.

Step 4: Create training plan

Training to meet certain major needs will usually be planned and agreed some time in advance (for example, health and safety training, retraining to cope with redundancies or redeployment of workers, or training to enable key workers to operate new technology). That apart, the training plan will be informal rather than heavily documented. A record should, however, be kept of the number and names of the learners, of training objectives, of the type, location and timing of the training, and of its timing, cost and outcomes related to objectives.

Step 5: Prioritise learning events

Although training, with the problem-centred approach, is done on a rolling basis rather than on the basis of an annual plan, attention must still be paid to prioritising events. Planning no more, probably, than a few weeks or months ahead, the training manager must still ensure that the training effort is put into those problem areas across the company where there will be the most significant return in terms of impact on the business. So, as with the prioritisation of departmental or divisional training needs, attention must be given first to those areas having a critical impact on the firm's survival, and crucial to its future stability and growth.

Step 6: Apply budgetary constraints

The training manager may not have a budget (or may only hold a small central budget for core training and development needs), but be paid from the budgets held by line managers. It is therefore particularly important that he or she has a clear idea of what the business overall, and particular departments within it, can afford for the training they are requesting. All training must be carefully costed. When line managers hold budgetary control, particularly close attention needs to be given to 'hidden' costs like lost opportunity and lost production, replacement or other costs involved in covering for people away from their jobs for a period of time. The training manager must be able to convince that training can offer the value needed to offset costs.

Step 7: Communicate results

With the problem-centred approach, initial requests for training must be acted upon quickly, and information about training and development activities that will be going ahead must be communicated to the managers concerned as soon as possible.

In situations where the problem-centred approach is used, certainty can rarely be built into any stage of the cycle. Even at the last minute action plans may have to be cancelled or postponed because of some contingency. Communications at that point must work particularly well in order to ensure that everyone is informed about the reasons for the changes, and that wherever possible alternative ways of responding to the initial request (assuming it is still valid) can be agreed.

Step 8: Monitor and evaluate implementation

Evaluation is essential in order to ensure that scarce resources (including time) are being used effectively. The initial clear specification of the nature of the problem and the exact outcomes training is intended to produce, together with agreement between training manager and line managers about how those outcomes will be measured, should ease the task of evaluation. Identifiable improvements in competences, and measurable impact on the indicators chosen beforehand – for example, material wastage rates, levels of employee absenteeism, turnover, learning times, indices of customer satisfaction, speed and quality of service provided – should all be used in order to assess the extent to which training has had an impact on the problems it was intended to resolve or reduce.

APPENDIX 5

Key Purpose

The key purpose for training and development has been defined as:

> Develop human potential to assist organisations and individuals to achieve their objectives.

This statement reflects training and development's dual role to assist both organisations and individuals.

To achieve this Key Purpose the Lead Body adopted the Systematic Training Cycle to define areas of competence.

The Systematic Training Cycle

The cycle was chosen because:

- it describes systematically and comprehensively the whole training and development process

- it is familiar in all sectors and to all parts of the training community

- most training and development roles can be located within it.

The Systematic Training Cycle still forms the basis of the revised functional map, which attempts to describe the functions carried out by trainers.

The Key Purpose is split into five *areas of competence* which, when taken together, constitute the achievement of the Key Purpose. You will see that Areas A, B, C and E correspond to distinct stages of the Systematic Training Cycle. Area D corresponds to the assessment and

The Systematic Training Cycle

FUNCTIONAL MAP: KEY PURPOSE AND MAIN AREAS

Develop human potential to assist organisations and individuals to achieve their objectives

A Identify training and development needs
- **A1** Identify organisational training and development requirements
- **A2** Identify learning requirements of individuals

B Plan and design training and development
- **B1** Design training and development strategies for organisations
- **B2** Design training and development programmes
- **B3** Design and produce learning materials

C Deliver training and development
- **C1** Manage the implementation of training and development
- **C2** Facilitate learning with individuals and groups

D Review progress and assess achievement
- **D1** Monitor and review progress
- **D2** Assess individual achievement
- **D3** Assess individual achievement of competence

E Continuously improve the effectiveness of training and development
- **E1** Evaluate the effectiveness of training and development within an organisation
- **E2** Evaluate the effectiveness of training and development programmes
- **E3** Improve own training and development practice
- **E4** Contribute to advances in training and development

progress of individuals only. It comprises the assessment and verification units, which are the cornerstones of the NVQ Quality Assurance System.

Some training and development occupations also require competence in occupational areas other than training. For roles such as training manager, training administrator and training centre manager, standards from other Lead Bodies are appropriate and might be combined with relevant units from the Training and Development framework to define the requirements of these roles.

'Standards and Qualifications for Training and Development' extracted from EMPLOYMENT STANDARDS OCCUPATIONAL STANDARDS COUNCIL (1996) *A Briefing Note*. Sheffield, Department for Education and Employment. p5.

'Functional Map' extracted from EMPLOYMENT STANDARDS OCCUPATIONAL STANDARDS COUNCIL (1996) *Functional Map – National Standards for Training and Development*. Sheffield, Department for Education and Employment. p1.

Both © Crown Copyright, by permission of the DfEE.

APPENDIX 6

A SEVEN-STEP APPRAISAL PROCESS

This approach can be used regardless of the particular type of appraisal scheme in an organisation, providing that the appraisal process:

- is based on self-appraisal (see Guidelines for the Seven-Step Approach below)

- has at its heart a formal appraisal discussion that takes place either annually or more frequently between managers and individual members of each manager's team

- is developmental in purpose, focusing on work review, forward work-planning, and support and development of individuals for their current job performance and for their future in the organisation.

OUTLINE

1 Agenda-setting meeting

Up to 15 (working) days before appraisal discussion – allow 30 minutes.

2 Producing the self-appraisal

Up to 10 (working) days before appraisal discussion.

3 Transmitting the self-appraisal

Up to five days before appraisal discussion.

4 The appraisal discussion

Allow at least two hours.

5 Meeting to finalise appraisal form

Up to five days later – allow 20 minutes.

6 Transmitting copy of the form

By (insert date).

7 First review of progress of action plan

Within three months of appraisal discussion.

GUIDELINES FOR SEVEN-STEP APPROACH TO THE APPRAISAL PROCESS

1 Agenda-setting meeting

Appraiser and appraisee go together through the organisation's written guidelines on the appraisal scheme and the appraisal form to be completed. They agree on dates for Steps 2 and 3, and on how the appraisal discussion itself will be structured. They check that they each have a copy of the appraisee's appraisal form and action plan from the previous appraisal discussion. They get spare copies of a new appraisal form to use in Step 2.

2 Producing the self-appraisal

Appraisee fills in the self-appraisal parts of the appraisal form for the coming period (using a spare copy). The appraiser does the same, trying to 'second guess' the likely responses of the appraisee in order to test his or her own understanding.

3 Transmitting the self-appraisal

The appraisee sends the appraiser a copy of the 'self-appraisal' produced in Step 2. Appraiser compares the appraisee's actual responses with those expected by the appraiser and reflects on any gaps here. He or she also identifies any further information needed from the appraisee or elsewhere before the appraisal discussion takes place.

4 The appraisal discussion

Performance review and work planning

This part of the discussion should be initiated by the appraisee, using the self-appraisal already completed. It should focus on reviewing the appraisee's job performance during the previous period, relating this to his or her key targets of performance set at the start of that period. Areas of achievement and any underachievement should be identified and discussed, together with aids and barriers to fully effective performance. This stage should lead to work targets being set for the coming period and agreement on necessary resources related to those targets.

Job-related and career-related support and development

This part of the discussion should focus on how best to support and enhance in the coming year not only job performance but also personal growth as part of long-term career development. The latter requires a discussion of the career path that the appraisee hopes to follow during his or her time with the organisation, and the generation of creative ideas on what might be done in the coming year to support him or her in moving along that path.

The action plan for support and development

A plan should be agreed outlining the actions of any kind that appraisee and appraiser agree as being the most feasible, most cost-beneficial and most likely to make a positive impact on the appraisee's (a) job-related performance and (b) longer-term development and personal growth.

Summarising the discussion and agreeing next steps[1]

The appraisee summarises his or her understanding of what has occurred and been agreed during the meeting; the appraiser agrees or explains any disagreement. Appraisee or appraiser confirms that he or she will write up the appraisal form accordingly, omitting a section for 'Final Comments' by appraiser and appraisee until Step 5. The appraiser confirms, where necessary, that he or she will confer with other parties whose approval may be needed in order to finalise the proposed action plan. The date is set for Step 5.

5 Meeting to finalise appraisal form

Appraisee and appraiser agree on the write-up of the form, or note in a 'Final Comments' section any disagreement. Their 'Final Comments' should also draw attention to any wider organisational issues that have emerged from the appraisal discussion. The appraisee asks the appraiser for confirmation of the action plan and for the date of the first check on its implementation.

6 Transmitting copy of the form

The appraisee keeps the original form, duly completed and signed by all the parties. The appraisee sends copy of the form to whoever is designated to receive it.

7 First review of progress of action plan

Appraisee and appraiser meet as agreed to review progress in implementing the action plan and take any action needed at that stage.

[1] Although the form can be written up by the appraiser at this stage, experience suggests that the appraisal process will be enhanced if the writing up is done later, and by the appraisee, with a further short meeting held to finalise the form, as suggested in Step 5.

APPENDIX 7

WHAT ROLE DOES THE MANAGEMENT DEVELOPMENT PROCESS PLAY IN YOUR ORGANISATION?[1]

> **Instructions**
>
> Give a score of **1** to each question where the statement made is **more true than it is false** of your organisation. Add up the scores for each section, and enter them on the 'Total' lines. To calculate the overall total, see notes at the end of Section C below.

Section A

The development of managers in my organisation seems to be:

- regarded by top management as a cost, not a value-adding process ____

- not linked to business goals ____

- a luxury, one of the first processes to be reduced or scrapped when belts are being tightened ____

- driven by HR specialists, with little line management responsibility ____

- mainly about training, as distinct from any other kind of development ____

- viewed generally as something 'they do to us', not 'owned by us' ____

- reliant mainly on training courses or picking the job up as you go along ____

  Section A total, expressed as *minus points*: ____

Section B

The development of managers in my organisation seems to be:

- characterised by a systematic approach to MD planning and design ____

[1] Based on themes in Sadler, P. and Barham, K. (1988). 'From Franks to the future: 25 years of management training prescriptions'. *Personnel Management*. Vol. 20. pp48–51.

- linked to managers' targets and to business goals, especially at unit and divisional levels   _____

- a responsibility of line managers   _____

- linked explicitly to the needs of the job   _____

- linked explicitly to appraisal of performance   _____

- done by 'them *and* us' – a feeling of shared ownership   _____

- focused mainly on developing knowledge and skills   _____

Section B total: _____

Section C
The development of managers in my organisation seems to be:

- seen as essential to the survival and advancement of the business   _____

- aligned with longer-term corporate goals   _____

- embedded in a formal HRD corporate policy and in business planning activity in the organisation   _____

- a major responsibility of every line manager, both in the planning and reviewing of strategy and plans   _____

- linked to individual needs through personal development planning and emphasis on personal initiative   _____

- focused on developing knowledge, skills and values   _____

- a process tolerant of errors, which are seen as vehicles for learning   _____

Section C total: _____

TOTAL SCORE: Add together the scores for B and C, and deduct from them any minus points entered in Section A   _____

KEY TO SECTION SCORES

Section A (maximum possible points: –7)
The higher the number of these 'minus' points, the more **fragmented** is MD likely to be in your organisation. Any impact it makes on business results is likely to be more by accident than by design, and individuals are unlikely to have much faith or interest in their training and wider development.

Section B (maximum possible points: 7)
The higher the score, the more **formalised and business-led** is MD likely to be in your organisation. A high score means that it is likely to be seen to make an impact on short-term business goals, especially at individual and unit levels, but unlikely to make any clear contribution to the long-term growth of the business. Individuals are probably motivated by the management development process (MDP), regarding it as valuable for themselves and for their unit.

Section C (maximum possible points: 7)

The higher the score, the more **strategically focused** is the MDP likely to be in your organisation. A high score means that MD is likely to be seen by the leaders of the business as essential in giving competitive advantage and in securing the growth of the business. It is therefore likely to be a central preoccupation of management at corporate and at divisional/unit levels. Individuals are probably self-directed in their learning, and development is likely to be seen as an integral part of their daily activity in the workplace.

KEY TO TOTAL SCORE (maximum possible points: 14)

The meaning of a total score depends on how that score is made up. The following are therefore generalised guidelines only.

A score of between 1 and 7 minus points suggests that MD is a fragmented process in your organisation, adding negligible value to the business and lacking business focus or strategic direction.

A score of between 1 and 4 suggests that the MDP is beginning to be business-led, but that there are significant gaps between what is needed here and what is actually being achieved. The gaps may be at corporate level, or it may be that corporate strategy is in place, but is not being effectively implemented at divisional/unit levels.

A score of between 5 and 7 suggests that MD is a business-led process, although not making much long-term contribution to the organisation's growth. This may be because it is not expected to do so, or because there are no processes or systems in place to ensure that it does.

A score of between 8 and 11 indicates that the MDP has a clear long-term, strategic role, although there are gaps between the contribution it could make here, and what is actually being achieved. The gaps could be at corporate, divisional or operational levels of the organisation – or in particular sections of the organisation.

A score of between 12 and 14 indicates that the MDP is both business-led and strategic in your organisation, and that it makes a powerful and recognised contribution to immediate business goals and to the long-term growth of the organisation and individuals.

Index

A-level standards 45–6
Academy of Human Resource
    Development 10
acquisitions 385–6
action learning 314–15, 372, 402
adaptive learning 398–9, 403
added value 5, 96–115
    Economic Value Added (EVA) 82
    human capital theory 10
    NHS case-study 112–14
    problems of measurement 108–10
    or 'value for money' 110–12
adult learning 50–51
    see also lifelong learning
affirmative action see positive action
ageing population 70, 348
Allied Domecq (case-study) 350–51
annual reports 107
AOL Time Warner 203
appraisal see performance appraisal
apprenticeship 72, 73
assessment of individuals 348–54
    assessment and development
        centres 349–53
    self-assessment 353–4
attitudes
    critical to job performance 262
    management development's
        concern with 362
audits of HRD activity 123–9

balanced scorecard 252
Baldridge National Quality Award 125
Barclays Bank (case-study) 151–2
Basic Skills Agency 29
basic training 22, 250–52, 276
    of HRD staff 178–9
    SmithKline Beecham (case-study)
        250–51
Beeton Rumford (case-study) 327–8
behaviour/behavioural attributes
    competency frameworks 247,
        269, 274

and job performance 262
Behavioural Event Interviewing 274
behavioural objectives 281–2
benchmarking 119–20, 121
best practice 97, 120–21
Best Value framework 96–7
boundary management 246
British Broadcasting Corporation
    (case-study) 325–6
British Petroleum (case-studies) 272,
    273–4, 338–9, 369
BTR (case-study) 380–81
budget management 189–97, 453,
    455
'bundling' of HR practices 3, 15–17
bureaucracy 137
business case, production of 250
business drivers 106
Business Excellence model 125
business-led HRD 5, 79, 80
    Hydro Polymers (case-study)
        409–13, 415, 416–17
    see also strategic HRD
Business Link 32, 232
business partnership see partnership
business performance see
    organisational performance
business strategy
    alignment of HRD with 106–7,
        133, 235, 321–2
    competency frameworks linked
        with 369
    definition of term 81
    effect on HRD of weaknesses in
        88–9
    implementation of 81
    integration of career development
        with 342
    integration of HR process with 3,
        4
    models coupling HR strategy with
        9–10
    strategic performance measures 82

strategically focused management development 370–72
see also strategic capability; strategic HRD

call-centre industry 215–16
capabilities of organisations 89, 383–9, 413
  Marks & Spencer (case-study) 390–92
  organisational 386–7
  resource-based 383, 385–6
  strategic 18, 107, 387–9, 392–6
capacity of organisations 89–90
career anchors 350
career breaks 343–4
  see also returners
career development 333–53
  assessment related to 348–53
  BP (case-study) 338–9
  career life cycle 346–8
  definition of 333
  of HRD practitioners 180
  mutuality of interest 334, 339–41
  planned career management systems 341–6
  processes 340–41
  SCO (case-study) 335–7
  triggers for planned approach to 335
career paths and patterns 334, 337, 346–8
Chartered Institute of Personnel and Development (CIPD)
  continuous professional development pack 180, 354
  professional standards 4, 6, 154–7, 158, 178, 366–7, 444–7
CIRO approach to evaluation 309, 311–13
City Academies initiative 43–4
codified knowledge *see* explicit knowledge
collective learning 393–4, 398–9, 412, 413
commitment
  of employees 19, 108, 269
  of line management 156
  of top managers 82, 88, 94, 126, 173, 231, 319
company performance *see* organisational performance
competencies and competency frameworks
  competency-based analysis 269–70, 271–4

competency-based management development 272–4, 366–70
  linked to strategic priorities 369
  use in performance management 246–7, 255
  see also national occupational standards; professional standards
competitive advantage 62–3
competitive environment *see* organisational environment
comprehensive approach to organisational HRD needs 451, 452–4
computer-based assessment 206
computer-based training *see* technology-based learning
confidentiality of records 201
Connexions programme 54
'consistency' in learning events 162, 302, 315
consultancy roles 151–2
consultants, use of by SMEs 233–4
continuous development 86, 182, 256–7
  see also self-development
continuous improvement, at Hydro Polymers 410–11
continuous learning 387
corporate strategy *see* business strategy
costing and cost-benefit analysis 111–12, 190–7, 310, 311
County NatWest (case-study) 121
'criterion' objectives 281
culture *see* organisational culture
Cummins Engine Co. (case-study) 103–5, 122

data protection 201
Dearing reports 46, 47–8
decentralisation of HRD function 171–2, 182–3
demographic changes 70, 348
Department for Education and Employment (DfEE) 30
development, definition of 2
  see also employee development; human resource development
development centres 349–53
development discussions 254–6
dialogic learning 242–3, 248
disabled people 323
discriminatory treatment *see* equality
disengagement policies 19, 87, 341, 347–8

distance learning 283, 291
  see also e-learning
'dominant logic' 390, 395, 415
double-loop learning 243–4, 329
dual educational system 69, 72

'E' factors 245
e-learning 203–7
  see also technology-based learning
earnings, related to skills 19–20, 64
Economic Value Added (EVA) 82
education, definition of term 2
  see also national education
    framework
educational standards 40–41, 42,
    43–4, 45–6, 47, 48
educational underclass 43, 50
employability security 18–20, 164,
    334, 337
employee development
  benefits of 1
  definition of terms 1–2, 79–80
  see also human resource
    development
employee relations
  in SMEs 221–2
  WERS survey 14–15
employee resourcing
  context 160, 252
  in HRD function 177–80
  in SMEs 223–5
employment law, training related to
    200, 322–3, 324
Employment Occupational Standards
    Council 149
empowerment 165, 393
English Nature (case-study) 121
equality
  in development opportunities 254,
    255, 324
  and record systems 200–201, 255
  role of HRD in achieving 322–6
ethics 155–6, 157
European countries, vocational
    education and training in
    70–74
European Union
  competitive advantage in 62–3
  implications of Social Chapter 159
  labour market flexibility 63–4
  unemployment rates 63
  VET policy 60–61, 69
evaluation of learning events
    308–15
exit interviews 249
exit policies *see* disengagement
    policies

experiential cycle *see* learning
    cycle
explicit knowledge 406, 407, 409
'external consistency' 162, 302, 315,
    377

failing schools 43–4
failure
  of learners 307
  tactical responses to 133–4, 144–6
financial incentives to participate in
    training 25
  see also individual learning
    accounts
financial management of HRD
    function 189–97
financial measures of performance 81,
    82
flexible workers, development of
    327–8
flexibility
  of labour markets 19, 63–4
  of the workforce 68, 75
'flexible firm' 13
France
  management education 364
  training tax 74
  vocational education 70–71, 72
functional analysis 153–4, 155, 366
functional performance of managers
    361, 362
further education 45, 48, 52, 54, 55,
    56

General Certificate of Secondary
    Education (GCSE) 40
general national vocational
    qualifications (GNVQs) 34, 45,
    46, 49
generative learning 399, 403
Germany
  dual educational system 69, 72
  education of managers 364
  incentives to participate in
    training 24
  level of workforce skills and
    qualifications 27, 33, 70, 73
goals
  of HRD 92, 99, 104–5, 106–7,
    110, 162
  organisational 79, 80, 85, 92, 94,
    98, 99, 100, 101, 106–8,
    159
government policies *see* national
    training policy; national
    vocational education and
    training (NVET) policy

'hard' human resource models 9
health service *see* National Health
    Service
Hewlett Packard 372
high-fliers 339, 373–4
high-performance/commitment work
    practices 15
higher education system 45, 47–52
    adult learning 50–51
    leadership and management issues
        51–2
    national policy and strategy 47–9,
        52, 56–7
    social profile of entrants 50
    vocational pathways 49–50
horizontal integration, in professional
    qualification structure 156–7
human capital theory 10, 23
human investment cultures 137
human resource development
    alignment with business goals
        106–8, 133
    assessment of value added 108–14
    attitudes to investment in 82
    barriers and facilitators to (case-
        study) 83–5
    business imperative theory 9–11
    business-led 5, 79, 80
    duality of purpose 7, 9, 10, 19,
        20–21, 107–8
    and employees' social needs 19,
        21–2
    failures in 3–4, 13, 133–4, 163,
        199, 318
    fit with organisational context 5,
        13–17
    history of 6–12
    HR context for 86–7, 88
    identification of role and
        contribution to business 101
    integration with HR strategy
        103–5
    marketing of 197–9
    model of impact on performance
        100, 102–3, 124, 125–6
    outcomes *see* outcomes of HRD
    political issues 132–46
    research methodology issues 21
    strategic aspects *see* strategic HRD
    tasks for, in relation to
        organisational
        capability 386–7
    tasks for, in relation to resource-
        based capability 385–6
    terminology 2, 7–8, 79–80
    theories and concepts 8–12
    trends in 3, 12–13
human resource development
    function
    decentralisation of 171–2
    employee resource planning for
        177–8
    financial management of 189–97
    leadership within 182–6
    line management responsibility
        for 164, 172–5, 181–2
    organisation of 170–77, 182–3
    outsourcing of 175–7
    record systems 199–201
human resource development
    practitioners
    appraisal of 179
    career development 180
    core tasks xiv
    impact of 82–3
    induction and basic training of
        178–9
    management of 177–80
    occupational standards for 8,
        149–50, 152–4, 158
    partnerships with others 4–5
    professional standards for 154–7,
        158
    recruitment and selection of 178
    retraining of 179–80
    role of *see* role of HRD
        practitioners
    self-development 180
human resource planning 86
human resource practitioners, status
        and impact of 83
human resource processes/practices
    'bundling' of 3, 15–17
    as context for HRD 86–7, 88
    fit with organisational context
        14–17
    'hard' models 9
    impact on organisational capacity
        90
    influence on organisational
        performance 15–16, 17, 108–9
    integration of HRD with 103–5
    integration with business strategy
        4
    and organisational change 108–9
    in SMEs 221–5
    'soft' model 9
Hydro Polymers (case-study)
        409–13,
        415, 416–17

implementation of strategy 81
incentives to participate in training
    for employers 26–7

for individuals 24–6, 87, 165, 263
individual learning accounts (ILAs) 25, 50, 52
induction 248–50
    of HRD staff 178–9
industrial training organisations 30
informal training 227–8
    see also on–the–job learning
innovative organisations 393, 406, 408
Institute of Personnel and Development
    see Chartered Institute of Personnel and Development
instrumental learning 242, 243, 248
'interim' objectives 281
'internal consistency' 302
internal consultancy 151–2
internal labour markets 66–7, 76, 335, 337
international careers 344
Internet
    use by call-centres 216
    use by University for Industry 53, 204
    see also e-learning
interpersonal and interactive skills analysis 271
investment in HRD, attitudes to 82
investment in VET 73–5
Investors in People 12, 30, 32, 53, 125, 223, 232

Japan
    funding of VET 73
    increasing short-termism 12
    integration between HR systems 15
    management development 364
job analysis 178
job components 262
job descriptions 178, 250, 265, 266–7
job design 16
job training analysis 261–75
    approaches to 266–70
    definition of 262
    job components 262
    processes 263–5
    techniques 270–5
job training specifications 265, 267, 275

key task analysis 267–8
knowledge, definition of 262, 405
'knowledge connectivity' 405–6
knowledge development 394, 404–13

knowledge economy 3, 207–10
knowledge management 207–8, 406–8
knowledge productivity 389–92, 408–13, 416–17
knowledge workers 207, 208, 334
Kolb's learning cycle see learning cycle
Kwik-Fit (case-study) 161

labour market
    flexibility 19, 63–4
    internal 66–7, 76
    matrix 61–2
labour productivity see productivity
law and legal considerations 25, 28–9, 200, 319, 322–3
leadership 86, 173
    within HRD function 182–6
'learndirect' 52, 53, 204
learners
    evaluation of reactions of 311–12
    motivations of 284–5
    production of profiles of 282–5, 289, 322
    selection of 296–7
learning 238–44
    areas of potential difficulty 245–6
    definition of 2, 238–9
    and knowledge development 404–13
    relearning 306, 389, 394, 395
    review of 241
    styles and skills 283–4, 304, 356, 357
    theories 239–40
    transfer of 265, 307–8
    types of 242–4
    unlearning 306, 389–90, 394, 395
Learning Age, The (1998) 23, 52, 57
learning and skills councils 32, 51, 54–5, 56
learning curves 306–7
learning cycle 188, 238, 239–40
Learning Environment Questionnaire 355
learning events
    delivery of 308
    design of 301–8
    establishing needs 261–5
    establishing purpose and objectives 241, 278–82
    media and methods 302–5, 326
    monitoring and evaluation of 308–15
    NRHA (case-study) 298–301, 313–15

outcomes *see* outcomes of learning events
production of proposals 275–6
retail store case-study 286–90, 292–4
stages in design and delivery of 261, 262
strategies 290–4, 301
timing of 276
learning needs
  Cummins Engine (case-study) 103–5
  of HRD personnel 179
  individual needs 107–8, 246, 254, 258
  of new recruits 248–50, 251
  NRHA (case-study) 298, 300
  organisational needs 99, 106–8, 451–6
  special HRD initiatives 318, 319
  Wesdale Acute Hospitals (case-study) 92
  see also assessment of individuals; job training analysis
learning networks 80, 234, 329
learning objectives
  case-studies 279–81, 286–7, 288–9
  and choice of media and methods 304
  establishing 278–82
  and evaluation of events 311, 312–13
  levels of 281–2
learning organisations 9, 18, 106, 179, 235, 400–404
learning strategy 290–4, 301
  case-study 286–7, 289–90, 292–4
learning technology 302
  see also technology-based learning
Learning to Succeed (1999) 30, 33, 54–6
levy-grants systems 27, 28, 74
lifelong learning 23–4, 39, 46, 48–9, 51, 52, 57, 72–3, 75
Lifelong Learning (1998) 23, 52
line managers
  commitment of 156
  development of HRD skills of 181–2
  responsibility for career development 343
  responsibility for HRD 92, 164, 172–5
Lloyds TSB 213

Local Education Councils (LECs) 31, 38
location of learning events 283
London Underground (case-study) 171
lost opportunity costs 191–2
low-wage economies 62–3

Management Charter Initiative (MCI) 366, 367
management development 359–77
  agendas for 361
  characteristics of effectiveness in 373
  competency-based 272–4, 366–70
  definition of managers 359–60
  design of 362–6, 370–72
  educational programmes 364–5
  linking strategic capability and 392–6
  management of 376–7
  NHS case-studies 112–14, 298–301, 313–15
  Open University report into 14
  role and contribution of (questionnaire) 462–4
  strategic focus 370–72
  succession planning 373–4
  tasks 361–2
  United Biscuits (case-study) 374–6
managerial role of HRD practitioners 167–86
managers, definition of 359–60
  see also line managers; top managers
Manchester Airport (case-study) 272–3, 274
Manpower Services Commission 29
manual skills analysis 270
marketing of HRD 197–9
Marks & Spencer (case-study) 390–92
Master of Business Administration (MBA) 365
McDonald's restaurants 242
measurement
  of organisational performance 81–2
  of value added by HRD 108–10
  see also evaluation of learning events
mentoring 179, 243, 248, 251
mergers *see* acquisitions
Metropolitan Police 318
milestones, strategic 94, 121, 315
mission 80, 87, 98

motivation 244, 246, 284–5
multiskilling 250–51, 263
mutuality of interest
    in career development 334,
        339–41
    in succession planning 373

National Advisory Council on
        Education and Training
        Targets (NACETT) 30, 34
National Council for Vocational
        Qualifications (NCVQ) 33
national curriculum 40, 41–2
National Education and Training
        Targets see National Learning
        Targets
national education framework 39–58
    post-16 provision 45–52
    school system 40–44
    see also national vocational
        education and training
        (NVET) policy
National Grid for Learning 214
National Health Service (case-
        studies) 91–3, 112–14,
        298–301, 313–15, 340–41,
        394
National Learning and Skills Council
        (NLSC) 53, 54, 56
National Learning Targets 39, 54,
        450
national occupational standards
        33–4
    in European countries 72
    in training and development 8,
        149–50, 152–4, 158, 178,
        457–8
National Record of Achievement 46
National Skills Task Force 13
National Traineeships 46, 54
national training organisations
        (NTOs) 29, 30
national training policy 24–9
    aims of 25
    incentives for employers 26–7
    incentives for individuals 24–6
    skills supply 27–9
national training strategy 29–35
    implementation framework 29–31
    NVQ system 33–5
    TEC system 31–3
national vocational education and
        training (NVET) policy 12,
        23–4, 29–33, 52–8, 65–6,
        75–6
    see also vocational education and
        training

national vocational qualifications
        (NVQs) 33–6, 448–9
    case-study exercise 35–6
    development of 33–4
    doubts concerning 34–5
    GNVQs 34, 45, 46, 49
    organisational competencies
        related to 269
    progress of 35
needs see job training analysis;
        learning needs; motivation
negative power 142
network organisational structures
        137–8
New Deal 26, 27–8, 55
Northern Ireland, vocational
        education and training 38
Northern Regional Health Authority
        (case-study) 298–301, 313–15,
        394
Northumbria Water 176–7
Nuclear Electric 176
objectives see learning objectives;
        targets
occupational standards see
        national
        occupational standards
on-the-job learning 242
    see also informal training
organisation development 399–400
organisation of the HRD function
        170–77
    decentralisation 171–2, 182–3
    line-managed 164, 172–5
    outsourcing 175–7
organisational advancement
        397–400
organisational capability and capacity
        89–90, 386–7
    Marks & Spencer (case-study)
        390,   391
organisational change 108–9, 398,
        399, 400, 403, 415, 416
organisational competencies 369
organisational culture 117–18,
        135–40, 159–60, 291, 294,
        386, 407
organisational environment 89, 159,
        168, 381, 382
organisational goals 79, 80, 85, 92,
        94, 98, 99, 100, 101, 106–8,
        159
organisational learning 400, 401, 408
organisational mission see mission
organisational performance
    influence of HR practices on
        15–16, 17, 108–9

measures of 81–2
and orientation of HRD strategy
    10
organisational politics 134–42
organisational strategy *see* business
    strategy
organisational structures 12, 135–40,
    159–60
organisational survival 397–8
organisational vision *see* vision
organisations as systems 8–9, 160
outcomes of HRD
    auditing 123–9
    measurement of 108–10, 130
    principles to aid assessment of
        129–30
    setting standards 118–23
    in SMEs 234
outcomes of learning events
    evaluation of 312–13
    and formulation of objectives
        281–2
    standards 276
outdoor development 248, 284
outsourcing 151, 175–7
'overarching competences' 368

part-time workers 327, 328
partnership 4–5, 28–9, 47, 80, 93–4,
    115, 328–9
pay-back approach 110–11
pay-forward concept 114
'perceptual distinctiveness' 305
performance
    influences on 245
    model of impact of HRD on 100,
        102–3, 124, 125–6
    organisational *see* organisational
        performance
    parameters of 244–5
    poor performance 246, 263
performance appraisal 86, 252–6,
    459–61
    appeals procedure 255
    discussions 252, 254–6, 460–1
    factors influencing 252–3
    of HRD staff 179
    as job training analysis technique
        274–5
    self-appraisal 255
    training for 255, 286–90
performance management
    best practice in 257–8
    definition of 237
    IPD survey on 14, 247
    key stages and elements of 237–8
    tensions between control and

development 246–7
person cultures 138–40, 142
personal development plans 248, 251,
    256, 338, 339, 355
personnel specifications 178, 250,
    276
police force 163, 199–200, 318
policy, meaning of term 80
politics
    case-study exercise 142–6
    of HRD 132–4
    organisational politics 134–42,
        361
poor performance 246, 263
positional capability 383, 385
positive action 323, 324–6, 335
power 141–2
power cultures 136–7
practice 306
pre-course assessments 313
probationary periods 179, 251
problem-centred analysis
    job training needs 268–9
    organisational HRD needs 451,
        454–6
productivity
    influence of HRM practices on
        15, 16
    measures of 81
professional standards, of the CIPD
    6, 154–7, 158, 178, 366–7,
    444–7
professionalism 155–6
profitability
    influence of HRM practices on 15
    measures of 81
proposal writing 275–6
psychological contract 334, 335
purpose of learning events 278–81
    case-study 286–8
pyramid structures 137

Qualifications and National
    Curriculum
    Authority 42, 46–7
Quality Assurance Agency 48
quality management, of HRD
    services 118–23

rail industry 4, 199
record systems 199–201
recruitment and selection 86
    of HRD staff 178
re-engineering 399, 413
regional development agencies 32
reinforcement of learning 240, 241,
    306–7

relearning 306, 389, 394, 395
resource–based capability 383, 385–6
    Marks & Spencer case-study 390
resource power 141
resources
    budgeting 189–97, 453, 455
    fit between learning strategy and
        291, 292–4
    intangible resources 187–8
    management of 187–97
    strategy for management of 197
    tangible resources 187
retirement policies 347–8
retraining of HRD staff 179–80
return on assets (ROA) 81
return on equity (ROE) 81
return on sales (ROS) 81
return on training investment 110
returners, training and development
        initiatives for 327
    see also career breaks
reward systems 87
    management development as
        reward 361
    as parameter of performance
        244–5
    and skill requirements 231, 263
role analysis 271
role cultures 137, 141
role of HRD practitioners 5–6
    consultancy role 151, 175–6
    at corporate level 162–4
    factors that influence 158–61, 176
    increasing the influence of 161–2
    job analysis 178
    managerial roles 167–77
    at operational/individual level
        164–5
    typologies 148–51
    at unit level 164

school system 40–44
SCO (case-study) 335–7
Scotland, vocational educational and
        training 38
Scottish Vocational Education
        Council
        (SCOTVEC) 38
self-appraisal 255
self-assessment 353–4
self-development 164, 174, 354–7
    of HRD practitioners 180,
        354–5
    see also continuous development
self-reflective learning 243, 248
shareholder activism 381
Shell 172, 395–6, 398, 408

short-termism 10, 12, 20, 26, 62–3,
        76
single-loop learning 243–4, 329,
        398–9
'skilled incompetency' 329
skills 262
    flexibility 19, 75
    integration of HR practices and 16
    and internal labour markets 66–7
    shortages and supply 27–9, 64,
        70, 226–7, 230
    tacit skills 228
Skills Task Force see National Skills
        Task Force
small and medium-sized enterprises
        (SMEs) 219–36
    (case-study) exercise 228–30
    characteristics of 219–21
    employment relationships 221–2
    external support for training in
        232–4
    human resource management
        222–5
    and New Deal programme 28
    outcomes of training and
        development 234
    training practice 225–7
    training provision 227–8
    triggers to training and
        development in 230–1
Small Business Service 232
SmithKline Beecham (case-study)
        250–1
Social Chapter 159
'social dialogue' 61
social motivation of learners 284–5
social needs of employees 19, 21–2
social profile of entrants to higher
        education 50
'soft' human resource models 9–10
special learning and development
        initiatives 317–31
    development of non-employees
        327–30
    equality initiatives 322–7
    issues requiring clarification
        318–19
    key principles in organisation
        of 330–31
    team development 319–22
'specific' objectives 281
spherical organisational structures
        138
standards
    educational standards 40–41, 42,
        43–4, 45–6, 47, 48
    for HRD outcomes 118–23

national occupational standards 8,
33–4, 72, 149–50, 152–4,
158, 178, 457–8
professional standards 4, 6,
154–7, 158, 178, 366–7,
444–7
for training event outcomes 276
stimulation to learning 240–41, 305
stimulus-response theory 240
strategic capability 18, 107, 387–9,
413
linking management
development
and 392–6
Marks & Spencer (case-study)
390–92
strategic HRD 5, 11–12, 17–18,
79–95,
106–8, 163, 382–3
characteristics of 101
at Cummins Engine Co. 103–5
definition of 7, 79
development of (case-study) 91–3,
340–41
and enhancement of strategic
capability 388–9, 392–6, 413
factors determining extent of value
of 81–5
identification of extent of 85–94
inhibitors to 87–9
related to learning organisation 18
scenarios that trigger introduction
of 89–91
in SMEs 234–5
trend towards 3, 12
at Yardley Cosmetics 320–22
strategic milestones 94, 121, 315
strategic progress 380–82
strategy see business strategy; learning
strategy
succession planning 339, 341, 373–4
supplier development programmes
329
support for HRD activities, gaining
132–3
systemic training cycle 152, 162, 302,
457

tacit knowledge 406, 407, 409
tacit skills 228
targets
job performance 244, 246, 251,
255
National Learning Targets 39, 54,
450
task analysis 266–8
task cultures 137, 142

Task Observation 297
teaching profession 42, 74
teamworking 86
in HRD function 182–6
team development 319–22
technology-based learning 185,
203–16
call centre case-study 215–16
concerns relating to 160, 210–12
e-learning concept 203–7
information sources on 214–15
knowledge economy and 207–9
stimulating interest in 213–14
success factors 110, 212–13
TVU case-study 209–10
temporary workers, development of
327–8
Thames Valley University
209–10
360-degree appraisal 252
time off for training 25
top managers, commitment of 82, 88,
94, 126, 173, 231
trade unions, role in HRD 5, 53, 56
trainability tests 296–7
training
basic training 22, 250–52, 276
historical starting point of 8
informal training 227–8
national training policy 24–9
national training strategy 29–35
plans 451, 453–4, 455
proposals 275–6
strategic tasks of 17
use of term 2
see also vocational education and
training
training and development
occupational standards 8, 149–50,
152–4, 158, 178, 457–8
practitioners see human
resource development
practitioners
professional standards 154–7,
158, 178, 444–7
resources see resources
roles see role of HRD
practitioners
see also human resource
development
Training and Enterprise Councils
(TECs) 29, 30–33, 54
'training by exception' technique 268
transfer
of knowledge 407–8
of learning 265, 307–8
transformational change 398, 399,

400, 403, 415, 416
trial and error 356
trust 19
turbulence 381, 382

'ultimate' objectives 281
underclass
    educational 43, 50
    in labour market 64–5, 70
unemployed persons
    company training programmes
        21–2
    New Deal 26, 27–8, 55
    training provision 56
unemployment, and labour market
        flexibility 19, 63, 64
unions *see* trade unions
Unipart University 403
unit level HRD planning 107–8, 164
United Biscuits (case-study) 374–6
United States
    historical development of HRD in
        8, 9–10
    income disparities 19–20
    labour flexibility 63, 64
    vocational education and training
        74
universities *see* higher education
        system
University for Industry 29, 52, 53–4,
        204
University Forum for HRD 10–11
unlearning 306, 389–90, 394, 395
unskilled workers, plight of 64–5,
        66, 70

value–adding *see* added value;
        Economic Value Added (EVA)
values, concern of management
        development with 362–3

vertical integration, in professional
        qualification structure 156
vision 80, 87, 98–103, 237, 408
vocational education and training
    consequences of lack of 67
    in European countries 70–74
    EU's vision for 60–61
    investment in 73–5
    reasons for 66
    as social engineering 65–6
    see also national vocational
        education and training
        (NVET) policy
vocational qualifications
    Dearing report 46
    in France 71, 72
    in Germany 33, 70
    GNVQs 34, 45, 46, 49
    harmonisation within EU 34
    NVQs 33–6
    rates of 33, 70
    for training and development
        practitioners 149, 157
voluntary workers, development of
        329–30

Wales, vocational education and
        training 38
women
    development programmes
        325–6
    returning to employment
        327
work-based learning 363–4, 389
work-sampling 297
Workplace Employee Relations
        Survey (WERS) 14–15

Yardley Cosmetics (case-study)
        320–21

The *People and Organisations* series
and
Core Management studies

The only route to a professional career in personnel and development is through the achievement of the CIPD's professional standards. One of the three fields that make up these standards, the new Core Management standards define the essentials for competently managing and developing people. They are compatible with an N/SVQ at Level 4 in management.

CIPD Publications has five new books in the *People and Organisations* series as textbooks for the new Core Management standards. The texts of these five books and their titles will closely follow the Core Management syllabus. The titles of the books are:

Managing Activities	Michael Armstrong
Managing Financial Information	David Davies
Managing in a Business Context	David Farnham
Managing People	Jane Weightman
Managing Information and Statistics	Roland and Frances Bee

Managing Financial Information

David Davies

Managing Financial Information is a practical explanation of the interface between the finance and HR functions in organisations. It analyses thoroughly many areas that managers may find daunting, and includes test questions and work-based exercises to assist competent learning.

It examines:

- balance sheets

- trading and profit and loss accounts

- budgeting

- costing.

David Davies is a principal lecturer in financial management at the University of Portsmouth. A qualified accountant with a Masters degree in management from Henley Management College, he previously spent 17 years in the private and public sectors. He currently lectures on post- and undergraduate courses, as well as undertaking consultancy work.

192 pages
1999
£14.99
0 85292 782 7

Managing in a Business Context

David Farnham

Managing in a Business Context illustrates the framework in which businesses are working in Britain today. Beginning with the nature of strategy and how strategy can be converted into practice, it then considers the issues of wider concern to HR practitioners and business managers in general.

It examines:

- economics, politics and political systems, and their effect on the workplace

- social and legal structures, and how they impinge on the private and public sectors

- the technological revolution and its effect on working practices

- business ethics and the impact of an international climate.

Professor David Farnham holds the chair in Employment Relations at the University of Portsmouth. He has also written *Employee Relations in Context*, published by the CIPD.

368 pages
1999
£16.99
0 85292 783 5

Managing Information and Statistics

Roland and Frances Bee

Managing Information and Statistics is a hands-on guide that explains how the apparently esoteric discipline of statistics can be an invaluable management tool. Tables, diagrams and graphs are explained in detail; surveys, forecasting and the principles of relationships between data each have their own sections.

It examines:

- how to produce reports and presentations to the highest standard

- how to use general statistical packages

- how to apply statistical thinking to people-management issues

- how to manage data effectively.

Frances and Roland Bee are experienced training consultants and have written five other highly successful CIPD books – *Training Needs Analysis and Evaluation, Constructive Feedback, Customer Care, Project Management* and *The Complete Learning Evaluation Toolkit.*

336 pages
1999
£15.99
0 85292 785 1

Managing People

Jane Weightman

Managing People is an approachable introduction to working with people and to understanding how people work. It discusses the psychology of the workplace, including its fundamental characteristics, differences between individuals, and how people learn. *Managing People* also studies issues of central concern to all managers, such as performance management, and training and development.

It examines:

- how to motivate your employees

- differing work patterns and their implications for the workplace

- how to manage work-related stress.

Jane Weightman is a psychologist and has been associated with UMIST since 1980. She has carried out research into a wide range of management-related topics and has written widely in a range of journals. Her books include *Competencies in Action* and *Managing People in the Health Service*, both published by the CIPD.

240 pages
1999
£16.99
0 85292 784 3